CANTUS FIRMUS

IN MASS AND MOTET 1420-1520

CANTUS FIRMUS

IN MASS AND MOTET

1420-1520

BY EDGAR H. SPARKS

UNIVERSITY OF CALIFORNIA PRESS

BERKELEY AND LOS ANGELES : 1963

UNIVERSITY OF CALIFORNIA PRESS
Berkeley and Los Angeles, California

CAMBRIDGE UNIVERSITY PRESS
London, England

© 1963 by The Regents of the University of California

Library of Congress Catalog Card Number: 63-15469

Designed by Adrian Wilson

Printed in the United States of America

ACKNOWLEDGMENTS

I<small>T HAS</small> been my good fortune, during the years in which this book was being written, to have had the help and counsel of many of my colleagues. Professor Gustave Reese has made numerous suggestions for improving and correcting the work, with regard to both matters of fact and matters of interpretation. Professors Edward B. Lawton, Charles C. Cushing, and Lawrence Moe have been kind enough to read the typescript, and Dr. Sydney Robinson Charles has checked it in great detail. My especial gratitude goes to Manfred Bukofzer, who guided the original dissertation and, before his untimely death, helped me prepare the first part of the book.

For permission to use transcriptions into modern notation, grateful acknowledgment is made to the following publishers:

American Institute of Musicology (Armen Carapetyan): examples 72 and 88, taken from Dr. Cornelis Lindenberg's edition of Johannes Regis, *Opera Omnia*, and example 104, taken from Dr. Bernhardt Meier's edition of Jacob Barbireau, *Opera Omnia*.

American Musicological Society: examples 53, 54, 60, 61, 62, and 89b, taken from Dr. Dragan Plamenac's edition of Johannes Ockeghem, *Collected Works*, Vol. II.

Mediaeval Academy of America: examples 93 and 94, taken from Dr. Helen Hewitt's edition of *Harmonice Musices Odhecaton A*.

Musica Britannica: examples 35, 37, 38, and 42, taken from Dr. Manfred Bukofzer's edition of John Dunstable, *Complete Works*.

W. W. Norton & Company, Inc.: example 92, taken from Dr. Gustave Reese's *Music in the Renaissance*.

E. H. S.

CONTENTS

PART III
Obrecht and Josquin des Prez

ABBREVIATIONS

Var. Prec.	*Variae Preces.* (Solesmes: E Typographeo Sancti Petri, 1901).
Vesperale	*Vesperale Romanum.* (Paris, Tournai, Rome: Desclée & Socii, 1936).

MANUSCRIPTS OF POLYPHONIC MUSIC

Aosta	Aosta Seminary Library, mensuralist musical codex without shelf number.
Apt	Apt, Treasury of the basilica of Sainte-Anne, 16*bis* (4).
BL	Bologna, Liceo Musicale, Q 15 (formerly 37).
Br. 5557	Brussels, Bibliothèque Royale, Ms. Mus. 5557.
Cambridge Ii.5.18	Cambridge, University Library, Cod. Ii.5.18.
Canonici	Oxford, Bodleian Library, Canonici misc., 213.
Capp. Sist. 14	Vatican City, Bibl. Vaticana, Cappella Sistina 14.
Capp. Sist. 51	Vatican City, Bibl. Vaticana, Cappella Sistina 51.
Chigi	Vatican City, Bibl. Vaticana, Chigiana, Cod. C.VIII.234.
Fountains	London, British Museum, Add. 40011 B (Fountains Abbey, manuscript fragment).
Mellon Chansonnier	New Haven, Yale University Library, the Mellon Chansonnier.
Mod B	Modena, Bibl. Estense, α.X.I, 11 (formerly Lat. 471; also VI.H.15).
Mod α.M.1, 13	Modena, Bibl. Estense, α.M.1, 13 (formerly Lat. 456; also V.H.11, 10).
OH	Old Hall near Ware, Catholic College of St. Edmund, manuscript without shelf number.
Pepys 1236	Cambridge, Magdalen College, Pepys 1236.
Segovia	Segovia, MS Catedral Archivo Musical, s. s.
Selden B	Oxford, Bodleian Library, Selden B 26.
Tr 87-92	Trent, Castello del Buon Consiglio, MSS 87-92.
Tr 93	Trent, Archivio capitolare del Duomo, MS 93.
Windsor	London, British Museum, Egerton MS 3307.

BOOKS AND MODERN REPRINTS OF MUSIC

Apt	*Le manuscrit de musique du trésor d'Apt* (XIVe-XVe s.), ed. A. Gastoué (Publications de la Société Française de Musicologie, Première Série, Vol. X [Paris: E. Droz, 1936]).
Doc. Pol. Lit.	*Documenta Polyphoniae Liturgicae S. Ecclesiae Romanae,* ed. Lawrence Feininger (Rome: Societas Universalis Sanctae Ceciliae, 1947-). ———— Series I, no. 1, G. Dufay, *Fragmentum Missae* (1947). ———— Series I, no. 2, L. Power, *Missa super "Alma Redemptoris Mater"* (1947).

DTO	*Denkmäler der Tonkunst in Österreich.* Publikationen der Gesellschaft zur Herausgabe der Denkmäler der Tonkunst in Österreich. (1894-).
DTO 14	———— VII. Jahrgang. *Sechs Trienter Codices. 1. Auswahl*, ed. G. Adler and O. Koller (Vienna: Artaria & Co., 1900), Vols. XIV/XV.
DTO 22	———— XI. Jahrgang. *Sechs Trienter Codices. 2. Auswahl*, ed. G. Adler and O. Koller (Vienna: Artaria & Co., 1904), Vol. XXII.
DTO 38	———— XIX. Jahrgang. *Sechs Trienter Codices. 3. Auswahl*, ed. G. Adler (Vienna: Artaria & Co., Leipzig: Breitkopf & Härtel, 1912), Vol. XXXVIII.
DTO 53	———— XXVII. Jahrgang. *Sechs Trienter Codices. 4. Auswahl*, ed. R. Ficker and A. Orel (Vienna: Universal-Edition A. G., Leipzig: Breitkopf & Härtel, 1920), Vol. LIII.
DTO 61	———— XXXI. Jahrgang. *Sieben Trienter Codices. 5. Auswahl*, ed. R. Ficker (Vienna: Universal-Edition A. G., 1924), Vol. LXI.
DTO 76	———— XL. Jahrgang. *Sieben Trienter Codices. 6. Auswahl*, ed. R. von Ficker (Vienna: Universal-Edition A. G., 1933), Vol. LXXVI.
Early Bodleian Music	*Early Bodleian Music. Sacred and Secular Songs*, ed. Sir John Stainer (London: Novello & Co., New York: Novello, Ewer & Co., 1901). Vol. I, facsimiles; Vol. II, transcriptions.
Marix	Marix, Jeanne. *Les musiciens de la cour de Bourgogne* (Paris: Editions de L'Oiseau Lyre, 1937).
MGG	*Die Musik in Geschichte und Gegenwart*, ed. Fr. Blume (Kassel, Basle, London, New York: Bärenreiter Verlag, 1949-).
Mon. Pol. Lit.	*Monumenta Polyphoniae Liturgicae S. Ecclesiae Romanae*, ed. Lawrence Feininger (Rome: Societas Universalis Sanctae Ceciliae, 1947-).
	———— Series I, Vol. I, fasc. 1-10 (1948). *L'homme armé* Masses of Dufay, Busnois, Caron, Faugues, Regis, Ockeghem, De Orto, Basiron, Tinctoris, and Vaqueras.
	———— Series II, Vol. I (1947). *Proprium Missae.* Anonymous settings of the proper of the Mass from Trent Codex 88.
OH	*The Old Hall Manuscript*, ed. A. Ramsbotham (London: The Plainsong & Mediaeval Music Society, 1933-1938). 3 vols.

INTRODUCTION

SEVERAL YEARS AGO my teacher, Manfred Bukofzer, suggested that I take *cantus firmus* treatment in the fifteenth century as a topic for a doctoral dissertation. The topic was significant because of the fundamental importance of cantus firmus in the history of polyphonic music; and the fifteenth century was the most interesting part of this history, for within it a long period of development came to a culmination and an end point.

Despite the interest of the topic, it had never been investigated systematically. The relevant literature consisted mainly of articles which were more or less limited in scope, and several of the authors had apparently been carried away by the fascinating aspects of the subject, for they had indulged heavily in speculation.

It seemed that a new study should stress what was done with the cantus firmus rather than what might have been done; it should be comprehensive enough to include all the customary methods of treatment; and it should be organized historically so as to show the development of these methods. A study so oriented was bound to be concerned, first of all, with the collection of facts, and this book which has grown from it is equally occupied with that tedious task. The facts are useful, however, because they have a bearing on historical developments. Better yet, the facts have to do with the voice which is the very heart of a composition, so they make an excellent starting point for analysis, and for the interpretation of the many kinds of musical expression we find in fifteenth-century compositions.

The term "cantus firmus" has a rather dull sound today, for it is best known to musicians from their studies in strict counterpoint. In its current and most widely understood sense, a cantus firmus is simply a brief melody in notes of equal value—one which is provided by the writer of a textbook, and which is to be copied out literally by the student and then used by him as a basis for writing exercises.

Cantus firmus usage in the fifteenth century is in every respect more diversified and more interesting. The term itself must be understood in a much broader sense than it has at present. The cantus firmus is any preëxistent melody which is used as the basis of a new composition. The source of the melody may be a Gregorian chant, or a popular song. It may be a voice of a sacred or secular polyphonic composition (a *res facta*, according to the definition of Tinctoris). The cantus firmus may also be an abstract subject.[1] (From here on, instead of "cantus firmus" I will use the abbreviation "c.f.")

Composers normally did not copy out the borrowed melody literally, but manipulated it in a great variety of ways. In many cases the preliminary manipulation was as important a part of the creative process as the writing of the counterpoints. Nevertheless, the composers sometimes proceeded as students do nowadays and laid out the part in long notes of equal value. They did this not often, but often enough that I have had to consider it as a category of treatment in its own right; when I came to discuss it, I found that I had to adopt a special, distinguishing term for the form of c.f. which is most familiar at present. (See p. 445, n. 22.)

Part I of this book discusses the methods of treating the c.f. in the period up to 1450. I am especially interested in the manner of quotation: the ways the composer alters the borrowed material, and the ways he remains true to it; the aspects of the original melody he respects, and those he ignores; the points of view implied by his choice of a certain type of treatment, and the musical procedures and characteristics that are apt to be the result of this choice.

There are not more than two truly different ways of treating the c.f. The notes are there, and the composer may choose to use them as the material for the formation of a new structure—as a foundational voice, or tenor. Or he may choose to use them as the basis of a melody part, and elaborate and remodel them to conform to some melodic ideal of his own.

The second—the melodic—type of c.f. is especially characteristic of the fifteenth century, so I take it up first and consider it in great detail. Detailed treatment is called for by the nature of the process of melodic elaboration, which is extremely variable and ranges from such slight elaboration that the borrowed melody retains almost its original form to such extensive reworking that it becomes almost a newly composed part. The border line between elaboration of a preëxistent melody and free composition is often vague, and in some cases it is extremely difficult to determine whether c.f. is being used or not. It was especially necessary to step carefully at these points, because I also criticize the opinions of others who, I feel, find c.f. in works which are freely composed, and who, in so doing, assume types of treatment which were never imagined by the composers of the fifteenth century. Most of these criticisms are reserved for the Appendix.

The first type of treatment—the use of the c.f. in the tenor as a foundation for a composition—is the traditional one, and I do not consider its use before c. 1430. My interest lies in the way it developed in the fifteenth century, so I pay little attention to its previous history, which goes back to the beginnings of polyphonic music.[2]

While the two types contrast with one another fundamentally, it is clear that composers did not feel that they were mutually exclusive, for we find modifications and hybrid types of many sorts. Some occur frequently enough that it is worth while to consider them as categories in their own right, and I have adopted terms to identify them. I have, however, not gone far in this, since I am interested in categories mainly as a means of organizing the discussion, and have tried to avoid a system of classification which might become burdensome.

In Part I compositions are selected which best illustrate the different types of treatment, without much regard to their musical quality. After establishing the main types of c.f. usage in existence before the middle of the century, I place more emphasis on tracing lines of development from period to period. In Part II, which covers the years from about 1450 to 1485, I devote most attention to the works of better-known composers and make no attempt at complete coverage of the material now available in modern editions. I do this as a matter of practical necessity, but I feel, also, that not much is lost with respect to c.f. usage at this period. The late works of Dufay, and the works of Ockeghem, Regis, Faugues, Busnois, and a few others, were widely admired and were taken as models by lesser composers, so that the use of c.f. in these works can be taken as representative for the period as a whole.

Complete coverage became even less possible as I approached the sixteenth century, and I had to choose between sampling the work of a large number of composers or concentrating upon a very few of the great names of the period. It seemed that comprehensive treatment was not so necessary here as in the period before 1450. The ways in which the c.f. was handled in the last half of the century are various and ingenious in the extreme, but there are no fundamentally new types of c.f. treatment which would require illustration from a variety of sources. This being the case, I chose to concentrate upon the works of two composers in whom I was interested—Jacob Obrecht and Josquin des Prez. I hope that the relatively thorough coverage of their output will make up to some extent for the lack of scope in this part of the book.

The field of c.f. is so vast that I have had to limit myself in other ways as well. I avoid the subject of the use of c.f. in secular compositions, except in the case of a very few pieces. As the title of the book indicates, I consider only serious and sacred music—motets, Masses, Mass movements, and other liturgical items such as antiphons, hymns, and sequences. (The term "motet" in the title can be taken in a loose sense to include these latter items.)

I have had to limit myself to a discussion of the use to which a given c.f. is put in a specific piece of music, and to exclude any critical discussion of the form of the chant itself or of its place in the liturgy. Also, since it was my intent to give a factual survey of the topic, I had to exclude works for which I could not find a reasonably good version of the original melody.

I have departed from this policy in only a few instances, one being the *Missa Graecorum* of Obrecht, in which the melody is stated so clearly that it is possible to analyze its use, even though its source is still unknown. Incidentally, the search for *cantus firmi* proved to be enormously time-consuming, and unsuccessful more often than not. Sometimes a composer quotes a chant no longer in use; sometimes he uses one that is known, but does not quote the beginning of it. In the latter case, no index will help in tracing the textual clue he gives. The c.f. used in the series of *Caput* Masses is a famous instance of this sort, *caput* being the last word of the antiphon *Venit ad Petrum*.

A few of the musical examples are transcriptions of my own, and a considerable number are transcriptions which Professor Bukofzer kindly made available to me.[3] The majority, however, are taken from modern editions. I have standardized the system of reduction of note values (4:1 for compositions before c. 1460, 2:1 for compositions after that date), have written all examples in treble and bass clefs, and have marked them liberally with brackets and *x*'s. I know that the reader can follow the notes of a c.f., and can detect unusual features of musical treatment as well as I can, but I wished to do everything possible to facilitate reading. In a work which contains as much description of music as this one does, the examples should be made as much a part of the text as possible. In fact, it seems to me that when examples are lacking the book must be read with score in hand if the running accounts of the compositions are to have any meaning.

I have, in general, accepted the indications of *musica ficta* as given in the editions from which I drew the examples. Likewise, I have not attempted to standardize Latin spellings, but have followed the orthography of the various sources. The result is some variety in the forms of words. (For instance, "*caelum*" appears also as "*coelum*" and "*celum*.") I have given texts in full in most of the passages quoted, but have omitted any repetitions of words introduced by editors.

E. H. S.

PART I

DEVELOPMENT OF

THE PROCEDURES

CIRCA 1420–1450

1

The Melodic Cantus Firmus
in the Conductus of
the Old Hall Manuscript

THE OLD HALL MANUSCRIPT CONTAINS by far the largest and most important collection of English music of the late fourteenth and early fifteenth centuries. As a result, it has been the object of an immense amount of study. The music has been printed in a modern edition which is provided with analytical essays and notes by the editors—Ramsbotham, Collins, and Dom Anselm Hughes.[1] In addition, a number of independent articles have appeared concerning the manuscript and its repertory, starting with that of Barclay Squire in 1901 and continuing to the present day. The largest and most detailed study was written by Manfred Bukofzer about ten years ago, and it has been followed by others. Recently, Frank Ll. Harrison has included valuable sections on the manuscript in his history of medieval British music.[2]

Every aspect of the Old Hall manuscript has been considered: its date, its organization, the composers represented in it, and the relation of the repertory to that of other manuscripts, both English and Continental. These investigations have thrown a great deal of light upon the history of English music around 1400, and, incidentally, when read in the order in which they were written, they make a fascinating record of the growth of musicology since 1900. In 1901, Barclay Squire could give no closer date for the manuscript than the middle of the fifteenth century.[3] Now, scholars are interested in exact decades, and contend for c. 1410 or c. 1420 as the date of

7

completion of the larger portion of the entries.[4] In 1933, the editor was "sometimes . . . forced to suppose that the members of the Chapel Royal who ventured to compose . . . were very imperfect or ill-trained musicians. Otherwise one must conclude either that the manuscript is so full of mistakes that it can never have been used as it now exists, or that musical ears tolerated in those days sounds which now strike us as thoroughly unmusical."[5] Now, the "thoroughly unmusical" procedures are not so puzzling. We have been taught to appreciate the competent and, at times, boldly original way in which many of the composers handled the contemporary idiom of the late *ars nova*.

This is not the place to summarize all the findings of the different scholars, partly because to do so would take up too much space, partly because the more important studies are readily available. Therefore I will review only such points as are pertinent to my topic and assume that the reader is already familiar with others, or can easily make himself so.

The chapter which follows adds no new knowledge, since it is merely an expansion of what has been stated briefly by Hughes, Bukofzer, Harrison, and others.[6] But because the Old Hall collection contains a large number of pieces in which the c.f. is treated as a melody voice—pieces written at a time when this type of treatment is found only occasionally in Continental collections—a detailed discussion of them is called for in a study of c.f. in the fifteenth century.

It happens that these compositions form a fairly unified group. They are related not only with respect to the manner of statement of the borrowed material, but also with respect to date, since the majority must have been written within a reasonably limited space of time. They were all copied by the scribe who originated the collection, the so-called Hand A. Scholars differ on the details of his dates, but all are in agreement that his activity ceased no later than c. 1420.[7] It is also agreed that some of the works in his hand date from the latter half of the fourteenth century, but since he was making a practical collection they must have been pieces still in use, which would indicate that most of them were written nearer 1400 than 1350. While the time span between the very earliest and the very latest works may be fairly large—approaching a half century—the indications are that a considerable number of them were written within the space of ten to twenty years. (See p. 40 below.)

The compositions are also related as to type, since most of them are conductus or derivatives of the conductus. Bukofzer has shown that the current of influence was running strongly from the Continent to England at this time.[8] French and Italian traits are clearly evident in the *caccia* Masses, the isorhythmic Masses and motets, the freely composed works in treble-dominated style, and in the pieces in "mannered" style, which in rhythmic complexity outdo even those written on the Continent. No matter how original these works may be, or how many English traits they may show, their dependence on developments of the late *ars nova* on the Continent is clear. With the conductus, the case is different. It became virtually obsolete in France after the thirteenth century, but continued to be cultivated in England throughout the fourteenth. The conductus of Old Hall, therefore, continue a tradition which is specifically English, and the treatment of the c.f., so far as it is motivated by the distinctive features of the type, can also be regarded as belonging to an English tradition. Certain parallels can be drawn with regard to Continental usage, but it is not necessary to assume a Continental origin for these usages.

The polyphonic conductus of the thirteenth century differed from the motet in several ways. It was provided with a single text which was pronounced simultaneously in all parts, while the motet was polytextual. The voices were written in approximately note-against-note style, as opposed to the rhythmic differentiation of the voices of the motet. The conductus was written in score, while the motet was written in *cantus collateralis*. (The voices were written individually, each being allotted a specific portion of the page.)[9] These features characterize the English conductus into the last half of the fifteenth century.[10]

Considering the limited period within which the conductus of Old Hall were written, it could be expected that they would be fairly homogeneous in style, but this is not the case. They show, in fact, considerable stylistic divergence amongst themselves—enough that they can be divided roughly into groups for the purpose of discussion.

First I consider the works in the simplest note-against-note style, written in longs and breves almost exclusively. Then I take up a fairly large number of works which show greater rhythmic variety. The parts are more independent of one another in rhythm, and note values shorter than the breve are used with some frequency. After these, I consider a few works which are relatively complex, both with regard to the rhythmic interrelation of the parts and with regard to the variety of note values used. Some of these are no longer written in score.

A classification on the basis of rhythm is necessarily inexact, but it is useful because other features of the writing can be related to it. On the whole, the works which are written in the simplest note-against-note style are the ones which display the most primitive harmonic traits[11] and the most conservative treatment of the c.f. They are the earliest in order of composition, and I have identified them as "simple conductus."

The works in which the voices have a greater degree of independence approach more closely the contemporary Continental style in harmony and rhythm. They are also the ones in which the c.f. was elaborated most freely. In the simple conductus the c.f. was quoted literally; the most that was done was to cause it to migrate from voice to voice. In the more complex conductus, the composer altered the contours of the c.f. to a greater or less extent by adding notes to it. Whether he knew it or not, he thereby raised his modest work to a position of considerable historical importance, for this type of elaboration was almost unknown in the fourteenth century, either in England or on the Continent, but became one of the most important ways of treating the c.f. in the second quarter of the fifteenth century.[12]

For the purposes of this study, then, the conductus of Old Hall are important largely because they are not a homogeneous group; because they show a stylistic development which indicates a desire on the part of the composers to bring the traditional English form into line with the style of the age; and because, in the field of c.f., they clearly show the transition from usages of the fourteenth century to those of the fifteenth.

The discussion which follows must be fairly detailed in order to demonstrate these developments, but I have kept it as brief as possible because it serves mainly as a preface to the following chapter, in which I consider this type of c.f. treatment after it has achieved widespread use.

The Simple Conductus

Example 1, an anonymous Sanctus, shows many primitive features. The c.f. is given to the middle voice, the one which usually carries it in these compositions.[13] The two other voices were added to it as counterpoints, but the writing is almost exclusively note against note, and the texture is chordal rather than contrapuntal. The shape of the added lines also indicates that the composer was much occupied with the vertical, harmonic aspect of the music. He chose the tones of the tenor to make proper intervals with the chant, the tones of the soprano to make proper intervals with the tenor,

EXAMPLE 1. Anonymous, Sanctus (*OH*, III, 28; *Gr. Sar.*, pl. 15+).

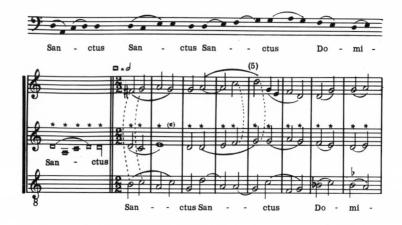

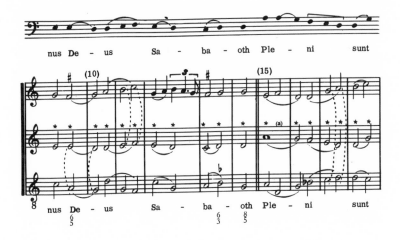

nus De - us Sa - ba - oth Ple - ni sunt

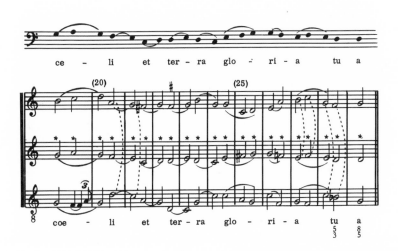

ce - li et ter - ra glo - ri - a tu a

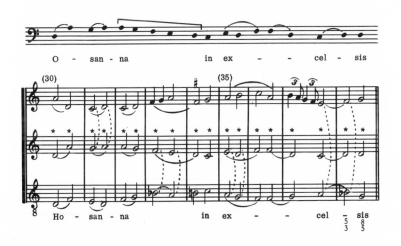

O - san - na in ex - - cel - sis

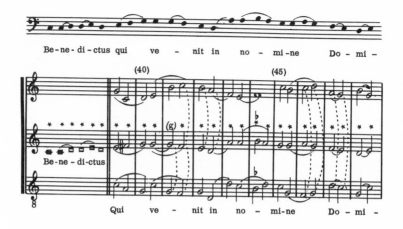

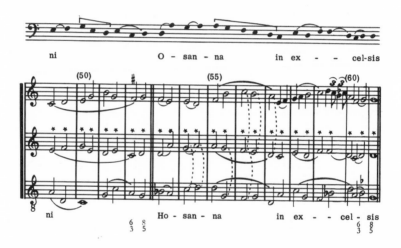

and obviously did not take much care with the melodic contour of these two parts. (See the disjunct lines of the bottom voice, m. 18-25, and the soprano, m. 22-28 and m. 39 ff.)

The respect he paid to the chant is quite remarkable. He retained its long phrases and allowed them to dictate the length of the phrases of the added voices, which do not pause at any points except the end of the sections of the chant. Harmonic cadential progressions can be found at other points (m. 9, m. 21, m. 25), but they do not break the flow of the lines. The distance between fully articulated cadences is unusually long in comparison with such distances in most music of the time.

Since the anonymous composer presented the c.f. almost entirely in notes of equal value (half notes in the example, breves in the original),[14] it may be that he was trying also to preserve the steady flow that he was accustomed to in performances of the Sanctus—whether chanted in monophonic form or sung in regulated values as a basis for improvised discant.

Furthermore, he kept almost exactly to the original ligatures, as can be seen by comparing the ligatures of the chant with those of the c.f.-bearing voice. The care taken to retain the entire outward appearance of the chant indicates the degree to which the original melody was respected. In setting it, the composer did nothing more than add harmonic sonorities.

The simplicity of the setting is matched by the primitive harmonic style. Parallel fifths are used freely and there are even some parallel octaves (indicated in the example). In measure 9 there is an instance of "differential" dissonance: the top and middle voices are both consonant with the bottom voice, but dissonant with each other.[15]

The treatment of the cadences indicates that the retention of the exact notes of the c.f. was not a passive procedure but a positive aim in this type of composition. At the time when the compilation of the Old Hall manuscript was begun (c. 1400, or shortly thereafter) the VII_6-I cadence had been firmly established as the definitive harmonic cadential formula (See ex. 2.)

EXAMPLE 2.
Cadential formula.

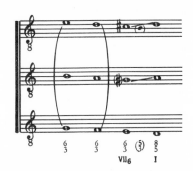

When the composer was free to choose, that is to say, when he was not occupied with a c.f., he used it almost invariably at important points such as the end of a composition or the end of a large section of a composition. It was used more than any other form at cadential points within a section, as well. Deviations from it are found chiefly at places where some type of deceptive or half cadence was wanted.[16]

The VII_6-I cadence calls for one or more sixth chords leading by downward scalewise motion to an $\frac{8}{5}$ on the tonic. In the two final chords, the essential movement of the top and middle voices is upward by step while the tenor—the bottom voice—moves down a step. Ornamentations may alter the details of this motion, but contrary stepwise motion remains the basic pattern.

The cadences of the Gregorian melodies, however, often involve the repetition of the final tone. Since this does not agree with the movement of any of the three voices in the standard harmonic cadence, the only alternatives the composer has are to change the chant or, if he wishes it to remain absolutely untouched, to alter the harmonic formula for the cadence. Also, many Gregorian cadences involve the descent of a second to the final tone, so that unless the c.f. is given to the bottom voice, rather than the middle, the composer is faced with the same problem and has the same alternatives for its solution. In these conductus settings, when an adjustment has to be made, it is made in the harmony, so that a variety of nonstandard cadential chords result. Only in the most complex conductus is the adjustment made in the c.f. (See ex. 13.)

In example 1, measure 52, the c.f. ascends a step at the cadence, so the normal harmonic cadence is made ($\frac{6}{3}$-$\frac{8}{5}$), but all the other phrases end with the repetition of a tone in the c.f., so an unusual harmonic form of the cadence is used (m. 13-14, 28-29, 38, and 60-61). The most unusual forms occur at measures 13-14 and 60-61, where all three voices deviate from the standard pattern of movement. The two upper repeat the same tone and the lower skips down a third. This amount of deviation is found only in the simplest settings.[17] In other conductus, the two outer voices are made to conform to the pattern of upward and downward stepwise movement, regardless of what the c.f. does. The result is that when the c.f. repeats the final note the harmonic cadence is $\frac{6}{4}$ - $\frac{8}{5}$ (see ex. 3a-b), and that when it descends a step to the final note the cadence is $\frac{6}{5}$ - $\frac{8}{5}$ (see ex. 3e-f). Various other cadences in which ornamentation of the lines causes a modification of the bald harmonic progressions are shown in example 3c, d, and g.[18] In example 3h, i, and j are shown other ways of making the cadence. Example 3j is one of the most unusual. The one thing common to most of the cadences is an $\frac{8}{5}$ chord as the final, but in this instance the c.f. is only a third above the bottom voice. This sonority must have been considered not very suitable for the end of a section, as a chord containing a third is seldom used in this location.[19] In this case, the fifth above the bottom voice is supplied by an added red note in the manuscript.[20]

Examples 4-13 supply many more instances of cadences, all of which have been marked with figures. It will be seen that, whenever the c.f. permits, the standard cadence is used. The freely composed conductus copied by Hand A give further proof that the variant forms are used only when necessitated by the c.f., for in them the standard form is used almost exclusively.

While settings of the Sanctus such as those quoted in examples 1 and 5 are, by every indication, products of the fourteenth century, the conductus in examples 4, 8, 9, and 11 must represent a style of writing which was cur-

EXAMPLE 3. (a) Leonel, Sanctus (*OH*, III, 8), (b) Typp, Sanctus (*OH*, III, 38), (c) Anonymous, Sanctus (*OH*, III, 26), (d) Anonymous, Sanctus (*OH*, III, 20), (e) Anonymous, Sanctus (*OH*, III, 19), (f) Lambe, Sanctus (*OH*, III, 11), (g) Anonymous, Sanctus (*OH*, III, 27), (h) Anonymous, Sanctus (*OH*, III, 18), (i) Leonel, Sanctus (*OH*, III, 16), (j) Leonel, Sanctus (*OH*, III, 37).

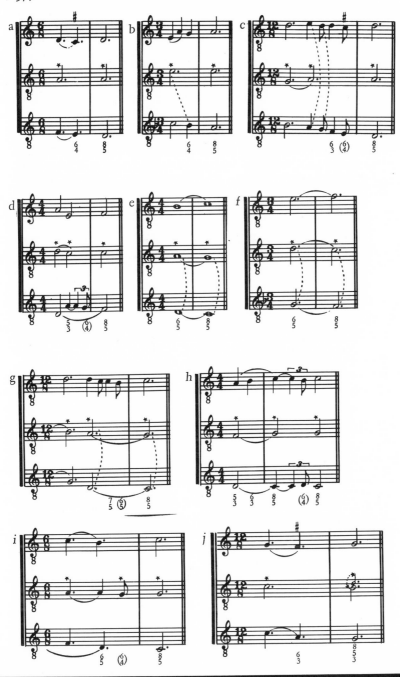

rent around 1400 and shortly thereafter. Chirbury, Typp, and Leonel are named as composers, and we are fortunate enough to know something about the lives of two of them. Leonel died in 1445,[21] so that, allowing him a creative career of forty to forty-five years, we can assume that his earliest compositions date from about the turn of the century. The first record of Chirbury is in 1421,[22] which indicates that he, too, did not start writing until about the same time.

In comparison with the earlier works, the compositions of these men show greater rhythmic activity in all the voices, especially in the treble. The c.f. does not flow steadily in notes of even length, but is expressed in a variety of values ranging from the minim to the breve and longa.[23] Under these conditions the ligatures of the original cannot be strictly retained, since only a limited number of note values can be expressed in ligature. Hence, the c.f. no longer keeps so closely to the original appearance of the Gregorian notation.

The phrases of the accompanying voices are not so completely determined by those of the c.f. There is a tendency to shorten them and increase the number of cadences. In example 4a, by Leonel, there is a cadence after almost every word of the text. (Phrases are indicated by brackets.) The outer voices not only come to a momentary standstill; they also perform the customary cadential movements (up a second in the treble, down a second in the tenor). A great variety of penultimate chords results, depending on the movement of the c.f. The placement of a cadence in the middle of a word (ex. 4b-c) shows an even greater degree of emancipation from the phrase structure of the c.f.

The harmonic style of these settings is also less crude. Parallel octaves largely disappear and parallel fifths become less common. The preference of the English for the conductus is often cited as evidence of their conservatism, but these traits are definitely progressive. The harmonic refinement, the shorter phrases, and the livelier and more varied rhythms indicate, in sum, that the composers were attempting to bring the conductus more into line with the style of contemporary Continental music.

Even though the c.f. does not completely dictate every aspect of the composition, and the accompanying voices have a greater degree of musical independence, the integrity of the chant melody is not seriously impaired. It is given note for note, and all of its important cadences are associated with cadences in the other voices. When the movement of the c.f. demands it, the unusual cadential forms are freely used.

THE MIGRANT CANTUS FIRMUS

Before taking up a further stage of the development of the conductus, it is necessary to consider certain other treatments of the c.f. which had been used by the English in the fourteenth century. Bukofzer has described the device of migration—the situation "where the plainsong wanders from one voice to another in succession"[24] instead of remaining in a single one—and has also pointed out the implications of this manner of statement with regard to the technique of composition. Migration would necessarily bring about certain modifications of the normal method of writing the voices in

EXAMPLE 4. (a) Leonel, Sanctus (*OH*, III, 8), (b) Typp, Sanctus (*OH*, III, 13), (c) Anonymous, Gloria (*OH*, III, [8]).

succession, so that it has historical significance as a forewarning "that the successive composition of superimposed voices, the traditional medieval technique of polyphonic composition, was nearing its end, and that composers were beginning to turn to simultaneously conceived parts."[25] My interest, however, lies not in the broad question of historical significance, but in the narrower one of the treatment of the c.f. itself.

Presumably it was necessary for the composer to devote some time and thought to planning the migrations before proceeding to write the remainder of the composition, and this fact alone brings up questions of various sorts. Why was the procedure used at all, and why was migration undertaken at some points and not at others? Was it used as a means of obtaining variety in the presentation of the c.f., which at the same time would not entail any drastic change that might impair its identity? Was the c.f. placed in another voice because of considerations of range? Was it because of considerations of the formation of the cadence? An analysis of several of the compositions with migrant c.f. will show that these questions, while they seem simple enough, cannot be given offhand answers.

An anonymous Sanctus (ex. 5a-h) given in two versions, one from the Old Hall manuscript and one from the Fountains fragment, is probably the most primitive, both harmonically and rhythmically, of the compositions in which the c.f. migrates.[26] In every case, migration downward occurs just before a cadence (compare ex. 5a-b with ex. 5c-d, etc.). The reason the c.f. migrates from the middle voice to the bottom cannot be because the range is too low for the former, as the c.f. only descends to f and that note is given to the middle voice twice (*OH*, III, 20, brace 1, m. 1, and p. 21, brace 2, m. 5). However, these f's both occur at the beginning of a phrase. Whenever the c.f. phrase ends on f there is migration to the bottom voice. When the c.f. phrase ends on c′ it remains in the middle voice. Since the tenor is always a fifth below the middle voice at the final $\frac{8}{5}$ chord of a phrase, it follows that all final chords are $\frac{8}{5}$ on f in this composition. Had the c.f. been left in the middle voice in the phrases ending on f, the tenor would have had to go down to B♭ to make the fifth below it. As it never goes below c, this would be one tone out of its range. Hence, if range is the reason for migration in this composition, the shift must have been made not for the sake of the middle voice, the main carrier of the c.f., but *for that of the bottom voice*.

The composer may have had other reasons for changing from voice to voice, but none that comes to mind seems very compelling. A possible one may have been concern for tonal unity, since he has arranged that all cadences shall be on f. Yet the restriction of the cadences to the tonic only is certainly not called for by the practice of the time. Cadences on both B♭ and f, degrees a fifth apart, would be quite consistent with the style, although it is also possible that the composer did not consider the note B♭ suitable for a cadence.

EXAMPLE 5. (*a-b*) Anonymous, Sanctus (*OH*, III, 20). (*c-d*) Anonymous, Sanctus from Fountains fragment (*OH*, III, [76-77]). (*e-f*) Anonymous, Sanctus (*OH*, III, 21). (*g-h*) Anonymous, Sanctus from Fountains fragment (*OH*, III, [77-78]).

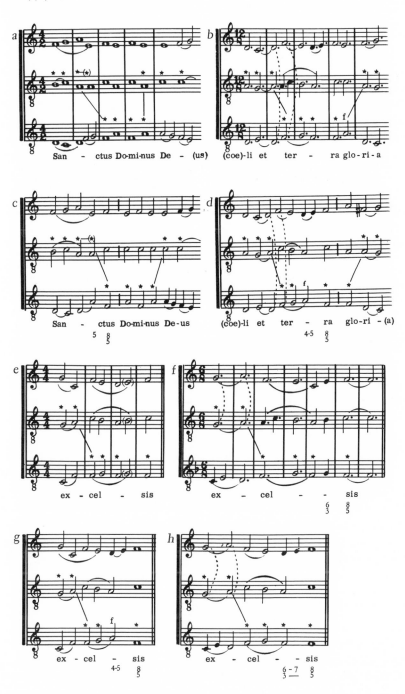

In any case, none of these explanations seems to be the only plausible one. Migration was apparently not undertaken in this composition to avoid some sort of practical problem, so the possibility cannot be excluded that it was employed for an esthetic reason—for the sake of gaining variety in the presentation of the c.f. This does not fit badly with the fact that the migration is not haphazard. A pattern can be observed, since it occurs at all places where there is a cadence on f.

Another anonymous Sanctus (ex. 6a-f) discloses no less than six points where migration takes place, although the last two are repetitions of two previous spots owing to the use of the same music for the two "hosanna" sections. (Compare ex. 6b-c and ex. 6e-f. I have used question marks to indicate doubtful c.f. notes.) Here, again, there is a consistent pattern— migration occurs whenever the c.f. has the notes e-f-e-d. This figure marks the low point of the range of the plainsong, but as the lowest note is d and as the middle voice descends as low as e (*OH*, III, 18, brace 2, m. 2) it hardly seems that range alone furnishes a very urgent reason for migration. In order to encompass every note of the chant the middle voice would have to descend only to d, a major second lower than it already does. One of these d's, however, is the final note of a cadence (ex. 6b). If it were kept in the middle voice the tenor would be forced down to G, a perfect fourth lower than the lowest note it touches. In this case it seems quite plausible that consideration of the range of the lowest voice caused the composer to choose migration. This choice may then have suggested the idea of the pattern of migrating every time the group of notes e-f-e-d occurs in the c.f.

The migration at the cadence (ex. 6b, m. 4) also allows the standard $\frac{6}{3}$-$\frac{8}{5}$ harmonic formula, as the c.f. descent of a step (e-d) is the proper tenor movement for the cadence. However, every migration is harmonized by one or more sixth chords leading to an $\frac{8}{5}$ on d, although there is no indication that they are cadential points. (See especially ex. 6d-e, where the $\frac{8}{5}$ comes in the middle of a ligature, and ex. 6a, where either the chromatic progression c'-c'♯ in the upper voice—m. 2-3 —or an e♭ in the lower would be required to make a cadence.) There is, then, no indisputable evidence that the desire for a standard cadence was a motivating factor in choosing the points of migration. Furthermore, the composer has no scruples about leaving the c.f. in the middle voice and using the variant $\frac{6}{5}$-$\frac{8}{5}$ form of the cadence when migration would produce the standard form.

Here, again, neither of the explanations advanced is sufficiently good to exclude the supposition that most of the migrations were undertaken for the sake of variety in the presentation of the c.f. (This composition also illustrates that migration may start and end in the middle of a ligature. The complete ligature must have been built up after the preliminary allotment of c.f. notes to the various voices. See ex. 6a, m. 4; ex. 6d, m. 3-4; etc.)

In the two preceding examples the shift of the c.f. to the lower voice does away with the need for crossing of parts. This is probably incidental, since voice crossing is not foreign to the conductus, and in an anonymous Agnus, which is about as primitive in style as the Sanctus cited in example 5, it is used interchangeably with migration. (See ex. 7a-c, *OH*, III, 113ff.) In three settings of the same phrase, the middle part sometimes carries the c.f. below the lowest voice, but at other times the c.f. migrates

EXAMPLE 6. (a-f) Anonymous, Sanctus (*OH*, III, 18-19).

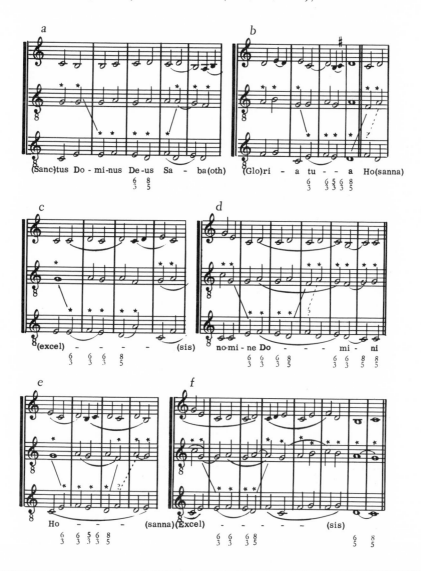

for the low tones. There is no technical advantage in stating the c.f. in one voice or the other, and the time spent in the new location may be brief. (Note migration for two notes only, ex. 7*b*, m. 5 and, in all probability,

EXAMPLE 7. (a-c) Anonymous, Agnus (*OH*, III, 113, 114, 115; Gr. Sar., pl. 17+).

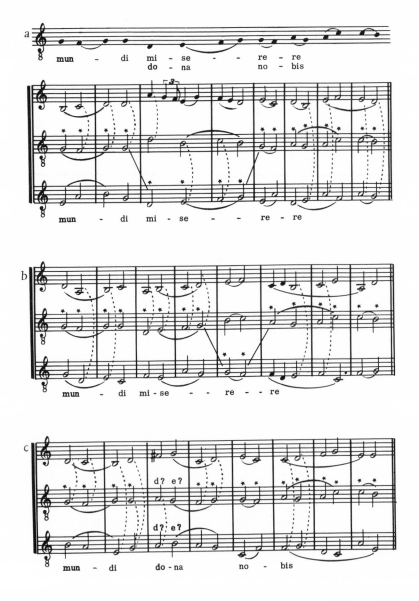

ex. 7c, m. 3.)[27] Migration does occur at the word "*miserere*" in every case, but, if this is a plan, it is a vague one.

The findings in these three simple conductus are clear enough with regard to what was done and what was not, and they throw some light on the question of *why* migration was used. We see that the c.f. is given only to the middle and bottom voices, not to the treble; the middle voice is still the chief carrier of the c.f.; migration is not undertaken because the c.f. goes completely beyond the range of the middle voice; migration may occur at any point in the phrase, although there is some discernible pattern in its use. Migration may be associated with the standard cadential pattern, but it is not always used in those cases where it would make a standard form possible (i.e., in order to avoid a variant form which will inevitably result if the c.f. is allowed to stay in the same voice). It does give a certain amount of variety in the presentation of the c.f. without genuinely altering its original shape, since all the notes of the melody are actually given; they are simply produced by one voice instead of another.

These are not the broadly organized patterns of migration which are found in the works of Dufay, and the conclusion is inescapable that at this early date the device was valued primarily as an ornament of composition; that formal and technical considerations were of secondary importance and did not dictate its use. Nevertheless, migration does at times aid in the solution of technical problems, as the following compositions show.

The first of these, a Sanctus of Chirbury (ex. 8a-c), is slightly more elaborate in style than those cited immediately above, and may well have been written after 1400. (See pp. 14-16.) Fewer parallel fifths are used, and many of the cadences are of the $\frac{6}{3}$-$\frac{8}{5}$ type. The voices are more varied rhythmically, the upper voice especially being given a number of notes of short value.

In addition, the technique of migration is extended in this work, since the c.f. is given at one time or another to all three voices, although the middle voice still carries it for the most part. Migrations to the top voice always occur at the high points of the range of the chant (the notes d′-e′-f′), but as the middle voice rises to e′ more than once (ex. 8b, m. 5; ex. 8c, m. 6), range can hardly be considered an imperative cause for migration. Low range can certainly be excluded as a reason for migration to the lowest voice, as the c.f. notes given to it force it a couple of tones higher than it goes anywhere else in the composition. It would seem to have been more natural to give these tones to the middle voice, as they lie completely within its range (see ex. 8b, m. 5-6; ex. 8c, m. 6-7), but when they are placed in the tenor the descending scale line of the c.f. can be harmonized by the commonly used progression of a series of sixth chords leading to an $\frac{8}{5}$, something which could not have been done if the notes had been placed in either of the upper voices.

Variant forms of the cadence are still used when the c.f. calls for them

EXAMPLE 8. (a-c) Chirbury, Sanctus (*OH*, III, 34-35; Gr. Sar., pl. 16+).

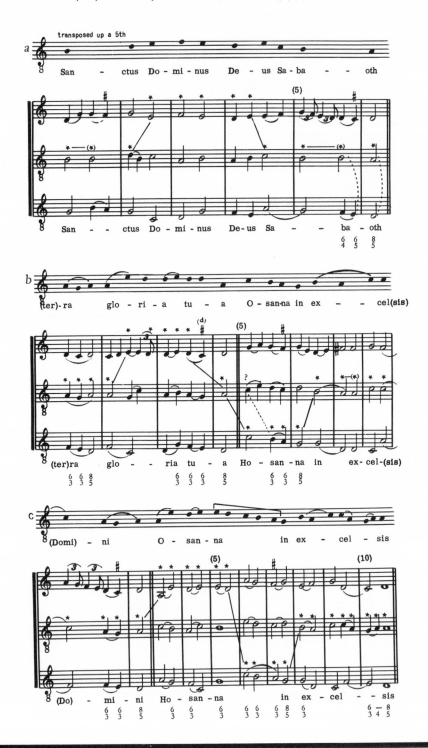

(ex. 8a, m. 5-6; ex. 8c, m. 9-10), except at one place where the c.f. cadences by the drop of a fourth, d′ to a (ex. 8b, m. 3-4). If the c.f. had been left in any one voice at this point, it would have created a very awkward situation, but by moving it from the top to the middle voice, the composer neatly solves the problem. This is the first clear instance of the employment of migration to assist in making a good cadence.

A Sanctus by Typp, written in a style about as advanced as the previous example, has migration from the middle to the bottom voice (ex. 9a-c).

EXAMPLE 9. (a-c) Typp, Sanctus (*OH*, III, 12, 13, 14; c.f. transposed up a second; Gr. Sar., pl. 15+).

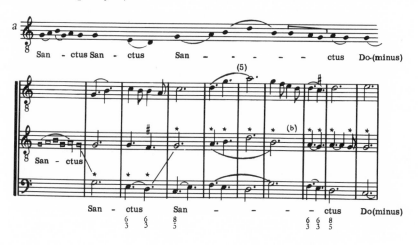

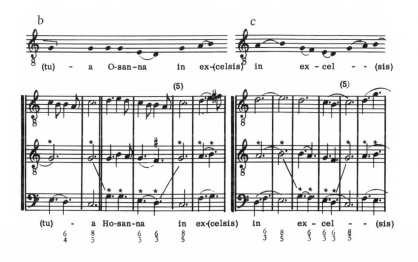

The shifts occur whenever the c.f. touches its lowest tones, and seem to be clear-cut cases of migration for the sake of range. Even though this may be the primary cause for migration, the composer contrives a good cadence in somewhat the same way as is shown in example 8b by returning the c.f. to the middle voice at a point where it leaps the interval of a fourth (ex. 9a, m. 2-3). He evidently felt this was a satisfactory way of treating the leap, for he repeats the procedure every time the fourth appears in the chant (ex. 9b, m. 4-5; ex. 9c, m. 4-5).

The interest in good cadences is also illustrated by the treatment of the chant in measure 8 of example 9a. The c.f. descends a step from a to cadence on g, a melodic movement which would lead to one of the variant cadential forms if both the a and g were harmonized. The composer, while literally stating every note of the original melody, actually violates its original form when he cadences on a (the penultimate note) and forces the real final note, g, into the position of a subsidiary melodic decoration, an anticipation of the following g on the word "*Dominus*." The possibility of making a standard cadence on the note a is evidently sufficient reason for a procedure which is not found in the simpler conductus. Nevertheless, variant cadential progressions are not excluded at the ends of phrases. (See ex. 9b, m. 1-2.)

The Change of Pitch Level in the Cantus Firmus

One other method of manipulating the c.f. is to change its pitch level. In most cases, the c.f. is raised a fifth or a fourth and is kept at that level throughout the composition. Such a change of pitch does not alter the outward appearance of the chant, but in most cases it brings about a real alteration in its sound, as accidentals necessary to keep the mode the same at the new level are not used. Thus a c.f. in the first mode (on D), a minor mode, when transposed up a fourth to G will be in the seventh mode, which is major unless the third is flatted. This is usually not done. Furthermore, whether the c.f. is transposed or not, accidentals foreign to the mode may be introduced. (See ex. 10, m. 2; ex. 1, m. 25 and 39; ex. 12d, m. 6; and also ex. 4a, m. 6-7, which contains a chromatic half step between f' and f'♯.)

It is apparent that composers felt no obligation to adhere strictly to the mode of the plainsong when they quoted it in a polyphonic work. They sometimes omitted necessary accidentals or signatures when they transposed it; they often added extraneous accidentals—whether they transposed it or quoted it on pitch. This is done in compositions in which every other aspect of the liturgical melody is scrupulously respected (individual notes, phrases, even ligatures). It is a reflection of the colorful "accidentalism" of the style. The addition or omission of sharps and flats did not represent as significant a change of the nature of the c.f. to them as it does to us, with our more regulated concepts of the modes.[29] (Irregularities of this sort become less frequent in the later fifteenth century, but they still occur. It is necessary to remember that when we use the term "transposition" we often have to understand it in a special sense, just as we do with many other terms proper to tonal music.)

EXAMPLE 10. Anonymous, Agnus (*OH*, III, 100).

The device of shifting pitch level is comparable to that of migration in a certain sense. It is a rather mechanical means which allows the composer to state the c.f. in a manner somewhat different from the original—since he alters its position on the staff—but it also allows him to remain true to it in the sense that he is not called upon to depart from its form or contours.

In those compositions in which the interval of transposition changes one or more times there is slight change of contour since, at the moment of "modulation," a melodic interval of the original must be changed. For instance, in example 11a, measures 3-4, the c.f. in the middle voice moves down a second only (d'-c'), owing to a change in "modulation," although in the original melody there is a skip down of a sixth at this point (a-c).

This Sanctus by Typp (ex. 11a-e) is fairly advanced in rhythmic and melodic style and displays migration to all three voices as well as change of transposition.[30] An attempt to find the reasons behind the changes of transposition brings the same indefinite results that were obtained in the investigation of migration. The transpositions were made so that the c.f. ends every important section on d', the tonic, although in the original melody the sections end on a as well. As mentioned before, there are too many compositions which cadence on other degrees than the tonic, both in this

group of conductus and in other early fifteenth-century music, to give satisfactory support to the idea that the composer felt bound to cadence on the
tonic only. Nor can excessive range of the original have forced the use of
"modulations," for they actually have the effect of making the range greater
—extending it from a ninth to a twelfth. (Incidentally, the extension of the
range makes migration a necessity at some points. At m. 1 of ex. 11*d*, the
c.f. is so high that it can only be given to the top voice.) The shifts of pitch
dispose of the downward skips of a sixth in the original melody (see
ex. 11*a*, m. 3-4; ex. 11*c*, m. 5-6), but skips of a sixth or greater may occur
in the style, so this, too, affords no convincing reason why the device was
used.

One cannot exclude the explanation that transposition, like migration, is
employed because it gives variety in the presentation yet does not interfere
with the proper succession of the c.f. notes.

With regard to migration in Typp's Sanctus, we find that demands of
range would not have forced the composer to shift the chant to the bottom
voice, since it goes no lower when in that voice than it does when in the
middle voice. Neither are the migrations made in order to achieve standard
cadential harmonies, as most cadences in the c.f. involve the repetition of
the final tone. In every case the composer uses the variant form, $\frac{6}{4}$-$\frac{8}{5}$. However, he contrives a cadence at the moment of migration (ex. 11*b*, m. 2-3),
at a point where it would have been impossible were the c.f. kept in one
voice. Except for the migrations to the treble, the device, in this work also,
seems to be used for the sake of the variety it offers.

The end of the composition (ex. 11*e*) offers a problem. It cannot be

EXAMPLE 11. (a-e) Typp, Sanctus (OH, III, 4-6; Gr. Sar., pl. 15+).

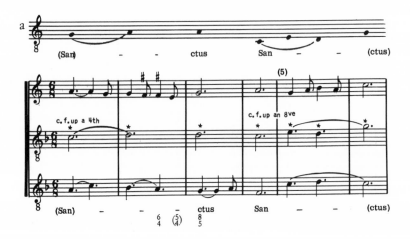

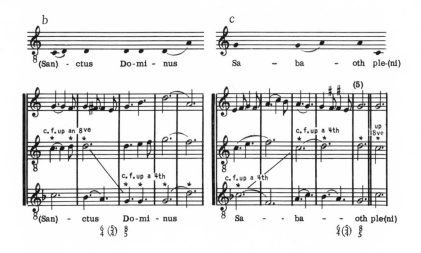

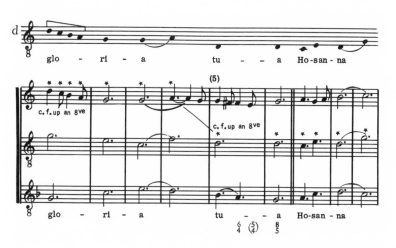

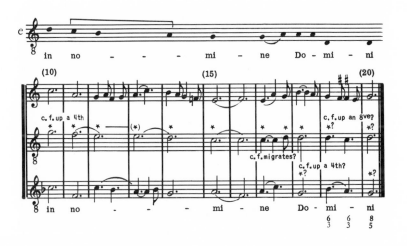

established with certainty whether the c.f. migrates to the bottom voice or whether it remains in the middle voice with a change in transposition. The latter alternative seems more probable, as in every other case in this piece transposition has been used wherever necessary to make the c.f. voice end the phrase on d. Whichever voice carries the c.f., the fact remains that it contains notes which are not given in the Gregorian melody. Furthermore, these notes make the standard $\frac{6}{3}$ - $\frac{8}{5}$ cadence possible. The question is whether they were interpolated by the composer or were present in the version of the chant he used. As is always the case with a few isolated notes, it is not possible to answer with certainty. It could well be asked, however, if the composer wishes so much to use the standard cadential progression that he is willing to interpolate notes, why he does not do so at all the other cadences. Why are they all $\frac{6}{4}$ - $\frac{8}{5}$ cadences?[31]

FREE TONES IN THE CANTUS FIRMUS

While the Sanctus of Typp remains an ambiguous case, a Sanctus and Agnus by Leonel (*OH*, III, 36, 118) and another Sanctus by Typp (*OH*, III, 38) give clear evidence of the addition of notes for the purpose of forming the standard cadence. It is noteworthy that in all the cases where this is done the extra notes either are added *after* a phrase is completed[32] or are written in red and sounded simultaneously with the c.f. (See ex. 12c, last measure. The red notes lie above the tones of the c.f. A single red note is also introduced above the c.f. in ex. 12e, m. 3.) By adding notes, the com-

EXAMPLE 12. (a) Leonel, Agnus (*OH*, III, 118; *LU*, p. 61). (b-c) Leonel, Sanctus (*OH*, III, 36, 37; Gr. Sar., pl. 17+). (d-e) Typp, Sanctus (*OH*, III, 39, 40; Gr. Sar., pl. 17+).

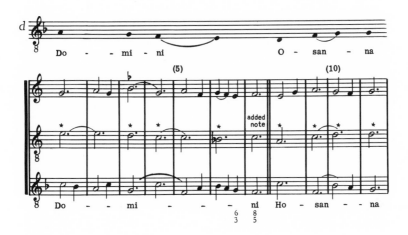

poser can maintain the integrity of the c.f. and at the same time satisfy the
harmonic demands of the style. He can give the cadence in proper harmonic form even in cases where the c.f. itself would prevent it (ex. 12a, c,
and d).

In the Sanctus by Leonel several notes not in the Sarum version of the
chant are used in the course of the piece. (See *OH*, III, 36 brace 3, m. 1 and 4;
p. 37, brace 1, m. 2 and 4, and brace 2, m. 5; also ex. 12c, m. 2.) Since there
are so many of these foreign notes, since they are always given the value of
a minim (the shortest note value used in the work), and since they have
the specific musical function of making standard cadences possible, it is
impossible to avoid the conclusion that they were added by the composer
himself. Granting this to be so, one must further admit that the composer's
purpose in adding the notes was to bring the conductus still closer to the
rhythmic and harmonic characteristics of the dominant style of the time.

Leonel's treatment of the c.f. in this Sanctus represents a significant step
away from the traditional methods shown in the conductus previously considered. The manipulations undertaken in those works—migration, "modulation," rhythmic variety, and even the addition of notes to the ends of
phrases—left the c.f. intact for the most part. Whether the notes were given
on a higher or lower pitch level, or whether they were given in part to one
voice and in part to another, there was a minimum of tinkering with the
internal details. There was nothing which could be considered a transformation or reinterpretation of the Gregorian melody by the composer. Certainly the few added notes in Leonel's composition do not bring about a
transformation of the chant melody, but they clearly suggest that this could
occur if the procedure were carried further.

In the most complicated (hence, presumably the most advanced) of the
conductus settings, the approach to the prevailing style of the age can be
seen even more clearly. The rhythms are more nervous (there is much more
use of rhythmic patterns such as ♪♩, ♪♩♩♪ ; etc.), the cadences are
mostly of standard form, and the c.f. is ornamented to a greater or less
degree. One of the most advanced of all is the setting of the Marian antiphon, *Nesciens Mater*, by Byttering (ex. 13a-d).[33] Here the composer
displays the whole bag of tricks. The c.f. migrates to all voices, and is transposed up a second and down a fourth as well as stated on pitch. The
middle voice is not the chief carrier of the c.f., as it has been in other compositions. Both the soprano and tenor are more important in this respect.
In addition, the original melody is ornamented by a considerable number
of interpolated notes, especially at the cadences, which are all of the regular
type. (See ex. 13a, m. 3 and 6-7; ex. 13b, m. 8-9, ex. 13d, m. 4-6.)
The voices display a rhythmic independence and a variety of rhythmic patterns more characteristic of the style of the ballade than of the
conductus. With these cross rhythms and syncopations come numerous

EXAMPLE 13. (a-d) Byttering, *Nesciens Mater* (*OH*, I, 157, 157-158, 158, 158; *Pal. Mus.*, XII, 32).

appoggiaturas and syncopation dissonances, also characteristic of the ballade and not of the conductus, which uses consonant chords for the most part. (See ex. 13c, m. 2-6; ex. 13d, m. 3-6.)

This composition is written in score. The composer conceived it as a conductus and therefore, by implication, as a relatively modest work. It is, however, no longer a harmonization of a simple statement of the c.f., but a contrapuntal setting of a c.f. paraphrase. It represents an advanced stage of the English conductus in its approach to the ballade style, and it is, in fact, a piece in Continental style notated in an English manner.

One more group of compositions remains to be considered. All are settings of Sanctus and Agnus for feasts and Sundays, and they bring up another point—the possible influence of the class of chant on the type of setting.

Dom Anselm Hughes has shown that the arrangement of Sanctus and Agnus in the manuscript gives evidence that "points to a discrimination in the minds of the musicians between what, for want of better terms, we might call Festal and Ferial chant . . ."[34] Scribe A has divided both Sanctus and Agnus into three subgroups. He entered first a series based entirely on festal chants, followed this with a series based on ferial chants, and finally entered another series based on festal chants.[35]

It might be expected that the discrimination which is apparent in the order in which the compositions were entered would also extend to the music—that the works would reflect the rank of the services, and that the settings of festal chant would be somehow more elaborate than those of ferial. But in the first two subgroups, both of Sanctus and Agnus, such a musical distinction is not apparent. (I leave the third subgroup out of consideration for the moment.)

Example 1 (a ferial setting) and examples 5, 6, and 7 (festal settings) are equally primitive in style. Examples 8 and 12b-c (ferial), and examples 9 and 11 (festal) are about equally advanced in style. (In addition to general aspects such as harmony and rhythm, they are similar with respect to ornamentation of the c.f., change of transposition, and migration.)

Furthermore, I find no evidence of attempts to elaborate the festal settings by other, more mechanical means. One such means is scoring in more than the usual three parts; but the only conductus in four parts is based on on a ferial chant. (*OH*, III, 133. I am referring, of course, only to works of the first two subgroups.) Migration is another sort of mechanical elaboration which could be undertaken even in musically primitive settings, and it is true that the musicians showed a preference for it in the settings of the festal chants of the Sanctus. (Migration occurs in five settings of festal chant, and in only one of ferial.) But, again, the evidence is not clear. The one ferial setting which employs migration (ex. 8) is fully as elaborate as any of the five festal compositions. The Agnus do nothing to clarify the situation. Migration occurs in one festal setting, but it also occurs in one ferial.

As far as I can see, the compositions of the two classes are about equal in character. Both ferial and festal settings which were written earlier are simpler in style, while those which were written later are more elaborate. The discrimination is purely one of organization up to this point, but the situation is entirely different in the third subgroup. Like the first, it consists entirely of settings of festal chants, but these settings are unquestionably more elaborate.

The series is fairly extensive, consisting of ten Sanctus, and two complete and one incomplete Agnus. Four of the Sanctus and one of the Agnus are written in score. The Sanctus of Sturgeon will be left out of consideration, because it is entered by a later hand and because it makes use of the plainsong only in the intonations. Another, a Sanctus of Excetre, was entered by Scribe A, but it will not be considered, because it may be freely composed. If a plainchant was used, it was probably given to the top voice, but its source has not been discovered. It may be mentioned that the setting is the simplest in the series and that this is not inconsistent with the fact that Excetre is listed as a member of the Chapel Royal during the reign of Henry IV (d. 1413). He is apparently one of the older composers of this group.

The three conductus of Olyver (two Sanctus settings and one Agnus) approach the style of the freely composed French chanson more closely than does the *Nesciens Mater* (ex. 13). In all of them the c.f. is in the top voice, the melody voice of secular song, and two are notably complex in rhythm: the Agnus (*OH*, III, 141), and one of the Sanctus settings (*OH*, III, 81). In fact, the Agnus approaches the chanson so closely that I discuss it in the next chapter. Olyver had already arrived at the stage of the later c.f. settings on the Continent, although he did not write in the smooth, flowing style of the 1430's. (See exs. 18 and 25.)

These works depart from the older conductus style, but they also develop certain aspects of it. The three voices are rhythmically equivalent, though independent, and together make a homogeneous texture which is altogether unlike the differentiated texture of the chanson. This is true, even though the two lower parts generally move more slowly than the upper.

Olyver remained true to the conductus in other respects as well. He wrote a middle voice which was melodic, not an erratic filler part like the contratenor of the chanson. The middle voice of the conductus had always been a melody part. Indeed, it had to be when it carried the c.f., and Olyver continued to write it so even when he placed the c.f. in an upper part. Also, the middle voice of the conductus differed from the contratenor in that it had a range of its own. It lay above the tenor, on the whole, and, as has been pointed out by Harrison, it was notated in a higher clef.[36]

What we find in these works is in part straight borrowing, in part adaptation. The style which results is something new—not the note-against-note writing of the conductus, nor the layered part writing of the chanson, but a counterpoint consisting of voices approximately equal in character.[37]

The remaining pieces of this series are not written in score, and so do not have the appearance of a conductus. In the case of a Sanctus of Tyes, (OH, fo. 99ᵛ; *OH*, III, 94), the manner in which the voices are entered may be the result of an accidental circumstance. Bukofzer has noted that Scribe A never wrote scores of more than three voices. In two instances where he had to deal with a four-voice composition he made the entry in a peculiar way by writing three voices in score and the fourth independently.[38] His reluctance to copy a score of more than this size may account for the separate entry of each of the four voices of the Tyes Sanctus, for the work has all the other characteristic features of a conductus. Much of the writing is note-against-note, as much as in many of the three-voice pieces in score. All voices are fully texted. The c.f. is carried by one of the lower parts and is entrusted with the intonations which ordinarily precede the polyphonic sections of a conductus. This voice can properly be called a tenor, but it is not so named. In fact, none of the voices is named— again characteristic of score format but not of *cantus collateralis*. These features lead me to believe that the piece was conceived as a conductus by the composer and that the exceptional form in which it appears in the manuscript may be due to a habit of the scribe.

An explanation of this sort will not suffice for five compositions of Leonel, since some of them are for three voices. They also show other features foreign to the conductus. In some instances, not all the voices are texted; in some, the lower parts are identified as tenor and contratenor; in some, full scoring is alternated with sections for two voices. Leonel approaches the motet more closely than Tyes in these external features; in addition, his idiom is more advanced, corresponding to Olyver's in the Agnus described above (i.e., in rhythmic texture, in melodic character of the voices, in free treatment of the plainchant, etc.). The pieces are of sufficient importance to justify describing each of them briefly.

A Sanctus for four voices (OH, fo. 96ᵛ-97; *OH*, III, 76) and its corresponding Agnus, also for four voices (OH, fo. 107ᵛ-108; *OH*, III, 136), have the plainchant in one of the lower parts. The borrowed melody is stated in its entirety in moderately ornamented form, and remains entirely in the one part, which is labeled tenor in the Agnus but is unnamed in the Sanctus. Three voices are provided with full text, while the contratenor has textual cues only. (The anonymous Gloria, OH, fo. 3, cited in n. 33, p. 435, is a parallel instance.) The rhythmic aspect of the two works is noteworthy. Words and phrases are constantly broken by short rests in order to produce a series of complementary entries in the different voices. This procedure reminds one of hocket to the extent that the voices rest alternately and then enter on a note of short value, but the entries are better described as rhythmic points of imitation. In any case, a procedure which focuses attention on alternating rhythmic patterns is as far removed as can be imagined from the simultaneous, complementary rhythmic movement of a normal conductus. Leonel uses elaborate French-style rhythms in many works, but here he deals with a feature of Italian style, in which imitative entries of this sort are common.

A Sanctus for three voices presents the chant, liberally ornamented, in the treble. (OH, fo. 94ᵛ-95; *OH*, III, 66.) The two lower parts are identified as tenor and contratenor, as they would be in the ballade, but all are provided with text when they are sounding. (This is not clear in *OH*, since the text of the contratenor is omitted in the first trio.) Possibly the most individual feature of this work is the treatment of the *Pleni* and *Benedictus* as duets. There is no such contrast of scoring in any of the conductus of Hand A. It is a feature which clearly met with approval, however, for duets are used in more than one of the conductus entered by later hands. Sturgeon follows Leonel exactly, by setting the *Pleni* and *Benedictus* as duets in his Sanctus. (It is written in score by Hand B, OH, fo. 92ᵛ; *OH*, III, 55 and [61].[39]

Another Sanctus for three voices (OH, fo. 93ᵛ-94; *OH*, III, 58) is so far advanced that I have found it convenient to discuss it in the next chapter among the later Continental settings of the c.f. (See ex. 24a-b. Note that Leonel is still using the dissonant style of the late *ars nova*, just as Olyver is in the Agnus of exs. 18 and 25.) The c.f. is stated in its entirety, divided between treble and contratenor, and treated most freely. Leonel calls the latter part a contratenor, even though it bears c.f., and presumably merely because it is a middle part. The lowest voice he calls tenor, apparently for no other reasons than its range and harmonic function. It does not share in the c.f. statement,[40] and is untexted except where it performs a duet with one of the upper parts—at *Dominus Deus* (ex. 24a) and *Gloria tua*. In sections for three voices it is provided with textual cues only. (See ex. 24b.)

All these works seem to me closer to the conductus than to the chanson or motet, despite the assimilation of many of the features of the two latter types. It seems correct to speak of them as advanced conductus or as conductus derivatives.

Another composition, a Sanctus for four voices (OH, fo. 95ᵛ-96; OH, III, 70), crosses a vague dividing line and I would prefer not to call it a conductus at all—even an advanced one. It is, rather, a movement in motet style which has some of the characteristics of conductus. The treble does carry the complete plainsong, but the two lower parts are slower-moving instrumental supports to the two upper. They are of equal range (they are written in the same clefs), they cross one another constantly, and, while they are not excessively disjunct, they make much more use of disjunct motion than the upper two. In short, the piece lacks the homogeneous texture which is the outstanding feature of the advanced conductus and the one which must be taken as decisive for purposes of classification.[41]

The last work of the group, a Sanctus of Pycard (OH, fo. 100ᵛ) is apparently incomplete and was not included in the edition of the manuscript. Only two voices are written out—a superius on the top half of the folio, fully texted, and a tenor on the lower half, untexted except for cues. As has been mentioned earlier in this chapter (n. 2), Harrison has shown that the work is actually complete as it stands, since the superius is written to be performed as a three-voice canon at the unison, and the tenor makes a fourth, supporting part. Pycard was partial to canon, but this one is of especial interest because it is based on a Sanctus melody which he quotes almost without alteration. The structure of the work sets it apart from the c.f. settings of this group, however, and relates it to the other canonic compositions of Old Hall.

These settings of Sanctus and Agnus bring to an end the account of the conductus entered by Hand A. They are all found in the first layer of the manuscript, but it can be seen that this layer itself consists of many layers of works of widely different character.

With respect to the treatment of the c.f., the works give us a detailed picture of progress, step by step, from an insular manner of setting which had been established in the fourteenth century to a well-developed paraphrase type in the style of the early fifteenth. One trait which runs throughout is the tendency to preserve the integrity of the original melody. This trait is clearest in the primitive settings where the composers cling to the exact form of the plainchant. The more advanced settings depart from the exact form, but they do present all the notes in their original order. In addition, most of these settings retain the original phrase structure, which indicates that the chant was considered as something more than a series of tones. (See chap. iii for a discussion of the manner of quotation in the tenor of the isorhythmic motet.) A cadence in the c.f. does not invariably call forth one in the setting, but it does so often enough that we can conclude that composers viewed the original as a melodic organism and that they wished to preserve this aspect of it. (As mentioned above, Leonel consistently ignored the phrase structure of the chants in a Sanctus and an Agnus, but here he had a special purpose in mind.)

Simple manipulation by means of migration does not interfere with the note order or the phrasing of the c.f., although it allows a certain variety in manner of presentation. Presentation at a pitch level different from that of the original does not interfere, either, although from our viewpoint it often brings about an important internal alteration, because it frequently changes the mode. Change of pitch level during the course of the piece does alter intervals of the chant, but only at the points where change occurs. The addition of free tones to the c.f. allows great opportunity for variety in presentation, but, even though it is possible by this means to convert the c.f. into an almost entirely new melody, the process need not, and usually does not, lead to a denial of the two aspects mentioned above.

With respect to harmony, we can see progress in the tendency to exclude parallel perfect intervals and abandon deviant cadential forms. On the other hand, the amount of dissonance increases with the approach to the complex rhythmic style of the late *ars nova*. The dissonance which results from syncopation appears especially arbitrary and crude, since it is not harmonically controlled. This aspect of the later works may seem to be a step backward from the relative consonance of the simple conductus. However, clarification of dissonance treatment was yet to come, even though it came very soon. The compositions of Sturgeon belong to the main body of the Old Hall repertory, and in them the dissonance is harmonically oriented. In this respect and many others, his works compare favorably with those of Dunstable. This is not surprising, since Sturgeon died in 1454, the same year as Dunstable, and was, therefore, probably of about the same age. Both men apparently were younger than Leonel and Olyver.

The development of other aspects of the writing can be summarized best, perhaps, by negative statements. On p. 9, above, I listed three points characteristic of the conductus. They fit the early works very well. They describe the later works poorly, however, for in these the music need not be written in score, all parts need not be provided with text, and the voices need not move in simultaneous rhythmic patterns. The one characteristic that all the compositions have in common is a relative melodic equality of voices.

The rate of development increases so rapidly in the later works that the composers can be seen for what they are. They are resourceful innovators, certainly not conservatives clinging stupidly to a traditional form. The extent of the development can be judged by reviewing two of the works of one man, the Sanctus of Leonel quoted in example 4a and that quoted in examples 24a-b. The first carries on directly the manner of the fourteenth century in the archaic forms of the cadences, the exposed parallel fifths, the unornamented c.f., and the compound duple meter. The second, much more refined in harmonic idiom, reveals the new concept of counterpoint, the new and far more sophisticated treatment of the plainsong, and the fusion of elements of motet and conductus. In addition, it shows a striking increase in Leonel's powers as a composer. The start-and-stop movement of the first is replaced by a continuous, expansive rhythmic flow, the short-breathed phrases by lines of great amplitude.[42]

It would be of great interest to know the precise number of years which intervened between the two works, but at present it is only possible to give maximum and minimum estimates. Leonel's death in 1445 makes it improbable that the first Sanctus was written much before 1400; the style of the work makes it improbable that it was written much after that date. According to Harrison, the second Sanctus would have been completed by 1413; according to Bukofzer, it could have been written as late as 1422.[43] This gives, then, a minimum time span of about ten years and a maximum of twenty, more or less. The lack of exact historical information is regrettable, but it does not prevent us from concluding that the music shows an advance of impressive magnitude even if we allow the maximum number of years.

We know also that other composers of the group were as progressive as Leonel, and that several men were involved in an upsurge of creative activity. Their work gives evidence of an inventiveness and a mental vigor which is surprising in view of the relatively quiet course of the fourteenth century, but which also explains how the English would be able, within the next few years, to take a leading position in music outside their own country.

It is generally agreed that the chief contribution the English made to European music was in the field of harmony, and it is known that they were making their influence felt in the late 1420's, when Dufay wrote the last movement of the *Missa Sancti Jacobi* as a *fauxbourdon*. It is difficult to avoid the conclusion, also, that their interest in melodic c.f. stimulated a corresponding interest among Continental composers, for it was just at this time that the latter began to write large numbers of compositions in which ornamented plainchant was used as a melody voice.

In the conductus of Old Hall the English anticipated a long future development in the field of c.f. treatment and probably established the pattern for it. They were to match this accomplishment later—and in the same general field—when they developed the Mass cycle on c.f. and established the main types of structure in this category.

2

The Cantus Firmus Elaboration

THE METHODS OF HANDLING the c.f. which are found in the conductus of Old Hall become of great importance in Continental composition in the second quarter of the fifteenth century. Judging from the manuscripts, it was not until about 1430 that ornamented c.f. was much used, but it then gained rapid and widespread popularity.

There are compositions of earlier periods which more or less clearly do anticipate the use of the c.f. as a primarily melodic part. The use of un-adorned Gregorian melody in the top voice of a composition was known in England as early as the late thirteenth century.[1] In a few compositions of Continental origin dating from the late fourteenth century the c.f. not only is used as a melody but is embellished as well.[2] These are isolated cases, however, and the treatment of the c.f. as a freely flowing melody may be considered as preëminently characteristic of the fifteenth century.

To distinguish between various ways of handling the c.f. current at the time, I have adopted the terms "c.f. setting," "c.f. paraphrase," and "struc-tural c.f." By "structural c.f." I mean one which is laid out in a rigid pat-tern, and which serves as a skeleton or "framework" upon which a compo-sition can be erected. This is the traditional type and up to this time was the most important one. Since such a framework was usually given to the tenor, I also refer to it more loosely as "tenor c.f."

I use the terms "c.f. paraphrase" or "c.f. elaboration" to describe the process by which a composer quotes a melody faithfully enough, but elabo-rates it freely as he goes along. By "c.f. setting" I mean to indicate a work in which the borrowed melody is provided with accompanying voices. The

42

first two terms, then, refer to the way in which the composer manipulates the borrowed melody itself; the last, the c.f. setting, refers to an entire polyphonic complex with c.f. as leading melody part. The techniques of elaboration and the various kinds of c.f. setting are taken up in this chapter. The structural c.f., which is entirely different in nature, is treated in the chapter following.

I have chosen 1450 as a convenient dividing line to separate works (in all categories) of the earlier part of the century from those of the latter part. Most of the works cited as examples in this chapter were written before that date. Since many compositions continued to be written in the older style after 1450, and since the discussion is mainly concerned with style and techniques, I have not hesitated to introduce some works which were written later.[3]

THE TREATMENT OF THE FREE TONES IN THE CANTUS FIRMUS SETTING

The c.f. setting normally consists of three voices, with the embellished c.f. in the highest part. In this position the c.f. functions much as the superius does in the three-voice chanson of the time. It is a melody part, often the most important one, and it is supported by the contrapuntal accompaniment of the two lower parts. The c.f. is, also, occasionally allotted to the tenor and, in a few instances, even given the position of the contratenor. Further details with regard to the settings, and especially with regard to the problems that arise when the c.f. is given to a voice other than the superius, will be taken up as the individual cases arise. The manner in which the composer embellishes the c.f. by adding free tones to it presents the most interesting problems and will be investigated first.

A number of studies have already been made of this aspect of c.f. treatment,[4] but while they have been conducted with great care, and often in great detail, they are in many ways unsatisfactory—partly because of dubious methods of analysis and partly because of a misconception of the function of the tones added to the chant by the composer. An instance of the latter is Ficker's term for the practice, "*Kolorierungstechnik*," which implies that the composer's intent is to add coloraturas or ornamentations to the given melody and brings to mind the techniques of instrumentalists and vocalists of the sixteenth century. Obviously, the procedures of both periods have in common the feature that notes are added to a preëxisting composition; it is also true that the chant is often highly ornamented by composers of the fifteenth century. The ornamentation, however, is an incidental result, not the chief end in view.[5]

In order to show this it is only necessary to adopt the methods of Ortiz and others who treat of the art of diminution in the sixteenth century. These writers organize their presentation by listing melodic intervals in order—from small to large—and by citing a number of suitable diminutions for each. This method can be applied to the chant settings of the fifteenth century, and that has, in fact, already been done briefly by Orel.[6] A list can be made of the various ornamentations of the unisons, seconds, thirds, and other intervals of the Gregorian melodies, and conclusions can be drawn as to the common and uncommon ways of treating each interval. This is an exact method of analysis and would be sufficient provided the technique actually were no more than one in which various more or less standardized figures were applied to a given melody. An analysis of a few compositions will show its virtues and shortcomings.

A start can be made with a list of the treatment of all the intervals of a second in the anonymous setting *Francisci patris*, the second verse of the hymn *En gratulemur hodie* (ex. 14). The hymn melody itself contains eighteen seconds, and in the setting eleven of these are left unornamented. Of the remaining seven, two rising seconds are ornamented by the fall of a second and the rise of a third (b-c′ in m. 3, d′-e′ in m. 6), and three falling seconds are ornamented by the fall of a third and the rise of a second (c′-b in m. 7-8, a-g in m. 8, a-g in m. 13). Two of them, however, are treated very elaborately. The second g-f (m. 8-10) is ornamented by the fall of a second, the skip up of a fourth, the scale-line descent of a sixth, and the skip up of a third. The second a-b (m. 13-14) displays a descent of a second, skip up of a fourth, further ascent of a second, and scalewise descent of a third. However, even these few measures show that certain ways of ornamenting a given interval are preferred and will be used more than once.

An anonymous Kyrie (ex. 15) shows a similar type of treatment. The fragment of chant quoted contains ten seconds, and in the setting three are left unornamented (a′-g′, m. 1; a′-g′, m. 4; and g′-f′, m. 4-5). Two rising seconds are ornamented, just as in example 14, with the fall of a second and rise of a third (g′-a′, m. 1-2, and g′-a′, m. 3-4). Three falling seconds are given another favored form of ornamentation, the anticipation of the final note of the interval (c″-b′, b′-a′, a′-g′, m. 2-3). Once more, as in example 14, two of the intervals are given somewhat more elaborate treatment. The rising second d′-e′ (m. 5-6) has the rise of a third, the rise of a second, and the fall of a third. The rising second g′-a′ (m. 7-9) is given a scalewise rise of a fourth followed by the drop of a third; in both cases the final inserted tone anticipates the final note of the interval.

Puer qui natus est by Benoit (ex. 16) shows traits similar to the two preceding compositions. A fair portion of the chant intervals are unornamented (three out of seven seconds in m. 1, 1-2, and 6). One second (m. 8-9) has the drop of a second and rise of a third seen in example 14, and another (m. 9-10) has the anticipation seen in example 15. Two others are given slightly more complicated treatment (m. 4 and 9).

There is a crucial difference between the methods of ornamentation in these examples and the improvised diminutions of the sixtenth century. The diminutions listed by Ortiz, Ganassi, Cerone, and others are designed to fill up specific spaces of time, a necessity since they are intended for the ornamentation of measured music. The purpose of diminution in the six-

EXAMPLE 14. Anonymous, *Francisci patris* (Mod B, fo. 33; c.f. *ibid.*, also, *Ant. Rom. Seraph.*, p. 729).

teenth century is quite uncomplicated: the added tones give the performer a chance for the display of virtuosity and add interest and brilliance to a composition by filling up space with short note values. No such simple statement can be made about the elaboration of a c.f. in the fifteenth century. The composers are using nonmensural source material, and a part of their technique is a very irregular spacing of the notes of the chant in the polyphonic setting. In one place, several tones of the c.f. may come in quick succession without intervening notes; in another, a dozen or more tones may be added. The larger number of tones in a given spot does not

EXAMPLE 15. Anonymous, Kyrie (Tr 90; *DTO*, 61, p. 63; *LU*, p. 25).

necessarily call for a display of virtuosity; the chief effect is to expand the phrase, or to convert one phrase into several, by widening the distance between tones of the c.f. The aims of the improvising musician of the sixteenth century and the composer of the fifteenth are quite different. In the earlier period the composer's manipulations may bring about some virtuoso display, but this is incidental to his main purpose.

While this type of analysis reveals a difference in intent, it also shows a resemblance in the techniques of both periods by indicating that certain standard methods of ornamentation were in use in the fifteenth century.

EXAMPLE 16. Benoit, *Puer qui natus est* (Mod. B, fo. 55; LU, p. 1505).

Examples 14, 15, and 16 show certain favored ways of filling out the ascending and descending seconds of the melody line. As they can be listed and categorized, these set figures lend themselves well to statistical treatment; however, the analysis also shows a good-sized residue of more elaborate, lengthier ornamentations which resist categorization because each one is different from the others. With regard to the three pieces analyzed, this is a somewhat minor difficulty—they are comparatively simple in style; but the minor difficulty becomes a major one in compositions where the ornamentation is elaborate and there is a much higher percentage of lengthy insertions. The same difficulty is encountered when one proceeds to classify the treatment of the intervals larger than a second. Each set of inserted tones tends to be different in some respect from the others, so that the statistical method leads to a list of unique cases. The precision which is the greatest virtue of the method is in this case its greatest fault, for it leads to a mass of results so cumbersome that they lose most of their value.

Experience shows another and opposite fault. The method is not only too discriminative; it is at the same time too blunt to give information of the most fundamental importance. A statistical analysis of a composition of the fourteenth century, an anonymous setting of the hymn *Christe redemptor omnium* (ex. 17), shows close agreement in methods of ornamentation with those already seen. Of twenty intervals of a second, seventeen are treated in familiar ways,[7] while only three show differences in ornamentation. The statistics give only a shadowy notion of the completely different character of this melody in comparison with the other three. The fourteenth-century hymn displays all the characteristics of freely composed ballade melodies of the late *ars nova*: the nervous, irregular rhythms, the ♪ ♩ ♪ syncopations and chains of syncopations, the appoggiaturas and rather jagged melodic outline. The three others, all from the fifteenth century, show the traits of Burgundian chanson style: the undulant melodic line, the flowing and varied rhythms in which the beat is not always sharply accented (as it is apt to be in the fourteenth-century ballade), frequent use of hemiola in triple meter, etc.

Any analysis which does not clearly reveal these differences is unsatisfactory because it fails to bring out a most essential point: that the Gregorian melodies have been adapted to dissimilar styles of writing and that the added tones have aided in this adaptation, regardless of whether they do or do not also serve to ornament the melodies. Statistics on melodic interpolations alone must fail to show this, as they are directed toward only a single aspect of a single element of a style—the intervallic make-up of the melody line. Nothing less than a consideration of all the elements which combine to make up a style is sufficient to make the discrimination. Despite the attractions of the statistical method, which has the outward appearance of the most careful scholarship, it must be rejected in favor of a general stylistic analysis. The broader, general approach, though it seems much less rigorous and painstaking, hence much less "scholarly," is the only one inclusive enough to give a real insight into the technique.

One further objection may be raised to the statistical approach. The accuracy of the method depends on the accuracy of the data and, unfortunately, this is often not all that could be desired. The setting of *Christe*

EXAMPLE 17. Anonymous, *Christe Redemptor omnium* (Apt, p. 56; *Hymns Anc. & Mod.*, p. 72).

Redemptor omnium (ex. 17) furnishes a good illustration. In this case the Sarum version of the hymn agrees more closely in certain respects with the elaborated melody of the setting than does the Roman,[8] so I have used it for purposes of analysis. Had the Roman version been used as a basis of comparison, the result would have been a somewhat different set of statistics. Neither set can be truly accurate, however, for it is apparent that the composer used a form of the tune which differs from both the Sarum and the Roman. Sometimes the c.f. is given in the source, as in example 14, but in a large number—possibly a majority—of cases, we do not have the exact version of the chant used by the composer and any statistics we might gather would be bound to be partially in error.

The discovery of the cumbersome and inadequate aspects of this method has, even so, given a clue for further investigation. Other compositions can be examined to determine whether they, too, give evidence of stylistic adaptation of the chant melody. A fragment of an Agnus by Olyver (ex. 18)

EXAMPLE 18. Olyver, Agnus (*OH*, III, 141; *Gr. Sar*, pl.18+).

from the conductus stratum of Old Hall shows how the c.f. is treated by an English composer of the early part of the century. A comparison with the previous compositions (exs. 14-16 and even ex. 17) does show differences in the character of the melodies. In this case it is possible to go a little farther, since we have other compositions by the same composer. The superius of a freely composed Credo by Olyver (ex. 19) shows remarkable similarities in melodic shape to the paraphrased Agnus. Both move busily within a very narrow range, using the small intervals of seconds and thirds exclusively, and circling around and touching the highest note of each phrase several times before leaving it. Rhythmically they are also very similar. Both are characterized by alternations of $\frac{3}{4}$ and $\frac{6}{8}$ meter and by sudden, short rests (ex. 18, m. 5, and ex. 19, m. 3). The freely composed melody and the elaborated chant melody, written by the same composer, are as alike as possible, so that the supposition arising from stylistic differences in pieces of different periods is also supported by stylistic identities in the freely composed and paraphrased compositions of a single composer.[9]

As the Burgundian chanson style was dominant in the first half of the century, its characteristics will be shown by many of the c.f. paraphrases from this period if the supposition on which we are working has general validity. A comparison of a few chansons by Binchois, which suitably represent this style, with examples 14, 15, 16, 21, etc., reveals abundant similarities. The harmonic style is generally identical. The same types of cadence are used, the dissonance treatment is the same, and the rhythmic patterns

EXAMPLE 19. Olyver, Credo (*OH*, II, 27-28).

are alike. The phrases of the chanson are apt to be short, and one of the features of the c.f. elaboration is the breaking-up of the Gregorian phrases into shorter ones by the interpolation of cadential formulae.

More to the point, in the superius of the chanson the phrase typically begins rather simply and then gradually expands in range and becomes rhythmically more active as the cadence is approached. This is exactly what is done when the c.f. is paraphrased. The ornamentation is sparing at the beginning of the phrase and becomes richer and more active as the cadence is approached. The superius line of the chanson tends to rise to a high point, which is more or less emphasized, and then descends gently to the cadence. This swelling line is attained in the c.f. settings by means of the c.f. notes themselves if they allow it, but more often by the liberal addition of free tones. For instance, in example 14, measure 4, the c.f. itself rises to a high point before the cadence, so it is little ornamented. In measures 9 and 14 it does not, so the composer adds sufficient notes to achieve the desired melodic climax. In example 16, measures 4 and 9, the c.f. descends to the cadence, but the composer adds one higher note in each case to emphasize the climax and descent. Example 15 shows similar procedures. In all these cases, the most extended interpolations are introduced in such a way that they give the c.f. the swelling character of the chanson melody.[10]

The free tones in an Agnus setting by Binchois (ex. 20a-20b) show the intentions of the composer most clearly. For the most part, the c.f. is very little ornamented, but in measures 4-5 of example 20a and measures 15-16 of example 20b he interpolates six notes in succession. If his intention were merely to ornament the Gregorian melody so as to make a florid variant of it, this bunching together of the added notes would seem a strange and arbitrary procedure. It would be expected that the ornamentation would be distributed evenly among the c.f. notes rather than concentrated in a single spot. By putting the free tones all in one place he does not ornament the melody at all in the sense of florid variation. What he actually does is to *transform* it, and he transforms it so that it becomes remarkably like

EXAMPLE 20. (a-b) Binchois, Agnus (Tr 92; *DTO*, 61, p. 50; *LU*, p. 63).

one of his freely composed chanson melodies. The interpolated notes not only supply the high point before the cadence and the fluid rhythmic approach to it; they spread out the syllabic, steadily moving Gregorian melody to fit the more leisurely, less direct course of a Burgundian melodic phrase.

The more of these settings that are examined, the more apparent it becomes that stylistic adaptation is the key to the whole technique, even though complete transformation is by no means intended in all cases. In the hymns of Dufay the chant is quoted almost unornamented. Yet even in these simple compositions the added notes are placed at the cadences so as to bring these crucial harmonic spots into line with the current style.[11] The degree of adaptation, of course, depends on the liberality with which the free tones are used, but in all the varied manifestations of the paraphrase procedure there is this common intent. When the chant is treated as a melody by a composer of the fourteenth-century French school, it is adapted to the ballade style and transformed into a melody similar to one which he would freely compose; when it is treated by one who writes in the style of the fifteenth-century Burgundian school, it is transformed into a melody of the chanson type; and so with other styles. Orel's opinion that the principle of ornamentation is taken over from the later development of the Gregorian Chant is not convincing.[12] Even to consider this procedure one of coloration or ornamentation obscures the issue, as it places emphasis on a secondary feature, an incidental result, rather than on the primary reason for which it is employed. If florid melody lines were all that were desired, many of them could be found in the responsorial chants. Yet these melismatic chants are fitted out with interpolated notes just as the syllabic ones are. Many examples can be found in *Mon. Pol. Lit.* (Ser. II, Vol. I); an examination of them shows that the composer is not trying to produce an ornamented version of an already ornate melody, but is bringing the Gregorian melismatic melody into line with a melodic type with which he is familiar. Only in so far as the style itself includes an element of floridity, and this is an important aspect of fifteenth-century style in general, can it be said that the free tones are employed primarily for ornamental purposes. Certainly, many compositions have highly ornamental melodies, but the type of ornamental line which the composer uses is determined by the style in which he writes.

It seems also that Ficker's strange idea that free composition was learned by practice in making polyphonic settings of the chant[13] not only has no foundation in fact, but is the exact opposite of the facts. The whole technique is a reflection of free composition and is a direct outgrowth of it.

THE TREATMENT OF THE CANTUS FIRMUS TONES

The next step is to determine how the c.f. notes themselves are employed and how they stand in relation to the added tones in the elaborated line.

In the majority of compositions written before 1450 by the English and Burgundians there is little evidence of an intention to obscure the identity of the original melody. Obviously, the more restrained the ornamentation, the more clearly the chant melody shows through. A setting of the hymn *Gloria, laus, et honor* by Binchois (ex. 21) illustrates this. The processional hymn for Palm Sunday starts with an initial figure, common in melodies of the first mode, which is set in long values and without interpolations. Since this figure is uncharacteristic of Binchois's chanson beginnings,[14]

EXAMPLE 21. Binchois, *Gloria, laus, et honor* (Tr 87; Marix, p. 194; Proc. Pred., p. 29).

the melody reveals itself quite clearly as a borrowed one. It is only after the statement of the initial figure that notes are added to produce the smooth curves of the Burgundian type. Even then, the c.f. notes are allotted sufficiently long rhythmic values to assure them an important position in the melody line. This clear method of paraphrasing the c.f. is typical of Dufay, Binchois, and Dunstable, as well as of most of their contemporaries.

The number of notes to be added to the c.f. is, however, a matter of the discretion of the composer. An anonymous Kyrie (ex. 22) and a Sanctus

EXAMPLE 22. Anonymous, Kyrie (Tr 90 and 93; *DTO*, 61, p. 65; *LU*, p. 25).

(ex. 23—attributed to Binchois in Tr 92) indicate an approximate maximum of elaboration. In example 22 the remodeling of the melody starts with the first note. Nevertheless, the c.f. notes occupy positions of some prominence in the line. They are distributed fairly evenly (about one per measure) and are generally given the value of a semibreve or greater. Exceptions are found in measure 3, where the chant tone is given the value of a minim on count 1, and in measure 8, where the composer takes advantage of the stepwise rise of the chant and incorporates it into the standard superius cadence figure. Hence the g of the c.f. is expressed by two semiminims in the superius.

The Sanctus (ex. 23) is even more elaborately paraphrased. The first phrase is six measures long and contains only two notes from the c.f., yet their importance is assured by long metrical values and by their position at the beginning and end of the phrase. In the second and third phrases the c.f. notes come at fairly regular intervals and, again, they are given impor-

EXAMPLE 23. Binchois, Sanctus (Tr 92; *DTO*, 61, p. 53; *LU*, p. 58).

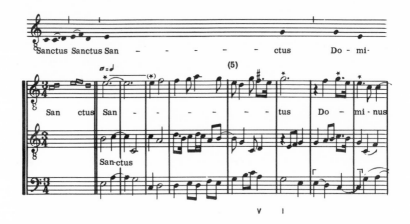

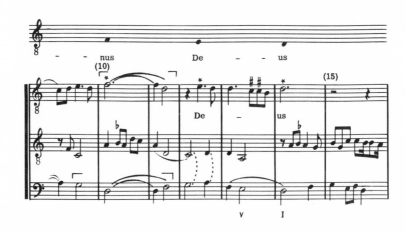

tant positions in the line, rhythmically and melodically. As in the previous examples, the note ending a phrase of the c.f. is, in every case, the one chosen for a cadence in the paraphrase setting. The note which begins a phrase of the chant is also normally chosen to begin the phrase in the setting, although exceptions to this are found, especially in very elaborate paraphrases (ex. 23, m. 7). Further, the notes of the chant melody, even though separated widely, are quoted without omissions and in exact order.[15] The composer does not disturb the original succession of notes by repeating any phrases of the chant or by developing any figures or motives derived from it. This is significant because it means extension is not gained by development out of the substance of the chant itself. The technique is simply one of quotation and of interpolation of fresh material.

Although the previous examples show that the technique is extremely variable, it is not entirely without bounds. There are innumerable degrees of simplicity and complexity of elaboration, yet they fall within certain limits. The setting of *Gloria, laus, et honor* (ex. 21) represents an approximate norm and the Sanctus (ex. 23) represents about the extreme in complexity. These, together with examples 14, 15, 16 and 20, show fairly enough the scope of the ornamentation in a majority of the compositions, as well as the position in which the borrowed and the newly composed elements stand in relation to one another. It seems that when the composer fashions the paraphrase he strikes a compromise between the old and the new. He keeps the original melody prominent, but at the same time he presents it in the garb of his personal style. His procedure may be compared to the action of a sculptor who throws a garment over a body: the drapery hides the details of its outline to a greater or lesser extent, but does not alter its essential structure.

There are a few cases in which the internal structure of the chant is altered to a certain degree by very long interpolations which have the effect of separating elements that are closely associated in the original melody. The point is illustrated by a Sanctus setting of Leonel (ex. 24a-b). The c.f. itself is stated simply, but a long free section is inserted before the final note of example 24a. Although in the light of Continental practice this procedure seems excessive, it can be considered a logical development from the short insertions before the cadence seen in some of the other conductus of Old Hall. Example 24b shows the same sort of long free passage, but here the insertion is made in the middle of the c.f. phrase and completely separates the first part from the last.[16] Interpolations of such length are not common in Continental music before the middle of the century, one of the few works which can be compared to the Leonel Sanctus being the Sanctus of the plainchant Mass of Liebert. In measures 54-85 of Liebert's work the chant is treated in a very irregular manner. The c.f. notes sometimes are separated by a great number of free tones; sometimes they come

EXAMPLE 24. (a-b) Leonel, Sanctus (OH, III, 59, 64; Gr. Sar., pl. 15+).

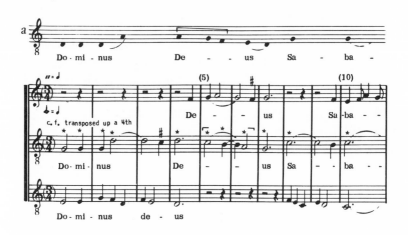

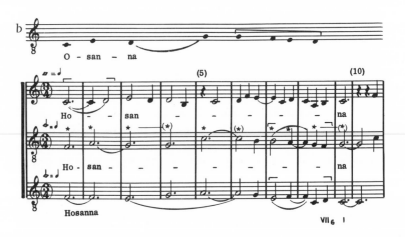

in immediate succession in an utterly unpredictable manner. (See *DTO*, 53, pp. 16-17).

In the second half of the century we find a great many more instances of unrestrained, irregular treatment of the c.f., but these early compositions of Leonel and Liebert are sufficient to show that it is not merely an outcome of the growth of a technique from a simpler to a more complex stage. The elaborateness of the paraphrase is much more intimately connected with a composer's style than with date of composition. Example 17, from the Apt manuscript (late fourteenth century), shows a fair amount of added notes although the hymn tunes of the other settings of this source are hardly elaborated at all. The Sanctus of Leonel and that of Liebert are very extensively elaborated, yet both these men were older than Dufay, who, for the most part, preferred to add very few free tones to the c.f. (This is not so true of Dufay's latest works, which may have been influenced by the development of a highly elaborate melodic style around 1460-70.)

Within the limits of a composer's style, other factors also affect the amount of elaboration. Dunstable, like Dufay, prefers to add only a moderate number of tones, yet there is a notable difference between the number used in the setting of the hymn *Ave maris stella* and that in the Marian antiphon *Regina caeli*.[17] The reason for this seems to be found in the type of composition. Composers evidently felt that it was appropriate to keep hymn settings unassuming, and Dunstable is following a general practice in keeping the ornamentation at a minimum. The rich ornamentation of *Regina caeli* can be attributed to the intent to make an impressive work, comparable in its beautifully melismatic style to the most elaborate of his cantilena motets to the Virgin.

Likewise, the function of the c.f. within the composition may affect the amount of elaboration. In the setting of the processional antiphon, *Crux fidelis*, Dunstable places the c.f. in the middle voice in the three-part sections and in the top voice in the duos; when it functions as a middle part it is treated very simply, but when it is taken by the superius there is a sharp variation in treatment and it becomes highly elaborated, in keeping with the soloistic nature of the duo sections.[18]

TREATMENT OF THE TEXT AND OF THE FORM OF THE CHANT

The Sanctus of Leonel (ex. 24*b*) strongly emphasizes another important feature of the treatment of the c.f. The words "*in excelsis*" begin in the treble at measure 14, but in the middle voice they are delayed for some time, not appearing until measure 32. This looks liks an ordinary instance of haphazard text underlaying, but in this case the displacement is motivated by a very sufficient reason. The middle voice, which carries the entire c.f., is occupied at measure 14 with the freely composed interpolation mentioned above. At measure 32 the interpolation is finally completed and the quotation of the c.f. is resumed. The reason for withholding the words "*in excelsis*" now becomes clear, since before this point they could not have been placed under the notes of the chant to which they properly belong.

The care taken to associate the words in the paraphrase with the notes to which they belong in the original is one of the most consistent features in this type of composition, regardless of school or date, and is especially noteworthy in view of the inexact manner in which the text was ordinarily underlaid in the manuscripts. There is, of course, not the close relation of note and syllable of the sixteenth century. The words of the c.f. are often displaced by a note or two, but anything more than this is rare.[19] I do not know of any instance where a c.f. is clearly present and the text of one phrase is intentionally and consistently allotted to the notes of another.[20]

With regard to the form of the chant, it has already been shown that the notes are quoted in their original order, though they may be widely separated, and that cadential points are kept as cadential in most cases. In addition, the larger, sectional organization of the chant is considered by the composer, who customarily uses either the entire chant or an integral portion of it. For example, a gradual may be set as far as the verse, an antiphon as far as the psalm, the remainder being left for monophonic performance. (The exceptions to this—that is, partial or fragmentary quotation—will be considered in the next section.) Furthermore, the completion of the quotation represents, for all practical purposes, the completion of the composition itself. In some cases a work may be continued for a time by free extension, but there is no such thing as the multiple cursus, the repeated fragment, of the traditional tenor. No more repetitions of the chant are used than would be made in a normal performance in the service.

In works of this type, the preservation of the proper relation of text and notes—as well as the avoidance of any manipulation which would disturb the proper order of the notes or distort the over-all sectional structure of the chant—can be laid to a certain degree of respect for it as a liturgical entity. Although the composer may expand the melody when he elaborates it, he does not disturb those primary characteristics of text and form having to do with the practical function of the chant in the service.

It seems, then, that the procedures of elaboration are variable but not entirely free. Two considerations combine to limit them: (1) the liturgical nature of the chant is respected, and (2) the purely musical structure of the chant is acknowledged with regard to phrase, section, and sequence of notes.

Once again the fact that the practice of the composers is extremely variable should be stressed. It is quite evident that they did not feel bound by rigid restrictions. The characteristics noted are those of a majority of the compositions, and they indicate widely held points of view, but there is no indication that these views were ever formulated in terms of specific rules.

Respect for the chant as a musical organism and as a portion of the liturgy accounts for many of the procedures of paraphrase, but by no means for all of them. As was mentioned before, the settings offer no proof of a general attempt to concentrate or pattern the original musical material by motivic means. On the contrary, the paraphrase procedure—as used—dilutes this material and spreads it out.[21] In the first half of the century, even the device of imitation is rarely used to concentrate the c.f. material, yet imitation was well known at this time and was used as an important structural means by Hugo de Lantins, Dufay, and others in the chanson.[22]

Before the time of Busnois the free tones are added in such a way as to produce a continuously changing melodic flow in which the fancy of the

EXAMPLE 25. (a-c) Olyver, Agnus (*OH*, III, 141, 142, 144; Gr. Sar., pl. 18+).

composer is restrained only by the necessity of giving the c.f. notes a position of some prominence in the melody line.[23] It is true that instances of
patterning by sequence or repeated rhythmic groups can be found both in
freely composed works and in works with c.f. These show that such practices were not unknown. However, the infrequency with which they are
used and the small part they play when they are used indicate—more clearly
than if they were entirely absent—the indifference of English and Burgundian composers to them.[24]

The tendency to avoid organization by means of repetition—evident on
the level of the motive—can also be observed on the level of the phrase and
section. The disinclination to state the same idea twice in the same way is
illustrated in the handling of the repeated passages which occur in many
chants. The degree to which repetition is obscured depends, of course, on
the richness or the poverty of the elaboration. For instance, in example
25*b-c* the composer adds but few tones and the repetitions in the c.f. remain quite clear. An even clearer instance is provided by example 20. Here
the superius of example 20*b* is a direct repetition of that of example 20*a*,
in that the added notes are kept exactly the same; yet even this literal
melodic restatement is denied the effect of exact repetition, since the
harmonization is changed.

Ordinarily, however, the repetitions are more disguised. The commonest
treatment is fairly represented by the *Alleluia, Posuisti Domine* (ex. 26)
which has the form AABA.[25] The ornamentation is quite restrained, and
the chant melody shows through clearly, yet it is presented in different
guise in each statement. There is no positive attempt to cover up the repetitions; neither is there an effort to emphasize them. In the setting, these
passages are scored sometimes as duos, sometimes as trios, and are rehar-
monized to a greater or lesser degree as well, so that their relationship with
one another is even less clear than would appear from the quotations in the
example. This is repetition under the aspect of a continuously unfolding
line.

When the ornamentation is extensive, the repetitions are obscured to an
even greater extent. A whole new paraphrase is constructed on the second
phrase of *Salve Regina* (ex. 27), so that the repetition is almost completely
hidden in the continuous progress of the melody. This shows a complete
disregard for the organizational value of exact, clearly discernible restatement. Further, while the restatements are undoubtedly varied, it is doubtful that they should be considered as variations. These phrases are "variations" only because of the necessity of following out the notes of the c.f.,
and this is managed so that the resemblances are of the most diffuse and
general nature. No succinct, clearly defined relationships enable the ear to
grasp affinities between the passages. Instead of indicating a desire for a
tightly knit structure, as implied by variation, they point in exactly the

EXAMPLE 26. Anonymous, Alleluia—*Posuisti Domine*, superius only (Tr 88; *Mon. Pol. Lit.*, 2nd ser., I, 88; *LU*, p. 1148).

EXAMPLE 27. Anonymous, *Salve Regina*, superius (Tr. 88; *DTO*, 53, p. 47; *LU*, p. 276).

opposite direction toward an apparent attempt to loosen it and to obscure whatever elements of unity are present in the original chant.

Furthermore, an examination of the contemporary freely composed works leads to the conclusion that any such tight structural procedure was foreign to the style as a whole.[26] In the paraphrases, the method of treating the repeated elements of the c.f. should be interpreted as a reflection of this peculiarity and as another instance of stylistic adaptation. Instead of "variation," it seems desirable to use the term "variant" with reference to c.f. phrases which are newly elaborated when they are repeated.[27]

Cantus Firmus Elaboration in Voices Other than the Superius

The superius, the text-bearing voice of the chanson, is the part usually chosen to carry the paraphrased melody. There are, however, a fair number of instances where it is given to the tenor, which is also a melodically important part in secular works, even though its line is plainer than that of the superius.[28] In agreement with the previous observation that the style of the elaboration is largely determined by practices of free composition, it is found that the tenor paraphrases are generally similar in character to freely composed tenors. They are melodically quite smooth and rhythmically flexible, but on the whole they move more slowly than the superius. A *Benedicamus Domino* by Dufay (ex. 28) is fairly typical. Although points of imitation (m. 6-8) carry the c.f. into all three voices for a few notes, the tenor remains the actual c.f. voice. To it Dufay has added an elegant, chansonlike superius and a contratenor which carries out the normal function of that voice by filling in the harmonies.

Most tenors which carry a c.f. are of the framework type, and in them the borrowed material is treated according to concepts which are different from those behind the paraphrase. (See the distinctions made at the beginning of this chapter, p. 42, and those at the beginning of chap. iii, p. 83.) Discussion of instances in which the categories overlap will be deferred until these mixed types can be considered more profitably, after the pure scaffolding type has been described.

The paraphrased melody is used even less often in the middle voice than in the tenor by Continental composers. The reason is, possibly, that there is no true middle voice in the typical writing for three parts at this time. The two indispensable structural voices are the superius and the tenor.[29] The contratenor is added later as a harmonic filler. As it is forced to skip about to complete the three-part sonorities, the resultant erratic motion effectively denies it a melodic character. In range it is not a true middle part; it lies as much below as above the tenor.

When a third voice of this type is replaced by one bearing a c.f., the whole concept of the function of each of the three parts is disturbed and, with it, the normal method of composing them. As the carrier of the c.f., this voice must come first instead of last, and the tenor and superius must be written in relation to it. This abnormal situation is sometimes indicated by the unusual names of the parts and by features remindful of composition practices of the English. For instance, in the setting of the sequence *Veni Sancte Spiritus* by Dufay (ex. 29a) the middle voice and the tenor cross occasionally and move much in parallel thirds in the manner of the gymel. Furthermore, the top voice is given the archaic designation *triplum*, while the c.f. voice is not called the contratenor even though it replaces that part.

EXAMPLE 28. Dufay, *Benedicamus Domino* (Tr 87; DTO, 53, p. 24; LU, p. 124).

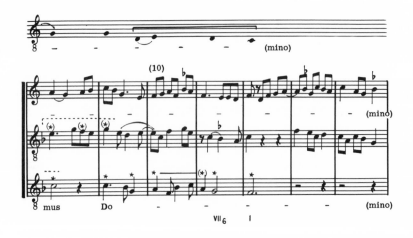

Ordinarily, the voices are designated in the usual way. A *Kyrie* setting by Binchois (ex. 29b) retains for the middle voice the name "contratenor" even though it carries the c.f. It, too, shows characteristics of the gymel.[30] The presence both of a c.f. in the middle voice, and of the gymel produced by that voice and its lower partner, suggests English influence on these writers, although it does not prove it.[31]

EXAMPLE 29. (a) Dufay, *Veni Sancte Spiritus* (Tr 92; *DTO*, 53, p. 29; *LU*, p. 880). (b) Binchois, *Kyrie* (Tr 87, 92; *DTO*, 61, p. 48; *LU*, p. 37).

On the grounds of tradition, it would not be surprising to find the English writers making considerable use of c.f. in the middle voice, but this practice apparently died out almost completely.[32] Even in Old Hall and the Fountains fragment there are no examples of pure middle-voice c.f. outside the conductus. There are none whatsoever in Selden B 26 and Egerton 3307, both of which date from about 1450. In the Pepys manuscript, c. 1470, however, there are several instances, one of which, a setting of the prosa *Sospitati dedit*, is written in an archaic, conductuslike style.

Migrant Cantus Firmus—Partial Statement—Transposition

Migrant c.f. is found in Continental music, but it is not so plentiful as in the conductus of Old Hall, a fact which may be accounted for, at least partially, on the basis of the mechanics of writing.[33] Even without contemporary evidence, practical considerations make it reasonable to assume that the conductus were composed in score much as they appear in the choir books.[34] In these circumstances it would be no more difficult to distribute the c.f. between the several voices—as a step preliminary to writing the counterpoints—than to lay it out entirely in one part. In other types of composition, where the parts are believed to have been written separately, as well as successively, such a distribution of the c.f. would have caused considerably more inconvenience. A difficulty of this type would not be a major obstacle to a composer who seriously wished to use migration, however, and these considerations probably indicate why it was natural for the technique to have developed in the conductus—not why it was used so little in other types of composition. There must be other reasons for the rather sparing use of this technique, and one that comes immediately to mind is that migration to the middle voice would cause the disturbance in procedures of composition which has been noted above with regard to middle-voice c.f.

In compositions of the second quarter of the century, migration is apt to occur at the end of phrases or sections, and when the c.f. moves from one voice to another it tends to remain in its new position for an entire section.[35] There is an important difference between this manner of statement and that observed in Old Hall, where migration occurs at any point in the phrase. In the former case, migration is related to the structure of the composition and shows an inclination toward simple and broadly sketched musical architecture. The latter reveals the typically Gothic pleasure in fanciful, intricate, and apparently unmotivated detail. Since such widely different points of view are involved, it is useful to distinguish between the two types, and to speak of "structurally motivated" and "structurally unmotivated" migration, referring respectively to that which occurs at the end of phrases or sections and that which is unrelated to the phrase structure.

In compositions in very elementary style, structurally unmotivated migration has the advantage of adding variety. It gives a necessary element of interest to the more primitive conductus of Old Hall—works so simple that they run the risk of being dull. In those cases where the c.f. is partially obscured by paraphrase, as it is in more complex styles, the irregular and unexpected changes of structurally unmotivated migration tend to obliterate it completely. This can be seen in the Kyrie of the Liebert Mass (ex. 30).[36]

A comparison of this Kyrie with a composition of approximately equal

EXAMPLE 30. Liebert, Kyrie (Tr 92; *DTO*, 53, p. 3; *LU*, p. 40).

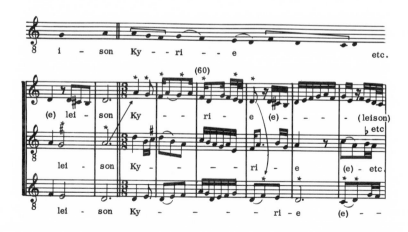

date (both come from Tr 92), in which the c.f. is treated with the greatest variety, but in which migration is by section only, shows the essential differences between the two types. In the setting of the Gloria from Mass IX with the trope *Spiritus et alme*[37] by Dufay, sections for a single voice are opposed to others in three parts and polyphonic writing is contrasted to passages of block chords. The c.f. is taken by all three voices at one time or another. The Gloria melody is given in alternate sections: as a paraphrase by the uppermost of the three voices, and in simple form by the tenor sounding alone. When the trope enters, it is always set in three parts, alternating with the phrases of the Gloria which are now given monophonically by the tenor. In addition, the three-part writing of the trope sections is alternately polyphonic and homophonic. In the polyphonic sections the tenor paraphrases the c.f.; in the chordal ones the c.f. is sung by the contratenor in simple form.

There is no lack of imagination or variety in this composition, yet the complex treatment follows a rational pattern. The Gloria melody appears always in the superius, or monophonically in the tenor. The trope melody is given to the contratenor in chordal sections and to the tenor in polyphonic ones. The c.f. remains in a single voice for a complete section, and each presentation is clear and straightforward. The artistic aim of presenting the c.f. clearly, but in as many lights as possible, is quite obvious and in direct contrast to the obscure and crotchety method of Liebert. As stated above, the relative formal clarity of one and the element of fantasy in the other represent divergent artistic viewpoints. Structurally unmotivated migration—a device developed in the fourteenth century—lent itself readily to an elaborate, irrational type of expression; Liebert apparently adopted it in its entirety as well suited to his ends. But most composers of the fifteenth century preferred to link migration with the structure of a work and to shift the c.f. from one voice to another only at the end of a section.

In example 31 migration occurs at points where there is no specifically indicated change of section, but it is structurally motivated, nevertheless, since it takes place at the beginning of duets which are heard as formal units in contrast to the preceding parts for three voices. (See m. 27 and 49.) Further, the treatment of the c.f. is perfectly clear. In the duet beginning at measure 27 it is given to the highest-sounding voice (the contratenor), so it is clearly audible. Even the entry of the third voice (m. 40) does not necessarily obscure it.[38]

A different usage is found in a Credo by Zachara da Teramo where the liturgical melody and its text are sung in alternation by the two upper voices.[39] Migration in this work is apparently used not so much for the sake of the technique itself as to preserve in the polyphonic setting the original antiphonal manner of singing the chant. Zachara's connection with Eng-

EXAMPLE 31. Anonymous, *Christus factus est* (Tr 88; *Mon. Pol. Lit.*, 2nd ser., I, 50; *LU*, p. 655).

land has been suggested,[40] and this composition may indicate an interchange of ideas. If so, it is another instance of the modification of the technique to suit the special purposes of the composer.

Migration continued to be used in the second half of the century. It can still be found in some of the works of Josquin, and it is used to a considerable extent by Ockeghem and his contemporaries. Its late manifestations will be taken up with the work of those men.

Migration represents a relatively complicated form of c.f. statement for composers of the later fifteenth century, just as it did for those of Old Hall. But the basic attitude that the c.f. is to be stated faithfully, note after note, remains the same in all works, regardless of whether they were written early or late. Likewise, statement at some pitch level other than the original one does not interfere with the presentation of the notes in proper succession, nor does the less common practice of changing the pitch level during the course of the composition. Faithful statement, note by note, does not include faithful retention of the original mode, which may be violated in a number of ways.

The only major deviation from the practice of faithful quotation is found in those works which state only a portion of the c.f. and then abandon it to continue as free compositions. There are not a large number of instances of partial statement at this time, but in those which have come down to us we find that the c.f., as long as it is present, is stated as faithfully as in any setting where it is given complete. There are various types of partial statement: the c.f. may be used only for the intonation and the whole composition be free,[41] it may be paraphrased for a greater or lesser time and the remainder of the piece be free,[42] or it may disappear and reappear from time to time.[43]

Problematical Cases of Cantus Firmus Elaboration

Since many compositions with sacred text were freely composed, it is always necessary to determine, as a first step in the analysis of one of these works, whether a c.f. is or is not present. In a great number of cases an affirmative or negative answer can be given easily: the c.f. is clearly stated, or it is obvious that one is not being used. There are, however, instances which are not at all clear. A few of these will be discussed, since they show the problems involved in this type of investigation and the precautions that must be taken.

When dealing with doubtful cases it seems reasonable that the analyst should accept as possibilities any of the c.f. treatments which are known to have been widely, even though not frequently, used (e.g., migration, partial statement of the c.f., change of pitch level within the composition). It must be remembered, however, that any chant—and, likewise, the melody voices of any of these compositions—may make much use of scale-line progressions and small skips. Hence, between many *cantus firmi* and any given composition there are bound to be points of agreement which are purely fortuitous. By indiscriminately assuming modulation and migration, the chances of finding agreements are so extended that the notes of practically every chant can be found somewhere in the voices of any composition which is at all florid or extended. This is especially true if the c.f. is in the same mode as the piece with which it is being compared, for the chances are that many of the cadences will be similar. Unless some rational check is applied, the procedure of comparison will degenerate to a point where anything can be equated with anything. Valid checks are provided by the common characteristics observed in a large number of compositions written at this time which are undoubtedly based on c.f.

A list of these characteristics, based on the practices observed in these works, can be drawn up as follows:

1. The notes of the c.f. follow each other in the order which they have in the original.

2. The c.f. notes themselves are usually given some importance in the elaborated melody line. Short notes, especially those in weak rhythmic positions, are usually free, added tones.

3. The first few notes of the phrase usually outline the c.f. melody rather clearly. Farther on in the phrase, a greater number of free tones are apt to disguise it more or less thoroughly.

4. The phrase of the elaborated melody usually concludes with the same note that ends the corresponding phrase in the c.f. The frequent occurrence of cadences which do not agree with those of the chant is sufficient reason for requiring confirmatory evidence that a c.f. is actually being used.

5. The structure of the c.f. is loosened by cadences in the course of the phrase as well as by free interpolations.

6. The relationship of text and melody in the original is retained in the setting, at least to the extent that the phrase of text is almost invariably associated with the phrase of music to which it belongs. Hence, the words are seldom displaced more than a few notes from their proper position.

7. Migration may be either structurally motivated or not. The c.f. usually remains for a fair amount of time in one voice before shifting to another, although in migration which is not structurally motivated it may remain in a given voice for only a couple of notes. Nevertheless, any analysis would be suspect which showed the c.f. constantly jumping about, with only one or two notes in each voice.

8. Fragmentary quotations of the c.f. are faithful to the original while they last; text is given to the proper notes as in complete statements.

9. Change of pitch level (transposition) during the statement of the c.f. can be found, though it is not common.

10. These methods of statement (nos. 7, 8, and 9) need not be used according to a rational plan.

11. The style of the school or individual composer, when known, should be considered in judging a case of c.f. statement. For instance, the rich ornamentation and casual method of statement which are found in works of Regis, and are accepted without question, would be sufficient to raise doubts concerning the presence of c.f. in a work of Dufay.

This list of characteristics is the result of observation of a large number of paraphrases of English and Continental composers. It is a summary of the customary procedures of these men, not a set of hard-and-fast rules. There are so many variations in individual practice that each item is subject to some qualification. On the whole, however, the items are valid, and they are useful checks to analysis—even though it is not possible to settle every doubtful point through them.

When allowance is made for the possibility that the composer is using a somewhat different version of the c.f. than the one available to the analyst, it can be seen that in many cases no final judgment can be passed. Also, it goes without saying that nothing is to be gained by trying to force a c.f. onto a composition which may be a freely composed work. It seems clear that the evidence must be weighed, and that if it is conflicting the case must be admitted to be doubtful.

In illustration of the problems which sometimes come up, a few compositions will be analyzed. The first two represent cases where, although c.f. is actually used, at first sight the elaborate treatment makes for difficulty in tracing the borrowed melody and thus causes doubts as to its actual presence.

The first, the anonymous setting of the hymn *Aeterne Rex altissime*, is the simpler. (See ex. 32a-b.) It presents some problems, but none of a very serious nature. Quite certainly it is a paraphrase, since, even though there are many inserted tones, most of the c.f. notes are given prominent positions in the melody line. At measures 17-18 there is apparently migration for only two notes. In any case, the c.f. notes are not promient in the treble line, and by assuming migration to the tenor the problem is solved very satisfactorily. The five-note figure a-g-f-g-g occurs at this point on the word *altissime*; it occurs once more at the word *gracie* (ex. 32b) and again at *deperit* (not quoted); but it is impossible to find convincing evidence that all the c.f. notes are used. Since the difficulties occur always at similar spots in the c.f., it is less likely that they are instances of temporary departure from the melody than that the version of the hymn used differs at these places. This in turn would cast doubt on the analysis at measures 17-18, which otherwise seems satisfactory. It appears that the piece should be classified as a paraphrase with doubtful passages. It is impossible at present to say whether they are freely composed.

The second, the setting of the sequence *Sospitati dedit* by Walter Frye

EXAMPLE 32. (a-b) Anonymous, *Aeterne Rex altissime* (Selden B; Stainer, *Early Bodleian Music*, II, 163, 164; *Hymns Anc. & Mod.*, p. 237).

al — — — — — — tis —
al — — — — — — — —
al

- si — — — —
tis - si — — — — — me
tis - si — — — — — me

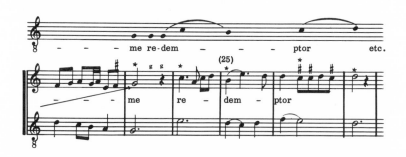

- — — me re-dem — — — ptor etc.
- — — me re - dem - ptor

gra — — — ci — — e
gra — — — — ci — e
gra — — ci — — — — e

(ex. 33a-c), presents more difficult problems. It is apparently a c.f. elaboration in certain places and is freely composed in others. The c.f. is outlined clearly enough at the beginnings of verses one and two (ex. 33a, superius, m. 1-5), five (ex. 33b, superius, m. 11-15), six (ex. 33b, tenor, m. 23-27), and seven (ex. 33c, tenor, m. 33-34, to superius, m. 34-37).[44] Although measures 6-9 may be free, if migration to the middle voice be assumed at measure 6, we find that all of the c.f. notes appear in proper order in the first verse. The second half of verse five (m. 15-22) is somewhat more ambiguous. It is granted that all the notes of the c.f. can be found easily enough in the superius, but the phrase does not begin with the right notes. There is no e' until the end of measure 16. Furthermore, the presumptive c.f. notes are often unimportant in the line. When it is considered that the superius has thirty-five notes, that it covers the range of a sixth (from c' to a') and runs up and down several times within these limits, while the c.f. has seven notes and covers the range of a fourth (c' to f'), agreement between them is almost inevitable. Practically any c.f. phrase of seven notes falling within a similar range would agree as well as this one, providing it came to a cadence on d'. The one certain point of similarity is the cadence. The only other sound reason for entertaining the idea of c.f. is that the piece apparently starts as a paraphrase, and so may be assumed to continue as one. But the corresponding phrase of verse six (m. 28-32) is, certainly, freely composed. Verse seven likewise apparently starts as a paraphrase and ends freely (m. 37-42), and verse eight is free throughout, so the argument that the paraphrase is apt to continue after it is once started loses

EXAMPLE 33. (a-c) W. Frye, *Sospitati dedit* (Pepys 1236, fo. 84ᵛ-86; Ant. Sar., pl. 360, also Var. Prec., p. 62).

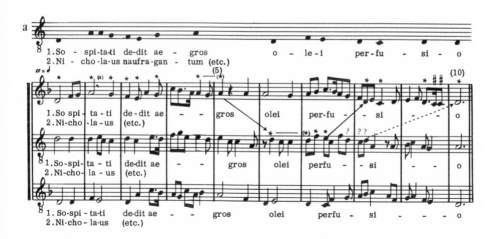

5. O quam pro - bat San - ctum De-i far - ris aug - men - ta - ci - o
6. Vas in mari mer - sum Pa-tri red - di - tur cum fi - li - o

5. O quam probat sanctum Dei far - ris augmenta - - ci - o

5. O quam probat sanctum Dei farris augmenta - - ci - o

6. Vas in mari mersum patri re dditur cum fi - li - - o

6. Vas in mari mersum patri redditur cum fi - li - - o

6. Vas in mari mersum patri redditur cum fi - li - - o

7. Er - go lau - des Ni - cho - la - o con - ci - nat hec con - ci - o
8. Nam qui cor - de po - scit il - lum pro - pul - sa - to vi - ci - o

7. Ergo laudes Nichola - - o concinat hec con - ci - o

7. Ergo laudes Nichola - - o concinat hec con - ci - o

8. Nam qui corde poscit illum propulsato vi - ci - - o.

8. Nam qui corde poscit illum propulsato vi - ci - - o

8. Nam qui corde poscit illum propulsato vi - - ci - - o

force. It seems fairly certain that the last half of verse five is free and quite probable that the last half of verse one is too. (This is merely an individual judgment of what is probable and what is not, but it seems better to err on the conservative side, if an error must be made, as any method of comparison loses force in proportion to the degree with which one thing can be equated with another—as the point is approached where everything can be equated with everything, it ceases being a method altogether.)

Despite the excursions into free writing, the cadences at the middle and end of each verse of the setting correspond with those of the sequence. This may be purely coincidental so long as the cadences in the c.f. are on the first and fifth degrees of the mode, because the cadences in freely composed music are most frequently on these degrees also. If migration is assumed, the chances of agreement are extended, since the fifth degree can be found in the contratenor in the final chord of a cadence on the first degree. For example, in the Dorian mode, the final chord of a cadence on the first degree is d-a-d. If the c.f. cadences on either tonic or dominant, the appropriate note can be found in this chord; mere agreement in mode between a c.f. and a polyphonic composition can account for many similarities between cadences.

This is not the case in two-part writing, and agreement carries more weight in those sections. When cadences on the less frequently used degrees of the mode agree in both c.f. and polyphonic setting, the probability of accidental similarity is further reduced, so it must be admitted that the concurrence of the cadences on the fourth degree (m. 37 and 47), when added to those on the first and fifth degrees in the two-part sections, can hardly be coincidental.

While much of this piece is freely composed, the agreement, without exception, of every cadence of the setting with a corresponding point in the c.f. gives strong reason to believe that Frye had the sequence melody in mind throughout, although he often adhered only to its important structural points. This would represent the extreme of freedom in paraphrase treatment, short of wholly original composition. It is a wide departure from the principles which have been previously observed, but it does not actually negate all of them. When a c.f. note appears, it is at the proper place musically and textually. The relationship is tenuous, but the method is still a horizontal one of melodic extension and transformation.[45]

In contrast to these two cases—which appear at first glance to be free compositions, but which can be shown to be based on c.f.—two other works may be cited to illustrate the reverse situation. These works have been said to be based on c.f., and at first glance they seem to be as clear instances of paraphrase as the two just analyzed. Examination will show that they deviate from common practice sufficiently to make it probable that they are freely composed.

The superius of the motet of Dunstable, *Alma Redemptoris Mater*,[46] begins in a way which calls the antiphon to mind. The melody emphasizes the first, third, fifth, sixth, and eighth degrees of the mode in ascending order (m. 1-7). The tones of the c.f., however, appear very irregularly in the remainder of the composition. After the beginning they can be found only at widely scattered spots and they are consistently dissociated from their proper text. Furthermore, the cadences of the setting disagree with those of the chant in the majority of cases. These deviations from normal methods are so marked that it is doubtful that a c.f. is being elaborated. At the most, the antiphon melody is present only in the first few measures of one version of the motet (a different version of the opening measures is given in Tr 93), and even this resemblance may result from the English practice of emphasizing certain degrees of the scale (first, third, fifth, and sixth) at the beginnings of phrases.[47]

Another attribution which seems doubtful has been made in the introductory duo of the Credo of Dufay's Mass *Se la face ay pale*. It has been suggested that the superius and contratenor—which are freely imitative—are paraphrases of the tenor of the chanson.[48] The manner in which the notes of the tenor are presumed to appear in the Mass is shown in example 34. (A comparison is made only between the chanson tenor and the

EXAMPLE 34. Dufay, tenor of chanson, *Se la face ay pale*, and contratenor of *Missa Se la face ay pale*—Credo (J. F. R. and C. Stainer, *Dufay and His Contemporaries* [London, 1898], p. 140; Dufay, *Opera*, III, 13).

contratenor of the Credo in ex. 34, since the presumptive paraphrase is clearer in that voice than in the superius; however, since the superius imitates the contratenor, it too contains notes which may be related to the chanson tenor. Note that in the musical example as given by Erickson,[49] m. 10 and 11 of the duo are missing.)

To begin with, it seems quite plausible that the tenor melody should be paraphrased here, as an anticipatory statement of the c.f. can be expected in an introductory duo. The analysis showing the tenor phrase expanded to several in the derived voices is also plausible, since the paraphrase technique involves making several phrases out of one. (In ex. 34, phrase A of the chanson extends through phrases A′-B′-C′ and into D′ of the voice from the Mass.) These two points, however, complete the evidence in favor of paraphrase. As the example shows, the structure of the tenor phrase is ignored in a variety of ways: c′, the cadential goal, must be located as a tone which starts a phrase (ex. 34, m. 14, contratenor, phrase D′); the top note of the tenor line—the subdominant f′—is treated as an altogether unimportant note, a passing tone to the dominant g′ (ex. 34, contratenor, m. 6); also, a, the lowest note of the first melodic curve of the tenor, is omitted altogether (ex. 34, contratenor, m. 5). I am strongly inclined to believe that the agreements are of the fortuitous type which, as mentioned above, are bound to occur betwen two stylistically comparable lines of the same mode and of similar range, especially when, as is the case here, one has a considerably greater number of notes than the other. These two lines center on c′ and move within the octave g-g′, and one has a total of twenty-six notes while the other has only fifteen.

None of these observations constitutes negative proof. All that can be said is that this instance is significantly different from the usual procedures of Dufay and his contemporaries. Their methods reveal a consciousness of the superior importance of the cadential tones and a strong tendency to retain them as structural points in the paraphrase. Further, they reveal a desire to retain the identity of the original line to the extent that they give its tones fairly prominent positions in the elaborated version. The composer converts the given melody more or less completely to his own style, but in so doing he tends not to negate these features of the original in as thorough a manner as is supposed to be done in the elaboration of *Se la face ay pale*.

The characteristics of paraphrase listed above (pp. 73-74) are no more than norms of behavior. These norms, however, not only reveal how the composer converts a melody; in an indirect manner they give some insight into the way he views it, what he feels is of its essence and is, therefore, to be retained. That these feelings remained relatively inarticulate, that they were not codified in the sense of clear regulations and strict prohibitions, is indicated by the variability in practice.

Because of variability in practice, there are areas where no certainty can be achieved; hence, two analysts are apt always to be in disagreement on certain pieces. It must be recognized that the nature of the technique makes impossible a final decision as to whether c.f. is or is not being used in some cases. For a study of c.f. treatment, however, nothing could be more futile than to assume c.f. where none is used. It is imperative to recognize doubtful instances for what they are.

3

The Structural Cantus Firmus

THE C.F., either as a paraphrased melody or as a structural tenor, occupies a position of central importance in the polyphonic composition, but its relation to the work as a whole differs fundamentally according to which of the two forms it assumes. In the works with paraphrased melody, the composition exists for the sake of the c.f. In the works with structural tenor, the c.f. is employed for the sake of the composition. The structural tenor functions as the foundation or starting point for the erection of a polyphonic whole; the paraphrased melody is merely supported and adorned by its polyphonic setting. The structural c.f. is the established, traditional type; the paraphrased c.f. is a newcomer in the field.

In the early fifteenth century the structural c.f. is represented chiefly by the framework tenors of isorhythmic Mass movements and motets. A comparison of these tenors with c.f. paraphrases shows that the differences in their function are attended by many differences in treatment.

The proper voice of the structural c.f. is the tenor, the traditional starting point since the twelfth century for the process of polyphonic composition. The elaborated c.f. belongs above all to the superius, the text-bearing voice of the secular song.

The total length of the c.f. quotation in the framework need not correspond to the over-all extent of the composition. The quotation is typically a fragment which is repeated until the composition ends, in accordance with development), it is fragmentary in the sense that it may be broken off a practice which dates back to the multiple cursus of the thirteenth-century motet. Even when the c.f. quotation is long enough to extend the entire length of a work (a rather unusual case which shows up in a later stage of development), it is fragmentary in the sense that it may be broken off

83

abruptly at the conclusion of the composition without regard for the structure of the original Gregorian melody.[1] The paraphrase, on the other hand, does not deal with a fragment. It is based on a complete chant or an important section of one. The setting of only certain sections of the chant means that alternate monophonic and polyphonic rendition is desired.[2] There is no intention that the whole chant should not be performed, although it often appears so in the manuscripts, since the music for the parts to be sung monophonically is usually not included.

Multiple texts are often used in a composition with framework tenor. The relationship between them is one of content. This tradition likewise goes back to the thirteenth-century motet. The text of the paraphrased c.f. is the text of the setting, and all voices which have words are given it.

The Gregorian chant, being monophonic, exploits above all the melodic aspect of music. Yet, when a chant excerpt is used as a tenor frame, the excerpt is stripped of the minimum essential of melody—continuous movement to recognizable goals. Continuity and movement are interrupted and destroyed by the use of notes of long value frequently separated by extended pauses. The goals of motion, the phrase ends, are not taken into consideration.[3] All that is preserved is a succession of pitch levels which are literally correct but are not melody. The notes of the tenor are tokens or symbols of the original musical organism. This comment does not, however, apply to all types of c.f. treatment. The simple paraphrase settings give evidence that the composer viewed the c.f. as a melody, and even the elaborate paraphrases show him preserving the important structural goals—the ends of phrases and larger sections.

The repetitions of the framework tenor may be literal, but they are often subjected to some kind of schematic manipulation. Exact diminution of the rhythmic values is the most common, although melodic inversion and retrograde motion are sometimes employed. Mechanical treatment of this sort is, of course, foreign to the c.f. paraphrase, which is above all a process of free elaboration.[4]

The Isorhythmic Tenor

Although the principle of isorhythmic organization has been applied in a great variety of ways, the treatment of the c.f. itself can be described in comparatively few words. The isorhythmic tenor is typically an exact quotation of a fragment of the original melody. It is laid out as a true framework, with notes of long value interrupted by rests. These are organized into a rhythmic pattern (*talea*) which is repeated a greater or less number of times, often with diminutions of time value. It is the *talea*, the pattern of fixed rhythmic durations, which is the basic structural unit. The group of tones quoted from the c.f. (*color*) may correspond in length to one, two, or more *taleae*, or it may cover one and a half *taleae*, etc.[5]

Except for the occasional addition of a note or two at the final cadence, it was not the practice to insert free tones. Hence an isorhythmic tenor does not present the same type of problems that an elaborated c.f. does. In some ways, despite the outward simplicity of these tenors, the problems are more puzzling. The disregard of the most obvious, organic aspect of the chant—that it is melody intended to be sung and breathed—is one of the most noteworthy features and gives evidence of an approach to music which in some respects is utterly foreign to us.

The composers seem to distort the chants arbitrarily and incomprehensibly, yet a parallel to these distortions may be found in the work of their contemporaries in literature. The medieval scholar recognized several approaches to the written word. First of all, he could view a text in the historical sense, i.e., in the primary sense of its obvious, straightforward meaning. This was considered, characteristically, an inferior approach suitable for the vulgar but hardly worth the attention of the serious reader. Of much greater value to the educated man were the meanings hidden behind the text—the allegorical, the anagogical senses—and these he must fathom by construing the words and letters as symbols, often of a mathematical nature. This procedure involved not only the disregard of the obvious meaning of the text but also a complete disregard of the integrity of sentences, phrases, and even individual words.[6] The process—so ridiculous to us, so significant to medieval man—involved a destruction of the original sentences just as complete as that of the phrases of the chant in an isorhythmic tenor.

The primary sense of the chant—its obvious musical appeal as a melody—may well be compared to the historical sense of literature. This sense was recognized, and straightforward quotations of the chant are found in simple compositions, such as the English conductus. In serious compositions, such as the isorhythmic motets, the chant is treated in a way analogous to that accorded a literary text when it was searched for deeper meanings. It is possible that the educated musician, conditioned by the medieval intellectual environment, had when he treated the chant in this way some speculative intent which was similar to that of the scholar pursuing his exegetical labors.

Whether the comparison with literature is valid or not, these compositions owe some of their features to viewpoints unfamiliar to us. The isorhythmic structure as a whole is the result of the medieval interest in the proportional aspects of music, something that is of minor concern to musicians of later periods. The isorhythmic tenor, especially, is an intellectual construction to which proportional duration is basic, and its does not necessarily depend on those elements of organization—tonality, rhythmic pattern, melodic repetition—which we regard as fundamental to any musical structure.

The rhythmically organized tenor is the core of the motet, yet in many works written for more than three voices the tenor may be replaced by an optional voice, the *solus tenor*. This was a synthetic part, a combination of the original lowest voices, the tenor and contratenor. It consists only of the notes of either voice which happen to be on the bottom at any time; since these cross each other constantly, the *solus tenor* is a thorough mixture of the two. Containing only the lowest-sounding notes, it could provide a proper harmonic foundation by itself and could be used in performance to replace the voices out of which it was constructed.[7]

The practical value of the *solus tenor* is clear enough, for it reduces the number of performers necessary to give a harmonically correct rendition of a work. The substitution of this voice for the original parts, however, can only be interpreted as a serious vulgarization of the music, since it covers up the liturgical and intellectual foundation. The isorhythmic organization of the lower parts is frequently destroyed, and the succession of notes of the c.f. is almost always obliterated, because the substitute part has only those notes of the chant that the tenor sounded when it was below the contratenor.

It is evident that works were actually performed with the reduced number of voices made possible by this part, but it is certainly unjustifiable to publish only the *solus tenor* and omit the tenor and contratenor, as van den Borren has done in the case of a motet by Carmen, *Venite adoremus Dominum*.[8] His edition gives a deceptive picture of the structure of the whole composition[9] and makes it quite impossible to determine whether or not the tenor carries a c.f.

The lively interest in isorhythm in the first three decades of the fifteenth century is attested by the large number of motets and Mass movements which were organized in this manner, as well as by the variety of ingenious ways in which composers handled the rhythmic schemes.[10] This was undoubtedly a flourishing period for isorhythm, but it was also a late one, for deterioration set in rapidly in the 1430's.

The waning of interest and the attempts to replace the old structural means by new ones can be seen clearly in the isorhythmic motets of Dufay. The earlier ones are invariably isorhythmic in all parts, but of the five which can be definitely dated in the 1430's four have only the tenor rhythmically organized—the other voices are either free or organized according to some different principle.[11] In one of these works, *Nuper rosarum flores*, the rhythmic element of organization is supplemented by others of a different type. The two lower parts are written in a "canon" of a sort,[12] and the upper parts are isomelic in the sections for four voices. Melodic repetition, both strict and free, is used in another of these motets, *Ecclesie militantis*. The contratenor sings the same melody three times over (m. 25, 61, 97) and the effect of repetition is emphasized by repetition of the text, *Bella canunt gentes*. There are also traces of isomelism in the upper parts, although the melodic correspondences are not as extensive as in *Nuper rosarum flores*. (Compare superius I, m. 34-44; superius II, m. 69-78; superius I, m. 106-116.)[13] Although Dufay continued to write motets which were rhythmically organized in all parts, it is apparent that he was abandoning this strict type in his early maturity. The tenor, as the structural part, continues to be rhythmically organized, but the upper parts lose the long, complex rhythmic schemes which had formerly controlled them.

With Dunstable, who was apparently about twenty years older than Dufay, the case is somewhat different. Of the motets which have come down to us, nine are fully isorhythmic. Two of the nine, *Veni Sancte Spiritus* and *Salve scema sanctitatis*, give every indication of being late works.[14] Both are written for four voices and the handling of the parts indicates that they could not have been written before the 1430's. Before this time, four-voice writing involved the use of a considerable number of parallel fifths and octaves, especially at the cadences, where the successive perfect intervals are so prominent as to have the effect of reducing the texture to only three real voices.[15] In these two motets we find that the cadences are for four real parts and that the voices are handled throughout so as to produce consistent, full, four-part harmony. In *Veni Sancte Spiritus* although the isorhythmic ordering is never relinquished, paraphrased c.f. is used. This fusion of the two kinds of treatment in the same work also indicates a late stage.[16] In *Salve scema sanctitatis* the bottom voice (called tenor in the manuscript) is a true bass line which seldom crosses the tenor bearing the c.f. In this work, then, there is not only competent four-voice writing: the four parts are supported by a real bass. It is, harmonically, one of the most advanced of Dunstable's works and quite possibly was written in the 1440's.

The works of these men give us a fairly clear picture of a historical process. They show that composers did not abandon isorhythm all at once, nor did they abandon it completely, but in the course of ten or fifteen years they modified the method of organization to a point where only the tenor was rhythmically bound. It is also noticeable that Dufay, the younger man, is the more actively experimental and uses the modified structure in some of his most magnificent works. Dunstable, the older, is by no means reactionary, but his tendency is to compromise by absorbing new procedures into the older form. He seeks a conservative solution and accommodates the traditional form to newer artistic aims, while Dufay is more radical and tends to reject the older procedures and to replace them with newer ones.

INCIDENTAL ISORHYTHM—THE NONISORHYTHMIC TENOR

There are framework tenors which have a more or less significant resemblance to the isorhythmic type but which are either not based on a rhythmic scheme (e.g., Dunstable's "Nesciens Mater") or are, at least, not organized according to such an exact scheme of repetition as that of the true isorhythmic tenor. Although few in number, they show a great variety of treatments.

The tenor of the motet of Dunstable, *Specialis Virgo–Salve parens inclita*, is partially rhythmically organized as an incident in the statement of the entire fourth verse of the sequence *Post artum Virgo Maria*.[17] There is no repetition of c.f. material, the statement of the verse continuing throughout the motet. The tenor is not rhythmically organized at either the beginning or the end, and the upper voices are almost entirely free, showing only occasional brief correspondences of rhythmic pattern. The motet *Veni Sancte Spiritus–Consolator optime–Sancte Spiritus assit nobis gratia* is isorhythmic in the tenor only, because of an exact restatement of the c.f. which, of course, causes the rhythmic pattern to recur. As in *Specialis Virgo*, the c.f. consists of an entire stanza of a sequence (Dunstable, *Works*, p. 177), but in this work it is stated three times—first normally, then in inversion, and finally in retrograde motion and transposed down a fifth. The *color* is not broken into *taleae*, and rhythmic repetition occurs between the first and second statements only because melodic inversion does not interfere with rhythmic values. The third statement, in retrograde motion, gives a different succession of note values, showing that Dunstable did not consider repetition of rhythmic pattern the basis of the structure. He did not write the tenor as a rhythmic palindrome, which would produce the same pattern whether read forward or backward, since he is primarily interested in manipulating the tenor melodically by means of transposition, inversion, and retrograde motion. Traces of isorhythm are, however, found in the upper voices, since the introductory duos of the first two periods as well as their cadences correspond. (M. 1-10 in superius and contra agree with m. 32-41; m. 28-31 agree with m. 59-62 in the superius only.)

In a third motet, "*Nesciens Mater*," there is considerable recurrence of rhythmic pattern in the tenor, but this is entirely due to repetition of the melodic fragment upon which it is based. A canonic prescription directs that the five-note pattern be stated four times, each time a tone higher. The two last-described works stand aside from the fully isorhythmic motets of Dunstable because (1) they are not laid out on a broad scale, (2) the tenors are not organized into *taleae*, and (3) they both make use of some manipulations of the tenor of a melodic nature. Whatever isorhythmic features they possess seem incidental, brought in to bolster tenor layouts which find their logic in other features of structure.

An Agnus of Dufay (*DTO*, 14, p. 153) also uses a framework tenor which is subjected to repetition in retrograde motion, as well as to rhythmic manipulation. The tenor quotation is not a real fragment, as it covers a whole section of the chant (the whole first Agnus of Mass IX). The section of the chant is itself fragmented, since it is broken into three parts, but significantly, each of these is a complete phrase. Dufay was nurtured in the late *ars nova* but, as indicated above, he adopted viewpoints of the Renaissance in his early maturity. He tends to consider melodic factors even when he is constructing a framework tenor.[18] In laying out this tenor he causes each of the phrases to be repeated before the next is taken up, so that, if the phrases are lettered A, B, and C, the entire scheme is: O A, A retrograde; ₵ B, ₵2 B, cadence;[19] O C, ₵ C, ₵ C.

This composition, like *Specialis Virgo* and "*Nesciens Mater*" of Dunstable, does not have isorhythmic organization of the upper voices. It need hardly be added that the manipulations of the c.f. in all of them are of a type not found in c.f. paraphrases.

THE STRUCTURAL ELABORATION

There are a number of instances of mixed types of c.f. which show features of the framework and of the melodic elaboration as well. A mixture of elements of this kind is presented by the tenor of the composition of Forest (Dunstable?) *Ascendit Christus–Alma Redemptoris Mater* (ex. 35). The Marian antiphon in the tenor[20] functions as a structural c.f. because it is the foundation upon which the composition is built. The phrase structure of the original is honored more in the breach than in the observance (see m. 101 of ex. 35 for one instance), and the c.f. is broken off in the middle of a sentence when the composition ends (m. 110). The antiphon text is completely ignored except for the indication given at the beginning. These are all features of the framework c.f.

On the other hand, the c.f. is elaborated in such a way as to bring it into line with the character of the other voices. Hence it does not agree with the

EXAMPLE 35. Forest (Dunstable?), *Ascendit Christus–Alma Redemptoris Mater* (Mod B; OH; Dunstable, *Works*, p. 149; LU, p. 273).

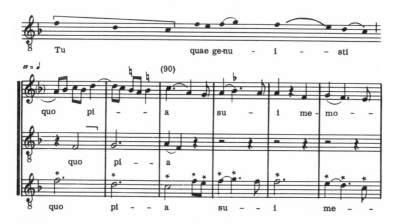

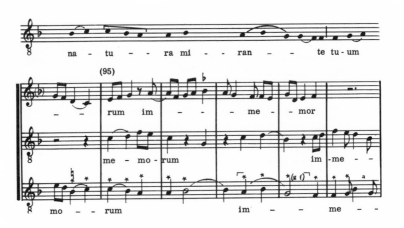

na - tu - - ra mi - ran - - te tu - um

(95)

- - rum im - - me - mor

me - mo - rum im - me -

mo - - rum im - - me - -

san-ctum Ge - - ni - to-rem Vir - - -

(100) (105)

ne - - qua quam e - xi - - - -

- - - mor ne - - qua-quam

- - mor ne - qua - - quam e - xi - - -

- - - go pri - - - - us

(110)

stat.

(e) - xi - stat.

stat.

definition of a framework tenor, as it does not have the rigid outline or the characteristic long note-values of such a part. It is, in fact, an elaborated c.f. used as a structural voice and will be called a "structural elaboration," or "structural paraphrase." The antimelodic features of these structural para-phrases, which are often very striking, differentiate them sharply from the settings of elaborated c.f. melodies. It seems that they must be explained as the result of a partial transfer of the process of elaboration to the frame-work tenor which yet does not displace all the characteristic antimelodic features of the type.[21]

The development of the rigid framework into the structural paraphrase represents the final triumph of the impulse to free, unhampered linear ex-pansion which has been seen as an essential characteristic of the elaborated melodic c.f. The strength of this impulse probably accounts for the fact that the framework c.f. is largely displaced by the structural paraphrase in the writing of the third quarter of the century; it may even account for the highly elaborate melodic style which arose at that time. An urge to unre-strained linear expansion lies at the heart of the style of Ockeghem, condi-tioning every aspect of his writing.

THE STRICT CANTUS FIRMUS

In a fairly large number of compositions the c.f. is presented in long notes of equal value. This method of stating the c.f. evidently never was as impor-tant in the written compositions of the fifteenth century as the statement in elaborated form, yet, strangely enough, it has persisted as a pedagogical aid, filtering down through the writings of a long line of theorists until at the present day it represents c.f. as such to every student of strict counter-point.[22]

In compositions of the fifteenth century these *cantus firmi* look and sound like frameworks, especially when used in the tenor, merely because that voice provides a foundation of notes that move more slowly than the upper voices; however, as the c.f. quotation is not a mere fragment of a chant, as the whole composition ends when the quotation of the c.f. is com-pleted, and as the words of all the voices are those of the c.f., a work based upon a quotation of this kind partakes of the nature of a c.f. setting. On the other hand, the length of the notes and their mechanically steady progres-sion lessen the feeling of melodic flow. The method of stating the chant in notes of equal values is the same as that used in the simple settings of the English conductus, but these compositions differ from the English since they are not c.f. harmonizations. They are best described as c.f. with contra-puntal setting since the plainchant is set off sharply from the more rapidly moving notes of the added parts.

Two settings of the gradual *Salve sancta parens*, one by A. de Lantins (ex. 36a) and one by Lymburgia (ex. 36b), have tenors which resemble each

EXAMPLE 36. (a) A. de Lantins, *Salve sancta parens* (BL, fo. 1; LU, p. 1263).
(b) Lymburgia, *Salve sancta parens* (BL, fo. 178ᵛ). (c) Anonymous, Alleluia,
Virga Jesse (Pepys 1236, fo. 33; *Ege Grad.*, fo. 88).

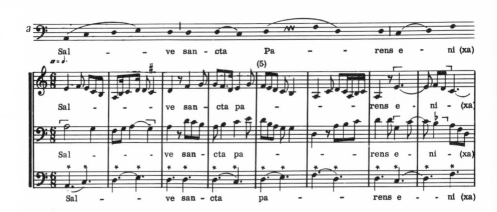

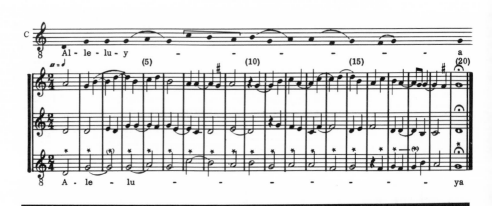

other very closely. Both quote the gradual down to the psalm, and even the forms of the ligatures agree. The melodies are presented continuously, without rests, so that there is no clear phrase division. This can be seen between the words *parens* and *enixa* (ex. 36a, m. 7; ex. 36b, m. 8-9). If a cadence is intended, it is not at all clear at either point. As in the unornamented settings of Old Hall, the composers are faced with the fact that the chant often will not fit the standard harmonic cadence. When the shape of the c.f. allows, as at the end of the first phrase in example 36a, a very clear harmonic cadence is made (m. 2-3). It may be that one was attempted at the end of the next phrase (m. 7) and was prevented by the repeated d's in the chant. At the corresponding spot in example 36b (m. 8), there is no indication that a cadence was even attempted.

Examples from the second half of the century are more plentiful. The Alleluia, *Virga Jesse*, of an anonymous English composer (ex. 36c)[23] also belongs to this type, although it approaches the c.f. paraphrase in character because of the free notes of shorter value at measures 16-18. An anonymous *Salve Regina* from Tr 91 presents the c.f. in the superius.[24] Some variety is gained by stating it in both breves and semibreves, although the two values are not mixed in the same phrase. Another anonymous *Salve Regina* from Tr 91 occasionally mixes the two values in the same phrase and also employs migration between the superius and tenor.[25] In both cases phrases are articulated by rests. A number of other examples of this type of setting are included in the Trent codices[26] and in manuscripts of German provenience.[27] From the evidence of the published works, it is a preferred usage with Adam von Fulda, but the examples given above show that it cannot be solely a German usage. It is probably not even a characteristically peripheral one, since it is found fairly often in the works of Obrecht.

4

Cantus Firmus in the Mass

FREQUENTLY POLYPHONIC SETTINGS of the Gregorian melodies of a given service, of both the Ordinary and the Proper of the Mass, are collected together. Examples of this are the Liebert Mass and Dufay's *Missa Sancti Jacobi*. The appropriate c.f. is not set in all the movements (e.g., the Gloria and Credo of the Liebert and Dufay Masses are freely composed),[1] nor are all the movements of the Ordinary always included.[2] In Tr 88 there are a number of sets which include Propers only for certain days.[3] The scheme of such a Mass does not provide for tonal or thematic unity; the chants on which the movements are based are not musically so unified;[4] but, since the chants all belong to the same service, the movements have an ·extramusical, liturgical unity. Works of this type will be referred to by the term, admittedly inadequate, of "plainchant Mass."[5]

THE MASS CYCLE

At some point not later than the first decade or two of the fifteenth century the practice arose of relating the movements of the Ordinary by musical means. It seems that at first· only pairs of movements were related, the Gloria-Credo and Sanctus-Agnus. In Old Hall there are occasional instances of relationship of a rather general nature between two movements, although they are not copied in immediate succession in the manuscript.[6] The practice of pairing movements was more clearly defined in Italy at this time, or slightly later, as is shown by the numerous Gloria-Credo combinations in BL.[7] In some cases the movements were written by different composers and the pairing must have been done by the compiler of the manuscript,

94

but in others the movements are conceived from the beginning as a related musical couple. The relationships are often vague, consisting of no more than similarity of texture, meter, or scoring. In contrast, a pair by Ciconia may be cited as an example in which the intent of the composer is unmistakable: passages from the Gloria are quoted in the companion Credo.[8] The passages are quoted haphazardly in the body of these two movements, but in other pairs quotations are often given a specific position, either at the end or, more commonly, at the beginning of the movements.[9]

THE CYCLE BASED ON CANTUS FIRMUS

A further step in the direction of unifying the Mass is made when all five movements of the Ordinary are related by means of some common musical material. The idea of relating the movements by means of a common c.f. in the tenor, it is now clearly evident, is of English origin. The lists of contents of five important manuscripts dating from about 1440 or earlier[10] disclose two complete Mass cycles by Leonel or Dunstable,[11] both of which are based on tenor c.f.—one on *Alma Redemptoris Mater*[12] and the other on *Rex saeculorum*.[13] In contrast to these are four complete cycles by known composers—one each by G. Dufay,[14] A. de Lantins,[15] Pyllois,[16] and J. de Lymburgia[17]—none of which makes use of tenor c.f. The movements are related by common musical material, most often in the form of initial motives. To these cycles may be added four Mass movements by Grossim (Kyrie, Gloria, Credo, and Sanctus)[18] which show the relationship of a common structure and scoring. Each movement consists of duos accompanied by *"trompetta"* alternating with the customary three-part writing. The Gloria and Credo also have clearly related initial motives which are, in addition, possibly related to the beginning of the Kyrie.

We can deduce not only that the Masses with tenor c.f. are English, but also, judging from the names of the composers, that the others are Continental. There are so few complete cycles at this time that evidence for two typical practices, Continental and English, would be meager were it not for the fact that there are a number of instances of Mass movements related in pairs. These paired movements show, as clearly as do the cycles, that it was primarily the English who cultivated the c.f. Mass[19] while Continental composers were apt to use mottoes or other devices.[20]

Neither group restricted themselves absolutely to one type of treatment. Bennet wrote a pair related by a very clear motto in the tenor, and there are a few single Mass movements with a tenor c.f. by composers with French and Italian names.[21] It seems that Continental composers were not slow to take up the idea of the c.f. Mass cycle, although there is a definite time lag. Stylistic considerations make it improbable that they composed many before 1450. Heinrich Besseler suggests that the *Missa Caput* of Dufay was written in the 1440's and that the remainder of the c.f. cycles of this master probably were written between 1450 and 1465, the last period of his life.[22]

Certain elements in the tradition of the English may account for their priority in the field of the c.f. Mass. This method of unification presupposes the use of foreign c.f., since a single c.f. must be foreign to at least four of the five movements. For instance, if a Gregorian Kyrie melody were used because it would be liturgically correct as tenor of the Kyrie, it would still be foreign to the four succeeding movements. In actual practice, chants of the Ordinary were avoided, chants of the Proper or Office being selected, so that the c.f. is foreign to all five movements (in the strict sense). Now we find the practice of using foreign c.f. established for the single Mass movements of Old Hall and the Fountains fragment. Each of these manuscripts contains a number of isorhythmic Glorias and Credos; in every case where the c.f. has been identified, it is not a chant of the Ordinary.

It has been shown that there was some thought of pairing isorhythmic movements even as early as the time of these manuscripts,[23] and, considering the widespread efforts to unify the Mass in the immediately succeeding years, it does not seem a surprising development for a composer familiar with isorhythmic movements with foreign c.f. to establish a specific relationship between more than one by writing them over a common tenor. There are indeed, in the Continental sources mentioned above, pairs with isorhythmic tenors (Dunstable's *Jesu Christe fili Dei* and *Da gaudiorum premia*) and an entire cycle (Leonel's *Alma Redemptoris Mater*). The later dates of these works, in comparison with the single movements of Old Hall, is indicated by the modifications of isorhythmic structure as used in them. In none is the *color* of the tenor divided into *taleae*, nor are the upper voices rhythmically organized.

The English also use tenors which are not isorhythmic. In the *Missa Rex saeculorum* by Dunstable (Leonel), the tenor is a structural paraphrase, the treatment being much like that of the motet *Ascendit Christus* (ex. 35). It is possible to trace this type of treatment back to individual Mass movements of Old Hall also. A Sanctus and Agnus of Leonel with ornamented tenor c.f. may be cited,[24] although they seem rather remote from *Rex saeculorum*, in that they do not make use of foreign c.f. and are stylistically much more primitive.

Sacred and Secular Cantus Firmus

The few Mass cycles that have come down to us from the fourteenth century show that composers at that time used c.f. in some of the movements of the Ordinary and that they chose the appropriate, traditionally prescribed melodies for this purpose. They were in the habit of writing a Kyrie over a Kyrie melody, an Agnus over an Agnus, and so on. For this reason, these Masses correspond to the definition of plainchant Mass given above and may be considered direct forerunners of the plainchant Mass of the fifteenth century. They can hardly be so directly related to the unique product of the early Renaissance, the c.f. cycle, inasmuch as they differ completely on the crucial point of choice of c.f.

The very existence of the cycle of the fifteenth century is predicated on the use of foreign c.f. and hence upon the disregard of strict propriety of the borrowed melody. Foreign c.f. as such was neither new nor strange, since it had the whole motet tradition behind it, yet the decision to use it as the basis for settings of the Ordinary involved more than a simple shift of procedure from one category of composition to another. Purely artistic considerations would not suffice as an explanation. Since the chants of the Ordinary form the very heart of the liturgy, the seriousness of dissociating the prescribed melody from its words cannot be ignored.

Whether composers in the fifteenth century felt that there was a question of liturgical propriety is not known; if they did, it is obvious that they must have judged that the advantages of foreign c.f. far outweighed the objections to it. These advantages were both aesthetic and liturgical. On the one hand, the repetition of the c.f. gives a specific musical relationship between the five movements; on the other, a c.f. chosen from the Proper or one of the offices of a service gives the Ordinary a close connection to the service as a whole. The polyphonic Ordinary becomes uniquely related to a given service, in contrast to the Gregorian Ordinaries which are common to many.

The lack of concern for outward appearances of liturgical propriety is, of course, most evident in the use of secular *cantus firmi*. True, in certain cases the relationship of the secular text to the sacred service is clear enough,[25] but in the majority it is difficult to conceive of a satisfactory connection between the secular love songs and the words of the Ordinary with which they are associated. For all the subtlety and the devious modes of thought of the fifteenth century, it is doubtful that composers ever seriously tried to maintain that there was any such connection in the case of many of their works (e.g., in Obrecht's *Missa Carminum*).

This being the case, it is quite reasonable to suppose that liturgical considerations often played little part in the selection of secular *cantus firmi* and that the composer was left free to base his choice on a variety of other factors, among them the purely musical qualities of a melody. Before this time the aspect of melodic conformation was of minor importance and the value of a c.f. lay in qualities which are not now considered as essentially musical. *Cantus firmi*, whether intended for use in the church, for state occasions, or for whatever purpose, were chosen primarily because of their text, not because of their inherent musical qualities. The way was, however, now being opened for a new attitude, one whose significance can hardly be overemphasized.

Although it is aside from the purposes of this study, the question of the propriety of the use of secular *cantus firmi* in sacred works should be mentioned. It has been the subject of much discussion, and opinions about the practice have ranged from complete condemnation to understanding acceptance. Nowadays it is recognized as simply one of the many ways in which the sacred and secular spheres were mixed in the fifteenth century.[26]

However, it is not necessary to refer to other cultural aspects of the period to account for the mingling of the two. From the point of view of musical style alone, it seems a natural enough development for secular art song and sacred music to be brought into such intimate association. The use of a popular tenor, identified by name, as basis of a Mass is only an overt manifestation of the spirit latent in the whole procedure of paraphrase—one of the most characteristic developments of the fifteenth century. It has been suggested above that the aim in paraphrasing or ornamenting a c.f. was to bring the Gregorian melody more or less closely into line with a melodic ideal, an ideal which was valid for secular as well as sacred music. There is but little difference between bringing the element of the familiar into the Mass in the form of a secular melody, or bringing it in under the form of a Gregorian melody which has been reworked to approximate the familiar type.

It was formerly often pointed out, in excusing the use of secular music, that the identity of a popular melody was lost in the many works where it was laid out in long note values. The secular melodies were, however, often used in direct quotation, in such a way that their identity could not possibly be mistaken. It seems that all we can say of their employment is that it is exactly on a par with that of sacred melodies—both might be quoted exactly, converted into a framework of pedal notes, or ornamented at the will of the composer. On the whole, his choice of secular or of Gregorian c.f. had little influence on the musical quality or the musical character of his work. The high or low origin of the c.f. he would consider scarcely relevant to the question of the appropriateness of the music to its solemn purpose.

In the latter part of the century Tinctoris made a very definite distinction between the styles proper to the Mass, the motet, and the chanson.[27] Characteristically, he based these distinctions on *varietas*—on the number of different ways in which the composer should handle his material in the different categories. He had nothing whatever to say about secular or sacred c.f., and, when citing a work of Dufay as a model of Mass composition, he did not choose one of the great masterpieces based on Gregorian c.f. (*Ave Regina caelorum* or *Ecce ancilla Domini*)—he chose *L'homme armé*, the work in which Dufay manipulated the material in the greatest variety of ways.[28] Tinctoris makes it clear that the Mass was indeed respected—that it was considered the highest category of composition—but respect was to be expressed through devoted workmanship and the most elaborate and ingenious treatment of which the composer was capable.

DETAILS OF CANTUS FIRMUS TREATMENT

Certain structural details of the early Mass cycles and pairs merit discussion. In the tenor of the Leonel *Missa Alma Redemptoris Mater*, the antiphon is quoted without ornamental notes up through the syllable *"po"* of *populo*, at which point it is broken off abruptly. (See chap. 3, n. 1.) It has other features characteristic of the framework tenor, such as arbitrary rests, frequent use of notes of extreme length, and a general disregard of the phrase structure of the original. Because the tenor is repeated exactly, both rhythmically and melodically, in each movement, historians have come to call it isorhythmic.[29] Yet it is not an isorhythmic tenor of the old type, as it is not internally organized into *taleae* and does not have the diminutions normally found in tenors of the older isorhythmic structures. Various proportional indications are used during the course of the statements, but they affect only the manner of reading the notes and apparently have no structural function.[30] The upper voices are not related to the c.f. musically, nor are there any other devices for connecting movements, such as mottoes, repetitions of material in the body of the movements, etc. Dunstable's Credo-Sanctus pair on *Da gaudiorum premia*[31] shows the same traits as the Mass of Leonel in all respects except that the phrasing and text have an influence on the placement of the rests in the tenor. In all cases they are placed so as not to contradict the phrase and word structure of the respond, except for the last word, *federa*, which is split by a long rest (*Works*, p. 43, m. 124-125, and p. 46, m. 136-139).

The treatment of the c.f. in Dunstable's Gloria and Credo, *Jesu Christe, Fili Dei*, is somewhat closer to the traditional methods. The whole tenor excerpt is given twice in each movement, although it, too, is not organized into *taleae* and it consists of an entire section of the chant. It is, however, subjected to the standard type of rhythmic manipulation; the note values of the first statement are twice as long as those of the second.[32] Initial motives are not used, nor are the upper voices related in any way to the tenor. In the works of both Leonel and Dunstable the upper voices are not isorhythmically organized.

Unlike these three tenors, that of the *Missa Rex seculorum* of Dunstable (Leonel)[33] is freely elaborated and falls into the class of tenors illustrated by the motet *Ascendit Christus* (ex. 35). It furnishes a very good example of the reluctance to employ exact repetition which has been commented upon in the discussion of paraphrase technique. The melody is quoted once in its entirety in each movement, but each presentation is different in rhythmic pattern and ornamentation. (See ex. 37a). Free extensions, such as have been noticed in other works of Dunstable and Leonel, are provided at the end of the Sanctus and Agnus (ex. 37b).

This Mass differs from those with repeated rhythmic scheme in another important respect. In at least one movement an upper voice is derived from the c.f. The superius of the introductory duet of the Credo clearly paraphrases the tenor melody for thirty-three measures, thus anticipating the statement of the c.f. by that voice. (See ex. 38*b*). When it is ascertained

EXAMPLE 37. (*a*) Dunstable (Leonel), *Missa Rex seculorum*—tenors only (Tr 92; Aosta; *Works*, p. 47, ff; *Pal. Mus.*, XII, 301a). (*b*) The same—endings of movements, tenors only.

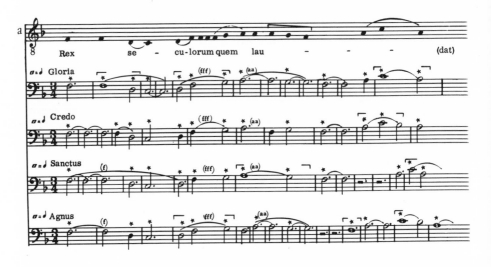

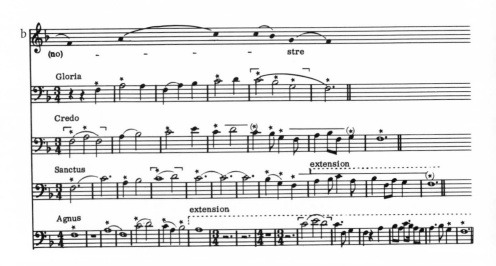

that this procedure was used in one movement, the question naturally arises as to whether it was used in the others. That it was used is unlikely. Example 38a shows that the first few notes of the c.f. can be found in the contratenor of the Gloria, which starts with a duet just as the Credo does. They can be found also in the superius of the Sanctus and Agnus, although

EXAMPLE 38. (a-d) Dunstable (Leonel), *Missa Rex seculorum*—upper voices, Gloria, Credo, Sanctus, and Agnus (Tr 92; Aosta; *Works*, p. 47, ff; *Pal. Mus.*, XII, 301a).

these two movements have no introductory duets. (See ex. 38c-d.) The tenor enters immediately with the c.f., and the superius has to be written as a counterpoint to it. Also, it is a customary feature of the English melodic style to emphasize the first, third, fifth, and sixth degrees of the mode. Here the first four notes of the c.f. are the first, sixth, and fifth degrees, so that the agreement may as well be accidental as intentional. In example 38b, the large number of notes which agree with the c.f. and their generally prominent position in the melody line make it certain that this is a c.f. paraphrase. In example 38a, c, and d, the few notes which agree, as well as the irregularity of their appearance and their occasional unimportant position in the line, make it appear very doubtful that they constitute a paraphrase.

Two other English Mass pairs are of interest because one, and possibly both, have mottoes—in addition to the customary tenor c.f. All three voices are exactly the same in the opening measures of the Sanctus and Agnus *Regnum mundi* by Driffelde (ex. 39a-b),[34] and the Gloria and Sanctus

EXAMPLE 39. (a-b) Driffelde, *Regnum mundi*—Sanctus and Agnus (Tr 90, no. 973, 92, no. 1552).

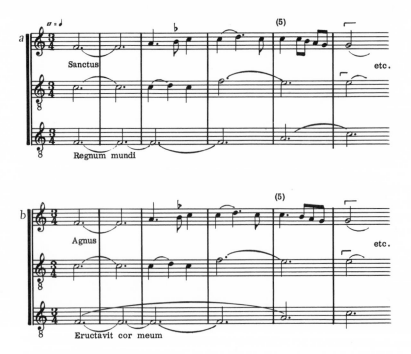

Jacet granum by Bennet[35] have exactly the same notes in the first two measures of the superius as well as general similarities in the contratenor (ex.
40a-b). These are two different pairs, by different composers, yet the initial
motives of both are similar. They illustrate well the English preference for
triadic melody outlines, and give some point to the preceding comments on

EXAMPLE 40. (a-c) Benet, *Jacet granum*—Gloria, Sanctus, and Sanctus (Tr
87, no. 21; 92, no. 1379; 90, no. 969).

the Leonel Mass. Another Sanctus on *Jacet granum*, by Bennet, has a similar beginning (ex. 40c), as do yet another Sanctus and Agnus by the same
composer.[36] Since beginnings such as these are stereotypes, they are not
good evidence of musical relationships unless supported by agreements in
other respects, as in example 39a-b, where the entire first section of the
Agnus is substantially the same as the first section of the Sanctus.

In the case of the two movements of Driffelde there may be a temptation
to propose that the superius is derived from the first three notes of the
tenor c.f., *Regnum mundi*. The use of tenor material in the superius of
the Credo *Rex seculorum* would tend to give the supposition some support.
Yet it is likely that the similarity is, again, simply an incidental result of
the English preference for triadic figures.

Another English Mass, an anonymous Gloria, Credo, and Sanctus on
Requiem aeternam,[37] presents the c.f. in melodically identical form in all
movements. As long as the tenor sounds, the rhythmic setup is also identical.
The only relaxation of the rhythmic scheme occurs between major divisions
of the tenor (marked by double bars in the original) where duos of different
length are introduced while the tenor is silent. Otherwise the treatment
does not differ from that of the framework tenors of Leonel and Dunstable
(the same use of very long note-values, arbitrarily inserted rests, etc.). This
Mass is probably a little later than those mentioned above. It is found in a
manuscript which is somewhat more recent than Tr 87 or 92; but the chief
reason for believing that the work is later is found in the writing for four
voices. The tenor functions as a real bass and stays constantly below the
other parts. The harmonic style is not noticeably advanced—parallel fifths
can be found in the cadences and the composer does not always avoid
unisons and octaves, but on the other hand, the maintenance of a strict
rhythmic scheme only when the tenor is sounding also indicates a later
stage. The method corresponds to that which Dufay follows in his Masses
Se la face ay pale and *Caput*. Some imitation is used in the two upper voices,
noticeably at the beginning of the movements. These imitative passages
outline triads, so it is possible, although not certain, that head motives were
intended.

The anonymous *Missa Quem malignus spiritus* is found in an English
manuscript and, with one movement lacking, in Trent also.[38] At first sight,
owing to the way rests are introduced, the very long note values, and the
identical rhythmic pattern of the first seven notes in every movement, it
appears that this is a rhythmically organized tenor. The continuation of the
c.f. quotation, however, is different rhythmically in every movement; also it
gives evidence of ornamentation (the original melody has not been located).
Hence it appears to be partially rhythmically organized and partially paraphrased. The rhythmically organized parts, because of their position at the
beginning of the movements, act as tenor mottoes. There are none in the

other voices, although the superius of the Kyrie, Gloria, and Sanctus and Agnus bear a general resemblance to one another.[39] It has been seen that the English tend to rely entirely on the tenor for purposes of unification. The only completely straightforward use of head motives in other voices has been found in the pair by Driffelde. The method of handling the tenor in *Quem malignus spiritus*, so that it also acts as a head motive, is a peculiarly English adaptation of a Continental practice.

There can certainly be no head motive in the superius of the Credo, since it begins with a quotation from the Gregorian Credo (ex. 41). It is broken

EXAMPLE 41. Anonymous, Credo, *Quem malignus spiritus* (Cambridge, Ii. 5. 18, fo. 223ᵛ-224; Gr. Sar., pl. D).

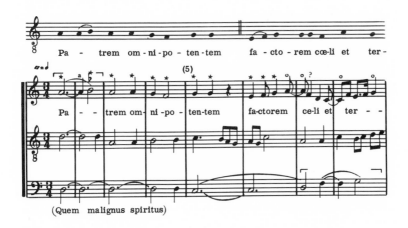

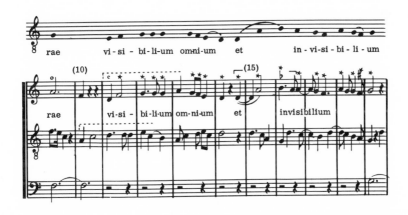

off when it cannot be fitted to the tenor easily (m. 6 ff.), and it is taken up again in the duet (m. 11 ff.). The combination of the correct plainchant melody with the one used in the tenor is uncommon at this time, although it becomes one of Josquin's favorite procedures. Quotations of the plainchant in freely composed sections are not infrequent, as will be pointed out from time to time.

The importance of these early Masses can hardly be overestimated. Not only is the general concept of writing a cycle on a single c.f. established; the most important specific methods of handling the c.f. are developed as well. The structural principles which are laid down in this period persist until well after the turn of the century despite the development of many new procedures of composition.

The two commonest means of handling the c.f. in the tenor are employed in basically the same ways that they are by Obrecht and Josquin. In the isorhythmic type, the notes and rhythmic patterns are repeated exactly or subjected to schematic manipulation (diminution, inversion, etc.); in the elaborated type, the c.f. is presented in differing guises on each statement. In at least one of the early English Mass pairs, mottoes are used in conjunction with the c.f.; in one movement of Dunstable (Leonel) there is anticipatory statement of the c.f. in an upper voice; and in another work there are quotations of excerpts from the Gregorian Credo.

The device of anticipatory statement—of anticipatory presentation of c.f. phrases by a voice other than the one which carries the complete melody— is of especial interest. It represents a significant stage in a leisurely historical process during the course of which the role of the c.f. became ever more important. Compositions in which anticipatory statement is used hold an intermediate position between works of the early part of the century, in which the c.f. was restricted to a single voice, and works of thirty or forty years later, in which it permeates every voice and dominates every aspect of the music.

5

Cantus Firmus in
More Than One Voice

IN CERTAIN OF THE EARLIER WORKS the c.f. is taken into more than one
voice. This is done in various ways, some of which were not generally
adopted later, so that a certain number of these works must be classed as
experiments.

1. *Alternating Statement.*—The isorhythmic motet *Veni Sancte Spiritus*
by Dunstable (*Works*, p. 88) uses material from the hymn *Veni Creator
Spiritus* in both the tenor and superius. The second and third phrases of the
verse (*mentes tuorum* and *imple superna*) make up the framework tenor.
The superius paraphrases one phrase at a time in each of the duets at the
beginning of the isorhythmic periods. Since there are six duets and only four
phrases to the hymn stanza, the first phrase is paraphrased anew in the fifth
duet and the second phrase in the sixth.[1] In general, no more than one voice
has the c.f. at any given time as the superius is freely composed when the
tenor enters. Even the appearance at one point of a few notes of the third
phrase in the superius while the tenor is sounding[2] does not alter the fact
that the over-all plan is one of *alternating statement* of the c.f. by superius
and tenor. If the phrases are lettered A, B, C, and D, the scheme of c.f.
usage is as follows:

Superius   (free)
paraphrase A (free) B (free) C (free) D (C?) A (free) B (free)

107

Tenor scaf-
folding   (rest) B (rest) C (rest) B (rest) C (rest) B (rest) C

(See also ex. 42a-e, tenor and superius only; first five duets with tenor notes
immediately following are given. The phrases of the c.f. are lettered as in
the diagram above.)

Anticipatory statement does not play a part in this arrangement of the

---

EXAMPLE 42. (a-e) Dunstable, *Veni Sancte Spiritus* (Tr 92 and OH, late addition; Dunstable, *Works*, pp. 88, 89, 90, 90, 91; *LU*, p. 885)

c.f., for the phrase given to the superius is never immediately restated by the tenor. While there is doubtless a musical relation between the superius and tenor (they are both derived from the same c.f.), it is not especially close, nor can it be easily heard, owing to (1) the musical differences of paraphrasing and scaffolding treatment and (2) the fact that the two voices proceed according to two different schemes, one presenting the c.f. melody phrase by phrase (although separated by free material) and the other repeating the same two phrases. Dunstable has, however, achieved here a union of the two common methods of treating the c.f. in one composition and has introduced the paraphrase method into the isorhythmic structure.[3]

It is possible that there is a similar union in the *Agnus Dei, custos et pastor* by Dufay. The composition is not isorhythmic but is based on a framework tenor which carries the first third of the Agnus of Mass IX.[4] At points where the tenor is silent, the c.f. is presented in other voices. The first Agnus is presented by the superius alone as an intonation, the second Agnus is paraphrased in the superius (ex. 43a), and the third is given to both of the voices of the duo (ex. 43b). The triadic outline of the beginning of the chant could cause doubt as to the actual presence of paraphrase in the duets, but since in both cases the melody is associated with the proper words and the first nine notes of the c.f. are clearly presented in succession, it is reasonably certain that this is not a coincidence.

A new pattern of tenor structure is gradually emerging in these works. The intent to increase the importance of the c.f. in the composition is clear. The method of doing so is basically one of alternating statement; i.e., the main c.f. statement is supplemented by subsidiary ones in a contrapuntal voice when the tenor rests. Even so, the idea of anticipating the material of the tenor in the contrapuntal voice, a standard feature of the later tenor Mass and motet, is not clearly defined. The combination of alternating and anticipatory statement which is found in the Credo of Dunstable's (Leonel's)

EXAMPLE 43. (a-b) Dufay, *Agnus Dei, Custos et Pastor* (Tr 92; DTO, 14, pp. 154, 156; LU, p. 42).

Missa Rex saeculorum is the final step to the fully developed tenor structure. As these works of Dufay, Dunstable (and Leonel?) must have been written by 1440 (all are found in Tr 92), it is evident that the great form of the fifteenth century was developing at the same time that the isorhythmic motet, the great form of the fourteenth, was dying out.

2. *Simultaneous Statement.*—Two other early works of Dufay make extensive use of the same c.f. in more than one voice, but paraphrase and scaf-

EXAMPLE 44. Dufay, *Nuper rosarum flores* (Tr 92; *DTO*, 53, p. 25; *LU*, p. 1250).

folding treatment are not mixed in the same composition.[5] Both tenors of *Nuper rosarum flores* carry the melody simultaneously in the form of isorhythmic scaffoldings. From the point of view of strict canon, the technical means by which this is achieved are not very imposing, as the notes are more or less pieced together, apparently being dropped in wherever they happen to fit well (see ex. 44). There is no strict imitation until the last few measures.

Dufay's motet *Anima mea liquefacta est* is a much more ambitious effort, the c.f. being given to all three voices. The chief carrier is the tenor, which presents the c.f. continuously, usually in long notes, and in but slightly ornamented form. The other two voices present it phrase by phrase with freely composed passages inserted at convenient spots. (See ex. 45). There are places where all three voices sound notes from different parts of the c.f. at the same time (ex. 45, m. 22-23, 31-33), so it is evident that the composer had to spend some thought on fitting them together. Yet this work is in no way comparable to the great technical tours de force of Josquin and his contemporaries, as the writing is not subjected to any rigid compositional procedures.[6] The composer avoids any severe restrictions by the use of freely inserted tones and passages. Even with these freedoms, the idea is not carried through without certain harshnesses, and this composition, therefore, is hardly typical of Dufay's normal manner of writing. Further, the idea of bringing the c.f. into all voices evidently did not seem of enough value to cause him to repeat the experiment.[7] It might be thought that lack of technical skill deterred him, for such a procedure would be bound to bring up problems comparable to those encountered in writing in imitation, but this cannot be the whole answer, as he was rather partial to the latter device. His competence is proved by the quality of the imitative lines, which

EXAMPLE 45. Dufay, *Anima mea liquefacta est* (Tr 87; Canonici; BL; *DTO*, 53, p. 20; *Proc. Mon.*, p. 275).

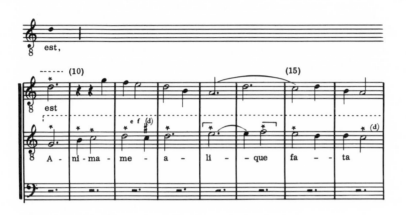

are melodically not inferior to those which are free.[8] Imitative passages occur fairly frequently in his sacred compositions and sometimes involve the c.f., but they appear incidentally, here and there, and do not usually follow any over-all plan.[9] Initial imitation is common only in the secular works.

Even though imitative writing is not of primary importance in his style, Dufay makes more use of it than most of his early contemporaries. It is not too common in free writing, and, not surprisingly, any extended use of the

EXAMPLE 46. Binchois, *Ave Regina caelorum* (Mod B; Marix, p. 189; *LU*, p. 1864).

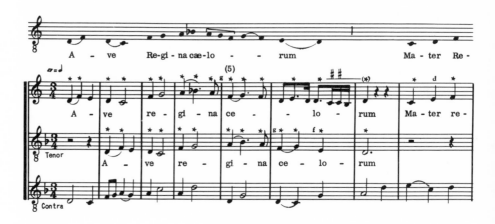

c.f. in imitation is a real rarity at this period. The first two phrases of a motet by Binchois, *Ave Regina caelorum* (ex. 46) provide an instance. Only two voices, the tenor and superius, are imitative, and the contratenor is free, a typical procedure of the chanson.

This is a surprising composition in more than one way. Even in his chansons, Binchois uses imitation much less frequently than Dufay. Also, the c.f. is present for only the first two phrases, which at the same time are the only ones wherein the superius and tenor are in imitation. The rest of the composition is free. This is a complete reversal of the customary experience, according to which the c.f. is much less apt to be present in passages where imitation is used than in those where it is not.

An instance of strict three-part canon on c.f. has been mentioned above (p. 38), but the conclusion to be drawn is that these are more or less isolated phenomena. There was a slight interest in using two types of c.f. treatment in the same composition. Imitation, a device that was well known in secular and freely composed sacred compositions, occurs rarely in connection with a c.f., and, on the whole, devices which bring the c.f. into more than one voice were not especially appealing to composers. The reverse is true in the third quarter of the century, so that a large part of the discussion of that period will be devoted to c.f. in more than one voice, especially to the first method that was widely adopted—alternating statement.

PART II

THE MASS
AND MOTET FROM
CIRCA 1450 TO 1485

6

The Masses of
Dufay, Ockeghem, and
Their Contemporaries

IN THE SUCCEEDING CHAPTERS, I make a great deal of the fact that certain composers prefer to proceed according to a plan in laying out the c.f. and to organize the counterpoints by means of short motives and points of imitation. Others, in contrast, prefer to state the c.f. freely and to avoid using motives and imitation in the other voices.

Historians have interpreted the two types of writing in various ways and have coined a number of descriptive terms for them. Of the many terms that have thus come into use, I have chosen "rational" and "irrational" as the most suitable for this work. They describe the musical situation sufficiently well, and they have the advantage, for a study of c.f. usage, of emphasizing the difference between planned (rational) procedures and those which are apparently unplanned (irrational).

I am aware of the objections that can be raised to the second of the terms. It is obvious that to call an art work irrational is to deny its essence. If the term is to be used at all, it must be used in the limited sense of apparent irrationality, and it is this sense that I employ. Also, I do not wish to make a sharper distinction between the two approaches than the facts warrant. The music of Ockeghem has often been characterized as irrational, yet instances of typically rational procedures are to be found in it. Similarly,

119

Busnois often copies the fanciful procedures of Ockeghem, although his approach is on the whole of the rational type.

In this period the c.f. is treated in a greater variety of ways than it had been before. The older types of treatment continue to be used, but the distinctions betwen them become less clear. Composers mix types, they use more than one type in a single composition, and they invent new ways of stating the borrowed material. Consequently it is impractical to set up a number of categories of c.f. treatment and cite compositions to illustrate them, as I did in Part I. The individual work must be used as the starting point and a summary made of the c.f. usages found in it. In Part II, I group works according to form and according to composer, starting with the cyclic Mass and laying especial emphasis on the Masses of Dufay and Ockeghem. After this I take up the motet and other smaller forms.

The Late Masses of Dufay

The five Mass cycles of Dufay which may be termed late are *Caput*; *Se la face ay pale*; *L'homme armé*; *Ecce ancilla Domini–Ne timeas Maria*; and *Ave Regina caelorum*. They are all scored for four voices and each bears a c.f. in the tenor, the c.f. being stated at least once in each movement.

There is some difference of opinion as to the dates of composition of these works, since we have very little historical information upon which to base a chronology. Judging from the style (the use of imitation, the place of the c.f. in the polyphony, etc.), it seems that *Caput* and *Se la face ay pale* are the oldest. *L'homme armé*, *Ecce ancilla Domini*, and *Ave Regina caelorum* are stylistically more advanced and so presumably younger.

Van den Borren at one time estimated that *Se la face ay pale* was written about 1460, and later suggested approximately the middle of the century.[1] *Ecce ancilla Domini* was copied at Cambrai in 1463, so we are sure that it was written before that date. The Kyrie of the *Missa Caput* was copied in the same year, which was formerly interpreted to mean that the entire Mass was as late a work as *Ecce ancilla*. It is now felt that this merely indicates the Kyrie was a later addition to an original work in four movements only.

Some indication of the date of composition of the *Ave Regina caelorum* Mass can be gleaned from the fact that the funeral motet of that name was copied at Cambrai in 1464. A striking passage for three voices is used in both at the word "*miserere*" (in the second Agnus of the Mass, and at the trope *miserere supplicanti Dufay* in the second part of the motet).[2] This quotation would indicate that both works were written at about the same time but it does not inform us as to which was the earlier. Van den Borren is inclined to believe that the Mass came first: ". . . the fragment of the motet appears copied in the Agnus of the Mass, or the other way about, which is the more probable."[3] There is equally good reason to believe that the passage was originally inspired by the text of the motet, for it sets off the trope from the rest of the words in a musically very striking way by a sudden change of tonality. It has no such obvious artistic justification in the Mass, where it is only one of many passages in which the tonality is altered by the use of accidentals.

The latest investigation into the matter has been made by Besseler in conjunction with the edition of the complete works. He places *Caput* in the 1440's. (Bukofzer suggests the 1450's as a likely date.)[4] *Se la face ay pale* is not much later, and *L'homme armé* comes next, occupying a place more or less by itself. *Ecce ancilla* and *Ave Regina* are the latest works, and are closely connected to one another stylistically and to a certain extent by musical material. A few measures of Agnus II of *Ecce ancilla* are actually quoted in Kyrie V of *Ave Regina*.[5]

Other points with regard to the Masses are not so debatable. It is clear now that Dufay did not originate the cyclic Mass. What he did in the later years of his life was consolidate the structural procedures which had been developed separately as English and Continental types. All of the works under consideration make use both of head motive and of preëxisting melody in the tenor voice in all movements. These two means of unification had apparently grown up separately and had seldom been combined, but Dufay uses them together consistently. He also makes use of both isorhythmic tenors and structural paraphrases, as Dunstable and Leonel had done. His use of a secular song as tenor for a cycle (in *Se la face ay pale* and *L'homme armé*) also seems to be a combination of English and Continental practices.[6]

The tenor of the chanson *Se la face ay pale* serves with practically no change as the tenor of the Mass.[7] It is rhythmically identical in the Gloria and Credo, so that these two movements are more closely related to each other structurally than to the other movements and form a pair within the cycle. The Kyrie and Agnus are also laid out similarly, but the rhythmic organization is modified as it was in the *Missa Requiem aeternam*. (See p. 104.) The voices are isorhythmic in relation to one another only when they are sounding, because the rests between different sections vary in length. The Sanctus has a different tenor layout, although again the rhythmic scheme of the tenor is identical with that of the other movements so long as that voice is sounding, because the original rhythmic patterns of the chanson are carefully retained.[8]

The scheme of diminutions in the triple statement of the tenor in the Gloria and the Credo represents a position as close to the isorhythmic motet as that occupied by Dunstable and Leonel, who also use this device in their isorhythmic Mass tenors. While there is a clear relationship to true isorhythmic structure, Dufay has selected from it only those elements which suit his purposes. He makes use of the possibilities of extension afforded by the augmentations and repetitions of the precomposed melody, which allow a short chanson tenor to support a lengthy movement, and he exploits also the integrative value of direct repetition and the climactic effect of progressive shortening of the note values. Otherwise there is no relation to the older form. The tenor is not organized into *taleae*, nor can it be, because its rhythmic patterns stem directly from the chanson. It hardly needs to be added that there is no isorhythmic ordering of the upper voices.

There is little that needs to be said about the *Missa Caput*[9] for it is thoroughly treated in Bukofzer's study on the Masses of that name by Dufay, Ockeghem, and Obrecht.[10] The tenor is a long closing melisma from the antiphon *Venit ad Petrum* which is given a double statement, first in triple meter, then in duple and with a new rhythmic arrangement. It is an isorhythmic tenor because the time values and notes are kept the same from movement to movement. It has no scheme of augmentation or diminution like that found in *Se la face ay pale*, but it does show a certain disregard of the structure of the melisma in the way in which rests are inserted and the original phrases arbitrarily cut up. This is a feature of the scaffolding tenor which is not present in the other Mass.[11] Only in one respect does the composer recognize the phrase structure: he shortens the statement in the Agnus by omitting a complete phrase of the original. (The phrase is repeated in the original melisma and Dufay omits the repeat in the second statement in duple meter.)

It is impossible to characterize the treatment of the tenor in the *Missa L'homme armé*[12] in a brief statement, partly because we do not know "the" original version of the tune, partly because of the variety of treatments Dufay uses.

The melody is sometimes stated quite literally—in *integer valor* in Agnus III (m. 113 ff.), in doubled values in *Osanna II* and in Agnus I. It is stated nearly literally in the Kyrie, although with a certain amount of ornamentation. In the Gloria, Credo, and Sanctus (through *Osanna I*), however, it is presented with a very irregular freedom. In these movements considerable ornamentation is introduced at the ends of sections of the c.f., while at the beginnings of sections the notes are quoted unornamented and in greatly extended values. The long values are not achieved by precise augmentation, but nevertheless the original patterns show through here and there, and this is true even of the statements in duple meter (*Christe, Qui tollis, Et incarnatus, Osanna I*).

Certain statements are regulated by canonic instructions calling for halved values and the omission of certain rests (Kyrie II and *Et incarnatus*), or for retrograde motion (Agnus III). The c.f. is not stated exclusively by the tenor. It is duplicated by the bass for a time in the Sanctus (m. 35-51), and in Agnus II, where the tenor is silent, it is stated in its entirety by the three contrapuntal voices. (See p. 129.)

The statements vary in form from movement to movement, but there is nevertheless some attempt to relate movements by repetitions of the c.f. The tenor of the Gloria is partially repeated in the Credo, so that these two movements form a pair within the cycle. There is no question that Dufay uses repetition here as a unifying factor, but he avoids restatement that is completely literal. *Osanna II* and Agnus I are based on tenors which are very similar simply because both are reasonably exact quotations of the original, and for this reason they may not constitute good evidence of intent to unify the structure by repetition. The intent is strikingly clear, however, when the composer repeats all four voices of the close of Kyrie II to form the close of Agnus III. This is a rather noteworthy procedure for Dufay, but one may well question its effectiveness to the ear, considering that the repeated passages are only five measures long and that they are situated at such a distance from one another. (Cf. Kyrie, m. 80-84; Agnus, m. 127-131.)

The sequence of statements from movement to movement is briefly as follows: The entire tune is used as basis for the Kyrie, fitting naturally into the tripartite structure of the movement because of its form of ABA. The A section is used for Kyrie I, the B for the *Christe*. Kyrie II is based on two statements of A, the second in halved values.

The Gloria is based on two different statements of the entire melody, the second one being used for the *Qui tollis*, the second half of the movement. The tenor of the Credo is in large part a quotation of the two statements of the Gloria, but, as indicated above, neither is quoted complete. In the first statement the repetition is exact through the A and B sections, but the final A is different. (Cf. Gloria, m. 67 ff.; Credo, m. 81 ff.) The situation is similar for the second statement in the *Et incarnatus*. The melody as it appeared in the *Qui tollis* is repeated into the final A, but once more Dufay deviates at the close. (Cf. Gloria, m. 167 ff.; Credo, m. 223 ff.)

The Credo is a longer movement than the Gloria and requires a third statement of the c.f., beginning measure 238. This statement is not new, but is derived from the second by a canon calling for halved values and omission of long rests. When it is completed, Dufay adds a short, freely composed passage to bring the movement to a close (m. 270-281).

The Sanctus is based on A and B, the B section being duplicated in canon at the octave between tenor and bass (m. 35-51). *Pleni* and *Benedictus* are free, as usual, but the final A appears in *Osanna I*. In *Osanna II* Dufay abandons ornamentation and alteration of rhythmic values and gives a simple quotation of the tune. So far as we know, the chief alteration consists in doubling the original values. He also adds brief imitative statements in the bass as details (m. 170-172, 173-176).

The entire melody is given again unornamented in Agnus I, the statement being the same as that of *Osanna II* except in minor points. Even the brief imitation in the bass at measure 170 of the latter submovement recurs in the Agnus at measure 13. The entire melody is stated twice in Agnus III in accordance with a canon directing that it be given first in full values in retrograde motion and then repeated in normal motion and in halved values (m. 113 ff.) The halved values would be the actual values of the original, so that the Mass ends not only with a relatively fast statement of the entire melody, but also with the melody substantially in its original form.

This is possibly the earliest *L'homme armé* Mass, but it is not the simplest use of the melody. Even though Dufay keeps reasonably close to the original, as can be told by referring to Robert Morton's setting of the tune,[13] he by no means stays as close to it in all statements as Busnois does in his *L'homme armé* Mass. Dufay's setting also holds a unique place among his own Masses because of the variety of treatments of the c.f. It was probably this feature which caused Tinctoris to select the work for special commendation. (See p. 98 above.)

The treatment of the c.f. in the two remaining Masses is simpler and more consistent than it was in *L'homme armé*, but the manner of quotation is not without points of interest. The *Missa Ecce ancilla Domini–Beata es Maria*[14] is based on more than one borrowed melody, and so stands as the first instance of a type that was later to become fairly common.[15] The two antiphons Dufay uses are related liturgically[16] and, to a certain extent, musically. In the Mass the musical relationship between them is clearer than in the versions of the Vatican edition, since Dufay uses a form of *Ecce ancilla* which starts with an ascending fourth (g moving up to c) and is thus identical with the beginning of *Beata es Maria*. The use of two *cantus firmi* does not give rise to any complicated procedures of composition, for they are always quoted singly. They are given paraphrase treatment, although the figuration is less extensive than that used in the *Missa Ave Regina caelorum*.

Three of the movements—Kyrie, Sanctus, and Agnus—reveal differences in rhythm and ornamentation of the statements as well as dissimilar schemes of quotation of the two antiphons. For the sake of brevity they can be designated A and B. Kyrie I is written over A, *Christe* is free, Kyrie II is written over B. The first half of A is used for the Sanctus, *Pleni sunt caeli* is free, *Osanna I* has the second half of A, *Benedictus* is free, and *Osanna II* makes use of B. In the Agnus, B is given twice through, once in Agnus I and again in Agnus III, which is an exact repetition. Agnus II is free.

The Gloria and Credo show much greater similarity to one another than do the other movements. There are only minor differences in the c.f. statements, at cadences and at points where the tenor rests. The scheme of quotations for the two movements is AB in the Gloria, ABA in the Credo. Not only are A and B practically identical in both movements: the final A of the Credo is an almost exact repetition of the first, so there can be no doubt as to Dufay's intent to pair them.

It has been pointed out that the four Masses already discussed show marked differences in c.f. treatment, but in all of them the tenor layout tends to make a pair of the two central movements. Pairing within the cycle is clearly an important secondary means of organization.

In the *Missa Ave Regina caelorum*[17] the tenor presents the entire antiphon in every movement except the Agnus. In that movement it states the first two phrases in Agnus I, is silent in Agnus II (omitting a phrase of the antiphon), and resumes it at Agnus III, quoting to the end.[18] The phrase of the antiphon omitted in Agnus II is not entirely missing, however, for it is presented prominently by the contratenor as the highest part of a duo (*Opera*, III, 119, m. 47-63). In a general way, then, the second Agnus of this Mass is similar to that of *L'homme armé*, where the c.f. is also taken by parts other than the tenor (p. 129, below, and ex. 50). Otherwise the tenor presents the antiphon with different rhythmic patterns and different ornamentations in every movement, so that the Mass stands as a typical example of paraphrase treatment in the tradition of Dunstable's *Rex saeculorum*.

Van den Borren is of the opinion that the treatment is much freer than that found in the ordinary paraphrase. He states that the proper phrase of the chant is not present in the *Qui tollis* of the Gloria (i.e., *Gaude virgo gloriosa . . . speciosa*), but is replaced by "a very free variation of the incise A" (i.e., *Ave Regina*).[19] Since at this point in the manuscript the tenor is given the correct textual cue, *Gaude gloriosa*, and since it is quite easy to follow the original notes of that phrase, it is impossible to agree with him. (See ex. 49b, below. He probably based his statement on the fact that it is possible to find the notes of phrase A in the tenor from measure 84 onward, but this is due to internal agreements within the phrases of the chant itself.) He says, further, that the distribution of the phrases of the c.f. in the Credo, Sanctus, and Agnus is likewise such that it is not always possible to determine precisely which one is being employed; that Dufay has not attempted to state the tenor so that the different periods appear in orderly succession; and that he uses the melodic fragments of the tenor with complete freedom.

The facts do not bear out these statements. Throughout the Mass the tenor phrase being used is carefully indicated in Br 5557 (the manuscript to which van den Borren especially refers) by the words *Ave Regina, gaude gloriosa, vale*, etc. These show definitely that the antiphon is quoted from beginning to end and that, although there may be omissions, the order of the phrases is not altered. Granted that the ornamentation is often rich, that there are numerous free extensions, that phrases are omitted in a few places—still, the tenor is not treated in the form of "free variations."

The precise textual cues leave no room for speculation along these lines. It is true that certain sections of this Mass and of *L'homme armé* are based on the c.f. when the tenor is not sounding, but in such cases the quotations are extensive and exact enough that there can be no room for doubt. Free treatment of the c.f. is characteristic of Ockeghem, but the manner in which he handles the structural voice is one of the noticeable points in which he differs from Dufay. The latter may ornament the c.f. to a considerable extent, but he is not inclined to disrupt its original structure as Ockeghem does or in the manner that van den Borren's analysis of this Mass would indicate.

The variety in rhythmic presentation of the c.f. gives opportunity for extreme, although free, diminution. Example 47 shows that the phrase *Gaude gloriosa* is presented in the space of fifty-two semibreves in the Credo as against seven in the Sanctus.[20] The latter presentation of the c.f. is in its conciseness reminiscent of the strict diminution of the scaffolding tenor. There is, however, nothing strict in this case, which might be called a "compression" of the subject. A similar compressed statement is found in

EXAMPLE 47. Dufay, *Missa Ave Regina caelorum*, tenor (Br 5557, fo. 115ᵛ, 118ᵛ; *Ant. Mon.*, p. 175).

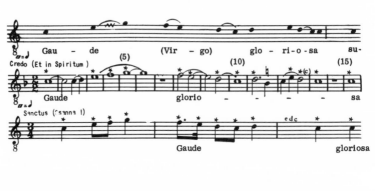

the second *Osanna* of *Ecce ancilla Domini*. In works of later composers these free diminutions are commonly found at the end of a movement, where they have an obvious formal function—they aid in bringing the composition to a climactic close. It is not clear that Dufay had such a function in mind. At least, the passage quoted in example 47 comes in the middle of a movement, not at the end.

The head motive of *Ave Regina caelorum* must also be mentioned, since it includes statements of the c.f. In the other Masses the head motives are neither quoted from the tenor material nor even written completely as counterpoints to that voice.[21] In this work the introductory passage includes an anticipatory statement of the c.f. in the bass and the first five bars of the tenor statement as well. (Ex. 48a, m. 1-3 and m. 4-8. The head motive of the Sanctus serves as illustration for the four remaining movements, since the passage appears in identical form in each of them.) It is also the only head motive which involves all four voices, those of the other Masses concerning at most only the two upper ones.

In addition to the elaborate identification badge which Dufay prefixes to each movement, there are several instances where interior sections of movements begin in a related manner. The second statement of *Kyrie eleison* in Kyrie I, Kyrie II (ex. 48b), *Qui sedes*, Agnus II, and other places in the Mass are marked by a descending scalewise passage in the superius which links them musically with one another and with the head motive as well. (Compare the superius lines, ex. 48a-b.) That these passages contribute to the musical unity of the work cannot be gainsaid. Whether they are to be considered as an extension of the device of the head motive—that is, as secondary head motives—is open to question, since they are placed irregularly in the various movements and are by no means exact quotations of one another.

Examples 48a and 48b give instances of anticipatory statement, but these are not the only places in the Mass where the c.f. is used in a voice other than the tenor. The final notes of the antiphon are brought into all four voices by means of imitation at the end of the Sanctus. (Ex. 49a, m. 1-5, tenor and superius; the imitative passage is then repeated exactly in the contratenor and bass, m. 6-10.) Another phrase is brought into two voices by the same means in the short introductory duo to the *Qui tollis* section of the Gloria. (Ex. 49b, tenor and bass voices; the imitation in the bass is rhythmically free from m. 4 to the end of the example.) The c.f. appears again in the bass for a few measures at the end of both the Gloria and Credo in the form of a simple restatement. As is shown in example 49c, a duo between superius and tenor (m. 4-9) is repeated by the contratenor and bass (m. 9-14). Incidentally, it is this passage which has the effect of making a pair of the Gloria and Credo. It was pointed out above that these two movements were paired by means of the similarity of the entire tenor layout in the other Masses, but in *Ave Regina caelorum* all five movements stand on an equal plane in this respect, since there is a different paraphrase of the c.f. underlying each. Also, in *Ave Regina* caelorum there is no greater similarity in the head motives of these two movements than in the others, because the head motive itself is identical in all. The means chosen here

EXAMPLE 48. (a-b) Dufay, *Missa Ave Regina caelorum*—Sanctus and Kyrie II (Br 5557, fo. 117ᵛ-118, 110ᵛ-111; Ant. Mon., p. 175).

for relating the two movements—by identical closing passages—is unique for this group of Masses, but it is not altogether new to Dufay.[22]

Ave Regina caelorum is noteworthy for the extent to which c.f. is used outside the tenor, and in this respect, as well as many others, it shows an advance over *Caput* and *Se la face ay pale*. However, it would be unsafe to assume a steady progress on the part of Dufay toward a style of writing which becomes standard in the next generation. His *L'homme armé* Mass is presumably earlier than *Ave Regina caelorum*, yet it is in this work that we find the most extensive use of c.f. material in voices other than the tenor. It is worthwhile to return to it for a moment in order to illustrate the point.

From measure 26 of the Sanctus of *L'homme armé*, the c.f. appears in the bass in canon at the octave with the tenor, and in the second Agnus it is taken altogether by the other voices. As usual in that section, the tenor drops out and the remaining voices join together in duos and trios. They are not, however, entirely composed of fresh material in the usual manner, since one or the other of them states clearly recognizable phrases of the chanson tenor in the order in which these phrases appear in the original. Between them, the three voices present the complete melody. (See ex. 50. The version of the tune found in Naples, *Bibl. Naz. VI. E.* 40 is used for purposes of comparison since it is closer to Dufay's tenor than Robert Morton's version. Breve and longa rests are omitted, and the phrases are marked A, B, and A.) The change of pitch level in the quotation (ex. 50, m. 39) and the imitation (m. 40 ff. and 47 ff.) represent a very elaborate and advanced degree of c.f. treatment for Dufay. On the whole, he and his contemporaries still treat the c.f. as an entity in itself and do not regard it as a source of material for the other voices.

Any summary of the Masses of Dufay must take account of the variety in the treatment of the c.f., and of the change in status of that voice in relation to the contrapuntal voices. In *Caput*, *Se la face ay pale*, and *Ecce ancilla Domini* the material of the c.f. is restricted entirely, or nearly entirely, to the tenor itself. In *Ave Regina caelorum* and *L'homme armé* it penetrates the other voices from time to time. There is no question that in this respect these two works show a stylistic advance pointing toward the early works of Obrecht and Josquin. There is also a certain growth in the amount of manipulation of the c.f. In *Caput* the tenor is simply restated in its original form; in *Se la face ay pale* it is manipulated by augmentation; in *L'homme armé* there is an instance of manipulation by retrograde motion. Also, in *L'homme armé* the tenor is at times ornamented and at other times laid out in pedal notes, a mixture of treatments that is found constantly in Josquin. In *Ave Regina caelorum* and *L'homme armé* there are quotations between movements in addition to the motto which appears at the beginning of each.

EXAMPLE 49. Dufay, *Missa Ave Regina caelorum* (Br. 5557, fo. 118ᵛ-119, 113ᵛ-114; Ant. Mon., p. 175). (a) Sanctus—final 13 bars. (b) Gloria—*Qui tollis*. (c) *Gloria*—final 17 bars.

EXAMPLE 50. Dufay, *Missa L'homme armé*—Agnus II (Mon. Pol. Lit., 1st ser., I:1, 32; *Zeitschrift für Musikwissenschaft*, X [1927-28], p. 612, facsimile.)

These works show, as does Dufay's entire output, that he is one of those composers who are constantly evolving, who do not fall into stereotypes even in old age. Nevertheless, in summarizing his attitude to the structure of the cyclic Mass one should take care not to overweight the furthest developments.

Van den Borren, in his beautifully written appreciation of Dufay, says:

> . . . the new style of the Ockeghem epoch evolves toward a concept which tends to make the tenor the spiritual center of the work. In this system, the tenor is no longer satisfied to be the foundational material, the backbone of the whole. It aspires, in addition, to become its nutritive substance, to impregnate the musical structure in its entirety with its quintessence.[23]

This is true, but in judging the Masses of Dufay it is well to emphasize the aspect of evolving *toward*. Only in the late works of Ockeghem and Obrecht can we comfortably show that the c.f. is impregnating the musical structure at all extensively. The passages quoted from Dufay take up very little space indeed when compared to the total length of the Mass movements, and in relation to the general method of writing on a c.f. they are clearly exceptional. The standard procedure of the older master is to give the c.f. to the tenor and to add to this tenor other voices which have, on the whole, no other relation to it than that of good counterpoints. The contrapuntal voices are customarily not organized in any other way, the only restriction to their free flow being that of the limitations of the style. When the tenor is sounding, imitations among the counterpoints are infrequent and cursory. The mere statement of the c.f. is the important structural factor.[24] But when the tenor is silent, imitation is used liberally. (See ex. 51.)[25] The organization is thus on two planes: the statement of the c.f. in the tenor provides one, and, when it is absent, imitation between the free voices provides a substitute. One at a time is deemed sufficient. The combination of the two—c.f. statement and imitation—is, as yet, a possibility which is not often realized in practice.[26]

Masses with Bipartite Tenor

A group of anonymous Masses published in conjunction with four late ones of Dufay[27] may be considered at this point because they are based on tenors of the rather unusual structural type found in the *Missa Caput*.

The first of these Masses, *Veterem hominem* (Tr 88), resembles Dufay's *Caput* in many ways, quite aside from the obvious point of tenor layout. It is scored for four voices, the c.f.-bearing tenor being written as an inner part; the counterpoint is nonimitative; there is no, or extremely little, use of c.f. in any voice outside the tenor; all movements are introduced by a motto. In short, the procedures generally correspond to those of Dufay in his earlier cycles and, except for the one point of tenor layout, the work is a quite average example of Mass structure from the middle of the century.

The form of the tenor in *Caput* and *Veterem hominem* is not only strikingly similar, it is practically identical. In both Masses the voice is organized into a double cursus with the first statement in triple meter, the second in duple; both of the borrowed melodies are of English origin, since they are

EXAMPLE 51. Dufay, *Missa Ave Regina caelorum*—Credo, *Qui propter* (Br 5557, fo. 114ᵛ-116).

chants of the Sarum Use; in both Masses the entire tenor is stated once in each movement and the text of the various sections of the ordinary is allotted to the bipartite tenor form in an almost identical way. Such differences as there are occur mainly in the Sanctus.[28] Because of these similarities of structure it is of the greatest interest that *Veterem hominem* is not by Dufay, as the editor maintained, but is the work of an anonymous Englishman.[29] This goes to show that the peculiar type of tenor layout used in *Caput* was familiar to the English, and further strengthens the supposition that Dufay borrowed his tenor from an earlier and now unknown English work.

The *Missa Christus surrexit* (Tr 89) lacks Kyrie and Agnus, but of the three remaining movements the Gloria and Credo are practically identical in tenor layout and allotment of text with the corresponding movements of *Caput*. The chief difference is once more in the Sanctus, and in this work it is substantial, since cursus A is stated twice (once with the Sanctus and again with the *Pleni sunt–Osanna I*). Cursus B underlies the *Benedictus* and *Osanna II*. The c.f. is the German *Leise, Christ ist erstanden*, which often appears with Latin text.[30] The use of a German melody is especially interesting, since the editor also attributed this anonymous Mass to Dufay.

The bipartite tenor layout of two more of these Masses shows that the use of this type of c.f. was reasonably widespread. *Pax vobis ego sum* (Tr 88) consists of only a Gloria and Credo.[31] In this case the c.f. is given in alternation by two tenors. Each phrase is given by one of the voices and is immediately restated by the other at a pitch a fifth away, so that the entire melody actually receives two statements in each cursus. Variety is gained in this tenor antiphony by having each voice alternate as the leading one. In cursus A the lower tenor (which is also the lowest part of the score) takes the lead and is followed by the other tenor at the fifth above. In cursus B, the higher tenor leads and is followed at the fifth below. The statement of the c.f. can hardly be considered canonic, seeing that each phrase is merely repeated. The two tenors never overlap, with the result that although five voices are involved the scoring is actually for four parts, and no more than four parts ever sound at one time. As in *Veterem hominem*, the counterpoint is substantially nonimitative and does not partake of the melodic material of the c.f. Moreover, as in that work, the final chord of each big section is a full triad, complete with third.

The fourth Mass of this type, *Sine nomine*, does not have Trent as a source but Cappella Sistina 14. The scribe does not give any clue to the origin of the tenor, but probably it is a borrowed voice, not a newly composed one.[32] As the editor points out, it is somewhat notable tonally, being written in F but ending on a G. The manner in which the words of the Ordinary are fitted to the two cursus differs considerably from that in

Caput—much more than in the other Masses of this group—and the writing shows stylistically rather more advanced traits. There is a certain amount of imitative counterpoint (for example, Kyrie, m. 21-22; *Qui tollis*, m. 33-40; Sanctus, m. 66-68; Agnus III, m. 13-20), and there are a few brief *ostinato*-like repetitions of a motive (Agnus I, tenor, m. 12-16 and m. 19-20). Also, whether conscious quotation or not, the material of the tenor appears from time to time in other voices (for instance, Kyrie, alto, m. 1-4; superius, m. 27-29; *Christe*, alto, m. 6-10; *Et incarnatus*, alto, m. 1-9). The first six or seven notes of the tenor appear in each of these places, although it must be admitted that the agreement may simply mean that this is a favored melodic figure (c-d-f-e-d-c). Bukofzer rejects Feininger's suggestion that Dunstable is the author of the work, on the grounds that the style is too advanced.[33]

The *Missa Puisque ie vis* (Cappella Sistina 14) is based on the tenor of a chanson and is not related to the others in this publication by reason of double cursus. Here, again, no extended discussion of the c.f. layout is necessary, since the editor has given the chanson and a complete diagram of the tenor as it appears in all movements.[34] The analytic tables show that the tenor is newly ornamented in each of its appearances. This work also does not present anything radically new. The first four movements have a motto of four measures which is reduced to two in the Agnus. The counterpoints are occasionally organized by brief scraps of imitation which do not appear in a planned manner; however, long passages of imitation do occur in the duos when the tenor is silent and when there is, therefore, no c.f. to direct the counterpoint. The work is, on the whole, similar in technical features to the later Mass cycles of Dufay and to many other works of the third quarter of the century, some of which will be discussed below.

THE O ROSA BELLA MASSES

An anonymous Mass cycle, based on Dunstable's famous chanson O rosa bella and appearing in Tr 88,[35] is stylistically less advanced than any of the cycles of Dufay. This fact, however, by no means proves that it is an earlier work.[36] It is written for three voices, and the contratenor is a typical vagans which leaps back and forth above and below the tenor. The tenor of the chanson is taken as the tenor of the Mass, although it is not quoted exactly. (See ex. 52.) The melody line is ornamented and the original rhythmic patterns are altered in a different manner in every movement. The anonymous writer also goes a step farther than Dufay in the extent to which he makes use of the material provided by the chanson for he quotes the first few notes of the superius as the head motive in the superius of the Mass.

A second Mass for three voices on O rosa bella, from Tr 90,[37] shows another of the numerous possible ways of employing material borrowed from a polyphonic composition. In this case it is not the tenor that is borrowed, but the superius of the chanson. What is more, the superius is given to the contratenor of the Mass. The result is that the middle voice of *O rosa bella II* is not a contratenor at all in the strict sense (although the scribe labels it so, following the custom for works in three voices). It crosses the tenor freely, but it does not have the disjunct motion of a normal voice of this type, such as the contratenor of *O rosa bella I*. On the contrary, it is just as melodic as the newly composed superius. The equalization of the character of the different voices is an important aspect

EXAMPLE 52. Anonymous, *Missa O rosa bella I*—Kyrie (Tr 88; DTO, 22, p. 1), with tenor of Dunstable's *O rosa bella* chanson (*Works*, p. 134).

of stylistic development around the middle of the century, and one which goes hand in hand with the practice of displacing any part into any other. For instance, it is easily possible for Ockeghem to place a borrowed superius melody in the bass, since his bass lines are not essentially different from those of any other part. In this case the use of the superius as a contratenor causes no difficulties. When the c.f. has a superius cadence formula it is put between the two other voices, and when it has a tenor formula it crosses below the tenor or makes a unison with it.[38] Wagner points out that in looking beyond the tenor of the original composition as the source of material, as well as in choosing voices other than the tenor to carry that material in the new composition, these works represent an advance over the standpoint of Dufay. Otherwise they offer little that is new. In *O rosa bella II* the melody is quoted exactly in every movement except for rests of different lengths between phrases. There are some extended passages in imitation when the contratenor is not sounding[39] but they are simple canons at the distance of two-and-a-half bars and four bars, respectively, which show none of the refinements found in Dufay (see ex. 51). Imitations of c.f. material are rather inconsequential (e.g., Gloria, m. 24-28). Every movement starts with duple meter, which differs from Dufay's practice of starting in triple and shifting to duple meter later, but this is accounted for by the fact that the chanson is in duple meter. Another interesting point is that the time values of the notes quoted are kept exactly as in the original even when a change is made to triple meter in the short passage which closes each statement of the c.f. Ockeghem frequently does this also.

A four-voice Mass on *O rosa bella* from Tr 89[40] is, in the general features of c.f. usage, a more highly developed counterpart of *O rosa bella I*. Like the latter, it makes use of the tenor of the chanson in an altered form as tenor of the Mass.[41] It also uses the superius in the superius of the Mass, but instead of limiting the quotations to a few notes for a head motive, there are paraphrases of long sections in several of the duets preceding the tenor entries.[42] In addition, the bass gives an anticipatory statement of the tenor entry in several spots,[43] but when the tenor enters the other voices, as usual, drop their reference to the chanson and are written as free counterpoints. On the whole, this work stands nearer to Ockeghem than to Dufay. The active voice lines and complex rhythmic patterns go beyond the bounds of the generally simpler chanson style. The free treatment of the secular tenor, the irregular and rather sketchy head motives, and the liberal use of other voices of the polyphonic original than the single one chosen for the actual c.f. are all features of Ockeghem's Masses.

The Masses of Ockeghem

When we compare the cycles of Dufay written after about 1440 with those of Ockeghem (whose earliest Masses must have been written at about this time), we are struck with the great variety of structural types employed by the younger man. Dufay, according to the five extant tenor cycles, settled upon a more or less standardized structural plan which takes as its point of departure the achievements in methods of formal unification developed up to about 1440 or 1450. He invariably uses both head motive and tenor c.f. in combination as the basis of the structural scheme. Ockeghem's output includes examples of all the types cultivated in the first half of the century.[44] The plainchant Masses[45] and head motive Masses[46] perpetuate types which were in existence as early as the first third of the century. In the c.f. cycles he takes advantage of the many possibilities inherent in the tenor structure. Some of these correspond to works written by his older contemporaries after the middle of the century.

A scaffolding type of c.f. very similar to that of Dufay is used in *L'homme armé*. Of the works with paraphrased c.f., the ornamented tenor of a chanson is used as Mass tenor in *De plus en plus* much as it was in *O rosa bella I*. In *Ecce ancilla Domini* we find the same kind of structure on two levels as in Dufay's *Ave Regina caelorum*.[47] The late works show the impress of the developments which were occupying the minds of composers in the 1470's and 1480's. In the *Missa Fors seulement* there is an extensive use of recombinations of c.f. material. The Masses *Cuiusvis toni* and *Prolationum* are of a type not seen before. The unifying factor in both is an abstract idea, a procedure of composition, as each is devoted to the solution of a particular musical problem.[48]

The broad scope of these works, as compared to those of Dufay, can in part be explained on chronological grounds. Whereas the cycles of Dufay belong to a limited span of time at the period of his greatest maturity, those of Ockeghem must cover a much greater number of years. His career as a composer of significant works probably began before 1450 and lasted at least through the 1480's.[49] His formative years were passed at a time when the cyclic structural methods were not completely consolidated, when head motive and c.f. Masses were cultivated as separate genres, and his career ends on the verge of the period when c.f. treatment is becoming so concentrated that it is merging with the techniques of parody.

The plainchant Masses

The treatment of the c.f. in the plainchant Masses is quite straightforward and does not break with traditional methods.

Two of the three movements of the *Missa sine nomine* (No. 14 of the collected works)[50] are certainly based on c.f. The Gloria clearly has the melody of Gloria XV of the Vatican edition. It migrates between the superius, tenor, and contratenor, the point of migration always coinciding with the beginning of a phrase. The c.f. is given on pitch for the most part, but the contratenor presents it a fifth higher in measures 8-12 (pp. 77-78).

There also seems no doubt that in the Credo the tenor carries a simplified version of Credo I. The case is not so clear in the Kyrie, although there are strong indications that a melody similar to Kyrie XVI is used. This movement is a marvel of compression. The first three supplications—*Kyrie eleison*—are based on the threefold statement of a migrating motive which appears first in the superius, then in tenor I, then in tenor II. This takes up but three measures of the modern score, as the motive itself is only one measure long. Measures 4-6 contain the threefold statement of a new motive, first in tenor I, then in the contratenor, and again in tenor I, and this comprises the *Christe*. The final Kyrie is extended to six measures in length. The motive of Kyrie I reappears in tenor II (m. 7, duplicated at the tenth above by the superius) and is restated by tenor I (m. 8). The leading voices of the final four measures are probably the superius (m. 9-12) and tenor I (m. 11-12).

The motives are apparently c.f. material drawn from a chant which parallels Kyrie XVI both in melodic outline and in structure. We are of course not warranted in drawing definite conclusions until the original Kyrie is identified. Ockeghem, as usual, does not always repeat the motives exactly. Those for the Kyrie, in measures 2, 7, and 8, are identical, while those in measures 1 and 3 differ in detail although the relationship is clear enough. Each of the three for the *Christe* (m. 4-6) differs from the others in some respect. Partly because of these variations in statement, but mostly because of the thick, low scoring for five voices, the structure as a chain of motives is not clearly apparent to the ear.

The Requiem Mass[51] makes most extensive use of the plainchant. The appropriate c.f. is used in every movement,[52] although it is present only in the first five notes of the tenor of one section of the Offertory, *Quam olim Abrahae*. (Does the composer drop it because he is occupied with proportional intricacies?) In another section of the Offertory, *Sed signifer*, it is given entirely to the tenor, and at the beginning of this same movement of the Mass, *Domine Jesu Christe*, it migrates between treble and bass. The c.f. also migrates between treble and contratenor (and to the tenor at the very end?) in the verse of the Gradual, *Virga tua*. The *cantus firmi* are clearly presented, on the whole, and in no way break from traditional paraphrase treatment. Example 53 illustrates this clearly, as well as the movement of the c.f. from voice to voice. From measure 148 the upper voice imitates the lower, freely to be sure, but sufficiently accurately that the notes of the c.f. can be found in it also. It will be noticed that migration occurs at natural division points of the original melody. There is considerable misplacement of the words in the lower voice, resulting from the running underlay of text in Chigi, the only source for the Mass. (Further illustration of the sketchy way in which text was entered in this sumptuous manuscript, and of possible error in the notes as well, is given in ex. 72.)

EXAMPLE 53. Ockeghem, Requiem Mass, Gradual, *Si ambulem* (*Works*, II, 88; Grad. Sar., pl. 62).

The Credo *Sine nomine*[53] (No. 12 of the collected works) also is based on a c.f. which is extremely similar to Credo I. It migrates to all four voices at one time or another, and also changes transposition during the course of the movement. It is stated a fourth (or an eleventh) above the original pitch of the chant at times. The notes of the c.f. are marked in the edition so the extremely clear way in which the c.f. is presented can readily be seen.

EXAMPLE 54. Ockeghem, Credo *sine nomine* (Works, II, 59; *LU*, p. 64).

Even though it changes voices, it is quoted continuously, and again we see that migration takes place at incises. On the basis of this observation, I will venture to suggest that at the words . . . *lumine, Deum verum de Deo vero* Ockeghem did not lay out the c.f. in the way indicated. (See ex. 54. Editor's analysis indicated by asterisks, my suggestions by circles.) This passage is difficult because there is no way in which all of the notes of Credo I of the Vatican edition can be satisfactorily accounted for in Ockeghem's composition. When the c.f. is treated as simply as it is here, we can be sure that the reason for trouble in finding any of the chant notes is that the composer has used a version which differs in some respects from the one we are referring to. No solution can be more than guesswork until the correct version of the c.f. is found. It seems that the editor's solution, which leaves measure 31, and most of measures 30 and 32 without c.f. and also assumes an overlap in the statements of the superius and contratenor measure at 26, is not completely satisfactory. It is suggested that migration to the bass and contratenor be assumed at bars 26-32. The result is more consistent with the manner in which Ockeghem has set the c.f. in the remainder of the composition, as both overlaps and breaks in the presentation are avoided. At the same time, no more notes are left unaccounted for than in the analysis of the editor, although that is not a consideration of much importance in a case of this kind. Another overlapping migration, at measure 66 of the movement (*Works*, II, p. 61), suggests that at this place also the melody used by Ockeghem differs from the Vatican version. Credos are characterized by repeated melodic fragments, so it is likely that at *Crucifixus* and *Et resurrexit* the original melody contained the notes g-a-g-e-f. The contratenor outlines these notes at both places (*Works*, II, p. 61, m. 64-65 and 77-82), and the figure appears in conjunction with the same words in Credo settings of other composers, notably in the *Missa de Beata Virgine* of Josquin.

These compositions reveal nothing new in the treatment of migrant c.f. In fact, Ockeghem's choice of migration points between phrases follows the Burgundian tradition. It is also apparent from the number of times he uses the device that he had a greater liking for it than his Burgundian predecessors. This can be readily understood, as the similarity in character of all the voice lines openly invites its employment. It is a natural concomitant of the tendency toward the equalization of parts.

Before turning to the c.f. Masses proper, another practice may be mentioned. During the course of the Credo, Ockeghem (and Obrecht and Josquin as well) occasionally will introduce a fragment of the Gregorian tune without warning and as suddenly drop it out. Example 55, measure 64 ff., is an instance of this sort of spot quotation. The scoring leaves no doubt that he intended the reference to the traditional melody to be clearly heard. This practice may be more common than is suspected, for it is very easy to overlook such passages. There is no reason to suppose that it is limited to the Credo, although it happens to be easier to identify references in that portion of the Mass than in others because there are comparatively few melodies for it.[54]

EXAMPLE 55. Ockeghem, *Missa Au travail suis*—Credo (*Works*, I, 35; LU, p. 64).

The cantus firmus Masses

The strictly traditional methods of treating the preëxistent material which Ockeghem adopts in the plainchant Masses give no inkling of the state of affairs in the c.f. cycles. There we find a fanciful variety and flexibility in the handling of the c.f. not equaled by his predecessors. Although the borrowed material is given to the tenor much of the time, it is by no means bound to that voice. It may be given entirely to another voice or change parts from movement to movement.[55] Migration is also used within a movement, and in some cases the procedure may be said to be raised to the second power. In *Ma maîtresse* and *Fors seulement* the borrowed material not only moves from one voice to another in the Mass, it is also taken now from this voice of the chanson, now from that. Migration is involved at both ends of the procedure: in the act of borrowing and in the application of the borrowed material to the derived composition.[56]

The quotation is often not direct in other respects. The composer may omit phrases,[57] or repeat them, or he may double back on himself in a most unpredictable way. He also may state the c.f. faithfully at the beginning of certain movements, only to abandon it completely after a few measures. In *Au travail suis* the entire tenor of Barbingant's chanson is presented by the tenor in the Kyrie, but in the following movements the quotations last for a few measures only, after which the composition is entirely free.

Even so, not every element of c.f. treatment is without precedent. To the extent that Ockeghem copies the *Caput* c.f. of Dufay, his tenor shows all the traditional elements mentioned above (p. 133). *Caput* is his only Mass in which the c.f. is presented according to a rigid rhythmic scheme.[58] This should not be taken as an archaic trait in Ockeghem. Tenors which are organized according to a strict rhythmic pattern continue to be used through the time of Josquin. Nevertheless, the fact that only one of the Masses is based on a tenor of this type shows very clearly his disinclination to strict scaffoldings. (Even in this case the layout of the c.f. is not Ockeghem's own but is borrowed from Dufay.) All the remaining works show his definite preference for free treatment of the c.f.

L'homme armé approaches *Caput* in rhythmic strictness of presentation simply because the chanson tenor is quoted very literally. In fact, the melody as it appears in Ockeghem's Mass is closer to the chanson as we know it than is the tenor of Dufay.[59] As in Dufay, no two movements have a rhythmically identical tenor, partly because the rests between c.f. fragments differ and partly because individual note values are changed here and there, so that there is an extraordinary combination of strict quotation and constantly varied shift of detail. Also, as in Dufay, free extensions are added at the ends of important sections of the Mass. This is the only Mass in which the c.f. is subjected to anything approaching strict proportional treatment. (See the augmentations in the *Osanna* and the final Agnus.) Schematic organization is simply not a favorite device with him, although it remains one of the mainstays of the tenor structure, as can be seen in the works of Obrecht.

The general similarity of *De plus en plus* and *O rosa bella I* has already been mentioned. *Ecce ancilla Domini* has also been compared to Dufay's *Ave Regina caelorum*, but the freedom in the details of c.f. treatment in Ockeghem's work is purely his own and merits some consideration. As in Dufay's Mass, the c.f. is paraphrased differently every time it is presented, but in *Ave Regina caelorum* the melody is at least gone through from beginning to end every time, even though a phrase is omitted in a few places. Ockeghem is not inhibited by even such a minimal consideration of regularity, except in the Kyrie and Gloria of his Mass.[60] In the Credo the antiphon is quoted quite regularly as far as the *Alleluia*. It is then restated from beginning to end,[61] but this time according to a phrase order different from the one that has been established.[62] That order is never used again. In the Sanctus it is A-B : C-D-C'-D, without *Alleluia*, and in the Agnus, A-B-C D-D (plus part of the *Alleluia?*). This goes beyond any irregularity that has been seen before and is a reflection in the use of c.f. of the "irrationality" which characterizes Ockeghem's style. It is a negation of the general method of writing a movement in accordance with some sort of preconceived plan of c.f. statement, however loose that may be.

Example 56a (from the Gloria: Qui tollis to the end of the movement) shows further individualities of treatment. From measures 122-131 the c.f. drops out and is replaced by a freely composed section. It is taken up again at measure 132 and continues without further incident to measure 170. It is barely possible that there is no omission of c.f. material, as the notes lacking in the tenor can be found in the superius in measures 133-138. It is not at all certain that this is a case of intentional migration, because some time elapses after the c.f. statement ceases in the tenor and before it begins in the other voice. In the other instances of migration noted in Ockeghem the statement starts in the new voice without delay. Also, in the Gloria under consideration, the notes in the superius sound simultaneously with the renewal of the tenor c.f. statement at measure 132, another uncharacteristic procedure for Ockeghem. At the corresponding point in the Credo the same notes are omitted from the tenor (m. 195-208), and in this case there is even less evidence of migration; however, some of the missing notes can be found in the superius at measure 199-201 of that movement. If, as seems probable, there is no migration, the absence of these notes can only be accounted for on the grounds of Ockeghem's generally unpredictable methods of c.f. treatment.

The free extension at the end of the Gloria (ex. 56a, m. 171 ff.,) is rather longer than those used by other composers. Equivalents can be found more easily in English compositions than in Burgundian.

EXAMPLE 56a. Ockeghem, *Missa Ecce ancilla Domini*—Gloria (Works, I, 85; Proc. Mon., p. 247).

The course of the c.f. in the final Agnus is difficult to follow, but it seems that phrase C' is omitted and D is repeated, with the omission of some notes. (See ex. 56*b*.) There may be the usual free passage at the end (m. 92 ff., ex. 56*b*), but it cannot be denied that in this case the tenor reproduces the general outline of the next phrase of the antiphon (starting at m. 92), though several notes are omitted and the quotation definitely ceases at measure 96. If it is granted that these bars are not freely composed, this passage again exceeds in freedom any of the paraphrase treatments of a c.f. that have so far been seen.

EXAMPLE 56b. Ockeghem, Missa Ecce ancilla Domini—Agnus III (Works, I, 98; Proc. Mon., p. 247).

The beginnings of the movements of *Au travail suis* and *Ma maîtresse* present a different method of treating borrowed material. The procedure employed in the chanson, the presentation of the voices in imitation, is used as the point of departure for constructing the first few measures of each movement of the Mass. (See ex. 57a and ex. 57b-f.) In *Au travail suis* every moment shows a different scheme of imitative entry. Sometimes four, sometimes two or three voices are concerned; the imitations are now at the unison, now at the octave or fifth; the order of entry of the voices and the time interval between entries also frequently change. No longer mere quotations, these are explorations of further possibilities inherent in a procedure of composition, and so are true examples of musical development. These passages, however, make up but a fraction of the entire length of each movement. After they are completed there is a reversion to older procedures. In the Kyrie only the tenor continues to quote the c.f.; the other voices are written as free counterpoints to it, as usual. In the following movements the c.f. is abandoned entirely after a half-dozen measures or so, with the result that the Gloria, Credo, Sanctus, and Agnus are largely freely composed.

EXAMPLE 57. (a) Barbingant, *Au travail suis* (Ockeghem, Works, I, 42); (b) Ockeghem, *Missa Au travail suis*—Kyrie, (c) Gloria, (d) Credo, (e) Sanctus, (f) Agnus (*ibid.*, pp. 30, 31, 33, 38, 40).

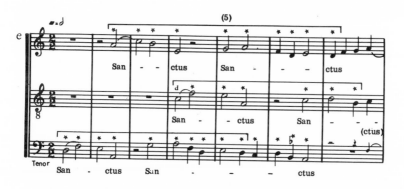

In the two movements of *Ma maîtresse* the imitative entries of the beginning of the chanson are also developed. (See ex. 58a-b.) In both of these Masses the developmental treatment of the points of imitation exceeds the normal limits of c.f. technique, since several voices of the original are involved. Properly speaking, the procedures followed should be classified as parody.

While parody treatment at this time is usually limited to comparatively brief passages, these passages occur with increasing frequency, so that it becomes necessary to take them into consideration at this point in order to

EXAMPLE 58. Ockeghem, *Missa Ma maîtresse*. (a) Kyrie I (*Works*, I, 117), with his *Ma maîtresse* chanson (*ibid.*, p. 124). (b) Gloria, with same chanson (*ibid.*, pp. 119, 124).

distinguish them from c.f. treatment proper. The distinction is not always easy to make in works of the late fifteenth century, despite the fact that the essential features of the two techniques have been described in numerous studies.

In an article devoted to the subject, Father Lenaerts distinguishes between c.f., which is a "monodic element of construction," and parody, which "is of a harmonic nature," presupposing "an auditory perception focused on the consonances rather than on the independent lines of the voices." "The *parodia* . . . is based on a polyphonic composition, the preexistent material consisting not only of themes but of consonances, successive entries, subjects and countersubjects, of phrases having a harmonic dimension, and cadences showing an accentuated tone color."[63]

The crucial point, then, is the introduction of the harmonic element of the preëxisting work into the new composition. For a passage to qualify as parody, more than one voice must be carrying borrowed material at the same time.

The harmonic, or vertical, dimension is most simply introduced by direct quotation of the voices in a block, but it can also be brought in as part of a developmental section provided more than one voice is involved. In such a case the harmonic element is present, even though it may be subsidiary in importance to the elaboration of melodic material. The expanded points of imitation mentioned above are instances of this type of parody.

Historically speaking, it is well known that parody gradually becomes of greater importance until it finally replaces c.f. as the leading structural technique in the generation of Clemens non Papa. In recent years it has also been shown that parody is of much earlier occurrence than was previously suspected. Mass movements from the fourteenth century, as well as a number of works by Italian composers writing during the second and third decades of the fifteenth century, have been discovered which show clear applications of the technique.[64] It appears that the Italians had no hesitation about using secular material in the Mass and that they employed more than one parody technique. Most commonly they merely quoted passages from the model composition, but in some cases they developed phrases on melodic fragments taken from it. The first-mentioned method—simple quotation of entire passages—is not far removed from the *contrafactum* in a technical sense. In the *contrafactum* the music is simply quoted in its entirety and only the text is changed (which, in itself, may call for minor adjustments in the music). In the Italian parody, such as the Gloria of Bartolomeo da Bologna, the quotations are of this type but newly composed sections are added. Dufay, in the use of the passage "*Miserere*" in both the motet and the Mass *Ave Regina caelorum*, was dealing with this type of parody and was employing a technique with which he must have been familiar from boyhood.

Parody apparently was not favored in the mid-decades of the century, although Pirrotta suggests that there may have been a continuing tradition and cites the *Missa Deuil angouisseux* of Bedingham as a possible case of its introduction into the cyclic Mass.[65] As far as can be told at present, however, it played an insignificant part in the work of Dufay, Dunstable, and their contemporaries. The interest of these men was centered on the c.f. and the possibility it offered of unifying elaborate works of several movements. It is not until the last thirty years of the century, more or less, that parody resumes a position of some importance, and at this time it makes its appearance not as an independent technique but, most commonly, *in conjunction with c.f.* The early Italian parodies which have so far been discovered are parodies from their inception and use that technique only. In the last half of the fifteenth century we find a c.f. which persists throughout the work and forms its foundation. Those passages of parody which may be introduced from time to time are subsidiary to it in importance as constructive elements.

The simple technique of quoting a block of voices is occasionally used (for instance, in the Sanctus and Agnus of Driffelde, cited as ex. 39, and in the anonymous *Missa Quant che vendra* from Tr 89),[66] but more often the composer elaborates on a procedure—he expands a point of imitation, prolongs a canon, or places material into new contrapuntal combinations. Such passages in parody are a natural outgrowth of the interest of the late fifteenth century in contrapuntal combination and motivic elaboration of all sorts. Hence it is not necessary to account for the resurgence of the technique on the basis of a continuing tradition even though further research may show that one in fact existed.

Questions of nomenclature constantly arise because so many of the works fall more or less between the two types, but the definitions quoted above make it possible to classify them with some consistency. There are many Masses in which all voices of a chanson are used but are quoted singly, the tenor being used in one movement, the superius in another, and so on. By definition, these works are not parodies. That a composer views an entire composition as a suitable source for material does not alter the fact that he is using a c.f. technique so long as he uses the material to form a single line only in the new composition. Of course, c.f. technique is not restricted to the quotation of a *single line*, since it is possible to have multiple c.f. Obrecht's *Missa Sub tuum praesidium* is a c.f. Mass even though four different chants are brought together and sounded simultaneously. There is no possibility of parody because there is no harmonic element to borrow from the Gregorian sources.

I will make it a rule to call the treatment parody whenever more than one voice of a preëxistent polyphonic work is sounded with another. Even this criterion becomes rather arbitrary at times, because the question of intent arises. According to the definition quoted above, parody presupposes an interest "focused on the consonances rather than on the independent lines of the voices." There are bound to be cases in which it is not clear just where the composer's interest is focused. For instance, in the passage quoted by Besseler from A. Agricola's *Missa Je ne demande*,[67] it is doubtful that the composer had the harmonic dimension of the chanson in mind at all, even though he does state two voices from it simultaneously. Since he consistently displaces them from their original relation to one another, it seems far more likely that his intent was to demonstrate skill in contrapuntal recombination. His technical problem is closely related to that of the composer who combines two or more Gregorian *cantus firmi*, and it can be maintained that this passage is, in reality, an instance of double c.f.

When analyzing a work, a question such as this should be taken up, but in assigning a work to a category, I believe it is better to leave it out of consideration, because there could well be disagreement about the answer. The passage agrees with the conditions of the simple definition given at the beginning of the preceding paragraph, so I will group it with parody.

In most works of this period it is clear that the structural basis is a c.f., even though there are occasional outcroppings of parody. Because of the mixture of techniques, it is necessary to admit the existence of a hybrid type—of a c.f.-parody structure. It is to this type that the *Missa Le serviteur* of Faugues and *Ma maîtresse* and *Fors seulement* of Ockeghem belong.

To return to the work being discussed, after the imitative entries illustrated in the quotation from the Kyrie of the *Missa Ma maîtresse* (ex. 58a, opening measures) the tenor of the chanson proceeds alone, being quoted in the bass. A bit later on, however, the chanson superius appears in the tenor of the Mass, so that the two structural voices of the chanson are taken up into the Kyrie and used as a double c.f. As stated above, this sort of quotation falls within the domain of parody, for the two voices are kept in their original relation to one another, merely being shifted downward into the bass and tenor. The pair continue this way for only two measures before the chanson superius migrates from the tenor to the contra, where it stays for the remainder of the very brief Kyrie. (Only the first eleven measures of the chanson are quoted in Kyrie I, corresponding to the first two lines of the *virelai* text.)

Although there is no double quotation in the *Christe*, the third phrase of the chanson tenor simply continuing in the bass, there is a statement in the contratenor of tenor material which anticipates the true entry in the bass. (The first six notes of the chanson tenor appear in the contra, m. 15-16, before the true entry in the bass at m. 19.)

In Kyrie II the bass continues with the quotation of the chanson tenor, starting with a repetition of the final note of the c.f. of the *Christe*. This is another one of those tiny, unpredictable details which are so characteristic of Ockeghem. Before long the tenor resumes the quotation of the superius of the chanson, so that there is again double c.f. and, as in Kyrie I, the superius soon migrates to the contratenor. The double statement continues to measure 35 of the Mass, where the contratenor gives up quoting the superius. The bass holds to its quotation of the tenor until the first half of the chanson is completed. At this point Ockeghem adds an F and brings the Kyrie movement to an end.[68]

In the Gloria there is a hint of double c.f. also. In this movement the superius of the chanson is the favored voice, being quoted throughout by the contratenor.[69] The tenor of the chanson is not wholly forgotten, however; there is a brief reference to it in the superius (chanson tenor, m. 35-37, Mass superius m. 110-112).

The two movements of *Ma Maîtresse* do show certain features of structural regularity. The first notes of the superius are the same in both Kyrie and Gloria, and may constitute head motives.[70] The movements are also based on a c.f. which persists throughout, but on the whole the work is a typical example of the irregular and complex usage which Ockeghem favors. Not only is a different voice of the original used as the structural voice of each of the movements; in addition there is intermittent quotation, repetitive quotation, migration, and an important element of parody—just about all the devices which he had at his disposal.

In some cases the purpose behind unpredictable procedures can be seen. For instance, the disregard of the phrase structure of the original (Kyrie, ex. 58a, bass, m. 8, 12, and 14) is harmonically motivated in two places. By interrupting the line at G (in m. 8), a V-I cadence on C is made possible. At the end of Kyrie I, a cadence is made on F (m. 14). F is the tonal center of the whole movement (the final Kyrie cadences on this note) and C is an important subsidiary center (the *Christe* ends on it), so these two cadences are understandable as elements of a simple tonal scheme. Since the F chosen for the final note of Kyrie I appears on count three in the chanson, it is necessary to shift it to count one in order to make a satisfactory cadence. This is done by means of the rest in measure 13. The choice of a rest as the means of shifting the rhythmic position of the final notes (rather than lengthening the time value of one or more of the notes of the chanson) is not untypical of Ockeghem, who rather frequently drops out the bass before a cadence.[71]

The late Mass, *Fors seulement*, crowns the series of works based on borrowed material. On the side of c.f. statement it is packed with quirks and subtleties, and on the side of musical development it represents the composer's most extensive attempt at recombination and expansion of the material of the original composition.[72] Ockeghem's music is often compared to Late Gothic architecture, and it seems true that in such a work as *Fors seulement* the detail is equal in intricacy to the decoration of the "Flamboyant" style. An analysis of the Mass indicates, moreover, that the composer was able at times to surpass the architect in richness and variety of structural scheme.

The Credo is the least involved of the three movements, and for this reason will be considered first. It starts with a short, slightly rearranged quotation of material from the beginning of the chanson.[73] The superius is used as c.f. in tenor I up to *et resurrexit*. The original notes and note values are scrupulously observed, although presented in the Mass in triple meter, rather than in the original duple, and interrupted by rests which, in at least one place, distort the phrase structure. (Compare Credo, m. 12, and chanson, m. 20.) In the second half of the movement, tenor I changes over to the chanson tenor for the source of its material, and again quotes very literally in short snatches interrupted by rests; however, instead of going all the way through from the beginning, it makes use of only the last portion of the chanson tenor (from m. 49 of the chanson, starting at m. 101 of the Credo). The quotation proceeds to within a few measures of the end of the chanson (to m. 61), long before the end of the Credo is in sight, and in order to gain the necessary length, the entire fragment is repeated. The tenor then occupies itself with freely composed material (m. 158-167 of the Credo).[74] After an extended rest it finally presents the last phrase of the chanson to bring the movement to a close.

The Kyrie is more complicated than the Credo in some ways, but the c.f. layout is simpler. The superius is quoted from beginning to end without any repetitions of phrases (chanson, m. 10-70; excerpts from the chanson are given in ex. 59). It starts with the tenor entry (ex. 60, m. 11 of the Mass) and continues in the tenor to measure 52 of the Mass, where it is transferred up to the contratenor and is carried through to the end by that voice. It is given literally and is not interrupted by rests so often as in the Credo. As mentioned above, there are some complications. At the points in the chanson where the superius rests while the other voices continue to sound, the tenor does not quote the rest, but temporarily makes use of one of the sounding voices. Thus the bass is quoted at measures 30-32 of the Kyrie (see ex. 60), and the tenor at measures 47-52. (The quotations are from m. 28-30 and m. 42-47 of the chanson, respectively.) The shift of the c.f. to the contratenor at measure 52 is not necessarily an arbitrary procedure, for it reproduces exactly what happened in the chanson. At this point in the chanson *the voice above the tenor, the superius,* enters again. In the Mass the superius is also brought in, and in a voice above the tenor— the contratenor. Although these usages fall within the limits of c.f. techniques, it is clear that Ockeghem looks beyond a single voice of the chanson to the polyphonic whole as the source of his material.

The secular composition does not begin with overlapping imitation, but the superius does restate the tenor entry (ex. 59, m. 10 ff.). In the Kyrie, however, this tenor entry, which is ten measures long, is treated in close imitation at the fifth above at the distance of one measure. This is accomplished without a single significant change in the notes of the original line.[75] In addition to the extensive quotations for the c.f. of the Mass, Ockeghem makes use of various brief figures of the chanson. The most noticeable of these is a scalewise descent of a fourth which appears repeatedly in both chanson and Mass and which is usually given in the rhythmic pattern ♩. ♫♩ ♩ .[76] Other quotations are not so obvious, or

EXAMPLE 59. Ockeghem, chanson *Fors seulement l'attente*. (*a*) Beginning and (*b*) end of chanson (Gombosi, *Jacob Obrecht*, Appendix IX, p. 12).

are completely insignificant,[77] but the total effect is to bind the derived composition closer to the original than has been done in any of Ockeghem's previous works.

Of all three movements, the Gloria is the high point, both in complexity of c.f. statement and in extent of elaboration and recombination of source material. An examination of the first dozen bars of the movement shows the tenor and superius combined in simultaneous statement (ex. 61,

EXAMPLE 60. Ockeghem, *Missa Fors seulement*—Kyrie (Works, II, 65).

m. 1-5), an extra statement of the introductory motive (m. 7-9), and a quotation of the tenor in the superius (m. 9 ff.). All this is accompanied by free imitations and numerous appearances of the descending scale of a fourth. A comparable passage appears later in the Gloria after an extended, freely composed trio (ex. 62, m. 97-111). The c.f. in the tenor is accompanied by a maze of imitations, scalewise descents of fourths, and even a short sequence on a new figure (ex. 62, m. 107-110, vagans).

These two pages represent the ultimate degree of concentration and integration of material achieved by Ockeghem in the Masses. Such concentration of motives could be expected of Josquin, but Ockeghem does not approach the style of Josquin in his use of them. Indeed, he is never more characteristically himself than at this point. The imitative passages and short quotations are swallowed up in the thick stream of low sonorities. They are jumbled together without discernible order, often obscured by free voices, frequently led almost unobserved out of preceding material, and they are partially deprived of individuality because of freedoms of statement. Owing to the presence of specific, identifiable ideas, the musical relationships are not so generalized as in most of his output, but, as in all of his mature works, the total effect of this rich concentration of material is a homogeneous, continuous, almost undifferentiated stream of sound. A startling difference in attitude toward what is desirable as a total musical effect is revealed by a comparison of these passages with a composition such as Josquin's motet for six voices, *Benedicta es caelorum Regina*.[78] It, too, is a complex work in which numerous musical ideas are combined, but in it we find an orderly plan of presentation. The elements are clarified and firmly established in simple, thinly scored statements before more complicated combinations are introduced. For Josquin, the material must first be elucidated so that its subsequent concentration may be aurally comprehensible. For Ockeghem, concentration of material is sufficient. There is no intent to highlight the detail, and the ear is continually occupied with the entire contrapuntal web and its profusion of intermingling elements.

In the *Missa Fors seulement*, with minor exceptions, direct quotations from the chanson are given to only one voice at a time, even in the passages from the Gloria just described. The sum of these quotations can be said to make up the c.f. element in the structure of the Gloria, as distinct from the parody element. In both Kyrie and Gloria any voice of the chanson may be

EXAMPLE 61. Ockeghem, *Missa Fors seulement*—Gloria (*Works*, II, 67).

(Tenor or Superius-first motive-down 5th)   Tenor, bars 1-10 of chanson, down 4th, direct

(Tenor, bars 1-7 of chanson, free quotation

Sequences

(? Superius, bars 12-15 of chanson, down 10th

Imitates Tenor

Sequences

quotation)   (15)

(Superius, bars 18-22 of

Free section- - - - - - - - - - - - - - - - - - (20)

chanson, down 15th

(25)

(Superius, bars 18-21 of chanson

(Superius, bars 21-41 of chanson, down 12th, some free interpolations later

down 12th

etc.

etc.

drawn on as c.f. material, but while the quotations appear in a simple and orderly succession in the former movement they by no means do so in the latter. The course followed by the quotations in the Gloria is tortuous, complicated by twistings and turnings, and often interrupted by free interpolations; even so, it is not aimless. In its own way, it does lead from the beginning to the end of the chanson as the following analysis shows.

Example 61 shows the first statement of the superius in the vagans (m. 1-6), followed immediately by statements of the first phrase of the tenor in the superius (m. 7-15 of the example) leading to measure 10 of the chanson. There is then a skip to measure 18 of the chanson as the bass takes up material from the superius (ex. 61, m. 15-18). Musically this skip amounts to very little, as the melodic material omitted has already been thoroughly treated. An apparently free section follows, and after this the vagans repeats the material of the superius from measure 18 of the chanson (ex. 61, m. 23). The quotation is soon transferred to the tenor of the Mass (m. 25 of the example), which continues to present the superius very exactly down to measure 41 of the chanson (m. 39 of the Mass).[79] After a short free section, at measure 45 of the Mass the tenor again takes up chanson material, going back to measure 30 and this time quoting the tenor to measure 41, which is the precise point at which it had dropped the superius. Now that these two voices are brought up abreast of each other, the section concludes (on a typical Ockeghem cadence: VI_6-I).

The second section (*Qui tollis*) starts with scale-line imitations which may be derived from measures 20 ff. of the chanson, although they are not exact quotations. The thread of the c.f. is picked up again at the point where it had been dropped in the previous section of the Gloria (chanson, m. 42; Mass, m. 63), with the tenor continuing with the tenor (to m. 68 of the Mass, m. 47 of the chanson). The contratenor and tenor then treat the following tenor phrase of the chanson in imitation (m. 68 ff. of the Mass). At measure 77 of the Mass the material of the chanson tenor is trickily hooked onto the chanson superius of a couple of bars previous (see chanson, tenor, m. 55, and superius m. 53). The chanson tenor line is dropped provisionally, and the tenor of the Mass quotes the superius until a free trio interrupts (m. 85-96 of the Mass). Example 62 shows the course of the c.f. from that point forward. The tenor continues to carry the superius with various repetitions. Most interesting are those following

EXAMPLE 62. Ockeghem, *Missa Fors seulement—Gloria, Tu solus* (*Works*, II, 70).

bar 114 of example 62, which should be compared with the final measures of the chanson, given in example 59. Several times the tenor approaches the final cadence of the chanson, only to interrupt its progress, return to a point further back, and then approach it again until, finally, it pushes through to the end. This extraordinary behavior is mimicked in the contratenor, at a pitch a second above the tenor. The vagans (ex. 62, m. 125) then goes back and picks up the tenor (m. 60 of the chanson) and quotes it to the end of the chanson, thus again bringing the tenor abreast of the superius as it had done in the previous section.[80] In general, then, the c.f. for this movement is the material of both the superius and tenor of the chanson presented in a series of alternating statements, chiefly by the tenor of the Mass, although with substantial assistance from the other voices. The freedoms of usage are the final stage of the fanciful, irrational tendencies which appear to a lesser degree in the c.f. statements of Ockeghem's other Masses.

In evaluating this aspect of irrationality as it is revealed in the c.f. statements, we must note that while the methods are unpredictable they are not purposeless in a larger sense. There is a strong tendency to present the c.f. most simply in the Kyrie, so that this movement functions as a sort of exposition of the borrowed material. In the following movements it is given various treatments, sometimes being stated more casually, sometimes more intensively. In the Gloria of *Fors seulement* the repetitions of the cadential phrases approach the status of a development.

The use of any part of the chanson as source for borrowed material, the presentation of this material by voices other than the tenor of the Mass, the reworking of the form of the original melodic part, and the concentration and recombination of the borrowed material all represent advances on previous c.f. usages. On the other hand, the attitude of Ockeghem's predecessors—that the other voices are to be written as free counterpoints when the c.f. is stated—holds for the most part. This attitude is maintained to a large extent even in the Gloria of *Fors seulement*, despite the advanced type of treatment. In addition, many of Ockeghem's freer methods of treatment, such as migration, partial quotation (dropping the c.f. and continuing freely), intermittent quotation (dropping the c.f. and then returning to it), are firmly based on tradition, especially that of the English.

In the treatment of the Gregorian chant in the *Missa Ecce ancilla Domini* Ockeghem not only follows the traditional custom of transforming it melodically; he also reworks it formally. By thus compounding the alteration to which the chant is subjected, he achieves a degree of sophistication in c.f. presentation which could hardly be surpassed. Indeed, this seems to be the final stage in the evolution of the technique of c.f. paraphrase, at least in the sense in which it was used in the first half of the century. The practice of adding notes to a c.f. continues in use, but melodically transformed statement becomes less and less an end in itself. Rather it becomes an aid to new methods and new techniques of composition which are developing at this time.

A survey of procedures such as the one just completed is only a first step in dealing with Ockeghem. Many problems remain to be solved, even though the completion of the publication of the Masses has helped to clear away some of the grossest misinterpretations.

The writings of the theorists give evidence of the esteem in which he was held by his contemporaries and successors, and the practical results of his influence are visible everywhere. Yet, in many respects, he is not a leader in developments which take place during his lifetime. Many of the procedures of composition which come to full development in the works of Obrecht and Josquin are hardly to be found in his music, even in rudimentary form. The proper placement of this man, acknowledged as the leading musician of his time and undoubtedly one of the most original of all composers, is the task of a special study in which all aspects of his work, not just a single one such as the c.f., can be considered.

Miscellaneous Masses

Only a fraction of the Mass repertory of c. 1450-1485 has been published, but enough works are available to indicate certain shifts in emphasis with regard to the treatment of the c.f. and to make possible a beginning on the task of determining the position Ockeghem holds in relation to these trends. The procedures of Dufay will still be taken as a point of reference, both because his Mass cycles were written early in the period and because he was the chief figure of the Burgundian school and hence stands in close relation to Regis, Busnois, and other younger members of that group.

It has been shown that, in the broadest sense, Dufay's statement of the c.f. is predictable to the extent that he is apt to quote the notes of the borrowed material from beginning to end in the original order, while the c.f. statements of Ockeghem do not show even this small degree of regularity. Several other Masses which will be taken up show greater irregularities than those of Dufay in this respect, and at least one of them, the *Missa Deuil angouisseux* of Bedingham, equals or surpasses Ockeghem in unpredictability. The evidence provided by this group of works indicates that irrational usages were common to many composers and were not restricted to Ockeghem, although he may be regarded as the leading exponent of the irrational style.

On the other hand, many composers are evidently interested in rational methods. They tend to quote the c.f. in a reasonably simple and straightforward manner, to regulate the structure of their compositions by some sort of exact repetition, and to apply rational procedures to the c.f. (i.e., to state it in canon, to use it as a basis for imitations, etc.). Such procedures have been found in rudimentary form in the works of Dufay, and one of them, the use of the c.f. in imitation, appears in a much more advanced form in those of Ockeghem. There are indications that in this respect Ockeghem is not the leader, but is under the influence of the rationalists. For one thing, a great deal of imitation on c.f. material is not found until the very late work *Fors seulement*. For another, the imitations are not so articulated and highlighted that their integrative effect is clearly audible; they tend to be submerged in the undifferentiated flow of the music. Other composers quite obviously strive to make the most of the formal value of imitation, since they bring in the entries after rests and by various means attempt to make these passages stand out from the remainder of the music.

Altogether, the situation is complicated by cross influences, rationalistic procedures being found in works of the irrationalists and irrational ones in those of the rationalists, yet it is clear that some composers tend to one side and some to the other.

The first aspect to be considered here is that of the c.f. layout. We find that the Masses of Ockeghem are by no means the only ones in which the c.f. is quoted fragmentarily, or with repetitions of various sorts, instead of straightforwardly from the beginning to end.

Certain movements of the anonymous *Missa Grüne Linden*[81] show considerable flexibility in the c.f. layout of the tenor. In the Gloria the c.f. is given only halfway through (m. 17-55), after which there is a return to the beginning and the melody is presented twice in its entirety. In the Sanctus the first phrase is presented straightforwardly only to measure 8. The tenor is then free to the end of the section (m. 24). The c.f. is taken up again at the second phrase in the *Osanna* (m. 46) and continued without excessive ornamentation or interpolation to the end. (As usual, the tenor is silent in the *Pleni sunt caeli* and *Benedictus*.) Only the first phrase is used in Agnus I (m. 16-26 of that movement), while the remainder of the c.f. is presented in Agnus III. It is a very common procedure to split the c.f. between these two sections, but it happens in this case that the second Agnus is not entirely freely composed. It starts as a duo, but at *Miserere* (m. 54) the tenor reënters and presents the c.f. in its entirety. The result is a statement within a statement; the entire melody is interpolated between its own first and last halves. (The presentations are more regular in the Kyrie and Credo. The melody is stated twice in the former, once through in Kyrie I and *Christe*, and once again in Kyrie II in a varied form. It is given four times in the Credo, once in m. 1-51, again in m. 93-122, in a telescoped form in m. 123-144, and lastly in m. 148-177. *Et homo factus* and the very end of the movement are freely composed. The repetition at m. 123 does not coincide with a formal division of the Credo.)

The anonymous *Missa Le serviteur*[82] presents the c.f. one and one half times in the Kyrie, Sanctus, and Agnus. The return to the beginning of the c.f. with a partial restatement of it has been seen before. The internal treatment given the Dufay chanson tenor is more interesting. It is stated faithfully with regard to pitches, but it is subjected to extreme rhythmic distortion. For the most part this is not allowed to interfere with the original phrase structure, but in two cases phrases are broken in a most arbitrary fashion. At measure 35 of the Sanctus the fourth phrase of the chanson is not quite completed, yet a cadence is made and the freely composed *Pleni sunt coeli* is given. The tenor reënters at the *Osanna* (m. 66) with the final four notes of the uncompleted phrase—but they are given a third too high! It seems that this must be intentional (not an error in transcription) as the notes would make parallel fifths with the contratenor if they were stated at the original pitch. The c.f. then reverts to the correct pitch and is continued to the end. The fourth phrase of the chanson tenor is also broken at the end of Agnus I. After the statement of Agnus II the tenor is again picked up from where it was dropped, but is given this time at its proper pitch (Agnus III, m. 62 ff.). Similarly arbitrary breaking up of phrases can be found in Ockeghem and Busnois, but the transposition of only four notes in the midst of a statement, otherwise all at the original pitch, is a quirk which has not been noticed before. (The c.f. is given twice through in both the Gloria and Credo, and the phrase structure of the original is retained for the most part. It is, however, disregarded at m. 134 of the Gloria and m. 100 of the Credo.)

Although the freedoms in the statement of the c.f. in these two Masses exceed those found in Dufay, they are rather mild in comparison with the procedures of Ockeghem. But, as mentioned above, the Bedingham *Missa Deuil angouisseux* is comparable to *Fors seulement* in irregularity of c.f. layout. The Bedingham Mass is found in Tr 88 and Tr 90, so was probably written a quarter of a century or more before the late work of Ockeghem.[83] The c.f. passages are fairly extensive and are clearly recognizable beneath the ornamentation. There are freely interpolated passages (see ex. 63a from the Gloria) and sections where the c.f. apparently disappears completely. These are not uncommon procedures in themselves, although the free passages are unusually long. Even the occasional doubling back on the c.f. is not unprecedented. (See ex. 63b from the Sanctus, where it seems that m. 46-48 of the chanson tenor are immediately followed by m. 43-52.) The feature that distinguishes this work is the extreme amount of irregular quotation. Bedingham begins each movement with the first phrase of the chanson tenor in the tenor of the Mass, and ends each with closing material, but during the course of the movements he chooses passages at random from the chanson tenor and mixes them indiscriminately with freely composed sections.[84] It is difficult to make an evaluation of the degree of freedom of the quotation, but it appears that Bedingham states the c.f. more irregularly than Ockeghem ever does. In any case, the manner of statement is similar to Ockeghem's and as unlike Dufay's as possible.[85]

Bedingham's melodic style is more discursive than Dufay's. In this respect, also, he is closer to Ockeghem than to the Burgundian master. (See ex. 80a.) The irregular treatment of the c.f. and the florid melodic style often associated in works of this period apparently represent two different aspects of the general tendency to irrationality.

EXAMPLE 63. Bedingham, *Missa Deuil angouisseux,* with Binchois's chanson *Deul angouisseux.* (a) Gloria (*DTO,* 61, p. 128) and chanson (*ibid.,* 14, p. 242). (b) Sanctus (*ibid.,* 61, p. 131) and chanson (*ibid.,* 14, p. 242).

As mentioned above (p. 153), the work contains elements of parody, since Bedingham quotes from the superius of the chanson as well as from the tenor. His method of elaboration often makes it difficult to determine when he is using borrowed material, but quotations of the first phrase of the superius can be identified with reasonable certainty because of two distinguishing features. The phrase begins with the outline of an F-major triad and cadences on a', a third above f' in the tenor, rather than making the more customary cadence at the unison (chanson, m. 9).

Both features appear in the opening phrase of the superius of each Mass movement and serve to prove intentional quotation even though the chanson melody is often distorted to a considerable extent. (Compare the superius of the chanson, m. 1-9, with the superius of the Gloria, m. 1-4, the Credo, m. 1-5, the Sanctus, m. 1-4, and the Agnus, m. 1-4.) The superius of the second section of the Credo (*Et incarnatus*) may begin with a simplified form of the second section of the chanson (m. 20 of the Credo may be derived from m. 20-27 of the chanson). Fragments of the final phrase also appear in the Mass, but the quotations of the superius, so far as I have been able to determine, are considerably less extensive than those of the tenor.

Because of the simultaneous statement of two borrowed voices, *Deuil angouisseux* may be considered a continuation of the Italian tradition of parody. It is equally a continuation, or expansion, of the later tradition of paraphrased c.f., for Bedingham's interest is centered on the rewriting and reinterpretation of the borrowed material. He is definitely not interested, as the Italians were, in the literal quotation of entire blocks of the model composition.

There are many other Masses in which the c.f. is stated more simply than in *Deuil angouisseux*. In the *Missa L'homme armé* of Basiron,[86] which was written about the same time as Ockeghem's *Fors seulement*, the c.f. is retained in the tenor throughout. It is moderately ornamented, and some free extensions are added at the cadences, but with minor exceptions the tune is quoted straightforwardly every time it appears. In general, the method of utilizing the c.f. is the same as that of Dufay. The most important exception is the rather frequent duplication of the statements by means of canon. (The contratenor imitates the tenor canonically in three sections, Kyrie II, *Et unam sanctam*, and the final *Osanna*.)

Busnois treats the *res facta* even more literally in his *Missa L'homme armé*,[87] since he quotes it directly, much as Dufay had done with the tenor of *Se la face ay pale*. An abbreviated form of the melody is, however, used in the *Confiteor*, both A sections of the chanson tenor being stated only in part. Also, instead of breaking the quotations at the structural divisions of the melody, he divides it in halves, interrupting the statements at some point in the B section. This feature is an unpredictable element in the c.f. usage, as he does not break the melody at a fixed point but interrupts it now on one note, now on another.[88] Variety in the presentation is gained largely through schematic manipulations. The c.f. (in minor mode, with B♭ in the signature) is given in various augmentations and in various meters, although these do not interfere with the relative durations of the original notes. In the Credo it is transposed down a fourth, from G Dorian to D Aeolian, and in the Agnus it is stated in inversion. Both of these treatments are indicated by written-out instructions. The inversion of the c.f. in the Agnus causes it to become an actual bass voice although the name of tenor is retained.[89]

Schematic manipulations of this type are usually associated with quotations in which the composer does not ornament the *res facta*, or otherwise quote it irregularly, but is content to state it literally. It seems that one type of treatment at a time—the fanciful (in the form of ornamentation or irregular quotation) or the literal (in the form of schematic manipulation)—was deemed sufficient. Certain compositions can be found, however, in which both types appear. In the *Missa Pour quelque paine* of Cornelis Heyns[90] the c.f. is not given a completely regular exposition in the Kyrie. In Kyrie I the chanson tenor is quoted down to measure 8, after which there is a free cadential extension. The statement does not continue from measure 8 in the *Christe*, but doubles back and starts at measure 6, after which it proceeds to measure 14. There is also a slight overlap in the c.f. quotation at the beginning of Kyrie II (the *Christe* ends with the notes a-g; Kyrie II begins with the notes g-a-g), after which the quotation is continued to the end of the chanson and the end of the movement. The chanson tenor is not ornamented, but the quotation is not entirely literal— there are minor changes in the values of the notes. The whole tenor is freely augmented in such a way that the original values are generally doubled in Kyrie I and II and quadrupled in the *Christe*. In any case, the result is a framework-type tenor. In the Gloria there is a quotation in free triple augmentation to measure 14 of the chanson (to m. 85 of the Mass), then one in free quadruple augmentation from measure 13 to the end of the chanson (m. 113-189 of the Mass), and finally, one in generally doubled values which again proceeds from measure 13 to the end of the chanson (m. 190 to the end of the Gloria).

This c.f. layout is repeated identically in the Credo and in the Sanctus as well, except that in this movement it is presented in inversion (again in accordance with a written-out canon). In Agnus I the first thirteen measures of the c.f. are given in retrograde motion. The tenor is silent in Agnus II, but in the middle of this section the contratenor ceases to be freely composed and becomes the carrier of the same section of the c.f. (m. 1-13), this time in forward motion. (See m. 80-99 of the Agnus.) In Agnus III there is a recapitulation of the entire c.f. in the exact form it has in the original. In this one section the quotation is completely literal and loses the fanciful traits displayed in the others. Both rational and irrational attitudes are displayed in the Mass. The method of quotation is in many respects quite unpredictable, yet the statements are frequently manipulated according to a strict plan. Such a mixture of traits can be found in other works, but there is a growing tendency at this time for rational methods of treatment of all sorts to be associated with statements of the c.f. which are relatively simple and straightforward.

Busnois, however, applies the rational procedures to which he is especially partial even to the treatment of an elaborated c.f. In the *Missa O crux lignum* he starts with an ornamented form of the sequence melody. On its first appearance in the Kyrie, then, he gives the c.f. an essentially non-schematic type of treatment, but instead of continuing to ornament the tenor anew each time it appears, the customary way with c.f. elaborations, he chooses to go no further in the direction of ornamentation. He takes the first statement as a model and quotes it exactly from then on. As he would with a strictly quoted *res facta*, or with a strictly quoted Gregorian melody such as Dufay's *Caput*, he applies schematic treatments only—in this Mass changing only the mensural and proportional indications from section to section.[91] Obrecht also prefers to curb the never-ending elaborations; in his Masses on c.f. he often takes one ornamented version of the Gregorian melody as the basis for several movements, achieving variety in the presentation by schematic means just as Busnois had done. (See the discussion of his Masses on Gregorian *cantus firmi*, p. 268, below.)

The various ways of manipulating the c.f. which were used at the time of Busnois (augmentation, diminution, retrograde statement, etc.), are modes of treatment which were known as far back as the fourteenth century. They are not new developments of the High Renaissance, but were used by the "rationalistic" composers of that period more extensively than ever before.

Further evidence of the tendency toward rational procedures of composition is found in the frequent use of exact repetition of two or more voices. This amounts to a new development since repetitions of blocks of counterpoint are rare in the sacred music of the first half of the century.

It has been pointed out that Dufay repeats the last few measures of the Gloria at the end of the Credo in his *Missa Ave Regina caelorum* (see ex. 49c). Repetitions of much greater extent are found at the end of the Gloria and Credo of Faugues's *Missa Le serviteur*.[92] (M. 250-287 of the Gloria are the same as m. 239-276 of the Credo.) Dufay also uses the last few measures of the Kyrie of his *Missa L'homme armé* to bring the work to a conclusion by restating them at the end of the third Agnus. Faugues, in his *Missa L'homme armé*,[93] once more outdoes the older man in this respect. He uses the music of the second Kyrie for the final section of the Gloria (*Cum Sancto Spiritu*), for the final section of the Credo (*Confiteor*), and for both

Osannas as well. This means that four of the five large divisions of the Mass end with the same music and indicates his unusual interest in clear structural relationships. Regis likewise emphasizes this aspect in his *Missa L'homme armé*.[94] He repeats the final section of the Gloria, almost literally, as the final section of the Credo. Also, at the beginnings of the two movements he uses identical c.f. quotations. (The tenor sounds the complete c.f., which has the form ABA. The contratenor imitates the A sections canonically, but not the B sections. In the Credo, when the tenor is silent, the contratenor is written freely and is not a repetition of what has been heard in the Gloria.) Furthermore, in the first Agnus there is a rather extensive quotation of the three lower voices of the Sanctus (down to p. 16, m. 28 of the Sanctus).

These works further illustrate the divergent interests of the younger contemporaries of Dufay. Ockeghem is little concerned with formal regularity, but many of the others show considerable interest in the matter and so take advantage of the device of exact repetition.

The increasing use of imitation in the Masses is another indication of the interest in rational procedures. Imitations on c.f. material may be divided into three main types: *a*) canonic, *b*) freely introduced, and *c*) parodistic.

a) The structural c.f. may be duplicated by means of canon. The canons may be of greater or less length and used more or less frequently in a given work. One short example has been pointed out in Dufay's *L'homme armé* and others in the Masses of the same name by Basiron and Regis. Faugues carries the process to its logical conclusion in his *Missa L'homme armé*, since he states the c.f. in canon between the two lowest voices throughout the cycle.[95]

b) Freely introduced imitations may bring material from the c.f. into other voices. These imitations appear infrequently and irregularly in the tenor Masses, for the principle established in the first half of the century that the other voices are written as free counterpoints when the tenor is sounding remains valid for this period. The only places where the c.f. can be expected to appear in the other voices is in the duos and trios preceding the tenor entries. These, of course, are anticipatory statements which seldom involve imitation of the c.f. material. Some imitations based on the c.f. are found during the tenor statement. For instance, there are a fair number of short entries in Ockeghem's *Missa L'homme armé*, and a few examples have been pointed out in Dufay's *Ave Regina caelorum*. Most of the imitative writing in these Masses is not concerned with the c.f. and is found in the freely composed sections where the tenor is silent, such as the *Benedictus* or *Pleni sunt caeli*. One such movement, however, the second Agnus of Dufay's *Missa L'homme armé*, does make use of c.f. material and gives it fairly extensive imitative treatment (see ex. 50).

The consistent use of initial imitation had long been known in the chanson[96] and may have been taken into it from Italian models of the first part of the century. In the chanson the imitative entries chiefly concern the two structural voices, superius and tenor, while the contratenor either is completely free or only occasionally joins in with a point. This manner of writing shows up also in a limited number of Masses, and is probably taken directly from the chanson. One of the best-known examples is the *Missa sine nomine* of Ockeghem (No. 2 of the complete edition), which is not based on c.f. A few which are based on c.f., however, are written in a similar manner, the points being derived from the borrowed material.

An anonymous Kyrie *Fons bonitatis* (Tr 89, No. 649) is an instance. The tenor carries the complete c.f., but the superius consistently imitates it at the beginnings of phrases (see ex. 64). The contratenor takes no part in

EXAMPLE 64. Anonymous, Kyrie *Fons bonitatis* (Tr 89, no. 649; LU, p. 19).

the imitations so that the technique is identical with that of the older chansons, and also agrees with one of the c.f. settings previously examined.[97] Even though this work is included in one of the younger Trent codices, there is nothing advanced in its style. It could easily have been written around 1450, or before, and hence may be regarded as a rather early instance of the literal transfer of this aspect of secular style to the Mass. This work, it also should be noted, is only a Mass section, not a cycle.

The *Missa Grüne Linden* is a more extensive and, stylistically, somewhat more advanced instance. It is found in Tr 88,[98] so the date of composition cannot be later than that of the Dufay Masses and probably falls within the period 1450–1465. It cannot compete with the Masses of the Burgundian master in musical merit, or even in sheer size; it is a comparatively short work, modestly scored for three voices; but it is interesting because of the extent to which material from the tenor is brought into other voices by means of imitation. Initial imitation is used most frequently in the syllabically set Gloria and Credo. In the *Confiteor* the contratenor joins in, so that there are entries in all three voices; this is also the case in the third Agnus.

The Kyrie of Johannes Martini's *Missa Dominicalis* represents a still more advanced stage of the technique.[99] The tenor carries the whole c.f., but owing to the frequent imitations a great deal of it appears in other voices. Indeed, in measures 11-16 (ex. 65) it is given most clearly in the superius. The system of entries is not consistently carried out; in the *Christe* imitation is replaced by anticipatory statement, a device of the

EXAMPLE 65. Martini, *Missa Dominicalis* (Mod α M.1, 13, no. VII; *LU*, p. 46).

typically nonimitative tenor Mass and motet. A similar instance of the mixing of chanson and tenor techniques is found in the setting of the hymn verse *Collaudamus venerantes* (ex. 75) which appears to be of approximately the same date.

These pieces have a forward-looking appearance because they display methods of writing cultivated in the sixteenth century. Yet it is possible to overemphasize their importance in a retrospective view. As has been pointed out, the method of beginning successive phrases with points of imitation had been known in the first half of the century, but was at this time (the third quarter) still restricted to secular music, to unpretentious sacred works such as song motets, or to Masses of the type illustrated above. The great works of the time—those upon which composers expended the utmost care and ingenuity—were tenor structures, and in these compositions points of imitation were not used consistently; they appear, rather, as elements of detail. One must conclude that this method of writing, while long and widely known, was still limited in its application. It took on major importance only under the impact of certain new concepts which arose around the beginning of the sixteenth century.

c) Imitation of a parodistic type occurs in Masses built on a polyphonic work. In these there is a tendency to take over and expand upon points of imitation which are found in the original. Tentative beginnings of this practice may be seen in the imitative passages based on triadic figures which occur in *Se la face ay pale* and *O rosa bella II* and *III*.[100] These amount to little more than direct quotations of the imitative passages in the respective chansons. Similar cases in Busnois's *L'homme armé*[101] represent a somewhat more advanced stage of development as the passages in the original are considerably expanded.

The *Missa Le serviteur* of Faugues (*DTO*, 38, p. 95) is especially remarkable because points of imitation from the chanson are brought in so often throughout the Mass and, in addition, because of the amount of expansion they undergo. This work appears in Tr 88, the same codex which contains the *Caput* Masses of Dufay and Ockeghem and the *O rosa bella I* and *Deuil angouisseux* of Bedingham, none of which makes any use of imitation worth mentioning.[102]

In the chanson of Dufay[103] from which the Mass takes its tenor each of the last three phrases (corresponding to the last three lines of text) starts with initial imitations in all three voices. The final one of these continues with imitative passages between tenor and superius. (See ex. 66a.) Examples 66b-f show how this concluding tenor phrase and its attendant point of imitation are treated in the five movements of the Mass. In three places— the Kyrie, Credo, and third Agnus—the point is expanded to include all four voices (exs. 66b, d, and f). Example 66f, from the third Agnus, shows that the imitative treatment may be extended to include the figures which follow the head entries in the chanson. (M. 165-168 of ex. 66f correspond to m. 27-28 of ex. 66a; m. 169-171 to m. 29-30.) In the Gloria (ex. 66c) the point is reduced, being made shorter and given to only two parts. In all of these spots, whether the point undergoes expansion or contraction, the interval of imitation at the unison or octave which was used in the chanson is left unchanged. The passage from the *Osanna* (ex. 66e) is somewhat ambiguous. The tenor is probably not imitated at all, although it is just possible that there is imitation at the fifth between it and the superius (compare superius, m. 154, and tenor, m. 155). Except for this dubious spot, it can be seen that there is no genuine attempt to form completely new combinations, since neither the contraction to two voices nor the expansion to four necessitates real rewriting of the original points. The most that can be said is that they are not copied exactly. Also, imitations are not introduced every time this section of the tenor is quoted. Nevertheless, they are used often enough to show the unmistakable interest of the composer in reproducing them in various forms in the new composition. This is emphasized by the fact that the imitative points for the third and fourth lines of the chanson are used in the same manner, i.e., expanded and rearranged to a certain extent, but not recombined in any technically striking way. The *Missa Fors seulement* of Ockeghem is much more advanced in this respect, but it must have been written fifteen or twenty years later than the work of Faugues. *Le serviteur* still represents a primitive stage in the development of the hybrid form of the late fifteenth century, the c.f.-parody (see p. 154, above), but it also shows that the composer takes a very lively interest in the question of combining the two structural procedures. This work and the others cited indicate, moreover, that the possi-

EXAMPLE 66. (a) Dufay's chanson, *Le serviteur* (DTO, 14, p. 239). (b-f) Faugues, *Missa Le Serviteur*: (b) Kyrie, (c) Gloria, (d) Credo, (e) Osanna, (f) Agnus III (DTO, 38, pp. 99, 107, 110, 120, 128).

(165)

etc.

Tenor

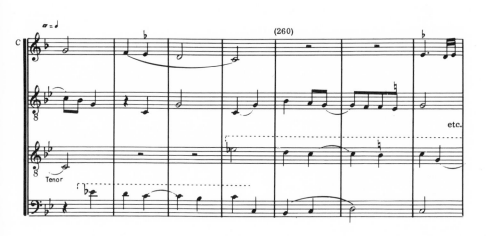

(260)

etc.

Tenor

(70)

Tenor

etc.

bilities of such a combination were generally recognized, and that the idea of grafting parody onto a basic c.f. structure need not be attributed to any one man. The type was not invented, it grew. It was natural to all who dealt with the new style.

A fourth possibility of imitation may be mentioned, although it does not directly concern the c.f. The counterpoints to the tenor may be organized independently among themselves by this means. This is done only in brief passages as yet, but the instances, even though fleeting, are worth mentioning because of the future importance of the procedure. (See ex. 67 of Faugues[104] and ex. 71*b*, m. 14-17.)

EXAMPLE 67. Faugues, *Missa Le serviteur*—Sanctus (*DTO*, 38, p. 116).

There is evidence that composers were not so much interested in imitative procedures per se as they were in recombination of musical material in general, for at this time there are increasingly numerous instances of the use of two different *cantus firmi* in combination. Examples of this have been found in the music of the first half of the century, but the number of compositions in which more than one c.f. occurs and the determination with which the process of combining them is carried out increase noticeably from this time forward. The two Mass cycles of Regis must be considered in relation to this development, since each makes use of several *cantus firmi*.

In the *Missa Dum sacrum mysterium (L'homme armé)* the *L'homme armé* melody is used in every movement and is the most important unifying factor.[105] There are fragmentary presentations of the melody in only one voice, but the majority of statements are in canon for two voices. The canons are all at the fifth, they are only partially strict, and, while they differ among themselves in detail, they fall essentially into two groups, one in triple meter and one in duple. Despite the fact that the canons show many irregularities, it can be seen that Regis is proceeding on the premise that the main c.f. shall appear in two voices.

He complicates the structural plan of the Mass by using, in addition, several of the chants of the office from the service *in dedicatione S. Michaelis Archangeli.*[106] In many cases he quotes only the texts. They are written into the tenor and contratenor and are generally set to *L'homme armé* or to freely composed lines. This is the situation in the Kyrie and Agnus, but in the Gloria, Credo, and Sanctus he quotes the melodies of two of the chants and states them simultaneously with *L'homme armé*. (These combinations are also interesting because they join sacred and secular *cantus firmi*—a rather unusual procedure.)

In the Gloria, the contratenor presents a portion of the responsorial verse *Milia milium* in the first section and later continues it in the *Qui sedes (Ant. Sar.,* pl. 553). The c.f. layout is as follows (the sections of *L'homme armé* being represented by the letters A, B, A):

Gloria

	(m. 9-16)	(m. 21-26)	(m. 30 to end of section)
Contra:	A) in canon at	*Milia milium . . .*	A) in canon at
Tenor:	A) the fifth below	B	A) the fifth below

Qui sedes

	(m. 68-81)	(m. 83-97)	(m. 102 to end)
Contra:	A) in canon at	(. . . *et decies . . .*)	A) in canon at
Tenor:	A) the fifth below	B?	A) the fifth below

Since the c.f. layout is the same in the Credo, these quotations are repeated in the corresponding parts of that movement. Both the melodies are freely ornamented when they are combined, and in *Qui sedes* the B section of *L'homme armé* is so distorted that there is room for doubt that the tune is being used at all. (Several measures of this "B" appear previously in the *Christe,* but not in conjunction with any Gregorian c.f. Compare the tenor of the Gloria, m. 83-87, with the tenor of the Kyrie, m. 35-39.)

Portions of the antiphon *Dum preliaretur Michael* are quoted in the Sanctus and *Pleni sunt caeli (Ant. Sar.,* pl. 557). This time the antiphon is stated by the tenor while *L'homme armé* is taken by the contratenor and stated on E instead of D, as it had been in the first three movements. In addition, the bass states *L'homme armé* since it imitates the contratenor. This means that three of the four voices are occupied with c.f., a high percentage even for Obrecht and certainly noteworthy for a Mass of this period. The details of the layout are as follows:

Sanctus

	(m. 9-14)	(m. 27-33)
Contra:	A	A
Tenor:	*Dum cerneret belli . . .*	*. . . audita est vox . . .*
Bass:	A (free imitation of Contra)	A (free imitation of Contra)

The c.f. layout of the Sanctus is repeated in Agnus I, measures 7-13, while the statement in Agnus III is in large part a repetition of a passage of the Gloria (m. 68-78) and the corresponding passage in the Credo (m. 82-92). According to the c.f. usage, then, the cycle includes a Gloria-Credo pair, while the Agnus is related in part to this pair and in part to the Sanctus.

In all probability there is another passage in which three voices are occupied with c.f. In the *Osanna*, *L'homme armé* is stated in imitation by the contratenor and bass while the tenor evidently quotes a Gregorian melody. It has not been identified, but it is apparently a chant of the first mode.

The same composer's *Missa Ecce ancilla Domini–Ne timeas Maria*[107] is an even more imposing attempt at c.f. combination. Dufay, as we have seen, used two Marian *cantus firmi* in a Mass (*Ecce ancilla Domini–Beata es Maria*), although he presented them in alternation, never in combination.[108] Regis combines the two antiphons he has chosen, giving them to the two lowest voices simultaneously. In addition to these (LU, p. 1417, the Annunciation of Mary), he uses five more Marian antiphons during the course of the work: *Beata es Maria quae credidisti* (Visitation, LU p. 1538[v]), *Beatam me dicent* (Visitation, LU, p. 1542), *Spiritus Sanctus in te descendit* (first Sunday of Advent, Ant. Mon., p. 189), *Angelus Domini nuntiavit* (first week of Advent, second Feria, Ant. Mon., p. 191), and *Missus est Gabriel Angelus* (Annunciation, LU, p. 1416). This makes a total of no less than seven *cantus firmi* for the Mass.

The liturgical relationship of the melodies is obvious, and is emphasized by the fact that complete text is given for all. (In addition, the text of the Ordinary is included in the tenor parts, underneath the appropriate c.f. texts.) There is also a musical relationship between the first four antiphons named, so they can be classed in one group on this basis. *Spiritus Sanctus in te descendit* and *Missus est Gabriel Angelus* are also alike musically, so could be classed in another group, but *Angelus Domini nuntiavit* stands alone in this respect. There is, however, no evidence from the way in which the *cantus firmi* are employed that Regis took these relationships into account. It is apparent that the selection of the seven melodies was governed solely by liturgical considerations.

Never more than two *cantus firmi* are sounded at once, and they are combined in various ways. A certain plan is observable in their appearance.

If they are numbered 1 to 7 in the order in which they were named, the scheme is as follows (numbers in the top line indicate the c.f. carried by tenor I, in the line below that carried by tenor II):

Kyrie I	Christe	Kyrie II
1.	3. (first half)	3. (concluded)
2. (transposed fifth and octave below)	Tenor II free	Tenor II free

Gloria	Qui tollis	Cum Sancto Spiritu
.1.	4. (on pitch)	1.
2. (transposed fifth below)	4. (transposed fifth below)	Tenor II free

Credo	Et incarnatus	Et resurrexit
1.	4.	freely composed
2. (transposed octave, then fifth below)	5. (transposed fourth below)	

Cujus regni			
6. (transposed fourth up and on pitch)	3. (on pitch)	1.	
7.	3. (down fifth) (alternating, not simultaneous statement!)	Tenor II free	

Sanctus	Pleni	Osanna
1.	Tenor I free	freely composed
2. (first half; octave below)	2. (concluded)	

Benedictus	Osanna
5.	1.
5. (transposed fifth below)	Tenor II free

Agnus I	Agnus II	Agnus III
1.	Tenor I free	1.
2. (first half; fifth, then octave below)	2. (concluded)	Tenor II free

Every movement starts with *Ecce ancilla–Ne timeas* in combination (although each combination is different in some respect), and all but the Kyrie end with *Ecce ancilla* alone. These two, then, dominate the work and give a certain unity despite the multiplicity of borrowed melodies. The remaining antiphons do not appear in such regular order. The Credo is the only movement in which all seven are used and, in fact, is the only one in which the sixth and seventh appear at all.

The general layout testifies to a strong desire to present antiphons in combination; however, the aim may have been more to get a concentration of texts than of melodies, since the integrity of the latter is not always carefully maintained. The melodies are clear enough at the beginnings of movements (see ex. 68a), but in other places their outlines are obscured to a great extent. For instance, phrases often start with non-c.f. tones (see ex. 68b, m. 10, tenor II; ex. 68c, m. 2 and 7, tenor II); they often end on

EXAMPLE 68. Regis, *Missa Ecce ancilla Domini—Ne timeas Maria* (Br 5557, fo. 121ᵛ-122, 128ᵛ-129, 134ᵛ-135). (a) Kyrie (LU, p. 1417). (b) Credo (Ant. Mon., p. 191; LU, p. 1416). (c) Agnus (LU, p. 1417).

a note different from the last one quoted from the c.f. (see ex. 68*b*, m. 13, and ex. 68*c*, m. 7 and 11, tenor II; 68*c*, m. 4, tenor I); the pitch level of the c.f. may be changed (ex. 68*c*, the second tenor is a fifth below the original until m. 7, where it shifts to an octave below); the ornamentation is often fairly elaborate; there are free interpolations of considerable length; etc.[109]

The work is more impressive in the ambitiousness of the plan than in the maner of its realization. The consistent and extensive working-out of

such combinations is in general a later development. In both of these Masses the basic attitude toward composition remains one of free elaboration even though it is not so clearly the all-controlling factor that it is in the work of Ockeghem. Regis does show an interest in orderly musical procedures which exert a certain control over the course of the work, but their appearance is somewhat sporadic and their effect is diluted by the pervading tendency to free fantasy. It is only in certain works such as the Masses of Faugues and the motets of Busnois that such procedures are used rigorously and consistently enough to condition the structure of the composition and to show clearly a turn toward the attitudes of the next generation.

Summary of Cantus Firmus Treatment in the Masses

The Masses of this period show three main types of structure. The first, the plainchant Mass, is simply a series of c.f. settings. The second, the chanson-style Mass, need not have a c.f., but when it does the c.f. is ordinarily presented in its entirety in a single voice. Characteristic of this type is the use of points of imitation in a manner comparable to those found in secular songs. Since the imitations bring c.f. material into other voices than the one which has the chief task of bearing the c.f., this type of Mass has a higher degree of musical integration than is found in the plainchant and tenor Masses.

The third class comprises by far the largest number of works. These are the tenor Masses or derivatives of the type. The tenor Mass of Dufay may be said to be based on two main principles or attitudes: (1) the tenor lying in middle range is taken for granted as the voice proper to carry the c.f.—the borrowed material is always given to it, whether paraphrased or laid out as a framework; and (2) positive musical integration between the tenor and other voices is not considered essential—superius, contratenor, and bass are normally written as free counterpoints to the tenor and literal restatement of tenor material in them, by imitation or otherwise, is only incidental to the main scheme.

A further important feature follows from the habit of delaying the tenor entry at the beginning of a work and preceding it with duos or trios of the other voices. In some cases one of these voices anticipates the tenor by stating the c.f. material; since the anticipatory statement is immediately followed by a restatement in the tenor itself, an element of repetition is brought into the form. There is no doubt that any repetition tends to tighten and unify the structure, yet it cannot be assumed offhand that these restatements indicate a desire for increased formal unity.

The evidence will not support any such uncomplicated assumption because in some cases anticipatory statement does not entail repetition of material at all. In works in which the tenor is derived from a polyphonic composition the anticipatory statements may be derived from other voices of the original (as in *O rosa bella III*). In this case the material is entirely different from that of the tenor and the statements can be called anticipatory only by virtue of their position. They stand before a tenor entry, but they do not anticipate its content.

In the majority of cases, however, there is repetition of a sort. The tenor actually restates the material of the anticipatory voice, but the effect of repetition is veiled by differences of ornamentation. There may be a desire for integration of material here, but its expression is ambiguous at best. It is much more in accord with evidence of the majority of cases to conclude that the repetition of c.f. material is an incident which is allowed to interfere as little as possible with the free unfolding of the elaborated voice lines. This is readily understood as a continuation of the practice of varying repeated phrases of the c.f. which was found in the settings of the first half of the century.

If we ignore later attempts to achieve formal clarity by exact repetition and view the evidence of the earlier works objectively, we find that what they do indicate is a desire to create a form wholly dominated by c.f., since in these works the quotations are extended even to points where the tenor is resting. Repetition may be a result of this, but it is not a main objective. The anticipatory statement is, however, occasionally exactly the same as the tenor entry, so it cannot be said that the possibility of literal repetition is excluded from the earlier tenor structures. (See the *Missa Ave Regina caelorum* of Dufay, ex. 48a, for one instance.)

The Masses of Ockeghem show that the tenor plan is capable of much variation without denial of its fundamental principles. There may be irregularities of c.f. statement (partial statements; arbitrary rearrangement of the original form of the c.f.; in the case of a polyphonic source, the choice of other voices than the tenor for quotation). Other voices than the tenor may be used as carriers of the structural c.f. It may be given to another voice for a whole movement or for a whole Mass, or it may shift within a movement to as many different voices as the composer desires. Such fanciful play with the structure is characteristic of the Ockeghem Masses. But no matter how numerous or surprising the deviations are, they only extend, they do not break with, the traditional assumption that a lengthy movement is to be built up on a foundation of borrowed material.

This structural attitude, in either its strict or its free manifestation, holds until after the turn of the century. We see, however, with the introduction of extensive imitation into the writing (such as the canonic duplication of the tenor in the *L'homme armé* of Faugues, or the initial imitations of his *Le serviteur* and the *Missa Fors seulement* of Ockeghem) the beginnings of the abandonment of a viewpoint of the Early and a turn toward that of the High Renaissance, since integrated texture is as characteristic of the latter as nonintegrated is of the former. Likewise, the appearance of long repeated sections in various Masses written at about this time indicates a new interest in formal clarity. Regularities of this type can be easily impressed upon the tenor structure, although they were not formerly an essential feature of it. They are completely absent from the majority of the works of Ockeghem and are not a pronounced feature of those of Dufay. In this period of transition, new stylistic concepts are coming into being, but they do not call for the development of an essentially new type of musical structure—the traditional one is sufficiently flexible to provide a medium for their realization.

There is as yet no sharp differentiation between the older and newer attitudes. Both are widespread and are found in varying combinations in all the works of the period. The Masses of men of lesser rank than Dufay and Ockeghem show that these two are not unique representatives of certain opposing styles and, furthermore, that they are not undisputed leaders in the new·developments. The examples cited above leave no doubt as to the alertness of the secondary composers, and testify to the first-rate importance of their contributions to the process of stylistic development. The motets of this period, to be considered in the next chapter, demonstrate likewise the broad basis upon which the style of the following generation was formed.

7

The Motets
of Dufay, Ockeghem,
and Their Contemporaries

IT IS CONVENIENT to discuss the Mass and the motet separately, although the differences between them result chiefly from differences in size. The Mass cycle is laid out according to a very extensive plan which entails multiple statement of the c.f. This calls for a greater display of means than would be necessary or appropriate in a shorter composition. No specific technique, however, is peculiar to one category or the other. Every procedure found in the Mass, whether it applies to the c.f. or to the free parts, can be found at some point in the motet. Indeed, it seems that the works of more modest dimensions are used as the proving grounds for new developments, as it is in them that the most advanced procedures are found.

The anonymous motet for five voices *Adoretur–In ultimo–Dies datur–Lilia nunc flores–Pacem Deus reddidit* was written in 1451 at about the time that Continental writers were beginning to cultivate the Mass cycle based on c.f.[1] The c.f. of this motet is a portion of the versus of the Alleluia *Virga Jesse* and is treated as a structural paraphrase. It is differently ornamented for each of the two statements it receives, although in the manner of the ornamentation it shows some resemblances to the older, framework-type tenor. The statements include many long notes and are frequently interrupted by rests which destroy the melodic quality of the voice. (See *DTO*, 76, p. 78, m. 67-84). Harmonically the composition is quite up to date, but the treatment of the c.f. is conservative and the work is of interest here largely because it can be dated accurately.

Settings of the plainchant continue to be written, although this category is not so important in the third and fourth quarters of the century as it was in the second. An anonymous setting of the *Salve Regina* (Tr 89)[2] is scored for four voices in a way which indicates it was written after 1450, but here again the treatment of the c.f. is conservative. There is little new in the method of presentation of the c.f. or in its function in the composition, so that the work is essentially the same as the three-voice settings written in the first half of the century. (This is from the point of view of c.f. treatment only, since the harmony in four parts is considerably in advance of the earlier three-part scoring.) In this setting the simply paraphrased plainchant is carried by the superius for the most part, although there is migration to the tenor and contratenor (e.g., the tenor carries the melody at the section *O clemens*, the contratenor at *O pia*, and the superius again at *O dulcis Maria*). A special feature is the abrupt alternation of florid c.f. statement with completely unadorned presentation in notes of fairly long value. (See m. 50-55, 84-87, 110-116.) Fluctuation between elaborate and simple presentation is found rather commonly in the c.f. elaborations of the period and is the one feature of the treatment of the c.f. itself which indicates a date later than the middle of the cen-

EXAMPLE 69. Anonymous, *Salve sancta parens* (Tr 89, no. 674; *LU*, p. 1263).

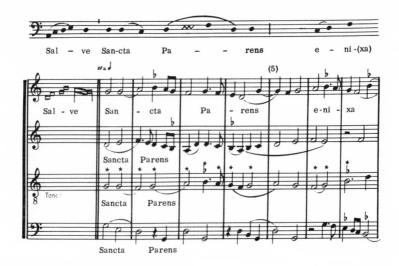

tury.[3] A similar type of c.f. setting is shown in an anonymous *Salve sancta parens* (ex. 69), but in this case the tenor carries the elaborated melody. Again, the treatment of the c.f. is of the traditional type while the setting is for four voices and the harmonies are supported by a real bass.

Two compositions from Tr 91 provide instances of strict c.f. in which the tenor moves in notes of equal value.[4] (See exs. 70 and 71a-c.) Example 70, an anonymous *Regina caeli*, is written in a rather simple style although it is scored for four voices and has such forward-looking features as movement in parallel tenths between bass and superius (m. 7-8) and rather frequent use of deceptive cadences (m. 8). (The c.f. used in this composition is simpler than that of the *LU*, several notes before the end of the phrase being omitted.) The anonymous *Salve sancta Parens* (ex. 71a-c) is much more advanced. The low register alone puts it outside the Burgundian chanson style. The approximate melodic and rhythmic equality of the voices other than the tenor, as well as the tendency to treat them as figurated harmonies over the long c.f. tones, reminds one of certain motets of Busnois. The parallel tenths between the bass and an upper part (ex. 71a, m. 2-3, bass and contratenor; ex. 71b, m. 20; and ex. 71c, m. 66-67, bass and superius) become an even more prominent feature of writing in the last quarter of the century.[5] This is also true of the use of imitation between the parts written over the c.f. (ex. 71b, m. 14-17; see also ex. 67). The sum of these characteristics leads to the opinion that this work could hardly have been written earlier than c. 1480. That

EXAMPLE 70. Anonymous, *Regina caeli* (Tr 91, no. 1214; *LU*, p. 275).

many of its stylistic features were still generally acceptable as late as the turn of the century is shown by some of the compositions included by Petrucci in the *Odhecaton A.*[6]

Two works of Dufay which were written after 1450—*Lamentatio sanctae matris ecclesiae Constantinopolitanae: Très piteulx–Omnes amici eius*[7] and the funeral motet *Ave Regina caelorum*[8]—are based on the principle of alternating statement of the c.f. which is familiar through its frequent use in the Mass. In each work the ornamented chant is carried by the tenor

EXAMPLE 71. (a-c) Anonymous, *Salve sancta parens* (Tr 91, no. 1233; LU, p. 1263).

throughout, so that it functions as the leading structural voice. Duos or trios precede the tenor entries and give opportuniy for anticipatory statements of the c.f. in one of the other voices. As usual, the ornamentation of the anticipatory statements is different from that of the main statement. The two works represent a type of composition which is based on the same structural principles as the individual movements of the tenor Mass, so they are quite properly called tenor motets.[9]

Johannes Regis cultivated the tenor motet more extensively than Dufay, and his compositions in this form merit careful consideration. Seven of them have been preserved—five complete, two lacking one of the voice parts.[10]

All were originally written for five voices, and Stephan suggests that it was Regis who established the practice of scoring tenor motets for five or more parts.[11] Stephan also places Regis's entire motet output not long after the middle of the century, which would indicate that the works were approximately contemporary with Dufay's funeral motet, *Ave Regina caelorum*, or of only slightly later date. It is certain that *Clangat plebs* must have been written before the middle of the 1470's, since it is mentioned by Tinctoris in the *Liber de arte contrapuncti* as a model of motet composition.

Not all the *cantus firmi* used by Regis have been identified, and even the name of the melody underlying *Salve sponsa* is unknown, for the voice which carried it has been lost.[12] The remaining six works, however, give evidence of the variety of ways in which Regis used the c.f. In four of them he placed it in a middle voice, following the practice of his master Dufay. In *Ave Maria . . . Virgo serena* he caused it to migrate, and in *O admirabile commercium* he placed it in a high register, as Busnois and Ockeghem sometimes did.

The c.f. of *Celsi tonantis* is stated once in the *prima pars*.[13] It is written in triple meter and is apparently ornamented toward the end. It is repeated in its entirety in the *secunda pars*, but the note values are reinterpreted in duple meter. The ornamented melody is thus treated as a framework since it is restated exactly except for the one point of change of meter. This is a type of treatment which Busnois uses throughout the *Missa O crux lignum*, and which Obrecht uses in several works, but Regis uses it only once in the motets. Another noticeable feature of the c.f. statement is its discontinuity. Regis breaks it into fragments and separates them by long rests, thereby giving ample time for the other voices to perform quartets, trios, and duos.

There is apparently no anticipatory statement of the c.f. at the beginning of the motet, but it is possible that tenor material is given out by one of the top voices at a few other points. (Compare the superius, m. 21-23, with tenor, m. 25-29; the *secundus puer*, m. 31-34, with the tenor, m. 36-40.) There is a point of imitation between the two upper voices at the beginning of the *prima pars*, and again at the beginning of the *secunda pars*, but the counterpoint is free for the most part.

The text of the tenor of *Lauda Syon* comes from the feast of Corpus Christi, although the melody or melodies used by Regis are not the ones in the *Liber Usualis*.[14] As in *Celsi tonantis*, the tenor statement is broken by rests which give opportunity for variety in scoring. The frequent contrast of full, five-part writing with a great variety of smaller combinations is not peculiar to these two works; it is one of the most noticeable features in all of Regis's tenor motets. His scoring, in this respect, is more advanced than that of Dufay and looks forward to that of Josquin. The treatment of the counterpoints in *Lauda Syon*, however, reminds one much more of

Dufay or Ockeghem than it does of Josquin. Aside from an anticipatory statement of the tenor in the superius (m. 1 ff.), and occasional imitation between two voices (m. 5, m. 23, m. 31, m. 75-79), the parts are conducted freely. Another significant feature of the work, one which is characteristic of Ockeghem rather than Dufay, is its low range. The superius never ascends above a' and the bass frequently descends to D.

The tenor of *Clangat plebs* is stated three times, each time differently ornamented.[15] The first statement underlies the entire *prima pars* and extends twenty-four measures into the *secunda pars*. The statement closes on a weak cadence and does not mark a formal division of the work. It would be difficult to find a similar instance in Dufay, since he prefers to bring a c.f. statement to an end at an important structural point, such as the final cadence of a section. Here, again, Regis shows himself more closely related to Ockeghem and other irrationalists than to his Burgundian master.

During the *prima pars* of the motet Regis quotes the antiphon in long values and breaks it up with long rests in his usual way. In the *secunda pars* he quotes the remainder of the melody in short values and again breaks it with rests, but in a noticeably regular way. He makes each fragment of c.f. two measures long and separates each of them with two measures of rest. Since all voices sound when the c.f. sounds, and only the two upper ones continue when it rests, there is a contrast of sonority every two measures. (There is a total of six duos and six tuttis in twenty-four measures.) In this passage Regis is obviously striving for an effect of structural regularity, and it seems especially characteristic that he should choose to achieve it by means of sonorous contrast. It is equally characteristic of him (and of his time) to proceed immediately to a passage which is differently and much less regularly organized (m. 61-84).

The tenor rests at measure 60, after having completed its first statement, and the passage from measure 61 through measure 84 consists of duos alternating between the two highest and two lowest voices. The duos are irregular in length and are written as freely evolving counterpoints, yet they do not completely lack repetitive organization. The material of the *bassus* (m. 65-67) is repeated by the *contratenor altus* (m. 70-72), and there is a short imitative passage between the two upper parts (m. 75-78).

The tenor enters again at measure 85 with the second statement of the c.f. The reëntry of the tenor is usually a signal for the resumption of full scoring, but in this case Regis continues with alternating duos, the tenor and superius forming one pair, the *contratenor bassus* and *contratenor altus* the other. In these duos the c.f. material of the tenor is echoed by the *contratenor bassus*. The tenor gives a full statement of a phrase of the c.f. in each duo with the superius, and in the answering duo of the two contratenors the *contratenor bassus* refers to the tenor statement in some way—sometimes it gives but a few notes of the tenor phrase, sometimes it gives the entire phrase, but it never repeats a phrase exactly in every detail. In this passage Regis approaches a type of statement which is favored by Josquin, but he carefully avoids the exact symmetry which Josquin attains by the simple expedient of repeating phrases literally.

Scoring for five voices is resumed at measure 109, and the third statement of the c.f. begins at measure 110. Since this statement is in short note values and is not broken by rests, it takes up only thirteen measures and brings the work quickly to a close. (The third statement of the c.f. may easily be overlooked in the complete edition, for the editor gives the tenor only a portion of the text of the antiphon, m. 110-120.)

Imitation occurs sporadically in the counterpoints and, as stated before, material from one duet is sometimes repeated in an answering duet, but free conduct of the voices is the rule, just as in the other motets. The scoring is very low, the ranges of the superius and bass being identical with those of *Lauda Syon*. (In both works the highest note of the superius is a′, the lowest note of the bass is D.)

The tenor of *Lux solempnis adest* is based on the respond *Repleti sunt omnes*.[16] The Gregorian melody is quoted down to the versus and is rather sparingly ornamented. It is a long melody, and Regis breaks it frequently with long rests, so that a single statement without any repetitions is sufficient to underlie the entire motet.

This motet, possibly more than any of the others, shows Regis's fondness for contrasts in scoring. One long section (m. 36-51) consists entirely of alternating duos between the two highest and the two lowest voices. The duos are short, and most are of the same length (a measure and a half in the complete edition). The resulting impression of regularity is strengthened by a consistent alteration of cadences on d and on a, and by tiny bits of melodic repetition.

In the *secunda pars* melodic repetition becomes a prominent feature of the organization. A rhythmic pattern, ♩ ♩ ♩ , appears several times in the superius at the beginning of phrases. It is given out on a repeated note (a′ most often) so that it is clearly heard as a consistent element in the counterpoint. Otherwise the counterpoints in this work are handled much as they are in the others. The bass is organized briefly by means of sequence (m. 112-116), the two upper voices imitate one another for an entire phrase (m. 138-144), and material of the vagans reappears in the superius (m. 62-63 and 67-68), but these are mere details which have none of the effect of consistency imparted by the recurring pattern of repeated notes mentioned above. *Lux solempnis* is the third of the motets which is scored low. As in the other two, the bass voice (*Barriphanos*) descends frequently to D.

It is unfortunate that one voice of the motet *Ave Maria . . . Virgo serena* is lost, for the work is constructed differently from any of the other tenor motets.[17] The sequence melody is not given out by the tenor alone;

it migrates to all the voices at one time or another. The c.f. can be followed throughout the motet, although there are gaps in the statement which, in all probability, mark points where the melody was given to the missing *contratenor secundus*.

Since the c.f. is a sequence, it consists of a series of repeated phrases, and Regis sometimes takes advantage of this feature to introduce exact repetition into the motet. The most striking instance occurs in the duos of measures 56-62, where he repeats both text and music much in the way Josquin would. (Compare m. 56-59 with m. 59-62.) In the duos (m. 44-49) he repeats the text, but only one of the voices. (Compare the superius, m. 44-47, with the bass, m. 47-49.) In a similarly scored passage (m. 98-103), he repeats one of the voices, but not the text. In both cases, the repeated voice is the one carrying c.f. In another passage he repeats all four voices of the phrase *de lacu faecis et miseriae* in the parallel phrase *theophilum reformans gratiae*, but with a number of minor changes. (Compare m. 90-93 with m. 94-96. Note that the repeated phrase is displaced by one count so that count 4 of m. 90 reappears as count 1 of m. 94, etc.)

In other places he carefully avoids emphasizing the repetitions of the c.f. He does this by changing the ornamentation of the c.f. quotation, by changing the counterpoints to the c.f., and by changing the scoring. (Compare the parallel phrases, *Benedicta tu . . .* , *quae peperisti . . .* , and *Et benedictus . . .* of m. 13, 17, and 25.) More passages could be cited, but those already mentioned are sufficient to show the vacillation between free and strictly regular procedures which is characteristic of this composer's style.

Because Regis uses so much repetition in this motet and because he causes the c.f. to migrate, it is possible to determine the outline of a few phrases of the missing *contratenor secundus*. A reconstruction of the voice can be made with a reasonable presumption of accuracy at measures 70-71, a point at which the bass sounds entirely alone. It is unlikely that Regis intended a bass solo here, and very likely that the missing part joined the bass in a duet. There is also in these measures a gap in the statement of the c.f. which indicates that the *contratenor secundus* must have carried a phrase of the sequence melody (to the text *Tu floris et roris*). This tells us a number of notes which must have appeared in the voice, but because Regis ornamented the c.f., it does not tell us the exact shape of the line.

Information with regard to the nature of the ornamentation is provided by the passage which immediately follows (m. 72-73). It is a duo between superius and *contratenor primus* in which the text given to the bass in measures 70-71 is repeated. Also, the *contratenor primus* repeats the notes of the bass almost exactly, and the superius gives out the same phrase of the c.f. which the missing voice of measures 70-71 must have carried. These facts indicate that the entire passage, from measure 70 through measure 73, consisted originally of a pair of repeated duos similar to those of measures 56-62, and we are justified in assuming that the superius reproduces the missing voice almost note for note. (It is difficult to see how it could fail to do so, for the known notes of the c.f. will fit the known counterpoints in only a certain way. The ornamentation cannot be radically different, since it is limited by the counterpoints and the c.f. notes as well as by considerations of stylistic congruity.) We cannot assume, however, that Regis would write an exactly literal repetition. It is very probable that the missing fifth part, if ever discovered, would differ from the superius in minor details.

A similar reconstruction can be made in measures 74-75 from the duo which immediately follows. Likewise, from the first two measures of the duo beginning at measure 113 we can get some idea of the shape of the missing voice in measures 109-110.

Only a very few measures can be reconstructed with any degree of exactitude, but these few give an idea of the character of the *contratenor secundus* and help to answer a question raised by the editor, who suspects that it may have been the real bass and low in range. He says that the lost part "is supposed to be a *contratenor secundus*. The *bassus* (after Petrucci, *Motetti a cinque*) has a rather high pitch and a melodious character. It is possible that this voice is the original *contratenor bassus* and that in fact the real *bassus* is missing."[18]

This is a plausible suggestion, because Regis often writes low bass parts and because he designs them as harmonic supports which move more disjunctly than the other voices. There are, however, several reasons for answering it negatively.

In a work for five voices it is to be expected that all five will sound together in certain places. One of the most likely places for this to occur is the final cadence, yet the two final chords of the work (V-I) have roots in the *bassus* as it is given in the score, and a still lower voice would have nothing left to do. The spacing of the two chords indicates that there is a missing part, but it is a middle part. The note needed is a d′, the fifth of the G-major tonic chord. The final cadence of the *prima pars* also has a correct bass and apparently lacks a middle part. There are other V-I cadences scored for four voices in the work, and in every case the lowest sounding voice provides a perfectly correct bass. One must assume either that the fifth voice is a middle part or that there were no cadences for five voices in the motet.

Also, the reconstruction of the duos indicates that the missing part is of medium range. (This is most apparent in m. 109-110.) There is no need to assume a voice lower than any of the others, and the *bassus* as given in the edition of Petrucci can be accepted as the original bass part. Its unusually melodic nature may be accounted for on the basis of the unusual treatment of the c.f. Because Regis quotes the sequence in all the voices at one time or another, every one must function as a melodic part. With respect to range, the bass of this work does not resemble those already discussed, but it is not unique, for the bass of *O admirabile commercium* is also high.

The Christmas motet, *O admirabile commercium*,[19] is divided into three large sections. In the first two the tenor has the textual incipit, *Verbum caro factum est*. It is probable that a c.f. is used and ornamented differently on each presentation, but the melody has not been identified. The last section begins with the Introit to the third Christmas Mass, *Puer natus est*, although the text diverges later and the c.f. is dropped. (It cannot be followed in the tenor after m. 66.)

There is some use of c.f. in voices other than the tenor. There is a reference to the antiphon *O admirabile commercium* in the superius at the very beginning of the work (m. 1-3), and the third section begins with entries in all voices on the first few notes of the Introit *Puer natus est*. (See ex. 72. The d' of the *contratenor bassus*, m. 46-47, makes an unlikely six-four chord. It should almost certainly be changed to g', to

EXAMPLE 72. Regis, *O admirabile commercium* (Opera, II, 55; LU, p. 408).

ª d' in the complete edition. Since the *contratenor bassus* is the lowest-sounding voice at this point, d' makes a prolonged six-four chord which, to say the least, is unusual for this period. I have changed it to g' to form a root position chord and to give a proper statement of the first three notes of the c.f. The dissonant fourth at the end of m. 47 can be explained as a passing tone.

form an acceptable chord and to give a proper statement of the c.f. I have made this correction in ex. 72.) A similar use of a tenor motive in other voices occurs in the second section of the work, measures 22-26, so that with respect to concentration of c.f. material this is one of the most advanced of the motets.

A second work entitled *Ave Maria* uses the well-known antiphon as c.f.[20] It is a song motet and is scored for three voices, the typical number for the genre. Also typical is the considerable amount of imitation it contains. The use of c.f. is, however, unusual in a song motet. The antiphon melody appears in both upper voices when they imitate one another, but it can be traced only to measure 27. It is apparently not used from this point to the end of the piece (m. 47).

The Masses and motets show Regis's great debt to Dufay, his awareness of the achievements of other composers, and his progress beyond Dufay toward the more complex and varied style of the seventies and eighties. His style is characteristic because he develops given traits in original ways. For instance, the motet *Lux solempnis* begins with melody lines which are related to those of Dufay in contour and rhythm, but it proceeds with lines which are in some places more elaborate than Dufay's, in others simpler and more syllabic. An example of the latter is found at the words *Imbuit, illustrat* . . . (superius, m. 82 ff.). The superius line takes on the character of a psalm tone at this point, owing to the repeated notes and restricted range, but it is written so that it stands out from the other parts and the text is produced with a dignity and emphasis which is noteworthy for a work of this period.

Regis advances beyond his master in harmonic idiom also. Like Dufay, he spaces individual chords carefully to produce a clear, resonant effect, his interest in this aspect of harmony being especially apparent in those works where he proceeds beyond the medium range which Dufay preferred. His use of low registers has been compared with Ockeghem's, but the similarity is no more than a surface one. Ockeghem, who thinks linearly, allows basses and baritones to intertwine and to crowd closely together even in the lowest reaches. Regis, who thinks harmonically, treats the bass as a harmonic support and conducts the other parts with constant regard to spacing and chordal resonance. His exploration of the bass regions is not so much an imitation of Ockeghem as it is an expansion of his own harmonic resources.

The interest in the sound of individual harmonies may also explain Regis's habit of indicating sharps more freely than was customary at the time. By specifically notating F♯'s, C♯'s, and G♯'s, he assures the presence of major triads which would not normally appear in the mode and which would not necessarily be produced through the application of the rules of *musica ficta*. In some cases he creates a major tonic chord by sharping the third of a minor triad (*Lux solempnis*, m. 61 and m. 157); in others he insures strong dominant chords by the same means (m. 54 and m. 52). In yet other cases his intent is apparently to sustain harmonic interest through colorful progressions. At measures 3-4 and again at measures 55-56 of *Lux solempnis*, he writes an A-major chord and immediately follows it with a C-major chord, while in measure 146 he writes an A-major chord immediately followed by A minor.

The motets are unfailingly interesting in everything that has to do with sonority—whether it be the fullness of the scoring, the variety of the scoring, the low or high register, the resonance of individual chords, or the colorful variety of harmonic progressions. Regis shows a sensitivity to sonorous effect which, in an age devoted to effects of line and of rhythm, is sufficient to mark him as a musical thinker of unusual independence. He is not as much of an experimentalist as Busnois, whose works foreshadow future stylistic developments more clearly, but his music is more consistent in quality. It is not surprising that it won the praise of Tinctoris and a continuing repute which led to publication by Petrucci thirty years later.

The motets of Ockeghem, like those of Regis, show considerable variety in the employment of the c.f. One is a setting of the Marian antiphon *Salve Regina*, which is paraphrased in the superius.[21] In a second *Salve Regina*[22] the c.f. is laid out in much the same way that it is in the late motets of Dufay, but it is given by the lowest part rather than by a middle one.[23] Characteristically, it is a bass part in range only, since it has the same melodic qualities as any of the other voices. (See ex. 73.) Two other points worthy of note are the ornamentation of the anticipatory statement of the superius, which is remarkably elaborate, and the imitative entry of the tenor on the opening motive of the chant (ex. 73, superius, m. 1-7; tenor, m. 10-12).

EXAMPLE 73. Ockeghem, *Salve Regina* (Capp. Sist. 14; Besseler, *Musik des Mittelalters*, p. 238; LU, p. 276).

The motet *Alma Redemptoris Mater*[24] differs from any of the others.
(See ex. 74a-b.) According to our categories it must be called a c.f. setting,
since the antiphon melody is paraphrased without interruption from beginning to end and is carried by one voice only; but it is a highly evolved
example of the type. Evidence of the high degree of adaptation of the c.f.
to the composer's style is found in the quality of the paraphrase, where
the original melody is converted into a typical and very fine line in the
manner of Ockeghem.[25] Stylistic adaptation is also revealed in the placement of the c.f., which is not given in the superius as would have been

expected in the Burgundian style, but in the next-to-the-highest voice. This is not only possible, but a very natural thing in a style where every voice is of equal melodic importance. It is another instance of the expansion of traditional uses made possible by the new features of Ockeghem's writing. Also quite in keeping with a work of this size are the external resemblances to the form of the tenor motet—the typical structural scheme for works of large dimensions at that time. These are exemplified by the duets and trios introducing the tutti sections and the division of the work into two parts.

The works cited up to this point show that certain new stylistic developments may cause changes in the detail of the manner of presentation of the c.f., but that they do not alter it in its fundamental aspect—in its role in the structure as a whole. There are, however, some practices developing at this period which point to the time when the role of the

EXAMPLE 74. (a) Ockeghem, *Alma Redemptoris Mater* (Besseler, *Von Dufay bis Josquin*, p. 21; *LU*, p. 273). (b) The same (Heinrich Besseler, *Altniederländische Motetten* [Kassel: Bärenreiter Verlag, 1929] p. 8; *LU*, p. 273).

c.f. in the structure will be changed—when it will be more than merely the central line of a composition and will become the generator from which the whole work springs.

The c.f. is a generator to the extent to which its material is used in voices other than the tenor. This spreading of the material is normally, but not always, the result of imitation. Points of imitation occur in Ockeghem's *Alma Redemptoris Mater* (ex. 74a, m. 9-10; ex. 74b, m. 56-59), and they have been pointed out in the motets of Regis and in certain Masses (e.g., *Grüne Linden* and the *Kyrie Dominicalis* of J. Martini). Imitation is also found to an increasing extent in other works,[26] even though it is by no means generally used as yet. Even when used, the points

usually do not involve all voices, and they are introduced in only a few
of the total number of phrases of a work. The anonymous hymn setting
Collaudamus venerantes,[27] a late addition to Modena B, is of especial
interest because the c.f. is brought into the other voices both by head
imitation and by anticipatory statement of a differently ornamented form
of a phrase. (See ex. 75a, m. 1-6, and ex. 75b, superius, m. 13-16, tenor,
m. 16-20.) After the first set of entries there is no more use of imitation,
which is quite usual.

EXAMPLE 75. (a-b) Anonymous, *Collaudamus venerantes* (Mod B, fo. 81ᵛ-82—
late addition; Ant. Mon., p. 547).

Motets are also written over secular *cantus firmi*. Stephan lists several which are not published.[28] Little need be said of the anonymous *Salve Regina* with tenor *Hilf und gib Rat*,[29] since the original melody has not been identified and, furthermore, since Orel has already discussed it in some detail.[30] It is apparently stated twice in different rhythmical forms, and the duos preceding its entries do not contain quotations from it or from the Gregorian *Salve Regina* melody.

Compère uses the tenor of Ghizeghem's chanson *De tous biens pleine* as tenor of his motet *Omnium bonorum plena*, the so-called "Singer's Prayer."[31] The borrowed melody is given note for note in its entirety in the first part. While there are some differences in rhythmical layout, they arise in large part from the reinterpretation in triple meter of the note values of the original duple meter. For example, the figure □◇◇□ indicates the rhythmical pattern $|{}^2_1 \square|\diamond\diamond|\square$ in the chanson, which is in imperfect time (chanson, m. 11-13), but when these same notes are taken into the motet, which is in perfect time, they indicate $|{}^3_1 \square\cdot|\diamond\square|\square\cdot|$ (motet, m. 36-38). The second part of the work is introduced by long duos, the first between tenor and bass, the second between superius and contratenor. These begin with a c.f. reference in the tenor (m. 109-c. 120 of the motet equal m. 1-c. 13 of the chanson); they then continue freely. With the reëntry of the tenor at the tutti (m. 182), duple meter becomes the rule and the entire chanson tenor is presented almost exactly in original form. There are minor deviations which have chiefly to do with differences in the length of rests between phrases. In addition to the tenor statements there are some quotations by other voices. For instance, the alto of the duo (m. 157 ff.) presents the beginning of the tenor of the chanson. (M. 157-c. 167 of the motet equal m. 1-c. 13 of the chanson.) The superius of this duo is also closely related to the superius of the beginning of the chanson. At another point, the alto quotes a short section of the chanson superius. (M. 12-14 of the motet equal m. 29-34 of the chanson.) Also, the final bars of the bass of the motet are a quotation of the bass at the end of the chanson. (M. 262-274, motet, equal m. 51-61, chanson.) There are other references of a less exact nature.[32] For instance, the beginning of the superius may be derived, although the relationship with the chanson superius is not too close. When compared to the Masses *Fors seulement* or even *O rosa bella III*, these quotations appear rather sketchy.[33] They do show, however, that the attitude which claims the total original as a possible source of material holds in the motet as well as in the Mass.

The anonymous *Salve Regina* with tenor *Le serviteur* (Tr 89, No. 638; DTO, 53, p. 52, No. 5) is of somewhat more interest. The chanson tenor (DTO, 14, p. 238) is again quoted in the tenor of the motet. It is transposed up a second and is stated once entirely through, then again from the beginning to the middle of the fourth bar of the chanson, where it is broken off abruptly as the composition ends. The first statement is an exact quotation of the original and, to a large extent, the second is also, even though there is a difference in meter between the motet and the chanson. (The motet changes to duple meter in the second half, while the chanson is in triple throughout.) Differences are found at the very end of the tenor statement and at its entry on a series of sustained chords. The practice of retaining original rhythmic values with a change of meter is common enough, but so is the opposite procedure, the reinterpretation of values in the new meter according to the notational rules of that period. (The latter possibility was illustrated in the motet *Omnium bonorum plena.*) The duets preceding tenor entries are apparently freely composed. However, during the first statement of the tenor, at every point where there is an imitation in the chanson a corresponding one is introduced in the motet. This is not done on the second statement. (See m. 37 ff., superius and tenor; m. 44 ff., all four voices; m. 58 ff., superius and contra-tenor I.) While the process is not so consistently or extensively carried out as it was by Faugues in the *Missa Le serviteur*, it shows that the seeds of the future parody technique were rather widely scattered—certainly not restricted to the Mass.

Another procedure which has been observed in the Mass, the extensive, simultaneous use of c.f. in more than one voice, is also found in the motet. The anonymous motet *Alma Redemptoris Mater* with tenor *Et genitorem* and *Ave Regina caelorum*[34] is a remarkably successful solution of the problem of combining two given melodies. At certain points the composer departs from them, at least from the form in which they are given in the Vatican edition, but for the most part their identity is carefully main-tained. (See ex. 76a. A comparison of the chant with the superius shows the deviations, the most noticeable of which are at m. 11-12.) The restraint of the ornamentation is noteworthy, as a greater amount would have simpli-fied the technical problem of fitting the melodies together.[35] The work is smooth and full harmonically, despite the fact that it is for only three voices. This is largely due to the skillful handling of the contratenor, which amply performs its function as a harmonic filler and yet maintains good melodic contours and a lively rhythmic independence. (See ex. 76a-b.) On the whole, the combinations are made much more adeptly in this work than they are in Regis's *Missa Ecce ancilla Domini–Ne timeas Maria*.

It seems that the tenor of the first part of the motet is made up of a plainchant phrase which is repeated six times, in whole or in part, although the source of the c.f. is unknown to me. It has the character of a psalm tone (see ex. 76a) and may be taken from some text which is recited psalmodically. (*Et genitorem*—the second half of a verse?) In text and music it is strongly suggestive of the phrase *tuum sanctum genitorem* of

EXAMPLE 76. (a-b) Anonymous, *Alma Redemptoris Mater* (Tr 91; DTO, 53, p. 37; LU, pp. 273, 274). (c) The same—tenor only.

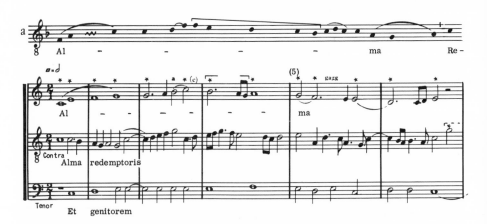

the antiphon which is paraphrased in the superius. This phrase is quoted above the tenor in example 76c. It is not the actual c.f., but as multiple *cantus firmi* are commonly related in some way, it is possible that these similarities induced the composer to choose the one he did.

The possibility must not be overlooked that the repetitions demonstrated in example 76c occurred in the original and that the composer merely copied them into his tenor. However, if they did not occur in the original—and this seems more probable—and the composer purposely organized the line by means of repeating a figure, he is anticipating here the *ostinato* technique of Obrecht, Josquin, and their contemporaries. Among the works already examined, the only passage that can compare with this one is the close of the Gloria of Ockeghem's *Missa Fors seulement*, where a fragment of the c.f. is repeated again and again. The motet holds a slightly more advanced position, however, as there is some attempt in it to produce a progressive increase and intensification of the motion of the tenor which is not evident in the Gloria of Ockeghem. (Note the shortening of the repeated phrases and the faster note values of the last two statements.)

In the second part of the motet the tenor introduces the antiphon *Ave Regina* while the superius continues with *Alma Redemptoris Mater*. The two *cantus firmi* are handled with the same skill shown in the first part. (See ex. 76b.)[36] The work is significant as a harbinger of accomplishments such as Josquin's *Alma Redemptoris Mater–Ave Regina caelorum,* in which every voice carries c.f. It is in every way a worthy early representative of an era which delighted in clever recombinations of material and in the solution of the attendant technical problems.

THE MOTETS OF BUSNOIS[37]

Of the motets of Busnois which are known today, five are based on Gregorian c.f.[38] One is a c.f. setting with the chant melody in the upper voice; three are tenor motets or variants of that form; the fifth practically defies classification, although it, too, is a tenor structure.

Conditor alme siderum is a four-voice c.f. setting with the hymn melody in lightly ornamented form in the superius. It is not of great interest from the point of view of c.f. treatment, since it shows nothing new in the manner of handling the borrowed melody. It is primarily an exercise in mensural combinations. Each of the voices is written in a different mensuration and in some of them the mensuration signs change from time to time. The individual lines are not elaborate and the harmonies give an impression of great solidity since they are preponderantly root position chords and complete with third.

Anima mea liquefacta es–Stirps Jesse is a very simple example of tenor motet. It is written for three voices, the lowest being the tenor and the bearer of the c.f. There are the usual anticipatory statements when the tenor is silent, one at the beginning and one near the middle of the composition, but the work is not formally divided into two sections by cadences and double bars in the way in which most tenor motets are.

Regina caeli I resembles one of Ockeghem's arrangements of *Salve Regina* in several of its structural features. (This is the *Salve Regina* from which Besseler quotes an excerpt in *Musik des Mittelalters,* p. 238; see also ex. 73, above.) In both of these works the c.f. is carried by the lowest voice rather than by one of the inner ones. In Busnois's motet the next-to-the-bottom voice (the tenor) briefly imitates the c.f. statement of the bottom voice (the *theumatenor*) just as it does in Ockeghem's. (Compare ex. 77, m. 15 ff., and ex. 73, m. 9 ff.) The anticipatory statements at the beginning are also comparable in certain ways. Both are very extensive, owing to the introduction of long free passages before the final c.f. note. Busnois's introductory duo is even more complex than Ockeghem's, since it combines migration with the very elaborate ornamentation of the melody lines (see ex. 77, m. 4-6).[39] This is all relatively unusual for Busnois, who normally treats the c.f. in a fairly simple manner; the similarities thus may well be the result of conscious imitation. It is quite possible that Busnois is copying the work of his illustrious contemporary.

There is also a certain relationship between Busnois's *Victimae paschali*

EXAMPLE 77. Busnois, *Regina caeli laetare, I* (Br 5557, fo. 86ᵛ-87; LU, p. 275).

laudes and Ockeghem's *Alma Redemptoris Mater*. In both, the entire c.f. is given by the next-to-the-top voice. (See exx. 78b and 74a-b.) The exterior similarity ends here, however, for in Ockeghem's work the c.f. is carried in one voice throughout, even in the duos. Busnois holds closer to the pattern of the tenor motet at first, as an anticipatory statement is given by one of the contrapuntal voices (the *basistenor*) at the beginning of the work. There are also introductory duos to the second part, but in the first of these the c.f. statement is made by the c.f. voice itself. It then rests while the c.f. is presented by the soprano in the second duo as a *restatement*. (See ex. 78a, m. 66-73 and m. 74-81.) This represents a genuine overthrow of the traditional structure, even while apparently following it. In the tenor motet and Mass the duos are merely preliminary. The c.f. statements are *anticipatory*, and the entry of the chief structural voice is reserved until they are completed. In this case the desire for clear structural relationship is unmistakable, since the c.f. statement is exactly repeated in the soprano instead of being given the usual fresh ornamentation.

Regina caeli II is similar in structural background to the *L'homme armé* Mass of Faugues, since the entire c.f. is stated in canon at the fourth by the lowest voices (ex. 79a-c). The motet departs further from the usual

EXAMPLE 78. (a-b) Busnois, *Victimae paschali laudes*—second part (Br 5557, fo. 85ᵛ-86; LU, p. 780).

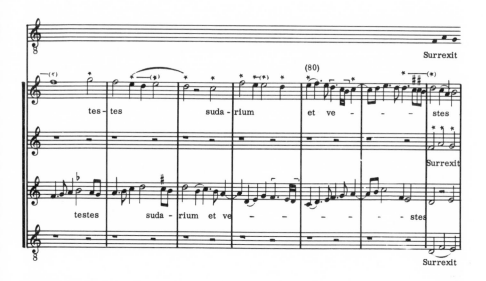

tenor structure than does Faugues's Mass, since there are no duet sections before the tenor entries. The canonic voices start the work off and
are shortly joined by the superius with a brief imitative passage (ex. 79a,
m. 3-5). The canon continues without interruption, so that the only duet
of any length in the body of the work occurs between the lowest voices
(at *ora pro nobis*) while the upper voices rest. This is also somewhat
unusual in that the tenor is the voice which ordinarily rests, allowing
duets and trios to be freely composed in the other parts.

The canon itself is rather crude. It is broken into short phrases of one
to eight measures in length and the time intervals of imitation vary

EXAMPLE 79. (a-c) Busnois, *Regina caeli laetare*, II (Br 5557, fo. 88ᵛ-89; LU, p. 275).

from one half to three-and-a-half measures. (Compare ex. 79a, *b*, and *c*.) At the longer distance of imitation the following voice of the canon sounds as though it were repeating the phrases of the leading voice rather than imitating them. Otherwise the imitation is exact as to interval and rhythm. It is managed also with noticeable regard for the architecture of the whole composition. The canon is kept continuous for the first seven measures, and in the third measure, where Busnois contrives to have the superius make an imitative entry, the c.f. is present in three voices for a short time. Then follows a shifting series of quartets, trios, and duets with one or both of the c.f. voices always taking part. Following these and a canonic duet for the two lowest voices comes the final section, which is the sonorous climax of the composition. Since this section is scored for four voices throughout, the two lowest parts have to run in continuous canon for eighteen-and-a-half measures. In order to accomplish this the composer introduces a phrase not derived from the c.f., but he treats it canonically also and the guiding principle is not relinquished at any time.

In order to carry out his plan Busnois had to ornament the c.f. more than he generally does, and here and there he has to drop in an isolated note to fill out the chords (ex. 79a, m. 4, alto; also m. 16-17, bass, not in the example). The imitative writing also causes the harmony at the beginning to be very static (ex. 79a, m. 1-4). The work lacks refinement, but it does not stand alone in this respect. Most of the contemporary efforts of a similar type are equally crude and their value is chiefly that of forward-looking experiments.

Anthoni usque limina and *In hydraulis* are both laid out according to the plan of the tenor motet, but the tenors do not present borrowed material in either case. The content of these tenors is not melodic material at all; it is contrived especially to serve as a scaffolding for the composition. These are interesting as early examples of a type[40] which was very popular during the generation of Josquin. The notes for such tenors were often chosen from syllables of the text (*Ut Phoebe radiis*),[41] from a person's name (*Hercules Dux Ferrariae*), or from some other source that struck the composer's fancy. It has been suggested that the notes of the tenor of *In hydraulis* were chosen so as to agree with the musical intervals mentioned in the text: the fourth, fifth, and octave. (The tenor notes are D-C-D, rests, A-G-A, rests, d-c-d, etc. The second statement is a fifth higher than the first, the third a fourth higher than the second and an octave higher than the first.)[42] The tenor of *Anthoni usque limina* consists solely of the repetition of the note d' (*nete synemenon*), either struck by a bell or produced in some manner in imitation of a bell.[43] This also has a relation to the text since the bell is traditionally associated with Busnois's patron saint, to whom the work is addressed. The tenor frameworks of both motets are laid out according to a strict rhythmic scheme,[44] a procedure which was even rarer in the motet than in the Mass at this time. The tenors have no melodic influence on the other voices, although the repeated d' in *Anthoni usque limina* restricts the choice of harmonies in that work. Any elements of organization other than the rhythmical plan imposed by the tenor must be provided by the counterpoints themselves. Few and scattered, they are of an interesting type as they consist mainly of sequences and passages in imitation.

The foregoing analysis of motets and Masses has shown many instances of new types of c.f. usage. Some of these types, such as imitative and canonic statements and exact repetition of passages of greater or lesser length, are obviously not peculiar to c.f. treatment alone. They are the result of a growing interest in rational procedures and must be considered as a reflection of a general stylistic trend in this period.

Also new is the highly elaborate figuration of the chant found in works of Ockeghem, Bedingham, the later Burgundians, and other writers. It has been suggested that this, too, is not an independent development in the field of c.f. The change in treatment *is* the change from the melodic style of the Dufay generation to that of Ockeghem and Busnois—from the relatively simple melody of c. 1440 to the elaborate melody of c. 1480.

As we approach the latter date we find more frequent use of c.f. in deliberate contrast to the other voices—as a bare, unornamented framework. Frameworks may be constructed from preëxistent material, or be contrived especially for a new composition. Such structures also are the result of the new interest in regulated form. In addition, the new developments in methods of organizing the contrapuntal voices seem to have some relation to the use of *cantus firmi* of this type.

Since c.f. treatment is not a thing apart, but is intimately associated with the style of a period, and since changes in the treatment of the c.f. are the direct result of general changes in the manner of writing, it is necessary to devote some time to an account of the advances, especially in the field of melody. The following chapter will be concerned with the change in melody type which occurred in the second half of the century, and also with the development of methods of controlling the elaborate lines by means of melodic patterns. The investigation will largely pertain to the motets of Busnois, in which the new features can be seen most clearly.

8

The New Trends

HEINRICH BESSELER gives a summary of the differences between the Burgundian and Netherlandish[1] styles (Dufay versus Ockeghem, Obrecht, and others) which can serve as a starting point for the discussion.[2] Besseler points out that in Netherlandish compositions, especially those of Ockeghem, the polyphony is homogeneous, for all voices are of the same melodic character. In contrast, the sacred music of the late Burgundian composers clearly derives from the nonhomogeneous polyphony of the Burgundian chanson of the first half of the fifteenth century, which in turn derives from French secular art song of the fourteenth. There is a marked opposition in character between the melody-carrying voice, or voices, and the supporting parts.

Furthermore, there is a distinct difference in the melody type of the individual voices in the compositions of the two schools. The Burgundian composers tend to retain the clearly outlined, self-sufficient, chanson-type melody. Such melodies are divided into distinct phrases, each of which has a definite cadence as its goal. The meter is generally triple, and although the rhythms are fluid, with constant employment of hemiola, the basic meter is heard as prevailing. There is a strong tendency to avoid extreme rhythmic complications, such as chains of syncopations and rhythmic groups starting on subdivisions of the unit beat smaller than one half (i.e., smaller than the minim).

The sacred works of Ockeghem are in noticeable contrast. The lines do not have the balanced shape of the Burgundian chanson melodies. They do not necessarily proceed to a cadence as a stopping point, but break off anywhere. They are rhythmically much more complex because they make much use of the smaller subdivisions of the beat. Displacements of accent with regard to the unit of beat are the rule. Lines often reach their climax on an "offbeat." All voices hold over from one tactus into the next, etc.[3]

Yet, any statements concerning the differences between the styles of Ockeghem and the late Burgundians must be carefully qualified. It is undeniable that in the late works of Dufay, and in many of those of Regis, the distinctions become somewhat less sharp. The old characteristics of clarity of melodic outline and definite delimitation of phrases remain, but the differentiation between the voices becomes less pronounced, the polyphony tends to be more homogeneous, and complex rhythms appear more frequently. Nevertheless, the superius and tenor remain as the smoothest parts, melodically. Traces of the old treatment of the contratenor, which was made to skip about to fill up gaps in the harmonies, are still discernible, and the bass moves more slowly and in a more disjunct manner than the melody voices since it is given the function of supporting a clear succession of harmonies.

We find that these differences between the voices are present to a much lesser degree in Ockeghem. Even the bass has much the same melodic character as the other parts, with the result that it loses in effectiveness as a harmonic support and much of the music has no clear harmonic structure. Occasionally, in his most animated moments, Dufay approaches the elaborate style of Ockeghem quite closely, although such passages serve as contrasting episodes and by no means alter the fact that his style is essentially simpler and more song-like. However, they may be the result of Netherlands influence.[4]

THE FIGURAL MELODY

Others of the period, including Burgundians, are even more inclined to write elaborate voice lines. The melody lines of Bedingham, illustrated in example 80a, are more discursive and elaborate by far than those of Dufay. In their rhythmic irregularity they are much closer to Ockeghem. Bedingham is English; but Faugues is probably not, and his works also show a definite break with the older style in melodic and rhythmic aspects, as well as in a general tendency toward greater equalization of the parts. (See ex. 80b and exs. 66 and 67.)

The same tendencies may be observed in the anonymous *Missa Le serviteur*, which is also remarkable for its extreme rhythmic energy (ex. 80c-d). It is doubtful that any of these excerpts could ever be taken for works of Ockeghem, yet in general they differ from the older Burgundian style in the same respects as his. Balanced and reserved melody lines are replaced by elaborate and rhythmically intricate ones; functional distinction between parts is disappearing in favor of equality of voices. In all

EXAMPLE 80. (a) Bedingham, *Missa Deuil angouisseux*—Benedictus (Tr 88; DTO, 61, p. 133). (b) Faugues, *Missa Le serviteur*—Agnus II (Tr 88; DTO, 38, p. 127). (c-d) Anonymous, *Missa Le serviteur*—*Pleni sunt caeli* and Benedictus (Tr 88; DTO, 38, pp. 152, 153).

probability, no one carries the process of equalization as far as Ockeghem, and in none of these works does the harmonic aspect suffer so much as it does in his motets and Masses. This is especially noticeable in the treatment of the cadences. Nevertheless, the conclusion is inescapable that the Burgundian style was generally breaking down during the 1460's and 1470's.

The process of change can be traced in the works of Busnois. Some of the motets start out with typical, although not too distinguished, song lines of the older Burgundian type. These may be freely composed, as in the case of *In hydraulis*, or they may be elaborations of a c.f., as in *Anima mea liquefacta es–Stirps Jesse* and *Regina caeli II*. (See exx. 81 and 77.) Busnois is evidently not at his best in the writing of sustained, songlike melodies, as his do not have the elegance of those of Dufay or Regis. There is a certain restlessness and angularity in the upper voice of example 77 (rhythm of bar 10, octave leap in bar 11) which is even more noticeable in the lower parts.

It is probable that these are among the earlier motets. *In hydraulis* must have been written before 1467, because the Count of Charolais mentioned in the text became Duke of Burgundy (Charles the Bold) in that year. Pirro[5] suggests 1461 or 1465 as probable dates of composition, since Charles was in Paris with his retinue in those two years and on either occasion Busnois could have presented the work to Ockeghem.

As mentioned before, Br 5557 was compiled before 1481 and the motets in it were written no later than about 1475. Internal evidence indicates that *Anima mea liquefacta es–Stirps Jesse* is the earliest of these. It has no real bass line and the contratenor is treated as a harmonic filler, moving as often below the tenor as above. The melody of the soprano (ex. 81) shows certain Burgundian characteristics. It starts in a quiet way, the phrases are not excessively long, and they come to definite cadences. However, the interval of a ninth covered by an ascending octave and second (m. 17) is somewhat too vigorous for the standard Burgundian manner. Likewise there is in the lower voice of the duo a rhythmic restlessness

EXAMPLE 81. Busnois, *Anima mea liquefacta est—Stirps Jesse* (Br 5557, fo. 83ᵛ-84; *Vesperale*, p. 129).

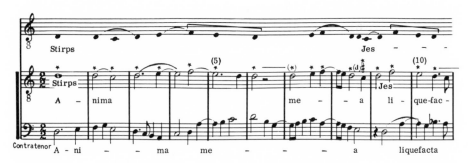

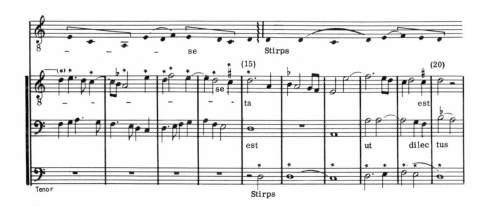

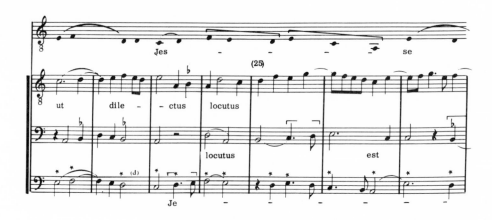

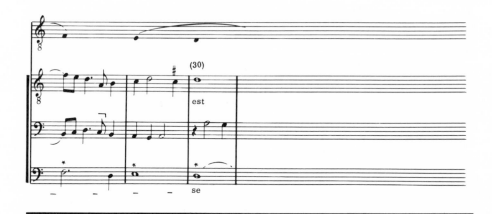

which is not characteristic of the beginning of a composition of Dufay. This voice has the character of a counterpoint and is more like a Flemish than a Burgundian line. (Ex. 81, m. 1-14, contratenor.)

The lines of more highly developed and hence apparently later works display a rhythmic and melodic vigor that can hardly be called "Burgundian" at all. The upper voice of the duet at the beginning of example 78a (*Victimae paschali laudes*, second part) is quiet enough, although it starts with hemiola figures instead of emphasizing the basic triple meter and in measures 72-73 the bass has a series of short figures which contradict the beat consistently (marked by dotted brackets in the example). The lower voice of this duet is obviously not in the older style. It is impossible to conceive of Dufay writing a line such as this, with its startling increase of speed, angular leaps, and rapid syncopated patterns (m. 70 ff.). The disjointed effect of this is entirely foreign to his style, where ornamental lines have the character of light and graceful filigree.

The new method of writing is evident in all voices of *Regina caeli laetare* (ex. 82). The unit beat is constantly broken into small values;

rhythms based on the pattern ♩♩♩ abound (ex. 82, m. 39 ff.); the melody contains vigorous leaps; and no one part can be called the melody voice. The contrapuntal texture is quite homogeneous, as all voices are about equal in character, although the lower ones move slowly enough to provide for a clear succession of harmonies in most cases.

EXAMPLE 82. Busnois, *Regina caeli laetare, II* (Br 5557, fo. 88ᵛ-89; LU, p. 275).

In *Anthoni usque limina* the voices are as active as in the example above, yet the chordal background is even clearer because the lines frequently have the character of figurated harmonies. (Owing to the single note d' of the tenor, the chords are almost entirely restricted to those on D, B♭ and G.)

So we find this late Burgundian, who was a member of the court of Charles the Bold at the time, moving forward from the style of Dufay and fusing elements with it that are more characteristic of Ockeghem and other composers of the last quarter of the fifteenth century. By giving up poised, songlike melody, while generally retaining clear harmonic structure, he makes a choice that is the same as that made by his successors Obrecht and Josquin.

IMITATION IN BUSNOIS

The counterpoint of Busnois, like that of most of his contemporaries, is to a large extent nonimitative,[6] and many of the imitative passages which do occur in his works do not represent any new practice.[7] In certain respects, however, he uses imitation in a highly individual manner, one which has a direct bearing on further developments in melodic style at this time. The imitative lines of Dufay are apt to be extended and lyric in nature, but Busnois tends to write brief figures, often of a cadential type.

EXAMPLE 83. Busnois, Magnificat *Quinti toni* (Br 5557, fo. 70ᵛ).

The imitations often involve three voices and are employed in such a way that short sections are extremely tightly integrated. Ockeghem also sometimes uses short, incisive figures which call attention to themselves in no uncertain way (see ex. 74*b*, m. 56-58), but their effect is of momentary contrast, of accentuating the generally independent, unrestrained flow of the voices by the fleeting restriction they impose.

One of the most significant aspects of Busnois's writing is the skillful employment of the effect of climax. He tends to place climaxes in structurally important positions, and he achieves them by means of stretto—by concentrating *ostinato* and sequential figures in close imitation.

In *Anima mea liquefacta es–Stirps Jesse* there are rather simple sequential passages treated in imitation in two voices (ex. 84a, m. 95-101, and ex. 84b, m. 119-124.)[8] In *Victimae paschali laudes* and *Anthoni usque*

EXAMPLE 84. (a-b) Busnois, *Anima mea liquefacta est—Stirps Jesse* (Br 5557, fo. 83ᵛ-84; *Vesperale*, p. 129).

limina there are imitations which have the total effect of *ostinato* (ex. 85a-b). In both cases the constantly reiterated high A's have an emphatic, climactic effect which is a new element in the music of that time. There is apparently nothing to equal these passages in music of the generation before Busnois. In example 85b the imitative entries start on the beat in measures 80-81 and off the beat in measures 82-84. The melodic figures also gradually increase in length. The bass is especially regular in this

EXAMPLE 85. (a) Busnois, *Victimae paschali laudes* (Br 5557, fo. 85ᵛ-86; LU, p. 780). (b) Busnois, *Anthoni usque limina* (Br 5557, fo. 49ᵛ-50).

respect, increasing exactly three fourths of a beat on its second and third entries. Characteristically, the lines are brief and vigorous and have strong harmonic implications. They serve very well to arouse a strong expectation of a cadence while at the same time delaying its appearance.

The Patterned Line and the Drive to the Cadence

The organization of the line by means of repeated rhythmic patterns and sequences is not peculiar to Busnois. Sequential passages are common in Italian compositions of the fourteenth and early fifteenth centuries. They are found in the works of Dufay's first period (in the 1420's), when he was strongly under Italian influence, but after c. 1430 such passages are ordinarily not found in compositions of the Burgundians and English.[9] In their secular music these composers apparently took over certain Italian characteristics (witness the frequent use of imitative entries at the beginning of phrases), but they pointedly ignored this most striking element of sequence. After the middle of the century, however, they begin to readmit it to their works.[10]

Instances of rhythmic patterning of the individual line are found in certain short compositions of the Trent codices which apparently date from Busnois's time or a little earlier. (See ex. 86.)

As is customary, the patterns in measures 3-4 of example 86 emphasize the offbeats. These are not true sequences, there being no repetition of

EXAMPLE 86. Anonymous, *Cantate Domino* (Tr 88; *Mon. Pol. Lit.*, 2nd ser., I, 100; *LU*, p. 408).

melodic figures. Slightly more extended instances of the same type are found in Faugues. (See ex. 80b, m. 131-135 and m. 142-146. The latter passage makes use of figures of three eighth-notes in duple meter.) Bedingham uses groups of five eighth-notes in one voice and three in another (ex. 80a), and greatly increases the effect of patterning by making the melody sequential (m. 69-70). The composer of the anonymous *Missa Le serviteur* most closely approaches Busnois in the extended and effective use of the device. Not only are the sequences clearly heard; their effect is increased in some places by imitation (ex. 80c, m. 48-51; 80d, m. 111-117) and by following up longer patterns with shorter so as to get an increasing rhythmic climax (ex. 80d, m. 119-122). Although passages such as these take up but a small portion of the total length of the compositions, the fact remains that they appear much more frequently at this period than they did a few years earlier.

It happens that all of the compositions cited are contained in Tr 88, which would suggest that the practice of patterning the lines was developing around 1460. This belief is supported by the appearance of several such passages in Busnois's *In hydraulis*, which, as mentioned before, was written not later than 1467. A very few instances appear also in the late works of Dufay, showing that he, too, was not unaware of this trend. Example 87 from the *Missa Ecce ancilla Domini* shows that it was used by him with characteristic attention to balance of lines and restraint of rhythm (e.g., the descending phrase, m. 5-9, following an ascending phrase, m. 1-5; hemiola or displaced hemiola are the only rhythmic patterns). While this is quite an extended passage, and while another appears in the Credo of the same Mass, these never become an important element of Dufay's later style. Rather, they form contrasting episodes to the rest

EXAMPLE 87. Dufay, *Missa Ecce ancilla Domini–Beata es Maria—Osanna I* (Br 5557, fo. 57ᵛ-58; LU, p. 1417).

of a work and seem to be the result of outside influences. He certainly never uses them with the vigorous effect of Busnois.

The closing section of a song motet by Regis (ex. 88) contains sequential passages which approach those of Busnois, but the quietly descending scales are quite different from the terse, energetic, chordally influenced figures of the latter.[11]

It is noticeable to a greater or less degree in all of these examples that

EXAMPLE 88. Regis, *Ave Maria* (*Opera*, II, 61).

not only are the individual figures of the sequences syncopated in relation to the beat—they are also syncopated in relation to one another when used concurrently in more than one voice. Their rhythmic impact is thus increased out of all proportion to the amount that could be attained by the mere duplication or triplication of the patterns without the conflict and stress of syncopation. It is also prophetic of their future use that most of them occur before final cadences or near the end of important sections.[12]

One thing is strikingly clear—sequences are not a significant feature of Ockeghem's writing. The instances which can be found represent the exception rather than the rule for him, just as example 87 does for Dufay. In the case of Dufay this sparing usage can readily be explained on the ground that his creative career was coming to an end around 1460, just about the time that interest in such procedures was growing up. This does not apply to Ockeghem and the reason must be sought elsewhere. The answer seems to lie in the nature of the procedure itself, since it binds the voices to the repetition of fixed patterns, deprives them of a measure of their contrapuntal independence, and tends to throw some passages into high relief in relation to others, thus disrupting the continuous, smooth flow of the polyphony. Motivic usages such as these contradict the very premises of a style in which continuity is prized above articulation; in which joints are covered over, even at the expense of destroying the cadence; and in which anything of a formulary nature is avoided, whether it be in the conduct of an individual voice or the layout of a c.f. for a whole Mass. Nevertheless, Ockeghem occasionally writes patterned lines (see ex. 89a-d). The first two citations are passages from the Masses *Au travail suis* and *Mi-mi* which contain voices related by imitation and organized by repeated, complementary rhythmic patterns. (Ex. 89a, superius and tenor, m. 33-35; ex. 89b, superius and tenor, m. 251-254.) The presence of motivic organization cannot be

denied, but it can also be seen that Ockeghem's employment of it is
strictly conditioned by the demands of his style. Whereas Busnois develops such passages and makes sure that they stand out in sharp contrast
to their surroundings, Ockeghem minimizes them and integrates them
into the polyphonic continuum as much as possible. The motivated lines
in *Au travail suis* (ex. 89a) are partially obscured by the surrounding
voices, while the corresponding lines in *Mi-mi* (ex. 89b) are smothered,
so to speak, by the profusion of similar rhythmic figures which appear on
all sides (marked by x's and brackets in the example). A somewhat
clearer instance of sequential organization, from the *Missa Quinti toni*,
is given in example 89c but even here the repeated figure does not take on
a rhythmically striking shape and it is imitated only once. Another passage from the same work (ex. 89d), with its insistence on triadic figures
in the two top voices, comes as close as any to the usages of Busnois.
Ockeghem repeats these figures at the same pitch level, but he only
approximates the effect of an *ostinato*. Under his hand the figures are
fluent and flexible in shape. They are not the hard, clear-cut entities
that Busnois uses (ex. 85a-b). The result is that the passage does not
make an emphatic contrast with the rest of the work.

Examples of motivic usage in the music of this period could be multi-
plied, but those cited are sufficient to show that interest in the various
devices of sequence and *ostinato* is widespread. The examples also show
that Busnois exploits these devices most fully, employing them far more
effectively than do his contemporaries at this time (c. 1475). He fully
perceives the possibilities they offer for contrast with the normal type of

EXAMPLE 89. (a) Ockeghem, *Missa Au travail suis*—Kyrie II (*Works*, I, 31).
(b) Ockeghem, *Missa Mi-mi*—Credo; (*Works*, II, 14). (c) Ockeghem, *Missa
Quinti toni*—Agnus II (*Works*, I, 14). (d) The same—Osanna (*Works*, I, 11).

flowing polyphonic line, and he makes these effects of contrast a central element of his style. To be sure, he uses such passages for merely momentary effect. In his works they appear suddenly, without preparation, and disappear just as quickly, without a trace. The longest and most complex ones are, however, placed at or near the end of the composition, where they have a broader formal significance and bring the whole work to a brilliant close. Both in appearance and function they are direct forerunners of the motivically organized sections which are such a striking feature of the works of Obrecht and Josquin. In this aspect of their style the later composers certainly owe much more to Busnois than to Ockeghem.

Around 1475 the practice of emphasizing the final cadence of the composition is by no means limited to Busnois. The passages quoted from his works are simply special cases in which the desired effect is achieved in a most emphatic way by means of powerful rhythmic strettos. Other, less drastic means are used by him and by other writers as well. Often there is merely an increase in the speed of all the voices—probably the simplest way in which a drive to the cadence can be achieved. This is the characteristic device of Ockeghem, Regis, and Dufay, and it is also employed by Busnois in some cases (as at the end of *Anima mea liquefacta es* and *Regina caeli II*).[13] Other devices are also employed, usually in conjunction with an increase in speed, such as the rise to a high note,[14] the use of close imitation (ex. 89b), or harmonic extension.[15]

Lines of Development

The motets of Busnois showed a marked development from the most primitive to the most advanced. An example of the former is *Anima mea liquefacta es–Stirps Jesse*, which displays a rather undistinguished Burgundian melodic style, contrapuntal and harmonic procedures definitely related to those of the first half of the century, and rather tentative use of sequence and imitation. Instances of greater technical advancement are found in *Victimae paschali laudes* and *Anthoni usque limina*, which are presumably later works. They disclose a highly characteristic boldness in the melody lines, considerable homogeneity in the counterpoint, well-defined harmonic background, the use of sequence and imitation to achieve brilliant climactic effects, and a tendency to repeat phrases and short groups of notes identically, rather than in differently ornamented form, so that the formal relationships are clearly audible.

The *cantus firmi* of these motets (and the two Masses as well) are of the two usual types—the ornamented melody and the unornamented framework. Busnois likes the unornamented tenor which functions as a structural skeleton, but he bases a number of works on elaborated c.f. Since his contemporaries prefer to ornament the c.f., so far as we can judge from their available works, his preference for the simple type is worth pointing out. When Busnois elaborates the borrowed melody, however, he does essentially the same thing as all the others, converting it into a line which approaches in character the figural melody of the added voices. (See ex. 82, m. 37–42.) A comparison of his ornamented lines with those of Ockeghem shows differences of detail, but these differences appear in the freely composed lines of the two men as well. They are to be expected because of general differences in style.

It is noticeable that the motivic figures which are such an important feature of the contrapuntal lines of Busnois do not often appear in the elaborated c.f. They are not altogether absent from this part, and, on occasion, the ornamenting notes are cast into sequential form when the shape of the c.f. itself permits. Instances are found in *Anima mea liquefacta es–Stirps Jesse* (ex. 84a, m. 96-101, and ex. 84b, m. 119-124). In both cases the melodic outline of the c.f. offers opportunity for the construction of sequences and Busnois takes advantage of this fact when adding the free tones. Nonetheless, sequence and *ostinato* are normally devices of the free counterpoints. This is necessarily the case when the tenor is totally unornamented, as in *Anthoni usque limina* (where imitations on an *ostinato*-like figure take place when the tenor is silent—see ex. 85b), but it is also true of the ornamented c.f. of *Victimae paschali laudes.* The voice carrying the sequence melody takes no part in the climactic imitations of the closing section until *after* it has completed its quotation. (See ex. 85a, m. 114-116.)

It should be noted parenthetically that the sequential passages in the more primitive work, *Anima mea liquefacta es–Stirps Jesse,* have a decorative rather than a structural function. In the two works which are more advanced in style, the passages are not only more concentrated—they occur at critical structural points. (Ex. 85a is a final cadence; ex. 85b immediately precedes the final cadence.)

As stated above, Busnois shows an interest in plain, rhythmically organized scaffoldings which is unusual for this period. When he deals with this type of tenor his methods are much further removed from those of Ockeghem than is the case when he elaborates a c.f. This can be shown by comparing the framework tenor of Ockeghem's motet *Ut heremita solus* with the tenors of *Anthoni usque limina* and *In hydraulis.* Ockeghem's tenor is not a simple one. Externally—in its aspect as a musical line—it is a long and aimless series of notes. Internally—in its aspect as an intellectual construction—it is doubly complicated. First, the composer has provided instructions for deriving the tenor notes which are obscure in themselves; second, the means for deriving the notes is an involved and subtle computation.[16] In comparison to this many-layered complexity, Busnois's framework tenors are models of regularity and simplicity. The canon for *Anthoni usque limina* is obscure in certain respects,[17] but the part which results from it is completely straightforward—a tenor consisting of a single repeated tone. The tenor of *In hydraulis* is scarcely more complicated, consisting essentially of a repeated three-note figure stated at various pitches and in various mensurations.

Tenors such as these of Busnois not only provide strict frameworks which satisfy the rationalist's requirement for controlled form; they advertise their function by contrasting sharply with the other parts. In addition, they do not prevent the organization of the other parts by means of imitation or motivic patterns. Structural control is possible, then, on two levels, and in these motets Busnois is dealing with potentialities which become realities in a couple of decades. In works such as the Kyrie and Sanctus of Josquin's *Missa Hercules Dux Ferrariae* there is total organization, the scaffolding providing the external, over-all plan and the contrapuntal voices the internal, detailed order.

The two Masses of Busnois also give evidence of his preference with regard to type of c.f. In *O crux lignum* the Gregorian melody is ornamented, it is true, but it is not reornamented every time it is stated, as is usual with this kind of c.f. The form in which it first appears in the Kyrie is taken as a constant and is never changed in the succeeding movements. Busnois does not employ the technique of ornamentation in the usual way, to produce continuous flexibility and change, but treats the ornamented c.f. as a rigid framework. Variety is achieved in the way usual for frameworks, by means of change of mensuration. He handles the elaborated Gregorian melody, then, in the same way Dufay handles the *res facta* in *Se la face ay pale*.

The c.f. treatment of the *Missa L'homme armé* is not dissimilar. Busnois quotes the chanson tenor quite literally, in a manner which contrasts noticeably with the elaborated presentations of the *L'homme armé* tune in the Masses of Dufay, Ockeghem, Faugues, Regis, and others. He gives the unornamented quotations logical scaffolding treatment, laying out the tenor according to set rhythmic patterns and manipulating the statements schematically by augmentation, diminution, melodic inversion, etc.

These works, the two Masses and the two motets, show that an interest in traditional rationalistic methods is as important an aspect of Busnois's thought as are the experiments in melodic organization—the use of the c.f. in canon, the motivic organization of the counterpoints, the exact repetition of sections. None of the outstanding features of Busnois's style, (with the exception of the elaborate melody line and the correspondingly complex c.f. elaborations) are important aspects of the style of Ockeghem. As will be seen in the following chapter, however, every one of them appears in a more highly developed form in the work of Obrecht. Sequential passages, complicated rhythmic combinations, and brilliant drives to the cadence abound in Obrecht's writing. Even more than Busnois, he prefers to quote borrowed material literally and to present his *cantus firmi* as scaffoldings. In the scaffoldings he shows the greatest inventiveness in varying the methods of schematic manipulation. The conspicuous revival of the c.f. scaffolding in the works of Obrecht represents an important and characteristic aspect of the rational trend in the late fifteenth century. Furthermore, procedures which are found in works of Faugues, Regis, and others—such as the use of c.f. in imitation (especially in the anticipatory duos and trios), the simultaneous statement of two or more *cantus firmi*, and the use of c.f. in canon—make up an important element of his writing. And, like Busnois, he shows comparatively little interest in the free elaboration of the c.f.

There has been a tendency to view Ockeghem as the leader in these developments, and to overlook the achievements of other men. "The efforts of Ockeghem led the Netherlandish tendencies to complete victory in the second half of the century. The whole younger generation stands on his shoulders . . ."[18] However, the technical elements which make up the style of Obrecht show many more points of difference than of agreement with Ockeghem, and they can be found almost in their entirety in Busnois and Regis, who are both late Burgundians. If this member of the younger generation stands on the shoulders of any one man, it is far more likely that they are those of Busnois than of Ockeghem.

There are also strong points of similarity between Josquin and Busnois, but the relationship is not so unequivocally direct as it is with Obrecht. For instance, Josquin is not so partial to literal quotation of the borrowed material nor so apt to bind himself to rigid plans of statement as Busnois and Obrecht. The cantus firmi of Josquin's Masses *L'homme armé sexti toni, Gaudeamus* and *Ave maris stella* are given the most varied elaborations, certifying to a brilliant, imaginative quality of thought which makes Obrecht's literal presentations seem stodgy in comparison.

It can well be said that in some respects Josquin continues the fanciful practices of the irrationalists. In the earlier works, especially, there are similarities to Ockeghem—witness the undifferentiated flow of the counterpoint and the relative harmonic weakness of the *Missa Fortuna desperata*.[19] It seems, also, that the plan of the *Missa L'homme armé super voces musicales* could hardly have been executed by anyone who felt it necessary to maintain a modally appropriate harmonization of the c.f. As the c.f. makes its way up through the musical voices, it comes into highly unusual modal relations with the contrapuntal parts, which adhere to the minor mode on d that is the tonic of the Mass.[20] Such unusual relations would have been p ˜sible for Ockeghem, as is shown by the repetitions of phrases a whole tone ᴀ ˙rt in the *Missa Fors seulement*. (See ex. 62, m. 114-124.)

On the other ᴀnd, it goes without saying that Josquin uses all the rational devices of contrapuntal combination and motivic treatment which had been developed by his predecessors. In his work the rather primitive attempts of the 1470's are carried to a perfection which was never surpassed. He also by no means avoids the other means of organization offered by the c.f. framework. The *Missa Hercules Dux Ferrariae* is a model of strict construction and a supreme expression of the urge to rational music architecture which pervades the era.

Josquin will be seen, then, as combining and bringing to their highest realization both the rational and the fanciful trends of the preceding generation. He certainly "stands on the shoulders of Ockeghem," but he also stands on the shoulders of many of Ockeghem's contemporaries, both of the North and of the South.

Despite the differences in the music of Regis, Busnois, and Ockeghem, they are all Northerners. So far as is known, none of them spent any time in Italy. However, at this time traits which can only be interpreted as a reflection of Italian taste commence to make a rather tentative appearance in the music of Northerners living in Italy. The "substitution" motets of Compère were probably written while he was in Milan in 1474–1475. In them, simple chordal writing and syllabic setting of the text replaces florid counterpoint to a noticeable extent. Compère's motets are not of great artistic value—they present a rather primitive mixture of stylistic elements from the North and the South—but they are of some historical importance because the traits they show appear in much clearer and more elevated form in works of Weerbecke and of Josquin (who also worked in Milan, along with Agricola and Martini).[21] The Italian influence ultimately has an enormous effect on the development of music but during the 1470's it is still only of regional importance.

SUMMARY

The picture we get of this period is one of great variety and activity. The preceding chapters show that two opposing tendencies coëxist in the "Northern" style. Ockeghem is the chief representative of the irrational, or fanciful tendency, Busnois of the rational, or formalistic.

The mensural development, in which the semibreve loses its position as the unit of beat, may be credited to the irrationalists, since the constant use of the smaller note values is necessary to their elaborate melodic style.[22] Since these writers tend to make all the voices equally florid, they break down the old functional differences between them, and attain contrapuntal equivalence through similarity of melodic quality in all parts. They do not require, nor do they aim for, similarity of melodic content. With regard to musical form, they are chiefly concerned with varying traditional structures rather than with developing new concepts of organization. On the one hand, they loosen the fixed, traditional formal procedures (especially with regard to the tenor, which they no longer recognize as the only rightful bearer of the structural c.f.); on the other, they weaken the logical simplicity of those structures. In the realm of harmony they show an interest in exploring the low registers and in creating fuller, heavier sonority (writing for five voices). Harmonic clarity is minimized, however, and Ockeghem goes so far as partially to abandon the standard cadential forms. The result is that clear definition of phrase gives way to a continuous, largely undifferentiated stream of sound.

The rationalists, for their part, also abandon the quiet melodic style, with the semibreve as the unit of beat. Yet, while they cultivate the more elaborate figural style, they bend it to their own purposes: they subject the lines to detailed organization—using the various methods of patterning mentioned above—and they control the linear flow by means of a relatively clear harmonic rhythm. They also vary the older formal schemes, but in a positive way so that formal relationships are made even more clearly audible, either by exact sectional repetition or by concentration of material through imitation, sequence, *ostinato*, duplication of the c.f. in canon, etc. They also tend to equalize the voices, but not to the extent of denying their special functions completely. The bass continues to support a clear succession of harmonies, the tenor tends to retain its position as structural, c.f.-bearing voice. The tenor presents the quoted material continuously, although it may be duplicated by other voices which imitate it for a greater or less time or in some other way join in with subsidiary, fragmentary references to the c.f.

With all their differences, these two currents of musical thought show one trait in common. It is clear from the work of all writers that the older, "song-type" melody is no longer cultivated (except in compositions in secular style). The irrationalists may be given chief credit for this change, a change which is of lasting importance in the stylstic development of the time. It is also clear that the procedures of the rationalists with regard to formal integration are a contribution of equal importance to stylistic development, since they are the elements which receive the most striking expansion in the next generation. Other rationalist traits, such as the preference for a clear harmonic background and the retention of specific functions for the parts despite contrapuntal equalization, also continue on into the next generation. With the later writers contrapuntal equivalence of the parts is as much the result of similarity of content (achieved largely by means of imitation) as it is of a similarity of quality (achieved by making each voice an elaborate melody without differentiation of character).

Although it is possible to define the two currents of thought, in actual fact no one man writes purely in the rational or irrational manner. Regis, Faugues, Basiron, Busnois, etc., tend more or less clearly toward the former, and Ockeghem, Heyns, Frye, Bedingham, Caron, etc., toward the latter. Ockeghem, however, presents us with a Mass constructed entirely on a rational device, the mensuration canon.[23] Regis uses very low registers and scores for five voices. Busnois copies Ockeghem in taking the structural c.f. away from the tenor and giving it to other voices. Except for Regis, all of them abandon the elegantly simple chanson melody. Nevertheless, the tendency of each man toward one or the other type of thought is evident from the devices he prefers and from the way he uses the ones which belong essentially to the opposite outlook.

A thorough mixture of the characteristic traits of the two tendencies is presented by the *Missa L'homme armé* of Tinctoris.[24] The famous theorist, connoisseur, and admirer of Ockeghem, Busnois, and Regis creates a work in which there is a wilderness of effects. At times he starts by treating the c.f. as a scaffold and immediately shifts over to a high degree of ornamentation in a way which recalls the practices of Ockeghem and Regis (e.g., the *Qui tollis* section of the Gloria,); at times he forces the c.f. to skip from voice to voice, or he repeats phrases of it, or he omits phrases and replaces them with elaborate free sections quite in the Ockeghem manner (in the *Christe*, the first section of the Credo, and the first section of the Sanctus). At other times he treats the c.f. in canons of greater or less extent and varying degrees of strictness as do Faugues, Busnois, and Regis (in Kyrie II and *Et incarnatus*); he combines two different phrases (in the first section of the Gloria, where phrase A of the c.f. is given alone, and after a free duet phrases B and A are combined in the alto and tenor); he concentrates c.f. material by giving parts of it to other voices than the current structural one (at *Cum Sancto Spiritu*, where the c.f. is in the alto and there are references to it in tenor and bass), or he includes references to it and imitations on it in a section which has no structural c.f. (in Agnus II). At other points where there is a scaffolding c.f. he makes a definite attempt to organize the remaining voices among themselves (see *Osanna* and Agnus III). In the lack of simple plan, of a dominant structural voice, or of any regular method of c.f. treatment, the Mass belongs to the irrational school of thought as surely as do any of Ockeghem. Yet, it goes beyond Faugues or Busnois in the use of devices which are especially favored by the rationalists (and hence is probably a later work than any of theirs). Tinctoris, without doubt, is following his own recommendation that a composer make use of all artifices in a large composition such as a Mass, but the effect, on the whole, is rather jumbled. Even at this distance in time it is possible to detect in this Mass the work of an eclectic, of a man who is aware of all the current developments and who is making a conscious attempt to combine them in his writing. The contrasting elements which are brought together in this work are found also in the works of Josquin, but there they are combined much more successfully and on a much higher musical plane.

PART III

OBRECHT AND JOSQUIN DES PREZ

9

The Masses and Motets
of Jacob Obrecht

THE MASSES OF OBRECHT included in the great publication of Johannes Wolf[1] are apparently all based on c.f., with one possible exception.[2] The source of some of the melodies has not yet been ascertained, but in most cases this does not prevent trustworthy analysis, since Obrecht generally provides at least one literal, unadorned quotation of the borrowed material. For instance, the source of the c.f. of the *Missa Graecorum* remains a tantalizing mystery, yet it is stated so clearly at several different times that every note of it is known, and the various ways in which Obrecht manipulates it can therefore be determined readily enough. In the case of the *Missa Salve diva parens*, however, there may be no c.f., and if there is one, it is stated in such a way that it is impossible to be sure what the original notes are; analysis would be futile, as it would have to be based largely on speculation. For this reason a discussion of this work cannot be included in the following study—regrettably, because it is one of the very finest of the Masses.

In view of the developments in the 1460s and 1470s, it is not surprising to find the c.f. penetrating the polyphonic complex to a greater extent than ever before. This cannot, however, overshadow the fact that a specific voice, or group of voices, is still allotted the role of chief bearer of the c.f. This is the time-honored function of the tenor, and it is this voice which Obrecht chooses to carry the borrowed material in most of the Masses.

There are some exceptions. The c.f. is given to the superius in *Fors seulement*, *Sub tuum praesidium*, and *Malheur me bat*. In *Caput* it shifts to different voices from movement to movement: the tenor in the Kyrie, the superius in the Gloria, the tenor in the Credo, the alto in the Sanctus, and the bass in the Agnus. While it is exceptional for the c.f. to change voice in every movement, it is common for it to shift for a single movement only, usually the last one, or to shift partially during the course of a movement or section. Also, when c.f. is used in movements in which the structural voice is silent, it must of course be entrusted to one of the other parts. The shifting of the c.f. is certainly not an innovation of Obrecht's—witness the Masses of Ockeghem—but it occurs more frequently with him than with earlier composers.

Obrecht's method of treating c.f. in general gives evidence of a pronouncedly rationalistic turn of mind. He customarily lays out a c.f. according to a clear plan, and this he cleaves to, carrying it out consistently to the last detail. These plans do not preclude the unexpected or fanciful. Indeed, in some cases the plans themselves are fanciful, but his is a rationally controlled fancy which is of a completely different order from that of Ockeghem. As has been seen, in Ockeghem's works it is possible to discover only a general method of c.f. treatment; the nature of the details is absolutely unpredictable. It is characteristic in the *cantus firmi* of Obrecht that events are foreordained, sometimes down to the last minim rest. His penchant for the procedures which I have labeled "rational" is also quite obvious in the way he adopts and develops the motivic devices of his predecessors and older contemporaries. There is no doubt that he makes greater use of them than has been observed in any composer up to this time. This is true even of the very earliest works.

There are comparatively few instances of paraphrase treatment in the Masses, as that method normally calls for a constant variation in detail which runs counter to the rationalist's tendency to keep everything under the control of a predetermined order. This may explain why, when Obrecht does paraphrase a melody, he is apt to repeat it in the same form from movement to movement rather than proceed to new elaborations in the traditional manner.

Peter Wagner classifies the Masses into three types according to method of treatment of the c.f. The types he recognizes are: the simple scaffolding (*L'homme armé*, *Graecorum*, etc.); the scaffolding made up of successive fragments of the c.f. (*Je ne demande*, *Malheur me bat*, etc.); and multiple c.f., as found in several Masses for special services in which a number of chants of the Proper are used (*Sub tuum praesidium*, *de Sancto Martino*, etc.)[3]

This classification is quite correct as far as it goes, but it does not cover all the types of c.f. usage. For that reason it will be followed only in part in this study. I will take up the Masses individually and consider first those which are based on *res facta*. The sequence is roughly in order of increasing complexity of the manipulations of the c.f., which, by the way, does not necessarily correspond to the chronological order of composition, so far as that can be ascertained.

Masses Based on Res Facta

In the incomplete *Missa diversorum tenorum*[4] a number of secular *cantus firmi* are given one after the other.[5] These are stated most often by the tenor, although they are occasionally carried by other voices.[6] So far as it is possible to check, the c.f. quotations are quite exact, in keeping with Obrecht's practice in other works. In general, he shows great respect for the original rhythmic and melodic form of a *res facta*, and he often quotes it directly without any alteration whatsoever. Since he does not manipulate the melodies used in this work in any way—i.e., he does not augment them or invert them, or do anything else of that kind—it is probable that he feels the successive statement of a large number of different melodies gives sufficient variety in itself. All he does is write new counterpoints to the melodies in the other voices. The Mass consists essentially of a series of new settings of the chanson melodies, and because different ones are quoted one after another the work can hardly be considered as a unified Mass cycle. Rather, it is more in the nature of a potpourri of popular tunes.

The conservative attitude toward *res facta* is also illustrated in an early Mass for three voices, *Fors seulement*.[7] The greater part of the c.f. material consists of exact quotations of the chanson superius by the superius of the Mass. The most important exception occurs in the *Pleni sunt caeli*, where all the rests of the original are omitted. Otherwise, deviations from the original form of Ockeghem's melody are rare.[8]

Obrecht also takes over other features of the chanson into the Mass. For instance, in the original work, the tenor gives the first statement of the melody, the superius not entering with it until the tenth bar. This procedure is copied in every movement except the Credo and *Pleni sunt caeli*; the superius entry is delayed until the tenth bar and is preceded by a quotation of the chanson tenor in the tenor of the Mass. Some use is made of other voices of the chanson,[9] but on the whole the Mass consists of a series of new settings of the soprano melody of Ockeghem.

In the other Masses based on *res facta* the borrowed melodies are often not copied directly, but in these cases we generally find that the original form is taken as the point of departure for some consistent plan of manipulation, so that, in the final analysis, the resultant musical lines are a direct product of the original and are strictly controlled by it. There is little of the arbitrary change of rhythm or free ornamentation of the *res facta* which has been seen in *O rosa bella III* or the anonymous *Le serviteur*. (See pp. 138 and 168, above.) Obrecht rather adopts the attitude of Busnois as seen in his *Missa L'homme armé* or especially in his *Missa O crux lignum*.

It has been mentioned above that Obrecht makes use of the tenor of Busnois's *L'homme armé* Mass as the basis of his own.[10] He remains very faithful to his model, as is his custom. Except for the final longs, he takes over the rhythmic schemes of Busnois's c.f. in their entirety, even to the rests preceding the tenor entries. (It should be remembered that in cases like this the relative values of the notes and rests are retained; the absolute values of the original may be increased or decreased by augmentation or diminution.) In addition, he goes so far in his imitation of the model as to hold the movements without tenor to exactly the same number of measures used by Busnois (Kyrie II, *Pleni sunt caeli*, *Benedictus*, and Agnus II). In derived works of this kind it is customary for a composer to try to outdo his predecessor in some way; so even though Obrecht borrows very literally, he manipulates the material more extensively than Busnois had done. For instance, where Busnois converts the original major melody (G Mixolydian) into G Dorian (Kyrie, Gloria, Sanctus, and Agnus) and D Aeolian (Credo), Obrecht states it in E Phrygian (Kyrie, Gloria, Sanctus, and Agnus) and A Aeolian (Credo). (The tonic of Busnois's Mass is G, the same as that of the majority of the c.f. statements; the tonic of Obrecht's is A, despite the statements in E Phrygian in four movements.) In the Agnus, where Busnois gives the tune in inversion, Obrecht gives it in retrograde inversion; however, he uses the first half of the tune in Agnus I and the second half in Agnus III just as Busnois does. He generally presents the *L'homme armé* tune in augmentation, sometimes increasing the values very greatly. He gives it in sextupled values in the *Qui tollis*, *Et incarnatus*, and *Osanna*, and in doubled values in Kyrie I and II, Gloria, Credo, *Confiteor*, and Sanctus. As it appears in *integer valor* but once—at *Tu solus altissimus*—it can be seen that the Mass is largely based on scaffolding type c.f.[11]

Taken together, these manipulations cause a considerable departure from the original sound of the tune, but this is accomplished without relinquishing the direct relationship to the original. There is no change whatsoever in relative rhythmic values or relative position of the notes, so that, despite a great deal of variety in the treatment, everything is rigidly controlled. There is nothing free in the treatment of the details of the *res facta*—free, that is, in the sense of being unexpected, or of having occurred to Obrecht on the spur of the moment.

Similar types of treatment are found in a late Mass, *Fortuna desperata*.[12] In general, the borrowed material is presented in one voice at a time and in a form very close to the original. (An important exception

to this is found in the Kyrie.) The manipulations are restricted for the
most part to the presentation of material by retrograde motion.[13] In these
cases, as in *L'homme armé*, Obrecht does not always simply quote the
tune straight from the last note to the first. In the Gloria only the first
half of the tenor is given in reverse; the remainder is presented in normal
motion. That is, he quotes first from the *middle to the beginning* (m. 31
to m. 1) and then from the *middle to the end* (m. 31 ff.). The same
layout is used once more in the *Qui tollis*. In the Credo the procedure is
reversed; the last half of the chanson tenor is presented in retrograde
and the first half in forward motion. This layout, too, is repeated at *Et
incarnatus*. Otherwise the c.f. usage resembles that of *Fors seulement* or
Diversorum tenorum, rather than *L'homme armé*, because the original is
quoted in *integer valor* rather than in augmentation. The tenors of these
works are not distinguished by long note values and so do not appear as
scaffoldings, as they do in *L'homme armé*.

As these works show, the favored methods of manipulating c.f. are
augmentation and diminution, quotation in retrograde motion or in inversion, or some combination of two or more of these. Other, less com-
monplace methods are used also in the following works. (One of this
type—and they are extremely varied in character—has already been encountered in the *Pleni sunt caeli* of *Fors seulement*, where all the rests of
the original were omitted.)

It has been noted above that the source of the tenor of the *Missa
Graecorum*[14] is still unknown. It has never been finally proved to be a
secular melody,[15] but because of the ways in which Obrecht manipulates
it, it is convenient to consider that it is, and to discuss it among the Masses
based on *res facta*. As in the *Missa L'homme armé*, there is frequent use of
augmentation and consequently a large number of scaffolding tenors.[16]
There are, of course, a variety of types of schematic manipulation other
than augmentation. At *Et resurrexit* the entire tune is given first in retrograde inversion and immediately thereafter in forward motion, although
still in inversion. In Agnus I it is given in inversion and in Agnus II in
retrograde motion. The most unusual treatment is found in the Credo,
where the notes of the c.f. are presented in order according to their value,
following the canonic instruction "*digniora sunt priora*." First the longs
are given; then, reading from the beginning of the tune once more, all the
breves are selected and given in order, then the semibreves, and finally the
minims. (Ex. 90a-b.)[17] Each of these note values is raised to the next higher
one (i.e., minim becomes semibreve, semibreve becomes breve, etc.) and
placed in triple meter.[18]

Whimsical as this method of treating the c.f. may seem, it is not unprecedented in Obrecht's works. A similar procedure is found in the Credo
of the *Missa De tous biens pleine*.[19] In this case the tenor is written out

EXAMPLE 90. Obrecht, *Missa Graecorum*. (a) Tenor. (b) Credo—tenor.
(*Works*, I, 62.)

almost exactly as it is found in the chanson; the special method of reading
it is indicated by the canonic inscription "A maiori debet fieri denomi-
nacio." The same tenor is used for the *Et incarnatus*; the notes are again
performed in order of their value, but this time they are to be read from
the end to the beginning of the voice part according to the instruction
"*Ut prius, sed dicitur retrograde.*" Another fanciful, yet rigidly schematic,
procedure is found in the Sanctus of the same Mass. In this movement
the tenor of Hayne's chanson is broken into eight short sections which
are given in the order 1, 8, 7, 6, 5, 4, 3, and 2. Yet another plan is found
in the Gloria. The tenor and superius of the chanson are given out by
the tenor and superius of the Mass respectively, each voice presenting a
phrase of its part in alternation with the other. The superius gives out the
first phrase of the superius, then the tenor gives the first phrase of the
tenor; the superius then gives the second superius phrase, the tenor follows with the second tenor phrase, and so on until the final phrase is

reached; this they give out simultaneously. Example 91a-b illustrates
the treatment of the first two chanson phrases, and example 91c that
of the final one. This is a clear attempt to bring the c.f. material into
more than one voice and, in the first part of the movement, comes as
close to parody treatment as is possible while still remaining c.f. The
final phrase is genuine parody, according to the definition given above
(p. 153), so that this movement illustrates once again how easily composers at that time passed over from one type to the other. It is clear
that they felt no need to keep them separated; so in all probability they
did not distinguish clearly between the two methods of treatment as yet.
There is good evidence that the concept of a single, leading c.f. voice
is not relinquished at all in this movement, despite the fact that borrowed material is consistently used in more than one part. A difference
in the type of quotation can be discerned, depending upon whether it is
in the tenor or the superius. Quotations of the tenor are more strict than

EXAMPLE 91. (a-c) Obrecht, *Missa De tous biens pleine*—Gloria (*Works*, V,
159; Hayne van Ghizeghem, chanson *De tous biens pleine*, Gombosi, *Jacob
Obrecht*, No. XIV, p. 24; superius and tenor).

Superius, phrase 2, m. 16-18

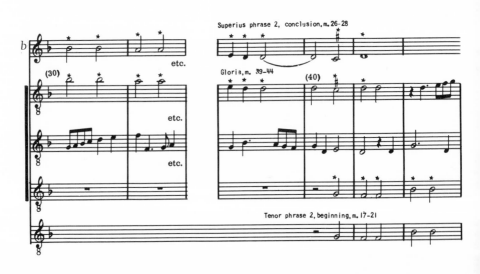

Superius phrase 2, conclusion, m. 26-28

Gloria, m. 39-44

Tenor phrase 2, beginning, m. 17-21

those of the superius; wherever an adjustment must be made, it is the superius which is forced to yield. (That is, the tenor quotations direct the course of the music; the quotations of the superius must be altered from time to time to conform to this course. See ex. 91a, m. 14-15 of the Gloria; ex. 91c, m. 90-94.) Furthermore, the tenor presents nothing but borrowed material, since it rests between statements; the superius has freely composed phrases between its quotations of borrowed material, and so is not purely and completely a c.f. voice. (Ex. 91a, m. 18-28; ex. 91b, m. 42-44.)

These Masses show Obrecht as an uncompromising rationalist who prefers to use for the structural voice either a literal quotation of the original melody or a schematically manipulated version of it based directly on the original. Scaffolding *cantus firmi* had traditionally been literal quotations of the original, so it is not surprising to find that alterations are infrequent and of comparatively minor importance in the scaffolding tenors of the Obrecht Masses; but in the class of *cantus firmi* which function as melodic parts (i.e., *cantus firmi* which do not consist chiefly of pedal notes), Obrecht's habit of quoting literally is noteworthy because elaboration, or stylistic transformation, had formerly been standard procedure in the statement of the c.f. as a melody. Interest—no longer centered on the transformation of a given melody—has shifted to the working-out of a multitude of integrative devices, motivic and otherwise. In Obrecht's case these devices are largely matters for the contrapuntal voices; they are of small concern to the structural voice.

I have placed a great deal of emphasis on Obrecht's habit of faithful quotation since it presents such a contrast with older practices. There are, however, a few places where he may be said to be following those practices by taking some liberties with the original. Slight alterations have been noted in the tenor of the *Missa Graecorum*. Even more are found in the *Missa sine nomine (Pfauenschwanz)*,[20] where, for example, the tenor statement of the Kyrie differs noticeably from that of the Gloria. But changes as far-reaching as those in this work are rare indeed. The Gloria of the *Missa Ave Regina caelorum* provides one of the few additional instances.[21] The rhythmic form of the derived voices in this Mass differs noticeably from the original form of the tenor of the motet (ex. 92a-d), and it is immediately apparent that there is a specific reason for these changes. They are introduced not merely for the sake of melodic transformation, but, in every case, for the sake of the motivic or contrapuntal devices in which Obrecht is so interested. In examples 92a and 92d the rhythmic and melodic changes allow the simultaneous presentation of the c.f. in more than one voice in a freely imitative manner; in example 92c they make possible a short section of strict imitation between tenor and bass. In example 92b the stretching-out of each note of the descending scale in the c.f. makes possible the introduction of that most highly favored device, a passage in sequence. However, except in the last example, it is remarkable how close Obrecht keeps to the original. The alterations, especially those in the tenor, are only changes in the value of the rests. On the whole, the tendency is to achieve organization through devices similar to those in example 92a-d, but with an absolute minimum of change in the c.f. or, preferably, with no change at all.

Possibly the most extreme instance of free treatment of a *res facta* is found in a *Missa Adieu mes amours* which is not included in the series of Masses of the complete works.[22] The tenor of the chanson upon which the Mass is based has an extremely simple form, being an ABA in which each section consists of two phrases. The entire structure may be labeled A_1A_2B B A_1A_2.

EXAMPLE 92. (a-d) Obrecht, *Missa Ave Regina caelorum*—Gloria (*Works*, III, 145; Walter Frye, motet *Ave Regina caelorum*, Reese, *Renaissance*, ex. 24, p. 94; tenor).

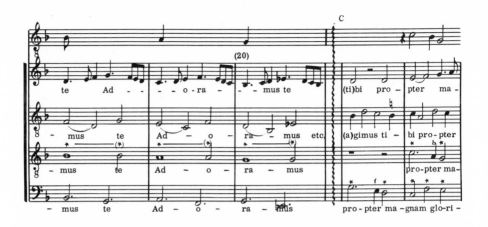

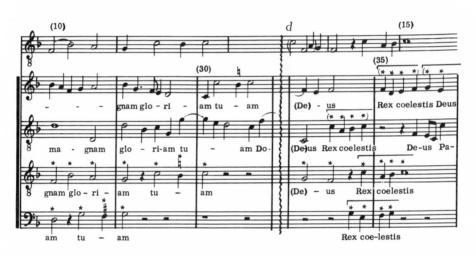

This tenor is treated in ways more favored by Josquin than by Obrecht. It is quoted, sometimes unornamented and in extremely long values, sometimes in shorter values with lively ornamentation, and these types of quotation are placed side by side in the same movement with a maximum effect of contrast. The borrowed voice is also not subjected to schematic manipulation as frequently as it is in the other Masses based on *res facta*. Rather, Obrecht directs his attention here to musical manipulation through *ostinato* and imitation.

Kyrie I is comparable to the Kyrie from Josquin's *Missa Gaudeamus*. It is built upon a strictly laid out *ostinato* bass, the repeated motive consisting of the first five notes of the chanson. The motive is stated six times, each statement being separated from the next by two measures of rest. Over this extremely regular framework the other voices make as many statements of the first phrases of the chanson as Obrecht can contrive to fit in. The tenor is given nothing but the material of the A section, ornamented sufficiently to enable it to fit the bass. (Specifically, the tenor makes two complete statements of phrase A_1 and one of A_2.) The other two voices are also concerned with borrowed material, although not so exclusively as tenor and bass. The superius presents the opening notes of the chanson once (the same motive as that in the bass) and the contratenor presents it twice, so that, even though these two voices are largely written as free counterpoints, the fact remains that all four parts have something to do with the chanson tenor.

In the *Christe* the tenor is silent, but, nevertheless, a statement of A is included in the contratenor (m. 43 ff.), sandwiched in between two freely composed sections (the first of the free sections being written in non-imitative counterpoint and the second being an elaborate sequential construction which brings the movement to a close). In Kyrie II, the quotation which had been started in Kyrie I is continued. There is no attempt at motivic or imitative elaboration this time. The tenor alone is concerned with the *res facta* and states B B A_1A_2 in ornamented form to complete the tenor melody.

The method of dividing the chanson in the Kyrie—allotting A to the first section of the Mass movement, BA to the second—is followed in general in the Gloria and Credo. The Gloria is based on A, the *Qui tollis* on BA. Likewise, the Credo is on A, the *Et incarnatus* on BA, but this time BA is elaborated and stated twice. The tenor of the Gloria is uneventful except in one respect. In the interim between the statement of A_1 and A_2 Obrecht does the unpredictable thing and gives the tenor a few notes which apparently are not from the original voice at all but are added for the sake of sonority, in order to make a full cadence in four voices in a section which is otherwise all duos and trios (m. 35-37). A corresponding spot appears in the *Qui tollis* after the statement of B, but this time the unexpected notes are from the c.f., being a restatement of the last half of B (m. 80-87). The statement of the final A (phrases A₁ and A₂) contrasts with the extremely long note values of B by a comparatively rapid movement, and it differs also by being given to both bass and tenor. The bass merely repeats the tenor statement in the case of phrase A₁, but actually imitates it in A₂ since its statement overlaps the tenor.

The tenor of the Credo is comparable to that of the Gloria in that it begins with long values which contrast with the shorter values of the ending. The ending is, also, given a richer ornamentation than that of the Gloria. The tenor of the *Et incarnatus* likewise corresponds to that of the *Qui tollis*. The final A is treated in imitation here also, this time between tenor and superius in phrase A₁, tenor and bass in A₂. The whole idea of imitating the tenor material is now expanded. B is restated (m. 92) and cleverly imitated in all parts, and then A is given once more (m. 100) in all voices and in closer imitation than before. The whole passage is something of a tour de force for Obrecht and ranks with his most thoroughgoing attempts to bring the c.f. into all parts.

The general scheme of layout of the preceding movements is continued in those sections of the Sanctus which are scored for four voices. At the beginning of the movement the tenor presents the A part of the tune in newly ornamented form. (A₁ is quoted in a notably free manner, A₂ quite simply.) The *Osanna* repeats the music of Kyrie II, so that the method of dividing the quotation established in the Kyrie is retained in the Sanctus as a matter of course. The sections for three voices also contain c.f., but the quotations do not follow the regular tenor pattern. *Pleni sunt caeli* begins with a fourteen-measure introduction—an imitative fantasy based on a phrase which is an elaboration of the first four notes of the c.f. The chief quotation then begins in the superius, and consists of phrases A₁, A₂, and B (m. 46-70), followed by a second statement of B, transposed down an eleventh in the contratenor (m. 72-78). A closing section, free of c.f., provides a melodic and rhythmic climax to the movement. *Benedictus qui venit* is largely free, although it contains a citation of A₂, beginning in the superius and completed in the contratenor (superius, m. 113-116, contratenor m. 117-121, and again at m. 138-142).

The tenor quotation in Agnus I consists, as might be expected, of a new statement of A₁ and A₂, the latter immediately restated by the superius. However, the most interesting use of c.f. is not in the main statement, which does not begin until measure 15, but in the introductory measures. Here phrases A₁ and A₂ appear in the superius and contratenor, in imitation at the octave, and with entries at the distance of a perfect breve. The phrases move sedately enough, in semibreves for the most part, and come to a cadence at measure 10. Then, surprisingly, these same phrases reappear, hurrying along in halved values, and in close imitation in three voices. This sudden flurry of activity lasts but three measures, when normal movement and texture are resumed. As mentioned above, Obrecht shows considerable interest in elaborating c.f. material by means of imitation in this Mass. He has already demonstrated various possibilities of imitation at the fourth, as well as at the octave, but even the extensive imitations at the end of the Credo are for two voices only. The possibility of stretto imitation in three parts he has held in reserve until the final movement, but when the time comes to make use of it he does not develop it into a climax. He enunciates it once, allows it to make a temporary contrast, and then lets it go.

It is not until Agnus II that he makes a statement of the type he most favors. Here he gives the entire chanson once through—unadorned, in *integer valor*, and in inversion.

One further point may be mentioned—so small it would call for no comment at all in the work of most composers. Obrecht uses two versions of the chanson tenor which differ from one another by the matter of a single note in the B phrase. In some movements he uses one or the other of the versions exclusively; in some he uses both indifferently. But it is possible that even this tiny point of quotation is regulated by plan, for he gradually shifts from one form to the other. In Kyrie and Gloria he uses only the first version, in Credo and Sanctus he uses both, and in the Agnus only the second version.

On the whole, the treatment of the chanson tenor in the *Missa Adieu mes amours* is as free as in a Mass of Josquin, but for all the freedoms of treatment, the work does not offer enough evidence by itself to reverse the opinion which has been formed concerning Obrecht's preferences in handling the *res facta*. The other Masses are sufficient to show the strength of his inclination to literal statement and schematic manipulation; however, *Adieu mes amours* does make clear to us that his methods cannot be described by a single, unqualified statement.

MASSES BASED ON SEGMENTED CANTUS FIRMUS

A group of mature works gives evidence that Obrecht's powers of organization become more impressive as time goes on. In these Masses he reverts, in a restricted sense, to the rationality of the *ars nova* for the method of organizing the structural voice, while at the same time he retains all the methods of organization of the new style in the contrapuntal voices. In each of the Masses the structural voice is a rhythmically organized scaffolding based on a *segment of a c.f.*, and this segment is stated first in long values and then repeated in proportionally related ones. These are features of the tenor of the isorhythmic structure of the fourteenth and early fifteenth centuries which may never have fallen entirely into disuse, but which certainly do not appear often in works of the period c. 1450-1480.[23] In the very advanced works of Obrecht they have a definitely archaic appearance. The tenors are, of course, not genuinely isorhythmic in the older sense, yet they, more than any others of Obrecht, reveal that primary concern with rational organization which was characteristic of the *ars nova* but can hardly be said to have existed in the ·middle decades of the fifteenth century. These works of the latter part of the century betray a distant but real kinship to those of the late Middle Ages.

The names of the Masses displaying this treatment read like a catalogue of the composer's most impressive efforts. The group includes *Si dedero, Rosa playsante, Je ne demande, Malheur me bat*, and *Maria zart*.[24] As indicated above, instead of following the common method of using the complete c.f. or an extended portion of it in every statement, Obrecht divides the original melody into a desired number of short sections, or segments, and each of these is repeated several times before the next one is taken up.

The structural voice of the *Missa Malheur me bat* will suffice to illustrate the general aspects of the procedure. In this work the superius of the Ockeghem(?) chanson is given to the superius of the Mass (although in the other works of this type the c.f. is given to the tenor).[25] Example 93a-e shows that the original voice is segmented and that each segment, taken in order, provides the material for a rhythmically organized framework. These frameworks, in turn, are used as the bases for the successive important divisions of the Mass. (The segments are labeled A, B, C, D, etc.; immediately below each is given the framework of the entire Mass movement to illustrate the repetitions and the various mensural manipulations.)

EXAMPLE 93. Ockeghem (?), chanson *Malheur me bat*, and Obrecht, *Missa Malheur me bat*. (*a*) Chanson, segment A—superius, and Mass, Kyrie I— superius. (*b*) Chanson, segment B, and Mass, Kyrie II—superius. (*c*) Chanson, segment C, and Mass, Gloria—superius. (*d*) Chanson, segment D, and Mass, *Qui tollis*—superius. (*e*) Chanson, segment E, beginning, and Mass, Credo—superius. (Hewitt, ed., *Odhecaton*, p. 353; *Works*, I, 141 ff.)

The examples show that the natural phrase divisions of the melody are often ignored in the process of dividing it up. Various reasons for this come to mind, one of them being that Obrecht wishes each fragment to end on a note which will fit into a cadence appropriate to the tonal scheme of the Mass. Also, his purpose is to apportion the fund of notes provided by the original melody in such a way that it will not be exhausted until the entire Mass is substantially completed. In this way a melody of quite modest length is converted into a huge arch which springs across a work of extremely large dimensions. This is a new way of using a c.f. to achieve continuity in a work of many movements. While it gives impressive evidence of the consistency of Obrecht's thought, such a manner of c.f. statement strengthens only the ideal relationship between the members of a Mass; it does not supply actual musical connections, because no provision is made for repetition of material from movement to movement.

This lack of connections is, however, made up in other ways. The scaffoldings do not extend quite to the end of the work in any of these Masses. In *Je ne demande, Rosa playsante,* and *Malheur me bat* the material is exhausted in the first Agnus (although in *Rosa playsante* it is restated in the third Agnus, which is merely a literal repetition of Agnus I). In *Maria zart* the scaffolding material extends only to the end of the Sanctus. In *Si dedero* it extends to the first Agnus but is carried into the third by repetition of the final tenor fragment. However, the termination of the plan of the scaffoldings at the point where the last note of the original melody is reached does not put a stop to c.f. quotation in the Mass. The sections which remain are also generally based on a structural voice. In *Malheur me bat*, for instance, the bass presents the entire tenor of the chanson in original form in the second Agnus, and in the third Agnus the superius gives the entire superius once again. At the very end of the Mass, then, there is a double recapitulation of the entire material which has been distributed along the length of the work—in the scaffoldings and in the intervening movements based on the tenor. Double recapitulation occurs also in the last two movements of *Je ne demande*, both statements being given by the tenor.[26] The plan of recapitulation in *Maria zart* is more elaborate. The bass states the entire melody in the first Agnus. In the second, which is a trio, the melody is again given in its entirety but distributed among bass, alto, and soprano by means of sectional migration.[27] In the third Agnus the soprano presents the entire c.f. for the last time; when it is completed the tenor repeats the final phrase to bring the movement, and the Mass, to a close.[28]

As indicated above, the case is somewhat different with *Si dedero*, for the scaffolding extends into the final movement of the Mass. The tenor gives a single, closing statement of the last segment in the third Agnus. In addition to the complete quotation of this voice, Obrecht quotes fragments of the other voices of Agricola's motet[29] from time to time. (He does this at places where the tenor is silent.) When the Mass nears a close, however, he gives straightforward statements of the entire motet, one voice at a time. The alto gives a direct quotation of the tenor of the motet in the *Pleni sunt caeli*, the soprano gives the soprano in the *Benedictus*, and the bass gives the bass in Agnus II. In this way he provides a recapitulation or, better, a summation and explication of all the quotations he has distributed across the entire Mass.[30] He does the same thing in *Rosa play-sante*, giving the chanson tenor to the contra in *Pleni sunt caeli*, the soprano to the soprano in the *Benedictus*, and the bass to the bass in Agnus II.

Traditionally, certain sections of the Mass were freely composed, the c.f.-bearing voice being marked *tacet*. These movements without c.f. ordinarily are the *Christe, Pleni sunt caeli, Benedictus*, and second Agnus (although there seems to have been no set rule as to which parts of the Mass were to be written in this way). Although Obrecht often follows the traditional practice, in the group of Masses under discussion he generally chooses to supply these sections with c.f. also, but not of the framework type; he supplies, instead, exact quotations of an entire voice of the original.[31] The result is a double plan of structural c.f. statement. The chief element of the plan is the segmented scaffolding which arches across the whole series of movements and serves the Mass in its entirety. Direct quotations, in *integer valor*, are used to serve single movements only, and are the subsidiary element of the plan; yet they have an irreplaceable function in the whole, of concentrating material which is otherwise very thinly spread out, and of providing a unity which the scaffolding cannot. Without them these Masses would hardly be cyclic at all.

Concentration of material is increased by the liberal use of c.f. references in the form of anticipatory statements, *ostinatos*, imitations, and so forth. These references may sound simultaneously with the chief c.f. statement or they may be inserted in the intervals when the c.f. voice rests. Hence they are especially common in the Gloria and Credo, as the general layout of these movements is quite like that of the traditional tenor motet or Mass movement, the tenor statements being preceded by long pauses. In contrast to the archaic-appearing tenors, the subsidiary statements of the other voices show the most advanced types of treatment. These statements may be made in more than one voice and the c.f. material may be recombined or developed in any way that strikes the composer's fancy.

The Gloria and Credo of *Malheur me bat* give some idea of the possibilities that Obrecht finds. The introductory trio of the Gloria (ex. 94a, m. 1-10) begins with a brief working-out by means of imitation of a portion of the chanson superius. (Obrecht chooses a portion of segment

C; ex. 93c, above.) This trio provides an anticipatory statement in the traditional sense, as the same phrase, segment C, is used for the scaffolding of this movement. Before the trio is concluded, however, segment A is stated by the bass in combination with segment E in the alto (ex. 94a, m. 17-20). Segment A is the beginning of the chanson and has been used as the scaffolding of the first Kyrie; segment E is not used as a scaffolding until the following movement, the Credo. The whole Mass is integrated by a system of cross references such as these, which frequently bring material from any portion of the chanson to the attention of the listener.

In the introductory trio to the Credo, segment A is treated again. (See ex. 94c.) The material is presented in imitation at the octave between tenor and superius in the chanson, and this treatment is retained in the Mass. It is, however, varied by being given to different voices (bass and alto), and expanded by the insertion of a third imitative entry in the tenor at the fifth above (ex. 94c, bass and alto; also ex. 94c, tenor, m. 4). The trios in the body of the movement also contain c.f. references.[32] In the one between the first and second c.f. segments in the Gloria, the bass merely quotes a part of the chanson tenor while the two other voices are written as free counterpoints (ex. 94b). This happens to be that por-

EXAMPLE 94. Ockeghem (?), chanson *Malheur me bat*, and Obrecht, *Missa Malheur me bat*. (*a*) Mass, Gloria (*Works*, I, 145), showing quotation of segments of chanson (Hewitt, ed., *Odhecaton*, p. 353). (*b*) Chanson, tenor, and Mass, Gloria (*Works*, I, 148). (*c*) Chanson, superius, and Mass, Credo (*Works*, I, 156).

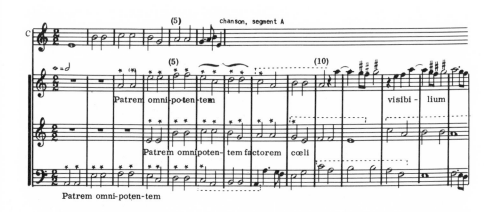

tion of the tenor which, in the chanson, forms a counterpoint to the superius segment used as the scaffolding in this movement of the Mass, so there is a close relation between them in the original composition. However, even though the chanson tenor imitates the superius for the first four notes at this point, it is not sufficiently similar to it to have the effect of increasing the musical coherence of the Mass.

It is clear from these examples that the effect of the trios is not so much to integrate a given movement by means of anticipatory statements as it is to increase the total c.f. content of the Mass. In this way the trios help make up the deficiencies of the scaffolding c.f. as a unifying factor. The scaffolding certainly gives continuity from movement to movement, but it does not permit the repetitions of material which are a feature of the cyclic Mass; as in so many Renaissance structures, the unity is intellectual rather than musical. The subsidiary and recapitulary quotations, then, have a very important function in the Mass, for they provide the purely musical unity which the scaffolding cannot.

On the other hand, the layout of the scaffolding *cantus firmi* represents a high level of constructive thought. The organization of a work where an entire movement is but a stage in the realization of a plan of grand dimensions is admittedly on a higher plane than an organization where individual movements depend from a series of approximately coequal plans, closely interrelated it is true, but each plan complete in itself. In the late fifteenth century, attempts to increase the continuity of a Mass become more and more common, although they often consist of no more than an unusually brilliant or weighty final movement to bring the work to a climactic ending. These works, then, are part of a historical trend, but they are among the most important representatives of it because of the scope of their plans and the consequential way in which the plans are carried out. It should also be noted that these three types of c.f. quotation bring about a most intimate relation between the Mass and the work from which it is derived and present yet another stage in the transformation of c.f. Mass into parody Mass.

Rosa playsante is one of the finest of this group. Because it has not yet been published in its entirety, a discussion of some of the details of its structure seems in order before we proceed to the next group.[33]

The chief structural element is, as usual, a voice of the chanson which is divided into sections, each section then being used as a framework for a portion of the Mass. In this case the tenor of the chanson is divided into nine sections which form the tenor of Kyrie I, Kyrie II, Gloria, *Qui tollis*, Credo, *Et incarnatus*, Sanctus, *Osanna*, and Agnus I respectively. The second structural level is found in the statement of all three voices of the chanson—in their entirety and without manipulation—in movements near the end of the work. The tenor is silent in the *Pleni*, *Benedictus*, and second Agnus, and in these sections are heard all three voices of the original, i.e., the superius in the superius of the *Pleni*, the tenor in the contratenor of the *Benedictus*, the bass in in the bass of Agnus II. Lastly, there are numerous statements of material from the chanson, but they are relatively short and fragmentary and do not occur in any regular order, so that they are adjuncts to, rather than integral parts of, the grand scheme of the cycle.[34] In all these respects the work is a quite normal member of its class.

Another typical device, well illustrated in *Rosa playsante*, is the frequent change of mensuration in the tenor.[35] The tenor fragments are stated more than once in each movement—twice in Kyrie I and Kyrie II, three times in each of the following movements—and each fragment contains two or three shifts of mensuration. The tenor of the first Agnus is typical, having as it does three shifts of mensuration in each of three statements, or a total of nine changes. (Ex. 95.) The result is a degree of rhythmic dissimilarity between statements that is not characteristic of framework tenors as a class. The liberal occurrence of mensuration signs gives the *cantus firmi* of *Rosa playsante* an aspect of variability, with regard to rhythm only, that makes them approach the freely elaborated tenors which are characteristically written so as to be different in some respects on each statement.

EXAMPLE 95. Obrecht, *Missa Rosa playsante*—Agnus I, tenor (MS Segovia, fo. 34ᵛ-35).

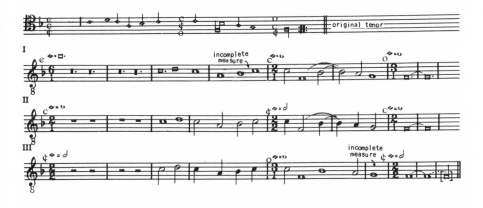

With regard to the choice of mensurations, it is generally true that those which will produce longer values are used at the beginning of movements, while those which produce shorter values occur nearer the end. For this reason the tenors follow the usual course of beginning with long note values and gradually speeding up as the movement proceeds. Other than this, however, the order in the choice of mensurations is not apparent to me.

It is also hard to say what Obrecht's reasons were for many of the other details of the treatment of the tenors. As in the other Masses of this class, there seems to be no imperative reason for cutting the tenor of the chanson at the precise points where he did. No considerations of mensuration, harmony, or phrase structure satisfactorily account for the divisions in the sense that one can say, "they must occur here and nowhere else." It seems merely that Obrecht wanted nine fragments to support the nine sections of the Mass based on c.f. and so divided the tenor into nine approximately equal parts.

Since a framework tenor is an essentially rational construction, one tends to expect a reasonable explanation for all its details. In this case, however, and in many others, one finds that the composer's intent in planning a tenor cannot always be fathomed. It may well be that in the making of this plan there is much that is fortuitous and unpredictable. The Masses of this group leave no doubt as to Obrecht's urge to logical construction; but he is a child of his time, and one of the aspects of that time is a love of the unexpected. This is always given free play in the added parts—the contrapuntal voices—but it is also apparent that the unexpected enters to a certain extent into the architectural voice as well. With all the careful planning, we constantly run into loose ends which may, of course, be only apparent loose ends because we do not fully understand the plan. On the other hand, they give evidence of a certain carelessness which may be connected with Glareanus's report of the extreme rapidity with which Obrecht composed.

The parody element in this Mass is of especial interest in the form in which it appears in three movements without tenor: *Pleni*, *Benedictus*, and Agnus II. As stated above, in each of these movements one of the voices of the chanson is quoted completely unadorned and exactly in the form in which it appears in the original. Thus, each of these movements has a leading *part* which must have been set down first and which can only be described as a c.f. The other two voices provide counterpoints to this c.f., but the interesting thing about the counterpoints is that they, too, are not completely new—they coincide with the corresponding voices of the chanson from time to time. There is no pattern to the coincidences, although the chanson material tends to appear most completely near the cadences. The technique is extremely fluid. A voice will quote a number of notes of the chanson and will then proceed freely, only to refer to the chanson again, a bit later. There is an air of nonchalance about the whole proceeding, but the quotations are frequent enough and extensive enough to make it clear that Obrecht is consciously applying a parody technique to a c.f. structure. These movements are further examples of those hybrids, characteristic of the period, where parody and c.f. join together and result in a work which is neither wholly of one type or the other.

MASSES BASED ON GREGORIAN MELODIES

The Masses discussed so far prove that Obrecht was more interested in other methods of c.f. treatment than the one which had chiefly occupied composers for the previous half century—the melodic elaboration, in a single voice, of borrowed material which is itself but a single voice. He does not, however, completely neglect the older technique. There are a small number of Masses constructed on tenors which are paraphrased versions of the original tunes. With the exception of *Adieu mes amours* these are all Gregorian melodies, so that it appears he applied the technique of paraphrase chiefly to material which is nonmensural. In this group are the *Missa Beata viscera* (*Works*, V, 97), *Petrus Apostolus* (III, 189), *O quam suavis* (III, 61),[36] *Sicut spina rosam* (III, 104), and *Libenter gloriabor.*

When the c.f. is used as a tenor for a Mass cycle there is a tendency to present it rather simply. In the *Missa super Petrus apostolus* the antiphon is ornamented moderately in the first Kyrie. (Ex. 96a, line 1: the c.f. is given on the top line; the tenors of the various movements are given below on the lines numbered 1, 2, 3, etc.) At the beginning of the Gloria the version used in the first Kyrie is restated exactly. It is then repeated, starting at measure 38 of the Gloria. This statement differs

EXAMPLE 96. Obrecht. *Missa super Petrus Apostolus.* (a) *Cantus firmus* and (lines 1-8) tenors of the various movements. (b) Inverted c.f. in *Qui tollis* and *Osanna*; retrograde inversion in Agnus III. (c) C.f. in Kyrie II. (d) Motto for soprano and alto—Kyrie I, Gloria, Credo, Sanctus, and Agnus I. (e) *Christe.* (*Works*, III, 189-228; *LU*, p. 1547.)

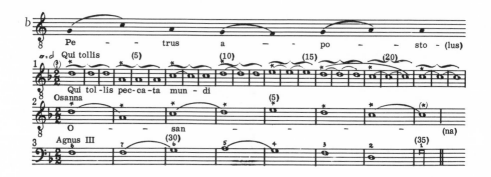

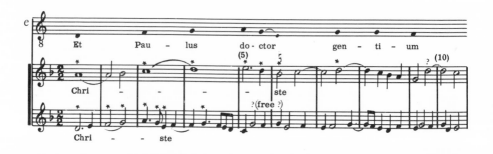

from that of the Kyrie in only one respect: the first note is given the value of an imperfect rather than a perfect breve, so that the whole melody is shifted over by one count. (Compare ex. 96a, lines 2 and 3. Apparently, the mensuration has been changed from *tempus perfectum* to *tempus imperfectum*, a procedure which would affect the value of the first note only.) The tenor of the Credo has a quite different appearance from the preceding ones, but on examination it proves to be simply an augmented form of the same elaborated melody in which the individual notes have been broken into shorter values in order to accommodate the syllables of the text (ex. 96a, line 4).

The repetition of a single ornamental version of the c.f. is not at all the practice of Obrecht's predecessors, who, on the whole, prefer to provide a new ornamentation with each new statement. The procedure followed in this Mass again points to his preference for regulated, orderly statement over the traditionally irregular, semi-improvisatory type. Further indication of a certain disinclination to elaborate the c.f. freely is found at *Et iterum venturus*. Here he abandons ornamentation altogether and states the Gregorian melody twice in succession in simple form. In example 96a, line 5, it can be seen that while the c.f. tones may be divided and repeated for textual reasons, each of them is allotted the time span of a perfect breve. On the repetition of the melody these values are exactly halved. Each note of the c.f. is given the value of a dotted semibreve (ex. 96a, line 6). These statements turn out to be of the type which I have called "strict" c.f.,[37] and are related to the statement in the Sanctus (ex. 96a, line 7).

In the first Agnus Obrecht reverts to c.f. paraphrase, but, as might be expected, this proves to be not a new version but a restatement of the one used in the first Kyrie. It is changed somewhat by being transposed down a fourth and given to the bass voice. (The transposition causes the c.f. to end on a D, but a G is added at the very end, so that the movement comes to a close on the same tone as do all the others.)

Strict c.f. is found in three other sections, although in each of them the original notes are also subjected to familiar manipulations. In the *Qui tollis* and *Osanna* the melody is inverted (ex. 96b, lines 1 and 2) and in the third Agnus it is given in retrograde inversion. As in the first Agnus, it is transposed down a fourth and given to the bass. (The final phrase is given in ex. 96b, line 3, as it contains the notes which correspond to the first phrase of the c.f. quoted on the top line.) In the second Kyrie the bass also shares in the presentation of the c.f., as it repeats each phrase of the tenor, again at the fourth below (ex. 96c). A certain number of free tones are interpolated, and in places where the statements of the two voices overlap they even substitute for the original ones (ex. 96c, m. 9, tenor; m. 12, bass). It is obvious that despite the preferences indicated above Obrecht is willing to sacrifice literal statement for the purpose of combining material.[38]

Each of the five main divisions of the Mass is provided with a head motive stated by the soprano and alto (ex. 96d). The soprano carries a paraphrased form of the first phrase of the c.f., but it is again the same as that of the tenor of Kyrie I.

The sections *Domine Deus, Et incarnatus, Pleni sunt caeli, Benedictus,* and Agnus II are freely composed duos or trios which are organized for the most part by imitative procedures of one sort or another. The *Christe* is a simple mensuration canon in which the top voice moves twice as slowly as the bottom. It, too, is probably free although it may be influenced by the c.f., since a relationship can be found between it and the phrase *et Paulus Doctor* (ex. 96e).

To summarize, even though this Mass begins with paraphrased c.f. and makes considerable use of it thereafter, orderly repetition and schematic manipulation predominate in the treatment of the c.f. Forms of statement not controlled by a simple guiding plan occur only when necessary to achieve some combination of materials, as in Kyrie II. Freedoms due to the same cause have also been observed in the case of a *res facta* (Gloria of the *Missa Ave Regina caelorum*, ex. 92a-c, above), so it appears that either in the case of a Gregorian chant or a *res facta*, combination of material was regarded as a sufficiently worthy object by Obrecht to induce him to depart occasionally from his usual strictly regulated methods.

The Masses *Beata viscera* and *O quam suavis* give further illustration of the methods of treatment seen in *Petrus Apostolus*. In *O quam suavis* the ornamented form of the c.f. fixed upon in the Kyrie is repeated in other movements also. In this case, however, it is used in all the movements instead of a few, and so forms the total structural c.f. for the Mass. It is occasionally augmented and there are some minor deviations in notes and values of rests, but the relationship to the original version is always clear. In fact, the tenor quotations at the beginning and end of each of the five main sections are exactly the same. (As a partial illustration of this, compare the tenor of Kyrie I, ex. 97a, m. 9-15, with that of Agnus I, ex. 97b, m. 1-7.) Considerable use is also made of head motive, and the treatment is the same as that in the *Missa Petrus Apostolus*. That is, the head motive consists of a statement by a single voice of the first phrase of the antiphon and this phrase is given exactly the same form of elaboration found in the tenor. (Compare the superius, ex. 97a, m. 1-9, with the tenor, m. 9-17.) It appears in every movement except the Agnus (see ex. 97b); however, the voice carrying it varies from movement to movement and the counterpoints written to it are changed, also.

In the *Missa Beata viscera*[39] the ornamentation varies in the restate-

EXAMPLE 97. Obrecht, *Missa O quam suavis*. (a) Kyrie I (Works, III, 61; Ant. Mon., p. 548). (b) Agnus I (Works, III, 94).

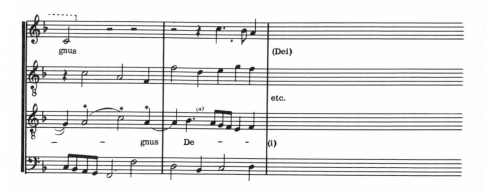

ments of the c.f. so that this work stands more in the line of tradition than the two already discussed. Ornamentation is restrained, in general, and most of the Gregorian notes are given long values. At *Et unam sanctam* the quotation takes the form of strict c.f., as the melody is presented entirely in semibreves. Hence, in the utilization of both strict and elaborated c.f. in the same work, this Mass resembles *Petrus Apostolus*. The c.f. is given in a freely canonic statement in the Sanctus and *Osanna I* and *II*, as was also done in *Petrus Apostolus* (Kyrie II). However, the occurrence of the latter device does not, in itself, indicate any noteworthy similarity between the two works, since it is found in many of the Masses. Head motive based on c.f. is also used in every movement except the Sanctus.

Obrecht keeps to the original form of a *res facta* most carefully when he quotes it. In the aforementioned Masses based on Gregorian chant he keeps just as carefully to the original ornamented version of the c.f. when he restates it. In this respect he treats it as he would a *res facta*.

The c.f. of the *Missa Sicut spina rosam* is given much more varied and irregular treatment than the three which have already been discussed. In this work also, however, there is a tendency to view a previous statement of the c.f. as a *res facta*. The section of the respond *Ad nutum Domini (Proc. Mon.*, p. 187)[40] used as c.f. is stated once in its entirety by the tenor in the Kyrie–Christe–Kyrie. The section given in Kyrie I (stated twice, the second time in diminution) is taken as the basis of the tenor statement of the Gloria; the one given in the *Christe* serves in the *Qui tollis* and that of Kyrie II in *Qui sedes*. There are minor alterations in the statements of the two latter sections, but there is no question of their relation to the *Christe* and Kyrie II. All three of the sections are provided with anticipatory statements, but the one in the alto at the very beginning of the Gloria is especially long. It is, in fact, a new paraphrase of the entire c.f. In the Credo this alto paraphrase appears again, repeated exactly as an anticipatory statement in the superius. It is now taken as the model for the structural voice and is quoted by the tenor in its first statement in this movement (m. 21-41). A familiar form of the c.f. returns in the Sanctus, where the tenor of the first Kyrie is used again. It is stated three times, the last two in diminution.

Otherwise, the freedom and variety of treatment reminds one of Josquin or Ockeghem. The second statement in the Credo (starting at m. 44) is in the form of a canon at the octave between the tenor and superius. The canon displays certain freedoms, the most noticeable of which is the variation in the time interval between the voices. The *Et incarnatus* starts with a statement of the first phrase of the c.f. in the alto, but the c.f. is abandoned in favor of a canon between the two upper voices—alto and superius—which is accompanied by occasional statements of an *ostinato* figure in the bass. The abandonment of the c.f. is extremely unusual for Obrecht, but again is not uncharacteristic of Ockeghem and Josquin. The next section, *Et resurrexit*, is written in a more familiar manner, as the phrases of the c.f. are repeated by the alto and tenor in alternation. *Et in Spiritum* starts with imitative entries on the first few notes of the c.f. in tenor, bass, and superius. It continues with a scaffolding made up of the remainder of the first phrase, which is given first by the superius (m. 212). As the scaffolding is then repeated exactly by the tenor (m. 225), alto (m. 238), and bass (m. 251), the section can be said to be founded on "migrant scaffolding." (Similar c.f. layouts are found in the *Missa Gaudeamus* of Josquin.) The superius paraphrases the complete respond in the *Confiteor* so that the movement ends in general as it began, with the c.f. as a melody in the top voice.

The structure of the first section of the Sanctus has already been mentioned. The *Pleni sunt caeli* is a free trio except for the last six measures, where the beginning of the second phrase of the c.f. is used. It is then quoted continuously to the end in the *Osanna*, so that between the Sanctus, *Pleni*, and *Osanna* the entire melody is utilized. (From m.

11-17 of the *Osanna* the c.f. is stated in canon at the fifth by soprano and alto. At m. 18, tenor and bass restate this canon, and continue with c.f. in canon to the end of the movement. As in the canon of the Credo, the time intervals of imitation vary.) The *Benedictus* is constructed on a migrant scaffolding of the same type used in *Et in Spiritum*. The first phrase is stated once by the tenor, twice in succession by the bass, and once each by the superius and alto. The melody is split into thirds in the Agnus, as it was in the Kyrie, and is stated in newly ornamented form in conjunction with the entire bass voice of the Kyrie of the *Missa Mi-mi* of Ockeghem.[41] (As both Kyrie and Agnus are tripartite in form, the Ockeghem bass fits very well. The bass of Ockeghem's Kyrie I is given as the bass of Agnus I, that of the *Christe* as the bass of Agnus II, etc.) The quotation from Ockeghem is not completely unprepared, for the *Mi-mi* motive (e-A-e-f-e) has already been heard in the first notes of the bass of the Kyrie and Sanctus. It does not seem too farfetched to assume that the many features of the c.f. layout which are uncharacteristic of Obrecht but characteristic of Ockeghem are in some manner intended as a preparation for the quotation in the final movement. The whole Mass seems to be conceived as a gesture of respect to the older master.

The *Missa Libenter gloriabor*[42] is comparable to *Sicut spina rosam* because in this work, also, Obrecht treats the c.f. rather casually. It shows neither the complexity nor the imaginative variety of treatment of *Sicut spina rosam*, however, as the following list of c.f. statements indicates. The antiphon *Libenter gloriabor* is stated once in the tenor of Kyrie I and imitated in the bass in a manner approaching strict canon. In Kyrie II it is given once again in the tenor with some imitations in bass and superius. In the Gloria it is given again by the tenor, in inversion and in long note values; the tenor restates it in the *Qui tollis*, right side up and slightly ornamented, and with some repetition of the phrases; there is another complete statement in the same voice, starting at *Tu solus Dominus*, which is in shorter values than the two preceding ones; the final section, *Cum Sancto Spiritu*, is free. In the Credo the c.f. is still entrusted to the tenor and is stated once through in schematically manipulated form in the first section; in the *Crucifixus* it is stated once more, but this time in strict canon between superius and tenor and in slightly ornamented form. The statement in the Sanctus is made by the bass, although with some imitations in the tenor; the *Osanna* is a repetition of Kyrie II, so the c.f. statement is once more made by the tenor. (*Pleni* and *Benedictus* are freely composed trios.) There is no Agnus as an independent movement, the manuscript simply containing the direction "Agnus Dei cantantur supra Kyrie," so that the c.f. is heard again in the tenor as it was in the first movement.

These ways of handling the c.f.—a majority of statements in the tenor, a statement in the bass in the Sanctus, statements in strict canon or in a manner approaching strict canon, an instance of inversion, manipulation in the Credo which completely alters the sequence of notes[43]—are familiar from the other Masses on c.f.

Also familiar are the numerous exact repetitions. Those already mentioned involve restatements of the entire polyphonic complex, but in addition to these there is an instance of repetition of the c.f. voice only. The tenor of Kyrie I appears an octave lower as the bass of Sanctus (but with the rests differing in length). Finally, there is repetition of fragments of the c.f.: the first few notes are used as a motto before the tenor entry of every movement except the Gloria. The form of the motto in the Kyrie is most often used, appearing literally in the Sanctus and in very similar shape in the Credo. (It appears in Agnus I as a matter of course, since this movement is merely a repetition of Kyrie I.) The versions of the motto in the *Qui tollis* and *Crucifixus* are somewhat different, although both are based on the first few notes of the c.f.[44]

Except for these instances of exact or approximately exact repetition, the c.f. is given in somewhat different form in each movement. It is re-ornamented several times, and also it appears that Obrecht is not so careful to quote the notes of the antiphon literally as he is in the other Masses of this type. There are certain small irregularities in the notes of the second incise, and the end of the chant is sometimes altered almost beyond recognition. The small irregularities are not easy to account for,[45] but the purpose behind the most far-reaching alterations is clear enough. It happens that the third incise (the next to the last of the chant) can be interpreted as containing the germ of a sequence and, as might be expected, Obrecht takes full advantage of the possibilities this offers. In Kyrie II he expands the incipient sequence into a full-blown formation of five patterns which takes up the entire final part of the c.f. statement and completely absorbs the original melody. Again, in the statements of the *Qui tollis* and *Crucifixus* he develops sequences at this same point in the c.f. with the result that the final incise is practically obliterated in both cases. These departures from the Gregorian melodic outline are further examples of his attitude, which permits him to deviate from literal statement for the sake of carrying out a logical structural device.

The Mass also includes noticeable freedoms with respect to the order in which the phrases of the antiphon are stated. In the *Qui tollis* the quotation proceeds quite uneventfully until halfway through the third incise (m. 67), at which point it is broken off. After several measures' rest Obrecht retraces his steps and repeats the last three notes (i.e., tenor of m. 65-67 equals m. 79-84) to form the first pattern of the sequence mentioned above. After the completion of the sequence (m. 103) the c.f. is apparently dropped and the tenor freely composed until measure 112, when an entire restatement of the antiphon in shorter values begins. This is completed at measure 128, and the final, brilliant section of the movement is again freely composed, depending on imitation and sequence for its organization. In the Sanctus the quotation of the c.f. in the bass also contains an element of the unexpected: it is extended beyond the last note of the chant by threefold repetition of the final phrase—first in the superius, then in the contratenor, and finally in the tenor.

In two respects—the extension of the c.f. by partial or irregular repetitions of phrases, and the use of different ornamentation in some of the statements—this work shows Obrecht using methods of treatment which are less typical of him than they are of most of his contemporaries. There is, however, enough of literal restatement and schematic treatment to show his special preferences, and in the Credo he makes use of a type of organized reshuffling of the c.f. notes which is entirely characteristic.

On the whole, it appears that the manipulations of the c.f. are of a rather routine nature for him and do not show the careful thought and the ingenuity apparent in the other Masses on a single Gregorian melody. These evidences of hasty or casual work are supported by the fact that he failed to write independent music for the Agnus, simply making the music of the first movement serve for the last.

MASSES BASED ON MORE THAN ONE GREGORIAN MELODY

Just as more than one secular c.f. is used in certain Masses, several Gregorian melodies may be employed. This seems to be a regular procedure in Masses for saints' days, as they contain many chants appropriate to the occasion, and many of these are used by the composer.[46] The treatment of the *cantus firmi* corresponds to the types noted above, since some are presented very simply (even as strict c.f.), some are ornamented (and a given ornamented form is often repeated), some are used in canon, etc.

The *Missa de Sancto Martino* contains several antiphons from the service for St. Martin Bishop and Confessor, and a quotation from the Litany of the Saints, *Sancte Martine, ora pro nobis*.[47]

The tenor presents the antiphon *Martinus adhuc catechumenus* as a strict c.f. in the Kyrie. The melody appears three times in its entirety, once for each of the sections. The first appearance is in perfect breves, the second in imperfect breves, and the last in imperfect longs. In the Gloria the tenor presents *Dixerunt discipuli*. While the c.f. notes are in general given long values, there is liberal ornamentation at the phrase ends. (The alto also gives an anticipatory statement in the opening duo.) In the trio, *Domine fili unigenite*, the bass repeats this antiphon at the fifth below and entirely in imperfect breves. A peculiarity of this strict statement is the insertion of rests between each word of the antiphon, even though only the text incipit is given. (See ex. 98. The text runs only to m. 19 of the

Mass; from there on, the relation of the rests can be checked against the antiphon itself, as it is given above the score of the Mass movement.) The c.f. is repeated in the *Qui tollis* in the same ornamented form in which it was introduced in the Gloria, except that it is now interpreted in duple meter (perfect breves become imperfect, etc.). At measure 69 of the movement the quotation from the Litany, *Sancte Martine ora pro nobis*, is introduced; it brings the entire Gloria to a close. In the Credo several new melodies are introduced. To begin with, the tenor states the antiphon *O virum ineffabilem* twice. The second statement is a repetition of the first, without rests and in notes of the next lower value (breve become semibreve, etc.). Since in this mensuration the prolation is imperfect while the time is perfect, there are the variations in relative value that have been mentioned before. In the *Et incarnatus* another (unidentified) melody, *Martinus episcopus*, appears in the tenor, again in the form of strict c.f. At the trio, *Et resurrexit*, still another strict c.f., *Oculis ac manibus*, is given in the tenor. At *Et in Spiritum Sanctum* there is a return to c.f. paraphrase. *O beatum virum* appears in strict canon between the tenor and bass.[48]

Another unidentified melody, *Adoramus Christum*, appears in the Sanctus. It also is apparently ornamented. The *Pleni sunt caeli* is an exact parallel to *Domine fili unigenite*, as it, too, is a trio with strict c.f. in the bass. Once more, rests separate each word of the text, *Ego signo crucis*. The Osanna makes use of *Martinus adhuc catechumenus*, which has already been heard three times in the Kyrie. Each note is given the value of an imperfect long, just as it was in the second Kyrie. There is no textual indication of c.f. in the trio, *Benedictus qui venit*, although it is possible one is used.[49]

The Mass ends with the antiphon *O beatum Pontificem*, which is divided between the three parts of the Agnus Dei.[50] The c.f. layout is unusual for Obrecht. In Agnus I the melody of the words *O beatum Pontificem . . . Christum Regem* is given, transposed up a fourth and ornamented in places. In Agnus II the melody of the words *et non formidabat imperii principatum* is given to the bass, on pitch. It is presented chiefly in long note values. At measure 33 it migrates to the tenor and is transposed up a fourth. It can be traced from the words *O sanctissima anima* to *gladius*, after which there is a free cadential section. In Agnus III the tenor goes back to *O sanctissima anima* and proceeds to the end of the antiphon as strict c.f. in semibreves. Migration is unusual, but the turning-back in the quotation is even more so for Obrecht. Otherwise, the Mass simply repeats types of c.f. usage which occur in many others.

In one sense this work belongs in the class of Masses on multiple c.f. such as have been found as far back as Dufay and Regis. In another, it belongs in the class of plainchant Masses. It does not have cyclic unity,

EXAMPLE 98. Obrecht, *Missa de Sancto Martino* (*Works*, II, 124; *LU*, p. 1748).

as did the works of the two older men, since the single restatement of the first c.f. used can hardly have much effect in binding the work together. As in a plainchant Mass, the cantus firmi bring about liturgical unity only.

The Marian Mass, *Sub tuum praesidium*,[51] exhibits structure on two levels. On the one it employs multiple c.f., but in more complex form than seen in the previous works, for the melodies are quoted simultaneously rather than successively. On the second level, it employs only the antiphon from which it gains its name. This melody is quoted in its entirety in every movement, being presented in the superius as an isorhythmic scaffolding of considerable length. The scaffolding retains the same form throughout the work except for two changes—the third section is stated in diminution in Kyrie II, and a rest of the value of a perfect breve is added in Agnus II.

At first glance the changes appear to be inexplicable departures from a carefully laid out plan, such as have been noted in some other works. In *Sub tuum praesidium*, however, they turn out to be neither arbitrary nor accidental, but directly related to one of the most significant features of the work—the mathematical background of the scaffolding. Van Crevel, who has discovered this aspect of the structure (see n. 51, this chapter), lists a host of points of numerological significance which he discerns in the structural voice. On the most extensive level, he demonstrates that the five movements of the Mass add up to the length of 888 semibreves. Furthermore, the first two movements—Kyrie and Gloria—total 333 semibreves, while the last three—Credo, Sanctus, and Agnus—total 555. Since 2 will not divide evenly into 333, 3 into 555, or 5 into 888, these totals would be impossible if the movements were based on an isorhythmic tenor of fixed length.

Obrecht has arrived at a clever compromise solution which enables him to stay as close as possible to strict isorhythm and yet obtain the totals he wishes. The lapses from pattern turn out to be the means he employs to solve the apparently insoluble, and to realize the fundamental plan.

Ingenious as the scaffolding of *Sub tuum praesidium* is, it is still no more than the starting point for the most ambitious scheme of c.f. combination in all the Masses of Obrecht.[52] The work is unique in another respect also, as the number of voices increases from movement to movement. Three are used in the Kyrie, four in the Gloria, five in the Credo, six in the Sanctus, and seven in the Agnus. The sole c.f. in the Kyrie and Gloria is the superius scaffolding, *Sub tuum praesidium*. (However, in the first half of the Gloria, numerous quotations from the beginning of the antiphon are fitted into the contrapuntal voices.) In the Credo a second Gregorian melody, *Audi nos, nam te filius*, is given in combination with it. In the Sanctus another melody, with the text *Mediatrix nostra*, is combined with it. However, as the new melody is given out in alternation by the second soprano and tenor, there are three voices occupied with c.f., even though only two *cantus firmi* are in use. In the first and second Agnus Dei, two more melodies are united with *Sub tuum praesidium*. The second soprano and vagans give the melody of *Celsus nuntiat Gabriel* in alternation and the first alto carries *Supplicamus nos emenda*, so that there is now a total of three *cantus firmi* occupying four out of the seven voices. The final Agnus also presents three *cantus firmi* in four voices. *Sub tuum praesidium*, which is divided between the three sections of the Agnus, is completed by the first soprano; the second soprano and vagans each present the Marian antiphon *Regina caeli* and the first alto gives out the final words of *Salve Regina (O clemens, O pia, O dulcis Maria)*.

In order to combine these melodies Obrecht has inserted rests freely, so that no more than three of the four voices sound at once. (See ex. 99. All four of the c.f. voices sound together only in m. 21.) Some ornamentation is used, although, considering the complexity of the task, the amount is very small. It has been necessary to transpose the melody of *Regina caeli* up a tone, as it is in the fifth mode and could not otherwise be made to fit that of *Sub tuum praesidium*, which is in the seventh. The excerpts from *Salve Regina* are transposed up a fourth in some places and up an octave in others. (Ex. 99, alto I, m. 21-22; the change in transposition occurs at *O dulcis*.) It is also possible that Obrecht has altered a few notes of this melody. (Ex. 99, alto I, m. 19-20; he may, of course, have used a form which varies from any of those available to me.) In addition to this, three free voices help to fill out the harmonies. It is noticeable that the bass part is taken almost entirely by a composed voice.

However, this Mass shows a steadily developing technical proficiency in achieving c.f. combinations. More important, it also indicates a broadening realization of the possibilities for using such a technique in a composition. With regard to the first point, Obrecht has provided an impressive example of contrapuntal ingenuity, even though he does not always carry off the combinations with great elegance, but, rather, forces the melodies to fit one another whether they will or no. As for the second, it is obvious that the combinations are not made for their own sake alone but for their contributions to the climactic musical structure, which depends in part on the progressive increase in complexity of the c.f. combinations (and in part, of course, on the increase in total number of parts).

In *Sub tuum praesidium* full thought is given to both aesthetic and intellectual aspects of structure. A great amount of care has obviously been expended on the plan of the scaffolding—a plan of numerical proportions which can be appreciated only by the intellect. Similar care has been devoted to the organization of the contrapuntal voices—under a plan of increasing climax which can be immediately appreciated by the ear. So far as can be told from the music, Obrecht considered the two of equal importance. Furthermore, both plans indicate his interest in structure on a very

EXAMPLE 99. Obrecht, *Missa Sub tuum praesidium*—Agnus III (*Works*, II, 38).

large scale. Here again, as in *Si dedero* and other Masses of its class, he deals with schemes that come to full realization only in the final movement of the work.

MISCELLANEOUS CHARACTERISTICS

Up to this point attention has been directed chiefly to the methods of laying out the c.f. for a complete Mass. Before leaving Obrecht it is necessary to consider a few of his procedures which affect the smaller details of the c.f. usage.[53]

Examples have already been given of one of his favorite procedures— the combination of two or more different *cantus firmi*. It is a central structural device in the *Missa Sub tuum praesidium*, which presents a series of combinations of increasing complexity. This is apparently one of his mature works, but interesting examples of the device can be found in earlier ones. Not surprisingly, in the earlier compositions the device is of an occasional nature and does not influence the formal design of a whole Mass.

The Credo of *Fors seulement* is a case in point, even though the presence in it of more than one c.f. is not immediately apparent owing to the

EXAMPLE 100. Obrecht, *Missa Fors seulement*—Credo (*Works*, V, 140; *LU*, p. 64).

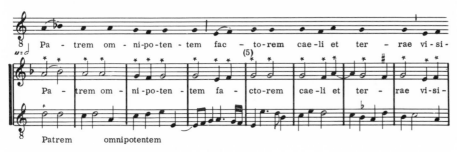

form in which the work is printed in the complete edition. As given by
Wolf, the first half of the Credo appears to have been written for only
two voices. This is unusual in itself, because the Mass is for three voices
and the Credo is not customarily scored for less than the full number.
Further, the upper of the two voices presents the Gregorian melody of
Credo I in a curiously haphazard manner. These and a few other peculiarities imply that the work must have been written originally with a third
voice. The *Qui tollis* also is given for only two voices in the complete
edition; fortunately, it is quoted by Glareanus in complete form and the

missing superius turns out to be the *Fors seulement* melody.[54] This gives an obvious clue for reconstructing the Credo, and a trial shows that the superius of the chanson fits the two lower voices perfectly, thus proving that this movement was originally written for three voices also. (See ex. 100.) The next section, *Et incarnatus*,[55] also has the *Fors seulement* melody in the top voice, and the middle voice continues with Credo I, so the entire Credo proves to be based on the combination of two different *cantus firmi*. If, as Gombosi suggests, the work was composed around 1470, it constitutes a very ambitious attempt in this direction.

Certain other devices, familiar in the compositions of Busnois and his contemporaries, are also found in *Fors seulement*. There is a short sequence in the bottom voice (ex. 100, m. 50-52), a brief figure is repeated and freely imitated (ex. 100, m. 63-71), the final cadence is emphasized by a deceptive progression and an extension, etc.[56]

Instances of extended combinations of c.f. are found in the other Mass for three voices, *De tous biens pleine*. In the *Qui tollis* the complete material of the chanson tenor is given by the tenor of the Mass and, at the

EXAMPLE 101. Obrecht, *Missa De tous biens pleine*—(a) *Qui tollis*, (b) Agnus III (*Works*, V, 163, 184; Gombosi, *Jacob Obrecht*, No. XIV, p. 24).

fifth above, by the superius (ex. 101a). The Mass tenor is clearly the
leading c.f. voice, as it adheres very closely to the original form of the
res facta. The superius states all the notes of the c.f. with a minimal
amount of ornamentation, but it is obviously the secondary voice which
is being fitted to the primary one, as all sorts of rhythmic adjustments
are made in it.[57] The same methods are used in the third Agnus, except
that in this case the tenor and superius are at the unison (ex. 101b).
These free duplications (not canons) are one of the several ways Obrecht
uses to increase and concentrate the c.f. content by getting it into two
voices. The method of statement is somewhat similar to that used by
Dufay in the two tenors of *Nuper rosarum flores*.

Other procedures which occur throughout the Masses are also found
in this early work. The Kyrie starts with the statement of some of the
tenor material in the superius (ex. 102), but this is very brief, and from
there on an attempt is made to organize that voice independently of the
c.f. by means of a figure which is repeated several times (marked by
letter A in ex. 102). The figure is emphasized by its position at the head

EXAMPLE 102. Obrecht, *Missa De tous biens pleine*—Kyrie I (*Works*, V, 157;
Gombosi, *Jacob Obrecht*, No. XIV, p. 24).

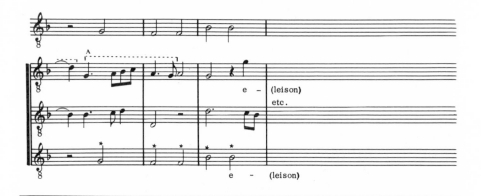

e – (leison)
etc.

e – (leison)

of the phrase, by its syncopated entry after a rest, and by its characteristic rhythmic outline. It even occurs twice within a single phrase at different pitch levels (ex. 102, m. 15-18). A similar type of organization is
found in the first Agnus, although in this case it is carried further. The
first four measures are occupied with imitative figures (marked A in
ex. 103a), but starting with measure 5 the superius states and restates a
certain figure in varying but clearly related forms. (See ex. 103a. The
related figures are marked B, B′, B″.) This figure is also made prominent
by its position at the beginning of the phrase and because it enters on the
offbeat. After numerous restatements it leads to a sequence which is based
on a new figure (marked C in the example). However, even this is similar
enough to the preceding figures to seem to have grown out of them, and
the line remains entirely consistent. The bottom line of the score is not
organized by such clearly recognizable motives, yet the constant recurrence of the rhythmic figure ♩. ♪♪♪♩ , first heard in measures 6-7, tends
to give it a general unity. There are also a few other repeated figures (ex.
103a, m. 30-33, 15-17). The devices used in the superius of this movement
are not new with Obrecht. Busnois occasionally organized a line by means
of free *ostinato*, and he used sequences very frequently, but there is
nothing in his works to equal the extended use of such figures by Obrecht
in this Agnus.

In parts of the Credo of this same Mass the counterpoints are given an
organization among themselves by means of imitation (ex. 103b, m. 1-6
and m. 7-9; ex. 103c, m. 7-10). The two upper parts imitate one another,
using simple triadic figures, as long as the tenor notes move very slowly.
The imitations are dropped when the tenor notes become shorter, and the
two upper voices continue as free counterpoints. This method of organizing the voices above the c.f. is not an innovation of Obrecht's—we have
seen a very brief instance of it in the *Missa Le serviteur* of Faugues (ex.
67, above). Nevertheless, these are presumably among the very earliest works
of Obrecht and so would have been written at approximately the same time

as the most advanced motets of Busnois. Whatever the exact date of compositions, it is clear that Obrecht was vitally interested in the procedures of his immediate predecessors and was actively concerned in developing them.[58]

Organization of the contrapuntal voices does not have the effect of

EXAMPLE 103. Obrecht, *Missa De tous biens pleine*—(a) Agnus I, (b) Credo, (c) *Et incarnatus* (Works, V, 179, 166, 168).

minimizing the importance of the structural c.f., which retains its traditional position as the backbone of the Mass. But the employment of means such as those discussed above, which bind the voices to a set procedure when the c.f. is sounding, is new. From the very inception of polyphonic writing, the voices added to a c.f. had been bound by no consideration except the general one of making acceptable counterpoints to it.[59]

These devices point in different directions. Those which bring the material of a single c.f. into more than one voice at the same time point to a type of composition which is totally integrated because its content is derived almost entirely from the melody on which it is based. Obrecht, however, never carries this trend to its conclusion; that is left to Josquin and other men who employ continuous imitation.

In Obrecht's hands, the independent organization of the counterpoints, rather than leading to the total integration of the polyphony, tends to make it break apart into two sharply opposed elements so that, in this sense, his methods point to an earlier style. In many cases it can be seen that he does everything to further the contrast between elements. The counterpoints are excessively active; they are apt to move by large leaps and in widely extended scale passages; they move rapidly and have enormous rhythmic vigor due to syncopations and cross rhythms.[60] The c.f., on the contrary, is often cut down to the plainest possible form; it generally consists of comparatively small intervals and has a restricted range; above all, it moves slowly.

EXAMPLE 104. Obrecht, *Missa sine nomine* (*Pfauenschwanz*)—Agnus III (*Works*, V, 49), with tenor melody in the setting of Barbireau—(*Opera*, II, 9).

These opposite ways of utilizing the chant are in themselves traditional. The sharply contrasted scaffolding comes down from the fourteenth century, although it had largely dropped from favor in the generation preceding Obrecht. The fashion of writing structural paraphrases, which developed in the first half of the fifteenth century, tends to integrate the c.f. into the polyphonic whole in the general sense that contrasts in rhythmic and melodic shape are eliminated. With Ockeghem the c.f. is, as it were, engulfed by the stream of sound. However, with the new methods of recombination of material and motivic organization, the composer is able to intensify either one of these effects according to his wish. In the case of paraphrased c.f., whereas the integration had previously been of a general nature (the texture was made homogeneous by similarity in rhythmic movement and melodic style between the paraphrased c.f. and the other voices), it can now be specific (the texture can be organically integrated, as all voices may be formed from the same material). In the other case, the scaffolding had been made to stand apart from the other voices mainly because of differences in rate of motion; now the composer is able to accentuate the opposing nature of the voices even more, since, by integrating the counterpoints among themselves, he can reduce the composition to two essential elements—one, the c.f.; the other, the group of counterpoints arrayed against it as a unified body. But the c.f. is the immutable voice, and, despite the teeming life of the others and their own rational mode of existence, it is the higher power which sets the terms of that existence.

In the works of Obrecht the organization of the upper voices may vary from a highly consistent to a rather loose one. In the example quoted from the *Missa de Sancto Martino* (ex. 98, above), no fewer than six different figures may be detected, and these are not all that are used in the movement. (They are indicated by brackets and the letters A to F.) In some cases they are varied slightly on restatement (compare B, m. 8-11, and B', m. 11-15) and are not always repeated in immediate succession (figure C, m. 14-18, recurs at m. 28 and not again until m. 76).[81] The section omitted in the quotation (m. 54-75) contains a couple of sequences, each with its own characteristic figure, so that the organization they contribute concerns individual spots rather than the complete composition. On the whole, the organization of the counterpoints is rather loose; even so, the contrast between them and the very plain, slowly moving c.f. is pronounced.

The third Agnus from the *Missa sine nomine (Pfauenschwanz)* is a good example of extended, consistent organization of the counterpoints. (See ex. 104. The *Pfauenschwanz* melody as it appears in the setting of Barbireau is included for purposes of comparison; it is very similar to the form used by Obrecht.)[62] The movement starts as a free harmonization

of the borrowed melody (it is possible that the first four notes of the bass
are derived from it) and leads to a full cadence on G (m. 13). There
follows a long section in which the voices are organized by means of a
repeated motive with the rhythmic form ♩ | ♪♩♩♩ ♩|♩ . (See m. 13-50.
This again illustrates Obrecht's habit of employing motives which begin
on the offbeat and gain rhythmic emphasis by means of the effect of
syncopation.) The motives are not put in haphazardly at whatever points
they may fit with the c.f. but according to a scheme of statement which
is given to the bass voice. The figure appears as a descending sequence in
that voice, beginning on the notes g, f, eb, and d (m. 13-21). This sequence is repeated, but not so regularly, as the notes on which the figures
begin are g, f, eb, and c (m. 23-32). The following appearances are still
less regular, the first notes of the figure being g, f, and c (m. 32-39) and
then g, g, d, and c (m. 39-50). Even so, because the bass is written
against an unornamented c.f., it can be seen that a serious attempt has
been made to achieve a consistent design in statement. The other voices
carry the motive in parallel sixths, tenths, or sixth chords with the bass,
although they add occasional independent statements. The final section
(m. 57-63) presents the usual drive to the cadence. There is a change
to triple meter, and the bass rapidly descends a tenth by scalewise motion
and then rises by means of a sequence before the final cadence. The c.f.
is very definitely of a different nature from the other voices, even though
it does not contain the extremely long pedal notes which Obrecht often
employs. (See ex. 105, below, m. 19 ff., for a scaffolding of the latter type.)

Instances in which the c.f. and the other voices are integrated into an
organically unified polyphonic texture are not common. Obrecht definitely
prefers to contrast the c.f. to the other voices. An instance has been seen,
however, in the Kyrie of the *Missa O quam suavis* (ex. 97a, above).
Complete integration is made the more feasible as the c.f. itself is orna-
mented. A rhythmic figure ♩. ♪♩♩|♩ appears in measures 3-4 as a part
of the ornamentation of the superius, the voice bearing the c.f. at this
point. It next occurs in the form of a descending scale-line in the alto at
measure 5 and again in the superius at measure 7. Starting at measure 9,
the tenor repeats the anticipatory statement of the superius, so these
figures appear again in it. In the meantime, the other voices take up the
scale-line figure. The bass and alto present it in canon at the distance of
half a beat (m. 13-15), while the superius and tenor each add a single
statement. This brief movement is an example of organic growth from a
single idea to an impressive, massed climax such as is often found in
Josquin. (See ex. 118, below. The difference is one of degree rather than
of method.)

Another aspect of Obrecht's work is the increasing importance of
parody in the later Masses, such as *Rosa playsante*, *Si dedero*, and *Je ne*

EXAMPLE 105. Obrecht, *Missa Si dedero*—Kyrie I (*Works*, III, 1).

demande. [63] The Kyrie of the *Missa Si dedero* starts as usual with points of imitation on material of the motet. (See ex. 105; borrowed material is indicated by brackets; measure numbers of the motet and the voice being quoted from it are also given.) The noteworthy point is that after the entry of the scaffolding tenor (m. 19) the quotations in the other voices are continued. Hardly a measure of this movement is free of these quotations, and in some cases they occupy two voices besides the tenor (m. 27-30).[64] The quotations are of fair length and for the most part are literal, even though the melodic fragments are transplanted into an entirely different harmonic context which is determined by the rigid tenor. The purpose of these contrapuntal feats is not to produce tightly organized lines over the c.f., nor to lead to any rhythmic climax. Nevertheless, the technique employed is essentially the same as in those works where the aim is to organize closely or to bring about climaxes. In all of the cases, the technical process consists of fitting together pieces of fixed shape and the outcome is a sort of musical mosaic work.

In writing of the sort seen in example 105, there is a lack of flexibility, which is attributable to Obrecht's inclination to hold to the exact form of any given piece of material, whether it be a short motive or an extended c.f. This seems to be a matter of personal preference, since many of the canons on c.f. material show that he was quite aware of the possibilities of altering a melody by means of ornamentation and thus making it more pliable for purposes of contrapuntal manipulation. Because of his preference for quoting exactly, his combinations often sound awkward, and give the effect of being patched together. Josquin, not sharing this literal attitude, varies his materials willingly and easily achieves smooth combinations.

Obrecht's musical mosaic work is illustrated in another way in *Rosa playsante*. In this Mass, he opens several movements by presenting an idea in one voice, immediately thereafter in a second, and then in a third. He does not make the series of statements in close imitation (i.e., the entries do not overlap, or if they do the overlap is slight). They resemble the entries of a fugal exposition, although with some significant differences. The first entry is made not alone but accompanied by counterpoint in one or more of the other voices; the entries are ordinarily made only at the octave or unison; and, finally, the subject usually does not appear in more than three parts, since it is ordinarily not derived from the c.f. and can be given to the tenor—the fourth part—only in those cases where it is so derived.

Quasi-fugal passages such as these are not uncommon in the Masses, but these are of interest at this point because they illustrate Obrecht's inflexible method of quotation and also show his concern with the dimensional aspect of musical architecture. The tenor is of the framework type in this Mass and the problem of dimension is ever present because the length of all the parts, including the rests, is predetermined. A framework almost invariably begins with a long rest which is utilized by the contrapuntal voices to make their introductory comments before the tenor joins in with its statement. It is during this rest that Obrecht makes the fugal entries in question, and he must, of course, accommodate them to the space the rest provides. Rather typically, he goes about this in the most methodical way, calculating the counterpoints so that they exactly fill up the rest, whatever its length may be.

The beginning of the *Qui tollis* shows his method. Here the tenor is silent for fifteen measures and he has three contrapuntal voices with which to work during this space of time. A simple calculation shows that a phrase five measures long appearing once in each part will exactly fill up the space. Accordingly, he writes a phrase five measures long for the bass, which he then gives to the superius and next to the contratenor; the passage thus ends neatly just at the point of the tenor entry. The five-measure phrase begins with the tonic and ends with the implication of dominant, so that this little piece of musical inlay work fits together smoothly enough because of the effect of perfect cadence at each of the junction points between phrases (m. 5-6, 10-11).

In filling out similar spots in other movements the continuity of the succeeding statements is increased by overlaps of one measure between statements. (The last measure of the first phrase is made to coincide with the first measure of the second, and so on.) Thus, in the Credo, a twelve-measure rest of the tenor (m. 107-118) is exactly filled out by a five-measure phrase stated three times since the overlap of one measure causes the entries to occur at the distance of four measures. In the *Et incarnatus* three nine-measure phrases exactly fill twenty-four measures of tenor rest, since the overlap of one measure brings an entry every eight measures (*Et incarnatus*, m. 1-24).

At the beginning of the Gloria there is a rest of twenty-seven measures and here, too, some mathematical computations must have preceded writing. Obrecht treats this space in two parts, one of twelve measures and one of fifteen. The first part is filled by an idea which appears in only two voices (bass, m. 1; contra, m. 7), the second by a new idea which appears in all three voices (bass, m. 13; contra, m. 18; superius, m. 23). Both ideas are of the type which overlap, so that the first twelve measures are filled out by two seven-measure phrases and the final fifteen by three of six measures.

Another instance in the Credo (m. 64-88) is just as carefully calculated, but Obrecht does not confine the statements to the space of the tenor rest (eighteen measures, m. 70-87). He brings in the idea six measures before the rest, concurrently with the sounding of the final longa of the preceding tenor statement, and fills a total space of twenty-four measures by two statements of thirteen measures each. (The first statement is in the bass, m. 64 ff., and is repeated in the superius, m. 76 ff. There is an overlap of one measure.) The whole passage is much more complex than the others mentioned. The phrase is much longer and, in addition, has a fairly intricate internal organization. As example 106 shows, the bass line is constructed as a broad arch arising from F to c′ and falling to F again, the rise being accomplished by means of a rising sequence, the fall by a complementary falling sequence. The counterpoints, which are different in the two statements, are fitted out with ingenious imitations and motivic figures, so that the passage is of great musical interest.

EXAMPLE 106. Obrecht, *Missa Rosa playsante*—Credo (MS Segovia, fo. 30ᵛ-31).

These trios show once more the master's rather matter-of-fact approach. It is evident that before setting down the music he had to do a bit of measuring and this not entirely because of the rigid tenor foundation. Habits of thought evident in all his writing made it necessary. Once he had an idea he was very apt to treat it as a unit for literal repetition, and just because the ideas are literally repeated they have no flexibility of dimension. The result is seen in those specimens of musical joiner's work in which the pieces must be cut to exact size before they are fitted to one another. The regularity of structure does not in all cases lead to dull musical effect, because Obrecht provides a wealth of curious detail from moment to moment, and because at times he builds up passages of great power. The section quoted in example 106, with its ample proportions and bursting energy, stands comparison with any of the brilliant phrases which illuminate his works and the works of his contemporaries. However, most of the passages discussed above cannot rank with this one in musical interest. They are shorter breathed, less striking in melodic outline, and in their harmonic aspect they are simple to the point of naïveté. The phrases always proceed to a cadence, so that each is a self-contained unit. Moreover, they are so short that they produce an effect of start-and-stop which can hardly be covered up, although Obrecht does what he can to force the movement onward by overlapping the parts and varying the constant dominant-tonic progressions with occasional deceptive cadences. Even so, the effect in many cases is something short of inspired.

It should be added that Obrecht is not always so much concerned with the exact measurement of dimensions. For instance, in the Credo of *Rosa playsante* the tenor begins with a rest of thirty-six measures which is treated in two sections. In the first sixteen measures the counterpoints are reasonably free, but the last twenty are more strictly organized, being developed out of three statements of an idea seven measures long. (The idea appears in the bass in m. 17; in the contra, m. 24; in the superius, m. 31. The final note of the third statement overlaps the tenor entry by one note.) The Sanctus begins with a rest of fifteen measures, and a phrase stated first in the bass (m. 1-7) is repeated in the contratenor (m. 7-13), but here the statements are not planned to fill the rest at all. They come to an end in measure 13; the remaining two bars are filled out by a free extension. (This passage differs from the others discussed in other ways. The phrase is restated not at the unison or octave but at the fifth above, and it is not newly invented but clearly derived from the first seven notes of the c.f.)

The final fact to be noted in this survey of the Masses is a negative one. None of these works presents an example of continuous imitation (*Durchimitation*) on c.f. material, although there are numerous examples of c.f.

in canon. We look in vain for a movement based on c.f. in which points of imitation are used regularly throughout—in which all, or a majority of the phrases, begin with imitative entries on c.f. material. The closest approach to such a continuous method of organization is found in certain duos and trios not based on c.f., or in such a movement as the third Agnus of *Salve diva parens*, in which the voices repeat melodic figures in a way that gives an effect resembling points of imitation. The older attitude that imitation is an alternate form of organization to be used when the c.f. is silent still persists to a considerable extent. Nevertheless, in so large a body of works, the absence of continuous imitation is noteworthy, and I will speak of it again later (pp. 310-311).

THE MOTETS OF OBRECHT

Many of the motets are of the traditional tenor type as it developed along the lines laid down by Regis. That is, they are big works for five or six voices and consist of two or more sections (with the exception of the motet for five voices, *Haec Deum caeli*, which is in one). While they are scored more fully than the Masses, they show essentially the same techniques of composition. They are based on one or more *cantus firmi*, and the *cantus firmi* are manipulated in various ways, although not in ways that differ noticeably from those already seen.

In the six-voice motet, *Salve Regina*, the antiphon is given in ornamented form in the tenor. In the first part it is duplicated in the soprano (*Primus Puer*) by means of canon. In the motet for five voices, *Factor orbis*, we find multiple c.f. Its text is put together from a number of chants for Advent and the Vigil of the Nativity, and the appropriate melodies for several of them are used.[65] In *Salve crux, arbor vitae* a part of the sequence melody *Laudes cruces attolamus* (verse 18, *O crux, lignum*)[66] is given three times in succession, ornamented differently each time. The second statement is joined with another melody, *Per lignum crucis* (melody not identified; not the same as either antiphon or communio *Per signum crucis*). In *Laudemus nunc Dominum*, a motet for the dedication of a church, we find the mixture of ornamented and strict c.f. seen in some of the Masses. The antiphon *Non est hic aliud* is given twice in differently ornamented form and is followed by the strict c.f. of *Vidit Jacob scalam* and *Erexit Jacob lapidem*.[67] Several of these works are polytextual.

Probably the greatest concentration of c.f. material in any of the composer's works is found in *Haec Deum caeli*,[68] the concentration being achieved by an extension of methods he often uses. He frequently duplicates material freely in a second voice which he fits to the main c.f. statement; here the main c.f. statement is already in two voices (tenor and secundus *discantus* in canon), so the somewhat freer statement of the alto is actually a triplication of the material. (See ex. 107a. The alto is so similar to the tenor and *secundus discantus* as almost to amount to a third voice in canon; however, it has rests of different length. See m. 11-13.) The steady motion in breves, the frequent rests between words,

EXAMPLE 107. (a-b) Obrecht, *Haec Deum caeli* (Motetten, pp. 46, 48; text of hymn, Var Prec., p. 103; melody, LU, p. 1196).

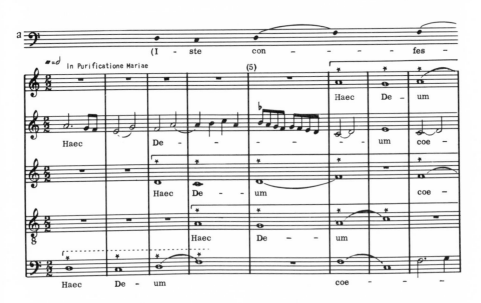

and the lack of ornamentation are all familiar features of c.f. voices. At the last word of the text the canon is broken, the melody is ornamented, and the piece ends with a free cadential extension. (See ex. 107b.)

The points noted in the motets for five and six voices hold true for those scored for four. These, too, have ornamented and strict c.f., multiple c.f. used in succession or in combination, and other devices seen in the Masses.

The motet *Ave Regina caelorum* is based on the tenor of Walter

Frye's motet of the same name;[69] it is the tenor on which Obrecht also bases his *Missa Ave Regina caelorum.* This voice is quoted literally in the motet, except that it is transposed down a third, which puts it in Dorian instead of the original Lydian mode. In the motet *Beata es Maria, Virgo clemens et pia,* the c.f.[70] is repeated in the second part of the work in exactly the same form it had in the first. Another c.f., the sequence *Ave Maria . . . Virgo serena* is combined with the second statement. It is not stated entirely regularly and ends with a repetition of the first line of text, but there is no mistaking the melody used.[71] Obrecht wrote the motet *Mille quingentis* (textless in the complete edition) on the occasion of his father's death in 1488.[72] The Introit *Requiem aeternam* is used as a scaffolding, being stated three times. It is transposed down a tone so that it is in Phrygian rather than the original Lydian mode. Continuous imitation is used no more in these works than it was in the Masses, or in the motets for five and six voices. Even the *Magnificat quinti toni*[73] contains no more imitation than do similar works of Busnois and Dufay. As in their works, several of the verses of the canticle begin with points of imitation but are not carried out consistently.[74]

We would expect to find examples of consistent use of initial imitation in the works for three voices, as that is the number of parts used in the song motets of the time. One of the three-voice works, *Si sumpsero,*[75] actually is a song motet and much use of initial imitation is made in it, although the points do not often involve all three parts. Like most motets of this class, *Si sumpsero* is probably not based on c.f.

The other two works for three voices are settings of the Marian antiphons *Alma Redemptoris Mater* and *Salve Regina.*[76] The first of these presents the melody in ornamented form in the bass throughout, although from *tu quae genuisti . . . mirante* (m. 110-136) the c.f. is duplicated in the superius by means of canon at the octave and there are a few short imitations in the other voices. The second motet, *Salve Regina,* is a very interesting and apparently early work. The c.f. is taken first by the tenor. It is ornamented in the erratic manner which became common in the third quarter of the century, sometimes being presented simply, in long note values, sometimes in a highly elaborated form. Starting at *et Jesum* (m. 130), the c.f. is freely duplicated in the bass (i.e., not in canon with the tenor); it then migrates to the bass alone, where it is presented entirely in longs and breves (*nobis post hoc . . . ostende,* m. 154-196). At *O pia* it is given as a scaffolding in the superius while the other voices are organized against it. Possibly the most interesting sections are *O clemens* and *O dulcis Virgo Maria* (ex. 108a-b). The first of these is a concentrated motivic development of the short c.f. phrase. It appears over and over in all voices, making up almost the entire content of the bass line and about half that of the other two. The second one, which is the final section of the work, is an extended and extremely elaborate fantasy. It opens with the first few notes of the c.f. phrase as initial entries in all three voices, but the antiphon melody is soon abandoned and there is a long free passage leading to a cadence (m. 250). The c.f. is picked up again at this point and appears briefly in all three voices in imitation (m. 250-253). It is then quoted to the end by the tenor (m. 254-258), but this does not end the section. The bass now becomes the structural voice and extends the composition by stating the notes of the final word, *Maria,* three times in succession. Even this does not bring the composition to a close, as an elaborate free coda in triple meter is added. This extraordinary outpouring is fitted with all the devices of the drive to the cadence: sequences, repeated figures, incisive rhythmic motives, etc. The variety of treatments of the c.f., the cadential extensions and the kaleidoscopic succession of rhythmic and melodic figures remind us of Busnois, but Obrecht outdoes him here on every count.

The Masses and motets of Obrecht show his great respect for the original form of a c.f. and his predilection for a planned employment of

EXAMPLE 108. (a-b) Obrecht, *Salve Regina* (*Motetten,* pp. 153, 155; melody, *LU,* p. 274, and *Studien zur Musikwissenschaft,* VII [1920], 91, *Salve Regina* VI).

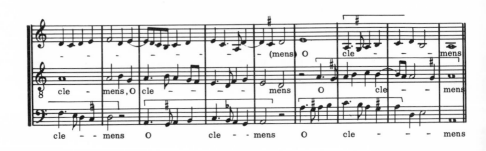

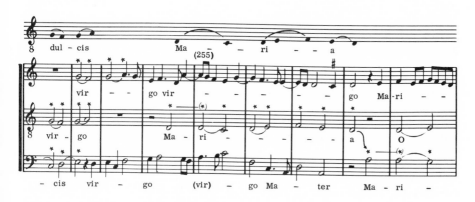

it. They also show that he uses a great variety of methods for concentrating and integrating material, some of them calling for a fair degree of contrapuntal ingenuity. These methods include the combination of the *same* material in more than one voice by means of canon, "free duplication," or imitative passages of more or less length and strictness. They also include the combination of *different* material, such as musically unrelated *cantus firmi* (e.g., in the *Missa Sub tuum praesidium*) or different parts of the same composition (as in the Kyrie of the *Missa Si dedero*).In addition, there are all sorts of motivic devices, the motives sometimes being derived from the c.f. (as in ex. 108a, above) sometimes being freely invented and used in combination with the c.f.

The Masses and motets abound in imitative passages of one sort and another, but it seems that a false significance may be attached to this very obvious fact. For instance, Peter Wagner says, *"His Masses repre-*

sent one of the last stages before the goal on the road from the c.f. Mass to the continuously imitative."[77] This is perfectly true from the chronological point of view, since Obrecht was nearer the sixteenth century than Dufay or Ockeghem, but it does not have the significance that Wagner's italics would indicate. As a matter of fact, not a single movement based on c.f. is "continuously imitative,"[78] nor does there seem to be any clear development in the direction of adopting the consistent, uniform procedures implied by this method of organization. An extension of the use of imitation is taking place in this period, but as a phase of the extension of the use of means of organization in general. Imitation as such is not the central issue. It is one of the well-known techniques in the field of secular music, and a comparatively old one—witness the chansons of H. de Lantins which in the second quarter of the century have already attained Wagner's goal of continuous imitation. Imitation of this type had also entered the field of sacred music in the form of the song motet. However, composers showed much greater interest in the exploration of the rich variety of possibilities of contrapuntal combination of all sorts, and especially of the possibilities of those devices by means of which a climactic type of organization could be achieved. This was a period in which lively movement and brilliant and various detail were greatly prized.[79] The consistent and uniform procedures of continuous imitation would probably have been considered unworthy of the c.f. Masses and motets of Obrecht. It is not until the delight in kaleidoscopic detail is lost and the interest in the drive to the cadence diminishes— when music becomes less colorful and less torrential in flow—that composers choose more and more to follow the consistent procedures of continuous imitation in their larger and more important works. The fact that Obrecht begins phrases with points of imitation very often, but as only one of a variety of possible ways of organizing his compositions, simply reveals him as a member of his generation.

10

The Masses and Motets
of Josquin des Prez

IN APPROACHING THE WORKS of Josquin it will be helpful to review once
more the two widely separated attitudes toward musical composition
which can be detected in the last half of the fifteenth century. Possibly
no greater contrast in style could be found between any two men who
are so nearly contemporary as that which exists between Ockeghem and
Obrecht. It is possible to show an almost direct opposition in every
aspect of their music. Obrecht not only prefers to quote the c.f. literally;
he makes a plan for the structural voice which he carries out consistently.
Ockeghem treats it fancifully, altering the form of statement at will.
Obrecht's music has clear contours; the counterpoint is written on a firm
harmonic background and phrase divisions are clearly defined, although
the phrases themselves are not necessarily regular in length;[1] important
sections are articulated both by harmonic means and by the primarily
rhythmic one, the drive to the cadence. Ockeghem strives for a continuous, undifferentiated flow—only in the very latest works is there any evidence of interest in providing a solid, clearly-defined harmonic element;
the joints between phrases are smoothed over and almost negated by
harmonic and melodic means; the drive to the cadence is restricted almost
entirely to a general increase in speed of all voices.

Obrecht experiments constantly with the new devices of c.f. combination and motivic organization. His intent, in dealing with motives, is to

312

make clearly audible units. He generally makes them short and gives them a clear, arresting rhythmic outline; by starting them on an offbeat, after a short rest, he makes sure that they will stand out sufficiently to attract attention. Examples of recombination of c.f. material are found in the later works of Ockeghem also, but he makes comparatively little use of motivic devices. When he does use motives, he does not emphasize them as individual units but incorporates them as smoothly as possible into the continuously flowing line. Far from using motives for the characteristic effects which they, as units, are capable of producing, he does what he can to inhibit any such manifestations.

THE MASSES OF JOSQUIN

It has seemed necessary to point out the above differences once more, since the two manners of musical thought come together in the early works of Josquin. The five Masses included in Petrucci's publication of 1502[2] give proof of this in almost every measure.

In the manner of laying out the c.f., Josquin inclines toward the varied, irregular methods of Ockeghem in all but one of these works. The *Missa L'homme armé super voces musicales* is the exception.[3] Josquin uses an elaborated and rhythmically varied form of the melody—as had Dufay, Ockeghem, and most other composers—instead of quoting it directly from the chanson as Busnois and Obrecht (copying Busnois) had done. But he does not provide a new elaboration for each statement, as Dufay and Ockeghem did. He takes a single statement of the c.f. as the basis of all the others in the work. This is a characteristic procedure of Obrecht.

Variety is attained by the usual schematic manipulations. Josquin chooses transposition as his chief means of manipulating the melody, but instead of confining himself to transposing it one or two times, as was customary, he goes to the final possible limit by stating the *L'homme armé* tenor on every degree of the hexachord. In the Kyrie it is given out by the tenor of the mass on C. (The A section of the tune is given in Kyrie I, the B section in the *Christe*, and the final A in Kyrie II.) The note values are especially long in the *Christe* and final Kyrie, so that the c.f. is given the character of a true scaffolding. In the Gloria the tenor states the entire tune on D. The first and last A sections are given as in the two Kyries, but the B section has shorter values. The diminution is exact, for a perfect long of the *Christe* becomes a perfect breve.[4] Indeed, all augmentations and diminutions are exact throughout the Mass, the tenor remaining in triple meter regardless of the meter of the other voices. There is no reinterpretation in duple meter as was seen so often in Obrecht. In the *Qui tollis* the c.f. used in the Gloria is given in retrograde motion. The Credo and *Et incarnatus* have the same c.f. layout as the

Gloria and *Qui tollis* with the exception that the tenor states the tune on
E rather than on D. The c.f. of the Credo (or Gloria) is repeated at
Et in Spiritum, and once again at *Confiteor* in reduced values. (Breve
becomes semibreve.) In the Sanctus the tenor gives the A and B sections
of the tune on F. The rhythmic layout is the same as in the Gloria.
The complete tune is given in the *Osanna* in reduced values as it was in
the *Confiteor.* In *Confiteor* and *Osanna* the c.f. loses the character of a
scaffolding because the tenor notes move as rapidly as those of the other
voices. The c.f. is stated on G in the first Agnus. As in the Sanctus, only
the first two sections of the tune are given. In the third Agnus it appears
on A, the highest of the transpositions, and is given to the highest voice,
the superius. The whole tune is given in doubled values and without rests,
according to the canonic instruction *clama ne cesses.* The tenor entries
are preceded by anticipatory statements of the melody in various voices,
usually in imitation.

From the point of view of c.f. layout this is a rationally constructed
Mass, the borrowed voice being handled in ways made familiar in the works
of Obrecht. The contrapuntal voices are motivically organized against the
tenor, also in the manner of Obrecht rather than of Ockeghem. Sections
which are free of c.f. have their own type of organization. The trio, *Pleni
sunt caeli,* makes considerable use of initial imitation. The three duos
making up the *Benedictus* as well as the trio, Agnus II, are mensuration
canons. Even in these comparatively early Masses, Josquin shows a greater
interest in initial imitation as a means of organizing the free sections
than Obrecht ever does, and in the mensuration canons an immeasurably
greater ability to handle difficult contrapuntal problems.

These features simply indicate a technical advance over Obrecht, but
there are others which are at variance with his practices. One of the
most striking of these is a rather free-and-easy attitude toward modal consistency. Without such an attitude it is doubtful if the idea of transposing the c.f. to every degree of the hexachord would even have been entertained by Josquin, as it runs directly counter to the general practice of
making a Mass a tonal unit. Despite the c.f. layout, Josquin does regard
tonal unity; all five movements are made to end on D, and the important
inner cadences at the ends of sections are made on D and A (with the
exception of the *Christe,* which ends on E). The whole Mass is so harmonized as to have a minor color, yet three statements of the c.f. are in
major modes (those on C, F, and G). Furthermore, in several of the
movements the c.f. must be dropped before the end in order to make the
final cadence on D. This is done, quite in the manner of Ockeghem, even
in the Gloria where the c.f. is in D and it would have been natural to use
it in the final cadence. The only movement where the c.f. continues to
the final chord is the third Agnus. As it is stated on A, it makes the fifth

above the bass. (It also forms part of one interior cadence, since, at the end of the Sanctus, the tonic of the c.f., F, is used as the minor third above the bass! Even in this cadence the influence of Ockeghem can be seen: the bass drops out a few measures before the end and only comes in again for the final chord.)

The contrast in modes becomes acute in the case of the anticipatory statements. These are made to agree with the tonal scheme of the Mass as a whole; that is, they are on D, A, and, rarely, E. Most unusual relationships to the tenor entries result from this, for the anticipatory quotations of the c.f. are often a second or third removed from the tenor in pitch. The second Kyrie illustrates this sufficiently well (ex. 109). The bass states the c.f. on A while the tenor enters with it on c (m. 67). Such a colorful relation would have been possible for Ockeghem, as is shown by the canon *"pausans ascendit per unum tonum"* of the *Christe* of the *Missa Prolationum*, or by the repetitions of phrases a whole tone apart in the *Missa Fors seulement*. (See ex. 62, p. 164, above.) Obrecht, however, holds to the tonally consistent relations of the unison, fifth and fourth. Another procedure characteristic of Ockeghem is the formation of cadences in which it is impossible to introduce a leading tone (ex. 109, m. 69-70, superius).

This Kyrie gives some indication of traits which are found throughout Josquin's work and which may be considered as a commingling of the rational and nonrational tendencies of his predecessors. He constantly makes use of motives for the purpose of linear organization and often repeats them literally (ex. 109, m. 74-76, superius and bass; m. 67-69, superius). However, he applies them with a brilliant nonchalance, shifting them in relation to the underlying beat, or changing the melodic and rhythmic patterns to a greater or less degree. A hint of this is given by the alto voice (ex. 109, m. 74-76), and there will be occasion to point out much more vivid instances as other works are taken up. In any case, this shows that an element of fantasy, of the unexpected, is apt to be present when he is dealing with a repetitive type of organization. Compared to these imaginative variants, the more literal motivic repetitions of Obrecht seem rather stodgy. Each man gains a special kind of effect. Obrecht, by the mere insistence on a given idea, attains a massive vigor; Josquin, though equally vigorous, is never heavy-footed. In these works he is the virtuoso who moves smoothly from one scintillating effect to another.

The *Missa L'homme armé sexti toni* is totally unlike its companion in c.f. layout.[5] While the one tends toward the regulated methods of Obrecht, the other displays all the fancifulness of Ockeghem. The melody is given rich ornamentation which is changed at every statement. The notes are sometimes excessively long, sometimes of about the same value

EXAMPLE 109. Josquin, *Missa L'homme armé super voces musicales*—Kyrie II (*Missen*, I, 3).

as those of the other parts. The c.f. is given to various voices. The tenor has it in the two Kyries, Gloria, Credo and Agnus I; the bass in the *Christe* and *Qui tollis*; the superius repeats the B section of the melody four times in the *Et resurrexit* as an isorhythmic scaffolding; the c.f. migrates between tenor, superius, and bass at *Et unam sanctam*.[6] In the Sanctus the tenor and alto carry the A section as a highly elaborated melody in canon in conjunction with a statement of the same section by the bass. In the *Osanna* the A section and parts of the B are given in strict canon between tenor and bass. In the third Agnus the A and B sections, stated in pedal notes, are combined as a double scaffolding. The tenor states the B section in normal motion while the bass gives the A section in retrograde. There is a rest of one measure exactly in the middle of the movement (m. 115), after which the entire scaffolding is restated in retrograde motion. This means that the B section in the tenor is actually given in retrograde while the A section in the bass is given in *retrograde of the retrograde*, which is, of course, normal motion.

Along with all this variety—the mixture of ornamented and scaffolding statements, canons and c.f. combinations, complete and partial statements of the c.f., change of voices between movements and migration within a movement—there is the usual rational organization of the other voices. Anticipatory statements are usually imitative and concern more than one voice; imitations are not limited to these preliminary passages, but also occur during the course of the main statement of the c.f. The contrapuntal voices are also organized by motives not derived from the c.f., which is customary, and in certain places these same motives are used to make up part of the ornamentation of the c.f., linking it tightly to the counterpoints, which is not so common. (See ex. 110a.) In addition to this, Agnus III is one of the most ambitious and complex canonic structures attempted in this period. The number of voices is increased from four to six and, over the double scaffolding described above, Josquin writes two two-voice canons at the minima! The two canons are independent, although they use similar material. At the end of the movement they are treated in the manner of a stretto; the melody lines are so similar and the statements are made so close together that the effect is of a canon in four voices, each voice imitating at the minima. (The end of the Agnus is quoted in ex. 110b.) This Mass, so full of freedoms, ends climatically with the most strictly bound type of rational writing.

In the course of the *Missa Fortuna desperata*[7] each of the four voices is used as the carrier of the c.f., and every one of the three voices of the chanson is made to serve as c.f. at one time or another. As has been pointed out in connection with some of the Masses of Obrecht, this weakens the cyclic unity of the work, by tending to eliminate repetitions which would bind the whole together. The voices of this chanson are

EXAMPLE 110. Josquin, *Missa L'homme armé sexti toni*—(a) Credo, (b) Agnus III (*Missen*, I, 122, 130).

related to each other primarily as counterpoints. As there is very little duplication of the material of one part in another, there cannot be sufficient repetition of ideas to provide a unity that can be immediately apprehended by the ear when the chanson is taken over voice by voice into the Mass.

The tenor of the chanson is given by the tenor of the Mass in the first two big divisions, the Kyrie and Gloria. It is quoted literally in the *Christe* and *Qui tollis* since they are in duple meter like the original. In the two Kyries and the Gloria the quotation is also literal, with the exception that the chanson tenor is interpreted in triple meter. The entire melody is given once in the Kyrie–*Christe*–Kyrie, once in the Gloria and twice in the *Qui tollis*—the second time in halved values. In the Credo the superius of the chanson is given to the superius of the Mass. The first statement is in doubled values, the second *(Et incarnatus)* in unit values, the third *(Et in Spiritum)* in unit values and triple meter, and the final one *(Confiteor)* in halved values. In the Sanctus the bass is used as c.f., but is stated by the alto voice at a pitch a fifth higher than the original. It is given once in this section and once again in the Osanna, in halved values. The *Pleni sunt caeli* and *Benedictus* are free trios, organized by means of head imitation. The first Agnus not only has a scaffolding c.f. consisting entirely of pedal notes, it is also schematically manipulated. The bass states the superius of the chanson in inversion and quadruply augmented. In the final Agnus the bass again has the c.f., but this time it gives the tenor of the chanson an octave below original pitch and in unit values.

As usual, the other voices are organized for the most part by means of motives which are not derived from the c.f. In the first Agnus these motives are used a great deal in imitation, although not to the extent that there is a point at the beginning of every phrase. The contrapuntal voices make use of c.f. material as well, sometimes treating it very freely. For instance, the bass develops on the first four measures of the chanson in measures 1-32 of the Credo. The fragment is not repeated literally, as it would have been by Obrecht, but is expanded in the most unrestrained manner (ex. 111). The treatment is free, even for Josquin, but just for this reason it may be taken as another example of the mixture of traits in his early work. The devices of the rationalists are constantly used but in a flexible, imaginative manner which lends them some of the character of the unhampered, freely flowing lines of Ockeghem.

On the other hand, there is a tendency to quote the entire material of the chanson in a block, a procedure which is exactly that used in the

EXAMPLE 111. Josquin, *Missa Fortuna desperata*—Credo (*Missen*, I, 88, chanson, *ibid.*, p. 105).

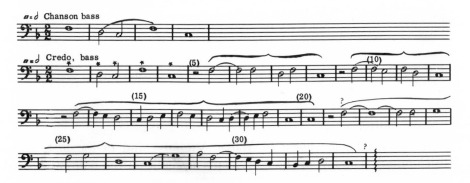

"*Missa parodia.*" (See ex. 112, superius, alto, and bass, m. 1-5 of the Kyrie.) Similar beginnings are found in the Gloria and Credo, and in the *Qui tollis* (m. 74-81) both the bass and tenor of measures 8-15 of the chanson are quoted literally. (Quotations of a similar type are also found in the *Missa Malheur me bat*, p. 350, below.)

EXAMPLE 112. Josquin, *Missa Fortuna desperata*—Kyrie I (*Missen*, I, 81; chanson, *ibid.*, p. 105).

The *Missa Gaudeamus*[8] is based on the Introit *Gaudeamus omnes in Domino*, a chant used in several services, among them the Assumption of Mary. (It no longer appears in this service in the 1952 printing of the *LU*.) As in the other Masses, the c.f. is given varied uses. It is stated by the tenor in the Kyrie, Gloria, and Credo, the superius in the Sanctus, and the alto in the *Osanna*. The tenor takes it in the first Agnus, and in the third it migrates to all voices.

The Introit is given entire only in the Gloria and Credo. It is partially quoted in the Kyrie (down to *Mariae Virginis*) and in the first Agnus (to *Domino*). The rest of the movements are built on the notes associated with *Gaudeamus*, the first word of the chant. In every case this motive is treated as an *ostinato* which may be either strict or free. In the third Agnus it is stated eighteen times by the various voices at various pitch levels; an effect of stretto is attained by a general increase of the speed of the statements. In the *Osanna* the alto gives four statements on the pitches c, g, c, g, and in the Sanctus the superius gives the motive three times as a strict *ostinato* scaffolding. The first section of the Gloria is also devoted to this portion of the c.f., the tenor stating it eleven times. It is not until the *Qui tollis* that the tenor proceeds into the second phrase, but then it quotes the introit to the end.

As in *L'homme armé sexti toni* the amount of ornamentation given the c.f. varies a great deal. For instance, at *Et in spiritum* the tenor presents the c.f. in pedal notes (ex. 113, m. 163 ff.). This sedate method of statement proceeds for some time, when, quite without warning, it is interrupted by an outburst of rather rapid ornamentation (m. 197-201, tenor). The ornamental passage runs its brief course and the tenor at once resumes its slow notes as though nothing had occurred to interrupt them. These few measures illustrate well the utterly unpredictable nature of much of the detail in the Mass. The notes f'-e' (tenor, m. 194-196) do not stand out in the tenor line any more than those which precede or follow, yet Josquin drops the method of statement in pedal notes and proceeds to elaborate on these two tones, repeating them six times over in two two-measure groups. Why he singles out just these notes for development it is impossible for me to say. This little passage evidently was introduced as an interesting detail, valued in and for itself, not

EXAMPLE 113. Josquin, *Missa Gaudeamus—Et in spiritum* (*Missen*, I, 69; *ibid.*, p. v).

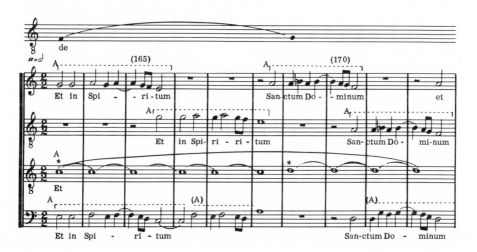

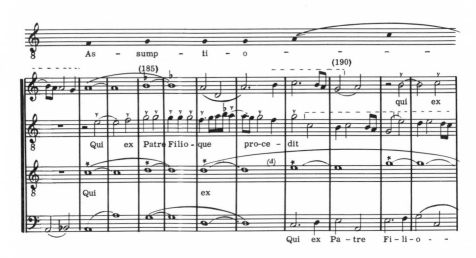

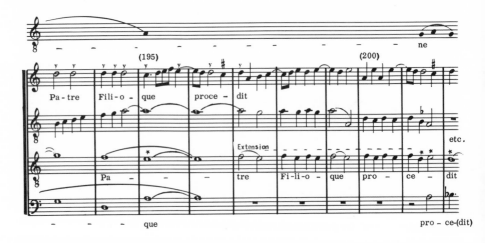

because it has any continuing influence upon the course of the movement. It need hardly be mentioned that this ornamentation, which is developmental in nature, is of a type entirely different from the melodic elaborations of Dufay and Ockeghem. (Ex. 111, above, is another instance of the development of ornamental extensions out of previously stated material.)

Organization of the other voices is of the types seen in the other Masses, although it is more intensive. The first Kyrie (ex. 114) starts with initial imitations on the material of the first three measures of the tenor entry (the *Gaudeamus* motive), and this motive is then taken by the bass as an *ostinato*. Tenor and bass are thus strictly controlled while the two upper parts play freely above them in a most intricate fashion (ex. 114, m. 5 ff., superius and alto). The contrapuntal voices of example 113 are organized by repeated figures in measures 163-172 (marked by the letter A in superius, alto, and bass). Although these also are derived from the c.f., the fact is not so obvious as it is in the bass *ostinato* of the Kyrie. The tenor moves up and down on the major second c'-d'-c'-d'-c' (m. 163-178), and the repeated figure in the other voices shows a similar outline although in greatly reduced note values and in somewhat ornamented form. Other repeated figures are freely composed (ex. 113, m. 173-182, soprano, alto, and bass; the figures are marked by the letter B). As with Obrecht, the contrapuntal voices are given a motivic organization of their own, but there is a noticeable growth away from the position that the counterpoints are to be freely composed and organized on their own terms against the c.f. There is a tendency for the c.f. to penetrate all voices, a tendency which takes the form, in part, of motivic derivation. This derivation, however, cannot always be heard (witness the figure A of ex. 113); the intent to draw the counterpoints from the c.f. is evident but the effect is not other than it would be if the motives were freely composed. One can regard this Mass as a halfway station between the standpoint of Obrecht in works such as *Caput* or the Agnus of the *Missa Pfauenschwanz* (ex. 104) and that of Josquin in late Masses such as *De Beata Virgine* or *Pange lingua*. In *Gaudeamus*, freely composed and derived elements are so intermingled in the counterpoints that at times they can hardly be distinguished; the two principles— derivation and free composition—are in nearly complete balance.

The marked effort to concentrate and organize material causes Josquin to use a great deal of imitation, but he does not apply it—or any other one type of organization—for long in any given way. For instance, he will not begin more than a few phrases in succession with points of imitation. The free section, *Pleni sunt caeli*, may be taken as an illustration. The first phrases begin with points, but they are soon given up in favor of sequential motivic statements which are employed in a forceful drive to the cadence. The keynote of the organization is still variety. The advances in this Mass are clear, but they are all predicated on the viewpoints of the late fifteenth century, upon the fondness of that age for lively movement and for multitudinous, brilliant, and intricate detail. Indeed, if any one feature of the work were to be singled out as showing especially marked advancement it should be the cadential drives. The one at the end of the Credo takes up almost the entire final section (*Et unam sanctam*) and in extent and brilliance surpasses any others yet seen. In this feature there is clear indication of steady development, yet it is an aspect of style which will be extinct within a generation.

EXAMPLE 114. Josquin, *Missa Gaudeamus*—Kyrie I (*Missen*, I, 57; *ibid.*, p. v).

Josquin, even more than other composers, is inclined to quote fragments of the Gregorian Credo in the Credo of his Masses. In the one
under consideration he goes so far as to drop the c.f. *Gaudeamus* altogether in the *Et incarnatus* and use the Credo melody instead. It is not
stated continuously by a single voice; it migrates and is occasionally
interrupted by free passages. It also crops up at other points in the
movement where it is quoted in conjunction with the introit melody.
(For instances of this see ex. 113, alto voice, m. 183-189; superius, m.
191-197. The notes of the Credo melody are marked by the letter y.)
  Attention has been called to the direct movement of the contrapuntal
lines in many of the works of Obrecht (chap. ix, n. 60). Comparatively
speaking, the lines of Josquin wind about more elaborately and are much

less firmly directed toward set goals. The soprano and alto voices of example 114 are characteristic illustrations of this; the alto of example 115a is similarly florid. (Another instance is found in ex. 117, alto, m. 18 onward.) Both men are apt to write parts which are very complex rhythmically, and in this they simply reflect the taste of the time. There is, however, a characteristic difference in the complexity also, which is easier to hear than to analyze. Obrecht's lines are apt to show a whimsical complexity of pattern which may be uncouth and even unclear. Josquin's patterns are organized and rationalized by skillfully varied repetitions, and, further, every statement is clearly audible, even though each may be different in some way. The effect of complexity comes in large part, also, from the overlap of patterns in more than one voice. The individual parts are not so perversely complex as they sometimes are in Obrecht; they are more grateful to perform, and the over-all effect is both more brilliant and more elegant. Comparisons such as these should not be too strictly applied, for there is much variety in the writing of both men; but in general Obrecht lacks the graceful ease we observe in these Masses of Josquin. Measures 9-10 of the alto of example 114 provide an instance of the type of rhythmic complexity the performer is called upon to deal with in Josquin. The underlying triple meter is shattered and any feeling of the semibreve as a unit of beat (the half note in the example) tends to be obliterated by the shifting series of rhythmic groups. In lines of this type a trend which began with the successors of Dufay comes into the final state of development. This stylistic feature, too, will disappear within a generation.

In the *Missa La sol fa re mi*[9] Josquin expands the normal scope of motivic usage by concentrating on one motive alone, which he retains not merely for a single more or less extensive passage but for the duration of the entire work. In the most comprehensive sense, this Mass belongs with those other contemporary works which spring from a single device or procedure and reveal the interest of composers in planning, and their capacity for realizing, an all-embracing organization of the several parts of a Mass. Ockeghem had used a single device, mensuration canon, as the basis of the *Missa Prolationem*, and Obrecht bases the *Missa Sub tuum praesidium* in part on the idea of c.f. combination. Such works differ widely, and the method of organization, as often as not, is on a level of procedural consistency which can be appreciated intellectually but hardly aurally, yet in each case a device of interest at that period is applied in a broad way to an entire Mass.

The germ of Josquin's Mass is a series of five notes[10] which is cast into motives of varying rhythmic design. Strictly speaking, the work is not a c.f. Mass at all, since no extensive guiding melody is used as a basis upon which to write the counterpoints; rather, the basis is motivic treatment in all its manifestations—sequence, *ostinato*, imitation, and probably most important of all, variation. An appropriate descriptive term for the work would be "motivic Mass."

EXAMPLE 115. Josquin, *Missa La sol fa re mi*—(a) Kyrie I, (b) Kyrie II (*Missen*, I, pp. 35, 36).

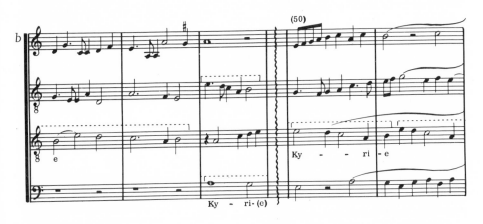

The five-note figure appears in almost every measure in one voice or another, causing a concentration of material and a degree of penetration of the entire contrapuntal fabric which surpasses anything seen in the *Missa Gaudeamus*. However, even though the motive is distributed liberally through all the parts, it is given most often to the tenor, which in many places states and restates it in an uninterrupted stream, so that it forces its way to a position of structural importance simply by insistence. It is evidence of the power of custom in a work as original in structure as this, in which there is no true c.f. and in which the crucial problem is motivic treatment, that the composer should nevertheless make a c.f. of a sort for himself in the traditional structural voice.

Motivic concentration is achieved in some movements by migration. The motive migrates to all voices in the first Kyrie (ex. 115a) and moves between the soprano, tenor, and bass in the *Benedictus*. It is even more concentrated in the *Christe*, being treated in imitation in all voices. However, in the second Kyrie, the entire Gloria and Credo, the Sanctus and two *Osannas*, and the first Agnus, it appears chiefly in the tenor. This voice is wholly composed of repetitions of the motive. As mentioned above, merely by dint of repetition the tenor attains the position of the most important voice and gives the impression of being a c.f. whether it rightfully is one or not. The motive makes up the material of all voices in the second Agnus, which is a duo, and in the *Pleni sunt caeli*, which is a series of alternating duos. (This is not true of the final measures of the *Pleni*, where all four voices join together, but even at this point the motive continues in the soprano and tenor.) In addition, it is used in anticipatory statements in the Sanctus, *Osanna*, and second Kyrie, and it is fitted into the various voices at numerous other points in all movements. (See the beginning of Agnus I for an instance.)

There is some relief from the incessant repetition. Independent motives are used in voices other than the one carrying *la-sol-fa-re-mi* as a c.f., and one short section, *Qui venit in nomine Domini*, is altogether free of it except for the last eight measures, where the five notes reappear in the tenor. The five-note motive itself is stated in varied ways, too. It moves from one hexachord to another and is presented in numberless rhythmic variations. (See ex. 115b.) In the *Pleni sunt caeli* new melodic outlines are achieved by mutation at some point within the motive. (See ex. 116. The motives which start in the *hexachordum naturale* change to the *hexachordum durum*, and vice versa. In the superius, m. 37, a single note is interpreted in both hexachords. Points of mutation are marked by *x*'s in the example.)

The musical problem in this Mass is an uncommon one for the period, as it arises from too little variety in the material. The work demands all the experience in handling motives which had been accumulated in this period, as well as Josquin's special flair for brilliant, interesting, yet consequential variation, in order that the innumerable repetitions not become intolerably dull. One will hardly find a work of comparable length based upon such a short fragment anywhere else in musical literature. In its own way, this work is as much of a breakneck feat as any of the canonic combinations attempted by the Netherlanders.

EXAMPLE 116. Josquin, *Missa La sol fa re mi—Pleni sunt caeli* (*Missen*, I, 50).

Considerable portions of the Gregorian Credo I are also quoted in the Credo of this Mass; in addition, portions of the Gloria of Mass XV are used in the Gloria. (Ex. 117. The notes of the Gloria melody are marked by y's in the superius, alto, and bass.)

The general comments on the *Missa Gaudeamus* apply to this group of Masses as a whole. Even if it were not known that they were published in 1502, analysis would show that they belong entirely to the late fifteenth century. They are more striking than the Masses of Obrecht

EXAMPLE 117. Josquin, *Missa La sol fa re mi—Gloria* (*Missen*, I, 37; *LU*, p. 57).

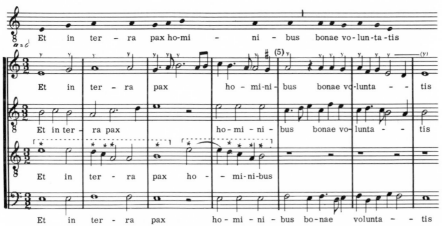

and, in some respects, more advanced. The attitudes are, however, similar to his. The movements are still constructed over a c.f. usually presented continuously in a single voice. The other voices may be free counterpoints, but they are apt to be concerned with c.f. material or, more frequently, with the working out of independent motivic ideas.

Advancement is found in just those devices which had begun to occupy the attention of musicians around 1460 to 1470. The various types of canon are more complex and more skillfully handled; ostinatos, sequences, and motivic devices of all sorts take up a larger part of the works; cadential drives become longer and more brilliant. The actual amount of organization increases, but its manner does not change essentially. For instance, imitation is used to an increasing extent, but for essentially the same purpose that it was used by Dufay—as an alternate form of organization when the c.f. voice is silent. It is commonly found in the anticipatory sections which precede the entry of the c.f. voice, much less frequently in the body of the movement. Initial imitation appears more often and is used to a greater extent in the free sections, such as the *Benedictus* and *Pleni sunt caeli*; but even in these it is apt to be dropped after two or three phrases in favor of some sort of motivic treatment. There is no doubt that Josquin makes more use of initial imitation in these Masses than Obrecht does in his, but if we look for signs that it is moving into the position of the primary means of organization the results of our searching will be negative or, at best, ambiguous. The situation is different in the motets and will be considered later (p. 339). Imitation absolutely does not hold the position in the organization of this music that it does later in the sixteenth century, nor is it the intention of the composer that it should. It is only one of many devices that he has at his disposal, and he shows as yet no inclination to give up a

fascinating variety of means in favor of a single procedure and the comparatively uneventful consistency in organization that he would gain by it.
Evidently, in these works Josquin shares the stylistic attitudes of Obrecht
and other contemporaries and predecessors. For all the differences in
detail, his and their works spring from an ideal of artistic expression which
is essentially the same. Furthermore, Masses similar in style continue to
appear in later publications of Josquin's works. Some surpass those of the
edition of 1502 in grandeur and breadth of conception, indicating that
they followed them in date of composition and must have been written
when he was well past fifty years of age.

On the whole, Josquin's works do not indicate a simple evolutionary
advance in which an earlier style is gradually supplanted by a later. Rather,
the situation is complicated by the category of the work. During the years
of his full maturity he cultivated the nascent style of the sixteenth century in the motets, while at the same time bringing the style of the
fifteenth to a glorious culmination in the Masses. He could simultaneously
cultivate two such different manners of writing because each had value
for him. As has often been pointed out, he deemed the elaborate, decorative style appropriate for impersonal Mass texts, but felt that the simple
style appropriate for motet texts called for a more intimate expression.[11]
In his Masses, then, the mere presence of older stylistic traits, or structural
means, is not evidence of early date of composition. In fact, Josquin
abandoned the old style only in very late Masses, such as *De Beata Virgine*
or *Pange lingua*.

The *Missa Hercules Dux Ferrariae* is contained in Petrucci's second book
of Masses of Josquin, printed in 1505.[12] The work is an outstanding example of the type of writing in which two opposed elements are placed in
conjunction with one another. The scaffolding—one of the best-known
examples of contrived c.f.—is sharply differentiated from the other voices,
which are independently organized among themselves. (On the whole, the
material of the scaffolding does not penetrate to the other parts, although
it possibly does so at the beginning of the Gloria and appears very clearly
in the bass of the *Osanna*.) The means by which the c.f. itself is formed,[13]
the manner in which it is laid out, and the degree of organization of the
other voices are all expressions of extreme rationalism.

The c.f. is given out primarily by the tenor and according to a fixed
plan. In its entirety, it consists of a threefold statement of a basic eight-
note phrase rising climactically in stages—the first statement being given
on d, the second on a, and the third on d'. As each note of the subject
is usually given the value of a breve, the single phrases are normally eight
measures long. Each of these is preceded by eight measures of rest, so
that the entire statement is unusually symmetrical. Repetitions are usually

isorhythmic, although some variations on the basic pattern are found; these variations are, however, achieved by schematic means.

The details of the layout are as follows. Two statements according to the plan outlined above are found in the second movement of the Mass (i.e., one in the Gloria and one in the *Qui tollis*). The same layout is used for the Credo and *Et incarnatus*. At *Et in Spiritum* the basic threefold statement is repeated, but in retrograde motion; it is fol-

EXAMPLE 118. Josquin, *Missa Hercules Dux Ferrariae*—Kyrie II (*Missen*, II, 20).

lowed by another statement in forward motion, but in halved values and without rests. In the *Osanna* the c.f. is given first as it was in the Gloria, but with halved values, and then in quadruple diminution and without rests. The *Benedictus* also contains a complete statement, as it consists of three duos each based on a single one of the three tenor phrases. The first Agnus is based on a statement in normal values but in retrograde motion. All of the statements so far mentioned are made by the tenor alone. The same tenor scaffolding—consisting of three statements divided by rests and on the pitches d-a-d'—is used in the remaining movements (Kyrie, Sanctus, and Agnus III), but it is amplified by alternating statements in other voices. A complete statement is divided between the Kyrie–*Christe*–Kyrie, but in the first Kyrie the superius also makes a statement, on d', during the eight-measure rest which precedes the tenor entry. In the two remaining sections of the movement the c.f. is carried by the tenor only, as usual. (See ex. 118, Kyrie II.) The Sanctus is laid out on the same plan as the first Kyrie, except that alto and tenor give the c.f. (ex. 119). This plan is carried out fully in the third Agnus, where the superius anticipates all three phrases of the tenor on the pitches d', a', and d''. (The two sections free of c.f. are both strict canons; *Pleni sunt caeli* is for two voices, Agnus II is for three.) On the whole, this is the most rigid kind of scaffolding and shows a close kinship to that of the motet *In hydraulis* by Busnois. (Busnois's motet is also based upon a contrived c.f., the elements of which, although much simpler than those of the *Missa Hercules*, are likewise stated on the pitches d, a and d'. See p. 217, above.)

In the Kyrie and Sanctus the organization of the voices other than the c.f. is carried out to the greatest possible extent, as they are composed almost entirely of repeated motives. (See exs. 118 and 119.) In both, a

EXAMPLE 119. Josquin, *Missa Hercules Dux Ferrariae*—Sanctus (*Missen*, II, 30).

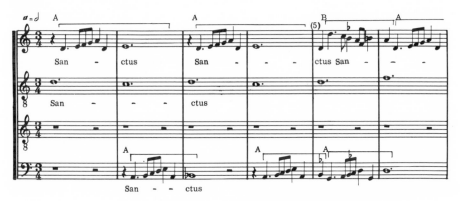

leading idea sounds uninterruptedly throughout (marked A in each of the examples). In example 118 it appears in only one part at a time, starting in the superius and shifting to the bass at measure 42, drawing an unbroken line from beginning to end of the section and from the highest to the lowest register. In example 119 it makes up the entire bass line and is further concentrated by alternating statements in the soprano. It appears on a limited number of pitches, not the notes of the descending scale, so that the motives associated with it are not organized sequentially as in the Kyrie. The effect is rather that of the insistent repetition of an *ostinato*.

The lines in these movements are comparatively simple and direct, quite unlike the irregular, florid ones found in the Masses of the edition of 1502. The motives are not subjected to infinite variation, but are combined in their original compact form into lines which move purposefully and economically to their goals. The solid harmonies and emphatic cadences combine to lend the movements something of the massiveness of Obrecht.[14]

As has been pointed out many times before, the composers of the late fifteenth century strove for brilliant, emphatic detail with which forcefully to attract the ear; strikingly syncopated patterns and cross rhythms between voices were the means chiefly relied upon. Josquin employs them as a matter of course, but in the Sanctus he finds another means to supplement the purely rhythmic ones. The crowded motivic statements are emphasized in the usual way by the impact of the offbeat beginnings, but this effect is outdone by the surprise endings. The e' in the superius (ex. 119, m. 2, 4, 7) is answered by a B♭ in the bass (m. 3, 5, 8), producing a startling tonal jar. Colorful tonal contrasts have been employed in other works as one of a variety of details, all of which go to make up an eventful and interesting composition (e.g., the *Missa L'homme armé super voces musicales*); in some cases they betray an excessive fond-

EXAMPLE 120. Josquin, *Missa Ave Maris stella*—Credo (*Missen*, II, 7; *LU*, p. 1259).

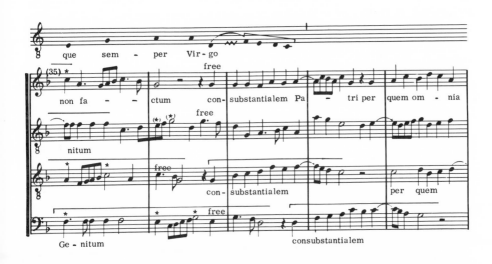

ness for startling effect (see p. 351, below). In this case, however, they do not appear as isolated and surprising events, but are used purposefully, in conjunction with all the other elements, to achieve a consistent and far-reaching effect. The tonal shock of the tritone by cross relation is essential to the character of the whole passage, and in combination with the rhythmic patterns produces a tension which makes the movement one of the most telling of its kind. Severe and compact, this work contrasts with the Masses of 1502, which are characterized above all by dispersal of means, by a dazzling succession of brilliant individual incidents.

The treatment of the c.f. in the *Missa Ave maris stella*[15] is more in accord with that found in the Masses of the edition of 1502. The statements include all the usual freedoms: repetition of phrases, free interpolations (see ex. 120, m. 36 ff.), great variety in the amount of ornamentation, etc. The tenor is the chief carrier of the c.f., although it is given substantial assistance by the other voices. Indeed, at one point in the Credo it does not have anything at all to do with one phrase, which is presented only in the alto and superius (ex. 120, m. 30-33).

The entire hymn melody is given by the tenor in the Kyrie. It is divided among the three sections, the final phrase being repeated three times in Kyrie II. It is given by the same voice in the Gloria and the last phrase is again repeated. In the *Qui tollis* the first phrase is given twice. It is followed by a free section, measures 79-84, and from measure 89 the remainder of the tune is quoted, although with considerable ornamentation. The treatment is much the same in the Credo. The entire melody is quoted but there are some free passages (see m. 24-30; also, in ex. 120, m. 36 ff.). As mentioned above, a section of the c.f. does not appear in the tenor at all, but only in the superius and alto (ex. 120, m. 30-33). In the next section of the Credo the tenor regains its position as the undoubted leader in the presentation of the hymn. Starting at *Et incarnatus* it presents the c.f. once straight through; another complete presentation begins at measure 78 *(Et resurrexit)*; a partial statement, including only the first two phrases, starts at measure 114 *(Qui cum Patre)*; after a short free passage (m. 124-130) a final statement of the complete melody is made, starting at measure 131 (*Confiteor*). The first two phrases, with a free cadential extension, are heard in the Sanctus. In the *Osanna* the entire melody is gone through again, beginning simply in long note values and ending more floridly. *Pleni sunt caeli* is a free trio; *Benedictus* and *Qui venit* are free duos. The entire melody is presented in canon between tenor and bass in the first Agnus and once again in canon in Agnus III, this time between tenor and superius. The final phrase is very freely stated in both movements. Agnus II is a canonic duo and free of c.f.

In the extent to which the c.f. penetrates the parts, this Mass surpasses any of the others examined except *La sol fa re mi*. The diffusion of the

EXAMPLE 121. Josquin, *Missa Ave Maris stella*—Gloria (*Missen*, II, 3; *LU*, p. 1259).

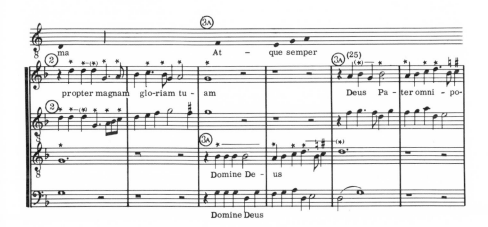

hymn material is not restricted to imitative entries at the beginnings of sections or to occasional short passages, but is carried out through large portions of a movement. Example 121, which includes nearly the entire first section of the Gloria, shows that the division of the material among the voices is achieved in a variety of ways. The alto and superius enter with a canon on c.f. material, but they do not use the hymn melody for long. (See ex. 121, m. 4 ff. The remainder of the canon, which is freely composed, has been omitted.) Tenor and bass also enter with a point of imitation, although it is dropped immediately in favor of freely imitative duplication of the hymn material. (Ex. 121, m. 13 ff.) Portions of the c.f. are then repeated by means of a series of alternating duos, some of which are freely imitative (m. 19 ff.). Despite the fact that all the voices share in the c.f., the tenor makes the most complete statement up to this point and at measure 27 it asserts itself sufficiently to carry a short part entirely alone. The bass and alto are momentarily organized by means of a freely repeated idea (m. 23-25, 25-27, and 27-29) which is derived, in part at least, from c.f. material (m. 18-19, 21-22). The movement ends with an imitative stretto in which all voices share in the last phrase of the hymn. (See m. 31 ff. The very last note of the hymn is reserved until the final cadential progression, m. 37-39.) This is truly a score of the late fifteenth century. It is highly organized, but organized in divers ways; imitation is used a great deal, but not in any methodical or systematic fashion. Variety is the keynote of the whole.

The voice lines are rhythmically active and of a highly florid character. They do not approach their goals directly, but postpone them as much as possible, occupying themselves with a great variety of motion. This is sometimes widely diffused, sometimes confined to a very restricted ambit. The superius of example 121 (m. 27 ff.) is a characteristic instance.

If anything, this work represents an advancement on tendencies found in the *Missa Gaudeamus*. It differs in almost every respect from *Hercules Dux Ferrariae*. In the *Missa Ave maris stella* the c.f. is amalgamated with the added voices; in *Hercules Dux Ferrariae* it stands in pronounced opposition to them. In the latter work all the statements are carried out according to set plan; in the former any procedure that suits the composer at the moment is adopted. One represents the extreme of control, the other the extreme of flexibility. The voice lines of *Hercules* tend to be stripped of unessential melodic movement and, in the place of the lively and varied rhythmic activity of *Ave maris stella*, they show purposeful and unremitting movement toward given destinations. Both Masses are mature examples of Josquin's work, but one gives clear indications of growing from the fanciful tendencies of the preceding generation, the other from the rationally regulated ones. One stands close to the tradition of Ockeghem, the other to the tradition of Busnois and Obrecht.

Imitation is used more than any of the other means of organization in *Ave maris stella*, although, as has been remarked, in a manner typical of the late fifteenth century. Josquin had, however, already written important sacred works in which this resource is employed in an orderly, consistent manner which suggests the method of the succeeding generation. The motet *Ave Maria . . . Virgo serena* (ex. 122) was published in the same year as the first book of Masses. (Petrucci, *Motetti A numero trentatre*. [Venice, 1502].) In the first four phrases each voice is treated in imitation; each duly enters with an initial statement of the melodic figure chosen for the particular phrase of text.[16]

It is obvious that imitation itself is the structural basis of this passage, but it is also true that the mere presence of imitation is not remarkable. The noteworthy facts are (1) that imitation is used alone (i.e., not intermingled with other devices as in the Gloria of *Ave maris stella*, ex. 121), and (2) that it is used methodically—a point of imitation is written for each phrase of text and all voices partake in each point, none being allowed a free line.

The consistent use of initial imitation is not the only way in which the work differs from the Masses. The flow of the music is much gentler. To be sure, the motet is in duple meter, which generally presents fewer rhythmic complexities than triple, but there is a difference in quality which cannot be entirely attributed to this. The lines are of a totally different character in this work—the sharply articulated patterns and the unpredictable floridities of the lines of the Masses are here replaced by melodies which move temperately, even in the melismatic spots. For example, compare measures 18-30 of example 122 with measures 25-31 of example 121, or with any of the excerpts given above from the Masses of the editions of 1502 or 1505.

The use of points of imitation in a regulated manner seems to be related to this type of rhythmic movement, as the two are generally associated. Some works of this type, such as *Rubum quem viderat Moyses* (ex. 134a-b, below), are based on c.f. Others, such as *Gaude Virgo, Mater Christi*, or *Ave, Christe immolate*, apparently are not. When we look about for other works which do not use much imitation but are similar in rhythmic quality, we find them among the declamation motets. Moreover, these works are notable from another point of view. They give clear evidence of a new kind of relationship between text and music in which, for the most part, stressed and unstressed syllables of the words guide the rhythmic shape of the music.

Probably the most obvious method for obtaining good musical declamation in all voices is to write in a chordal style; this insures the movement of all parts in similar rhythmic patterns. Another method of achieving the same end would be to make the melodic as well as the rhythmic patterns the same in all voices—but to allow the voices to follow each other rather than sound simultaneously. A consistent series of points of imitation would lend itself especially well to the realization of such a plan. Such a series not only provides a means of giving a correct rendition of the text in all parts; its has the further advantage of preserving the contrapuntal aspect of the music, which is to a considerable extent eliminated in the chordal style.

The first four phrases of example 122 seem to have been written with these aims in view. One voice after another makes its statement of the opening phrase, cast in a rhetorically acceptable form, and then pauses before going on with the next. (See m. 1-17. The bass concludes the second phrase in measure 17 while the upper voice has already started the third.) This is declamatory writing of a sort, but the voices, rather than producing the text simultaneously in vertical chord masses, overlap one another and produce it diagonally, as it were. The melismatic aspect does not fully come into its own until about measure 23, when four-part writing prevails and the individual lines are freely expanded. As is to be ex-

EXAMPLE 122. Josquin, *Ave Maria . . . Virgo serena* (*Motetten*, I, 1; Moberg, *Die Schwedische Sequenzen*, II, No. 34).

pected with Josquin, the type of setting varies after this first section. There are further points of imitation, but there are also canons, alternating duos, and chordal sections. The rhetorical inspiration of the music is, nevertheless, evident throughout the work. Remnants of the style of the Masses persist in the motets of this type, since *ostinatos* and sequences are not uncommon, but their rhythmic impact is greatly reduced.

Some of these motets are based on c.f., which means that a new element enters into the manner of treating the chant. The Gregorian melodies must now be ornamented and laid out rhythmically with reference to the declamation of the Latin texts. Musical and textual accent do not always coincide, but they do often enough to show that Josquin had the words well in mind when writing the vocal lines. (See ex. 121 and ex. 134.)

It is not necessary to demonstrate impeccable declamation to establish the fact that we have here a well-formulated attitude toward the text, and one that differs substantially from the attitude shown in the Masses considered so far. A comparison of these motets and the Masses serves to emphasize that in the latter the rhythmic patterns are commonly *not* generated by the words. Even where the words happen to fit the notes sufficiently well, as in the Sanctus of *Hercules Dux Ferrariae* (ex. 119), the rhythmic patterns are primarily musical events and are worked out on purely musical grounds. Their exclusively musical character is unmistakable in the more numerous places where, according to our standards, the text cannot be satisfactorily fitted to the notes in any way.

The manner in which the text is fitted to the music in the sources gives further evidence of the different attitudes toward the relation of text and music. In the Masses published in 1502 the text is so sketchily indicated that the editor of the complete edition has had to augment it throughout. Even so, all the problems are not settled. On the other hand, in the motet *Ave Maria*, likewise published in 1502, there is no need for any augmentation of the text and there are no insoluble problems of fitting syllables to notes. (Insoluble, that is, according to later standards.) This contradictory state of affairs cannot be explained on the grounds of carelessness, as both publications are by Petrucci, a printer known for careful editing. Helen Hewitt finds a similar situation with regard to the text underlaying of chansons of this period. "The latest compositions, which are largely syllabic settings of texts, are found for the most part in part-books in which the underlaying of the text is very carefully done. In the very compositions, therefore, where there could be little doubt as to how the text would be applied to the notes—there being usually one syllable for almost every note—the notes are widely spaced and each syllable is carefully set under its proper note. Yet where one feels less certain of how the underlaying should be done—in the more melismatic and florid style of setting texts—the manuscripts help little."[17]

There are many indications that opinions as to the relation of text and music which are now accepted as self-evident did not hold in the fifteenth century. For instance, it is taken for granted nowadays that the composer will make an effort to set texts so that they can be understood, yet the polytextual motet shows that, at least from the thirteenth to the fifteenth centuries, this attitude did not always prevail. It is also tacitly assumed that the composer intends a given syllable of text to be sung with a certain note of music, yet there is much evidence indicating that such an intent cannot be taken for granted on the part of a composer of the fifteenth century. It is true that many of the "problematical" places in the sources are the result of a text that is incomplete or corrupt (and they must be amplified or corrected, if possible). Many of these places are undoubtedly due to carelessness or ignorance on the part of the scribe, but even in the best manuscripts of the fifteenth century there is a generally haphazard, slipshod aspect to the text underlaying—haphazard and slipshod from our point of view, that is. If, as seems quite clear in a large portion of the literature, the musical rhythm is sufficient unto itself and is not an outgrowth of the rhythm of the text, the carelessness of the underlaying probably mirrors an attitude toward the relation of text and music which is entirely different from ours. In order effectively to produce this music, it is not necessary that any given syllable fit any given note; so it seems reasonable to assume that this was not considered an essential requirement by either musicians or scribes.

Much more depends on the clear presentation of the rhythmic groupings, so that they themselves can be heard and that their relations and conflicts with one another are plain to the listener. As they do not spring from the words, and as their effective production need not depend on words, they lose little or nothing if syllables are shifted or are even entirely absent. (This does not include all music of the fifteenth century—e.g., the declamation motets of Dunstable, the syllabic settings of certain Glorias and Credos, chansons, etc.) So far as possible, editorial additions to the text have been omitted from the examples in this book as a matter of policy. In many cases they are anachronistic, since they impose the viewpoint of the sixteenth century on the music of the fifteenth and in every case they tend to prevent a clear view of the situation as it appears in the sources.

If these remarks are accepted as valid, the question arises as to how much latitude was allowed in adapting the syllables to the music at the time the music was written. An answer can be given with regard to the c.f. voice, as it is possible to determine accurately what syllable belongs to what note. This question has been investigated above (pp. 60-61), and it has been shown that the amount of error varies but is usually not great; in most cases the syllables are placed within a note or two of the one they were associated with in the original Gregorian melody. With regard to the manuscript sources of the chansons of *Odhecaton* A, Hewitt finds that "the scribes were fairly careful to write a line of text directly beneath its proper musical phrase."[18] In a modern, practical edition it is not possible to leave the situation as vague as it is in the sources, where evidently the intent is only to fit an entire phrase of text to an entire phrase of music, not to fix the individual syllable in relation to a certain note. As the present-day singer must be given more specific indications, some choice must be made; it seems both justifiable and practical for the editor to make it, just as he indicates the necessary chromatic alterations. It seems, however, that augmentation of the text by repetition of words should be avoided if the purpose is merely to provide the notes with more syllables. This is the attitude taken by most modern editors and it is welcome, if for no other reason than that the melismatic nature of much fifteenth-century music is not disguised in their editions.

Around 1500 it is evident that a reaction was setting in against the older style which had been flourishing for thirty or forty years. A new style, the result of new interests and new goals in artistic expression, begins to re-place it in serious music. The humanistic interest in Latin declamation brings about the selection of certain preëxistent techniques, which are then used to the practical exclusion of others. The relationship of the *frottola* and polyphonic *lauda* to the chordal, declamatory motet has often been mentioned; a similar relationship exists between song-motet and chanson, and the large-scale imitative motet. There is, in fact, an upgrading of styles; traits appear in serious, large-scale motets which had formerly char-acterized secular, or modest sacred works.[19]

"Syntactic imitation," as text-linked imitation has aptly been called,[20] is a technique well suited to the requirements of just declamation,[21] but it is no more than one aspect of the new style. Far into the sixteenth cen-tury the highest value was placed upon simple, restrained, and balanced artistic expression. Aesthetic ideals of this type could not have underlain the effusive and asymmetrical productions of Ockeghem, nor the writing of Obrecht and Busnois which aims at multifold motivic detail and em-phatic rhythmic interplay of the parts. No more could they have under-lain most of the Masses of Josquin. However, the comparatively temper-ate spirit of *Ave Maria . . . Virgo serena* and other motets mentioned above—the suavity of movement, the organic relation of text and music, the renunciation of ever-varying means of organization—is wholly in ac-cord with the new concepts of propriety in artistic expression. These con-cepts have long been recognized through their manifestation in painting of c. 1500 and, with the flood of new editions in the past few years, it has become clear that there are exactly parallel manifestations in music of that time. Much as the two arts differ in medium and technical methods, the identity of the goals of expression is evident. In the one as in the other, the aim is to achieve a noble simplicity of expression and to create structures in which detail is subordinated to over-all design.

The new concepts are valid for Josquin, but not exclusively so. He opens the way to the new musical style, yet he never wholly relinquishes the old. He avoids weighty, massive harmonic effects; even his most ma-ture work retains a delicate linearity as a legacy from his earlier manner. In the composition of motets he does not altogether give up the stratified structure of c.f. with surrounding counterpoints, and in his Masses he writes relatively few movements which are dominated by the new style. Nevertheless, before 1502 he wrote the motet *Ave Maria*, a work in which it is clear that the ideal of *varietas* as expressed in the Masses is being replaced by new ones of *decorum* and *concinnitas* (to borrow terms from painting).

Edward Lowinsky has said that "the sixteenth century saw a process of interpenetration between the harmonious euphony of the South and the contrapuntal dynamism of the North . . . The first great synthesis took

place in the work of Josquin des Prez, recognized by his own, and remembered by many succeeding generations, as the outstanding musical
genius of his age, in whose work can be found the seeds of the bountiful
and diversified harvest of the new ideas, forms and techniques of Cinque-
cento music."[22] The synthesis only becomes complete in the works of the
composer's final period, but it is evident that it was being made at least
as early as the last decade of the Quattrocento.

The first two Masses of the edition of 1505 (i.e., Hercules and Ave
maris stella) appear to be advanced works, probably written around the
turn of the century. The third Mass of the collection, Malheur me bat,
apparently was written somewhat earlier.

The Missa Malheur me bat[23] is similar in at least one respect to many
works of Obrecht. In this Mass, in contrast to the previous ones based on
res facta, the quotations are scrupulously literal and manipulations are
based on a predetermined scheme. Josquin's plan for the treatment of
Malheur me bat does not have the huge scope of Obrecht's in his Mass
on the same chanson, but there is a simple order of procedure which gov-
erns the c.f. layout of the entire work. The tenor of the chanson is quoted
by the tenor of the Mass in Kyrie and Gloria, the superius by the superius
in the Credo, the alto by the alto in the Sanctus, and the tenor again by
the tenor in Agnus I; finally, in Agnus III, superius and tenor are quoted
simultaneously by the corresponding voices of the Mass. In this manner
every voice of the original is given an exposition in the Mass and a certain
effect of climax is attained at the end by the simultaneous quotation of
two voices.[24]

In the Kyrie the tenor quotes the entire material of the chanson tenor,
but it is supplemented by extensive statements in other voices. The first
phrase (to m. 11 of the chanson) is quoted literally by the superius and
then repeated by the tenor. In the Christe the alto picks up the chanson
tenor at measure 12 and carries it to measure 32; this, too, is repeated by
the tenor, which carries the quotation a bit further, to measure 35.
(Neither of these quotations breaks off at a clear phrase ending, and the
structural division of the rondeau at bar 28 is completely ignored.) In
Kyrie II the chanson tenor is picked up again at measure 35 and is quoted
to the end by the tenor of the Mass only. Because of this plan of quotation, the structure of the first two sections is notably symmetrical. In
Kyrie I the duo of superius and alto is repeated exactly by tenor and bass
(the two upper voices continuing as free counterpoints), so the section
falls into two exactly equal halves. The structure is thus even more symmetrical than the Kyrie I of Obrecht's Missa O quam suavis (ex. 97a).
The Christe is also divided into two parts by the repeated quotation, but
there are fewer elements of symmetry; the citations do not cover exactly

the same number of measures and the counterpoint to the first statement is not repeated at the second. Kyrie II, owing to the single quotation, consists of only one section and so lacks the symmetry of repetition.

In the Gloria—after an anticipatory statement of measures 1-11 of the superius of the chanson by the superius, with some imitation in the alto—the tenor takes up the main c.f. statement. Although the pitches and time values are given with the literalness which is characteristic of this Mass, the quotation is not straightforward but doubles back on itself time after time. The tenor quotes the chanson in this manner: following ten measures' rest it gives measures 1-7; after ten more measures of rest it starts over from measure 1 again, but goes as far as measure 10; it then goes back to measure 8 and pushes forward all the way to measure 16, then goes back to measure 11 and forward to measure 25, then presents measures 17 to 31, 26-32, 32-34, and 33-34. It can be seen that the layout is a series of interlocking repetitions, each of which moves forward a bit farther than the preceding one. An especially surprising point occurs at measures 83-84 of the Mass, where measure 32 of the chanson is stated twice in succession. At *Qui tollis* the chanson is picked up at measure 35 and the quotation proceeds in the same manner once more, even down to the statement of a single measure of the chanson twice in succession (m. 53 of the chanson at m. 139-140 of the Mass). Details of the quotation are as follows: measures 35-39, 35-42, 40-48, 43-52, 49-53, 53-58, 54-60, 59-60. At first glance one is reminded of the irregularity of the quotations of Ockeghem—e.g., the doubling back in the Gloria of *Fors seulement* (p. 165, above)—but closer inspection reveals an entirely regular plan behind this outward show of irrationality. The chanson tenor is merely quoted twice through, a customary procedure, but it is done in an exceptional way in two series of short fragments. The first series consists of measures 1-7, 8-16, 17-31, etc.; the second of measures 1-10, 11-25, 26-32, etc. The members of each series are stated in alternation and so give the impression of completely arbitrary twisting and turning in the c.f. statement. This rationally founded irrationality may be taken as symbolic of Josquin's position as inheritor and integrator of all preceding trends. Obrecht also segments *Malheur me bat* (soprano voice, however), but there is a great difference between his highly intellectual, far-reaching structural purpose and Josquin's ingenious method of stating the c.f. twice. Where the one is abstract and serious, the other is clever in effect. In order to appreciate the impression that Josquin's statement of the well-known tune must have made on the singers of his day, one should sing some well-known tune of the present day with the same sort of chain repetitions. The effect is whimsical, to say the least—and, no doubt, it was around the year 1500 also.

There is a system of double statement of c.f. fragments in the Credo also, but there are not two alternating series as in the Gloria. Each fragment is given first in doubled values and then repeated immediately in *integer valor*. The entire quotation for the Credo runs to measure 28, the point of repetition in the chanson, but while Josquin observes this structural point he entirely ignores the phrase divisions in the individual fragments of the quotation. At *Et incarnatus* the superius continues with re-

EXAMPLE 123. (a-d) Josquin, *Missa Malheur me bat*—Agnus Dei (*Missen*, II, 58-60).

peated fragments from measure 28 of the chanson to the end; this time all
are in unit values and the very last fragment is not repeated.[25] For the
third section of the Credo, *Et in Spiritum*, the c.f. is quoted straight
through; this section is simply a new setting of the chanson superius in
four voices.

In the Sanctus there are three entire quotations of the alto without any
changes from the original form of that part. It is given once in the Sanctus,

once in the duo *Pleni sunt caeli* and again in the *Osanna*. The *Benedictus* consists of three duos (alto-tenor, alto-bass, and superius-tenor) in which the first eleven measures of the alto of the chanson are given by the top voice in each case. In the first duo the alto quotes the chanson material on pitch, in the second duo it restates it a tone lower (beginning on d), and in the third the superius gives it a fourth higher than the original, starting on a'. In this way the characteristically Phrygian melody is heard in the two other minor modes, Dorian and Aeolian. The Sanctus begins with a trio (the bass does not enter until m. 11) which is an exact quotation of all three voices of the original. We do not know whether this type of three-voice quotation had any special significance to Josquin. It may be he felt that by introducing the alto in conjunction with the superius and tenor he could clearly demonstrate that the alto c.f. material of this movement comes from the same composition as the other borrowed voices, even though it has little or no melodic resemblance to them. However this may be, the quotation of a block of the original rather than a line is an instance of straightforward parody, and it illustrates once again the ease with which composers move from parody to c.f. technique in the same work.

The tenor again quotes the tenor in Agnus I, although in altered form owing to the canonic prescription "*De minimis non curat pretor.*" Following this instruction, all minims are ignored and only notes and rests of the value of a semibreve or greater are used. These are given in the Mass in doubled values; the result is a scaffolding tenor with no note of shorter value than the breve. (See ex. 123.)

Agnus II is a duo between alto and tenor. There is no c.f. and the two voices sing in strict canon at the distance of a semibreve and at the interval of a second above! In Agnus III the tenor quotes the tenor, the superius quotes the superius, and the borrowed material is fragmented once again. No repetitions are involved this time; there is merely an alternation of doubled and unit values in the quotation. (E.g., chanson m. 1-7 given in doubled values; m. 8-10 in unit values; m. 11-12 in doubled values; m. 13-20 in unit values; and so on.) Since two voices of the original are quoted simultaneously, the movement is, by definition, a parody and therefore outside the scope of this study. It cannot, however, be omitted, because the parody element—the simultaneous quotation of two voices—is the climax of a plan of c.f. layout. In this work, then, parody not only coexists with c.f., it is a consequence of c.f.

This Agnus is another of Josquin's great technical displays. It is scored for six voices and the counterpoints take the form of two canons, each for two voices and each at the distance of a minim. The movement is thus closely related to the final Agnus of *L'homme armé sexti toni*, as they are formally very much the same.

On the whole, the voices of the *Missa Malheur me bat* are rhythmically straightforward, lacking in the complications which are found in *Fortuna desperata, Gaudeamus*, and others. Because of the comparative directness and simplicity of the lines, the work stands closer to *Hercules Dux Ferrariae*. There is a great deal of motivic usage, but only that in the first Agnus need be discussed here. In this movement the motives contribute a sectional aspect to the structure over the continuous long notes of the scaffolding c.f. The movement actually falls into four fairly distinct sections, each identified by a characteristic motive of its own. (The third and fourth are fused together by an overlap of motives. See ex. 123a-d.) It will be noted that in some cases the rhythm of the motives is conditioned by the text, in others it is not. The attitude is transitional, neither entirely of the fifteenth nor of the sixteenth century.

EXAMPLE 124. Josquin, *Missa Malheur me bat*—Credo (*Missen*, II, 51).

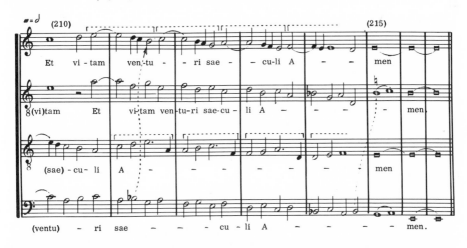

The final phrase of the Credo is harmonically striking because of the use of B♭ immediately before a close in E Phrygian (ex. 124, m. 214). The use of the flatted fifth degree so close to the tonic (just two measures before the final chord) is modally startling, but it is not entirely out of keeping with Josquin's practice. Nevertheless, none of the other instances of disregard of modal propriety which have been cited can match this one. (See p. 313.) Gombosi places this Mass after *Gaudeamus* and *Fortuna desperata* and suggests the last years of the fifteenth century as the date of composition.[26]

The remaining Masses of the edition of 1505 give quite a different picture from those already discussed. It seems that in order to fill out his publication Petrucci included works which were written many years before.

The *Missa L'ami Baudichon*[27] is apparently an earlier work than any in the edition of 1502. It is based on a very simple melody, a portion of which appears in the tenor of the anonymous chanson *Souviegne vous de la douleur–A bien amer.*[28] Smijers gives literary references which mention the tune in connection with dancing,[29] and in the form in which Josquin presents it in Kyrie I and *Christe* it does in fact show clear dance characteristics (ex. 125a). It is in straightforward triple meter and three-part form. (The phrases are marked $A_1A_2B_1B_2A_1A_2$ in the example. Phrases A_1A_2 appear in the chanson *Souviegne vous* in duple meter. If the assumption that this is a dance tune is correct, all the phrases probably were originally four measures in length.) The c.f. is given by the tenor in every movement; variety of statement is gained by such means as melodic and rhythmic alterations, transposition, statement in inversion, statement as strict c.f., and so forth.

As can be seen from example 125a, the entire melody is given in Kyrie I and the *Christe.* The *Christe* is written in duple meter ($\math161$), but this does not interfere with the actual triple meter of the tenor part. The first phrase (A_1A_2) reappears in Kyrie II, slightly ornamented and with values freely reduced. In the Gloria the first three tones of the melody, e' d' c', are presented in a strictly organized rhythmic pattern; they are cast into a phrase of eight measures in triple meter, in which each note is

EXAMPLE 125. (a-b) Josquin, *Missa L'ami Baudichon*—Kyrie I and *Christe,* and Agnus II (*Missen,* II, 67, 90). (c) P. de la Rue, *Missa de Sancta Cruce quinque vocum*—*Pleni sunt caeli* (*Liber Missarum,* p. 185). (d) Josquin, *Missa L'ami Baudichon*—Kyrie I (*Missen,* II, 67).

given the value of two perfect breves and which concludes with a rest of the same value; the entire c.f. statement is preceded by an introductory section of twenty-four measures and followed by a closing section of six. The eight-measure phrase is stated four times and each statement is made on a different pitch—first on e′, then on b♭, then g′, and finally e′. As a result, the succession of tenor notes is e′d′c′ (rest), b♭ a g (rest), g′f′e′ (rest), e′d′c′. This scalewise arrangement of notes gives considerable chance for harmonic variety. The b♭, in fact, introduces a markedly colorful effect, as it brings a g-minor chord into the predominantly C-major movement.

The *Qui tollis* is a free duo, in part organized by imitation. In *Qui sedes* a tenor scaffolding is used once more, this time based on the entire melody. A₁ and A₂ are presented in phrases equivalent to four perfect longs (of three imperfect breves). The remainder of the melody is given in a similar manner, but each note is a perfect breve, so that the phrases are equivalent to four breves this time. The entire melody is now restated in halved values, the notes and rests appearing as perfect breves in A₁ and A₂ and as perfect semibreves in the rest of the tune. The whole concludes with a cadential extension similar to the one used in Kyrie II.

In the Credo, after twenty-seven measures of introduction (nine longs of three perfect breves), the A and B sections are stated in inversion and in very long values as well, since the tenor continues in the metrical framework of *modus perfectus cum tempore perfecto*. *Et incarnatus* and *Crucifixus* are free duos (soprano and tenor, alto and bass) in which some imitation is used. There is a possible reference to the inverted form of *L'ami Baudichon* in the first few measures of the *Crucifixus*, although it must be admitted that, as the tune is scalic, any scale-line passage in the Mass would have some definable relation to it. In this passage, however, the notes of the scale line are also in triple meter, so that the similarity is very close. At *Et resurrexit* there is another strictly regulated scaffold based on the three descending notes of A. Each phrase is twelve measures long, as it consists of the equivalent of four perfect longs (of three imperfect breves). These phrases are transposed in regular order starting respectively on g′, f′, e′, d′, c′, and b. The set of six phrases is repeated and the entire movement ends with a pedal-note g′ in the tenor. The fact that the transposition is in six stages makes one wonder whether or not the pattern is based on the six tones of a hexachord. This is possible because, even though the beginning notes of the phrases (g′ down to b) do not compromise any normal hexachord, the ending notes make up a *hexachordum durum* (e′ down to g). Fragments of the Gregorian Credo I appear in the alto at *Et in Spiritum* and *et unam sanctam*; there may be other references, too, but none is so clear as these.

In the Sanctus, after a long duo, A₁A₂ is introduced as a scaffold. Each note is an imperfect long (two perfect breves) and the final c′ is greatly extended. The tenor sounds continuously, as there are no rests. *Pleni sunt caeli* is a very brilliant, freely composed duo. The Osanna has a tenor scaffolding once more, although the notes vary in value, some being perfect and some imperfect longs. B₁B₂ and A₁ are the parts of the melody quoted. The *Benedictus* consists of three duos (soprano and alto, *Benedictus*; alto and bass, *Qui venit*; soprano and alto, *In nomine*). The alto appears in each of the duos, singing always the same phrase while the other voices supply a different counterpoint to it each time. The alto phrase looks like a c.f. quotation, although no reference is given to identify it.[30]

In Agnus I and III the rhythmic form used in the tenor of Kyrie I returns, but the melody is quoted in slightly abbreviated form (A₁B₁B₂A₁).

Agnus II, a trio, is not based on a quotation of the c.f. and is organized largely by means of imitation. The lines are clearly in triple meter for the first couple of dozen measures, despite the fact that duple mensuration is used. Several measures of the bass part which are quoted in example 125*b* indicate the real triple nature of the meter and show also that the line is composed of a limited number of motives (marked a, b, and c). The soprano and alto are in imitation during a large part of the first phrase, so that they are more closely related to one another than to the bass, but they, too, are made up entirely of motives a and b. Hence all three voices are made up of the same material, and even though the motives appear in the two upper parts in another order than they do in the bass, they are all very tightly integrated.

The *Pleni sunt caeli* of the *Missa de Sancta Cruce quinque vocum* of Pierre de la Rue[31] is constructed in a strikingly similar way. It, too, is a trio in which the voices imitate one another more or less freely but are related chiefly because they are all made up of three short motives which are stated in a great variety of orders. The quotation from the bass part (ex. 125*c*) shows, furthermore, that motives a and b are the same as those of Josquin and that motive c' (la Rue) differs but slightly from motive c (Josquin). (Compare m. 31-32 of ex. 125*b* with m. 17-18 of ex. 125*c*; there is a difference in rhythm only.) Another characteristic common to both works is the frequent drop of a fifth between statements of the motives (ex. 125*b*, m. 22, 23-24, 28; ex. 125*c*, m. 9-10, 20, 24-25). There is no direct quotation of one work in the other, but it cannot be coincidental that the same material is used in both movements and that it is given the same type of treatment. It seems that one movement must have been derived from the other, although the derivation consists of the elaboration and expansion of material rather than literal restatement of it. The procedure corresponds to the elaboration of points of imitation which is a feature of many Masses based on *res facta* (for instance, Ockeghem's *Fors seulement*), or to the expansion of a structural device, such as la Rue himself undertakes when he extends his canonic motet *Ave sanctissima Maria* into an entire Mass. Since the *Osanna* of la Rue is more extensive and in that sense more elaborate than the Agnus of Josquin, it seems safe to consider it the derived work. The persistent triple meter and the constant reiteration of only three motives during a large part of a section of a Mass are features which do not fit in well with the style of the other works of la Rue available in modern publications. Hence there is a further reason to consider this *Osanna* an elaboration of a previous work; the supposition gives an explanation for an otherwise puzzling movement.

The *Missa L'ami Baudichon* has a head motive which appears consistently at the beginning of each movement (ex. 125*d*, m. 1-5). It takes the form of a duet and is restated with but very minor changes. (One note is rhythmically displaced in the Credo; in Agnus I a bass part is added.) The simple melodic design and uninvolved rhythmic patterns, in which the semibreve is clearly the unit of beat, are features which remind one of the head motives of Dufay—for instance, that of the *Missa Se la face ay pale.* The resemblances to Dufay, however, go so far beyond similarities in the head motive that a list of characteristics of this work reads as if it had been borrowed in large part from a description of a late work of Dufay. Simplicity of rhythmic and melodic pattern characterizes the entire work; the harmonies are clearly defined and the phrases clearly articulated by frequent and definite cadences; the music as a whole reveals the high, transparent sonority of the later Dufay. The introductory duos tend to be long and rather florid, while the entry of all four voices is emphasized by a solid chord and the four-voice writing continues in simpler less florid style. (See Gloria, m. 25 ff.; Credo, m. 28 ff.; Sanctus, m. 17 ff.)[32] The harmonic vocabulary is so similar to that of Dufay that certain passages remind one strongly of specific passages in his works. For instance, the kinship of the last half of his motet *Ave Regina caelorum* and the *Et resurrexit* or *Qui sedes* of Josquin is so marked that it can hardly be overlooked.

In this Mass Josquin seems as close to Dufay as Regis was, and even closer than Busnois. Like Regis and Busnois, he progresses beyond the style of the older master, but where they move to greater melodic and rhythmic involvement and to richer sonority, Josquin remains true to that ideal of clarity which pervades every aspect of Dufay's work. This quality is intensified in *L'ami Baudichon,* as the writing is even simpler and sharper in outline than that of Dufay. This is due in part to the motivic organization of the lines, which, along with the more involved manipulations of the tenor, indicates immediately that the work is more advanced than any of Dufay's. Nevertheless, the close stylistic association with the older master gives proof of a direct influence of the Burgundian style of the 1450's and 1460's on Josquin; it indicates also that this Mass is a very early work.

The *Missa Una Musque de Biscaya* is based on a tune which Josquin also treated as a chanson; Smijers includes it with the Mass for purposes of comparison. In both of these works the melody is given in an elaborated form; in the chanson it is treated in canon between the two upper voices, and in the Mass it is ornamented in a variety of ways. Although the lack of a simple form makes difficult the tracing of the tune in certain parts of the Mass, it can be followed for the most part with considerable certainty. The task is made much easier by the fact that both chanson and Mass quotations follow a similar scheme of phrases. The phrases of the chanson can be lettered ABABCA'BD.[33] The first two phrases (AB) are repeated in the chanson, as indicated, and in most of the quotations in the Mass as well. The tune is characterized by the scale-line rise of a fourth and this figure appears constantly in the Mass; the final cadence is on B♭ and interior cadences are made on G and F as well as the tonic.

The melody is presented in its entirety in the Kyrie. Phrases A and B are given by the tenor in Kyrie I. They are heard again in the *Christe,* which consists of four contrasting duos (superius and tenor, alto and bass, superius and tenor, and alto and bass). All the voices give out material from these phrases, but the superius gives it most accurately and completely. In the concluding measures of this section (scored for four voices) the superius continues with phrase C. In Kyrie II the tenor takes over again and states the melody from phrase C to the end.

The Gloria begins with long introductory duos and trios in which A and B are given in highly ornamented form by the superius. The tenor is again the leading voice, however, and on its entry (m. 17) it presents the first two phrases twice over. The first statement is in long values, the mensuration sign ₵ indicating augmentation; the second statement of the same passage is in normal values and the mensuration is changed to C. The next section (*Qui tollis . . . deprecationem nostram,* m. 50-72) is freely composed except for a florid statement of phrase A by the superius at the beginning. The third and final section (*Qui sedes*) begins with a free duo between alto and bass. The tenor reintroduces the c.f. when it enters (m. 78), taking it up again at the point where it had left it off in the first part and quoting it to the end (i.e., from phrase C to the end). The Gloria is thus based on one complete statement of the tune by the tenor which is interrupted by a free middle section.

The layout of the Credo is somewhat the same. After extremely long anticipatory duos and trios in which c.f. material is heard in superius and alto,[34] the tenor states the first two phrases twice (m. 47-159). Both statements are in augmentation, and the first one is in inversion. The second section of the movement (m. 160-174) is free, but at *Cujus regni* (m. 176) the tenor picks up the c.f. again at the point where it had dropped it and quotes it to the end. So far the layout of the c.f. is generally like that of the Gloria. However, at measures 206, the point which completes the quotation of the entire melody, the tenor moves to a cadence in g-minor instead of the proper one in B♭. From this point onward the tune of *Una musque de Biscaya* cannot be traced except for brief references to the scalewise rise of a fourth at measure 253 ff. The last part of the movement, then, may possibly be freely composed, but the tenor gives evidence of being a c.f., as it is rhythmically and melodically in simpler style than the other voices. As no textual reference is given, about all that can be said of it with certainty is that it is not one of the well-known Credo melodies. In any case, it leads the movement to a close in g-minor, although the Mass as a whole is in B♭-major.

In the Sanctus the c.f. migrates from superius to tenor. The superius states the first two phrases in the duo and trio at the beginning; the tenor enters at measure 17 with the third phrase and quotes through the next-to-last phrase to complete the section. Instead of continuing with the final phrase in the *Pleni sunt caeli*, the tenor starts the melody once more in notes of long value. The second phrase migrates to the superius (m. 50) and the c.f. stays in that voice through another statement of the first phrase. The second phrase is stated again also, this time by the alto at the fourth below (m. 65), and then by the superius on pitch (m. 69). These statements are followed by a free, cadential passage closing at measure 92. With the *Osanna* (m. 93) the tenor picks up the c.f. again at the point where the superius had left off (i.e., at phrase C) and quotes to the end of it to bring this part of the movement to a close. The superius carries the c.f. in the *Benedictus*, but the statement is not complete, the two final phrases not being given. (They are, of course, heard in the repetition of the *Osanna*.) The last fifteen measures of this section (m. 44-58) are freely composed, with the usual sequential drive to the cadence. It should be noted at the beginning of the movement that the first six measures of the quotation of the superius are identical with those of the alto in the Credo. This is exceptional for this Mass, as otherwise each statement of the c.f. differs from all the others.

The title, *Agnus super Kyrie*, indicates that the final movement of the Mass is an exact recapitulation of the first.

The c.f. usage in this Mass is not of unusual interest. In a general way, the manner of statement is consistent; the c.f. is given in its entirety in every movement although, as has been seen, the statements are often interrupted, or they are incomplete or are ornamented to the point where they cannot be followed with certainty.

There are a good many indications that this is an early work. The very long anticipatory duos and trios preceding the tenor entries, the rather limited use of imitation, and, above all, certain crudities in harmony point to an early date. Parallel fifths in the course of the phrase as well as in cadential suspensions in the manner of Isaac (Kyrie, m. 64-65, 67; Gloria, m. 88-89; Credo, m. 31-32, 230; etc.), barely covered parallel octaves and fifths (*Benedictus*, m. 50-51; Sanctus, m. 53-54; etc.), and unusual dissonance treatment (Credo, m. 152, 170-171; Sanctus, m. 118-119; *Benedictus*, m. 31-32), as well as other harsh-sounding combinations, occur more frequently in this Mass than in the others.

The widely different idioms of *Una musque de Biscaya* and *L'ami Baudichon* once more show Josquin to be receptive to divergent stylistic ideals. In the former his interest is centered on free and elaborate melodic movement and he is indulgent towards harmonic crudities arising from that movement; in the latter he maintains a high degree of harmonic clarity and in consequence shows a rigorously selective attitude towards dissonance. In later works he tends more and more to synthesize various traits into a personal style, but in these he writes quite distinctly in one style or the other—a fact which tends to support the assumption that they are youthful works.

The *Missa D'ung aultre amer*[35] is based on the tenor of the chanson by Ockeghem. It is a *Missa brevis*, quite unassuming in character, and in keeping with this Josquin has treated the *res facta* as simply as possible. It is not developed in any significant way in any of the statements. All quotations are completely literal except for prolongation of the final note in some movements and the occasional breaking-up of a tone into smaller values to fit syllables of text.

In the Kyrie and in the Gloria the tenor of the chanson is stated once through by the tenor of the Mass. In addition, in the Kyrie each section begins with a brief citation from the superius by the superius of the Mass (m. 1-4, 23-25, and 37-39). In the Credo the chanson tenor is given twice by the tenor and some extension is gained by considerably prolonging the final note of each statement. In the Sanctus and Agnus there is again but one statement of the chanson tenor per movement and, as in the earlier movements, it is entrusted to the tenor. The tenor is divided into thirds in the Agnus at exactly the same points as in the Kyrie. The Sanctus also begins, as the Kyrie had done, with a fragment of the superius of the chanson in the superius (m. 1-4).

An element of interest is added to this extremely straightforward lay-out by the quotation of the Gregorian Sanctus melody of the Mass for ferias of Advent and Quadragesima (Mass XVIII). It is stated by the alto in combination with the secular melody in the tenor, and, although it differs in a few respects from the Vatican version, the quotation is on the whole very simple and clearly recognizable. A similar procedure is followed in the Agnus. Agnus XVIII (again in a version that differs slightly from the Vatican edition) is cited by the alto up to measure 16, where the quotation breaks off. In Agnus II the bass starts with an imitation of the secular c.f. in the tenor (m. 24), but after three measures of this it proceeds with the Gregorian Agnus. In Agnus III the Gregorian melody starts in the superius and then migrates to the alto (m. 39), where it remains until the quotation breaks off (m. 44).

The brevity of the entire work is best illustrated by the Gloria, which is only forty-seven measures long. By skillful division of sentences and phrases between voices, and by judicious overlapping of them the entire text is presented. In the Sanctus, the *Benedictus* is entirely lacking and its place is taken by the first part of the motet *Tu solus qui facis mirabilia* (p. 465, note 21, below). Presumably the motet was chosen because the text is appropriate at this moment in the Mass. (It seems unlikely that the substitution was due to haste, as Pirro suggests.)[36] In any case, we cannot help but notice that the second part of the motet—which contains quotations from *D'ung aultre amer* and therefore would have a musical connection with the Mass—is not used.

D'ung aultre amer must have been a favorite of Josquin's, for he uses it in two other works. The superius of the chanson is cited in the motet *Victimae paschali laudes* (p. 395, below), and in a single Mass movement, a Sanctus from Petrucci's *Fragmenta missarum . . .* of 1505.[37] The Gregorian Sanctus from Mass XVIII is used in this movement also, being given to the tenor and combined with the chanson melody, which is quoted in its entirety in the superius. In the *Benedictus* the chanson superius is again cited in combination with the Gregorian melody, but not in its entirety. (The quotation breaks off at m. 33 of the chanson.) It is also converted into triple meter, which necessitates a few adjustments of note values. This Mass movement is followed by a freely composed chordal motet, *Tu lumen, tu splendor Patris*, which moves uninterruptedly in breves in all voices.

The *Missa Mater Patris* which opens the third volume of Masses of Josquin (Petrucci, 1514) is based on the motet of the same name by Antoine Brumel.[38] The work lies outside the scope of this study—it is a parody mass—so I will make only a few comments.

Most of the quotations from the motet involve more than one voice. Each of the five Mass movements begins with a version for two voices of the point of imitation with which the motet begins (in the Mass the third, or tenor, entry of the motet is omitted). The final passages of the Gloria and Credo, in triple meter, make use of the imitative *ostinato* figure with which the motet ends (m. 59 ff.).[39] In these passages, too, imitation is reduced from three voices in the motet to two in the Mass.[40] Agnus III is no less than the three-voice motet in its entirety, with two more voices added by Josquin to bring the total up to five. Unlike the final movement of the *Missa Malheur me bat*, this parody cannot be considered as incidental to a plan of c.f. statement. In the first place, most of the quotations are for more than one voice, so they are not of the c.f. type, and, in the second place, except for the quotations beginning and ending movements mentioned above, they are brief and erratically placed, so that it is difficult to speak of a general plan of statement.

Most of the quotations are short, so a large part of the Mass is freely composed or has a general rather than a literal relationship to the original. For instance, in the motet a simple effect of contrast is gained by alternating passages in imitative and note-against-note style, and the same thing is done in the Mass. As in all the other works of Josquin, there are points of individual interest which betray an original and lively mind. Possibly the most striking feature of this Mass occurs in the passages in which the three upper voices move in parallel $\frac{6}{4}$ chords while the bass moves about, touching appropriate roots or thirds. (In the Credo, m. 97, the bass makes parallel octaves with the superius!) These passages occur in Kyrie, Credo, and *Hosanna* and are related melodically as well as harmonically. Other points of interest are the canonic duos in the *Pleni* and *Benedictus* at the second above and below respectively.

The *Missa Faisant regretz* gains its name from the prominent use of a motive of four notes which is associated with the words "*faisans regrets*" which open the second half of a rondeau by Walter Frye.[41] Josquin uses the four-note motive, f-d-e-d, as a free *ostinato* in the tenor of the Mass. Further relationship with the chanson is achieved in the final Agnus by the use of the entire superius of the chanson in the superius of the Mass and, in addition, by taking over another four-note motive from the beginning of the tenor of the chanson (associated with the words with which the chanson begins, "*Tout a par moy*"). This motive (d-d-e-d in the Mass, d-e-d in the chanson) is reiterated in the alto while the tenor continues with its "*faisans regrets*" motive.

The innumerable restatements of a brief motive in ever-changing rhythmic guises remind one of the *Missa La sol fa re mi*, but in this case the motive is to a much greater extent restricted to a single voice— the tenor. Further elements of organization are provided by additional freely composed motives and by quotations from the Kyrie and Gloria of Mass XI (*in Dominica infra annum*) in the Kyrie and Gloria, and of Credo I in the Credo.[42] As a detailed analysis shows, this is one of the most complex of the Masses of Josquin in its variety of types of organization.

In the first Kyrie the superius carries the Gregorian melody in combination with the chanson motive in the tenor (ex. 126a). Further organization is gained by repetition of the final phrases (partly shown in ex. 126a, m. 7-9, 9-11), and by the use of the chanson motive in the bass and the Kyrie melody in the alto in the introductory duo (m. 1-3 of the Kyrie). In the *Christe* the alto takes over the Gregorian melody from the superius, although the first few notes appear in that voice (m. 15-18). These same notes are also taken up by the bass when it enters and given several statements as a free *ostinato* (m. 24-35). The tenor, of course, continues with the motive from the chanson, while a scalewise descending figure in the Kyrie melody of the alto is taken as an excuse to construct a sequence in all voices (m. 36-40). In the second Kyrie the motive is again carried by the tenor (with scattered appearances in alto and bass), while the very last phrase of the Kyrie (i.e., the music to the sixth statement of *Kyrie eleison*) is given in highly ornamented form in the superius again. The tenor motive is stated in different rhythmic forms and on different pitches as well. In Kyrie I it appeared on f′ and b♭; in the *Christe* on f′, b♭, and f; in Kyrie II on b♭ only.

The Gloria starts with imitative entries on the *Faisant regretz* motive between alto, bass, and tenor; the latter voice, as usual, continues to give out the four notes in various forms and on the pitches b♭, e♭′, and f′. The superius states the Gloria of Mass XI through *Gratias agimus*, but drops it at measure 23 and continues freely to the end of the section. It picks it up at *Qui tollis*, but at *suscipe deprecationem* (m. 54) drops it again and proceeds freely. The tenor states its motive rather sparingly on b♭, c′, and f′ until the closing section in triple meter (m. 84), where Josquin cleverly manages to get the motive into all voices in imitative, descending patterns (ex. 126b).

The Credo starts off with a statement of the chanson motive by the bass, immediately imitated by the tenor. After several statements on b♭, the tenor gives it in ascending line on c′, d′, e♭′, and f′ (m. 9-13); it is then stated many times on b♭, c′, and f′ according to no apparent order until measure 39, where it is again given in ascending line from b♭ to f′ to bring the section to a close. The superius starts out with the melody of Credo I, but Josquin evidently feels no compulsion to continue steadily with it, as it can be traced only in spots after measure 26 (*Deum de Deo*). In some places it is possible that he elaborates it by taking a few notes

EXAMPLE 126. Josquin, *Missa Faisant regretz*. (a) Kyrie (*Missen*, III, 33; *LU*, p. 46). (b) Gloria, (c) Sanctus, (d) Hosanna—tenor and bass only, and (e) Agnus I—tenor and bass only (*Missen*, III, 39, 46, 49, 52). (f) Agnus III (*ibid.*, p. 54), with superius of Walter Frye's chanson *Tout a par moy* (*MQ*, XXXVII, 530). (g) *Benedictus*—superius (*Missen*, III, 51), with superius of Frye's chanson.

b

(Spiri)tu in glo-ri - a De - i Pa - tris A — — — — (men)

(Spiri)tu in glo - ri -a De - i Pa - tris A — — — — (men)

In glo-ri - a De-i Pa-tris A — — — — (men)

In glo-ri - a De-i Pa-tris A — — — — (men)

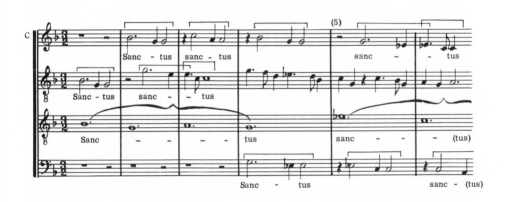

c

Sanc - tus sanc - tus sanc — - tus

Sanc - tus sanc - tus

Sanc — — — tus sanc — — (tus)

Sanc - tus sanc - (tus)

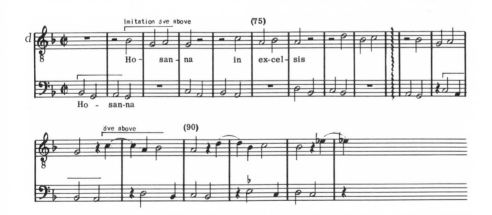

d

Imitation 8ve above (75)

Ho - san - na in ex-cel - sis

Ho - san-na

8ve above (90)

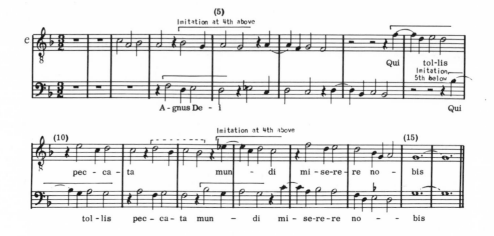

and repeating them, either on the same pitch or in sequence (m. 33-36, *Genitum, non factum*, and m. 40-43, *Qui propter nos*). Intermittent quotation of this type characterizes the movement to the very end. The Credo melody appears and fades away according to the composer's whim, rather than in accordance with any plan or from any correlation with the tenor statements. *Et incarnatus* starts with a canon between superius and alto which makes use of only a few notes of the Gregorian c.f. The melody becomes clear in the superius at measure 56 *(et homo)* and then migrates to the alto and bass, which present it in canon (m. 60). At measure 66 it returns to the superius, where it remains, with some imitations by the alto, until measure 80. From this point *(Et iterum)* it disappears. Meanwhile the tenor has been stating its motive with the usual variety of rhythms and pitches. *Et in Spiritum* begins with a free canon between alto and bass, but the superius introduces the Credo melody once more on its entry at measure 99 *(Qui ex Patre)*. The quotation stops at measure 103 and the c.f. does not appear again until measure 122 *(Confiteor)*; it soon disappears and the superius has a free imitation of the four-note tenor motive at measure 133. It continues freely until *Et vitam* (m. 140), where the Credo c.f. apparently makes its final entry. The statement is very free; the first four notes are ambiguous and can be explained either as free c.f. statement or as free imitation of the tenor motive. However, the phrase ends on the proper notes. The Amen (m. 151) is free except for the motive in the tenor.

The Sanctus is based on the tenor motive stated as a strict c.f. It is given out five times, on the pitches b♭, e♭', f', c', and b♭, in a steady succession of perfect breves uninterrupted by rests. It is not combined with a Gregorian melody but with two other, newly composed motives. These motives are used intensively and replace in a sense the element of organization which a c.f. offers. The bass line is exclusively composed of the motives; the first one, of a falling third, is used to measure 15 (ex. 126c) and the second, on a rising scale line, from measure 16 to the end of the section. The superius also uses the motives, although it does not hold to them so rigorously. The alto, as usual, is the freest, most florid voice (ex. 126c, m. 4 ff.). The *Pleni sunt caeli* is a trio, free of c.f. and organized by means of imitation. In the *Hosanna* the tenor and bass carry the *Faisant regretz* motive in canon at the octave. The figure is stated one step higher each time, moving from b♭ to f'. This scalewise ascent is then repeated, the time interval of imitation being shorter, however, so that the figures in the two voices are more closely interlocked (ex. 126d, m. 1-9 and m. 86-92). In the *Benedictus* the bass and tenor give answering statements of a phrase constructed out of the motive. The pitches of the statements change (b♭, e♭, c, f, b♭), but the rhythmic pattern remains the same until the final part of the movement (m. 41 ff.), where the plan gives way to reiterated statements of the motive in the tenor only and in lively triple meter. Over each of the structural statements in bass and tenor Josquin writes a flowing counterpoint, pairing the superius with the tenor and the alto with the bass. The movement, then, consists of a series of contrasting duos (until the final part, which is scored for four voices). The sense of contrast, of opposition between the duos, is heightened by bringing each to a clear cadence which overlaps but little or not at all with the succeeding phrase. Yet there is a sense of continuity also, as each statement of the superius or alto is in one way or another interrelated with the next.

The motive appears in Agnus I as a sort of free canon between tenor and bass much as in the *Hosanna* (ex. 126e), but there is a greater impression of stretto, and the motive also appears in the superius numerous times. The structural principle employed in the second Agnus is the same as that of the *Benedictus*, for the Agnus also consists of a series of alternating duos, each based on a phrase made out of the motive. The details differ, however—this time the motivic phrases are given to superius and tenor, and the duos are scored for superius and alto on the one hand and for tenor and bass on the other. The special feature of Agnus III, as mentioned before, is the combination of the *Faisant regretz* motive of the tenor with the entire superius melody of the chanson in the superius and the motive *Tout a par moy* in the alto. The motives of tenor and alto are fitted to the superius in a clever contrapuntal mosaic-work, the whole being supported by a bass which is written freely (ex. 126f).

The Mass also resembles the chanson because of a general similarity of melodic style. The lines, in their winding movement, return again and again to a certain note, as illustrated in example 126g. (For purposes of comparison, portions of the superius of Mass and chanson were chosen in which the reiterated note happens to be b♭.) This type of melody, which gives the impression of spinning out a single basic figure by means of a series of completely free variations, is characteristic of the last quarter of the century and is constantly found in la Rue, Josquin, and others. The stylistic relationship of the original and the derived work probably accounts for numerous spots in the Mass so similar to the chanson that they might possibly be considered as free quotations. (Instances occur throughout the Mass, but, taking only the *Benedictus* as an example, compare chanson superius, m. 1, to *Benedictus* superius, m. 1; chanson superius, m. 1-2, to alto, m. 26-29; chanson superius, m. 19-20, to superius, m. 34-35; chanson superius, m. 33-35, to alto, m. 36-40; etc.) Disregarding all instances of doubtful quotation, it is still true that the *Missa Faisant regretz* is one of the most complex in detail of all of Josquin's c.f. structures—one which, with its ornamented c.f., motivic c.f., migrant c.f., intermittent quotations, and c.f. combinations, just about exhausts the possibilities of organization of the nonschematic type.

The *Missa ad fugam*,[43] which follows *Faisant regretz* in the publication of Petrucci, is based on canon between superius and tenor and hence lies outside the scope of this study. Smijers has been unable to find that

Josquin uses a borrowed melody; aside from some quotation of the Credo I melody in the Credo, it seems probable that he has not, for the structural principle is provided by the canon itself.

The *Missa Di dadi*[44] takes its name from the *dadi* or dice. Two dice are pictured in the tenor part to indicate the proportional relationship of this voice to the others. In the Kyrie the proportion is 2:1, in the Gloria 4:1, in the Credo 6:1, and in the Sanctus 5:1. (It will be noted that the dice obligingly gave Josquin the proportion 6:1 in the Credo, the movement which requires the greatest extension of the structural voice in order to accommodate the text.) The Mass is based on the tenor of a chanson of Robert Morton, *N'aray je jamais mieulx*,[45] the quotations being of the most literal type. The treatment of the borrowed material is quite as simple in this Mass as it is complex and irregular in *Faisant regretz*. The tenor is given sometimes in triple and sometimes in duple mensuration, and in a variety of augmentations; it is transposed to the fifth below except in the last movement (the chanson is in D Dorian, the Mass in G Dorian); it is for the most part not quoted in its entirety, the whole tune appearing only in the *Hosanna* and Agnus I and III, while in the other movements only the first six measures are used.

In Kyrie I and again in Kyrie II the six measures of the chanson are given in doubled values. A rest, of the value of an imperfect long, precedes the quotation and is an integral part of the scheme of statement. It covers four measures in this movement, owing to the augmentation. The *Christe* is a freely composed trio. The first part of the Gloria gives the six measures in quadrupled values (the rest covers eight measures). The tenor is silent in the next three sections, which are a trio (*Domine Deus, rex caelestis*), a duo between alto and bass (*Domine fili*), and another trio (*Domine Deus, agnus Dei*). The tenor appears once more at *Qui tollis*; the quotation is exactly the same as in the Gloria. (The notes are twice as long in the score, but the increase in length is only apparent, since the other voices are in *proportio dupla*—₵.) The tenor of the Credo is fundamentally the same as that of the Gloria, but extension is gained not only by the augmentation of six to one but also by the insertion of a rest (in the middle of the quotation) of the same length as the introductory one (twelve perfect breves, or thirty-six semibreves, in this case). In the *Crucifixus*, as in the *Qui tollis*, the tenor is exactly repeated, but the notes once more take on an apparent increase in value because of the diminution of the other voices. The long rests are, of course, the cause of very long duos and trios in this movement.

The fivefold augmentation of the Sanctus is applied by Josquin only to the semibreves of the original, which are actually quintupled in value; all minims are doubled in value. In the *Hosanna* the mensural treatment of a fragment of the chanson gives way to a statement of the entire melody in *integer valor.* (The *Pleni sunt caeli* is a free trio, the *Benedictus* a free duo.) The entire tenor is stated again in Agnus I, this time in doubled values. Agnus II is a free duo. It is customary to give the c.f. some sort of special treatment in the last movement, and in Agnus III Josquin presents it on a different pitch and in another voice. It is stated on d, an octave below the original pitch, rather than on g, a fifth below, and by the bass voice instead of the tenor. As in Agnus I it is given in doubled values. Since the B-flat is retained in the signature, the mode of the *res facta* is changed in the final statement from D Dorian (as in the chanson) to D Aeolian. (The former statements are true transpositions from Dorian on D to Dorian on G as a result of the flat; the chanson tenor is altered with respect to pitch only.) Since the entire Mass is in G and the final statement of the *res facta* ends on a d, Josquin is forced to add a G in order to maintain tonal unity.

The simple style, comparable to that of *L'ami Baudichon,* indicates that this, too, is an early work. There is little use of c.f. material in any but the structural voice. (Agnus III forms an exception to this; it begins with statements of the first few notes by tenor and superius before the bass entry.) There is also comparatively little use of imitation. Even the free duos and trios have in most cases only a single point of imitation at the beginning and then proceed to passages based on motivic usage of one sort or another. (Exceptions to this are the *Pleni sunt caeli* and *Benedictus,* both of which start without imitation and proceed to passages based on that technique. There is quite extensive canonic writing in the *Benedictus* at very close time intervals.) The motives are on the whole brief and very clearly outlined; the final *ostinato* of Agnus III could well be a passage from a motet of Busnois, although the style is in general more straightforward, less crowded and intricate than his. Individual points of interest are the skip down of a fifth from the suspension of a ninth (Gloria, m. 47; also m. 41), parallel fifths between alto and bass (*Christe,* m. 27-28), and the extensive descending scale-lines between three voices in which each voice moves only in breves, one of them being syncopated so as to form a series of 7-6 suspensions. In such passages, with the boldness of complete simplicity, Josquin gets his most striking effects in this Mass and those others which resemble it.

A plainchant Mass, *de Beata Virgine,* is the final work of the edition of 1514.[46] The Kyrie and Gloria are based on the appropriate chants of Mass IX, *in festis B. Mariae Virginis, I,* the Credo on Credo I,[47] and the Sanctus and Agnus on Sanctus and Agnus from Mass IV, *in festis duplicibus, I.*

Imitation is used to a much greater extent in this Mass than in any of the others based on c.f. in the edition of 1514. The Gregorian melodies are carried into more than once voice by this means, and by means of duets and phrase repetition as well, so that in many places the texture is saturated with the borrowed material. In order to find a comparable work it is necessary to return to the *Missa Ave maris stella* of the edition of 1505.

The Kyrie begins with extended imitative entries in all voices on the Gregorian Kyrie melody, the first phrase being the only one that is used. The alto is the only voice which presents the entire phrase, carrying it to the end of the section and extending it by means of repeating the final cadence (m. 15-19 equal m. 19-23). The other voices, after the initial entries, are written chiefly as free counterpoints. The *Christe* opens with a canonic duo between bass and tenor on an ornamented form of the first phrase of the Gregorian *Christe*. This is exactly repeated by the soprano and alto (m. 16 ff.), and the section closes with all voices sounding, the two lower ones reëntering with a final statement of the cadences of the duos (compare m. 31 and m. 10 in the tenor, m. 33 and m. 12 in the bass). Kyrie II is based on the very last phrase of the original melody. The first incise is split into two halves, each of which is stated first by the alto and immediately repeated by the soprano in a series of duos and trios. The second incise (an exact repetition of the first) is presented similarly by bass and tenor (m. 16-27), following which the tenor carries the chant melody to the end (m. 30 ff.). This section also is rounded off by a repetition of the cadence (m. 41-43 equal m. 44-47).

The melody of Gloria IX is heard for the most part in no less than two voices and quite frequently in all four. As it moves freely from one part to another, no single voice, nor any pair of voices, can properly be called the structural ones. However, the c.f. appears in tenor and superius more frequently than in the other two. Superius and tenor carry it at the beginning (they are written in free canon at the octave up to m. 35), while the others sometimes take the form of free counterpoints, sometimes imitate the parts carrying c.f. (see m. 16-19 with imitation in all voices). The c.f. disappears entirely from the tenor at measure 67 and is carried by the two upper voices until the entry of the trope, *Spiritus et alme*, at measure 82. The trope enters as a musical as well as textual contrast, since it is scored for the lowest voices—the tenor and bass presenting the melody in an imitative duo. The two succeeding sections (Gloria text and melody at m. 93, trope again at m. 107) are scored for four voices, the borrowed melodies usually appearing in more than one part.

The *Qui tollis* continues in much the same unpredictable manner, for the method of presenting the *cantus firmi* is consistent only in its irregularity. The melodies appear in from two to four voices, and the tenor, the voice which usually carries the c.f., is often entirely without it. As if to make up for this neglect, the tenor is made the sole bearer of c.f. in the final measures of the section (m. 84-95). In *Cum Sancto Spiritu* all voices share equally in the borrowed material, presenting it in a series of imitative duos which lead up to a freely composed closing section scored for the full complement of parts (m. 15 ff., *Dei Patris, Amen*). The *Amen* is a brilliant drive to the cadence containing a long and elaborate sequence.

In the Credo the number of voices is increased from four to five and the tenor is given the entire chant, so that it once more becomes the main structural part. The increase in the number of voices comes about because the tenor is duplicated in strict, two-voice canon. Following the instruction *"Le premier va devant,"* it functions as *dux*, while the derived voice comes in two measures later at the fifth below. The canon continues in this form through the *Crucifixus*, but at *Et in Spiritum* a second instruction appears, *"Le devant va derriere,"* and in accordance with this the second voice of the canon takes the lead (still at the fifth below), while the tenor now functions as *comes* and follows at the distance of two measures. The other voices are written for the most part as free counterpoints, although there are occasional imitations of the c.f. (Credo, m. 15-21, *visibilum; Crucifixus*, m. 1-3; etc.).

The c.f. is treated in canon in the Sanctus, much as it was in the Credo. The tenor is again duplicated, the second voice following at the fifth above and at the distance of four breves according to the instruction *"Vous jeunerez les quatre temps."* The other voices are organized somewhat more extensively than in the preceding movement, sometimes imitating the canon, sometimes presenting patterns of their own (for example, m. 1, superius, and m. 5, alto; m. 16-18, superius, alto, and bass). *Pleni sunt caeli* starts with a point of imitation involving all voices, and the *Hosanna* also has a considerable amount of close imitation in all parts on the material of the c.f. This Sanctus is rather unusual because none of the sections is freely composed. The c.f. is treated in cannon throughout, which means also that the entire movement is scored for the full number of five voices. Contrast in sonority is achieved in the *Benedictus*, however, as it consists largely of duos and trios. This section, too, is integrated by imitations, especially from measure 25 to the end. The c.f. can be followed without much trouble, although in places it deviates from the version of the *Liber Usualis*.

Agnus I and III are constructed over a canon in the same way as the Sanctus and are therefore scored for five voices also. The organization of the noncanonic voices is especially close in Agnus I, the devices being the usual ones: sequential figures, imitations of the canonic entries (superius, m. 10, 17, and 22), imitations based on figures not derived from the canon, and a brief rhythmic figure. (This is a scale-line figure with the rhythmic form ♩. ♩ ♩ ♩ which is used liberally in all parts. It appears first in the bass and superius, m. 11, and many times thereafter.) Agnus II is a duo for alto and bass in which the c.f. is given to the upper voice alone for the first phrase. It is then carried into both voices by means of imitation (m. 16 ff.) and canon at the distance of a semibreve (m. 32-45). By measure 39 the c.f. statement is complete except for the cadential notes, but the movement is carried on for eighteen more bars in a free and beautifully florid cadential extension.

A problem of tonal organization presents itself in this work, since each of the *cantus firmi* is in a different mode; the Kyrie and Gloria are in the first and seventh respectively, the Credo in the fourth, the Sanctus in the eighth, and the Agnus in the sixth. Josquin does not put all the movements into a single tonality, but he does arrange them into a somewhat more unified scheme than they have in the original Gregorian Mass. The Kyrie is transposed down a fifth, so that both it and the Gloria have a tonic of G (the first movement is in G Dorian, the second in G Mixolydian). The Credo is in E Phrygian. The tenor is shifted up five tones (without change of key signature), but, as it is written as a canon, the second voice (at the fifth below) sings on pitch.[48] The Sanctus and Agnus are both in C. The former has a signature of one flat (i.e., C Mixolydian), as the tenor is transposed up a fourth from the original (the following voice of the canon is a fifth above, hence an octave above the chant). The latter is in C major, the tenor being transposed up a fifth. (The *comes* in this canon is also a fifth higher, thus a ninth above the c.f.) Complete diversity of tonality is in this way converted into a plan of a sort, in which the first two and the last two movements have tonics a fifth apart, while the middle movement, the Credo, falls in between with a tonic on E.

This Mass also is not completely uniform in range or scoring. As mentioned above, the first two movements are for four voices, the last three for five. Kyrie and Gloria are in medium range; the Credo is comparatively low, both because the superius goes no higher than d'' and because the canonic tenor is duplicated at the fifth *below*, thus causing a preponderance of voices in low register. The Sanctus and Agnus, on the other hand, are unusually high; not only does the superius often go to g'', the tonal center of gravity also lies high because the tenor is canonically duplicated at the fifth *above*. The high range, in combination with Josquin's thin scoring, produces movements of a crystalline sonority which contrast very effectively with the heavier sound of the Credo.

Despite lack of unity in c.f., in tonality, and in choral sonority, there is a uniformity of style which gives the work a distinctive character. With the exception of the Credo, the lines are consistently elaborate and in some places rhythmically very intricate (e.g., Sanctus and Agnus I). They are, however, so handled as to produce an effect of gentle movement; suavity and elegance are the outstanding characteristics of the work. There are a few moments of sharp contrast in the form of unusual harmonic progressions, of clusters of complex rhythmic patterns, or of drastic simplifications which stand out in high relief from the context. Forceful drives to the cadence do occur (see the end of the Gloria and Credo and the *Hosanna*), but they are surpassed by similar passages in other Masses. The *Missa de Beata Virgine* is notable, rather, for closing sections such as that of the Kyrie, where the rhythmic movement is handled with the utmost subtlety. There is an increase in momentum, but it is just sufficient to bring the piece to a quietly satisfying conclusion. Such a passage is an ultimate refinement of the traditional drive to the cadence. It is also more. The replacement of a spirited movement by a movement which is reposeful yet strong indicates once again the advent of new aesthetic ideals.

The quality of movement in this work is comparable to that of the motet *Ave Maria* which was discussed with regard to change of style around the turn of the century (pp. 337 ff., above). The fairly large amount of imitation and the resultant infiltration of c.f. material throughout the texture also remind one of the motet. With regard to text underlaying, however, the situation is different. Even in the syllabic writing of the Credo there is a great deal of evidence that the musical accent is not an outgrowth of that of the text. As for the rest of the Mass, the generally florid style of the lines indicates immediately that textual considerations could not have been a primary source of inspiration for Josquin. The *Missa de Beata Virgine* is not peculiar in this respect. Rhetorical considerations were simply not felt to be as important in the Mass as in the motet, and we find, even in the late works, that the Masses are more conservative in this aspect of style than are the motets.

EXAMPLE 127. Josquin, *Missa Pange lingua*—Kyrie II (*Missen*, IV, 3; *Hymns Anc. & Mod.*, p. 368).

The *Missa Pange lingua*[49] did not appear in print until eighteen years after Josquin's death (in Johannes Ott's *Missae tredecim*, 1539). There is no sure way of estimating the date of composition, but the Mass is generally regarded as a late work. No single voice can be called the chief carrier of the c.f. It is true that the tenor carries it many times while the other voices do not, but others often carry it when it is not given by the tenor. (Ex. 127, Kyrie II, m. 60 to end.) The first phrase of the hymn is presented in all voices by means of a point of imitation in Kyrie I; the second appears in all but the alto by similar means. Imitation likewise brings the next two phrases into all voices of the *Christe*, which is scored as a series of alternating duos. The second Kyrie begins with initial imitation in all voices, but the final phrase of the hymn is given by only the two outer voices. (Ex. 127, m. 60 ff.) The frequent points of imitation make this Mass very much like the imitative motets. The rhythmic and linear characteristics are, however, much closer to the majority of the other Masses. This is a much more vigorous work than the *Missa de Beata Virgine*. (See especially the extension, ex. 127, m. 65 ff., and sequential treatment of the c.f., m. 61-63.)

In the movements following the Kyrie there is no consistent use of points of imitation. As in the *Missa Ave maris stella* and the Gloria of the *Missa de Beata Virgine*, much imitation is used, but it is used rather

EXAMPLE 128. Josquin, *Missa Pange lingua—Qui tollis* (Missen, IV, 7, 8; Hymns Anc. & Mod., p. 368).

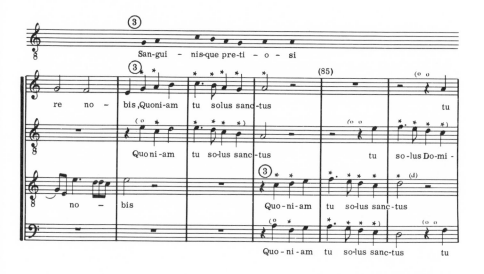

irregularly and in a variety of ways. In most of the movements the hymn is not used in its entirety. The first two phrases are given in the Gloria, starting with imitative duets in which the superius and tenor are the chief bearers of the c.f. The second line of the hymn is treated in the superius and alto (m. 14 ff.) and then in the tenor and bass (m. 23). The movement ends with a long free section based on short motives. The first three lines are given in the *Qui tollis*, the third one being developed at some length by repetitions in entirety or in part. (Ex. 128, m. 82-94.)

In the Credo the first phrase of the hymn appears in all voices in the imitative duos which start the movement off. After these the regular c.f. is dropped (m. 30) and a Gregorian Credo melody is used instead.[50] It appears in superius, alto, and tenor at first; then the chief carriers are tenor and alto (which are written in imitation, m. 43-73), alto and

superius (m. 73-75), and tenor alone (m. 83 to the end of the section).
These quotations are interrupted now and then by brief phrases free of
c.f. *Et incarnatus*, a chordal passage in the manner of a declamation motet,
uses the first line of the hymn once more. The melody is given out by
the superius in augmented and slightly ornamented form through *Virgine*
(m. 105). The following, solemnly declamatory phrase, *Et homo factus est*,
is apparently free. The first line of the hymn reappears immediately,
however, at *Crucifixus* (m. 111), and is given in alto and superius. From
measure 118 the c.f. disappears once more, the text being set syllabically
to a series of brief motives. From *Et iterum venturus* (m. 135) the
Gregorian Credo is used again, freely distributed among the voices. *Et in
Spiritum* is another motivic section in which the text is set syllabically
and which is without c.f. The first phrase of the hymn reappears at
measure 174 and is followed by phrases three (m. 183), four (m. 193),
and five (m. 200) given irregularly in one or more voices. Phrases two and
six are either not given or given in an extremely unclear fashion. From
measure 207 there is a free drive to the cadence.

The first two lines of the hymn are again treated in the Sanctus, appearing in all voices in imitative duets. The *Osanna* is based on the same
two phrases, but the treatment is much more elaborate and free. The
second phrase is given remarkably extended motivic treatment in the
long drive to the cadence (m. 113-138). The *Pleni sunt caeli* and *Benedictus* are free imitative duos.

The first Agnus presents the first line of the hymn in imitation in all
four voices, the second line in the superius and tenor, and then ends with
the usual free drive to the cadence. (It is possible that the final line of
the hymn appears in the superius, m. 20 ff., since all the notes can be
found. This, however, is probably coincidental; the entire passage is based
on a motive which appears in tenor and superius, and the last two statements of the motive in the top voice happen to contain the notes of
the last phrase of the hymn.) Agnus II is an imitative duo of great
beauty which, after a brief reference to the hymn, apparently proceeds
freely. (This duo is omitted in *Das Chorwerk*, following the edition of
1539.) A great part of the hymn is heard in the third Agnus. After a
preliminary point of imitation for all voices on the first few notes, the
entire first phrase is given as a scaffolding by the superius (m. 88 ff.).
The second phrase appears in the bass (m. 106) and then in the tenor
(m. 112). The third appears in tenor and superius in imitation (m.
121), and the fourth in all voices in two imitative duos, the first duo
between tenor and bass, the second between superius and alto (m. 129 ff.).
The first few notes of the point of imitation starting at measure 136 may
be a reference to the fifth phrase of the hymn, although there is no complete quotation of it in any voice. A free, motivated passage brings the

work to a close; as in similar passages in other movements, the text is set syllabically.

This survey of the Mass shows that the c.f. is treated quite irregularly; it is seldom quoted entire, it is interrupted by free sections, etc. The freedom with which it is treated in the *Qui tollis* is typical (ex. 128). The tenor carries it in a chordal, declamatory section (ex. 128, m. 67-73), tenor and superius have it in an imitative duo (m. 73-78) and they continue with it, either imitating one another or repeating statements, to the very end of the movement. Free sections, or sections which are only derived from some feature of a true c.f. statement, make up a considerable part of this work. For instance, the rising and falling thirds in the duets (ex. 128, m. 78-81) are an outgrowth of previous c.f. quotations (superius and tenor, m. 73-75). The figures which appear in all voices (ex. 128, m. 86-88) are a reduction of the c.f. statements in superius and tenor, measures 82-85; along with restatements of the third phrase of the hymn, they are reiterated in the closing section of the movement. A similar but more elaborate instance is found in the *Osanna* (m. 105 ff.). A freely elaborated form of the second phrase is stated in imitation in all parts and is then worked into a very long drive to the cadence during the course of which the second phrase is not only repeated in its entirety but also fragmented to form a sequence (superius, m. 121-126).

This sort of treatment, which involves numerous repetitions of c.f. phrases, is in the nature of a development on c.f. quotations and their derivatives. Certain works have a single voice made up of repetitions of a figure from the c.f.[51] The Gloria of *Ave maris stella* contains an entire closing section constructed on such a figure, which is stated over and over in all parts (ex. 121, m. 32-38). In the *Missa Pange lingua*, Josquin goes one step further. The c.f. quotation itself generates further motives, thus allowing more extensive and more flexible development of such passages and at the same time retaining the tight integration of literal repetition.

The numerous drives to the cadence and the vigorous rhythms of some of the melodic ideas (e.g., at *Et in Spiritum Sanctum*, the last section of the Credo) show that the older concept of Mass music was still much alive. In rhythmic quality this work is not so forward-looking as the *Missa de Beata Virgine*. In other respects it is more advanced: it surpasses that Mass in the number of passages in which care is taken with the declamation, and in the more regular use of points of imitation. The difference between these works is, however, more one of conception than of style or of stylistic advancement. Variety of style is an outstanding feature of many of the earlier works, but in them Josquin is dealing with issues he has inherited. Some works carry forward stylistic traits of $\longrightarrow$

Dufay, some stem from Ockeghem, and so on. Even such mature works as *Hercules Dux Ferrariae* and *Ave maris stella* show contrasted strains in the broad sense of systematic and nonsystematic structure,[52] although in every other respect they are in Josquin's own style. At the period of *Pange lingua* and *De Beata Virgine* the process of consolidation of influences has gone even farther, so that the very real differences between these two late Masses must be looked upon as different aspects of Josquin's personal musical thought. Relatively speaking, the *Missa de Beata Virgine* is decorative and gentle in tone, the *Missa Pange lingua* severe, virile, and much in the mood of *Hercules Dux Ferrariae*. Each in its own way is a masterpiece of great beauty.

The *Missa Da pacem* also appeared in Ott's publication of 1539. Of the five sources given by Smijers,[53] one attributes the Mass to Mouton and one to Noel Bauldewijn; the other three name Josquin as the composer. While the attribution is not conclusive, the evidence of the sources favors Josquin and the work has been accepted by Smijers, Osthoff, Pirro, Ambros, and other scholars as one of his late compositions.

In contrast to the *Missa Pange lingua*, the c.f. is treated most conservatively. The entire melody is divided between the three sections of the Kyrie, the tenor being clearly the chief carrier of the c.f., although each section begins with material from it in the other voices. In Kyrie II the final phrase of the chant is given three times, the superius making the second of these statements in a duo with the alto.

The c.f. is given again by the tenor in the Gloria, starting with breves and longs and then becoming more ornamented. The point of imitation between superius, alto, and bass on c.f. material with which the Kyrie begins is used as a head motive. (M. 1-5, Gloria, repeat m. 1-5, Kyrie). The contrapuntal voices are fairly tightly organized by imitations and motives after the tenor enters. The whole c.f. is restated in the *Qui tollis* in long notes with ornamentation at the phrase ends. As in the Gloria, the other voices are organized among themselves against the c.f., although the third phrase of the antiphon appears in the superius as well as the tenor (m. 80-94). The *Qui tollis* closes with a free, motivically organized section as had the Kyrie and the Gloria—(*Et in terra pax*, m. 43-51; *Qui tollis*, m. 114-122; Kyrie, m. 58-64).

The antiphon is stated three times in the Credo. In the first section it starts with very long notes (perfect longs) and again gradually becomes faster as it is more highly ornamented. The head motive of the Kyrie and Gloria is also used without essential change (Credo, m. 1-5). The third phrase of the c.f. is repeated by the bass after being stated by the tenor (tenor, m. 41-43; bass, m. 43-45). The first of these phrases is a duo between tenor and superius, the second between alto and bass. At *Et incarnatus* only the first three phrases of the tune are given. This is a chordal section and the slightly ornamented tenor moves at the same speed as the other voices. The *Crucifixus* is an imitative duo between alto and bass in which the last part of the third phrase (picked up at the point where it was dropped in the preceding section), the cadence of phrase four (m. 90-91), and phrase five—the final phrase of the c.f.—are used (m. 93-97). This duo is followed by another between cantus and tenor (*Et resurrexit*), which also uses imitation throughout, but which is not based on c.f. Both the thin scoring and the absence of c.f. are unusual at this part of the Mass. At *Et iterum* the whole c.f. is gone through again, and once more the tendency is to start with long values and proceed to shorter ones and a greater amount of ornamentation. The material of the third phrase of the antiphon (*quia non est alius*) appears in superius and alto as well as tenor, partly by means of imitation, partly by free duplication in the duos from measure 140 to measure 153. (Josquin's version of this phrase differs slightly from that of the Vatican edition. What is now given as a single phrase was apparently divided into two in the form of the antiphon he used.) The fifth phrase appears in imitation in tenor and bass (m. 169-182), but otherwise the voices are largely organized independently of the c.f.

In the Sanctus the melody is presented four times. The first section begins with an exact statement of the head motive; then the tenor presents the entire melody in note values approximately equal to those of the other parts. Material of the third phrase is again repeated in the superius and tenor in alternating duos (m. 10-18). The fifth phrase is also repeated by the tenor and in addition given by the bass at the fourth below (m. 25-33). *Pleni sunt caeli* presents a series of five duos alternating regularly between tenor-bass and superius-alto; these persist until the closing section, which is scored for the full number of voices. The entire c.f. is used again, given mainly by the tenor and superius, although bass and alto share in it—either by imitation or by repeating the material of the leading voice. The fifth phrase is stated thrice (superius, tenor, superius, m. 62-75). A free, motivated section ends this part of the movement. The *Osanna* begins with four voices, the tenor presenting the first two phrases of the c.f. This is followed by two repeated duos (superius and alto first, then tenor and bass), so that the third phrase of c.f. is given first by the superius and then repeated by the tenor. The tenor then gives the fourth phrase in a section for four voices, after which the fifth is presented first in the superius, then in the tenor in duos similar to those above, and finally in the tenor again in a section for four voices (m. 127). The *Benedictus*, like the *Osanna*, gives the entire c.f. once more in a series of duos between superius and alto, and tenor and bass, interspersed with a few sections for four voices. Again, the tenor and superius are the chief carriers of the c.f., although parts of it appear in all voices

at one time or another. *Pleni sunt caeli*, *Osanna*, and *Benedictus* end
similarly since each is given a free closing section consisting of a single
phrase exactly repeated.

The first Agnus[54] begins with a statement of the head motive, exact
except that the material of the bass is shifted into the tenor part. This
may be done to emphasize the fact that the bass as well as the tenor
carries the c.f. The lower voice freely duplicates the tenor statement,
except for the third phrase, which is given by the tenor only. The fifth
phrase is repeated and is also given in strict imitation, the bass leading
off at the fourth below (m. 25; see also the very similar passage at m.
25 of the Sanctus). The upper voices have occasional imitative figures,
some of which are related to the c.f. In the second Agnus the tenor and
bass are in strict canon and present the entire c.f. again. The canon
begins slowly and rigidly in breves, with frequent interruptions by rests,
but it becomes faster and more ornamented at the end. All voices start
with an imitative entry, and the superius actually gives the first two
phrases in ornamented form (to m. 46 in *Das Chorwerk*, m. 16 in the
complete edition). The final phrase of the c.f. is exactly repeated. The
third Agnus is written for six voices,[55] with the first superius, tenor, and
second bass joining in a strict canon on the c.f. (*superacuta vox*, cantus I,
and bass II in *Das Chorwerk*). The canonic parts are at the distance of
the octave and double octave (in *Das Chorwerk* the two top parts are at
the unison, the bass is two octaves below), and the entries are all two
measures apart. The whole c.f. is given unornamented (the third phrase
is apparently simplified), largely in breves, and so frequently interrupted
by rests that no more than two voices sound together most of the time.
Although the canon in three parts is something of a contrapuntal feat,
it does not equal many others of Josquin. The other three voices are
freely organized by melodic figures consisting largely of cadential formulae
and of scale-line movement in short note values.

The detailed analysis of the structure of this Mass shows a very
surprising regularity of procedure. The c.f. is stated again and again in
much the same way, commonly starting with long notes in the manner
of a strict c.f. and becoming somewhat more florid. The tenor is clearly
the main c.f. voice, although the other parts may share to a greater or
less extent in the statements. The antiphon is always given in its entirety
and the proper order of the phrases is retained, although certain of them
are occasionally repeated. Even this mild freedom has an element of
regularity not characteristic of the other Masses based on Gregorian
chant, since the same phrases, the third and the fifth, are always the
ones which are repeated. The techniques used in the Agnus—the free
duplication of the c.f. in the first, and the rigid canons in the second

and third sections of the movement, with their frequent interruptions by rests—recall the methods of Obrecht very strongly. (See, for instance, the hymn *Haec Deum caeli*, ex. 107a-b.)

The characteristic of regularity extends beyond the c.f. treatment to other aspects of the structure. Movements open similarly because the head motive is used much more consistently than is usual, while the similarity of many of the closing sections approaches the status of a formula. In eight sections of the Mass—Kyrie II, *Et in terra, Qui tollis, Patrem, Et iterum, Pleni sunt caeli, Osanna,* and *Benedictus*—a freely composed cadential passage is added on after the completion of the c.f. statement. The fact that six closing sections consist in whole or in part of a phrase which is exactly repeated makes the similarity even more striking. (The editor of *Das Chorwerk* has also pointed out that in four—Kyrie II, *Qui tollis, Pleni,* and *Osanna*—a melodic figure consisting of a descending second followed by a descending third is given a prominent position and thus adds a further element of unity to the Mass as a whole.)[57]

It is not the fact of repetition which attracts comment in this work. Repetition is one of Josquin's most useful devices, one which he uses to achieve symmetry and architectural clarity to an outstanding degree. What surprises is the tendency to routine, the lack of variety in handling the repetitions. With regard to the closing sections cited above, for instance, one can feel fairly confident that the c.f. statement will be completed before a movement is finished, that a closing section will be added on, and that this section will consist of a single phrase which will be stated twice.

It is enlightening to compare these closing sections with similar ones in the *Missa Pange lingua*—for example, with those in the Kyrie and Gloria. The closing section of Kyrie II is free and does *not* contain a repeated phrase; that of the first half of the Gloria is free and *does* contain a repeated phrase; the closing phrase at the very end of the Gloria repeats, but it is *not* free; in addition, in the two closing sections which contain a repetition there are numerous changes of detail. An examination of the *Missa de Beata Virgine* shows a similar situation. That is, in these two works general procedures can be discerned, but there are fresh points in the application of them which indicate a constant mental alertness on the part of the composer.

It can be said in general of the writing of Josquin that considerations of form do not lead to formalism, with its inevitable implication of a limited or sluggish mind. However, as outlined above, the manner of statement of the c.f. itself in the *Missa Da pacem* does show a tendency to routine. This work of his old age gives the impression of less alertness and less intellectual versatility than appear in the remainder of the works, which offer constant proof of an orderly intelligence that is yet brilliantly inventive.

In contrast to these aspects of the c.f. treatment (a tendency to archaism and routine procedures), this is, stylistically, the most advanced of the Masses. More consistent use is made of imitation, more attention is paid to declamation, and the lines are smoother and simpler in shape than in the other late Masses. (For example, the quarter-note motion generally takes the form of direct scale-lines rather than the winding patterns which are such a characteristic and beautiful feature of most of Josquin's writing.)

The heavier, firmer harmony also indicates progress toward the style of the second quarter of the century. Typical of this style is the frequent use of the six-five suspension. Josquin uses this sparingly in the other Masses, but in this work it appears again and again. It is an important part of the harmonic vocabulary, especially at the cadences. (In modern terms, there are many cadences in which the harmonic progression is II $_6^5$-V-I.)

On the other hand, there is a greater amount of unusual dissonance treatment than in the other mature Masses, and the sturdy Flemish idiom of Obrecht comes to mind once more. Taken as a whole, the work is in some aspects regressive, while in others it is definitely forward-looking. It stands away from the other works like a far-advanced outpost, yet it contains a baffling mixture of traits, some of which are novel, some outmoded.

THE MOTETS OF JOSQUIN

The motets form a most important part of Josquin's work. Each shows some feature worth close consideration, and to do them justice each should be treated in detail. That, however, is a topic for a separate study. Since a general chronology has been given by Osthoff,[56] the earliest motets have been systematically treated by Stephan,[57] and Reese has analyzed a large number of them,[58] a digest of the principal types of c.f. treatment is all that will be undertaken here. The motets can be roughly divided into classes: the traditional tenor motet, the declamation motet (chordal or imitative), the motets built on tenors contrived by the composer, those which utilize more than one c.f. in combination, and so forth. Although such classification has certain unsatisfactory aspects—it takes no account of chronology, and many of the motets fall into more than one category—it is adopted here for convenience of discussion.

Tenor *cantus firmi* of all types are found. The *Stabat Mater* is built on the complete tenor of the chanson *Comme femme desconfortée*,[59] which is quoted continuously throughout both parts of the composition.

It belongs to the type of composition in which the tenor scaffolding stands out in sharp opposition to the other voices. The chanson tenor is given in long note values while the four other parts move more fluently. As usual, they are organized among themselves, but not so much by motives as by short imitative entries. These sometimes occupy all voices, sometimes only a few. Some are independent ideas, some are derived from the c.f. (See m. 28-31 and m. 47-51 for instances of the latter.) The general smoothness and lack of assertive rhythmic combinations is worth notice since a fairly early date is suggested by the setting of the text, which is largely syllabic but far from perfect with regard to accentuation. This supposition is also supported by the shape of the imitative lines, which often are brief patterns of a triadic nature and sometimes do not enter at the beginning of a phrase but grow directly out of the preceding line. On the whole, they lack the extension and the character of independently composed melodies which mark the imitative lines in the more mature works.[60]

Missus est Gabriel Angelus[61] is similar in many respects. It is a long work in two parts, it is for five voices, the scoring is consistently full, and it, too, is based on a secular tenor. In this case Josquin borrows from a chanson of Busnois, *A une dame j'ay fait veu*,[62] but instead of freely augmenting the tenor as he did with *Comme femme desconfortée* he states it only in double augmentation and then repeats it once in order to gain the necessary extension. The result is that the tenor notes are not so long and do not stand out in such contrast to the other voices as they do in the *Stabat Mater*. The other voices, though very fluent and elegant in movement, are written mainly as nonimitative counterpoints.

The c.f. is also quoted continuously in the *Requiem*, or "Deploration on the Death of Ockeghem."[63] The subject of the work indicates it was written in 1495 or shortly thereafter. As in the *Requiem* of Obrecht, the Introit is transposed so that the original sixth tone is converted to Phrygian mode. The choice of the funereal Phrygian, the mode of mourning, was undoubtedly determined by the concepts of the aesthetic qualities of the modes which were current at that time and by the feeling that music and text should be brought into a general expressive relationship. The c.f. is little ornamented and in general moves more slowly than the other voices. It is quoted down to the psalm in the first part of the work, and in the second part the tenor gives out the short respond, *Requiescant in pace. Amen.* Aside from a head entry in the bass at the very beginning of the work, the other voices are written as free counterpoints to the c.f.

Huc me sydereo descendere jussit Olympo–Plangent eum is placed by Osthoff in the period 1485–1505.[64] It is a large-scale tenor motet for six voices. The tenor, a true scaffolding of the isorhythmic type, is stated three times. The rhythmic layout of the first statement is taken as the model for the two following in the usual way. It is in perfect mode and supports the whole *prima pars*. In the *secunda pars*, the mensuration of the tenor is reduced to imperfect time, and the perfect longs become imperfect breves in the second statement. The note values of this statement are exactly halved in the third, the imperfect breve becoming an imperfect semibreve. (As has been pointed out in the Masses of Obrecht, the change from a perfect to an imperfect mensuration prevents the reduction of all notes in the same mathematical ratio.)

The first tenor statement is preceded by rests of the value of sixteen perfect longs, the second by sixteen imperfect breves, and the third by sixteen semibreves. Hence, both the *prima* and *secunda pars* open in the traditional manner with long introductory passages in which the tenor is silent. There is, however, no anticipatory statement of the c.f. The voices are freely composed and each phrase of text is given a melodic figure which is presented in imitation exactly as in the imitative motets, so that in this work the method of organization by means of imitative entries is grafted onto the old tenor structure.

Ave nobilissima creatura–Benedicta tu in mulieribus[65] is very similar in structure. It, too, is based on an isorhythmic scaffolding tenor which is stated three times, the perfect longs of the first statement becoming imperfect longs on the second and imperfect breves on the third; the tenor is also preceded by rests of sixteen perfect longs at first, and these become sixteen imperfect longs and sixteen imperfect breves on the second and third presentations. The contrapuntal voices do not share the c.f. material, but are very extensively organized among themselves by points of imitation, so that the two works resemble each other in this aspect as well.

The motet *Lectio actuum apostolorum–Dum complerentur dies*[66] is also based on a tenor which is stated three times. However, while the statements are rhythmically similar, they are not exact. The second statement is a free diminution of the first and the third is a free diminution of the second; the second is also transposed up a fifth, while the first and third are on the pitch of the antiphon. In this work also, the other voices do not partake of c.f. material, but in this case they are not extensively organized by imitation. Considerable care is taken with the declamation, and the score often has the appearance of a chordal declamation motet.

The duplication of the tenor by means of canon is another traditional procedure used by Josquin. The motet *Homo quidam fecit*[67] shows more archaic features than the others in which the tenor is treated in this manner. Older methods of writing are evident in the short anticipatory statements at the beginning of each part (superius, m. 1-7; contratenor secundus and bass, m. 88-96), and in the presentation of the respond as

a strict c.f. (See ex. 129a.) The beginning of the c.f. statement is similar
to many of Obrecht's, as well as to the canon in the third Agnus of Josquin's own *Missa Da pacem*. In this work, however, the presentation
becomes rhythmically more animated toward the end of the *prima pars*,
which is quite in keeping with his usual manner of c.f. statement. (See
ex. 129b.) The *secunda pars* also begins simply, although the Gregorian
melody is not given as a strict c.f. and becomes florid in the final phrase.

The setting of the sequence *Veni Sancte Spiritus*[68] is much more ad-

EXAMPLE 129. (a-b) Josquin, *Homo quidam fecit* (*Motetten*, I, 147; *Proc.
Mon.*, p. 105).

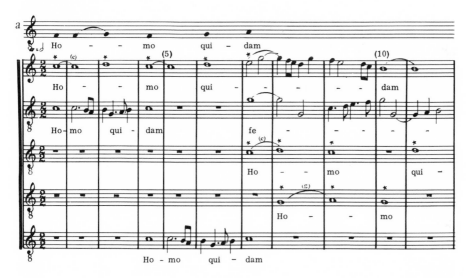

vanced in style. It is scored for six voices and the c.f. is presented in canon between the *quinta vox and discant*. It is, however, sufficiently ornamented so that it does not stand in complete contrast to the other voices. (See ex. 130.) In addition the tenor and bass are written in strict canon throughout, so that four out of the six parts are controlled by this means. Since the second canon is also partially based on c.f., the concentration of borrowed material greatly surpasses that which is found in the usual tenor motet. The two free voices are not set apart by any special means of organization; rather, they display strong similarities to the florid sections of the canonic voices, frequently imitating them briefly. The result is that, even though two voices are specifically entrusted with the presentation of the c.f., and even though the structural basis of two two-voice canons is maintained without any relaxation, this work closely approaches the most mature works in fluency of movement and in the extent to which the parts are integrated.

Continuous canon is a well-known feature of the chansons of Josquin. In fact, it occurs even more frequently in them than it does in the motets.[69] An exceptionally beautiful example is the chanson *Coment peult haver joye*, which may be mentioned here because it appears as a *contrafactum* motet, *O Jesu fili David*.[70] In this work the procedures of canon

EXAMPLE 130. Josquin, *Veni Sancte Spiritus* (*Motetten*, III, 37; *LU*, p. 880).

and head imitation are ideally combined; the gently ornamented c.f. is presented in strict canon between alto and tenor, and the two free voices are provided with head entries on c.f. material at the beginning of every phrase. The systematic use of imitation thus insures thematic as well as rhythmic integration of all parts. Stratification, in the sense that the c.f. is stated as an entity in itself and is surrounded by counterpoints which form a contrasting entity, is abandoned except in one respect. Josquin still entrusts the complete statement of the borrowed material to a certain bearer—here the two-voice canon.

Two other motets, *Alma Redemptoris Mater*[71] and *Inviolata, integra et casta es, Maria*,[72] are based on c.f. in canon, although in neither do the other voices share in the c.f. material to the extent seen in *Veni Sancte Spiritus* and *O Jesu fili David*. The Marian antiphon, *Alma Redemptoris Mater*, is presented in canon at the unison by alto and tenor at the distance of two measures; aside from an imitative entry on the first four notes the other voices do not share in its statement. The sequence, *Inviolata*, is presented by the first and second tenors in canon at the fifth above. The time distance of imitation becomes increasingly short—it is three measures in the *prima pars*, two in the *secunda*, and one in the *tertia pars*—and the statement becomes quite florid in the last phrase. Except at the beginning of the first and second parts, the other voices in this work, too, are written as free counterpoints with only the briefest of references to material of the canon. However, the beginning of the second part is somewhat different, as the alto and bass present a line of text and of the sequence melody in an imitative duo, and this material is not repeated by the tenor; at this point, alto and bass simply take over from the canonic voices.

Another method of c.f. statement which was used by Obrecht is found in those motets where each phrase of the borrowed melody is given by one voice and then repeated by another. Although the repetitions may be exact and may overlap slightly, so that the voices are actually canonic, the effect is not so much of imitation or canon as of duplicated, alternating statement. The repetition of each phrase makes progress through the c.f. very slow, so that works such as *Praeter rerum seriem*[73] and *Benedicta es, caelorum Regina*,[74] in which this method of statement is used, are among the lengthy motets.

The repetitive layout of *Praeter rerum seriem* is related to the form of the text in details as well as in the larger aspects. Each stanza of the sequence consists of two lines of four feet and a short concluding line of two feet. The *prima pars* of the motet covers the first pair of stanzas, the *secunda pars* the second and third pair. The third pair (stanzas five and six) is distinguished from the second by changes of meter and by note-against-note scoring. The layout of the sequence melody starts simply enough as a double scaffolding. The first tenor states the notes of the first line in long values, in slow triple meter. This line is immediately repeated by the superius an octave higher. The second line is given in exactly the same way, but at the third, short line of text the rigid scaffolding melts into an echoing series of statements which involve four of the six voices (m. 16-20, superius, tenor I, bass I, and bass II). With the second stanza the original plan of scaffolding is resumed, but with note values only half as great. The short closing line is this time given to a single voice only (tenor II, m. 27), completing the *prima pars*. The pattern set up in these two stanzas—scaffolding statement for the first two lines and free statement for the short closing line—is maintained consistently during the rest of the work.

The *secunda pars* is in duple meter (₵), but the scaffolding continues in actual triple meter. The first line of stanza three is given three times (superius; altus at the fourth below, m. 35; and tenor II at the octave below, m. 40); the second line is given, with a rhythmic outline similar to the first, by the superius (m. 45) and tenor I (m. 48), but in this case the strict regularity of the scaffolding is broken by a short overlap of the statements. Once more the closing line appears in several voices (m. 51 ff., superius, altus, and tenor I). The fourth stanza resumes the scaffold in triple meter—the first line is stated twice only (bass II, m. 61; tenor I, m. 65), the second line twice (tenor I, m. 70; superius, m. 73), and the third line three times (m. 76 ff., tenor I and superius). The form of the fourth stanza differs from all the others, since there is a short introductory passage in which the motive to be used against the c.f. is exposed. This motive is used interestingly in double counterpoint at the tenth (compare the altus, m. 60 ff., and superius and first bass, m. 64 ff.) and in such a way that the c.f. entry at measure 61 is harmonized by a B♭ chord while the answering entry at measure 65 is harmonized in g minor. The final line of the stanza is set as a cadential passage consisting of a short idea which is thrice stated with interchange of parts. Basses I and II call attention to themselves by repeating the leap of a tenth (m. 77, 79, and 81).

The third pair of stanzas is again in triple meter (*proportio sesquialtera*) and is written in a note-against-note style which forms a strong contrast to the intricate rhythmic interplay of the voices in the preceding sections. The first line of stanza five appears three times (superius, m. 83; tenor I, m. 86; altus, m. 89), the second line twice (tenor I, m. 92; altus, m. 95), the third line several times (in altus, tenor I, and tenor II, m. 98-104). The music to the first two lines of the sixth stanza (m. 104 ff.) is an exact repetition of the fifth (with some rescoring due to interchange of parts). The final line is different. There is a return to duple meter and a broad cadence is constructed to bring the entire work to a close. Tenor I and II state the c.f. and the other voices reiterate the final words, "*Mater ave*," in declamatory style.

On the whole, *Praeter rerum seriem* is written in the older style. Scaffolding statements stand out clearly from the counterpoints, which are constituted of a mass of motives disposed, as usual, so as to bring about all manner of cross rhythms. The motives are basically figurated triads, are stated in tight imitation, and have self-sufficient rhythmic configurations to which the text must somehow be adapted. When all voices are in use, the scoring is of great complexity and stirs with exuberant rhythmic activity. These features of fully developed late-fifteenth-century style need not indicate an early date of composition. The mere complexity of a double scaffolding and the flexible, hybrid form which is based on the fluctuation between rigid and free statement indicate a mature work from about the turn of the century. The uses to which repetition is put likewise indicate maturity. The element of repetition is carried far beyond the repetition of verses normal in a sequence and involves the restatement of nearly every line of the text. This leads to the architectural symmetry which Josquin seeks and also gives ample time for working out the motivic ideas placed against the c.f. The tendency to treat ideas comprehensively contrasts with the practice, noted in some of the earlier Masses, of moving quickly from one idea to another. Absolute symmetry is avoided; the repetitions of the c.f. are not always regular themselves and they are seldom attended by exactly repeated counterpoints; in fact, repetion of the c.f. gives opportunity for all sorts of contrast in scoring.[75] The indications are that, despite important work which we recognize as prophetic, Josquin continued on occasion to write motets in the older, rhythmically vigorous style just as he did with Masses. In any case, the long list of sources cited by Smijers[76] gives conclusive testimony of the great popularity of the work until well after the middle of the century and shows that the style of the late fifteenth century was appreciated for more than a generation after composers had abandoned it.

The plan of statement of the sequence *Benedicta es, caelorum Regina* is roughly the same as *Praeter rerum seriem* on the one hand and *Veni Sancte Spiritus* on the other. As in the former, the c.f. statement begins as widely spaced canon, and as in the latter, two other voices are related canonically (bass and *sexta pars*). The structure, however, is entirely flexible. The bass and *sexta pars* are not strictly canonic from the point of view either of melody or of time interval of imitation. Likewise, the alternating canonic statement of the c.f. is not long kept up. The c.f. statement tends to become more complex as the work proceeds. The c.f. phrases overlap more because they are written in closer imitation, other voices share in the quotation, and the ornamentation becomes richer.

As for the details of c.f. layout, the phrases of the first two verses of *Benedicta es, caelorum Regina* appear alternately in superius and tenor, but, as mentioned above, this regular order is soon abandoned. Starting at the third verse (m. 74), the c.f. appears in imitation in the three lowest voices. At measure 83 the tenor takes over, and at measure 87 the superius, which carries it to the end of the *prima pars*. The fifth verse is presented in an imitative duo built on c.f. material and terminating with a florid closing section. The sixth verse is set for six voices again, c.f. material being heard in the imitative entries with which each is provided. It is then taken by the superius and second tenor, and at measure 149 by the superius alone, the other voices providing a full harmonization. It soon migrates to the tenor, and the composition ends with a florid Amen.

The free voices are smoothly flowing and are completely integrated among themselves. At the very beginning they repeat an idea presented

EXAMPLE 131. Josquin, *Benedicta es, caelorum Regina* (*Motetten*, II, 11-12).

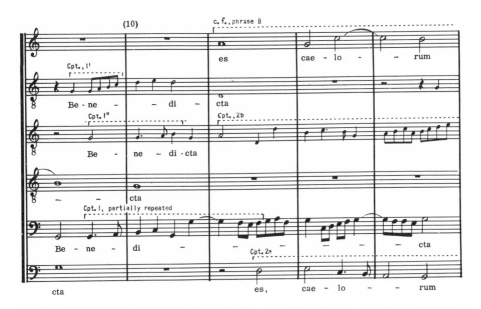

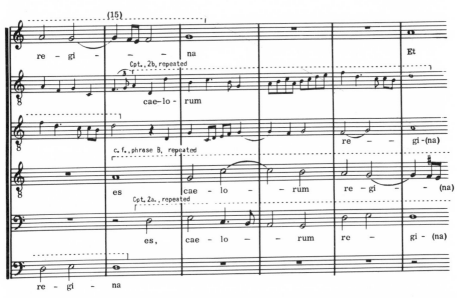

in the first measures (ex. 131, altus, m. 1-4; bass, m. 5-9; etc.) and then develop on it. The first twenty measures give the impression of a rounded musical unit, the idea first exposed being expanded and intensified and then brought to a satisfactory cadence. The next section presents a new set of ideas worked out in the same general way. In this sense *Benedicta es, caelorum Regina* resembles the motets which make consistent use of points of imitation as they, too, are comprised of a series of relatively short and self-sufficient units, in each of which an idea is presented and given a satisfactory working-out. Nevertheless, imitation is not the basic device in this work. It is still a tenor motet in which a given part, or parts, can be clearly heard as guiding the composition in its course.

Virgo salutiferi-Ave Maria[77] is based on another of these leisurely canons in which the two voices give the impression of answering back and forth rather than imitating one another. The work is in three parts, and the canons in the first and second parts are very much the same. Phrases of the c.f. are not repeated in the second as they are in the first, but in both the antiphon is quoted only down to *Dominus tecum*. In the third part the time interval of imitation becomes closer and the entire chant is given. (However, there is a departure from the notes of the Vatican version at *in mulieribus, Amen*, m. 197 to the end.) In another aspect of structure the work resembles the tenor motets *Huc me sydereo* and *Ave nobilissima creatura*. In the first two parts the structural voices are preceded by very long rests and their statement is interrupted by ample pauses between phrases. As in the tenor motets, the contrapuntal voices do not give anticipatory statements of the c.f. at these points but are extensively organized among themselves by means of imitation. Even though a single technique underlies the entire work (i.e., imitation in the form of canon or in the form of initial entries), the structural duality of c.f. versus counterpoints is retained.

Yet another traditional procedure favored by Josquin is the use of a repeated c.f. motive as the basis of the composition. This motive may be contrived by the composer or it may be a quotation of a fragment of chant, and it is usually disposed according to some orderly plan which involves statement on different pitches. The setting of the fiftieth psalm, *Miserere mei Deus, secundum magnam misericordiam tuam*[78] (in which the *tenor secundus* reiterates the first three words—the dramatic heart of the text), is structurally interesting, as the pitches of the statements exceed the scope of the hexachord. (This is true, too, of the *In hydraulis* of Busnois.) In the first part, the first statement is on e′ and each succeeding one is given a tone lower until e, the octave below, is reached. In the second part, the first statement is on e and the succeeding ones ascend scalewise until e′ is reached once more. The first statement of the third part is made on e′ again, but this time the scale-wise descent covers only a fifth, the final statement being made on a, the tonic of the work. The rhythmic pattern of the statements remains constant although they are presented at irregular time intervals. Both of these rhythmic aspects are a result of textual considerations; the pattern of the motive is determined by the accentuation of the words, while the irregular interval of appearance is the result of a dramatic plan in which the plea *"Miserere mei Deus"* is used as a refrain to each verse of the psalm. The crucial role of the text in the layout illustrates how the tenor structure, too, can become amenable to the newer artistic ideals. However, this means the abandonment of the time-honored approach in which structure is basically a matter of mensuration—of mathematical proportion as expressed in rhythmic durations. Earlier, the mensural plan for the tenor would have come first and the text would have been subordinated to it; it would have been made to fit in as best it could.

The earlier attitude is well expressed in the motet *Illibata Dei Virgo nutrix.*[79] The tenor fragment consists of three solmization syllables, la-mi-la, (Ma-ri-a?), which are stated alternately in the hexachord on F and in one on B♭. (The pitches are d'-a-d' and g-d-g.) In addition, they are laid out according to fixed rhythmic schemes, so that the tenor derives in every respect from some aspect of the musical system. As indicated above, such a tenor may have a relation to the text, but the relation is intellectual and symbolic, not dramatic.

In the *prima pars* each note is given the value of a perfect long and the motive is stated three times—once on d', once on g, and again on d'. Each statement is preceded by rests of the value of six perfect longs. In other words, the rests have twice the length of the motive itself, which covers only three of these notes. In the *Secunda pars* the rests preceding each statement of the motive are equal in value to it. When the notes are given the value of breves, three breve rests precede the motive; when given as semibreves, three semibreve rests precede it. The *secunda pars* begins with the meter signature ₵, and the motive is first stated four times in breves and then six times in semibreves. Following the meter signature ₵ 3, it is heard eight times in semibreves, and, after ₵ 2, eight times more in breves. The marks of the older style are especially noticeable in the first part of the work (which is in triple meter). Among other things, the rather bare sequences in imitation, the constant hemiola, and the other rhythmic groupings which tend to cover the basic meter may be pointed out. They indicate that this is a very early work.

The setting of the Marian antiphon *Salve regina*[80] is also constructed on an *ostinato* c.f. The work is scored for five voices, the c.f. motive being entrusted to the *Quinta vox*. The motive consists of the first four notes of the antiphon, each note being given the value of a breve. The statements are preceded by rests of the value of three breves and they begin alternately on the pitches g' and d'. Over this extremely rigid scaffolding, the entire antiphon melody is given in a freely elaborated form. It is given by the soprano for the most part, although there is migration in the third part of the motet[81] and the final phrase is so highly elaborated that it could well be considered free.

Ut Phoebi radiis[82] is based on a solmization scaffold which is more fanciful in its structure than that of *Illibata Dei Virgo*. The principle followed is illustrated in example 132a-b. The scaffolds are essentially a series of expanding scales, starting with a single note (*ut*) and adding one more note on every statement until the hexachord is covered. The scales are stated in canon between tenor and bass, and ascend in the *prima pars* and descend in the *secunda pars*. In both parts there is a cadential extension after the hexachords have finally been covered. (Ex. 132a, m. 62 ff.) Even though the motives do not have a set length, the rests between statements are always of the same duration, so that at least one aspect of the rigid rhythmic layout usually associated with these contrived tenors is found in this work.

The play on the syllables of the hexachord extends beyond the tenor, as the text of the upper voices is so contrived that each line begins with one or more of them in the expanding order of the scaffolding. For instance, in the first part the first line begins with *Ut* Phoebi . . . , the

EXAMPLE 132. Josquin, *Ut Phoebi radiis*—(a) tenor and bass, (b) tenor and bass, (c) superius and altus (*Motetten*, I, 110).

second with *Ut-re-ges* . . ., the third with *Ut re-mi* . . ., etc. The second part beings with *La-*tius . . . , then *Las-so lege* . . . , then *La sol fa ta mi na* . . ., etc. Each one of these syllables is, of course, allotted an appropriate note in the music, so that the free voices, too, are influenced by the scale motive. (See ex. 132c for one instance of this.) The significance of the isolated syllables which appear in the text of the second part is not clear to me. They add a fantastic aspect to a poem which begins quite seriously, despite its burden of punning.

Another traditional device, the statement of two or more *cantus firmi*, is found in some of the motets. The sixth part of *Qui velatus facie fuisti* is set to the sequence *Christum ducem*, the verses of which are so constructed that the final line of each consists of a quotation of the first line of some well-known hymn.[83] In the musical setting the melody of each of these hymns is given to the superius, so that the motet is based on multiple c.f. in successive statements.

In most cases, however, the *cantus firmi* are combined. Josquin does not state them plainly and piece them together as best he may, in the manner of Obrecht. He ornaments them freely, so that the simultaneous statements do not represent any great technical feat but the musical result is fluent and easy. In *O bone et dulcis Domine Jesu*[84] the tenor recites the *Pater noster* and the bass *Ave Maria, gratia plena*, while the two other voices are free. In *Victimae paschali laudes* the superius gives the superius of the chanson *D'ung aultre amer* by Ockeghem in the first part and that of *De tous biens pleine* by Ghizegem in the second.[85] Both quotations are literal. The sequence melody is stated continuously from beginning to end of the motet. It is moderately ornamented and instead of being given by a single voice migrates between alto, tenor, and bass.[86]

The motet *Alma Redemptoris Mater–Ave Regina caelorum*[87] is an even more thorough instance of c.f. combination. For the most part, all voices carry ornamented c.f., the two outer presenting *Alma Redemptoris*, the two inner *Ave Regina*. While this is the general plan, it is not carried out strictly to the last detail. For instance, although the second part of the motet (ex. 133, m. 57-67) starts out with statements divided between the voices according to this scheme, the alto is so highly ornamented in measures 69-79 that, even though c.f. notes can be found, it is for all practical purposes a free voice. At measure 80 the alto actually takes over material of the other antiphon, since it imitates the superius. (Ex. 133, m. 80.) Of the four voices, the two which present the c.f. most consistently throughout are the superius and tenor. This plan of c.f. usage incidentally results in double counterpoint in the opening duos, a type of contrapuntal manipulation not common at this time. (Compare m. 1-3 with m. 9-11.)

On the whole, the motets discussed above show Josquin in the aspect

of one who brings a traditional style to its culmination. Only a limited
number of others—those which make more or less regular use of points
of imitation, and at the same time dispense with an obvious structural
voice—show him fully in the aspect of innovator in the style which comes
to its zenith forty or fifty years later. The significance of the latter works
having already been discussed (p. 345), here only some details of interest
will be pointed out.

Speaking generally, all voices are imitative in these works, so all share
in the presentation of the c.f. Nevertheless, the old practice of entrusting

EXAMPLE 133. Josquin, *Alma Redemptoris Mater–Ave Regina caelorum—secunda pars* (*Motetten*, I, 107; LU, pp. 273-274).

a c.f. chiefly to a given voice persists; thus, despite the imitation, almost invariably the c.f. can be traced more clearly in one part than in any of the others, even though it does not stand out as an obvious structural voice. For instance, as far as it is possible to follow c.f. in *Ave Maria . . . Virgo serena*,[88] it is presented most clearly in the bass. A leading part can be found even in such a consistently imitative work as *Rubum quem viderat Moyses*,[89] where the tenor continues with c.f. at a point where the other voices drop it (ex. 134a, tenor m. 12-14; it is the only voice which has this part of the antiphon). On the whole, the c.f. is treated with some freedom in these works, and in this motet it is dropped in favor of free declamation at the end (ex. 134b, m. 57 ff.).[90]

The setting of *Mittit ad Virginem*[91] shows sufficiently consistent use of initial imitation to be classed with these works, yet the sequence melody can be followed most clearly now in one voice, now in another.[92] This work must represent the final stage in the history of the technique of migration, which now has no further reason for existence since the c.f. is brought into all voices much more consistently by means of imitation.

One other feature which places Josquin as a pioneer in the new style is this: his use of initial imitation does not become stereotyped, so it is never possible to predict with any certainty that a given phrase will begin with a point. The chances are just as good that it will not as that it will.

EXAMPLE 134. (a-b) Josquin, *Rubum quem viderat Moyses* (*Motetten*, I, 29; LU, p. 443).

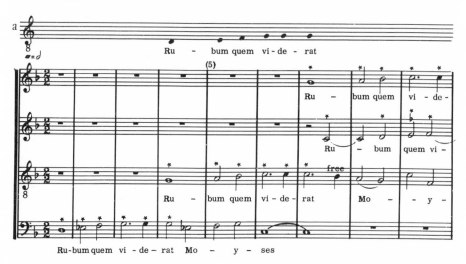

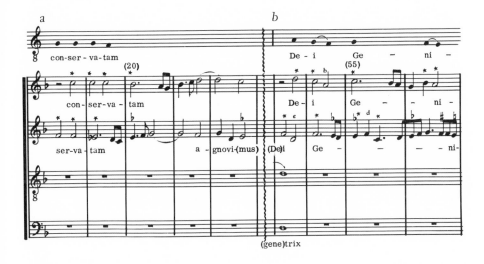

He still clings to repetition of c.f. phrases, usually in the form of duets. These may be imitative in themselves, but the effect is not that of the points of imitation of the next generation, which depend on fairly close entries of all voices.

A survey of the works of Josquin shows him bringing one stylistic era to its conclusion and also pointing the way very clearly to the one which is to follow without entering wholly into it. In these respects his career parallels that of Beethoven. Both men wrote expertly in the style of their predecessors and both had the creative imagination to go far beyond that style. Both had the unlimited esteem of their successors and both hold an important historical position because of the influence they exerted on those who came after them. Both, however, transcend history as individuals who have produced works of such quality that they rank among the most worthy achievements of the human mind.

APPENDIX

APPENDIX

Some Theories of Cantus Firmus Usage

Rudolph Ficker on Discant Coloration

Several articles propounding an elaborate theory of the use of c.f. in music of the fifteenth century and earlier have been published by R. Ficker and J. Handschin. Their ideas have achieved widespread circulation although their value has been questioned by many authorities, and they are now considered more or less outdated. I have hesitated to add further criticisms to those already expressed—first, because some difference of opinion is inevitable in this area of investigation, owing to the complex and often ambiguous nature of the subject of c.f. usage, and, second, because any sort of criticism introduces a contentious element which I would gladly avoid. There is, however, no way of avoiding the fact that these studies deal with the manner of quotation and layout of the c.f., which is precisely the subject of this book, and that the methods and conclusions of the authors differ widely from my own. It is impossible to leave them unmentioned, and a brief statement of disagreement would be profitless. Therefore I am appending a rather detailed analysis of a few of Ficker's and Handschin's writings.

Ficker's theories of discant coloration[1] have been seriously questioned by Wagner, Besseler, Bukofzer, and others.[2] It has been pointed out that his system of equating a c.f. with any given composition is so loose that it does not distinguish between accidental and intentional relationships. The system of c.f. usage he envisages differs from the practices observed in works which undoubtedly employ borrowed material,[3] and is never adequately connected with these practices.

Furthermore, it is a most serious weakness that the works he cites as examples of an advanced type of treatment by the English composers of the first half of the century never name the c.f. It is true that the c.f. is not named in every work of the fifteenth century based on borrowed material,[4] but the practice was to announce rather than to hide its identity. Hence, the total lack of any c.f.

403

references in the group of works which Ficker cites in support of his ideas raises questions in the reader's mind. It may be that these works were freely composed and, since Ficker never satisfactorily excludes this possibility, the proof of the presence of c.f. rests on no firmer basis than his conviction that one is being used. Even when he makes a convincing case for isomelism (i.e., where he shows that the melody of the second half of a work is a variant of the melody of the first half), he still fails to prove that the composer is varying *borrowed material* and not ideas of his own.

The method of the argument is open to question because one assumption is constantly used to prove another. Ficker has made important contributions in these papers, but he supports his central proposition—that a special type of discant coloration was used by the English—only by a series of unproved statements.

His article, "Die Kolorierungstechnik . . . ," starts clearly enough with a discussion of the plainchant Mass. The existence of ornamented c.f. in the discant of many movements of the Liebert Mass had been established by Koller, and tables illustrating its use are given by Ficker.[5] The analytic tables are satisfactory for the most part, although Ficker overlooks migration from the discant to the tenor in the fourth and sixth Kyries.[6] He accounts for the lack of agreement between the discant and the c.f. at these points by assuming that Liebert used a different form of the chant, which is reasonable, although it is a supposition which does not have to be made in this case.

Following the discussion of the Kyrie, the Alleluia *Ora pro nobis* is taken up and it is remarked that there are two places where the c.f. does not fit the superius (m. 46-51 and m. 70-81). The first of these is shown in example 135, where it can be seen that the c.f. is dropped at measure 46 and replaced by a florid, freely composed passage. It seems that this passage should not be described as one where the c.f. can *hardly* be followed, as Ficker does,[7] but as one where it cannot be followed at all, since it is simply not there.[8] It is taken up again at the structurally important d' (m. 52), the final note of the phrase. In another passage (m. 14-17) Ficker notes that the c.f. is also worked into a comparatively independent melodic shape in the discant, and he easily could have extended the observation to include the whole passage from measure 10 through measure 24. (See ex. 136, m. 7-27 of the Alleluia.) These measures are apparently extremely well suited to support his theories. According to his analysis, indicated by +'s in the discant, the c.f. is in fact used most irregularly. Two or three measures at a time seem to be totally independent, and the borrowed tones are often given melodically unimportant positions. For instance, the short ornamental d' at the end of measure 13 is supposed to be taken from the chant, while the structurally important f', the cadential note on the following strong beat, is supposedly freely composed. This certainly would depart from the methods observed in some hundreds of compositions with paraphrased c.f. The answer is plain, however, because at measure 9 the c.f. migrates to the tenor (marked by x's in the example). Two notes cannot be accounted for (m. 11, 25), but the same number were not found by Ficker in the discant either (m. 11, 19). Otherwise the c.f. tones almost totally dominate the outline of the tenor voice, quite in contrast to the small part they play in determining the shape of the discant. The passage is a quite ordinary instance of migration of the c.f. and is completely valueless as evidence of a very free, haphazard type of c.f. usage in the discant.

There is no question that Liebert's use of c.f. is extremely irregular. Ficker could hardly have chosen another work as well suited as this Alleluia to support his theories. However, as indicated in examples 135 and 136, it is doubtful that even this work actually supports his conclusions as to the nature of the coloration technique. It is possible to analyze critical passages differently from Ficker, and with the result that the freedoms appear as something very different from those he has in mind. With regard to the passage quoted in example 135, Ficker would have a strong argument except for the fact that intermittent statement of the c.f. is one of the features of works as irregular as this. The passage can be explained equally well on the assumption that at this point the c.f. is temporarily dropped and the superius freely composed. In the passage quoted in example 136 Ficker is on far weaker ground, since it can be analyzed more comfortably by assuming migration. It provides no evidence at all for the type of "purely constructive" usage he envisages, since by overlooking the migration he has missed the "constructive" feature the composer actually uses.

He says of these passages, "according to them, many parts of the upper voice of the Alleluia show a certain independence of the cantus firmus, an observation of importance for judging the technical methods used in the composition

EXAMPLE 135. Liebert—Alleluia, *Ora pro nobis* (*DTO*, 53, p. 7; Gr. Rouen, fo. 219b).

EXAMPLE 136. Liebert—Alleluia, Ora pro nobis (*DTO*, 53, p. 7; Gr. Rouen, fo. 219b).

of the Gloria and Credo of the Mass."[9] It seems from this that any questionable feature in his analysis of the Alleluia would weaken his further argument, but this is not really the case, since he has other reasons to support the c.f. usage he sees in the Gloria and Credo. His findings in the Alleluia are mainly useful because they make his following suggestions seem more plausible to the reader.[10]

The analyses of the Gloria and Credo of Liebert (and the Mass of Tournai as well) are presented in tables which make his methods of applying c.f. quite clear.[11] Among other things, they show that he equates notes of one phrase of the chant with those of other phrases of the setting, and that he assumes that notes forming important structural points of the chant may be used in completely unimportant positions in the ornamented melody. As stated before, he is aware that these usages are different from those normally found, but his interpretation implies far more than the existence in the fifteenth century of a different mechanical method of utilizing the notes of a chant in a superius line. Such usages, if they really existed, would indicate that composers adopted a basically different attitude toward the original melody from that implied in the more normal settings.

From the study of the c.f. settings made earlier in this book it is apparent that musicians viewed the chants as melodies with definite phrase structure, that they generally respected this phrase structure when they made elaborated versions, and that they maintained the relationship of text and music with some care. These are serious attitudes toward the musical and liturgical integrity of the chant which cannot be lightly dismissed, yet in Ficker's system they have no place. If his speculations are true, the original melodies were not seriously considered as musical organisms to be elaborated into more complex, but still related, organisms. Rather, they were no more than a source for a certain series of tones which could be fitted into the superius line quite haphazardly.

He gives plausible reasons for assuming the special type of treatment in the two movements of the Mass with longest text. Briefly stated, he feels that the plain syllabic declamation and repeated figures of the Gregorian Gloria and Credo melodies make them too monotonous for setting unless they are reworked considerably. However, elaboration of the normal type of these already lengthy melodies would make the settings too long for practical liturgical use. The reworking, then, must be of a different nature from that ordinarily encountered. It will still involve coloration, but, in order to counteract the excessive length which this brings about, unusable parts must be replaced by others or so altered from the original forms that almost nothing remains of them.[12]

It is true that there are not very many Glorias and Credos in which the chant is set in an ordinary way, but they can be found. Compositions from Old Hall and a few by Dufay[13] and Ockeghem show that such settings were occasionally made. Ficker's reasoning may well explain the scarcity of movements of this type, but it still falls far short of proving the existence of the kind of c.f. treatment he has in mind. He mentions that the upper voices may be freely composed in some instances,[14] but he never pursues this line of thought—although an indispensable first step in any investigation of c.f. technique is the development of some means for distinguishing between freely composed voices and those that make use of borrowed material. By failing to cope with the problem he has made it impossible to come to any secure conclusions. However, the reason for this critical omission is not far to seek. In order to demonstrate beyond reasonable doubt that c.f. is being used, he must show so many correspondences with the source that they cannot well be accounted for on the grounds of chance. From the nature of the treatment which he advocates, this is exactly what he cannot do, yet until it is done his arguments are no more than speculations.

An additional attempt is made to give a foundation for this type of treatment by assuming that it represents a stage in a hypothetical development from discant coloration to free composition.[15] We know now that there is no such development and that freely composed sacred music exists side by side with compositions based on c.f. throughout the fifteenth century. In addition, there are borderline compositions which contain c.f. references of greater or less length while the remaining parts are newly invented.[16] Furthermore, although the practice of turning a c.f. into an elaborated melody voice continues for at least fifty years after the time of the Liebert Mass, and the irrational melodic style of Ockeghem brings with it a correspondingly irregular ornamentation of the chant, there is still no evidence that c.f. treatment merges into free composition. Just the opposite seems to be the case, as there is a tendency to present the c.f. even more simply in the era of Josquin. On the whole, this supposed historical tendency seems to be no more than an assumption (based on an evolutionary idea) brought in to support another assumption.

After establishing to his own satisfaction that *cantus firmi* were used in the Gloria and Credo of the Tournai Mass and that references to this technique can be found in the Machaut Mass, Ficker investigates its further usage. A study of the thematic catalogue of the Old Hall manuscript leads him to the conclusion that the technique of discant coloration was in full bloom in England c. 1400. In the Trent codices, compiled several decades later, he finds it used much more frequently. Furthermore, in Trent it appears in a much clearer form in the works of Continental composers than it does in the works of their English contemporaries. This he takes as evidence that during the intervening years the composition technique of the English must have undergone significant development. He feels there must be some reason for the high esteem in which the English musicians were held, and for him, nothing lies nearer than the supposition that the significance of the English school rests above all in an alteration or further development of the c.f. technique.[17]

Because of lack of material from the earlier period, a study is then made of a much later work, the Mass *O rosa bella III*. The analysis of this is taken as confirmation of the previously stated conclusion that the essential characteristic of the new techniques lies *"in the simultaneous use of two cantus firmi, of which the one is treated in colorated form in the upper voice, the other, on the contrary, is generally taken in the tenor in unaltered form."*[18] The origin of this practice is then sought in various English works of the first half of the century.

Before taking up these English works, the analysis of the *O rosa bella* Mass should be considered, for it is an important link in the argument. Ficker's tables[19] merit fairly close study in order to gain a clear picture of his methods of applying the c.f., so I am presenting an abstract from them in example 137a-c.

The superius of the chanson is supposed to be used throughout in an upper voice of the Mass. Example 137a shows how a passage from the Mass which lies between the limits of the fifth d'-a' is equated by Ficker with one of the same range in the chanson. Only the note names d-e-f-g-a are used, although they do not occur in the same order in each passage. These differences in order are accounted for in the analytic tables by putting crossed lines above some of the notes to indicate reversed quotation. Thus g-f can be equated with f-g, and so on. Example 137b shows a-b equated with b-a of the chanson by the same means (m. 21-22 of the Agnus) and a-f-g with f-g-a by the use of a bent arrow (m. 27 of the Agnus). A single g of the chanson, which cannot be located on pitch, is correlated with one an octave higher (Agnus, m. 22). Migration opens up the contratenor as a field for hunting possible relationships. Example 137c shows that there may be long free sections (see m. 35-43 of the Kyrie), so that one measure of the chanson may spread over a great space in the Mass. On the other hand, several measures of it may be concentrated in a very limited area, since the migrations may double back and more than one part of the chanson be sounded simultaneously (m. 45-47 of the Kyrie).

Since the chanson melody has only a fraction of the number of notes contained in the two upper voices of any of the Mass movements, and since the voice lines are of approximately equal range, are similar (so far as they all move largely by step or small skips) in mode and melodic style, and, moreover, are counterpoints to the same melody in the tenor, it can be seen that many correspondences are bound to occur. Also, Ficker's objective is very limited, since all that he wants is to establish similarities in note names. As it is possible to reverse notes, to make an occasional octave transposition, to double back in the migrations, etc., it is clear that the chances are extremely good for finding the correspondences he is seeking. In fact, the odds are too much in his favor; he is largely playing on the fact that the two compositions are based on the same scale of seven notes. This is an obvious truth, but one that is completely useless for establishing the exclusive relationship that is desired, i.e., that the upper voices of this Mass are based throughout on a specific melody, the superius of *O rosa bella*.

Correspondences just as clear as those Ficker finds can be found between any

EXAMPLE 137. Anonymous, *Missa O rosa bella III*—(a) Credo, (b) Agnus, and (c) Kyrie (*Studien zur Musikwissenschaft*, VII, 46, 47, 45), with Dunstable's *O rosa bella* chanson (*ibid.*, p. 45).

melody and another one that is considerably longer, provided both are of equivalent range and mode. To substantiate the presence of c.f. one must adopt a process of exclusion. It is necessary to show similarities between the model and the derived line which are of so pronounced a nature that they cannot reasonably be accounted for as coincidences. The crossed lines, arrows, transpositions, etc., are devices of an inclusive nature. The more they are used, the more similarities the analyst will find in note names, but the greater the chances become that the similarities are merely accidental.

O rosa bella III is a typical tenor Mass. The tenor of the chanson is taken as the structural voice and is presented by the tenor of the Mass. At the beginning of movements, before the tenor enters, the Mass superius also quotes c.f., but in this work the quotations happen not to be simple anticipatory statements of the chanson tenor. Instead, the superius presents a portion of its counterpart voice, the superius of the chanson. In the tutti sections of each movement (wherever the tenor is sounding), the superius is written as a free counterpoint.

If it is true that the superius of the Mass quotes c.f. some of the time and some of the time is freely composed, this fact should show up in Ficker's analysis in one way or another, since he is trying to prove the continuous presence of the chanson superius in the upper voices regardless of whether the tenor is sounding or not. There should be a difference in the appearance of his analysis, depending upon whether the superius is part of an introductory duo or part of a tutti. As the examples given below indicate, this difference does show up.

In the introductory duos Ficker's analytical tables show a high concentration of c.f. notes, and the signs he has adopted to indicate rearrangement are notably absent. It is true that the composer takes many liberties in the elaboration of the c.f., but these consist largely of the omission of notes (see ex. 138a-b). In the most flagrant case, five notes are omitted (ex. 138b, m. 11-12), but even here the c.f. is so clear in the preceding and following measures that there is no doubt that it is actually being used. The other omissions have to do with ornamental notes and do not impair the relationships between the original and the derived voice.[20] In fact, they are the best possible proof of a nice awareness on the part of the composer of the melodic qualities of the original. By discriminating between the relative values of the individual notes, he is able to retain a convincing relationship between the chanson melody and the elaborated version

EXAMPLE 138. Anonymous, *Missa O rosa bella III*—(a) Credo and (b) Agnus II (*DTO*, 22, pp. 43, 66), with Dunstable's *O rosa bella* chanson (*Works*, p. 133).

without completely literal quotation.[21] Other freedoms have to do with an extreme shortening of ornamental notes (see the anticipations in ex. 138b, m. 14-15), rearrangement of the incises of the chanson in one place (ex. 138a, m. 3-4), and exceeding the range limits of the original to a certain extent (ex. 138b, m. 6-7). In making a thorough transformation of a rather plain tune into a much more elaborate one, the composer takes many of the liberties that Ficker assumes in his type of analysis. However, these liberties fall within the framework of an order which is provided by the melody of *O rosa bella*. The goals of motion provided by it, the phrase ends, become the goals of the paraphrase, so that the structure of the original determines that of the derived part. Within the phrases of the latter the minor melodic movements of the chanson are treated casually, but the major directions are retained in such a great majority of cases that the connection between the two melodies can hardly be doubted. In other words, the very number of c.f. notes in the Mass superius which appear in direct succession, in the original order, and which hold positions of some melodic importance, more than overbalance all the differences and thus exclude free composition as a likely alternative.

When we move from the duos to the tutti sections the whole picture changes. As an instance we can take the beginning of the Sanctus, which is scored for four voices (ex. 139). Ficker finds that the beginning of the chanson is used here, too, but, outside of the head motive of two or three measures, an essentially different attitude toward the original is revealed. According to his analysis, the evidences of a discriminative appreciation of the melodic qualities of the chanson suddenly disappear. The relative importance of the individual notes of the original is largely ignored; the structurally important cadence on g (m. 5 of the chanson) is destroyed (ex. 139, contratenor, m. 14, and superius, m. 11); the notes which agree with *O rosa bella*, instead of dominating the melody line, tend to be separated into little clusters of from two to four tones (ex. 139, m. 4, 6, 7, 12, 14, etc.); and it is necessary to assume big overlapping migrations. It seems significant that the whole apparatus of accounting for dis-·crepancies must be used in the sections where the tenor is sounding (as in ex. 137a-c and ex. 139), while there is no need for it in the duos. The analyses of the tutti sections require a larger variety of signs than the duos, which need only a simple series of x's, yet the appearance of complication in the former is merely one of drawing lines on paper.[22]

The treatment of the original is much more sophisticated in the duos, where the elaboration and transformation of a melody without destruction of its identity represents a musical achievement of a rather high order. In the tuttis, where every aspect of the c.f. except the note names is ignored, the treatment revealed by Ficker's analysis becomes a sort of naïve game of fitting in notes opportunistically, backward and forward and one on top of the other. It implies the improbability that within the same movement the attitude of the composer deteriorates from one that is musically mature to one that is rather childish.[23] At one point he attempts to give new life and meaning to the melody in terms of a more florid style, at another his treatment is no more than an arid and musically meaningless exercise.

It might be argued that such a change in treatment could be caused by difficulties of fitting the two *cantus firmi* together in the tenor and superius. Composers were, however, showing a growing interest in the problem of combining *cantus firmi*, and from the technical point of view it seems not to have been a

EXAMPLE 139. Anonymous, *Missa O rosa bella III*—Sanctus (*DTO*, 22, p. 56), with Dunstable's *O rosa bella* chanson (*Works*, p. 133).

difficult task for them, since they simply interpolated free tones when they had trouble putting the original ones together. Just because of this, their efforts are often technically unimpressive, but they do not contradict the normal attitude toward the c.f. There was absolutely no need for them to have recourse to the devices of Ficker, for they had at hand, in their ordinary methods of melodic elaboration, a simple means of circumventing practically any technical difficulty which might arise. An approximately contemporary instance (Busnois, *Regina caeli II*, ex. 79a-c) and one of much earlier date (Dufay, *Anima mea liquefacta est*, ex. 45) illustrate these procedures. Historically, these methods lead clearly enough to the procedures of Josquin, who also has recourse to interpolated notes in order to achieve new combinations of given material. His methods are technically more refined and more clearly subjected to an over-all plan, which puts them on a higher plane than the procedures of Dufay and

Busnois, but they do not constitute an absolute break. Where the procedures advocated by Ficker would lead is not clear. Josquin, for all his astounding feats of combination, does not sacrifice clarity of presentation of the c.f. It seems that according to Ficker's beliefs his relatively simple methods of coloration should represent a reversion to a more primitive stage of development.

It must be further considered that the tenor of the chanson *O rosa bella* is given as tenor of the Mass, and that the superius written over it will be bound to have some points of agreement with the chanson superius simply because they are both counterpoints to the same c.f. Thus a tenor cadence on G calls forth a superius cadence in measure 7 of the chanson and measure 9 of the Sanctus (ex. 139) which is substantially the same in both works. There is agreement of several notes in a row, but this results from the use of standard caden-

EXAMPLE 140. Anonymous, *O sanctissime presul–O Christi pietas* (DTO, 76, p. 82), with (a) original melody according to Ficker and (b) cantus-firmus reference (Proc. Mon., p. 119).

tial formulae and need not be accounted for on grounds of continuous quotation of the chanson melody in the Mass.

Another point of similarity between chanson and Mass occurs where a triadic
figure in the tenor is treated imitatively in both works. The figure is used as the
subject of a point of imitation involving three voices, although the arrangement
of the entries is somewhat different in the Mass from that in the chanson.
(The passage in the Mass is given in ex. 139, m. 8-12.) There are a fair number
of instances where a point of imitation is taken over and reworked in a derived
composition,[24] and this seems to be another instance of the practice. Ficker,
however, wishes to explain it in terms of coloration of the superius line. By
following example 139 closely, we find that he is on secure ground when he
equates the superius of the Mass at measure 10 with the superius of the chanson
at measures 8-9. He certainly is not when he attempts to relate the entry in the
contratenor (m. 8-9) to a part of the chanson superius which has nothing to do
with the imitative passage and which does not fit it conveniently at all. (In ex.
139 compare the chanson superius, m. 4-5, with the Mass contratenor, m. 8-9).
The contratenor at this point is obviously derived from the tenor (at m. 11)

or the superius (at m. 10), and the derivation from the superius at measures 4-5, which Ficker proposes, is so farfetched as to be unbelievable. Anyone who accepts his derivation would at least have to agree that, in order to work the imitation in, the composer was willing to distort the quotation into an unrecognizable shape. Continuous presentation of the superius could not have been so important to him here as the construction of an interesting but very brief incident in the counterpoint.

It is clear that there is an extensive plan of c.f. treatment in this Mass which is based chiefly on tenor statement of the tenor of the chanson. This is buttressed by anticipatory statements of the tenor by the bass, by quotations of the chanson superius by the superius when the tenor is silent, by a system of head motives based on the chanson superius, and by certain other c.f. usages.[25] These place the Mass in the traditional class of structures which are dominated by alternating presentation of the c.f., in one voice or other, while the other voices are written largely as free counterpoints.[26] Attempts to push the c.f. usage further than this immediately necessitate analytical contortions which strongly indicate that a plan is being forced on the work. Further objections can be raised on the grounds that the methods are so inclusive that anything they show can also be accounted for as the result of chance, and on the grounds that they make it necessary to assume two different attitudes toward coloration of the c.f., one of which is of some artistic validity, while the other is a purely mechanical exercise. These objections are based on improbability. It must be emphasized, however, that they are no more than objections and are not positive disproofs. No one can say at exactly what point improbability becomes so great that it must be accounted as impossibility.

CANTUS FIRMUS USAGE OF THE ENGLISH

From the inconclusive analysis of *O rosa bella III* Ficker leaps to a completely new idea for the English works of the preceding generation. In the compositions discussed so far, he has been able to name the c.f. and use it for purposes of comparison, but in the English works there are no c.f. references and he has no idea what the preëxisting melodies are. He finds, however, a way of circumventing this difficulty. If a number of note names in the first part of a composition correspond to note names in the latter part, he assumes that a c.f. is stated twice, differently ornamented each time.

The weakness of the method of comparing note names is that it does not always prove intentional repetition. For instance, Ficker shows that a certain series of notes can be found in both the first and second halves of the tenor *O Christi pietas*. (See ex. 140a. One tenor section of the motet is put below the other.) This is one of his more convincing examples, since the correspondences between the two parts are fairly close. However, a c.f. reference is given in this composition which Ficker evidently did not follow up. The composer uses the antiphon *O Christi pietas* and could have had no intention of repeating anything, since all he has done is to quote the melody continuously with very little elaboration. (See ex. 140b.)

The Gregorian melody does contain repeated figures, but there is no repetition at the point where Ficker supposes it to be, so that his presumptive melody is false in form. All that he has done is show that there are corresponding note names in the first and last parts of the tenor as well as in the antiphon itself, but this tells nothing of its true structure or of its specific melodic contours. In this one instance in which it is possible to determine the c.f. his method of arriving at one by presuming varied repetition turns out to be valueless.

There are certain obvious crudities in Ficker's application of the method. In the Gloria with tenor *Jesu Christe fili Dei* by Dunstable, he finds evidence that an ornamented c.f. in the superius sounds simultaneously with the tenor melody.[27] Note names which correspond in the first and second halves of the movement are again picked out and are supposed to represent the borrowed material. The results are not very satisfactory. For instance, the first note of the "c.f." does not appear until the middle of the fifth measure, and after this there are long sections which show no agreement with the second half of the piece. All this could be accounted for on the grounds that the composer is making an extremely free elaboration, but there is still another puzzling feature about the analysis. This has to do with the linear contour of the supposititious melody. The first dozen notes do not look like a c.f. (ex. 141a). What sort of original were they taken from? It is impossible to believe that the source of this series of tones is either Gregorian or a melody voice of a secular art song.

On the other hand, when Ficker reaches a point at which a cadence in the first half of the Gloria agrees with one in the second half the whole picture changes.[28] The "c.f." takes on a very familiar look, since it adopts the shape of the standard cadential formula of the superius (ex. 141b). This mixture of the familiar and the unfamiliar only deepens the mystery, since it means that the preëxistent melody is stylistically incongruous within itself. In one part it differs completely from any known source material of the type used by fifteenth-century composers, while in another it agrees exactly with one detail of fifteenth-century style—the cadential formulas of contemporary art music.

There is one way in which this mixture of stylistically familiar and unfamiliar elements can be easily explained. If a person were to set out simply to find corresponding note names in the superius of any given composition, the

EXAMPLE 141. Dunstable—Gloria, *Jesu Christe fili Dei* (*DTO*, 61, p. 114), with (a) cantus-firmus tones chosen by Ficker (first statement, m. 5-7 of the superius; second statement, m. 68-73), and (b) cantus firmus at cadential points according to Ficker.

chances are that he would get close agreement at corresponding cadences, while at other places he would get a succession of tones which would not necessarily make a melody that agreed stylistically with either a Gregorian or a fifteenth-century tune. This is what Ficker has done, and it seems to be the explanation for the conflicting characteristics of the basic melody at which he arrives.[29]

The analyses of these two compositions show the absurdities that cannot be avoided when such a musically undiscriminative system as the mere equation of note names is followed. However, despite the inadequacies of the system, some of the analyses are not so obviously improbable, and at least one or two are very convincing.[30] An anonymous Credo (*DTO*, 61, p. 90) shows melodic correspondences between the first and last parts which are so clear that they must be intentional. The case with a Credo by Markham (*ibid.*, p. 94) is just as obvious. The two examples are convincing because so many notes agree, and because they are distributed so thickly throughout the two sections of the respective Credos. Furthermore, they do seem to support Ficker's contention which has been criticized above, i.e., that note names are all that need be considered, since it is just in note names that the two halves of these melodies show the greatest similarities. So far as structure is concerned, the first half differs from the second at many points.[31] This is so striking that Besseler has suggested a name of "constructive" discant coloration especially for these pieces.[32] If a c.f. is ever found, Ficker's claims will be fully vindicated for a limited number of compositions. But until this is done, all that can be said is that the first part is used as a model for the second, and this, in itself, does not prove that borrowed material is used.[33] Ficker's contention for the use of double c.f. by the English before 1450 never rises above the status of a possibility, even in the examples where he has found good evidence of repetition.

In his search for an early example of English Mass cycle with tenors showing repetition of c.f. of the sort described above, he has found four movements of the ordinary which show sufficiently close relation to convince later scholars that they actually belong together as a cycle. Two of these movements, the Sanctus and Agnus, would doubtless have been generally recognized as a pair, since they stand together in the sources and have identical tenor incipits. It is doubtful, however, that the relation of the other two movements, the Gloria and Credo, would ever have been recognized without Ficker's diligent search for instances of his type of c.f. usage. Their placement in the sources would not have called attention to their possible cyclic connection with one another and with the Sanctus and Agnus, nor would their tenor incipits have betrayed it easily, since they have only a general similarity.

A general discussion of the cycle has been given by Bukofzer,[34] but it can be amplified here to show some of the difficulties which had to be overcome in establishing the relationship of the four movements, and to recapitulate some of the conflicts in the evidence which are of considerable interest.

Three of the movements come from Trent Codex 87—a Credo attributed to Leonel (No 26),[35] and a Sanctus and Agnus (Nos. 78 and 80).[36] The two latter are anonymous, but the Sanctus is attributed to Dunstable in Trent 90. The Gloria is anonymous and does not appear at all in Trent 87; it appears only in 90 and 93.[37] Thus there are already difficulties of two types: one, the separation of the movements in the sources; the other, the conflict in composers' names.

Only two of the movements are attributed to specific authors, the Credo and the Sanctus. However, it is safe to attribute the Agnus to the composer of the Sanctus, since the two are clearly a pair. The tenors of both start identically (see ex. 142d and e, m. 1-5) and they were entered in direct succession in Trent 90 and 93, proving that they were considered a pair by the compiler of the manuscripts. The case with the Leonel Credo and the anonymous Gloria is different, since they stand rather widely separated from the Sanctus-Agnus and from each other as well. In Trent 90 and 93, each appears in a section devoted to its respective class of Mass movement, so that the compiler gives no evidence that he considered them related, either to one another or to the Sanctus-Agnus pair.

The later discovery of the Aosta manuscript has added to the variety of evidence. In this source, the anonymous Gloria appears under the name of Bennet (No. 155, "Bonnet"). The Sanctus and Agnus also appear, and are attributed to Bennet in the index (Nos. 145 and 154). Not only does this add a third name to the list of contenders for authorship—the placement of the movements is confused since the pair is separated and the Gloria is placed *after* the Agnus. Nevertheless, the Gloria, which stood quite alone in Trent, is now brought closer to the Sanctus and Agnus by its position in immediate succession to the Agnus. The position of the Leonel Credo is not further clarified as it is not included in the manuscript.

Under these circumstances the proof of cyclic relationship must be provided by the music, and the first six notes of the tenor (c-d-c-f-g-a) do provide fairly

EXAMPLE 142. Tenors of Dunstable-Leonel Mass; and Cooke—Gloria. (a) Basic melody prepared by Ficker (*Studien zur Musikwissenschaft*, XI, 55). (b) Anonymous Gloria (Tr 90; attributed to Bennet in Aosta; DTO, 61, p. 119). (c) Credo (attributed to Leonel in Tr 87; DTO, 61, p. 121). (d) Sanctus (anonymous, Tr 87; attributed to Dunstable in Tr 90; attributed to Bennet in Aosta; DTO, 61, p. 123). (e) Agnus (anonymous, Tr 87, but attributable to Dunstable; attributed to Bennet in Aosta; DTO, 61, p. 125). (f) Cooke —Gloria (OH, I, 138).

convincing evidence. (See ex. 142a-e.) Ficker is looking for a c.f. which extends throughout each of the movements and which is stated twice, so he proposes as the basic melody a series of notes which at least has the merit of being a plausible melody line in itself (ex. 142a). However, the doubts which have been expressed before as to the reality of this type of usage apply here, too. The tenors show general similarities, since they are all based on a major mode with C as tonic, they all cover a range of a ninth or tenth upward from c, and they all move upward and downward several times across this range. Under these conditions the problem is still whether correspondences are accidental or intentional, because the Mass tenors have so many more notes than Ficker's presumptive c.f.

If the tenors were, in fact, all based on the same c.f. they would probably show the agreements they do, but it is also quite possible that many melodies of similar style, range, and mode could be found which would show a sufficient number of corresponding note names to allow the construction of a presumptive c.f. similar to Ficker's. The main requirement would be for the "derived" melodies to be considerably longer than the constructed one so that the laws of chance could operate.

To show that highly improbable conclusions can be reached by this method I have quoted the tenor of a Gloria by Cooke from the Old Hall manuscript and compared it with the Dunstable-Leonel-Bennet tenors (ex. 142f). This voice line has no formal connection with the cycle, but it is of the same mode, same range, and approximately the same length as the Mass tenors. From a purely statistical point of view, it and the Credo (ex. 142c) are equally close to Ficker's basic melody, since both agree with it in all but three notes. (Compare ex. 142c and f.) Neither is as close to it as the Sanctus and Agnus (each showing agreement in all but one note), or the first movement (the only one which includes the entire basic melody). It takes only a glance at the example to convince one that there is no real relation between Cooke's tenor and the others,[38] but the lack of relation is not to be established on the basis of a statistical comparison of note names.

The c.f. is presumably repeated in the second half of the movements (shown for the Gloria and Credo in ex. 143). In these two movements it can be seen that agreement is closest at the beginning of the section, since the first six note names correspond exactly.[39] The remainder of the two tenors corresponds to the basic melody about as well as in the first part. However, the continuation of the Sanctus and Agnus tenors can only be equated with the basic melody by assuming a great deal of rewriting,[40] so that it seems to be a considerable overstatement to call the relationships "*ganz evident.*"[41]

Viewing the evidence as a whole, the existence of a c.f. appears doubtful.[42] What can be quite comfortably shown is a relationship of head motives between tenors, since the best agreement comes in the first few notes of movements or sections of movements. Despite the plurality of authors,[43] the four movements may be considered as belonging together on these grounds. It has also been pointed out that the beginnings of the superius lines are similar in shape, although it is difficult to say whether this is evidence of relationship or not, since triadic beginnings like these are commonplaces of English style.

Heinrich Besseler has also expressed himself in general agreement with Ficker on this Mass:

> When the English treated previously composed melodies, they frequently used a technique which differs sharply from the Continental type. Instead of the beautifully rounded, plastic presentation of the Gregorian melodies by means of the conventionalized figures and cadences used by Dufay and his generation, there reigns here a boundless, fervent outpouring in which the c.f. tones form often only the framework (*Gerüst*) of a freely flowing melody of quite different structure (*ganz anders gegliedert*). In the tenor form also, the c.f. tends to be dissolved melismatically, paraphrased (*zersungen*) in flowing movement and continuous transformation. On the basis of a tenor which returns from movement to movement but in constantly varying form, the English have apparently undertaken the cyclic union of the individual sections of the ordinary into the "Mass" and have shown the way to the future Netherlandish Mass structure.[44]

As an instance of this he compares the tenors of the first half of the Sanctus and Agnus.[45] (Besseler's statement is partially outdated now, since much more is known about the origin of the c.f. Mass cycle. It is cited to show that both Ficker and Besseler believed in the priority of the English in this field long before conclusive evidence was discovered.)

In one other case besides the "Leonel-Dunstable" Mass, Ficker has combined movements separated in the manuscripts into a single cycle. The Gloria and Credo of the *Missa Deuil angouisseux* of Bedingham appear as a pair in Trent 90 (Nos. 1098-1099). All four movements appear in Trent 88, although they are presented as two separate pairs (Gloria and Credo, Nos. 214-215; Sanctus and Agnus, Nos. 208-209).[46] In this work there is better evidence for the presence of c.f. than there was in the other. In the first place, there is a reference to the Binchois chanson in the Credo of Trent 90. Next, there are substantial quotations from the chanson in each of the movements, showing that they are individually based on it. Finally, it is most probable that the four movements belong together as a complete cycle, since the beginning of the tenor of each deviates markedly from the version of the chanson found in Trent and the deviation is the same in each case, five notes of the chanson tenor being omitted (a'-g'-a'-f'-g'). Also, the tenors are related in a positive way at the beginning of each movement; each stresses the notes f-f'-e'-f'-d'. (See ex. 144.)

It seems that these considerations in favor of considering the work a c.f.

EXAMPLE 143. Tenors of Dunstable-Leonel Mass—Gloria and Credo (*Studien zur Musikwissenschaft*, XI, 55). (a) Anonymous Gloria (*DTO*, 61, p. 120) and (*b*) Leonel—Credo (*ibid.*, p. 122).

cycle cannot be outweighed by the uniquely irregular presentation of the chanson tenor. The free sections are of extraordinary length, the ornamentation is at times excessively elaborate, and the structure of the original is largely ignored. Similar factors were presented as evidence to support a decision against the presence of c.f. in the Dunstable-Leonel Mass, but it seems there is only an apparent contradiction in admitting its presence in the one work while rejecting it in the other. The earlier work has no decisive evidence in favor of a c.f. such as the reference to the original chanson in *Deuil angouisseux*, nor has it the extensive note-for-note quotations that are found in the latter.[47] Also, works with specific c.f. references written before 1450 do not show the type of freedoms in the plan of presentation which must be assumed in it. In the case of the later work[48] it is possible to cite similar usages in the Masses of Ockeghem which, while they may be somewhat later, yet belong to the same style. Ficker considers these characteristics as late manifestations of an earlier English technique.[49] Historically, it seems more likely that they are later developments which go hand in hand with the elaborate melodic style which is cultivated by many composers of the Ockeghem generation.

A few of Ficker's historical hypotheses remain to be mentioned, since they are linked with the theories of c.f. treatment. There has already been some mention of his belief that c.f. paraphrase was used far back in the fourteenth century, so that the English practice of the first half of the fifteenth century must represent a late and highly evolved stage in which complex ornamentation and the use of two simultaneous *cantus firmi* can be reasonably expected. The theory that the type of c.f. treatment found in the Gloria and Credo of the Liebert Mass is a stage in development toward free composition has also been mentioned. Another one is that the use of two *cantus firmi* simultaneously (the discant-tenor technique) led to the equalization of the voices which is seen in the next generation. Besseler[50] points out that this is not a necessary assumption, as the melodically conceived tenor-discant pair was already well known on the Continent in the Italian and Burgundian tradition. Indeed, the twin layout of these two voices makes the greatest distinction between the fourteenth-century French style and the fifteenth-century Burgundian.

Ficker also feels it necessary to explain why, after the development of the English type of coloration, which is supposed to represent an advanced stage of development over the old tenor technique, schematic tenors continue to be found in much later works. From several statements it seems that the discant technique, such as is seen in the Liebert Mass, is supposed to have developed out of the tenor technique; that when it is in turn applied to the tenor, as in the English Mass cycles, it gradually resumes the old schematic form.[51] From the evidence as it now stands, it seems clear that coloration technique developed independently and that it existed side by side with the older, framework-type tenor. The two techniques seem to have merged in the ornamented structural tenor, but the rigid framework tenor was never completely abandoned by composers, certainly not in the early English Masses.

Ficker shows a general tendency to give a rationalized rather than a factual account of historical developments.[52] His assumptions sound reasonable in themselves, but they are advanced without proof and then used to support other assumptions. All of these viewpoints are entangled inextricably with his ideas

EXAMPLE 144. Bedingham, *Missa Deuil angouisseux*—Gloria, Credo, Sanctus, and Agnus (*DTO*, 61, pp. 127, 129, 131, and 134); with tenor of Binchois's *Deul angouisseux* chanson (*DTO*, 14, p. 242).

on c.f. One makes the other seem more reasonable, but the fact remains that some are incorrect, some are unprovable, and some are merely unproved. Yet it must be remembered that he has been completely justified on one point—that the c.f. Mass cycle was an English invention.

THE CANTUS FIRMUS PARAPHRASE OF HANDSCHIN

The methods of c.f. paraphrase proposed by Handschin[53] need not occupy us so long as those of Ficker. Handschin goes beyond the latter in the variety of ways he assumes the c.f. was treated. The original melody may be fragmented and the fragments arranged in any sort of order (see ex. 145a), the c.f. may be quoted in reverse motion, there may be very rapid migration or simultaneous

EXAMPLE 145. (a) Anonymous, *Ave gloriosa*—tenor excerpt (*Zeitschrift für Musikwissenschaft*, X, 516; LU, p. 124). (b-c) Anonymous Gloria—*Iudea* (*Z. f. Mw.*, X, 549; LU, p. 41). (d) Anonymous Gloria (*Z. f. Mw.*, X, 553; LU, p. 41). (e) Anonymous, *Spiritus et alme* (*Z. f. Mw.*, X, 544).

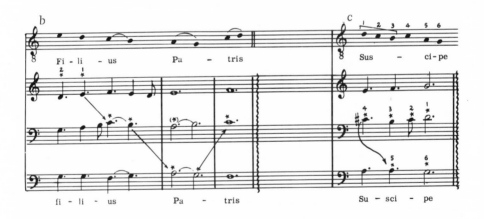

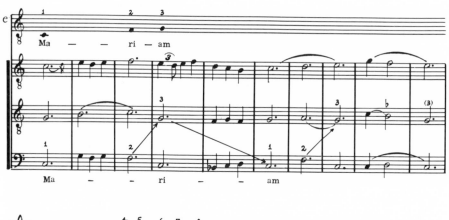

statement of two parts of a phrase (ex. 145b-c), there may be a great many
interpolated notes (ex. 145e), or the c.f. may be simplified to an extreme degree
(ex. 145d), etc. It hardly seems necessary to give a detailed criticism of these.
Such expansions of the possibilities of finding relationships defeat their own
purpose because, "given a certain mode and the restrictions of melody writing
of the time, almost any melody can be forcibly derived from plainsong of the
same mode simply because there are only seven notes in each and correspondences result merely from fortuitous agreement."[54] They are valueless as proofs
for his historical thesis, since they could be used equally well to support practically any idea anyone might wish to propose. It is my belief that this sort of
c.f. usage has no relation at all to genuine "paraphrase" in any style period.

In another article, Handschin presents the motet *Ascendit Christus* of Forest
(Dunstable),[55] saying, "the case is of significance with regard to the controversial issue of 'double paraphrase,' for which A. Orel (*Studien zur Musikwissenschaft* VII, p. 69) has already presented examples from the motets of
Trent."[56] I have been absolutely unable to fit the notes of the antiphon
Ascendit Christus into the upper voice parts of the motet in any satisfactory
way, in either the duos or the trios (where the tenor carries the c.f. *Alma
Redemptoris Mater.*) Many notes must be omitted, notes and text will not
agree, important structural points are ignored, etc. It is entirely different in
character from the works cited by Orel, which cannot be called controversial at
all, since the double c.f. in them is clear for all to see. Ficker also seems to dis-

agree with Handschin on this point; he makes no mention of double c.f. in his edition of the work (*DTO*, 76, music, p. 53, and editorial commentary, p. 102). Bukofzer also dismisses the idea as "unconvincing" (Dunstable, *Works*, p. 192).

Cantus Firmus Derivation in the Caput Mass of Dufay

The attempt to derive the superius of Dufay's *Caput* Mass from three phrases of the tenor rests on another conception of c.f. treatment—free, motivic derivation. (*DTO*, 38, p. xxii; tables, pp. xxiii-xxvii). The analyst conceives the superius as freely derived from motives which he picks out of the tenor part. The tenor phrases are subdivided into four sections, one containing one note, another two, and the third and fourth containing five notes each. Between them, these subsections contain ascending and descending seconds, thirds, and fourths. Since these happen to be exactly the intervals Dufay uses at least ninety-five per cent of the time in his superius lines, since the subsections are applied to the superius in any order, and since shortened or lengthened (ornamented) forms in the superius are considered as suitable equivalents to these tenor fragments, it is not surprising that the tenor melody is found to be "reproduced unceasingly throughout the discant of the whole Mass in an almost unbroken succession of variations which are in part very extended and free" (*ibid.*, p. xxii; translation mine). Further comment seems unnecessary.

Although they do not especially concern c.f. treatment, Riemann's theories of the use of variation by the English should be mentioned,[57] since they are typical of the misunderstanding of the style of the fifteenth century. One of his analyses, that of the superius of Dunstable's *Veni Sancte Spiritus*, has been disproved, since it is contradicted by the structure of the work.[58] His analysis of the superius of *Crux fidelis*, also by Dunstable, stands on no firmer ground, since this voice is in part a counterpoint to the c.f. in the middle voice, and in part carries the c.f. itself.[59] Even if there were no internal evidence against variation, the analyses would be doubtful, since not only must the variations be described as "free," but a very strong emphasis must be placed on that qualifying word. Ficker finds a "new and individual variation principle [which stands] in close connection with the coloration technique"[60] in a Gloria of Dufay (*DTO*, 61, p. 75). Here, too, aside from similar cadential figures the variations are free.

These three works certainly have a high degree of musical consistency, but the question arises whether words with such specific implications as "variation" or "development" should be applied. "Free" variation or "free" development can be applied to practically any work which coheres at all, depending on how elastically the adjective is interpreted, but the more emphasis that has to be put on the free aspect, the less meaning do the terms "variation" and "development" have. It seems that each case should be examined to see if it would not be better to attribute the qualities of unity and individuality to such factors as the use of a limited vocabulary of rhythmic and melodic patterns, and to considerations of tonal organization, melodic balance, and consistent manner of leading the voices. Such analysis is generally accepted as satisfactorily explaining the musical validity of the lines of Palestrina, and though their coherence could doubtless be explained in terms of free variation, it is unlikely that this would be accepted as appropriate or as a true description of the approach of the composer.

The danger of such terms as "development" and "variation" lies in reading the techniques of the eighteenth and nineteenth centuries into the music of the fifteenth century. Taken in their dramatic, symphonic sense, these devices do not apply to the earlier idiom; efforts to make them do so can be successful only if all sorts of freedoms are assumed. The results that can be obtained by such uncontrolled analyses are limited only by the imagination of the investigator.

To return to the specific subject of c.f., most of the criticisms already made of the analyses of Ficker and Handschin are based on similar grounds—lack of initial judgment and of objective control. A secondary criticism has been that both investigators often assume that the process of utilizing the c.f. was similar to the making of a mosaic in which one tiny piece is fitted to another. The compositions give evidence, however, that the composers did not think in terms of tiny fragments except in rare cases. In most works a notable feature of the c.f. usage is the broadness of the layout, whether the borrowed material is presented as a melodic paraphrase or as a nonmelodic framework.

It is also true that the c.f. theories often cannot be disproved categorically. All that can be pointed out is their improbability, and in this field lack of certainty is a serious defect. If we must err in our approach, it seems better to err on the side of caution, since nothing is to be learned from reading c.f. into a work when it is not present. Such a conservative attitude means ruling out of consideration those works in which the c.f. is not known, and this may cause us to miss much of importance. By restricting ourselves to those in which a c.f. is clearly present, however, we can feel certain that what we do learn is firmly based.

Even with these limitations there remains a rich literature of compositions which undoubtedly have c.f. These *cantus firmi* have been treated with much care and ingenuity, and the roles they play and the transformations they undergo in their polyphonic setting throw a great deal of light on the composers' attitudes. This is not to say that speculation should be excluded from an investigation. Coming from a qualified scholar, imaginative thought can be of the greatest value. It can also be misleading, and this means that the reader cannot avoid a critical attitude. No matter how attractive a new interpretation may be, it must be checked carefully to make sure that it correlates well with the known facts and that it solves more problems than it raises.

NOTES

NOTES

INTRODUCTION

[1]See the article "Cantus Firmus" in Willi Apel, *Harvard Dictionary of Music.* (Cambridge, Mass.: Harvard University Press, 1945), p. 117.
[2]For a factual account of the entire history of c.f. see Heinrich Husmann, "Cantus Firmus," in *MGG*, II, cols. 784-800.
For an interpretation of the significance of the c.f. as an element of musical style see Edward Lowinsky, "Music in the Culture of the Renaissance," *Journal of the History of Ideas*, XV (1954), 528 ff. This article is by far the best summary interpretation of musical developments during the entire period of the Renaissance which has yet appeared.
[3]Musical examples 16, 33, 36, 41, 64, 65, 69, 70, 71, and 75.

CHAPTER 1

[1]The Plainsong & Mediaeval Music Society, *The Old Hall Manuscript*, ed. A. Ramsbotham (Nashdom Abbey, Burnham, Bucks: The Plainsong & Mediaeval Music Society, 1933-35), Vols. I-II, and *The Old Hall Manuscript*, ed. A. Ramsbotham, completed by H. B. Collins and Dom Anselm Hughes (London: The Plainsong & Mediaeval Music Society, 1938), Vol. III. The Introduction to Vol I is by Hughes and Ramsbotham, and that to Vol. II by Hughes and Collins. Vol. III has an Introduction by Hughes and Musical Editor's Remarks by Collins.
[2]Barclay Squire, "Notes on an Undescribed Collection of English 15th-Century Music," *Sammelbände der internationalen Musikgesellschaft*, II (1901), 342. M. F. Bukofzer, *Studies in Medieval & Renaissance Music* (New York: W. W. Norton & Company., 1950), p. 34; hereafter cited as Bukofzer, *Studies*. Oliver Strunk, "A Postscript," *ibid.*, p. 80. Frank Ll. Harrison, *Music in Medieval Britain* (New York: Frederick A. Praeger, 1959), pp. 220-242, 245-249; hereafter cited as Harrison, *Music in Medieval Britain*. To Strunk's discovery of previously unrecognized canons in *OH* (see "A Postscript") should be added Frank Ll. Harrison's discovery of yet another one, a Sanctus by Pycard. *The New Oxford History of Music: Ars Nova and the Renaissance*, ed. Dom Anselm Hughes and Gerald Abraham (London, New York, and Toronto: Oxford University Press, 1960), III, 103.
[3]Squire, "Notes on an Undescribed Collection," quoted in *OH*, I, ix.
[4]Bukofzer, *Studies*, p. 78; Harrison, *Music in Medieval Britain*, p. 220.
[5]Ramsbotham, in *OH*, I, xii.

431

[6]For my purposes, the investigations into the employment of plainchant are most important: Hughes, *OH*, III, xiv; Bukofzer, *Studies*, p. 45; Harrison, *Music in Medieval Britain*, p. 230. In addition, the organization of the manuscript, the scribe who copied the music (four different hands have been identified), and the known dates of composers must be taken into consideration. See Ramsbotham, *OH* ,I, x; Bukofzer, *Studies*, p. 73; Harrison, *Music in Medieval Britain*, pp. 228, 245.

[7]See n. 4, above.

[8]*Studies*, pp. 38, 53.

[9]See the article "Conductus" in Willi Apel, *The Harvard Dictionary of Music* (Cambridge, Mass.: Harvard University Press, 1945), p. 179; hereafter cited as Apel, *Harvard Dictionary of Music*.

[10]I follow Bukofzer and others in applying the term "conductus" without further qualification to the pieces of Old Hall which show these external features of writing. Strictly speaking, the term indicates pieces used for "escorting" or "conducting," and these were not written for that purpose, since they are settings of items of the Ordinary of the Mass, votive antiphons, etc. For the history of the origin and development of conductus see Jacques Handschin, "Trope, Sequence, and Conductus," in *The New Oxford History of Music: Early Medieval Music up to 1300*, ed. Dom Anselm Hughes (London, New York, and Toronto: Oxford University Press, 1954), II, 171; Dom Anselm Hughes, "Music in Fixed Rhythm," *ibid.*, pp. 317, 326; hereafter cited as *The New Oxford History*. See also, the article "Conductus," by Jacques Handschin, in *MGG*, II, cols. 1615-1626.

[11]A clear exception is the Credo of Chirbury (*OH*, II, 36), in which extreme simplicity of rhythmic texture is combined with relatively advanced harmonic and melodic style.

[12]A few instances of the use of the c.f. as a melodic voice, but *unornamented*, are known from the thirteenth and fourteenth centuries. M. F. Bukofzer, *Geschichte des englischen Diskants und des Fauxbourdons* (Strassburg: Heitz, 1936), p. 115; hereafter cited as Bukofzer, *Geschichte des englischen Diskants*.

Examples of ornamented c.f. from the Apt manuscript (late fourteenth century) are referred to below; see n. 18 and chap. ii, p. 48).

[13]See the table of compositions with plainsong in Bukofzer, *Studies*, p. 47.

[14]Exceptions to the continuous movement in breves are found where two repeated notes on the same syllable of text are fused into one of double value (ex. 1, m. 2 and 15). The converse procedure—repetition of a single note of the plainsong—is also sometimes found in the simple conductus. See ex. 5a, m. 2, and the corresponding spot in ex. 5c.

[15]It was rather common in the three-part writing of the *ars nova* for two of the voices to be consonant with the third part, but not with one another. I am adopting the term "differential" used by Professor Bukofzer for this type of dissonance. In the case of the Sanctus under consideration the composer is concerned that the two upper parts be consonant with the lowest (which gives the clue to the order of composition of the parts as stated above). This is in agreement with the views expressed in the English tract *Quatuor principalia musicae*, written in 1351; see C .E .H. de Coussemaker, ed., *Scriptorum de Musica medii aevi nova series* (4 vols.; Paris: A. Durand, 1864-76), IV, 200-298; hereafter cited as Coussemaker, ed., *Scriptorum*. The anonymous author insists that in discant of more than two parts the upper voices must be consonant with the lowest. For this reason, if a singer is discanting below the plainchant, no one may discant above it unless he knows what the notes of the lowest voice are. "... *tamen dummodo discantaveritis sub plano cantu, nullus potest discantare supra, nisi fuerit expertus de gravium vocum sedibus, quia omnes superiores voces ad graviorem vocem habent reddere concordantiam, ad hoc quod consonantia bona sit.*" (*Ibid.*, p. 294.) In another passage he restricts voice crossing for the same reason. He forbids the singer to descend more than a third below the plainchant if others are discanting above it, and he may not do even this if the fifth or twelfth is sung above

the chant, because this interval makes the dissonance of a seventh (fourteenth) with the third, which is the lowest note. "... *non licet amplius descendere quam ad tertiam sub plano cantu, alio vel aliis discantantibus supra planum cantum; et hoc solummodo fiat, quando quinta vel duodecima supra planum cantum non modulatur; quae quidem consonantia ad illam tertiam quae gravior est nota, dissonat.*" (*Ibid.*, p. 292).

Of course, such restrictions on singing below the c.f. do not hold when the composition is written out. It may be added that, except for the placement of the c.f. in the middle part, this Sanctus reflects the teachings of the theorist of the mid-fourteenth century very clearly. Note the constant use of contrary motion, the lack of parallel sixth chords, the frequent parallel fifths, etc.

[16]Such cadences are uncommon in the Old Hall conductus. For examples, see *Regina caeli*, OH, I, 154, last measure of the page, and Credo, *OH*, II, 16, brace 3.

[17]See cadences of *Regina caeli* OH, I, 154, brace 2, m. 6-7, and 155, brace 4, m. 7-8. The tenor skips down a third and the two final chords can be called III-I. In both cases, however, the line of the superius is normal.

[18]Conductus of the fourteenth century other than those of Old Hall show similar treatment of the cadences when the c.f. does not permit the normal form. Stainer has edited a transcription of an Agnus of the late fourteenth century which differs in no important respect from the simpler settings of Old Hall, and contains $\frac{6}{4}$ - $\frac{8}{5}$ cadences. Sir John Stainer, ed., *Early Bodleian Music* (London, 1901), II, 46. Stevens has published four examples of Agnus and Sanctus which also contain variant forms, among them the $\frac{6}{5}$ - $\frac{8}{5}$ cadence. Denis Stevens, "A Recently Discovered English Source of the Late 14th Century," *Musical Quarterly*, XLI (1955), pp. 26-40, exs. 12-15. Harrison gives examples of a hymn setting (*O lux beata trinitas*) and the *Gloria patri* of the respond *Regnum mundi* which contain $\frac{6}{4}$ - $\frac{8}{5}$ and $\frac{5}{3}$ - $\frac{8}{5}$ cadences. (The latter corresponds to the III-I cadence mentioned in n. 17 above.) *Music in Medieval Britain*, p. 150, ex. 19, and p. 153, ex. 21. A similar situation is found in the hymn settings of the Apt manuscript, where a great variety of unusual cadences results from setting the chant melodies note for note. The $\frac{6}{4}$ - $\frac{8}{5}$ and $\frac{6}{5}$ - $\frac{8}{5}$ forms, however, do not figure prominently among them.

Likewise, these two cadential forms do not occur in the conductus of the English manuscript, Pepys 1236, written later in the century (after 1465). Sydney Robinson Charles, "The Music of the Pepys MS. 1236" (Doctoral dissertation, University of California, Berkeley, 1959).

[19]However, see Credo, *OH*, II, 53, brace 2, m. 6. Practically all the examples cited in example 3 are the ends of sections, so there can be no doubt as to their cadential function.

[20]In ex. 3*j*, note heads of smaller size are used to indicate the original red notes. Several red notes are used in this composition of Leonel. (See also ex. 12c.) Example 12e shows a red note in a Sanctus by Typp. A puzzling instance occurs in a conductus-type Gloria (*OH*, III, [10], brace 4, m. 4-5). The c.f. will not make an $\frac{8}{5}$ chord with the other voices. Red notes are added which do make a regular cadence with a final $\frac{8}{5}$ chord, but the final red note will not harmonize with the final c.f. note. Bukofzer, *Studies*, pp. 48-49.

[21]Harrison, *Music in Medieval Britain*, p. 42.

[22]Bukofzer, *Studies*, p. 79.

[23]Such a variety of note values is found also in conductus of the late fourteenth century. Stevens, "A Recently Discovered English Source ...," *op. cit.*, p. 38, ex. 13. Harrison, *Music in Medieval Britain*, p. 150, ex. 19.

[24]*Studies*, p. 46.

[25]*Ibid.* See also, in this connection, Edward Lowinsky, "Early Scores in Manuscript," *Journal of the American Musicological Society*, XIII (1960), 126-173. Further reference is made to the subject in chap. ii, n. 34.

[26]Of the two versions, that from the Fountains fragment is the simpler. For instance, in the final section all voices move in the same meter, while in the Old Hall version

the lower voice is in triple meter against the compound duple meter of the upper two. Also, Old Hall has several changes of meter while Fountains retains the same meter throughout. (See ex. 5a-h, where corresponding passages are placed below each other for ease of comparison.)

[27]In ex. 7c, m. 3, the c.f. disappears for two notes at a point corresponding to those where migration was undertaken before. In m. 2-3 there are parallel unisons between the bottom voices. Unisons are rare, even in this style, which permits parallel octaves. Since d and e, the two missing c.f. notes, would be harmonically satisfactory in either of the two bottom voices, there may be an error in the manuscript at this point.

[28]It will be noticed that the fourth count in the treble of m. 3, ex. 8b, is unaccounted for. The version of the c.f. used by the composer may have read d'-c'-a instead of d'-a, or he may have inserted the c' himself. Interpolations in the c.f. are very common; as it is impossible to make statements on the evidence of a single note, a discussion of them will be deferred to later examples.

[29]However, among the conductus with transposed c.f. there are three works of Leonel in which a fairly liberal use of accidentals tends to keep the original mode intact. They are: Agnus, OH, III, 128, c.f. up a fourth, containing B-flats; Sanctus, OH, III, 7, c.f. up a fifth containing F-sharps; Agnus OH, III, 118, c.f. up a second, containing F-sharps. (In the last work there are no C's in the transposed melody, so it is impossible to say whether Leonel would have provided them with sharps or not. In the free additions which he writes at the ends of sections, however, he uses C naturals.) The use of B♭—either in the signature or as accidentals—is common for modes transposed down a fifth, but the regular use of F♯ for the transposition up a fifth is unknown to me outside these pieces.

An anonymous Agnus in Old Hall (OH, III, 133) is interesting in this respect, for it shows clearly the unsystematic attitude of the composers. It is based on a plain-song which uses the same melody for each of the three sections of the Agnus (Sarum X, Vatican XVIII), and which is transposed up a fifth in the setting. In Agnus II the composer specifies the f♯ which is necessary if the mode is to remain the same, but in Agnus I and III, he not only does not specify the sharp, he harmonizes the chant in such a way that f′ natural is required. (Compare OH, III, 135, brace 3, m. 1 with p. 134, brace 2, m. 1.)

This lack of regard for the original mode of a borrowed melody persists throughout the century. Consider, for instance, Josquin's treatment of the c.f. in the Mass L'homme armé super voces musicales. (See p. 313.) Lowinsky states that composers, around 1500, "felt completely free to use a popular song in any manner they pleased." Edward Lowinsky, "The Goddess Fortuna in Music," Music Quarterly, XXIX (1943), 55.

[30]The scheme of pitch shifts is as follows: the c.f. is quoted a fourth above the original pitch through the first and second Sanctus; an octave above it in the third Sanctus; a fourth above, again, for Dominus Deus Sabaoth; an octave above from Pleni sunt through Hosanna in excelsis; a fourth above at Benedictus qui venit, with a possible change to an octave above at Domini; the final Hosanna is a repetition of the first, so the quotation is again an octave above the original.

[31]Ex. 11c, m. 2, offers another ambiguous spot. Is the f in the tenor interpolated or not? For other similar cases, see Credo, OH, II, 8 ff; also, ex. 5f, m. 5.

[32]In ex. 12a, b, and d the added notes bring the phrase to a close on a note different from the final one of the c.f. so there can be no doubt that they are appended, after the c.f. phrase has come to an end. In ex. 12e the phrase ends on the same note as the final c.f. note, and m. 6 and 7 could be considered as interpolated. The addition of notes which bring the phrase to a close on another tone than that of the last c.f. note is not very common, although there is an instance in an Agnus of Dunstable where the added ending cadences a third lower than the final c.f. note. John Dunstable, Complete Works, ed. M. F. Bukofzer, (Musica Britannica, A National Collection of

Music, VIII [London: Stainer and Bell, 1953]), p. 33; hereafter cited as Dunstable, *Works*.

[33]Other compositions of this type are: Typp, Credo, *OH*, II, 44 (which makes use of migration and change of transposition, as well as ornamentation of the c.f., and which has some deviations from the c.f.—Credo I—as given in the *LU*); an anonymous Gloria, *OH*, III, [8] (which has divergent cadential forms); Olyver, Agnus, *OH*, III, 141 (quoted in part as ex. 18 below). Harrison quotes a setting of *Conditor alme siderum* (written c. 1400) which corresponds to the pieces from Old Hall just mentioned, since it makes use of migration and melodic elaboration of the c.f. *Music in Medieval Britain*, p. 151, ex. 20. However, this is not so complex rhythmically as Byttering's *Nesciens Mater* or the Agnus of Olyver. (See my exs. 13 and 18.)

The hymn setting of the late fourteenth century quoted by Harrison, *O lux beata Trinitas*, is not a clear example of melodic elaboration of the c.f., although the statement that "the composer . . . put the plainsong in the highest part, slightly changed and ornamented" might lead the reader to believe it is. *Op. cit.*, p. 150, ex. 19. The statement is true as far as it goes, but does not make clear that the plainsong is stated in the usual way, unchanged (except for transposition) and unornamented in the middle voice, and that the appearance of portions of it in the upper voice is incidental to the sixth-chord style of the piece. The hymn melody does appear in the upper voice as long as that part moves in parallel fourths with the middle, but it disappears when other intervals are used.

[34]*OH*, III, xv. List of compositions, xiv-xv.

[35]In the Sanctus series Scribe A entered settings of festal chants on fo. 80ᵛ-85ᵛ, ferial on 86-89, and festal on 93ᵛ-100ᵛ. These are printed in *OH*, III, 1-25, 26-39, and 58-99. In the Agnus series he entered festal settings on fo. 101-104ᵛ, ferial on 104ᵛ-106ᵛ, and festal on 107-108ᵛ. These are printed in *OH*, III, 100-119, 120-135, and 136-144. (Incomplete compositions, or those believed by the editors to be incomplete, are not included in the main part of the edition.)

[36]*Music in Medieval Britain*, p. 246 and footnote 3; p. 248, footnote 2.

[37]A general discussion of the conductus is given by Harrison. *Ibid.*, pp. 230 ff.

[38]This fourth voice is not only unusual (for conductus) because it is written separately, but also because it is textless and is named contratenor. It is not a contratenor in style, however, because it lacks the characteristic disjunct motion. Bukofzer gives reasons for supposing that it is not a later addition. *Studies*, pp. 37-38 and ex. 1.

The second case is an Agnus (*OH*, folio 106ᵛ.; *OH*, III, 133). The voice written separately is texted and entitled "*contratenor de cantu feriali*." Note that this designation is placed over the wrong voice in *OH*. It should be above the third staff from the top instead of the second, as the latter is the voice which carries the c.f. The fourth voice in this piece is a real contratenor because it is a filler part that skips back and forth above and below the tenor. It contrasts rhythmically as well as melodically with the other parts and was apparently written as a later addition to them. It is a good example of an unassimilated borrowed element.

[39]Other instances are found in Damett's *Beata Dei genetrix* (*OH*, I, 164) and Cooke's *Ave Regina caelorum* (*ibid.*, p. 161).

[40]In the motet the tenor is the c.f.-bearing voice. Later in the century we find works of this type in which the c.f. is carried by the bass voice or one of the upper ones and these are called tenor regardless of range. The term does not have this significance in the settings of paraphrased c.f., in which the voice called tenor seldom carries the borrowed material.

[41]I leave out of consideration the Gloria of Excetre with c.f. in the upper voice (*OH*, I, 55), and an anonymous Credo with c.f. in the *cantus secundus* (*OH*, II, 176).

[42]The two works are also interesting because they show Leonel writing a simple and a complex setting of the same festal chant (Sarum I). The complexity of the

second setting may be due to the rank of the chant. This possibility cannot be excluded, if for no other reason than that we have no ferial setting comparable to it. But this cannot be the entire explanation, because the work is elaborate in a way which could not result from a momentary decision. It is more likely that in both cases Leonel wrote according to his capabilities. In the first his capabilities were limited; in the second they had matured and developed. It seems that the character of the second came about through the passage of time, and that no other considerations need to be taken into account in estimating the order of the works.

[43]See n. 4, above.

CHAPTER 2

[1]Bukofzer, *Geschichte des englischen Diskants,* p. 115. See also chap. i, n. 6.

[2]Heinrich Besseler suggests that hymns were first used this way. *Die Musik des Mittelalters und der Renaissance* (Potsdam: Akademische Verlagsgesellschaft Athenaion, 1931), p. 200; hereafter cited as Besseler, *Musik des Mittelalters.* As examples he cites a group of hymns from the Apt manuscript (p. 169 and ex. 117).

[3]It is, of course, not possible to determine the exact date of many of the compositions. In order to help the reader form some judgment on this point I have indicated one manuscript source in each example. Folio numbers are omitted, since the purpose is only to give a general indication of when the piece may have been written.

[4]Among the more extended articles are: Alfred Orel, "Einige Grundformen der Motettkompositionen im XV. Jahrhundert," *Studien zur Musikwissenschaft,* VII (1920), 48-101; Rudolf Ficker, "Die Kolorierungstechnik der Trienter Messen," *Studien zur Musikwissenschaft,* VII (1920), 5-47; Rudolf Ficker, "Die frühen Messenkompositionen der Trienter Codices," *Studien zur Musikwissenschaft,* XI (1924), 3-58. Also related, though not restricted to the field of fifteenth century music, is Jacques Handschin, "Zur Frage der melodischen Paraphrasierung im Mittelalter," *Zeitschrift für Musikwissenschaft,* X (June/July, 1928), 513-559.

[5]As stated above, I prefer "c.f. elaboration" and "c.f. paraphrase" as the general descriptive terms for this technique, although I do not feel that it is necessary to use them to the exclusion of others. The terms "ornamentation," and even "Kolorierung," may be used, although it is not desirable to employ them as general titles, since they overemphasize a more or less incidental aspect of the subject. I should mention that Handschin's use of the term "paraphrase" has given it connotations which do not apply here. Besseler has suggested that "figural melody" be used to denote the specific type of elaboration used by Ockeghem. Heinrich Besseler, "Von Dufay bis Josquin," *Zeitschrift für Musikwissenschaft,* XI (October, 1928), 14; hereafter cited as Besseler, "Von Dufay bis Josquin."

[6]He envisions a *"Kolorierungslehre des 15. Jahrhunderts"* and makes a start on a systematic presentation in which he discusses the treatment of each interval of the chant, starting with the second and proceeding to the larger intervals. "Einige Grundformen . . . ," p. 64-65. It seems inevitable that any investigator following him will undertake a more comprehensive investigation of this type, not only because the brevity of his treatment invites expansion, but because the method itself is attractive in its general appearance of scholarly thoroughness and exactitude. The advantages are so obvious that I have not felt that I could reject such a statistical method without a trial. Moreover, the time spent in demonstrating its inadequacies is not wasted, since various features of the paraphrase technique are at the same time clarified.

[7]Ten are unornamented, four descending seconds are provided with anticipations, one descending second has the fall of a third and rise of a second, and one rising second has the fall of a second and rise of a third, while one other is given somewhat more elaborate treatment. (In making these statistics I have accepted the two con-

jectural eighth notes added by the editor in m. 8, and have ignored slight differences between the ornamented melody and the hymn tune, such as occur at m. 4.)

[8]*Proc. Mon.*, p. 328.

[9]Other comparisons of freely composed and paraphrased c.f. lines can be made with similar results. Only a few need be mentioned here. One of the most interesting is the superius of Dunstable's isorhythmic motet *Veni Sancte Spiritus* which happens to contain both types within itself. Paraphrased c.f. alternates with freely composed sections, yet stylistically the line is completely undifferentiated from beginning to end. For an instance from a different period, compare the line bearing the c.f. in Ockeghem's motet *Alma redemptoris* (ex. 74) with the freely composed lines in the same composition.

[10]Two compositions not in the Burgundian style, the fourteenth-century hymn (ex. 17) and a Credo of Zachara da Teramo (*DTO*, 61, p. 18) also show a tendency to rise to a climax before the cadence. Yet the difference between them and the settings in Burgundian style is quite marked. It is one of time dimension. The Burgundian melodies unfold slowly and gracefully, while the lines of the other two drive rapidly and nervously to their cadential goals.

As applied to this style and to the men who wrote in it, the term "Burgundian" has been severely criticized, and with reason. As stated above, there was a dominant European style in the second quarter of the century which was by no means restricted to any one locality. (For example, one of the very finest of the writers of chansons, Hugho de Lantins, has never been shown to have had any connection with the court of Burgundy. Dufay, at the time he began writing in this manner, was active mainly in Italy. Binchois, however, was at the Burgundian court for many years.) For a summary of the question see Gustave Reese, *Music in the Renaissance* (rev. ed.; New York: W. W. Norton & Company, 1959), pp. 8-10, "Relative Musical Roles of France and the Low Countries"); hereafter cited as Reese, *Renaissance*.

I retain the term because I need one to contrast with the "English school," "English style," and "Italian style" of the early fifteenth century, etc.

[11]The same procedure has been shown in the more advanced conductus of Old Hall.

[12]"Einige Grundformen . . . ," p. 65.

[13]Ficker, "Die Kolorierungstechnik . . . ," p. 10 and elsewhere. See also, below, Appendix, n. 15.

[14]They begin with small melodic intervals and display a quiet poise which contrasts sharply with the energy of this initial Gregorian figure.

[15]I believe this to be substantially true, although it cannot be proved in a great many cases because of differences in the version of the chant used by the composer and the one available to the analyst.

The reversal of notes is one of the features of the technique which Ficker must assume to carry out his analyses. For this reason I go to some pains to point out my failure to find that it was actually done to any significant extent. This point is discussed further in the Appendix.

[16]It happens that the first eight notes of the c.f. appear in the tenor during this inserted passage (m. 13-25; the c.f. tones are marked by x's in parentheses). Because they are given long rhythmic values and are fairly prominent, they may possibly represent an intentional repetition of the c.f. phrase. If this is an instance of intentional repetition, it is most unusual for this period.

[17]*Works*, pp. 95, 101.

[18]*Works*, p. 103. Reese's remark that "this colored discant style was successfully developed in the early 15th century by Dufay and it may be from him that Dunstable learned it" needs some amplification. Gustave Reese, *Music in the Middle Ages* (New York: W. W. Norton & Company, 1940), p. 416; hereafter cited as Reese, *Middle Ages*. Emphasis must be laid on the word "discant." The technique of coloration was developed before Dufay's time, and Dunstable could hardly have escaped knowing it

before he left England. (See chap. i.) Continental writers show a strong preference for c.f. in the top voice; the English made relatively little use of it in this part. The fact that Dunstable does use discant c.f. almost exclusively can be attributed to Continental influence. If he learned anything, it was not a new technique, but a special application of a familiar one.

[19]For an instance of extreme displacement, see ex. 53, an excerpt from the gradual of Ockeghem's Requiem Mass.

[20]For similar findings on text underlaying in secular compositions of the last half of the fifteenth century, see Helen Hewitt, ed., *Harmonice Musices Odhecaton A* (Cambridge, Mass.: The Mediaeval Academy of America, 1942), p. 35; hereafter cited as Hewitt, ed., *Odhecaton A.*

[21]Concerning the lack of motivic elaboration in this music see Robert Erickson, *The Structure of Music* (New York: The Noonday Press, 1955), p. 61. Although this aspect of the music is generally recognized today, it seems to have been difficult to accept in the past. At any rate, the temptation to read into these works composition procedures which are not there has apparently been irresistible to many writers. See Appendix, p. 426. Since most music, especially that dating from the last part of the fifteenth century, exhibits a certain concentration of material by means of direct repetition, imitation, variation, motivic working-out, etc., and, since one of the chief functions of analysis is to discover these procedures, the analyst is apt to assume that it is his duty to find them in all music. There is a danger of his assuming that some sort of specific repetitive organization must be present regardless of the period of the music and that, if this cannot be found easily, it must still be assumed to be present in some obscure form.

[22]Lantins surpasses even Dufay in the amount of imitation he uses in the chansons. Charles van den Borren ed., *Pièces Polyphoniques Profanes de Provenance Liégeoise* (Publications de la Société Belge de Musicologie: Flores Musicales Belgicae, I [Brussels: Editions de la Librairie Encyclopédique, 1950]), pp. 36 ff.

[23]See exs. 14, 15, 16, 22, 23.

[24]For a few instances see: Dufay, Credo, Mon. Doc. Lit., Ser. 1, No. 1, p. 8, brace 4; Dufay, *Alma redemptoris mater*, HAM, pp. 70-71, at "*tuum sanctum Genitorem*"; Dufay, Credo, DTO, 61, p. 74, m. 56-60; Dunstable, Gloria, *Works*, p. 24, m. 69-73, and Credo, p. 28, m. 90-94 and 95-96 (bottom voice); Forest (Dunstable?) *Ascendit Christus*, in Dunstable, *Works*, p. 148, m. 103 ff.

Compared to the use of sequence and repeated motives in Italian compositions of the early part of the century, these passages are unimpressive. They probably should be considered as lingering traces of the Italian style of the late ars nova. Italian compositions were known in England before 1420. Bukofzer, *Studies*, p 40.

Dufay was strongly under Italian influence in his early period—see Heinrich Besseler, *Bourdon und Fauxbourdon* (Leipzig: Breitkopf & Härtel, 1950), p. 73; hereafter cited as Besseler, *Bourdon.* His earlier works show much clearer and more extensive use of motivic patterning than any of the pieces mentioned above. See, for example, the isorhythmic motet *Vasilissa, ergo gaude*, m. 56-61, 95-100. *Guglielmi Dufay: Opera Omnia*, ed. G. de Van and H. Besseler (Corpus Mensurabilis Musicae, I [Rome: American Institute of Musicology, 1947—three volumes out of six have appeared to date]), I, ii, pp. 3-4. A Gloria, which is likewise an early work, furnishes other instances. *Ibid.*, II:1, p. 4, m. 19-31; p. 6, m. 56-62; p. 7, m. 103-106. (Hereafter cited as Dufay, *Opera.*)

[25]In the example, the elaborated phrases are given directly below each other for purposes of comparison. The paraphrase of the first A section of the chant is labeled A in the example, the paraphrase of the second A section is labeled A′ and that of the final A is labeled A‴. A″ is allotted the final notes of A′ (the second section), since these notes are a partial quotation of the very beginning of the piece. This labeling complicates matters somewhat, but gives an opportunity to show the treatment of repeated material. The opening notes of the chant are given in Tr and indicate that

the composer was working with a somewhat different version than that of *LU*. This and the following example come from Tr 88, so were probably written after 1450; stylistically they belong to the period under consideration.

[26]Organizational elements are characteristically of the most general nature, such as stylistically consistent treatment of the lines, formalized cadential patterns, a rather simple tonal scheme in which the cadences are generally made on the tonic or dominant (not always true of c.f. settings, where the necessity of following the cadences of the chant may interfere), clear sectionalization of a composition emphasized by change of meter or by decrease or increase of the number of voices. This does not mean that repetitions of sections are not found. They occur frequently, but in the great majority of cases those of any length are the result not of musical, but of textual considerations. The form of the verse dictates the repeats in secular compositions. Exact repetitions in the prose text of the liturgy often call for repetition of the music, as the frequent occurrence of such a direction as "Osanna (Agnus, etc.) ut supra" testifies.

Repetitions of some extent which are not clearly textually motivated are hard to find in freely composed sacred works. One instance is a Kyrie by Dunstable (*Works*, p. 1). Another, a Gloria, has been found in the Fountains fragment (Bukofzer, *Studies*, p. 105). Isomelic repeats are not exact and are also not very common. Passages of one movement quoted in another in the mass pairs and mass cycles unmistakably exploit the integrative effect of repetition, but in relation to the total length of the movements, they are remarkably brief. Also the initial motives, or mottoes, are frequently stated in altered forms (Besseler, *Musik des Mittelalters*, p. 200, ex. 138), so that instead of providing a strong, heard connection between movements they act more as labels or tokens of relationship. In c.f. settings, repeated text and music in the original sometimes cause repetition in the setting itself (see ex. 20a-b and ex. 25b-c.); simple hymn settings also use the same music for each verse, and some or all of the verses of the Magnificat are set alike.

As noted on p. 62, lines organized by repetition of shorter musical ideas (*ostinato* figures, sequences, or any other type of motivic device) are rare. These devices are found, but outside the Italian compositions of the early part of the century they prove to be the exception, not the rule, when compared with the total musical output. The point is not that they were never used, which might indicate ignorance, but that they were so little used, which indicates that small value was attached to them. Those that occur catch the eye of the analyst, but the fact remains that the melodic norm of this style is a line in which organization by repetition, either of motive or of section, is not an important factor.

However, some of the more complex settings of the Magnificat form definite exceptions to these statements and reveal interesting schemes of repetition. The attitude is neither negative—with repetition disguised by new ornamentation, nor perfunctory—with repetition restricted to simple restatements of the psalm tone. A positive attempt is made to use sectional repetition in an imaginative way as a primary structural device. As an example of this period, see the Magnificat of Dunstable (*Works*, p. 95); an example of a later period is the Magnificat of Busnois mentioned above, p. 226.

Repeated structural tenors of the isorhythmic motet are not considered here; they belong to a type of composition which is entirely different from the c.f. paraphrase or from free compositions in chanson style.

[27]It should be mentioned that both Ficker and Riemann have attempted to show that some of the compositions of this period are built on a free variation principle or some other free application of procedures which were used in the eighteenth and nineteenth centuries. Hugo Riemann, *Handbuch der Musikgeschichte* (Leipzig: Breitkopf & Härtel, 1904-13), II:1, 113; Ficker, "Die frühen Messenkompositionen . . ."

Their use of the term "variation" is another reason I have turned away from it. It can be understood so broadly and in so many senses that it is almost useless. After all, any kind of restatement of a musical idea which is not literal repetition is a sort of variation—thematic development in a classical symphony, the episodes of a fugue, the thematic transformation of a symphonic poem, even the restatements of the row in dodecaphonic music. For this reason, again, I prefer to apply a special term such as "variant statement" to the newly ornamented statements of a c.f. in the early fifteenth century. In so doing I am merely following out a feeling that one should distinguish between types of "variation" and recognize the specific character and the expressive intent behind the procedure as it is used in works of different composers.

   [28]In certain Continental compositions of the fifteenth century, the use of the c.f. in the lowest voice has been attributed to the influence of the English discant. Bukofzer, *Geschichte des englischen Diskants*, p. 118, and his musical example No. 20, a Kyrie *Fons bonitatis* from the German manuscript of the mid-fifteenth century, Munich 3232a.

   [29]They provide the minimum essential intervals for the full cadence (one or more sixths followed by the octave) and are written to make correct two-part counterpoint with each other. Correct counterpoint in the fifteenth-century sense (more exactly, in the years of the dominance of the Burgundian three-part chanson) means that all the consonant intervals are used freely, parallel fifths and octaves rarely, and that dissonances are restricted in the great majority of cases to simple passing tones, appoggiaturas, syncopations, etc. Parallel fourths are not used between these two voices (superius and tenor). This is most convincingly illustrated in the progression of sixth chords leading to the $\frac{8}{5}$ cadence. The tenor takes the sixth and octave below the superius, and it is left to the contratenor to move in parallel fourths with it.

   [30]The two lower voices of Binchois's setting of the hymn *A solis ortus cardine* are written similarly. Jeanne Marix, *Les musiciens de la cour de Bourgogne* (Paris: Editions de l'Oiseau-Lyre, 1937), p. 188. See also the settings by Dufay of the hymns *Christe redemptor saeculi* (*DTO*, 14, p. 160) and *Audi, benigne conditor* (*Guillaume Dufay: Sämtliche Hymnen*, ed. R. Gerber [Wolfenbüttel: Möseler Verlag, 1937], p. 8—Vol. XLIX of *Das Chorwerk*, ed. F. Blume). Both compositions have c.f. in the middle voice.

   [31]An *Ave Virgo* of Dufay (found in Tr 92, published in Dufay, *Opera*, I, i, p. 19) apparently has c. f. in the middle voice, although the original melody has not been identified. The work is mentioned because the middle voice is actually the tenor, which happens to lie in this position simply because the contratenor is for the most part written below it. The clear bass function of the contratenor is interesting in view of the fact that the composition must have been written well before the middle of the century. There are a limited number of pieces from this period in which the contratenor stays in a low register; they are exhaustively discussed by Besseler (as part of an argument leading to the determination of the source of the term "fauxbourdon"). Besseler, *Bourdon*, chaps. ii-iii.

   [32]Two examples of c.f. in the middle voice by writers active on the Continent are the setting of the processional hymn *Crux fidelis* by Dunstable (*Works*, p. 103) in which the two lower voices are treated as a gymel, and the hymn *Ave maris stella* by Leonel (*DTO*, 53, p. 78). In the work of Leonel the contratenor is the highest voice and makes cadences with the tenor in the manner of a superius—a highly unusual procedure for this period.

   [33]Even in England, migration is uncommon among the compositions not written in score. There is only one instance in Old Hall, a Sanctus by Leonel (*OH*, III, 58). But the persistence of the tradition until late in the century is proved by the occasional occurrence of migrant c.f. in the manuscript sources. Two instances from the Pepys MS are known to me, fo. 28-29, 84-86.

   [34]These are not true scores in the sense of those used by Josquin and his successors. See Edward Lowinsky, "Early Scores in Manuscript," *Journal of the American Musicological Society*, XIII (1960), 126-173. They are not provided with bar lines, and the notes are not placed in exact vertical alignment. Nevertheless, the alignment is good enough to facilitate comparison between voices.

   [35]Some of the difficulties of laying out the c.f. would be avoided by this means, as

the sections are ordinarily clearly delimited by bars, rests, holds, etc. Instances are found in *DTO*, 61, pp. 62, 64 (c.f. indicated by the editor), p. 67 (migration to the tenor, m. 168-176), and p. 81; also *DTO* 53, p. 64, (m. 163 to the end) and p. 72 (m. 60-92 and m. 133-144).

[36]Besseler, *Musik des Mittelalters*, p. 223, quotes the *Kyrie ultimum* of this work as ex. 161. His analysis of Liebert's use of the chant results in an interpretation which is slightly different from that of my ex. 30. Liebert begins the sixth (final) Kyrie with an exact repetition of the fourth (ex. 30, m. 47-57), but, as the chant is given in the *LU*, the fourth *Kyrie eleison* and the first incise of the sixth do not repeat exactly. Part of the discrepancies between the two analyses result from this fact.

[37]*DTO*, 61, p. 81. The sources are Tr 92 and BL.

[38]Another example of migration at a duet is found in the anonymous setting of the Gradual *Constitues eos* (*Mon. Pol. Lit.*, II:1, p. 35, m. 55). Here, after a short free section, the c.f. migrates from the superius to the contratenor, which functions as the tenor in the duet. The same music, set to different words, is found (*ibid.*) on p. 20, m. 55 ff. See M. F. Bukofzer, review of *Mon. Pol. Lit.*, in *Musical Quarterly*, XXXV (April, 1949), 336.

[39]*DTO*, 61, p. 18. See also n. 10, above.

[40]Bukofzer, *Studies*, p. 40; Reese, *Renaissance*, pp. 31-32.

[41]See the Sanctus by Sturgeon, *OH*, III, 55.

[42]See the Credo of Dufay printed in *Doc. Pol. Lit.*, I, 5. The first few notes of Credo I are clearly harmonized at the beginning. The piece continues as a freely composed syllabic setting of the text. An anonymous *Salve Regina* (*DTO*, 53, p. 58) paraphrases the c.f. for about half the length of the piece, after which the chant disappears.

[43]See ex. 33, the setting of *Sospitati dedit* by Walter Frye.

[44]As usual in sequences, two verses are given the same music. In order to save space in the example, the c.f. is given only once. If the two verses have different settings they are put directly beneath the c.f., one under the other (as in verses 5 and 6, and 7 and 8). Verses 3, 4, 9 and all those following have not been quoted here.

[45]In the tenor, m. 23-25, there may possibly be a mild example of motivic treatment as the c.f. notes a-bb-a-f are given twice in succession by this voice. Frye worked at the Burgundian court around 1470, and Busnois was already experimenting with this means of musical organization. See chapter viii.

[46]Dunstable, *Works*, p. 106.

[47]Dunstable, *Works*, p. 179, editor's remarks. The work is quoted with presumptive c.f. tones in Reese, *Middle Ages*, p. 418, ex. 126.

[48]Erickson, *The Structure of Music*, p. 66.

[49]*Ibid.*, p. 67.

CHAPTER 3

[1]Leonel Power, "Missa super *Alma redemptoris mater*," *Doc. Pol. Lit.*, I:2. The disregard of the original structure extends to the text also. The tenor of the Mass is broken off on the note g, although the tonic is f, and at the syllable "po" of the word "populo." The few words found in the original manuscript, which are simply a reference to identify the original tune, have been supplemented with further text by the editor and the syllables have been shifted so the complete word "populo" is given. This is done for the sake of practical performance, although the editor recommends performance of the tenor by an instrument. For other examples of breaking off the c.f. see the Credo of Anglicanus, *Alma Redemptoris Mater* (*DTO*, 61, p. 92), which stops at the end of the word *genitorem*, on the tonic note at the end of a section of the chant, and *Ascendit Christus*, ex. 35, m. 110.

[2]Peter Wagner, *Geschichte der Messe*, I, Bis 1600 (Kleine Handbücher der Musikgeschichte, IX: 1 [Leipzig: Breitkopf & Härtel, 1913]), p. 53, n. 1; hereafter cited as Wagner, *Messe*.

[3]That is, the c.f. quotation may just as well break off at any point as at the end of a complete musical unit of the original. This may also involve the destruction of the original sense of the text, as shown in the tenors of the two isorhythmic motets with texts *Benedictus Mariae filius qui ve* and *(n)it in nomine Domini* (*OH*, III, pp. 40, 51).

[4]These characteristics of the framework tenor may be verified easily in the case of the isorhythmic Mass movements and motets of Dunstable. In the complete edition of Dunstable's works the editor reproduces the tenors in original form (*Works*, p. 162), and provides *cantus firmi* in versions very close to or identical with those used by the composer (*Works*, pp. 158-160).

(a) Pitch: As stated above, Dunstable's quotations are quite normal, in that they agree closely with the *cantus firmi* as given. The notes are not identical in every case, but the differences are no more than can be expected between slightly different versions of the same melody. There is no evidence that Dunstable used ornamental tones in these tenors, or intended to do anything but quote faithfully the pitches of the melody he had at hand.

(b) Structure: In some of the tenors the structure of the original is respected, the quotation consisting of a whole chant, or an integral section of one. (See nos. 15-18, 27, 31, and 33. Incidentally, this group includes the five tenors which are not divided into *taleae*. Another tenor, no. 24, while not comprising a complete section of a chant, does begin and end with a complete phrase.) However, the composer may ignore the element of phrase structure at will. Numbers 30 and 32 start midway in the course of a phrase, and numbers 25, 26, 29, and 32 break off before the end of one. Number 28 is an ambiguous case, the quotation ending on the penultimate note of a phrase, but the final note being given—outside the isorhythmic pattern—at the very end of the motet. Disregard of phrase structure may have important secondary consequences. In number 29, where the quotation misses reaching the end of the chant by two notes, a melody in third mode is converted into a tenor in fifth. In several instances the text suffers, since quotations begin and end in the middle of a word.

(c) Rhythm: All the tenors illustrate the preference for long note values (although pedal tones generally characterize only the first statement of a tenor, the diminutions in the repetitions reducing the notes to ordinary length). The tenors also illustrate that the succession of durations (longs, breves, and so on) is in apparently random order, that is, in an order which has not yet been satisfactorily explained. Likewise, rests are inserted apparently at random, and divide the quotations into groups of tones of varying lengths. It is in the latter feature of the layout—the placement of rests—that the disregard of original structure is most clearly seen. Rests are placed without regard to phrase or subdivision of the phrase, and, as a result, in the diminished statements they interrupt rhythmic flow in a completely arbitrary way. Rests are placed without regard to the text as well, a point which the editor makes clear by underlaying the text of the tenors exactly.

The differences in melodic and structural quotation of the c.f. can be conveniently reviewed in the motet *Veni Sancte Spiritus–Veni Creator Spiritus* (*Works*, p. 88). Here the hymn melody, *Veni Creator Spiritus*, is quoted as a structural voice in the tenor, as a melody in the superius. Fortunately, also, the c.f. given by the editor appears to be identical in every respect with the one used by Dunstable, so that a detailed comparison of the original and reworked versions can be made without the usual reservations. (The motet has so many interesting aspects that it will be mentioned several times. See pp. 87 and 107, and musical example 42.)

As to the structural quotation: it begins neither with the beginning of a phrase nor with the beginning of a word, but with the eleventh note of the hymn. It then proceeds with note-for-note accuracy in two groups of eleven tones each. Once again, neither group happens to begin or end with a word or phrase. (The splitting of words is not indicated in the sources, although it is made clear in the edition.) The groups of eleven (the *taleae*) are divided by rests into two groups of eight and three, causing more breaking of words. The tones are given proportional durations ranging from the breve to the maxima, the whole to be read in terms of *maximodus maior*, the ultimate formulation of the mensural system.

In the superius, preservation of phrase structure is a matter of primary concern; each quotation is exactly one phrase in length, no more, no less. The tones of the melody are quoted correctly but not literally. Rather, the melodic outline is somewhat enriched by ornamentation. Truncation of the text is not called for in a setup such as this, and is no more common than it would be in a freely composed melodic part. The procedures of quotation of this type preserve and develop upon the aesthetic values of the original. The primary appeal of the hymn to the ear is never forgotten.

In the tenor quotation, appeal to the ear is of no consequence. The long notes of the first statement can hardly qualify as melody; in fact, it takes a considerable mental effort to recognize the hymn at all when it is presented in this form. In the final statement, in short values, no effort is needed to recognize the hymn, but the factor of distortion becomes very apparent. Here, more than anywhere else, we are made aware of how little the quotation has to do with the aesthetic qualities of the original. In the tenor, the all-important goal is the construction of a new order—an order based on the intellectual values of number and proportion, and of such significance to the composer that it can supplant aesthetic values completely.

[5]Besseler describes the procedure, and gives musical examples to illustrate various aspects of it in the article "Ars Nova," MGG, I, cols. 708 ff. For further details see the article "Isorhythmic," in Apel, *Harvard Dictionary of Music*, p. 367; also, Reese, *Middle Ages*, p. 337. Most of the recent musical publications include analyses of isorhythmic compositions (e.g., the complete editions of Machaut, Dunstable, Dufay; *DTO*, 76; etc.).

[6]Henry Osborne Taylor, *The Medieval Mind* (4th ed.; Cambridge, Mass.: Harvard University Press, 1949), II, 67 ff. See also Vincent Foster Hopper, *Medieval Number Symbolism* (New York: Columbia University Press, 1938).

[7]Bukofzer, *Studies*, p. 62.

[8]Charles van den Borren, ed., *Polyphonia Sacra: A Continental Miscellany of the Fifteenth Century* (Nashdom Abbey, Burnham, Bucks: The Plainsong and Mediaeval Music Society, 1932), p. 167; hereafter cited as van den Borren, ed., *Polyphonia Sacra*. The editor explains exactly what he has done in the prefatory notes, p. xxxiv.

[9]On the basis of the edition of van den Borren, the motet has been cited as an example of a piece which is isorhythmically organized in the two upper voices only. See the article "Isorhythmic" in Apel, *Harvard Dictionary of Music*, p. 367. Actually, all four voices are isorhythmic; only the substitute voice, the *solus tenor*, is not. More recently the work has been published in its correct form. *Early Fifteenth-Century Music*, ed. Gilbert Reaney (*Corpus Mensurabilis Musicae*, XI:1 ([Rome: American Institute of Musicology, 1955]), p. 39; hereafter cited as Reaney, *Early Fifteenth-Century Music*.

[10]Bukofzer, *Studies*, pp. 56-73. The analysis of the isorhythmic motets and mass movements contained in a single source—OH—shows a surprising number of applications of the principle.

[11]The thirteen preserved isorhythmic motets are printed in *Opera*, Vol. II. The editor provides a chronological list in the Foreword, p. iii, assigning provisional dates to those works for which the exact date is not known and giving supporting evidence for each date in the Critical Notes, pp. x ff. Some of these dates must be modified. It now appears that *Magnam me gentes* was written in 1438, not 1443. H. Besseler, "Neue Dokumente zum Leben und Schaffen Dufays," *Archiv für Musikwissenschaft*, IX (1952), 167. The date of 1436 suggested for *O Sancte Sebastiane* is obviously

incorrect, the style of the work showing that it must have been written in the 1420's. H. Besseler, *Bourdon*, p. 186, n. 6. Likewise it seems that *O gemma, lux et speculum* should be placed in the 1420's, since it is stylistically similar to *O Sancte Sebastiane*. If these revisions are accepted, the works written between 1420 and 1430 are five in number: *Vasilissa, ergo gaude; Apostolo glorioso; Rite maiorem Iacobum canamus; O Sancte Sebastiane;* and *O gemma, lux et speculum.*

Five works can be exactly dated in the following decade: *Balsamus et munda* (1431), *Ecclesie militantis* (1431), *Supremum est mortalibus* (1433), *Nuper rosarum flores* (1436), and *Magnam me gentes* (1438). Of these, only the first is fully isorhythmic. The remaining three motets, *Salve flos tusce gentis, Fulgens iubar,* and *Moribus et genere Christo,* are all fully isorhythmic, but apparently were written in the 1430's or even in the 1440's. (The editor suggests the very late date of 1446 for the last one.) Further evidence of the tendency to write only the tenor isorhythmically at this time is given by the motet of Jean Brassart, *O rex Fridrice,* which can be assigned the date of 1440. G. de Van, "A Recently Discovered Source of Early Fifteenth Century Polyphonic Music," *Musica Disciplina,* II (1948), 14, 37. Bukofzer also mentions a fully isorhythmic secular song, *O potores,* which was apparently written shortly before the middle of the century in an intentionally anachronistic manner when isorhythm "was already a thing of the past." *Studies,* pp. 174 ff.

[12]Ex. 44, chap. v. It is, more exactly, a simultaneous statement of the c.f. in two voices.

[13]For a discussion of isomelism in several of the motets see Samuel E. Brown, Jr., "New Evidence of Isomelic Design in Dufay's Isorhythmic Motets," *Journal of the American Musicological Society,* X (Spring, 1957), 7.

[14]*Works,* pp. 88 and 81. Unfortunately, none of the isorhythmic motets of Dunstable can be given positive dates, so that decisions as to time of composition have to be made on stylistic grounds only, and evidence of this type must be used with considerable caution. For instance, the three works which have only the tenor isorhythmic cannot be adjudged late merely for this reason. These motets do not give evidence of an attempt to move beyond isorhythm as do the partially isorhythmic works of Dufay just mentioned, but rather belongs to a class of works where isorhythm appears incidentally, or where it appears sporadically as a sort of buttress to the structure as a whole. An anonymous Gloria from Old Hall can be cited as an earlier example of the type since it is partially freely composed, partially isorhythmic. *OH,* III, [37]. Dunstable's motet *Specialis Virgo-Salve parens inclita* can be included in the same category, since the isorhythmic elements are a partial encroachment on a scheme which is otherwise rhythmically free. *Works,* p. 86. In the other two, *Veni Sancte Spiritus–Sancti Spiritus assit nobis gratia* and *"Nesciens Mater,"* the repetitions of the tenor automatically bring about recurrences of rhythmic pattern, so that the isorhythmic features of that voice must be considered incidental. *Works,* pp. 92, 94. In these works, then, the combination of rhythmically patterned tenor and rhythmically free upper voices need not be interpreted as a progressive tendency as it was in the case of Dufay and Brassart. The two isorhythmic Mass pairs (with tenors isorhythmic and upper voices rhythmically free) probably do indicate that Dunstable was aware of the new modified form. See the pair on *Jesu Christe, Fili Dei vivi* and on *Da gaudiorum premia* (*Works,* pp. 35, 41).

[15]Examples can be found in Dunstable's *Preco preheminencie* (*Works,* p. 78, m. 149-150); in the final cadence for "five" voices of Dufay's *Ecclesie militantis* (*Opera,* II, 88, m. 133-134); and in the final cadence of Dufay's *Apostolo glorioso* (*ibid.,* p. 16, m. 93-95).

[16]For a detailed discussion of this work see p. 107. As the time of its composition Harrison suggests 1431, a date somewhat earlier than I would suspect from the style of the work. Along with the *Missa Da gaudiorum premia,* it may have been sung at the coronation of Henri VI as king of France. *Music in Medieval Britain,* p. 244. For further commentary on the motet see Bukofzer, *Studies,* p. 63.

[17]With regard to this work, and the two discussed immediately following it, see also n. 14, this chapter.

[18]A marked change of style, discernible in all aspects of his music, occurs about 1430. Besseler gives a thorough and brilliant analysis. *Bourdon*, pp. 121-138, and elsewhere.

[19]After the second B a few tones are added which proceed to a cadence (*DTO*, 14, p. 156, m. 165-171). They are not in the Vatican version of the chant and are not included in the scheme of repetitions, so were probably added by the composer. For further discussion of this work see p. 110.

[20]An unconvincing attempt has been made to show that the c.f. *Ascendit Christus* is also used in the superius. Jacques Handschin, "Gregorianisch-Polyphones aus der Handschrift Paris B.N. lat. 15129," *Kirchenmusikalisches Jahrbuch*, XXV (1930), 60-76.

[21]Another good example is the Anglicanus Credo on *Alma Redemptoris Mater* (*DTO*, 61, p. 92). The peculiarities of this tenor are thoroughly discussed by Rudolph Ficker in "Die frühen Messenkompositionen der Trienter Codices," *Studien zur Musikwissenschaft*, XI (1924), 44-48.

[22]Statements of the c.f. in equal note values were recognized by the theorists of the fifteenth century. Examples (labeled *cantus firmus*) are given by Guilielmus Monachus, c. 1475, in connection with a discussion of English musical practices. "De preceptis artis musice . . . ," in Coussemaker, ed., *Scriptorum*, III, 293, 295. Tinctoris also gives examples of *cantus planus* laid out in equal values. *Liber de arte contrapuncti*, bk. ii, chap. 21, (*ibid.*, IV, 130-131). But it was not until the sixteenth and seventeenth centuries that the quotation of a c.f. in notes of equal values became inseparably bound up with the writing of contrapuntal exercises in species. Knud Jeppesen, *Counterpoint* (New York: Prentice-Hall, 1939), p. 40. Since I have been using "*cantus firmus*" in a much broader sense (see Preface), it caused me some embarrassment to have to choose a special term, "strict," for this, its best-known sense at the present day.

[23]The source is Pepys 1236, fo. 33. Since the manuscript was probably compiled about 1470, the piece may well have been written about 1450.

[24]*DTO*, 53, p. 70, No. 11. Tr 91 was compiled about 1480.

[25]*DTO*, 53, p. 72, No. 12.

[26]Alfred Orel, "Einige Grundformen der Motettkomposition . . . ," *Studien zur Musikwissenschaft*, VII (1920), 68-69.

[27]*Ibid.*, pp. 80-81. Wilhelm Ehmann, *Adam von Fulda als Vertreter der ersten deutschen Komponistengeneration* (Neue Deutsche Forschungen, Abteilung Musikwissenschaft, XCIV [Berlin: Junker und Dünnhaupt, 1936], Teil I; hereafter cited as Ehmann, *Adam von Fulda*.

CHAPTER 4

[1]The reasons for concluding that the Gloria and Credo of Liebert are not based on c.f. are given in the Appendix, pp. 406 ff.

[2]Wagner, *Messe*, pp. 54 ff.

[3]Published in *Mon. Pol. Lit.*, II, 1.

[4]Wagner, *loc. cit.*

[5]For comments on the term "plainsong Mass" see Reese, *Renaissance*, p. 68 and and n. 180. He suggests naming the Masses according to the c.f. techniques used, but this limits the category a great deal and brings up problems of its own in the many cases where more than one technique is used in the same Mass. The common feature of these works is the polyphonic setting given to the texts of a number of items from a single service; the appropriate Gregorian melodies are used in most of the movements, but not necessarily in all. It seems that the only kind of term broad enough to cover this variety of treatment would be such a nearly meaningless one as "Gregorian service Mass."

[6]Bukofzer, *Studies*, pp. 44, 59-60.

[7]*Ibid.*, pp. 75, 219; Besseler, *Bourdon*, p. 148. Bukofzer mentions the pairs which also appear in the Cyprus manuscript (Turin, Bibl. Naz. J II 9).

[8]These movements are paired in the sources, Gloria, BL, Nos. 92-93 (71), "Jo. Ciconie," and Credo, Nos. 94-96, (73); Tr 87, Nos. 31-32, both anonymous. They are published in DTO, 61, pp. 1, 3. For passages of one quoted in the other, compare Gloria, p. 1, m. 22-28, and Credo, p. 3, m. 7-14; Gloria, p. 2, m. 57-59, and Credo, p. 3, m. 39-41; etc. (In this instance and in following ones I sometimes give more than one source reference. It is not my intent to give full concordances, but to choose sources which give some indication of the date of the composition.)

[9]Quotations at the beginning are too numerous to mention. Various terms have been used to designate them: "head motive" (*Kopfmotiv*), "motto," and "initial motive" (*motif initial*). An instance of relationship at the end of a movement, caused by similar final cadences, is found in a Kyrie, Gloria, and Credo by Dufay. *Doc. Pol. Lit.*, I, 1. Haphazardly placed quotations occur in these movements as well. Compare Gloria, p. 3, br. 3, m. 4 ff., with Credo, p. 6, br. 3, m. 5 ff.

[10]Oxford, Bodleian Library, Canonici Misc. 213; inventory of contents given by Gilbert Reaney, "The Manuscript Oxford, Bodleian Library, Canonici Misc. 213," *Musica Disciplina*, IX (1955), 73 ff. Bologna, Liceo Musicale, Q 15 (formerly No. 37); contents given by Guillaume de Van, "Inventory of Manuscript Bologna, Liceo Musicale, Q 15 (olim 37)," *Musica Disciplina*, II (1948), 231 ff. Trent, Castel del Buon Consiglio, MSS. 87 and 92; catalogue of six codices (87 through 92) in DTO, 14, pp. 31 ff. Aosta Seminary Library, mensuralist musical codex without shelf number; contents given by G. de Van, "A Recently Discovered Source . . . ," *Musica Disciplina*, II (1948), 5 ff.

[11]These cycles consist of four movements only—Gloria, Credo, Sanctus, and Agnus. It was the more usual English custom not to set the Kyrie.

[12]Found anonymously in Tr 87, Nos. 3-6, and under the name of Leonel in Aosta, Nos. 162-165. The discovery of the Aosta MS and publication of the list of contents with the attribution of this work to Leonel was the crucial point which, added to the previously known evidence, made quite clear the priority of the English in the c.f. Mass cycle.

[13]Tr 92, Nos. 1397, 1404, 1405, and 1446, "Leonellus." The movements are not written in direct succession in the manuscript although the first three are close together. The Gloria appears in Aosta in two places (Nos. 40 and 65) and is ascribed to Dunstable. Bukofzer decides in favor of Dunstable as the composer (Dunstable, *Works*, p. 171), with the reservation that "no final decision can be reached as to the author of this cyclic Mass."

[14]BL, Nos. 10-16 (9-15); published in Dufay, *Opera*, II:1, iii.

[15]BL, Nos. 172-176 (138-142) and Canonici, fo. 63-66, 70ᵛ-71, and 68 (Nos. 132, 133, 134, 149, and 142). The movements are written in direct succession in BL and partially so in Canonici. Published in van den Borren, ed., *Polyphonia Sacra*, pp. 1 ff.

[16]Tr 87, Nos. 153-157. The Gloria is attributed to Pyllois; the other movements are anonymous.

[17]BL, Nos. 161-165 (127-131). Beginnings of the superius line only of each movement are published in Besseler, *Musik des Mittelalters*, ex. 138, p. 200.

[18]Aosta, Nos. 50, 62, 85, and 100. Each movement is placed in its proper group of movements of the ordinary (the Kyrie with the Kyries, the Gloria with the Glorias, and so on).

[19]Pairs are found by: Dunstable, Gloria and Credo, *Jesu Christe fili Dei* (*Works*, pp. 35, 38). Dunstable, Gloria and Sanctus, *Da gaudiorum premia* (*Works*, pp. 41, 43). Bennet, Gloria and Sanctus, *Jacet granum* (Gloria in Tr 87, No. 21 [anon.], and Aosta, No. 70 [anon.]; Sanctus in Tr. 92, No. 1379 [Benet], and Aosta, No. 158

[anon.]). Driffelde, Agnus, *Eructavit cor meum*, Tr 92, No. 1552, and Sanctus, *Regnum mundi*, Tr 90, No. 973 (anon.); both c.f. references are to the same chant, the first being the text of the verse of the Respond *Regnum mundi*. It has the same melody as the beginning (*Ant. Sar.*, pl. 666). Anonymous, Kyrie and Gloria, *Alma Redemptoris Mater*, Tr 87, Nos. 133-134 (anon.); the fact that the Kyrie is set may well indicate that these movements are not written by an English composer.

[20]In support of this the following pairs can be cited: in section B of BL (*Et in terra/Patrem* section, inventory numbers 28-124 [27-95]) there are twenty-eight Gloria-Credo pairs, none based on common c.f., and the overwhelming majority attributed to Continental composers. The musical incipits of the Trent codices support the evidence of BL. A Gloria and Credo of Brassart, Tr 87, Nos. 74-75, apparently have related initial motives in superius and tenor. A Gloria and Credo of Dufay, Tr 87, Nos. 8-9, and BL, Nos. 138-142 (107-108), are provided with initial motives in all voices. An anonymous Sanctus and Agnus, Tr 87, Nos. 79 and 81, have three notes alike in the superius of both movements. Binchois makes a combination of types by using initial motives in a plainchant pair: Sanctus and Agnus, Mass IX (Tr 92, Nos. 1399-1400; published in *DTO*, 61, pp. 51, 53). He takes advantage of the similarities of the two *cantus firmi* to make the superius lines much alike in both and gives them nearly identical tenors. (M. 1-6 of the Sanctus correspond to m. 1-7 of the Agnus.)

[21]The movements of Bennet are published in Dunstable (*Works*, pp. 142, 144) as the last two movements of a *Missa sine nomine*, the famous Dunstable-Leonellus Mass. (The question of the disputed authorship is taken up in the editorial notes, *Works*, p. 189). While these show the use of motto beginnings by an English composer, the following movements show the use of foreign c.f. by Continental writers: Pugnare, Gloria, *Ave Regina caelorum*, Tr 87, no. 30; Jo. Franchois, Credo, *Alma Redemptoris Mater*, Aosta No. 31 and BL No. 158 (124) (Johannes de Gemblaco). To this group of single movements on foreign c.f. might be added an Anglicanus Gloria, *Alma Redemptoris Mater*, Tr 92, No. 1471 (published in *DTO*, 61, p. 92).

[22]Dufay, *Opera*, III, Foreword, p. iii. Further accounts of the early history of the cyclic Mass are given in Bukofzer, *Studies*, pp. 217 ff., *The New Oxford History*, III, 202 ff., and Reese, *Renaissance*, p. 66.

[23]Bukofzer, *Studies*, p. 107.

[24]*OH*, III, 76, 136. See also the ornamented tenor c.f. in a Sanctus by Tyes, *ibid.*, III, 94. These works are mentioned above, pp. 36, 37.

[25]Regis probably chose *L'homme armé* as c.f. for a Mass in honor of St. Michael because of the nature of the secular text. Likewise, Josquin undoubtedly chose *Comme femme desconfortée* as c.f. for the *Stabat Mater* for the same reason.

[26]The practice of using secular material in Mass settings began very early in the fifteenth century. For a discussion of folk-songlike material in two early Mass movements of Dufay, and of the esthetic implications of its use see Besseler, *Bourdon*, p. 213. A brief and interesting general historical account of "the excesses and abuses resulting from an extreme familiarity with things holy, as well as the insolent mingling of pleasure with religion" in the fifteenth century, which is yet a period "of unshaken faith and of a deeply religious culture," is given by J. Huizinga. *The Waning of the Middle Ages* (Garden City, New York: Anchor Books, Doubleday & Company, 1954), chap. xii.

[27]*Liber de arte contrapuncti . . .* , bk. iii, chap. iii, in Coussemaker, ed., *Scriptorum*, IV, 152. The importance of *varietas* to Tinctoris is sufficiently indicated by the heading of chap. viii: "*De octava, et ultima generali regula quae varietatem in omni contrapuncto exquierendam accuratissime precipit.*"

[28]An analysis of the Mass of Dufay is given on pp. 122 ff. See also the analysis of Tinctoris' own *L'homme armé* Mass, p. 241.

[29]A long note is split into two at one point (Sanctus, *Doc. Pol. Lit.*, I, ii, pp. 16-17,

m. 41-42). Also, the introductory duets of the Credo and Sanctus fall outside the general rhythmic scheme of the tenor. Otherwise the statements in each movement are the same in every detail.

[30]Thse are not indicated in Feininger's edition but are given by Oliver Strunk in a penetrating analysis of this Mass. "Documenta Polyphoniae Liturgicae . . . ," *Journal of the American Musicological Society*, II (1949), 107 (book review).

[31]*Works*, pp. 41, 43.

[32]*Ibid.*, pp. 35, 38.

[33]*Ibid.*, p. 47. (See n. 13, this chapter, concerning the question of authorship.)

[34]In this pair whole sections of one movement are quoted in the other with only minor differences. Agnus I, to *mundi*, is the same as Sanctus, and *miserere nobis* is the same as *Osanna in excelsis*. Agnus III is the same as *Benedictus qui venit*. For c.f. and manuscript sources, see n. 19, this chapter.

[35]The Gloria and Sanctus appear in both Trent and Aosta. See n. 19, above. The c.f. is given in *The New Oxford History*, III, 85.

[36]The first-named Sanctus, on *Jacet granum* (ex. 40c), is found in Tr 90, No. 969. The Sanctus-Agnus pair form the last two movements of the *Missa sine nomine* mentioned in n. 21, above.

[37]Contained in the English manuscript Bodl. Add. C 87, compiled c. 1450.

[38]Five movements, including the Kyrie, are written in succession in Cambridge, University Library, Ii. 5. 18 (fo. 219ᵛ-228). One folio which is torn out can be completed from Tr. Four movements (the Kyrie is lacking) are in Tr 90 (Nos. 897, 935, 962, and 963). The Gloria and Credo are not written in succession in Tr, but each is included in its proper group, as are several other Mass movements with tenor c.f. in this codex. In Cambridge it is clearly presented as a Mass cycle. This Mass and the Mass *Requiem aeternam* are analyzed by Bukofzer in *The New Oxford History*, III, 209 ff.

[39]The tenor begins on a long d (see ex. 41), so the upper voices naturally stress the notes d, f, a, and b.

CHAPTER 5

[1]As the text of the superius is the sequence *Veni Sancte Spiritus* and the notes are taken from the hymn *Veni Creator Spiritus*, there is here an exception to the general practice in paraphrases of associating the correct words and notes. Even though elaborated c.f. is used in this work, the textual procedures of the isorhythmic motet dominate.

[2]*Works*, p. 90, m. 113-114.

[3]So far as I know, this is the only isorhythmic composition in which this is done. See p. 87 for further comment on this work.

[4]The scheme of the layout of this tenor has been given in chap. iii, p. 89.

[5]The motet *Ecclesie militantis* will not be considered here. It makes use of two different *cantus firmi* sounded more or less simultaneously in the two tenors, but they are fitted together in a technically even less impressive way than the tenors of *Nuper rosarum*.

[6]There is no imitation in the strict sense of the word, although certain exact repetitions of the material of one voice by another are indicated in the example by brackets.

[7]No final statement can be made until after publication of the complete edition of Dufay's works. Of the works available at present, this is the only one with c.f. in all voices.

[8]See ex. 51 and the imitative passages in *Flos florum*, the tenor motet *Ave Regina caelorum*, etc. See also the canonic *Gloria in modum tubae*.

[9]Because of the repetition of verses, there is an over-all plan in the *Magnificat*

octavi toni (*DTO*, 14, pp. 174 ff.). More typical are those in ex. 28, m. 6-8; ex. 43b; and ex. 50, m. 39-44 and m. 47-49.

CHAPTER 6

[1]Suggestions made in works published in 1926 and 1941, respectively: *Guillaume Dufay, Son importance* . . . (Brussels: Lamertin), pp. 105-106, and *Etudes sur le xvᵉ siècle musical* (Antwerp: N. V. de Nederlandsche Boekhandel), p. 115. The latter is hereafter cited as van den Borren, *Etudes*. The author maintains this opinion as to the date of the Mass in a still later work, the valuable monograph on "Dufay and His Contemporaries," in *The New Oxford History*, III, 222.

[2]The passages are published in Dufay, *Opera*, III, 119, m. 72 ff., and in *Guillaume Dufay, Ave Regina coelorum*, ed. M. F. Bukofzer (New York: Music Press, Inc., 1949), MP-116, pp. 13-14, m. 86-96.

[3]*Etudes*, p. 164.

[4]M. F. Bukofzer, "*Caput redivivium:* A New Source for Dufay's *Missa Caput*," *Journal of the American Musicological Society*, IV (1951), 102 ff.

[5]Besseler discusses the whole question of chronology in his foreword to Dufay, *Opera*, III, pp. i ff., and repeats the stand he took on the *Missa Caput* in an earlier work (*Bourdon*, p. 157, n. 2, and p. 238, *These* 78).

[6]To my knowledge, the English used only liturgical melodies as cantus firmi for Mass cycles at this early period. But the use of secular melodies in the Mass was not strange to Dufay. Besseler, in *Bourdon*, p. 212, and Dufay, *Opera*, III, iv.

[7]Dufay, *Opera*, III, 1. Summary of c.f. treatment in Reese, *Renaissance*, p. 70.

[8]In both Gloria and Credo the tenor is stated three times, once with tripled time-values, once with doubled, and lastly with the original values. It is stated once only, with doubled values, in the other three movements. Owing to the tripartite form of the Kyrie and Agnus, it is split into two parts, one being used with the first and one with the third section. The middle section in both movements is free. In the Sanctus it is given in three parts, one each with the Sanctus, *Osanna I* and *Osanna II*. The *Benedictus* and *Pleni sunt caeli* are free. Also, in the Kyrie, Sanctus, and Agnus three notes are added at the cadence following the completion of the first half of the chanson tenor. (*Opera*, III, Kyrie, p. 2, m. 37; Sanctus, p. 26, m. 91; Agnus, p. 30, m. 43.) These notes do not belong to the chanson tenor; they are added to produce an extension of the tonic chord. This effect of trailing off at the cadence, in which one or more voices remain in motion after the others have come to rest on the final note, is much used by Ockeghem, Pierre de la Rue, Josquin, and others. (The added notes are incorrectly placed in the edition of the Mass in *DTO*, 14, and make parallel unisons with the contratenor.)

[9]Published in *DTO*, 38, pp. 17 ff.; also in *Mon. Pol. Lit.*, Ser. I, Vol. II, No. 1.

[10]See "*Caput*, A Liturgico-Musical Study," in *Studies*, p. 217. Bukofzer shows that the c.f. comes from the English liturgy, and indicates other English features in the Mass. This study establishes an essential link in the history of the cyclic Mass for it shows clearly how Dufay took over the English tenor-Mass cycle.

[11]It is not present in *Se la face ay pale*, since he takes over the rhythmic patterns as well as the notes of the original. The isorhythmic patterning is the inevitable result of quoting the original material exactly every time it is stated and is, in a sense, involuntary. Because Dufay interrupts the tenor quotation only at the end of a phrase, this scaffolding lacks the antimelodic features seen in the older ones where the rhythmic patterns are arbitrarily imposed. They are so imposed in *Caput* and the antimelodic aspect is present. This feature continues to show up in works of various composers, but its quality changes. Obrecht often interrupts a phrase, but his reason for doing so can generally be seen. For instance, in his *Missa Je ne demande*, the

interruption often occurs before a final note so as to delay the cadence. There is a whimsical instance in Busnois's *L'homme armé* Mass: the tenor of the first section of the Gloria breaks off in the middle of a short figure which is picked up and completed several measures later in the *Qui tollis.*

[12]Dufay, *Opera*, III, 33. Summary of structure in Reese, *Renaissance*, p. 72.

[13]Marix, p. 96. The tenor in Morton's setting is the same as that of the earliest known version in the Mellon Chansonnier. M. F. Bukofzer, "An Unknown Chansonnier of the Fifteenth Century," *Musical Quarterly*, XXVIII (1942), 19-20. Reese gives the Naples version of the tune with an English translation of the text. *Renaissance*, p. 73, ex. 18.

[14]Dufay, *Opera*, III, 66.

[15]Other instances are Regis's *Missa Ecce ancilla Domini–Ne timeas Maria* and Obrecht's *Sub tuum praesidium*, both of which quote several Marian chants, and Obrecht's *Missa de Sancto Martino*, which uses several chants from the Feast of St. Martin.

[16]At the present day, *Ecce ancilla* is found in the service for the Annunciation of Mary (*LU*, 1417), *Beata es Maria* in the commemoration of the Visitation (*LU*, 1538ᵛ). Formerly both were used in the same service, the Annunciation. (See *Pal. Mus.* IX, 379.)

[17]Dufay, *Opera*, III, 91. Analysis in Reese, *Renaissance*, p. 76.

[18]The section *Salve radix . . . orta* is omitted from the tenor statement, the c.f. being resumed at *Gaude gloriosa* in Agnus III. The original form of the melody is AABB'C and it is the B section which is omitted in the shortened form. (The omission of B does not entail the entire loss of any c.f. material by the tenor, since B' is retained.) It is possible that there is another omission in a tenor statement—at the word *speciosa* in Kyrie II, although it is difficult to decide definitely because of the ornamentation at that point. Another freedom, but of the opposite type, is found in Kyrie I and *Christe*. The Kyrie movement is unusually extensive, each of the nine supplications being given an entire section, the first *Kyrie eleison* being repeated for the third and likewise the first *Christe eleison* being repeated for the third. This involves repetition of the phrases of c.f. concerned, so that it is given in extended form for this movement: Kyrie, AAA; *Christe*, BB (*Christe* II is free); Kyrie, B'C (Kyrie II is free).

[19]Van den Borren, *Etudes*, pp. 158-159. Dufay uses one of the many variants of the antiphon which differ in some respects from the present-day version. In the *LU* and *Ant. Mon.* the text reads *Gaude Virgo gloriosa*, but in the Mass and funeral motet *Ave Regina caelorum* it is shortened at this point to *Gaude gloriosa.*

[20]This and the following examples of the *Missa Ave Regina caelorum* are taken from one of the manuscript sources, Br 5557. Comparison with the corresponding passages in Dufay, *Opera*, will show certain differences in key signature, accidentals, etc.

[21]The head motives appear in their full length only in the movements which begin with duet or trio while the tenor rests. In those where the tenor sounds from the very beginning (such as the Kyries of *Se la face ay pale* and *L'homme armé*), the head motives appear in a noticeably altered and shortened form. In several other cases they are identical in some movements and somewhat different in others. In *Se la face ay pale* the head motives are the same for the last four movements, and only that of the Kyrie is somewhat different. In *L'homme armé* there are two pairs, Gloria and Credo, and Sanctus and Agnus, while the Kyrie stands alone. In *Ecce ancilla Domini* the motive for the Gloria and Credo is the same, as is that for the Kyrie, Sanctus, and Agnus. The head motive is identical for all five movements of *Ave Regina caelorum.*

[22]See chap. iv, n. 9.

[23]Van den Borren, *Etudes*, p. 155.

[24]This may seem an ultraconservative evaluation, since even within the limited area of the five late Masses there is an increasing tendency for the c.f. to spread

from the tenor into other voices. Van den Borren analyzes the Masses in some detail (*ibid.*, pp. 144 ff.), and notes many more relations between the c.f. and the upper voices than have been mentioned here. I have not taken them into account because many of them are so brief and inconsequential that they can easily be no more than accidental similarities. The whole question is a matter for individual judgment, but it seems to me that there is danger of going too far in reading into works of an earlier generation aims which only become completely clear in works of a later one. Dufay does develop noticeably in the later Masses, but he only points the way toward the procedures of his successors. (Besseler indicates the ways in which Dufay laid the foundations for the style of the Ockeghem generation, but he also emphasizes the differences between Dufay and his successors. *Bourdon und Fauxbourdon*, Theses 80 and 82, pp. 238-239, and pp. 225-226.)

[25]The duet shows a considerable amount of initial imitation which is more subtly organized than is customary, as the distance between entries becomes constantly less (3 semibreves, m. 1 ff.; 2 semibreves, m. 8 ff.; 1½ semibreves, m. 14-15; and 1 semibreve, m. 16). When the tenor enters with the c.f. (m. 21), there is another brief point of imitation between the two upper voices. Even such a cursory one as this is extremely rare when the c.f. is sounding, and from m. 23 onward, the voices are free counterpoints as usual. The textual cue in the tenor is incorrect in the manuscript. It should read *Salve radix*.

[26]Other budding stylistic developments, such as rhythmic patterning of the voices, sequences, climactic passages at the end of compositions or important sections, etc., are to be found, but they, too, are exceptional incidents. The practice of breaking up the unit of beat (the semibreve) into smaller values is a standard procedure with Ockeghem, Busnois, and others of their generation and is also a feature of the late work of Dufay. The duets of ex. 51 (presumably for soloists) show a constant division of the semibreve into quarters with rhythmic patterns beginning on a fraction of a beat. Small hemiola (♩♩♩♩ , in contrast to the normal type, ♩♪♩♪) and other patterns which cut across the beat are indicated above the staff in the example. The simpler, more straightforward ternary rhythm of the tutti section (m. 21 ff.) harks back to the older Burgundian style of Binchois and A. de Lantins. The new stylistic feature which is most unreservedly adopted is the writing for four voices as the standard number, rather than three. The tenor is now an inner part, while the fourth voice is the lowest, and acts as a real bass line with the specific function of supporting the harmonies. The development of such a part—of epochal importance in the history of music—introduced the long period of bass-directed harmonic writing. Dufay's importance as one of the pioneers cannot be overestimated. In fact, some of his writing is deceptively advanced in sound and should not be taken as typical of the early four-part writing. The last section of the funeral motet *Ave Regina caelorum* gives us a strong sensation of a feeling for tonal propriety (due to the many successions of chords with roots a fourth or fifth apart, the simple rhythm, and the very clear cadences) which actually did not exist at that time. Most of the compositions give the impression of a rather featureless flow of chordal sonorities from which a concept of tonal direction is lacking, owing to the irregular subdivision of the beat and the consequent irregularity of chord changes, the avoidance of the cadence and the many deceptive cadences, the continued use of partial signatures, the use of accidentals in a nontonal manner (for instance, see the first few measures of ex. 48a), the successions of chords with roots a second or third apart, etc. This lack of tonal direction is especially noticeable in works of Ockeghem, where the melodic character of the bass is not essentially different from that of the upper voices.

[27]*Mon. Pol. Lit.*, Ser. I, Vol. II, *Missae octo cum duobus fragmentis*, ed. L. Feininger, 1951-53; No. 2, *Veterem hominem*; No. 3, *Christus surrexit*; No. 5, *Sine nomine*; No. 6, *Pax vobis ego sum*; No. 10, *Puisque ie vis*. These works are all anonymous, although the editor has ascribed some of them to Dufay. In addition the series includes four works known to be by Dufay (*Caput, Se la face ay pale, Ecce ancilla,*

and *Ave Regina caelorum*). Another work, the *Missa La mort de Saint Gothard*, is promised but not yet published. (Hereafter cited as Feininger, *Missae*.)

[28]In both works the statement in triple meter—cursus A—is given the texts of Sanctus, *Pleni sunt* and Osanna I. The statement in duple meter—cursus B—is given the texts . . . V*enit in nomine Domini* and Osanna II in *Caput*, while in *Veterem hominem* it is given *In nomine Domini* and Osanna II. This negligible difference is brought about by differences in the setting of the *Benedictus* in the duos which follow Osanna I. In the other movements the settings are identical. In both works cursus A is given to Kyrie I, cursus B to the *Christe*. There is no special section for Kyrie II. In the Gloria A is given to *Et in terra*, B to *Qui tollis*. In the Credo the *Patrem* is set to A, and B starts at *Et incarnatus*. In the final movement Agnus I and II are set to A, Agnus III to B.

[29]The authority for this is Thomas Morley, who quotes from the Mass in the *Plaine and Easie Introduction* . . . Thurston Dart, "Correspondence," *Music and Letters*, XXXV (April, 1954), 183. Morley's statement is not completely unambiguous, nor is he infallible, but there are several pieces of internal evidence which tend to corroborate what he says. There is the primary fact of the use of a Sarum chant for c.f., as well as of the use of the Kyrie trope *Deus creator omnium*. In addition, there is the use of full chords—complete with third—at important cadences (at the end of Kyrie I, *Christe*, *Et in terra*, *Qui tollis*, *Patrem*, *Et resurrexit*, etc.), the absence of imitative counterpoint, and several instances of complete breaks in the duos where pauses are given to both voices at the same time. All of these point to English and away from Continental authorship of the work. The Kyrie is also separated from the other movements in the manuscript source. Gloria, Credo, Sanctus, and Agnus are the first four items of Tr 88 (Nos. 199-202). The Kyrie, while in the same codex, appears a couple of hundred items later (No. 404). The separation of this movement from the others gives some reason for belief that the Mass may have been originally conceived as a four-movement work in the English manner and that the Kyrie was added later.

[30]The source of the c.f. was kindly pointed out to me by Dr. Louis Gottlieb, who discovered it when making a study of the cyclic Masses of Tr 89. Louis Gottlieb, *The Cyclic Masses of Trent Codex 89*. Ph.D. dissertation, University of California (Berkeley), 1958, unpublished.

[31]The entire tenor layout is given by the editor in the preface to the Mass, (Feininger, *Missae*, ex. 10, p. xi).

[32]A detailed plan of the tenor layout is given by the editor in the preface to the Mass, (*ibid.*, ex. 9, p. xi).

[33]Dunstable, *Works*, p. xv.

[34]The chanson is given in Feininger, *Missae*, Introduction, p. ix, the tenor layout on pp. x-xii.

[35]Nos. 475-479. Published in *DTO*, 22, pp. 1 ff., as *O rosa bella I*.

[36]Parts of *Caput* and all of *Se la face ay pale* also appear in Tr 88. The most that can be said is that they are all of about the same age. Wagner, *Messe*, p. 98, n. 4. Wagner expresses doubts concerning Riemann's conclusion that this Mass and *O rosa bella II* are definitely older than any of the Dufay Masses. In view of the recent tendency to place *Caput* before 1450, it seems even less likely that these two predate it. See n. 5, this chapter.

[37]Nos. 1114-1118; publishd in *DTO*, 22, pp. 13 ff., as *O rosa bella II*.

[38]See Kyrie, p. 14, m. 54-55; Gloria, pp. 15-16, m. 41-42 and p. 17, m. 100-101, etc.

[39]See Credo, pp. 21, 23.

[40]Nos. 715-719. It is also found in Modena, Bibl. Estense Cod. V. H. 10, No. 9. The versions of both manuscripts are published in *DTO*, 22, pp. 28 ff. For further discussion of this Mass, see Appendix, pp. 408 ff.

[41]The tenor of the Trent version gives evidence of corruption or reworking. In the second Agnus, a freely composed duo, the tenor is made to carry the lower voice

although it has nothing to do with the c.f. In Modena the tenor rests during this section (this is the general practice), while the lower voice of the duo is given to the contratenor. Likewise, the lowest part of the *Benedictus* and *Pleni sunt caeli*, both of which consist of freely composed duos and trios, is given to the tenor in Trent and, more properly, to the bass in Modena. The third Agnus is merely a repetition of the first in Trent. As the Agnus I uses only the first half of the c.f., this means that the borrowed melody is not given in its entirety as it is in all the other movements. In Modena, Agnus III has its own music based on the second half of the c.f. It is impossible to agree with Wagner, however, that the Trent version is an "unnatural procedure" and "not to be found elsewhere" (*Messe*, p. 100, n. 1), since comparable treatments are found in Ockeghem. Nevertheless, Modena is undoubtedly the better version and the appearance of free material in the tenor of Trent must be regarded as an error.

[42]There are clear examples in the Gloria, m. 1-15 (m. 1-18 of the chanson); *Qui tollis*, m. 56-67 (m. 27-34 of the chanson); Credo, m. 1-10 (m. 1-9, chanson); *Pleni sunt coeli*, m. 32-37 (m. 27-33); Agnus II (Trent versions), m. 34-60 (chanson, m. 1-27). In Agnus II (Modena version), m. 34-40 are a direct quotation of both superius and tenor of the chanson (m. 1-8). All these passages conclude with free sections of more or less length. It is possible, also, that the Benedictus, m. 83-87, is a simplified statement of m. 1-3 of the chanson.

[43]See Gloria, m. 17-21; *Qui tollis*, m. 73-80; Credo, m. 25-30; *Et incarnatus*, m. 98-111.

[44]The preserved Masses are published in two volumes, the first containing eight Masses and the second eight more Masses and Mass fragments.

Johannes Ockeghem, *Sämtliche Werke . . .* , ed. Dragan Plamenac (Deutsche Musikgesellschaft, Publikationen älterer Musik, I:ii [Leipzig: Breitkopf & Härtel, 1927]), I. A new, revised edition has been published recently. Johannes Ockeghem, *Collected Works . . .* , ed. Dragan Plamenac (2nd ed.; New York: American Musicological Society, 1960), I. All references in this book are to the older edition, hereafter cited as Ockeghem, *Works*.

The remaining Masses appear in Johannes Ockeghem, *Collected Works . . .* , ed. Dragan Plamenac (American Musicological Society, Studies and Documents, I; [New York: Columbia University Press, 1947]), II.

[45]The Requiem, *Missa sine nomine* (No. 14), and the Credo *sine nomine*.

[46]*Missa sine nomine* (No. 2), *Quinti toni*, and *Mi-mi*. It should be noted here that the structural type of the works has nothing to do with their order of composition. For example, *Mi-mi* is a late work unified by head motives only. So far as is known it is not based on a structural c.f. See Reese, *Renaissance*, pp. 131, ff.

[47]The structure is based on the c.f. voice alone when it is sounding; when it is silent, the other voices are often written in imitation. Characteristically, there is less imitation in the Ockeghem Mass than in Dufay's. But see Gloria, m. 79 ff., m. 90 ff.; the duets at the beginning of the Credo, m. 1-34, and at *Et resurrexit*, m. 94 ff., 103 ff., 118 ff. (free imitation); *Benedictus*, m. 104 ff., 112 ff., etc.; Agnus II, m. 37 ff., 39 ff., 47 ff., etc. Like Dufay, Ockeghem often imitates at a very close time interval.

[48]In a review of the first volume of the masses, Besseler says those for three voices are certainly early and stand nearer to the chanson than the motet. The Masses for four voices he divides into three groups. *L'homme armé* stands alone. It is the only one with a rigid, mechanically augmented tenor; it contains soloistic passages in the nature of improvised discant above sustained pedal notes; the movements do not have the introductory duos characteristic of the Burgundian motet. The whole work suggests that the roots of the Ockeghem style lie outside the Burgundian tradition, at least in part. *De plus en plus* and *Ecce ancilla* form a second group. The method of ornamenting the tenor is similar in these two; the imitative introductory duos show the influence of the central Burgundian motet and some relations to the Burgundian type of melody line can be observed. It is possible that they may have been written about

1454 or earlier. *Ma maîtresse* stands between them and the third group consisting of *Au travail suis* and the *Missa Cuiusvis toni*, both of which are mature works. The frequent contrast of duets with full homophonic sections, especially in *Au travail suis*, may be the result of the influence of younger composers. Besseler, "Von Dufay bis Josquin," pp. 10-13.

[49]He is known to have been in Antwerp in 1443-44, in France as early as 1446, and at the royal court in 1453, where he was employed until the end of his life over forty years later. For dates and contemporary references see André Pirro, *Histoire de la musique de la fin du XIVᵉ siècle* . . . (Paris: Librairie Renouard, H. Laurens, 1940), pp. 100 ff.; hereafter cited as Pirro, *Histoire*. See also Reese, *Renaissance*, p. 118.

[50]Ockeghem, *Works*, II, 77.

[51]*Ibid.*, p. 83.

[52]The editor states that the Gregorian melody enters with the bass in Kyrie III (*ibid.*, p. xxxii). It is true that the first five notes of that voice are the same as the Kyrie *Orbis factor*; however, this may be accidental, as the entire Kyrie proper to the Mass for the Dead is paraphrased by the superius.

[53]*Ibid.*, p. 59.

[54]Van den Borren (*Etudes*, p. 183, n. 1) says he has identified a Gregorian original for the long notes in the tenor of the second Agnus of *Missa Quinti toni* and gives as reference Agnus II, Missale, p. 2389 (not verified). He makes no mention of the Credo quotation in *Au travail suis* although he gives as a musical example the measures immediately preceding it (*ibid.*, p. 171). The Credo of *Missa Mi-mi* also begins with a brief quotation from the Gregorian. See Bukofzer's review of the second volume of the Masses in Music Library Association, *Notes*, V (June, 1948), 416.

[55]Ockeghem uses the tenor of Dufay's *Caput* as the bass of his Mass. This corresponds to the use of the superius of the chanson in the contratenor of *O rosa bella II*, but the procedure is musically more drastic, as the bass controls the progression of the harmonies. The c.f. is also given to the bass in the Credo and Agnus of *L'homme armé*, although the tenor has it in the remaining movements. Similarly, the c.f. quotation is clearest in the bass at the beginning of the Agnus of *Au travail suis*, although it is imitated by the tenor, which has carried it previously. In the train of this procedure of changing from voice to voice comes change of pitch level. The c.f. may be presented a fifth or an octave higher or lower in one place than in another. This occurs also in *Ecce ancilla Domini*, even though the c.f. remains in the tenor throughout. It is given a fifth lower in the Credo than in the other movements.

[56]In *Ma maîtresse* the tenor of the chanson is stated by the bass in the Kyrie; in the Gloria, the chanson superius is given by the contratenor and then by the tenor. In this case different voices of the chanson are used in different movements of the Mass, but in *Fors seulement* the idea is carried farther as now one, now another voice of the chanson is used in the same movement.

[57]This has already been seen in Dufay's *Caput* and *Ave Regina caelorum*.

[58]See the Gloria, Credo, and Sanctus. The only differences are found in the varying lengths of the rests between sections of the c.f. (compare m. 48-49 of the Gloria with m. 51-53 of the Credo, etc.). The Kyrie tenor differs from Dufay's because the c.f. is telescoped by the omission of repeated phrases. Nor is this completely original; the same method of shortening the c.f. was used by Dufay in the Agnus of his *Caput* Mass.

[59]See n. 13, this chapter.

[60]The c.f. is the final section of the antiphon *Missus est Angelus Gabriel* (*Proc. Mon.*, p. 246), although Ockeghem rearranges the order of the phrases. Those of *Proc Mon.*, can be lettered A-B-C-D. They are accompanied by the text *Ecce ancilla* . . . *verbum tuum* and are followed by an extended section on *Alleluia*. In both the Kyrie and Gloria, however, the order is A-B-C-D-C'-D-Alleluia. Ockeghem also starts the c.f. quotation with the notes d'c'-b-d' while in *Proc. Mon.* the passage begins with d'-b-c'-d'. In this respect he is in agreement with a manuscript source, so this is not an arbitrary alteration. See *Pal. Mus.* XII, 200, and Bukofzer, *Studies*, p. 308.

[61]Ockeghem, *Works*, I, starting p. 91, m. 140.

[62]It is given this time in the order found in *Proc. Mon.*, A-B-C-C'-D-Alleluia. The complete statement in the Credo is A-B-C-D-C'-D-A-B-C-D'-D-Alleluia.

[63]R. B. Lenaerts, "The Sixteenth-Century Parody Mass in the Netherlands," *Musical Quarterly*, XXXVI (July, 1950), 410.

[64]Leo Schrade describes two musically related Sanctus movements of the fourteenth century. They are apparently parodies not of one another but of an unknown original which was reworked in different ways by the composers. "A Fourteenth Century Parody Mass," *Acta Musicologica*, XXVII, fasc. i-ii (January-July, 1955), 13-19. For information concerning the possible original work, see Roland Jackson, "Musical Interrelations between Fourteenth Century Mass Movements," *Acta Musicologica*, XXIX (1957), 54-64.

It has also been shown that three Mass movements of Zachara da Teramo, in *BL*, are parodies of three of his own chansons. Nino Pirrotta, "Considerazioni sui primi esempi di Missa parodia," in *Actes du Congrès International de Musique Sacré*, ed. Higini Anglès (Tournai: Desclée & Cie., 1952), pp. 315-318, and Federico Ghisi, "L'ordinarium Missae n'el XV secolo ed i primordi della parodia," *ibid.*, pp. 308-310. Reese also points out the parody relationship of a *ballata* and a Gloria by Bartolomeo da Bologna, a contemporary of Zachara da Teramo. Both of these works are available in modern publications and can be easily compared for parody usages. Reese, *Renaissance*, p. 28.

[65]Pirrotta, "Considerazioni . . . , p. 318.

[66]Nos. 711-714. This Mass is based on the chanson of Busnois, *Quant ce viendra*, in the version for four voices which appears in the Mellon chansonnier (fo. 20-22). The tenor of the chanson serves as the tenor of the Mass, but, in addition, the entire four-voice version of the chanson is quoted at *Et in Spiritum*. (A short, free duo at *catholicam et apostolicam* is interpolated at the central division point of the chanson.) The anticipatory statements opening each of the movements also draw on more than once voice of the original, the superius and tenor being quoted by the superius and contratenor altus of the Mass. This information has been kindly supplied me by Dr. Louis Gottlieb. Bukofzer mentions a similar instance of parody of approximately the same date. This is the Mass *Summae Trinitati* of Walter Frye, which makes use of the tenor, the opening phrase, and other portions of a motet, *Salve Virgo*. *The New Oxford History*, III, 212.

[67]*Musik des Mittelalters*, p. 240, ex. 164.

[68]I attempt to clarify the quotations of chanson material in Kyrie I and II by means of a diagram below, in which the two halves of the chanson are placed directly above the corresponding sections of the Mass. The tenor is indicated by asterisks (***) and the superius *so far as it is used in the Mass*, is indicated by dashes (———).

Chanson:	Superius	—————	(m. 8-11)
	Tenor	********************	(m. 1-11)
Kyrie I:	Contra	——	(m. 13-14)
	Tenor	——	(m. 10-12)
	Bass	********************	(m. 3-14)
Chanson:	Superius	—————	(m. 19-26)
	Tenor	********************	(m. 18-34)
Kyrie II:	Contra	——	(m. 32-35)
	Tenor	——	(m. 28-31)
	Bass	********************	(m. 27-43)

[69]The quotation is quite literal with regard to the notes. The first half of the chanson (up to the sign of repetition) is used as far as *Domini fili unigenite*. Starting

from *Qui tollis* the second half is given complete, then quoted partially again (to m. 47 of the chanson). Ockeghem then skips back to the very beginning and states the first five bars of the original to bring the Gloria to a close.

[70]Head motives are used by Ockeghem, but they are not a standard device as with Dufay. When they are used they are often treated very casually—buried in a lower voice, or not presented in every movement.

[71]See *Mi-mi*, Gloria, m. 59-60 (*Collected Works*, II, 4) and Credo m. 63-66, (*ibid.*, p. 9).

[72]*Collected Works*, II, 65 ff. The version of the chanson which is used by the composer (*Fors seulement l'attente*) is given by Gombosi. *Jacob Obrecht, eine stilkritische Studie* (Leipzig: Breitkopf & Härtel, 1925), Appendix ix, p. 12; hereafter cited as Gombosi, *Jacob Obrecht*. Also given in F. J. Giesbert, *Ein altes Spielbuch* (Mainz: Schott, 1936).

[73]It is clear that the first few notes of the bass of the chanson are stated by the bass of the Mass, but in the first few notes quoted in the tenor of the Credo the composer plays with the similarity of tenor and superius entries in the chanson. See ex. 59, m. 1-4 and m. 10-13. It appears at first sight that the tenor I of the Mass quotes the opening figure of the tenor of the chanson because of the association with the bass, but as the c.f. continues (at m. 7) we find that the tenor is actually quoting the superius.

[74]Certain reminiscences of chanson material are possibly intentional. The ascending scale lines in imitation (Credo, m. 160 ff.) are fairly similar to m. 20 ff. of the chanson.

[75]It hardly seems possible that the tenor could have been written by accident in such a way that it could be imitated perfectly for so many measures. One can speculate that Ockeghem at first intended the chanson to have an imitative beginning and later gave the idea up, or even that he wrote the line so it would permit imitative treatment with the intention of using it later in a more elaborate type of composition. This supposition is not weakened by the fact that the bass of the chanson needs only slight alteration to make it fit the lines in imitation in the Mass. (Compare the bass of ex. 59, m. 1-7, with the bass of ex. 60, m. 1-7).

[76]This figure is marked by an inverted bracket in ex. 59, m. 3-4, 6-7, etc. Examples 60, 61, and 62 give a good idea of how often it is used in the Mass. However, aside from the fact that the figure is used so pointedly in the Mass, it has little significance, for it is a stereotype which appears in a large number of chansons at that time.

[77]The superius of the Mass (m. 30, count 4, to m. 32) quotes the tenor of the chanson (m. 28-30); the tenor of the Mass (m. 58, count 4, to m. 49, count 3) quotes the tenor of the chanson (m. 53-54), etc.

[78]*Werken van Josquin Des Prez*, ed. A. Smijers (Amsterdam: G. Alsbach, 1954), *Motetten*, III, 11.

[79]There is a short cadential interpolation at m. 29-30 of the Mass.

[80]Gombosi gives a detailed outline of the use of the c.f. in these movements. *Journal of the American Musicological Society*, I (Summer, 1948), 50 (book review). His references to the chanson differ by one bar from those given above. For instance, he calls the last bar of the chanson No. 71, while in the form to which I have access the last bar is No. 70. Table of c.f. usage and discussion are also given in Reese, *Renaissance*, pp. 126 ff.

[81]Tr 88, Nos. 482-486. Published in *DTO*, 38, pp. 159 ff. The c.f. is given in the introduction, pp. xxx ff.

[82]Tr 88, Nos. 406-41○· published in *DTO*, 38, pp. 141 ff. The chanson *Le serviteur*, by Dufay, is published in *DTO* 14, p. 238 (falsely attributed to Isaac). The tenor of the chanson is quoted in the tenor of the Mass.

[83]Published in *DTO*, 61, pp. 127 ff. The question of the date of composition of the Mass hinges on the dates of the manuscripts in which it appears. Both Tr 88 and Tr 90 were apparently completed around 1465. (*DTO* 14, p. xviii.) Besseler considers Tr 90 as probably the oldest manuscript containing Mass cycles on secular *cantus firmi*.

"It is conceivable that its contents may reach back into the 1440's." (*Bourdon*, p. 214.) See pp. 421-422 for further discussion of the c.f. treatment in this work and for details of its location in the manuscripts. The chanson is published in *DTO*, 14, p. 242, and I make use of the measure numbers of this edition in the diagram below. The work is written in the form of a rounded ballade, the final measures of the first part being repeated at the close of the second. The tenor is quoted in the tenor of the Mass, the superius in the superius.

[84]The following analysis of c.f. usage in the tenor is tentatively presented. It is only too easy to overlook c.f. when it is quoted in highly ornamented form; passages which I call free may well contain borrowed material. As mentioned in n. 83, the chanson tenor contains repeated passages.

MASS TENOR		CHANSON TENOR
Gloria		
measures 1-8	-----------	measures 1-14
8-16 free		
16-20	----------	36-42
21-22 free?		(21-33 reduced?)
22-23	----------	12-15
24-25 free		
Qui tollis		
measures 26-34	-----------	measures 22-42
34-41 free		
(Duo) 42-51 free		
Cum Sancto		
measures 52-57	-----------	measures 1-8
57-60	----------	36-47
61-63 free		
Credo		
measures 1-8	-----------	measures 1-13
9-11 free		
12-19	----------	34-47
Et incarnatus		
measures 20-28	-----------	measures 22-42
29-51 free		
Qui cum Patre		
measures 52-57 free		measures
57-63	----------	11-17
63-66 free		
(64-66	----------	19-21?)
Sanctus		
measures 1-8	-----------	measures 1-14
9-17 free?		
18-23	----------	46-48 (15-17)
23-27	----------	43-52 (12-21)
(Duo) 28-30	----------	22-27
(Duo) 30-45 free		
46-48	----------	1-7
(Duo) 57-76 free		
(Trio) 77-88 free		
88-91	----------	9-15
91-93	----------	17-21?

Agnus

measures	1-7			measures	1-8
	7-8 free				
	9-10		_____		34-3⁸
	11-12 free				
	12-13		_____		14-15?
	13-17 free?		_____		15-21?
(Duo)	18-44 free				
	45-56 free				
	57-62		_____		34-45
	63-65		_____		49-52 (18-21)

⁸⁵It is also closer to the style of the English as they, too, were apt to quote the c.f. more freely and elaborate it more richly than the Burgundians. See ex. 33 (chap. ii) by the Englishman, Walter Frye, who was active at the Burgundian court at about this period.

⁸⁶*Mon. Pol. Lit.*, I:1, fasc. 8. (For the chanson tenor see n. 13, this chapter. The Mass was possibly written in 1484. Dragan Plamenac, "A Postscript to Volume II of the *Collected Works of Johannes Ockeghem*," *Journal of the American Musicological Society*, III (Spring, 1950), 35.

⁸⁷*Mon. Pol. Lit.*, I:1, fasc. 2.

⁸⁸See also n. 11, this chapter.

⁸⁹Obrecht bases his *Missa L'homme armé* quite literally on the tenor of Busnois, taking over the rhythmic schemes in their entirety, including the rests in the tenor part. (He treats the final longs of each movement differently from Busnois, but the long is a value of indefinite duration when placed at the end of a composition.) In other respects he copies the dimensions so exactly that even the movements without tenor (Kyrie II, *Pleni sunt caeli*, *Benedictus*, and Agnus II) are given the same number of measures as those of Busnois. As is usual when a c.f. is borrowed from another composer, the material is manipulated differently. Oliver Strunk, "The Origins of the *L'homme armé* Mass," *Bulletin of the American Musicological Society*, No. 2 (June, 1937), p. 25. (See the discussion under the Masses of Obrecht, chap. ix, p. 248.)

⁹⁰Ockeghem, *Works*, II, 98. The tenor of the anonymous chanson, *Pour quelque paine*, (*ibid.*, p. 116) is used as tenor of the Mass.

⁹¹The *Missa O crux lignum triumphale* is found in Codex 51 of the Cappella Sistina, fo. 104ᵛ-113. Franz X. Haberl, *Bibliographischer und thematischer Musikkatalog des päpstlichen Kapellarchives im Vatican zu Rom* (Leipzig, 1888). The c.f. is the 18th verse of the sequence *Laudes cruces attolamus*. P. Aubry and E. Misset, *Les Proses d'Adam de St. Victor* (Paris: H. Welter, 1900), p. 260.

The treatment of the c.f. is extremely regular. It contains a cadence on the dominant note halfway through (at the end of the second phrase) and, when the melody is not quoted in its entirety, this natural division point is invariably chosen for the break. (In this way the quotations in this Mass differ from those of the *L'homme armé* tune in Busnois's Mass of that name.) The entire c.f. is given once in the Kyrie (the first half to Kyrie I, the second half to Kyrie II, *Christe tacet*). It is given one-and-a-half times in the Gloria (the entire melody to *Et in terra*, the first half to *Qui tollis*); twice through in the Credo (entire for the *Patrem*, the first half for the *Et incarnatus*, the second half for the *Confiteor*); two-and-a-half times in the Sanctus (first half only for the Sanctus and then twice in its entirety for the two Osannas, the second Osanna being merely a repetition of the first; *Pleni* and *Benedictus* tacet). The layout in the Agnus resembles that of the Kyrie. Agnus I is given the first half, Agnus III the second, while the tenor is silent in Agnus II.

Variety in presentation comes from the various proportions which are used. The c.f.

is given in *integer valor*, in diminution, and in various augmentations. There is occasionally a contrast in mensuration between the tenor and the other voices.

The counterpoints are for the most part of the free, continuously flowing type. They show occasional imitative writing, but little or none of the motivic treatments which make the motets so interesting. There is a well-defined head motive which starts off every movement, and in a few places the contrapuntal voices seem to be influenced by the shape of the c.f. (In the *Pleni* the two upper voices start with a brief imitative figure which is apparently derived from the first notes of the c.f., and in the *Osanna* the superius, contra I, and contra II form a point of imitation on the first tenor phrase.) For the most part, however, the writing is very conservative and expresses the point of view of the middle of the century. The ingenious, experimental, forward-looking traits found in the secular pieces and the motets are not even hinted at in this work.

[92]Published in *DTO*, 38, p. 95, where it is attributed falsely to Ockeghem. This Mass is discussed in greater detail on p. 177 of this chapter.

[93]My comments on the Mass are based on the version published in *Mon. Pol. Lit.*, I:1, fasc. 4. Reese discusses another and earlier version which has a different scheme of repetitions. *Renaissance*, p. 112. This version is printed in *Faugues*, ed. George C. Schuetze, Jr. (Publications of Mediaeval Musical Manuscripts, Collected Works, I. [New York: Institute of Mediaeval Music, 1960]).

[94]Johannes Regis, *Opera Omnia*, ed. C. W. H. Lindenberg (Corpus Mensurabilis Musicae, IX [Haarlem: N. V. Grafische Industrie, 1956]) IX, i, p. 1; hereafter cited as Regis, *Opera*. The use of multiple c.f. in this work is discussed on p. 182 of this chapter.

[95]This is said to be the earliest known Mass which is based entirely on canon. Laurence Feininger, *Die Frühgeschichte des Kanons bis Josquin des Prez* (um 1500) (Emsdetten: H. & J. Lechte, 1937), p. 33.

[96]The chansons of H. de Lantins are quite remarkable in this respect. Since those published by van den Borren come from the Canonici manuscript, they must have been written before c. 1435. (See chap. ii, n. 22, above.) Many of the chansons of Dufay from this manuscript also contain points of imitation. J. F. R. and C. Stainer, *Dufay and His Contemporaries* (London, 1898).

[97]*Áve Regina caelorum* by Binchois, ex. 46.

[98]Nos. 482-486; published *DTO*, 38, p. 159, anonymous.

[99]Along with other features, the passage in parallel tenths between superius and bass (ex. 65, m. 20-23) indicates a rather late date, probably after 1485. For biography of Martini and discussion of other compositions see Reese, *Renaissance*, pp. 220 ff.

[100]See ex. 94, m. 8-12.

[101]*Mon. Pol. Lit.*, I:1, fasc. 2, p. 7, m. 3-7 and 16-17.

[102]Codex 88 was completed around 1465. See *DTO*, 14, p. xviii.

[103]Published in *DTO*, 14, p. 238. See also Hewitt, ed., *Odhecaton A*, No. 35, p. 294.

[104]The two Masses of Faugues which have been discussed reveal him as an outstandingly progressive composer who shows an interest in consistent procedures not commonly found at this time. This aspect of his thought is indicated by the repetitions in both Masses, the recombinations in *Le serviteur*, and above all by the treatment of the c.f. in canon throughout *L'homme armé* which makes it one of the first works of the time to be placed entirely under the control of a single device.

[105]Regis, *Opera*, I, 1. The work is entitled by the editor "*Missa Dum sacrum mysterium*" because the text of this antiphon is used at the beginning of the Kyrie, Gloria, Credo, and at other points during the Mass. C. W. H. Lindenberg, *Het leven en de werken van Johannes Regis* (Amsterdam: N.V. Uitgeversbedrijf "De Spieghel," 1938), p. 18; (hereafter cited as Lindenberg, *Regis*). Lindenberg also points out the pertinence of the text "The armed man" to the Archangel Michael. *Ibid.* Reese

gives biographical details, bibliography, and commentary on the works of Regis. *Renaissance*, pp. 113 ff.

[106]An analysis of the text quotations and c.f. usages has been made by M. F. Bukofzer in *Musical Quarterly*, XXXVI (1950), 308, review of *Mon. Pol. Lit.*, I:1, fascicles 4-10.

[107]Regis, *Opera*, I, 25. The Mass must have been written no later than c. 1475, since it appears in the MS 5557 of the Bibliothèque Royale of Brussels (fo. 121^v-136). The compilation of this source is known to have been completed before 1481 and the repertory to date from the period of c. 1450-1475. Sylvia W. Kenney, "Origins and Chronology of the Brussels Manuscript 5557 in the Bibliothèque Royale de Belgique," *Revue belge de musicologie*, VI (1952), 75-100. See also Charles van den Borren, "Inventaire des manuscripts de musique polyphonique qui se trouvent en Belgique," *Acta Musicologica*, V (1935), 68. Van den Borren discusses the Mass in *Etudes*, pp. 203 ff., although his comments on the c.f. usage are incomplete. A thorough analysis is given by Lindenberg, *op. cit.*, pp. 20 ff., and in Regis, *Opera*, I, p. iv. I use my own transcription from Brussels 5557 in ex. 68a-c.

[108]Regis generally uses the form of *Ecce ancilla* beginning with the rising fourth, g-c', which was employed by Dufay, but in some of its appearances the c.f. begins on c', the form given in the Vatican edition.

[109]The style as a whole is closer to Dufay than to Ockeghem or even Busnois. The unit of beat is seldom divided into notes of less than half its value, cadences are numerous, and the movement of the harmonies is clear. The melody lines are of the swelling Burgundian type. Indeed, the whole of ex. 68a is so like Dufay that it might have been written by him; however, the simple hemiola tends to be supplanted by displaced hemiola (ex. 68a, m. 3-4, superius) or syncopations (ex. 68b, m. 5-6, alto; ex. 68c, m. 5-6, superius). The casual attitude towards the c.f. is another noticeable difference, and there is less use of imitation in the work as a whole than would be expected of Dufay. Regis's use of accidentals is interesting. In the Credo, at *Et homo factus est*, Eb's and Ab's lead to a Phrygian cadence on G! Notice also the phrases alternating between C major and minor, ex. 68b, m. 4-13. Modulation by the addition of successive flats was well known to Dufay and to the generation preceding. See Césaris's *Bonté bialté*, in Reaney, *Early Fifteenth-Century Music*, I, 30. This most striking trait of the older style tends to disappear later in the century, when the younger Netherlanders incline to diatonic writing. There are, however, some striking uses of accidentals in Josquin.

CHAPTER 7

[1]The work celebrates the surrender of Bordeaux to Charles VII. It appears in Tr 89, No. 585, and is published in *DTO*, 76, p. 77.

[2]No. 727; published in *DTO*, 14, p. 178, where it is ascribed to Dufay in accordance with the Trent Codex. The attribution has been contested by Karl Dèzes. "Das Dufay zugeschriebene Salve Regina eine deutsche Komposition," *Zeitschrift für Musikwissenschaft* X, (February, 1928), 327. The rather low register, the almost uninterrupted scoring for four voices, and the emphasis on complete triads (even the final chord of the cadences is supplied with a third) combine to give a full, rather dull sonority which differs from the thinner, more brilliant sound characteristic of the late works of Dufay. However, in the emphasis on clear harmonic progression, in the frequency of the cadences, the restraint of the c.f. ornamentation, and, above all, in the type of melody, it falls within the orbit of the Burgundian school rather than that of the group of exponents of the elaborate melodic style (Bedingham, Busnois, Caron, Ockeghem, etc.). The many deceptive cadences are quite characteristic of the harmonic style of this time, and the short sections of parallel sixth chords are not

uncommon. See Ockeghem, *Mors tu as navré–Requiem* "Deploration on the Death of Binchois") in Marix, p. 83, and G. Dufay, *Ave Regina coelorum*, ed. M. F. Bukofzer (New York: Music Press, Inc., 1949), p. 14, m. 101, etc.

[3]See *Alma Redemptoris Mater*, Tr 91, No. 1209 (*DTO*, 53, p. 36, m. 23 ff.) and *Salve Regina*, Tr 88, No. 235 (*DTO*, 53, p. 46, m. 158 ff.).

[4]Two works on *Salve Regina* from Tr 91 (published in *DTO*, 53, pp. 67 and 70 as *Salve Regina* Nos. 10 and 11, respectively) also make use of strict c.f. The melody appears in the tenor in one, in the superius in the other. There are minor relaxations of the steady movement of the tenor at the cadences in No. 10, while the superius in No. 11 moves in breves in some sections and in semibreves in others. Some irregularity in the note values was characteristic of the strict c.f. For instance, see the tenor of *Regali ex progenie* by Adam von Fulda. Ehmann, *Adam von Fulda*, pp. 10 ff.

[5]Charles Warren Fox, "Non-quartal Harmony in the Renaissance," *Musical Quarterly*, XXXI (January, 1945), 40-41.

[6]Hewitt, ed., *Odhecaton A*, p. 81. Example 71 was probably intended to be performed by instruments, and Hewitt's list of devices characteristic of the instrumental works of the *Odhecaton* is entirely applicable to it.

[7]This work was performed in 1454. The text of the upper parts is in French, but despite this I am including it among the motets since it has the structure of a tenor motet. For further details see Reese, *Renaissance*, p. 58. The music has been edited by Albert Seay as No. 4 of *Masterworks of Yesterday*, Series A (Boulder, Colorado: The Colorado College Music Press, 1958).

[8]Copied at Cambrai in 1463. See also Bukofzer's note in his edition, *op. cit.*, p. 2.

[9]The authoritative work on the motets of this period is the dissertation of Wolfgang Stephan, *Die burgundisch-niederländische Motette zur Zeit Ockeghems* (Heidelberger Studien zur Musikwissenschaft, VI [Kassel: Bärenreiter, 1937]); hereafter cited as Stephan, *Motette*. Here the complete repertory is considered, and is divided into four categories:

Tenor motets (chap. i, pp. 11-50) are large compositions for four or more voices, usually written for special occasions and hence lacking any specific liturgical function. They include the works of Dufay mentioned above and such others as Busnois's *Regina caeli* and *In hydraulis*, Regis's *Clangat plebs*, and Ockeghem's (*O*) *intemerata Dei mater*. The work by Ockeghem is without *cantus firmus*.

Song motets (chap. ii, pp. 51-59) are small works for three voices which hold a place midway between the large, festive tenor motet and the chanson. Touront is the chief exponent of the type. Aside from those by him, examples are the *Ave Regina coelorum* of Frye, *Si dedero* of Agricola, *In pace in idipsum* of Josquin, *Parce Domine* of Obrecht, and *O vos omnes* of Compère. For the most part they are freely composed works, although the *Ave Maria* for three voices of Regis has c.f. (Stephan, *op. cit.*, treats these on pp. 54 and 58, respectively.)

The Remaining Forms (chap. iii, pp. 60-70) includes analogies to the tenor motet and free, four-voice writing in Italy. An *Ave Maria* by Ockeghem, his ballade with Latin tenor, *Mors tu as navré–Requiem*, Compère's *O genitrix gloriosa*, etc., are grouped under these headings.

Chant Settings in the Motet (chap. iv, pp. 71-85) are written for four voices, no longer in the three-voice chanson style. The c.f. is often not in the upper voice. Examples are *Alma Redemptoris Mater* and two settings of *Salve Regina* by Ockeghem, Busnois's *Victimae paschali laudes*, the pseudo-Dufay *Salve Regina*, etc.

[10]Regis, *Opera*, II, contains all the motets which have been preserved. For an extensive analysis of them see Lindenberg, *Regis*, pp. 29-40.

[11]Stephan, *Motette*, p. 24.

[12]Regis, *Opera*, II, 1, and Critical Notes, p. 1.

[13]*Ibid.*, p. 5. The c.f. is unknown to me.

[14]*Ibid.*, p. 14. For comments on text and c.f. see Critical Notes, pp. 1-2.

[15]*Ibid.*, p. 21. The complete c.f., *Sicut lilium*, is given in *Pal. Mus.*, IX, fo. 456. The editor of the *Opera* does not make it clear that the tenor carries c.f. throughout the work. Critical Notes, p. 2.

[16]*Ibid.*, p. 30. (C.f. in *LU*, p. 875.)

[17]*Ibid.*, p. 42, (C.f. in *Var. Prec.*, p. 46.)

[18]*Ibid.*, Critical Notes, p. 5.

[19]*Ibid.*, p. 49. The editor gives references to the *cantus firmi* in the Critical Notes, p. 6.

[20]*Ibid.*, p. 60. (C.f. in *LU*, p. 1416.) For further mention of the work, see p. 231, chapter viii.

[21]Stephan, *Motette*, pp. 73-74. For discussion of all the known motets of Ockeghem see Reese, *Renaissance*, pp. 121 ff.

[22]The beginning is published in Besseler, *Musik des Mittelalters*, p. 238, ex. 163.

[23]Cf. the treatment of the c.f. in Ockeghem's *Missa Caput*. Stephan classifies this motet as a *C.f.-Bearbeitung*. *Motette*, pp. 75-76. For my purposes it is only incidental that the structural voice is the bass rather than the tenor. The work is considered here as another manifestation of structure based on alternating statement of the c.f.

[24]Published in Heinrich Besseler, *Altniederländische Motetten* (Kassel: Bärenreiter, 1927), p. 5. According to the editor's notes (p. 24), the original is a fourth lower than the transcription, which would put it into a very deep register. However, according to another transcription *in the original clefs*, also made by Besseler, the original is actually a fourth higher ("Von Dufay bis Josquin," p. 21). This is an important point, as the original *tessitura* is unusually high and shows that Ockeghem was interested in exploring the upper as well as the extremely low registers.

[25]In connection with an analysis of this work, Besseler suggests that the term "chant figuration" be used to designate the paraphrase of Ockeghem and "chant coloration" be reserved for that of the Burgundians. "Von Dufay bis Josquin," p. 14. He points out that quantitatively the coloration hardly exceeds that of Dufay in number of notes, but that it is different in essence. The one is an objective, the other a highly personalized expression. For instance, Ockeghem breaks a word by rests (ex. 74a, m. 2, 5, and 6), precedes the c.f. notes with added tones (ex. 74a, m. 9), gives the climaxes to "weak" beats, places the tones of arrival on any beat of the measure, covers caesuras at the cadence by bringing in other voices (ex. 74b, m. 56 and m. 58), suddenly alternates long and short notes (ex. 74a, m. 1; ex. 74b, m. 53, etc.). These procedures could be expanded on at length, and they would sum up to the difference between the total melodic style of Ockeghem and the Burgundians. Indeed, if the term "figural" c.f. is adopted, the Ockeghem melodic style could equally well be characterized in general as "figural." This motet shows that the impulse to transform and absorb the Gregorian melody into the composer's own personal style is as strong now as in Olyver's day. (See ex. 18, above.) Variations in style among composers go to show that this is the single constant factor governing the elaboration of the c.f. during this period.

[26]A distinction must be made between initial imitations—those that start phrases off—and incidental ones which may appear at any point during the course of a phrase. Initial (or "head") imitation can be found considerably more frequently in compositions on c.f. at this time than in those from the first half of the century. A few instances are found in *Salve Regina* settings from the younger Trent codices. See *DTO*, 53, *Salve Regina* No. 3, pp. 47 ff., (from Tr 88) m. 15 ff., 63 ff., 80 ff., 89 ff., etc. Some of the points involve all three voices. See also *Salve Regina* No. 4 (*DTO*, 53, p. 50; Tr 89), which starts with head imitations in all four parts, and No. 12 (*DTO*, 53, p. 72; Tr 91), which does the same in all three parts.

[27]The text is the second verse of the hymn *Tibi Christe splendor*, but the tune used is not the one given in *Ant. Mon.*, p. 1056. It is another of the melodies to which this text was sung, and I have quoted it in ex. 75 as it appears in *Ant. Mon.*, p. 547,

with the text *Pange lingua.* The date of the setting is probably somewhat after 1460.

[28]*Motette,* p. 23.

[29]Tr 89, No. 729; published in *DTO,* 53, p. 55, as *Salve Regina* No. 6.

[30]Alfred Orel, "Einige Grundformen der Motettkomposition im XV. Jahrhundert," *Studien zur Musikwissenschaft,* VII (1920), 67.

[31]Tr 91, No. 1161, and Codex 80b of the capitulary archives of St. Peter's in Rome; published in *DTO,* 14, p. 111. The chanson was published by Petrucci. Hewitt, ed., *Odhecaton A,* p. 263. Textual reasons obviously caused the composer to choose this tenor.

[32]Gombosi, *Jacob Obrecht,* pp. 34 ff.; Stephan, *Motette,* p. 23.

[33]Gombosi (*op cit.,* p. 34) places the motet in the early 1470's, which would make it somewhat earlier than the Ockeghem Mass. It should be noted that these dates are estimated, and so indicate only the probable decade of composition.

[34]Tr 91, No. 1319; published in *DTO,* 53, p. 37.

[35]Orel, "Einige Grundformen . . . ," p. 69.

[36]In addition to the imitation between contratenor and superius (ex. 76b, m. 35-38) there is a melodic relationship between tenor and superius at the same point (ex. 76b, m. 35-37, passages marked with dotted brackets). The similarity in shape between the two lines is quite clear despite the fact that each is carrying a different c.f. It may or may not be the result of an intentional effort to integrate the diverse material of the two voices.

[37]Most of the material which follows concerning the motets of Busnois has appeared in an article of mine, "The Motets of Antoine Busnois," *Journal of the American Musicological Society,* VI (Fall, 1953), 216. For further comment on these works see: C. L. Walther Boer, *Het Anthonius Motet van Anthonius Busnois* (Amsterdam: H. J. Paris, 1940); van den Borren, *Etudes,* pp. 212 ff.; Ehmann, *Adam von Fulda,* pp. 145 ff. Several of these works have not yet been published, two of them being the important tenor motets *Regina caeli* (I) and *Victimae paschali laudes* discussed below. Also unpublished, but less important, is the setting of the hymn *Conditor alme siderum.* This work, contained in a Perugia manuscript (M 36), was kindly called to my attention by Professor Gombosi. The *Magnificat quinti toni* and two small works not based on c.f., *Noël, noël* and *Alleluia, verbum caro factum est,* also remain unpublished. Of those that have been published, *In hydraulis* appears in *DTO* 14, p. 105; *Regina caeli* (II) and *Anima mea liquefacta est* in: *Van Ockeghem tot Sweelinck,* ed. A. Smijers (Vereeniging voor Nederlandsche Muziekgeschiedenis [Amsterdam: G. Alsbach & Co., 1939-]), pp. 16 and 22; *Anthoni usque limina* in Boer, *op cit.*

[38]The incomplete work, *Ad coenam agni providi,* also is based on c.f. The bass voice carries the melody of the hymn *Ad regias agni dapes, alter tonus* (*Ant. Rom. Seraph.,* p. 374).

[39]It deserves special notice that in this composition migration is indicated in the manuscript. The syllables of the text are written *on the staff* under the appropriate notes of the c.f. In addition, the text is written in *below the staff* in the usual way. (See ex. 77.)

[40]It is very likely that a yet earlier instance of this type exists in an isorhythmic tenor of Dunstable which is based on statements of the tetrachord. Dunstable, *Works,* No. 66, p. 156.

[41]The notes of the tenor of the motet of Ockeghem, *Ut heremita solus,* are at least partially derived this way. See the discussion, p. 236.

[42]Stephan, *Motette,* p. 22.

[43]The rhythmic placement of these notes is indicated by a canon, but its meaning is sufficiently obscure that several different interpretations have been offered. Van den Borren gives one of Fétis as well as another of his own (*Etudes,* pp. 239 ff.). Boer, in his complete publication of the work, follows van den Borren's suggested tenor

layout (*op. cit.*, musical appendix). Stephan offers still another solution (*Motette*, p. 22).

[44]Stephan gives complete outlines of the tenor layouts. (*Ibid.*)

CHAPTER 8

[1]See chapter 2, n. 10, for comment on the validity of the term "Burgundian." Similar criticism can be directed at the other regional terms such as "Flemish" and "Netherlandish." They are, nevertheless, useful at times for pointing up contrasts in style.

[2]*Musik des Mittelalters*, pp. 230 ff.

[3]A few instances of the contrasting melody types will do more than any number of words to make clear the differences in style. Compare exs. 48 (Dufay), 68 (Regis) and 73-74 (Ockeghem).

[4]A trio in the tenor motet *Ave Regina coelorum* is a good example of this. (Dufay, *Ave Regina coelorum*, m. 16-17). See also ex. 51.

[5]*Histoire*, p. 114.

[6]This is true despite the numerous examples of imitation that have been cited. There is always the danger of distorting the picture of the normal style when examples are chosen because of their significance in relation to future practices.

[7]None of the motets are written in chanson style; thus the regular use of points of imitation does not occur. The *Magnificat quinti toni*, however, has imitative entries in two or three voices at the beginning of eleven of its twelve verses. The Dufay *Magnificat octavi toni* also displays a great deal of head imitation. In many Magnificats, including these two works, there is much repetition of material, so that a point of imitation, once written, is apt to appear again. This is the case in the pieces of Dufay and Busnois, and there are not actually as many *different* points as the total number would suggest.

To return to the motets of Busnois, it should be noted that the imitation in the introductory duets of the second part of *Regina caeli I* and of *In hydraulis*, or even the short imitative passages in three voices which close the introductory trios of *Anthoni usque limina*, constitute nothing essentially new; such treatment is found in the introductory duos of motets as far back as the beginning of the century. They all occur at a time when the tenor is not sounding. The most fully developed point of imitation constructed to include the tenor, and based on the c.f. melody of that voice, is found in *Regina caeli II*, which begins with a statement of the c.f. material in three of the four voices.

[8]We have already seen instances of linear organization of a *single* voice by means of repeated rhythmic patterns which may or may not form part of a true sequence.

[9]See the end of *Ascendit Christus*, ex. 35, for one of the comparatively few instances of a clear and unambiguous sequential formation at this period.

[10]It may be that this is a renascence of an Italian style element which had lain dormant for nearly fifty years, although one is tempted to assume that it arose anew at this time in answer to a need of the music. With the breakdown of the melodic style of the second quarter of the century, and the general acceptance of the figural melodic style, some need may have been felt for formal control of lines which otherwise would tend to become undisciplined effusions. (See Bedingham *Missa Deuil angouisseux* and the anonymous *Missa Le serviteur*.) Rhythmic patterning and sequence would achieve this without inhibiting the activity of the lines.

[11]Regis, *Opera*, II, 60. The two upper voices imitate extensively; the bass also occasionally joins in to make a point for three voices (m. 9). A somewhat similar method of writing is found in a chanson by Busnois, *Ma plus qu'assez*. Knud Jeppesen, *Der Kopenhagener Chansonnier*, (Leipzig: Breitkopf & Härtel, 1927), No. 13. Because

of the liberal use of imitation the motet looks very advanced, an appearance common in sacred pieces of that time written in chanson style.

[12]Mary Clement, "The Approach to the Cadence in High Renaissance Music" (Master's thesis, University of California, 1945). In this study, the term "drive to the cadence" is applied to passages designed to emphasize the force of a cadence. Various methods are employed to achieve this emphasis, some being of a basically rhythmic type (these are seen in ex 85a-b), others being of a specifically melodic or harmonic nature.

[13]The increase in speed is also reflected in the elaboration of the c.f. if one is present. See ex. 56a-b.

[14]G. Dufay, *Ave Regina coelorum*, ed. M. F. Bukofzer (New York: Music Press, Inc., 1949), p. 12, m. 74-75, and p. 19, m. 167.

[15]This is a favorite device of Busnois. Striking instances occur at the end of *Regina caeli I* as well as in the two short works, *Noël, Noël* and *Alleluia, verbum caro factum est*.

[16]Arnold Schering, "Ein Rätseltenor Okeghems," in *Festschrift Hermann Kretzschmar* (Leipzig: C. F. Peters, 1918), p. 132. A condensed description is given by Reese, *Renaissance*, p. 124, n. 151. Petrucci, in his publication of the motet in *Canti C*, has given the tenor *ad longum* as well as in its enigmatic form so that the puzzle forms no hindrance to transcription.

[17]The work is published and discussed at length by C. L. W. Boer in his monograph *Het Anthonius Motet van Anthonius Busnois* (Amsterdam: H. J. Paris, 1940). Amusingly enough, the problem of transcribing this tenor arises from its very simplicity. The canon is not clear on how many times the tenor tone is to be sounded or at exactly what points. Since the tenor reiterates only the single note d' and since the harmonic background of the contrapuntal voices consists solely of chords on G, Bb, and D, the placement of the tenor notes cannot be determined merely by making a score and seeing where they will fit in. Unfortunately, they will fit at almost any point.

[18]Besseler, *Musik des Mittelalters*, p. 236.

[19]Gombosi, *Jakob Obrecht*, p. 112.

[20]For details see discussion of the Mass, p. 313.

[21]Loyset Compère, *Opera Omnia*, ed. Ludwig Finscher (Corpus Mensurabilis Musicae, XV [Rome: American Institute of Musicology, 1959], XV:ii. See the Foreword for a discussion of these works, and of the "substitution" motet.

[22]The *cantabile* melody of the Burgundian chanson persists in secular song, while the florid melodic style is applied to works of large scope. Rather paradoxically from our point of view, rhythmic liveliness and intricacy was considered appropriate to serious music.

[23]In the *Missa Prolationum*. Typically, the music is rational only on paper. The voices start together and soon get far enough apart so that their relationships are not audible.

[24]Published in *Mon. Pol. Lit.*, I:1, fasc. 9.

Chapter 9

[1]*Werken van Jakob Obrecht: Missen* (5 vols.), *Motetten, Wereldlijke Werken, Passio Domini Nostri Jesu Christe*, ed. Johannes Wolf (*Vereeniging voor Noord-Nederlands Muziekgeschiedenis* [Leipzig: Breitkopf & Härtel; Amsterdam: Johannes Müller, G. Alsbach, 1908-21]); hereafter cited as Obrecht, *Works*, I-V (Masses) and Obrecht, *Motetten*.

A new and altogether superior edition of the works has been inaugurated, originally under the editorship of the late Albert Smijers, now under M. van Crevel. *Jacobus Obrecht, Opera Omnia*, ed. A. Smijers and M. van Crevel (Vereniging voor Nederlandse Muziekgeschiedenis [Amsterdam: G. Alsbach, 1953-]); hereafter cited as Obrecht, *Opera Omnia*. Six instalments of Vol. I, *Missae*, 1953-1959, have appeared to date; of Vol. II, *Motetti*, two instalments have appeared, in 1956 and 1958. The new edition is especially welcome because Wolf's edition is faulty in many respects and a considerable number of Obrecht's work have been discovered since it was completed.

A manuscript of Segovia (Catedral Archivo Musical, s.s.) contains three Masses (*Libenter gloriabor, Sine nomine,* and *Rosa playsante* as items 3, 4, and 5), eleven motets (items 12, 15, 16, 20, 21, 23, 79, 96, 104, 137, and 153); and several secular pieces. Higini Anglés, *La Música en la Corte de los Reyes Católicos—I. Polifonia Religiosa* (Madrid, 1941), pp. 107-112. For an earlier description and catalogue, see H. Anglés, "*Un manuscrit inconnu avec polyphonie du XVe siècle conservé à la Cathé-drale de Ségovie*," Acta Musicologica, VIII (1936), 6. The *Missa sine nomine* in Segovia is actually a *Missa Adieu mes amours* which was known to Wolf, but only in muti-lated form and so was not included in the complete edition, where it would have made a second *Adieu mes amours* Mass. As it appears in the Segovia manuscript, it has only three movements, being without Sanctus and Agnus, but it is preserved in its entirety at the University Library of Jena, Choir-Book 32 (Reese, *Renaissance*, p. 196, n. 61). The Kyries of the three Masses and the chanson *Rosa playsante* have been published in: *Van Ockeghem tot Sweelinck*, ed. A. Smijers (Vereeniging voor Nederlandsche Muziekgeschiedenis [Amsterdam: G. Alsbach & Co., 1939-]), pp. 51-64; a portion of the *Pleni* of *Rosa playsante* is given by Reese (*Renaissance*, p. 203). Two of the motets occurring in the Segovia manuscript have been published: *Mille quingentis*, edited by Wolf, (Obrecht, *Motetten*, p. 179, under the title *Requiem aeternam*), and a *Salve Regina* for four voices, edited by Smijers (*Van Ockeghem tot Sweelinck*, p. 65).

Besides the substantial additions necessary to make a satisfactory complete edition of Obrecht, it is necessary to delete certain works included by Wolf which are now known to be by other men. The most important of these is a Passion according to St. Matthew. A. Smijers, "*Vijftiende en zestiende eeuwsche Muziekhandschriften . . . de Matthaeus-Passie van Jacob Obrecht,*" Tijdschrift der Vereeniging voor Neder-landsche Muziekgeschiedenis, XIV (1935), 165.

For all its shortcomings, the edition of Wolf is the most complete that we have, and the analyses of the music in his chapter have been made from it, unless otherwise noted.

[2]A study of the c.f. usage in the masses of Obrecht is given in: Maria Kvriazis, *Die Cantus-firmus Technik in den Messen Obrechts* (inaugural dissertation; Bern: Arnaud, 1952). The work is divided into four chapters: I. The effect of the c.f. on the formal unity of the mass. II. The setting-off of the c.f. from the other voices. III. Tendencies to unification. IV. The effect of the c.f. on formal articulation. The emphasis is not on the schemes of statement of the c.f. as such, but on their relation to general formal aspects of the Masses. (The insufficiency of this sort of treatment arises from the fact that the individual schemes of statement create their own formal problems, and these problems are not necessarily well covered when the author adheres to a stock list of headings for discussion.) The works are regarded strictly from the evolutionary point of view; Obrecht is considered as a transitional figure between the style of the mid-fifteenth century and that of Palestrina.

A more recent study of the Masses—as yet unpublished—has the great merit of viewing Obrecht as a composer in his own right, rather than as a figure representing a stage in music history. Arnold Salop, *The Masses of Jacob Obrecht (1450-1505), Structure and Style*. Ph. D. Dissertation, University of Indiana, 1959. The author undertakes a thorough, step-by-step analysis, and the result is that a clear picture of Obrecht's notably individual style emerges. The c.f. usage is examined in detail, and the methods of laying out the melodies are considered from the point of view of the notational practices of Obrecht's time. The dissertation was not written until after this chapter was completed, and so is not referred to as frequently as it deserves.

Two studies of Bernhard Meier likewise have the great merit of using concepts current in Obrecht's time as points of departure for study of the works. Bernhard Meier, "Die Harmonik im Cantus firmus–haltigen Satz des 15. Jahrhunderts," *Archiv für Musikwissenschaft*, IX (1952), 27-44, and "Zyklische Gesamtstruktur und Tonalität in den Messen Jacob Obrechts," *ibid.*, (1953), 289-310. The first of these concerns the manner of adding counterpoints to the c.f. and the results with regard to harmony and tonality. The predominant consideration in the choice of chords is the vertical relationship to the c.f. note sounding at the moment (usually in the tenor). The result is harmonic succession rather than harmonic progression, since the latter depends on tonally conditioned movements of the bass. In the second article Meier points out, with regard to the c.f. structure of certain Masses, that there are certain symmetries of *number* of statements. He also takes up problems of the "tonus," especially in those Masses where several *cantus firmi* of different tones are combined.

For further information, see the article "Obrecht" by Ludwig Finscher in MGG, IX, cols. 1814-1822, and Pirro, *Histoire*, pp. 192-194. Reese, *Renaissance*, gives a biography (p. 186) and summaries of a number of the motets and Masses pp. (190-205). See also Bain Murray, "Jacob Obrecht's Connection with the Church of Our Lady in Antwerp," *Revue Belge de Musicologie*, XI (1957), 125-133, and "New Light on Jacob Obrecht's Development—A Biographical Study," *Musical Quarterly*, XLIII (1957), 500-516; Suzanne Clercx, "Lumières sur la formation de Josquin et d'Obrecht," *Revue Belge de Musicologie*, XI (1957)—information on Obrecht on pp. 155-156.

³*Messe*, p. 116.

⁴The Mass lacks the Agnus. I follow Reese in using the title *diversorum tenorum* (*Renaissance*, p. 195 and n. 59), but the work appears in Wolf's edition as two incomplete Masses, *Adieu mes amours* and *Carminum* (Obrecht, *Works*, IV, 1, 85). Smijers has shown that certain of the movements included by Wolf do not belong. The second Sanctus of *Adieu mes amours* belongs to another Mass of the same MS; the second tract of the *Missa Carminum* (*Domine non secundum*) is by de Orto, not Obrecht, and the first one probably does not belong to this Mass either. A. Smijers, "De Missa Carminum van Jacob Hobrecht," *Tijdschrift voor Muziekwetenschap*, XVII:3 (1951), 192. Gombosi noted several years earlier that a part of the Sanctus of the two works of the Wolf edition is identical and suggested that they be combined into a single *Missa Carminum*. *Jacob Obrecht*, pp. 116-119. Smijers agrees, and further suggests that the missing Agnus may well have been sung to the music of the Kyrie, as in Josquin's *Una musque de Biscaya*.

⁵Gombosi has identified many of the *cantus firmi* and given a list of those which he could not locate. *Op. cit.*, pp. 116-119.

⁶For example, in the *Missa Carminum*, the superius is given *Scoen lief* in the Sanctus and the contratenor is given *S'en tel estat* in the *In nomine*.

⁷*Works*, V, 133. Gombosi suggests the early 1470's as the probable date of composition. *Jacob Obrecht*, p. 34.

⁸In the Credo the melody is quoted once in its entirety, then at *Et incarnatus* it is given part way through (down to m. 54 of the chanson), and then once again from the beginning to the very end (starting at m. 64 of *Et incarnatus*). In both the Kyrie and Agnus it is given once completely through, but is split into three sections because of the tripartite division of the movements. None of these is a serious alteration, and similar ones are found in many of the Masses.

⁹The superius is silent in the *Benedictus*, so the whole chanson tenor is given by the tenor of the Mass. There are also occasional references to the bass of the chanson in the bass of the Mass, but no extensive quotations. (See m. 7-11 and m. 22-24 in Kyrie I, and m. 1-11 and m. 67-70 in the *Qui tollis*.) The bass also carries tenor material in the *Osanna* (m. 1-10). In Agnus II (m. 17 ff.) it imitates the superius,

and hence presents superius material. This imitation is an extension of one already found in the chanson. For further discussion of the Mass, see pp. 285 ff.

[10]*Works*, V, 20. Oliver Strunk points out the relationship to the Mass of Busnois ("The Origins of the *L'homme armé* Mass," *Bulletin of the American Musicological Society*, No. 2 [1937], p. 25). See also Kyriazis, *op. cit.*, pp. 9, 42, and Reese, *Renaissance*, p. 197.

[11]Gombosi gives a complete c.f. analysis (*Jacob Obrecht*, p. 59). Also he suggests that the work was written in the 1470's, possibly before *Fors seulement* (*ibid.*, p. 61).

[12]*Works*, I, 85; *Opera omnia*, I, 113. According to Gombosi, ". . . it is a late mass, if not the latest preserved work of the master . . ." (*Jacob Obrecht*, p. 116). Busnois's chanson, upon which it is based, is printed in Josquin, *Missen*, I, 105. For further commentary on this work, and on Josquin's of the same name, see Myroslaw Antonowytsch, "Renaissance-Tendenzen in den Fortuna-Messen von Josquin und Obrecht," *Die Musikforschung*, IX (1956), 1-26.

[13]The tenor of the chanson is generally stated by the tenor of the Mass with the original note values. However, the bass carries it in the *Osanna* and the superius in the Sanctus. In the latter movement, after the superius completes the quotation of the chanson tenor it adds the first fifteen bars of the chanson superius to bring the movement to a close. In Agnus III the superius quotes the entire chanson superius twice, once in unit and once in halved values. A similar scheme is found in Agnus I, where the chanson tenor is given by the tenor, likewise in unit and then in halved values. An analysis of the c.f. treatment is given by Gombosi, *ibid.*, p. 112.

[14]*Works*, I, 49. *Opera omnia*, I, 69.

[15]In rhythm the c.f. gives the impression of being a vigorous secular melody. However, its melodic shape shows many resemblances to that of a much used melody type of the 7th mode. (See, for instance, the Antiphon *Urbs fortitudinis*, *Vesperale*, p. 76.) Because of the title of the Mass, it has been supposed that the c.f. comes from the Greek liturgy. Johannes Wolf and others have entertained this idea but have never identified the original melody. Pirro (*Histoire*, p. 194) suggests that the name may derive from the custom of reading the Epistle and Gospel in Greek in the papal chapel during the Mass of the Resurrection, and that the c.f. may be derived from the intonations of this "*modulation solennelle.*" He is led to this conclusion by the discovery that in the *Osanna* the superius quotes portions of the Easter sequence *Victimae paschali laudes* in combination with the c.f. in the tenor. See Smijer's Introduction, *Opera omnia*, I.

[16]Assuming that the tenor melody is given in unit values in Kyrie I, it would be stated in sixfold augmentation in the Gloria and in double augmentation in several other sections (*Et incarnatus*, Sanctus, Osanna, and Agnus I and III). In several cases the quotation of the melody ends with a restatement of the first four bars (Kyrie II, the three statements in the *Qui tollis*, and in the *Osanna*). In the Sanctus three notes are added at the final cadence. In the third statement of *Qui tollis* the tune is given in triple meter, but without alteration of the relative values. The tenor is normally the c.f. voice, but the superius presents the melody in Agnus II and the bass in Agnus I and III. The instructions for augmentation and other manipulations are given by Smijers (*ibid*).

[17]The notes have been numbered 1, 2, 3, etc., in ex. 90b and the same numbers are given to the corresponding notes in ex. 90a. They have not been numbered beyond 32 as that is sufficient to make the procedure clear. In order to explain every detail of the derived c.f. it is necessary to assume that there are some places where Obrecht deviates from the normal rhythmic form of the melody. For instance, it seems that the maxima rest (ex. 90b, m. 5-8) should be derived from a longa rest in the original (end of ex. 90a, marked 2?), yet out of all the statements of the tune a suitable rest is found only at the end of the Credo (*Works*, I, 71). The sixth measure of the c.f. (ex. 90a) is usually given in the rhythmic form ♩ ♪ ♪ , although the form ♩. ♪ is found in the Gloria (*ibid.*, p. 58, m. 150-151) and a few other places. Measure 22,

ex. 90a, is usually given as ♩ ○ ♩, although the form ♩ ♩ ○ is used in the Gloria (*ibid.*, p. 61, m. 212-213) and in some other places. The same is true of the brevis rest (ex. 90a, m. 12-13), which is sometimes given as a semibrevis.

[18]Owing to the perfection of the breves in triple meter, breves and semibreves of the original appear in the new mensuration as three times their former value. For instance, the breve in m. 4 of ex. 90a appears in m. 11-12 of ex. 90b as two dotted breves tied together (*longa, modus imperfectus, tempus perfectum*). The original note has the value of two semibreves, the derived one has the value of six, so it is triply augmented. However, the minims of the original are merely doubly augmented, as semibreves are imperfect in the new mensuration. (Compare the minims, ex. 90a, m. 3, with the semibreves, ex. 90b, m. 39-40.) Augmentation along with change of mensuration from imperfect to perfect, or vice versa, occurs constantly with Obrecht. This is the source of some ambiguity in description, as the augmentation may be either duple or triple, depending on what note value is being referred to. (See also n. 23, below.)

[19]Works, V, 166. It is entitled *Missa sine nomine* by the editor, the c.f. having been identified later by Gombosi. The work is for three voices and is apparently very early. Gombosi suggests a date somewhere between 1465 and 1474 (*Jacob Obrecht*, p. 47). On the whole, the c.f. usage corresponds to that of *Fors seulement, Fortuna desperata*, etc., as the tenor of the chanson is generally quoted exactly by the tenor of the Mass and without augmentation. It is used in diminution only once (in Agnus II) and is given in triple meter in *Osanna II* and at *Et unam sanctam*. It is given to the middle voice in the *Christe, Osanna II*, and Agnus I. It is used in both the tenor and superius in Agnus III and *Qui tollis* (see ex. 101). For further comment on this Mass, see p. 288.

[20]Works, V. 1. Gombosi has identified this c.f. also (op. cit., p. 116). The tenor statements in the Kyrie, Sanctus, and Agnus are quite similar, but those of the Gloria and Credo show many differences in rhythmic form as well as ornamentation. These seem to be in the class of arbitrary and unpredictable changes that are common in the works of Obrecht's predecessors, so that in this respect the Mass is somewhat exceptional. Although there are some augmentations, none is great enough to produce the pedal notes found in the *L'homme armé* scaffolding.

[21]Works, III, 141. The tenor of the motet *Ave Regina caelorum . . . Mater Regis*, by Walter Frye, is used as c.f. Bukofzer, *Studies*, pp. 309-310. It is carried by the tenor of the Mass except in the first and third Agnus, where it is given to the bass. The tenor c.f. is occasionally replaced by material from the superius of the motet, which is given to the superius of the Mass. This occurs in the *Benedictus* and at the end of the Credo, following the completion of a tenor statement (m. 58 ff.). The c.f. material is presented simultaneously in two voices in the *Qui tollis* (tenor and bass), Sanctus (tenor and alto), and Agnus II (tenor and bass). These are not canons. The strictest statement is in the tenor and it is freely duplicated by the second voice.

[22]MS Segovia, fo. 22ᵛ-27. (See n. 1 above.) Text is almost completely lacking, being restricted to incipits of sections. The Mass appears complete, and completely texted, in Jena, Universitäts-Bibliothek, cod. mus. 32, fo. 142ᵛ-158. The Kyrie, along with the tenor of Josquin's four part chanson, is published by Smijers (*Van Ockeghem tot Sweelinck*, p. 54).

[23]Obrecht subjects the c.f. fragments to diminutions in the successive statements, but, as pointed out above (n. 18), because of changes in mensuration the exact numerical ratios between the note values of the first statement are not always retained in the repetitions. (Ex. 93c gives further illustration of this.) The rhythmic values of the chanson superius are taken as the basis for all the statements in the scaffolding of the Mass. In the chanson the first five notes (b, g, a, b, c′) are all of equal value (imperfect semibreves). In the first statement in the Mass each semibreve is read as a long in perfect mode. According to the rules of the notation of the time, the first four of these longs must be interpreted as perfect and hence must have six times the

value of the original notes. The fifth one, however, must be interpreted as imperfect, so it has only four times the original value. In the second statement of the scaffolding each semibreve of the original is read as a breve in imperfect time, so that all the breves are imperfect and have exactly double the value of the original notes. If we compare the second statement of the scaffolding with the first, we find that the breves b, g, a, and b have one third the value of the corresponding longs, while the fifth breve, c′, has only one half the value of the longa c′.

[24]For detailed analysis of the Masses *Si dedero, Je ne demande, Maria zart,* and *Malheur me bat* see Kyriazis, *op. cit.,* pp. 14 ff.

The composer of the chanson *Malheur me bat* is not known for certain. In two manuscript sources the work is anonymous, in two it is attributed to Martini, and in one to Malcort. Ockeghem is named as the composer in one manuscript and in Petrucci's *Odhecaton A.* For details see Hewitt, ed., *Odhecaton,* p. 158. Aron also mentions Ockeghem as the composer in the *Trattato della natura e cognizione di tutti gli toni di canto figurato.* See Oliver Strunk, *Source Readings in Music History* (New York: W. W. Norton & Company, 1950), p. 214, footnote m. The weight of the evidence is slightly on Ockeghem's side, so far as the number of times his name is mentioned in connection with the chanson is concerned. I cite him as the composer, therefore, in the following discussion of Obrecht's Mass *Malheur me bat.*

[25]An example of the scaffolding tenor of *Je ne demande* is given by Wagner (*Messe,* pp. 116 ff.). A facsimile of the tenor of the *Missa Si dedero* in the Petrucci edition of 1508 is given by Willi Apel, *The Notation of Polyphonic Music* (Cambridge, Mass.: The Mediaeval Academy of America, 1945), p. 183. In the *Missa Malheur me bat* the tenor of the chanson is used in the *Crucifixus* and *Benedictus* when the main c.f. voice, the superius, is silent. Both movements are trios and the borrowed melody is given by the tenor; both are also identical, as Obrecht simply repeats the music of the *Crucifixus* note for note in the *Benedictus.* Agnus II is also a trio, and the chanson tenor is also given in it, but by the bass voice. Two other trios, *Christe* and *Pleni,* are freely composed.

[26]An alternate version of the second Agnus (*Works,* I, iv) is based on a much more complex c.f. layout. The tenor and alto quote phrases from the chanson in alternation and in a rather peculiar order. The tenor actually has an *ostinato* on c.f. material, owing to the fact that it repeats the first phrase of the tenor of Busnois's chanson ten times over. The alto quotes the phrases of the chanson tenor in reverse order, the last one first, the next-to-the-last second, etc. However, it does not present the very first one, which is used for the tenor *ostinato.* In addition, the soprano and bass move entirely in parallel tenths, called for by the canon in the soprano part: "*Qui mecum resonat, in decimis barritonisat.*" All four voices are thus strictly regulated in some way, making this movement exceptional among the works of Obrecht.

[27]This is one of the few instances of migration during the course of a movement.

[28]In addition, the tune has been twice quoted in its entirety in the Gloria. The bass gives it in *Domine Deus,* the alto in *Qui tollis.* (Both of these sections are duos.) Reese gives a detailed description of the c.f. usage, with musical examples. *Renaissance,* pp. 193-194.

[29]Hewitt, ed., *Odhecaton,* p. 339.

[30]There is no doubt that there is a tendency, in certain works, to end with a clear, concise presentation of the c.f. material which gives an effect analogous to recapitulation. In many Masses, moreover, we can detect a conscious effort to bring the entire work to a musically effective close. We find that this is done in many ways, the type of "recapitulation" mentioned above being only one of them. Josquin is inclined to put off the fullest scoring and the most astonishing contrapuntal feats to the very last, so that the whole work moves to a climax. Obrecht adopts a similar method in the Marian Mass *Sub tuum praesidium.*

[31]There are some exceptions to this. In the *Missa Maria zart* the *Qui propter, Pleni sunt caeli,* and *Benedictus* are either partially or entirely freely composed.

[32]In all movements such as this the trios before the final c.f. statement are very short, since the progressive diminutions greatly reduce the length of the rests in the tenor part. Possibly because of this, they often do not present any c.f. material.

[33]It appears in the Segovia MS, fo. 27ᵛ-35. The Kyrie and the chanson, *Rosa playsante*, are published by Smijers (*Van Ockeghem tot Sweelinck*, pp. 58, 62.).

[34]These brief quotations may come from any voice of the chanson. For instance, in Kyrie I, m. 1-5, superius and bass are quoted in the superius and bass of the Mass. Most of them come from the tenor of the chanson, although not directly; they result from bringing material of the tenor framework of the Mass movement into other voices. In Kyrie II, m. 81-89, a descending triadic figure of the tenor is imitated in all voices. In the *Et incarnatus* a melodic figure which may be derived from the tenor (m. 25-33) appears in the bass (m. 1-4), superius (m. 9-12), and contra (m. 17-20). In the Sanctus there is a similar occurrence, since the first few notes of the tenor (m. 16-32) occur in the bass (m. 1-7) and the contra (m. 7-13). In the first Agnus, a quotation in the initial phrase of the contra (m. 1-14) differs from those just mentioned since it is the initial tenor phrase of the chanson and hence is not related to or derived from the specific tenor fragment used as framework for this movement.

[35]The mensuration changes in this work outnumber those of *Si dedero* and *Maria zart*. The tenor of *Maria zart* is reproduced by Meier, "Zyklische Gesamtstruktur und Tonalität in den Messen Jacob Obrechts," *Archiv für Musikwissenschaft*, X (1953), 300.

[36]The melody used in the *Missa O quam suavis* differs in important respects from those available to me. However, there are so many clear resemblances that it is possible to observe Obrecht's paraphrase technique in the Mass, just the same.

[37]Following the lead of the editor of the complete works, I have barred the tenors in duple meter in ex. 96a, lines 5 and 6. While this barring is correct for the other voices, the tenors are obviously in triple meter and this I have indicated in the examples by placing braces above the staff.

[38]The music of this section is repeated at the end of the Credo (*et exspecto*). It should be mentioned here that several accidentals added by Wolf in the Kyrie are omitted by him in the identical passage in the Credo. This gives evidence of haphazard procedures in indicating *musica ficta* which strengthens my opinion that this aspect of the edition is open to serious question. On the whole, it seems that more accidentals have been added than are necessary and that in many cases the only purpose behind them is to bring the music into line with modern major and minor tonalities as much as possible. For instance, the Kyrie mentioned above is given a strong cast of g minor by the editorially suggested e flats and f sharps (see ex. 96c, m. 1-7). These are omitted in the Credo, and the passages simply remains in Dorian mode. The melodic diminished fourth (ex. 96c, m. 2-3), while often specifically called for in music of the first half of the century, seems quite out of place in music of the last half.

[39]The c.f., given by Wolf in the Introduction to the Mass, differs in some details from the Vatican version. Owing to the loss of a page in the sole manuscript source, some voices are missing in the sections *Qui tollis* to *Et incarnatus*. Kyriazis evidently mistakes this for intentional thin scoring on the part of Obrecht (op. cit., p. 60).

[40]Bukofzer, *Studies*, p. 309 and n. 158.

[41]Heinrich Besseler, "Musik des Mittelalters in der Hamburger Musikhalle," *Zeitschrift für Musikwissenschaft*, VII (1924/25), 44.

[42]MS Segovia, fo. 15ᵛ-22. The Kyrie is printed by Smijers (*Van Ockeghem tot Sweelinck*, p. 51). The c.f. is an antiphon for second Vespers, The Conversion of St. Paul Apostle. It is given by Smijers with the Kyrie and is also included in the *LU*, p. 1348.

[43]I am not sure that I understand how Obrecht manipulates the c.f. in order to obtain the series of notes which make up this framework. I assume that this tenor is

based on the tenor of Kyrie I, since it has the same number of notes (28 excluding the final longa), and since it contains all the pitches of that part in a scrambled order (with a difference of one note, concerning which see n. 45, below). The method of construction seems to be to choose one note from the beginning and then one from the end of the melody, so that we hear the first note of the Kyrie tenor, then the last, then the second note, then the next-to-last, and so on. However, the pattern is not kept quite consistent, which may well mean that my interpretation is incorrect. Assuming that it is correct, and numbering the notes of the Kyrie tenor in order from 1 to 28, the notes of the Credo would be selected in this order: 1, 28, 2, 27, 3; rest; 4, 26, 5, 25, 6; rest; 7, 24, 8; rest. Then the order of selection is reversed: 23, 9; rest; 22, 10, 21, 11, 20, 12, 19, 13; rest. The order of selection is reversed again: 14, 18, 15; rest; 16; rest; 17; rest.

Another feature of this tenor attracts attention. It is obviously a constructed voice (see the leap of a major sixth, m. 87-88), but it does not consist of a series of long values as most of Obrecht's frameworks do. The values are often reasonably short, giving the tenor a rhythmic aspect similar to the other voices. However, a second glance shows that these shorter values always repeat the same pitch and it turns out that, in every case, the notes on a single pitch add up to the value of a longa. The whole tenor was evidently originally conceived as a framework in which each note had the value of a longa and some of the longae were later subdivided into two or more notes of shorter value. The subdivision of the long notes does not noticeably facilitate the setting of the text; evidently it was done for reasons of texture and rhythm.

[44]The c.f. quotations in the mottoes, or head motives, are of sufficient importance to be listed in detail. In the Kyrie, the c.f. fragment appears in the contratenor and superius in close imitation and a few measures later in the bass and tenor, also in imitation. The Gloria is without a motto, but the *Qui tollis* presents the c.f. fragment, although in a different rhythm from that of the Kyrie. (It appears first in the contratenor and is then exactly repeated in the superius, m. 13.) In the Credo the original rhythmic form of the motto is picked up again, the fragment appearing first in the bass, then the contra (m. 8), then the superius (m. 15), and lastly in the contra again (m. 23). The motto of the *Crucifixus* is short, only five notes of the c.f. being used. These appear first in the contra, then in the bass (m. 9), then the superius (m. 17), and finally the tenor (m. 21). In its first appearance in the contra the motto is imitated in the bass at the fifth below. In the Sanctus the motto appears in imitation as it did in the Kyrie, first between contratenor and superius (m. 1-8) and then between tenor and bass (m. 15-22).

[45]Obrecht treats two notes near the beginning of the second incise variably, and in a way for which I can see no ready explanation. The *LU* version (transposed down a tone to agree with the Mass) is: f f a bb c' bb g. The version of the Gloria is identical with this. The version of Kyrie II is slightly different because it lacks one note. It reads f f a c' bb g. The version of Kyrie I differs by two notes and reads f f a a c' c' g. The scrambled framework of the Credo is evidently constructed out of the tenor of Kyrie I, but Obrecht for some reason reads the second phrase as f f a a c' bb g— a form which is a mixture of those of Kyrie I and II. (This means that in the order of notes suggested in n. 43, above, note number 14 is not c', as it should be if Obrecht had followed exactly the scheme I have proposed, but bb. This is a small point, and I would not mention it at all except that this is the one note which my explanation of the Credo framework will not account for.)

[46]The *Missa sine nomine* (*Works,* IV, 41) is apparently based on several *cantus firmi,* but unfortunately text references are given in only two cases. In the *Et incarnatus* the antiphon *O clavis David* (*LU,* p. 341) is presented in simple form and long note values. In the *Osanna* a melody with text *O beate Pater Donatiane* (unidentified) is used. It reappears in Agnus I and Agnus III and is also apparently used in Kyrie I, *Christe,* Kyrie II, and the Sanctus, differently paraphrased each time and without any textual reference to identify it. As far as can be told, the ornamentation is very

extensive at times, so that, without the original melody for comparison and without a textual clue, one can do little more than make conjectures. No other c.f. references are given, although it is probable other *cantus firmi* are used in the remaining movements. On the basis of the c.f. in the *Osanna* and *Agnus*, *O beate Pater Donatiane*, Gombosi identifies this Mass as one composed for Bruges in 1491 in honor of the patron saint of the city and suggests it should be called *Missa Sancti Donatiani* (*Jacob Obrecht*, p. 116).

[47]Obrecht, *Works*, II, 117. Most of the melodies have been identified: *Martinus adhuc catechumenus* in the Kyrie (*Pal. Mus.*, IX, 480); *Dixerunt discipuli* (*LU*, p. 1748), and *Sancte Martine, ora pro nobis* (*LU*, p. 837) in the Gloria; *O virum ineffabilem* (*LU*, p. 1749)), *Oculis ac manibus* (*LU*, p. 1749), and *O beatum virum* (*LU*, p. 1746) in the Credo; *Ego signo crucis* (*Pal. Mus.*, IX, 480) in the Sanctus; and *O beatum pontificem* (*LU*, p. 1750) in the Agnus. Melodies not identified are those to the words *Martinus Episcopus* in the Gloria (not the melody used in *Pal. Mus.*, IX, 485, or *Proc. Mon.*, p. 206) and *Adoramus Christum* in the Sanctus.

[48]The technical methods used in this canon are in many respects similar to those used by Busnois in the canon in the second setting of *Regina caeli laetare* (p. 214, above). In both, the bass enters first and the tenor follows at the fourth above. In order to fit the voices together a liberal amount of ornamentation is introduced, rests are used freely, and free sections of some length are interpolated.

[49]If there is c.f., it seems to be carried by the alto. Apparently there is considerable ornamentation at places, and there is possibly migration to the superius. It should be remembered, however, that the *Benedictus* is often freely composed, so there may be no c.f. at all.

[50]The antiphon text is given only for the portion of the c.f. used in the final Agnus. The reason for the omission of the first part of the text is unknown to me.

[51]Obrecht, *Works*, II, 1; Obrecht, *Opera omnia*, II, 1. The publication of this Mass in *Opera omnia* is an event of considerable importance, since it is the first work to appear under the editorship of M. van Crevel, and marks the initiation of a number of new editorial policies. (See the introductory remarks, *ibid.*, pp. I-LI.)

Van Crevel adopts a type of scoring in which the value of the *tactus* (semibreve) is given a fixed amount of space on the staff, and is further indicated by a small sign above the staff. By this means he is able to eliminate bar lines and yet maintain complete legibility. (See "Transcription and Scoring," *ibid.*, p. XII ff.) He makes a serious attempt to locate all the *cantus firmi*, and in forms as near as possible to those used by Obrecht. (The melodies are reproduced in the section "Building Material," *ibid.*, p. XLVI ff., and in some cases are closer to Obrecht's version than the ones to which I give reference in n. 52, this chapter.)

Finally, as the most important part of his analysis of the music, van Crevel interprets the hidden numerological structure of the tenor at some length. (See "Secret Structure," *ibid.*, pp. XVII-XXV.) The demonstration of an underlying order in *Sub tuum praesidium* is very welcome, not only because of the light it sheds on that work, but also because it raises the hope that explanations may be found for problematical features in other of Obrecht's planned structures. There is the possibility, also, that a mathematical approach of this sort may be profitable in the study of isorhythmic tenors in general.

[52]There are quotations from seven different *cantus firmi*. Three of them are antiphons: *Sub tuum praesidium* (*Var. Prec.*, p. 37), *Regina caeli* (*LU*, p. 275), and *Ave Regina caelorum* (*LU*, p. 274, or better, *Studien zur Musikwissenschaft*, VII [1920], 91, *Salve Regina* VI). Four others are taken from Marian sequences: *Audi nos, nam te filius* is the twelfth verse of the sequence *Ave praeclara maris stella*, while *Mediatrix nostra* and *Celsus nuntiat Gabriel* are the eighteenth and sixth verses of *Aurea virga*. Anselm Schubiger, *Die Sängerschule St. Gallens von 8. bis 12. Jahrhundert* (Einsiedeln and New York: K. & N. Benziger, 1858), pp. 54, 49, and 48, respectively. *Supplicamus nos emenda* is the last verse of the sequence *Verbum*

bonum et suave, Var. Prec., p. 95. (The *LU* version of *Sub tuum praesidium* is closer to Obrecht's than that of Var. Prec., at the phrase *libera nos*, and so has been used in example 99 for this one spot.)

[53]No more than a few aspects of Obrecht's style can be taken up here. For further studies see: Salop, *The Masses of Jacob Obrecht*; Kyriazis, *op. cit.*; Bukofzer, *Studies*, pp. 292 ff.; and Gombosi, *Jacob Obrecht*. Peter Wagner also points out some interesting features, in *Messe*, pp. 122 ff.

[54]*Works*, V, 133. Wolf states that there is only one source for the Mass, evidently overlooking the fact that Glareanus quotes the *Qui tollis* and Sanctus in the *Dodecachordon*. Henricus Glareanus, *Dodecachordon*, trans. Peter Bohn (Leipzig: Breitkopf & Härtel, 1888), pp. 179, 181. Gombosi also shows that the *Qui tollis* is for three voices (*Jacob Obrecht*, p. 33). The bottom voice of this movement moves entirely in breves, making it look like a strict c.f. It is possible Obrecht saw he could reduce the first eleven measures of Ockeghem's bass to one note per measure, and decided to carry on in this manner to the end of the movement. In any case, he has here set himself the task of writing a voice which may be called a "scaffolding counterpoint" rather than a "scaffolding c.f." It is common enough to reduce the c.f. to a series of long notes and then add florid counterpoints to it, but in this case the procedure is reversed. The c.f. remains florid while the counterpoint is written as a scaffold of equal, long values. Apparently to add some interest, the tenor is written in alternate white breves and dotted black breves, two ways of expressing the same temporal duration in *tempus imperfectum* (Glareanus, *Dodecachordon*, p. 179).

It hardly seems likely, as Gombosi has proposed (*Jacob Obrecht*, p. 33), that this Mass is an unfinished sketch. True, the bass of the *Qui tollis* is very bare, but one must ask: Why should Obrecht limit himself to writing a series of breves if he intends to elaborate the line in the future? Writing a series of breves is not a difficult task, but it is a definitely restrictive one, because in several measures only one pitch, and no other, will fit. (See m. 14, 23, 25, etc., of the *Qui tollis*.) Why impose such a restriction on the sketch if the eventual line is to be of a type for which the restriction has no meaning? The allegedly inferior quality of the line does not prove, in itself, that it was not intended to sound as it does. There are many other cases where the procedure adopted by Obrecht does not add to the musical beauty of the work. The theory that the Mass is a sketch becomes even less likely in the face of the ingenious construction of the Credo. When this movement is analyzed it will be seen that the composer must have expended a great deal of care on it.

[55]This section is printed in its complete form (i.e., for three voices) in the Works.

[56]Spot quotations of the Gregorian Credo are found in some of the other Masses. The superius has one in the *Missa Graecorum* from *Et incarnatus* to *et sepultus est*. In the *Missa de Sancto Martino* it also has one at the same words of the text. The same voice gives freer, but unmistakable references to the Gregorian melody in the *Missa Maria zart* (*Sedet ad dexteram* to *et in Spiritum Sanctum*). All these passages are quoted in combination with the c.f. of the Mass.

[57]In the Gloria of this Mass the tenor plays the leading part also. (See p. 251, above.)

[58]Reese points out further elements of organization. *Renaissance*, p. 199.

[59]This leaves out of consideration the various kinds of rhythmic organization of the thirteenth and fourteenth centuries. The striking feature of Obrecht's work (compared to the music of earlier periods) is the extent of the organization. Phrases organized by sequence or some other motive means are found in the organa of Notre Dame, as is well known, but they are isolated; the organization does not continue in force for any length of time.

[60]Another and important aspect of the free parts is well illustrated by the middle voice of the Gloria of the *Missa De tous biens pleine* (ex. 91a-c) and that of the *Qui tollis* of the same work (ex. 101a-b). It is obvious at once that Obrecht makes much more use of large leaps than do the late Dufay and Ockeghem. Skips of the

octave and sixth are common, and even larger ones can be found. He also makes much use of scalewise lines of extended range; these skips and scalewise ascents and descents are, however, apt to be given immediate compensation. Upward motion is immediately balanced off by downward, and vice versa. This is not the case in the filigreelike ornamental lines of Dufay. The melody can skip lightly over small intervals, and high and low points need not be accounted for immediately by motion in the opposite direction but are balanced only in terms of the entire phrase. Ockeghem pays even less attention to the aspect of melodic balance, for it is of the essence of his lines to be in a state of greater or less unbalance. The lines of Obrecht are at least as active and energetic as those of Busnois, but they do not give the sense of meaningless activity sometimes found in the latter. The reason for this is that they are not free to move in any direction at any time, as a given motion determines to large extent what the following one shall be. The principle of immediate compensation is applied in these lines, although not so strictly as it is used later in the sixteenth century. There is, moreover, considerable variation in strictness of application of the principle within the works of Obrecht himself.

[61]The harmonic succession of an e-minor, f#-minor and g-minor chord in the sequence lettered F (ex. 98, m. 46-48) is most unusual for Obrecht. It would have been a fairly ordinary occurrence in the colorful harmonic style of the earlier part of the century, but the tendency in the last half of the century was toward diatonicism, so that such progressions become uncommon. As the Mass is found in only one source (Gregor Mewes, *Concentus harmonici*), there is no way of checking on the reliability of the accidentals.

[62]Jacob Barbireau. *Opera omnia*, ed. Bernhard Meier (Corpus Mensurabilis Musicae, VII [Rome: American Institute of Musicology, 1957]), VII, ii, p. 9. For a somewhat different form of the same melody, see the setting of Paulus de Broda in the *Glogauer Liederbuch. Das Erbe deutscher Musik, Reichsdenkmale* (Kassel: Bärenreiter, 1936) IV, 89 ff.

[63]Kyriazis gives a detailed analysis of the quotations in this work. *Op. cit.*, pp. 25-26.

[64]It would hardly be possible to approach closer to the parody Mass. Even where there is no direct quotation, the voices are conducted so much in the manner of Agricola's motet that they seem to have grown out of it. Gombosi has remarked of the *Missa Malheur me bat* that so much of the chanson has been used that the songlike character of the melodies colors the whole Mass (*Jacob Obrecht*, p. 92). Likewise, the *Missa Ave Regina caelorum* shows similarities to the fairly simple style of Frye. In the *Missa Sicut spina rosam* the similarities to the style of Ockeghem are not caused merely by quotation. They are not involuntary but are conscious inmitations of his procedures. In this and other works, I feel that Obrecht shows sensitivity to the styles of other writers and reproduces these styles to a certain extent in his own work.

[65]Reese discusses the structure of the motet in some detail (*Renaissance*, p. 191). I have identified the following melodies: *Veni, Domine, et noli tardare* (Pal. Mus., IX, 26), *Canite tuba in Sion* (LU, p. 356), *Media vita* (Var. Prec., p. 106), *O clavis David* (LU, p. 341), *Erunt prava* (LU, p. 357), *O virgo virginum* (Pal. Mus., IX, 28). It is probable that a few more melodies are used, although I have not located them.

[66]P. Aubry and E. Misset, *Les Proses d'Adam de Saint Victor* (Paris: H. Welter, 1900), no. XVIII, p. 260.

[67]*Liber Resp.*, pp. 237, 241, and 238 respectively.

[68]The text is the second verse of the hymn *Quod chorus vatum*. It is given in Var. Prec., p. 103, but with a melody different from the one used by Obrecht. The melody he uses is associated with this and several other hymn texts, one of which is *Iste confessor* (LU, p. 1196). It is the one I have used in ex. 107a-b for purposes of comparison. It has been pointed out in the introduction to a popular edition of this work (*Vereeniging voor Nederlandsche Muziekgeschiedenis. Drie Oud-Neder-*

landsche Motetten. [Amsterdam: G. Alsbach & Co., 1936], Vol. 44) that the melody used is the same as that of the hymn *Ut queant laxis providi.* It is true that this is one of the melodies associated with it, but it is not the famous one on which Guido d'Arezzo based his system of solmization.

[69]Bukofzer, *Studies,* p. 310; Obrecht, *Motetten,* p. 64.

[70]I have not identified the c.f. According to Wolf, the same melody is used in Brumel's *Beata es Maria* in Petrucci's *Motetti Libro quarto* (1505). Obrecht, *Motetten* (Bundel II), p. x.

[71]Var. Prec., p. 46.

[72]*Motetten,* p. 179, under the title *Requiem aeternam.* Smijers gives the text in "Twee onbekende motetteksten van Jacob Obrecht," *Tijdschrift der Vereeniging voor Nederlandsche Muziekgeschiedenis,* XVI (1941), 129. Peter Wagner discusses it as a work of Josquin (*Messe,* p. 161).

[73]*Motetten,* p. 136.

[74]Although the *cantus firmi* used in some of the motets for four voices have not been identified by me, it seems that only one of these works is freely composed—the declamation motet *Quis munerare queat.* (*Motetten,* p. 12.) Another declamation motet, *Si oblitus fuero,* (*Ibid.,* p. 97), is not by Obrecht but Ninot le Petit. A. Smijers, "Vijftiende en zestiende eeuwsche Muziekhandschriften in Italië met werken van Nederlandsche Componisten," *Tijdschrift der Vereeniging voor Nederlandsche Muziekgeschiedenis,* XIV (1935), 180.

[75]*Motetten,* p. 175.

[76]*Ibid.,* pp. 157, 145.

[77]Wagner, *Messe,* p. 115.

[78]By this I understand Wagner to mean the type of writing that is generally taken to be the basis of the sixteenth-century motet. Phrases begin with a point of imitation, initial entries being allotted each of the voices. This is adopted as a consistent method of organization, occasional contrast being offered by passages in nonimitative style. For an extensive discussion of imitation in the Masses of Obrecht, see Kyriazis, *op. cit.,* p. 38.

[79]Interesting detail of all sorts was sought after; a model for this period is the motet of Obrecht, *Salve Regina,* just discussed. For fuller commentary on Obrecht's style see citations in n. 53, this chapter.

CHAPTER 10

[1]Bukofzer, *Studies,* pp. 292 ff.

[2]*Misse Josquin* (Venice, 1502). See Reese, *Renaissance,* pp. 228 ff. (biography), 235 ff. (analysis of Masses), 246 ff. (analysis of motets). The study of the Masses of Josquin by A. W. Ambros is old, but still good. (*Geschichte der Musik* [Leipzig: F. E. C. Leuckart, 1887-1911], III, 212 ff.) They are also discussed by Pirro (*Histoire,* p. 179).

Since I have written this chapter, two articles of first-rate importance have appeared. Sartori has produced evidence that Josquin must have been born before 1450 (the previously accepted date). His birth date may be as early as c. 1440, no later than 1445. Claudio Sartori, "Josquin des Prés cantore del duomo di Milano (1459-1472)," *Annales Musicologiques* (Neuilly-sur-Seine: Société de Musique d'Autrefois, 1956) IV, [55]-83. See also Suzanne Clercx, "Lumières sur la formation de Josquin et d'Obrecht," *Revue Belge de Musicologie,* XI (1957), 157-158, where an argument is presented for the later date.

Helmuth Osthoff, in the article *Josquin Desprez,* MGG, VII, cols. 190-214, has presented the most careful and complete chronological arrangement of Josquin's works which has yet appeared. He divides the Masses into three periods. The first runs to

c. 1485 (when Josquin would have been at least forty years old) and includes the Masses *L'ami Baudichon, Ad fugam, Di dadi, Allez regretz, Gaudeamus, Malheur me bat, Fortuna desperata, Una musque de Biscaya,* and *Mater Patris.* The second extends from c. 1485 to 1505 (when he would have been sixty years old, or more) and includes *L'homme armé super voces musicales, Faysant regretz, L'homme armé sexti toni, La sol fa re mi, D'ung aultre amer, Sine nomine, Ave maris stella,* and *Hercules Dux Ferrariae.* The third period extends from c. 1505 to his death in 1521. The three great Masses, *De beata Virgine, Pange lingua,* and *Da pacem* were then written when the composer was in his sixtieth and seventieth years.

It is apparent that Josquin retained his creative powers to a great age (one is reminded immediately of Verdi). It is also apparent that the great majority of works for which he is best known at present—those that point most clearly to the style of the sixteenth century—were not written until after he was fifty years of age. It is not only the music of this man that is extraordinary, his life is extraordinary as well.

As stated above, these articles did not appear until after I had written the section on the Masses. They do not disqualify what I have said, but had I been acquainted with them I would have made some of the statements stronger.

The musical examples of Josquin in this chapter are drawn from the edition (in progress) begun by Albert Smijers in 1921 and continued by him through 1956 and, since his death, prepared from 1957 on by M. Antonowycz. *Werken van Josquin Des Prez,* ed. A. Smijers (*Vereeniging voor Nederlandsche Muziekgeschiedenis* [Leipzig: C. F. W. Siegel, and Amsterdam: G. Alsbach, 1921; Leipzig: Kistner & Siegel, and Amsterdam: G. Alsbach, 1926-27; Leipzig: Kistner & Siegel, 1929-42; Amsterdam: G. Alsbach, 1948—]). My examples are from the four volumes of Masses and five volumes of motets issued so far; hereafter cited as Josquin, *Missen,* I-IV, and Josquin, *Motetten,* I-V.

[3]Josquin, *Missen,* I, 1. An analysis of this Mass is given by Gombosi (*Jacob Obrecht,* p. 51).

[4]This way of looking at it may well reverse the actual situation. It seems that the tenor statements of the Gloria and Credo are the models on which all the others are based. That is, the statement in the *Christe* should be viewed as an augmentation of the corresponding section of the Gloria. This Mass shows a clear tendency to pair the Gloria and Credo, and Sanctus and Agnus, which has been noted in some of the Masses of Dufay and Ockeghem.

[5]*Missen,* I, 109. Gombosi gives an analysis of the c.f. usage (*Jacob Obrecht,* p. 55). Various aspects, such as the harmony and the employment of motives for structural rather than purely ornamental ends, lead him to conclude that it is a later work than the other *L'homme armé* Mass.

[6]The tenor gives the A section; the superius states part of the B section four times on the pitches F and B♭ and the remainder of it twice. The alto takes over the final A section. It is questionable, at the very end of this movement, whether the c.f. is much elaborated and drawn out or whether it is dropped altogether.

[7]*Missen,* I, 81. Smijers makes a practice of appending the work upon which a Mass is based, so that no other reference than that for the Mass need be given. Gombosi has analyzed this Mass also, remarking that it shows the influence of Ockeghem, and pointing out the similarities of the beginning of Agnus II and the *Hosanna* of Obrecht's *Fortuna desperata* (*Jacob Obrecht,* p. 108). Lowinsky calls attention to the symbolism of the motto of the Agnus and its connection with the idea of the wheel of Fortune. The melody is shifted from high to low estate (the soprano is removed to the bass), and it is completely overthrown (inverted). E. Lowinsky, "The Goddess Fortuna in Music," *Musical Quarterly,* XXIX (1943), 76.

[8]*Missen,* I, 57.

[9]*Missen,* I, 35.

[10]Smijers cites the old account according to which the syllables *la, sol, fa, re,* and *mi*

represent the words *laisse faire moy* (*lasso fare mi?*). *Ibid.*, p. vii. Josquin is not the only one to use these syllables. (See Pirro, *Histoire*, p. 172; Reese, *Renaissance*, p. 238).

[11]The styles are not mutually exclusive; they mingle in various ways in many of the motets. However, the presence of older techniques is a better indication of early date of composition in the motets than in the Masses, although not decisive with them, either. (Take the case of *Praeter rerum seriem*, which is in very elaborate style but can hardly be an early work.)

[12]*Missen*, II, 19.

[13]It is a "*soggetto cavato dalle vocali di queste parole.*" The c.f. is formed on the solmization syllables *re-ut-re-ut-re-fa-mi-re*, which contain the same vowels as the syllables of Her-cu-les Dux Fer-ra-ri-ae. *Ibid.*, Introduction, p. v.

[14]Pirro points out that Hercules was known as an architect and warrior. He suggests that this may have caused the very strict architecture of the Mass, and following the conceit further finds the noise of chariots in the second Kyrie, the renewal of the attack in the Sanctus. *Histoire*, p. 181. Fanciful as this is, it gives some idea of the seriousness and force of the music.

[15]*Missen*, II, 1.

[16]Josquin, *Motetten*, I, 1. The melodic figures of the beginning are not freely invented, but agree with those of the beginning of the sequence *Ave Maria . . . Virgo serena*. The identity in text makes it certain that c.f. is used. It can be traced in all voices to m. 31, and apparently continues in the alto and bass to m. 37, even though after m. 31 the text Josquin uses is no longer that of the sequence. It is highly probable that the remainder of the motet is freely composed, although many of the ideas show certain relationships to the first phrase.

The sequence melody appears in *Var. Prec.*, (p. 46), but in a form which differs somewhat from Josquin's. In ex. 122, I use the melody as given by Carl Allan Moberg in *Die Schwedische Sequenzen* (Uppsala: Almquist & Wicksells Boktrykeri -A.-B., 1927) II, no. 34. Moberg cites several variant forms of the melody and one of them, from a *Graduale Basilense* printed in 1511, begins with the leap up of a fourth such as Josquin uses in the first phrase of the motet (ex. 122, m. 1 ff.). On the repetition of this phrase, however, Josquin uses the melody in its more normal form (ex. 122, m. 16 ff.). The variant form must have had some currency for an anonymous *Missa Ave Maria* in Jena choirbook no. 7 also makes use of the ascending fourth at the beginning. Karl Erich Roediger, *Die geistliche Musikhandschriften der Universitäts-Bibliothek Jena* (Jena: Frommann [W. Biedermann], 1935 II, 15 (no. 35). Jacquelyn Mattfeld gives the source of the remainder of the text and states that it was probably used as a votive antiphon. "Some Relationships Between Texts and Cantus Firmi in the Liturgical Motets of Josquin des Pres," *Journal of the American Musicological Society*, XIV (1961), pp. 171-173.

[17]Hewitt, ed., *Odhecaton*, Introduction, p. 35. Petrucci gives only the text incipits in his publication.

[18]*Ibid.*

[19]In discussing the profound stylistic changes which occurred about seventy years earlier, Heinrich Besseler emphasizes the factor of selection from preëxistent elements of those which are suitable to the new ideals of expression: "Ein solcher Wandel ist nicht mit 'Einflüssen' zu erklären. Er setzt eigenes Wollen und eine klare künstlerische Richtung voraus . . . *Eine schöpferische Zeit übernimmt nur, was der eigenen Art und dem eigenen Suchen entspricht.*" *Bourdon und Fauxbourdon*, p. 194 (italics mine).

[20]Charles van den Borren, "Quelques reflexions à propos du style imitatif syntaxique," *Revue Belge de Musicologie*, I (1946-47), 14.

[21]The reason that initial imitation and chordal declamation are not used so much even in the later Masses of Josquin may be that the familiar texts did not require clear

presentation. In motets, where the text is not so well known, or may even be unique, clear understanding of the words may have been considered more necessary. It should not be forgotten, also, that most musicians were not so impressed with the need for correct declamation as were the literati. The musical ideas do not slavishly follow the accent of the words and instances are not uncommon where the musical accent actually negates that of the text.

[22]"Music in the Culture of the Renaissance," *Journal of the History of Ideas*, XV (1954), 534, and 547.

[23]*Missen*, II, 39. The chanson of Ockeghem(?) is appended. It is also given in Hewitt, ed., *Odhecaton*, p. 353.

[24]Gombosi gives an analysis of the work in *Jacob Obrecht*, p. 88.

[25]Either Obrecht or Josquin may have got the idea of fragmenting the c.f. from the other, depending on who first wrote a Mass on *Malheur me bat*. This seems unlikely, however, as there is no direct quotation; the fragments of one work do not correspond with those of the other.

[26] *Jacob Obrecht*, p. 91. See also n. 2 above.

[27] *Missen*, II, 67.

[28]Stéphen Morelot, *De la musique au XVᵉ siècle. Notice sur un manuscrit de la Bibliothèque de Dijon* (Paris: V. Didron, et al., 1856), Appendix 6. The relation to the Mass of Josquin is noted by Morelot (*ibid.*, p. 24). The tenor of the chanson is a quodlibet consisting of quotations from five chansons. The final one consists of words and music from *L'ami Baudichon*.

[29]*Missen*, II, v.

[30]The difficulty in identifying this phrase, assuming that it is c.f., is that so many Gregorian melodies have the same shape.

[31]P. de la Rue, *Liber Missarum*, ed. Tirabassi (Milan: Carisch; Basle: Hug; Malines: Dessain, 1941), p. 185.

[32]*Missen*, II, 70, 76, 84, respectively.

[33]*Missen*, II, 93. In the superius of the chanson these occur at the following measures: A—m. 2, B—m. 6, A—m. 10, B—m. 14, C—m. 18, A'—m. 22, B—m. 26, and D—m. 31. Phrase D could well be labeled A″, as it is merely phrase A stated at the third above. *Ibid.*, p. 119.

[34]The alto states phrases A and B; the superius enters m. 16 with phrase B but drops it after a few notes. The bass also has a bit of c.f. material at the beginning, as it is written in simple mensuration canon with the alto. (The bass is a fifth below the alto and is written twice as fast. The canon is very brief, m. 1-3 of the bass equaling m. 1-6 of the alto.)

[35]*Missen*, II, 121.

[36]*Histoire*, p. 185. Reese's suggestion that the work is related to the "substitution" Mass and to the "custom of singing a motet in honor of the Sacrament, in connection with the transsubstantiation" is much more probable. *Renaissance*, p. 245.

[37]Smijers includes it with the *Missa D'ung aultre amer* as Appendix I. Josquin, *Missen*, II, 136.

[38]*Missen*, III, i. The motet is included by Smijers in an appendix (p. 29), and is also conveniently available in Hewitt, ed., *Odhecaton*, p. 351. Commentary by Reese given in *Renaissance*, p. 240.

[39]These two movements are related by identical closing sections in the same way as the Gloria and Credo of the Mass of Dufay, *Ave Regina caelorum*.

[40]Brumel brings his motet to a close with a passage which is very similar to drives to the cadence in some of the motets of Busnois (e.g., *Victimae paschali laudes*). The imitative entries of each voice are made on a short cadential figure of the type which Busnois often uses; in addition, they are stated at the unison in all parts and at the distance of one measure, so there is an effect of *ostinato* as well as of stretto.

[41]*Missen*, III, 33. The music of the rondeau of Frye, *Tout a par moy*, is readily

available: Dragan Plamenac, "A Reconstruction of the French Chansonnier in the Biblioteca Colombina–Seville—I," *Musical Quarterly*, XXXVII (1951), 530. The chanson of Alexander Agricola given by Smijers as an appendix to the Mass of Josquin (*op. cit.*, p. 56) is likewise derived from the composition of Frye. Agricola, in developing his four-voice composition, starts with Frye's tenor and states it throughout in doubled values. The contratenor of the first part he bases on the opening notes of the tenor: from m. 5-27 he uses the first eight notes and freely extends them; this figure he states four times as a free *ostinato*. From m. 31 to the end of the *prima pars* he states only the first four notes, just as Josquin does in Agnus III; this motive is brought in nine times at points where it will fit the tenor. The contratenor of the *secunda pars* is made up in a corresponding way: the four-note motive associated with the words "*faisans regrets*" (used by Josquin throughout his Mass) is stated ten times at points where it can be made to fit. The two outer voices, bass and superius, move more rapidly than the inner ones. They are written as free counterpoints on the whole, but with occasional motivic organization, brief imitations, etc. Both the Mass of Josquin and the chanson of Agricola draw their material from the composition of Frye, so one cannot be said to be derived from the other. They are, however, similar to the extent that both make use of the same four-note motives in combinaion with other borrowed material, and it is quite possible that one of the composers had the other's work in mind when writing his own.

⁴²Josquin uses Gloria and Credo melodies in *La sol fa re mi* also (p. 329, above).

⁴³*Missen*, III, 61.

⁴⁴*Missen*, III, 93.

⁴⁵*Ibid.*, p. 124.

⁴⁶*Missen*, III, 125. Also published in Das Chorwerk: Josquin des Prés, *Missa de Beata Virgine*, ed. Friedrich Blume (2nd ed.; Wolfenbüttel: Möseler Verlag, 1951), Heft 42.

⁴⁷Not Credo II as Blume states (*ibid.*, p. 2). For further information on the choice of melodies, see Reese, *Renaissance*, p. 242.

⁴⁸The *comes* evidently should be provided with a signature of one flat. Oliver Strunk, *Source Readings in Music History*, (New York: W. W. Norton & Co., 1950), p. 211, footnote d. For an even more striking instance of Josquin's use of different key signatures in different voices see Edward Lowinsky, "The Goddess Fortuna in Music," *Musical Quarterly*, XXIX (1943), 45 ff.

⁴⁹*Missen*, IV, 1. Also published without Agnus II in Das Chorwerk: Josquin des Prés, *Missa Pange Lingua*, ed. Friedrich Blume (4th ed.; Wolfenbüttel: Möseler Verlag, 1951), Heft 1. See the discussion of the Mass, p. 376.

⁵⁰It is similar to, but not identical with Credo I of the Vatican edition, so it is not possible to account for every note. In addition, it is probable that Josquin treats it freely, which would increase the number of discrepancies. In any case, it is closer to Credo I than Credo II (*Reese, Renaissance*, p. 244).

⁵¹For example, the bass line of the Kyrie of the *Missa Gaudeamus* makes use of a figure from the c.f. as an *ostinato*. In the *Et in Spiritum* of the same Mass the ornamentation of the tenor line is in one spot derived from a c.f. figure also (ex. 113, m. 194-201).

⁵²Systematic or nonsystematic treatment of the c.f. seems to depend on the personal preference of the composer. With Josquin it apparently has some relation to the source of the c.f. also. In general, he treats Gregorian melodies nonsystematically; those from other sources may be treated one way or the other. It is noticeable that all *cantus firmi* which are consistently quoted unornamented and which are given schematic treatment are voices from some polyphonic composition, either sacred or secular.

⁵³*Missen*, IV, xx. The work is also found in Das Chorwerk. (2nd ed., 1950), Heft 20. The Gregorian prayer for peace is given in *LU*, p. 1867.

⁵⁴This is given as the first Agnus by Blume in Das Chorwerk, Heft 20, following the

manuscript source München, Bayerische Staatsbibliothek, Mus. Ms. 7. As this movement does not occur in any of the other sources available to Smijers, he includes it only as an appendix (*Missen*, IV, 58). Whether or not it was written by Josquin, it was certainly intended to make a part of this Mass, for it starts off with the head motive heard in the preceding four movements.

[55]Friedrich Blume in the edition of the Mass in *Das Chorwerk* interprets the inscription "*Agnus secundum in superacuta voce sic incipit*" in the tenor part of the publication of Ott to mean that that part is to be performed an octave higher than written. This puts it into the same range as Cantus I, and Blume places it on the top staff of his score. "Superacuta vox" is not too fit a designation, as this part has exactly the range of the first cantus. Smijers, in his edition, leaves the tenor on pitch (following Stuttgart, Landesbibliothek, Cod. Mus. 46 and München, Bayerische Staatsbibliothek, Mus. Ms. 7).

[56]MGG, article "Josquin Desprez," VII, cols. 209-211. Osthoff suggests a chronology for the motets as he does for the Masses (see n. 2, this chapter). He places *Illibata virgo Dei nutrix* and *Ut Phoebi radiis* in the first period; *Praeter rerum seriem*, *Huc me sydereo*, the *Ave Maria* for four voices, *Alma Redemptoris Mater*, *Stabat Mater*, and others in the second; *Benedicta es, caelorum Regina*, *Pater noster–Ave Maria*, and others in the third.

[57]He discusses them under the formal categories he has established. See above, chapter vii, n. 9.

[58]*Renaissance*, pp. 246-260.

[59]*Motetten*, II, 51. Also in Ambros, *Geschichte der Musik*, V, 62. The chanson is printed by Eugénie Droz in: *Trois chansonniers francais du xve siècle* (Paris: 1927), 70. The work is attributed to Binchois in the Mellon Chansonnier. M. F. Bukofzer, "An Unknown Chansonnier of the Fifteenth Century," *Musical Quarterly*, XXVIII (1942), 18. Osthoff states that the tenor comes from a work of Agricola. *Op. cit.*, col. 213.

[60]The great popularity of this work is suggested by the number of sources in which it appears. Smijers lists eight prints dating from 1519 to 1559 and thirteen manuscripts. *Motetten*, II, viii-xii.

[61]*Motetten*, II, 89.

[62]The chanson is printed in Bukofzer, "An Unknown Chansonnier . . .," *op. cit.*, p. 39.

[63]*Motetten*, I, 152. The text is *Requiem aeternam*, and is given in the tenor only (Introit, *LU*, p. 1807; verse and respond, *LU*, p. 1815). Smijers also publishes it in the complete edition in its form as a motet-chanson with text *Nymphes des bois*. *Wereldlijke Werken*, 56. For a full discussion of the earliest known source of the work in this form, see Edward Lowinsky, "The Medici Codex, a Document of Music, Art, and Politics of the Renaissance," *Annales Musicologiques*, V (1957), pp. 79-81, and p. 154.

[64]*Op. cit.*, col. 213. The work is printed in *Motetten*, II, 11; c.f. in *LU*, p. 735.

[65]*Motetten*, II, 29; c.f. in *Ant. Rom. Seraph.*, p. 164.

[66]*Motetten*, II, 99; c.f. in *LU*, p. 884.

[67]*Motetten*, I, 147; c.f. in *Proc. Mon.*, p. 105.

[68]*Motetten*, III, 37; c.f. in *LU*, p. 880.

[69]Reese, *Renaissance*, p. 231.

[70]Glareanus, *Dodecachordon*; trans. Peter Bohn (Leipzig: Breitkopf & Härtel, 1888), p. 316. *Das Chorwerk*, Heft 30. The original secular song is published by Petrucci in *Canti B* (1502). (See Pirro, *Histoire*, p. 176; Reese, *Renaissance*, p. 256). Glareanus says the chanson is based on a German and a French song in the vernacular (*Dodecachordon*, p. 314). Osthoff gives the German song, *Wohlauf gut G'sell, von hinnen*, in *Das Chorwerk*, Heft 30, p. 2.

[71]*Motetten*, II, 77; c.f. in *LU*, p. 273.

[72]*Motetten*, II, 111. The sequence in honor of the Virgin Mary is in *LU*, p. 1861.

[73]*Motetten*, II, 21. The melody of this sequence for the Assumption of Mary is given in simple form in a two-voice composition of the late thirteenth century. J. H. Baxter, ed., *An Old St. Andrews Music Book*. (London: Oxford University Press, 1931), fo. 194ᵛ.

[74]*Motetten*, III, 11; c.f. in Anselm Schubiger, *Die Sängerschule St. Gallens . . .* (Einsiedeln and New York: K. & N. Benziger, 1858), *Exempla*, No. 24, p. 23.

[75]Oliver Strunk calls such repetitions with new elements "variation-chains." "Some Motet-types of the Sixteenth Century," in *Papers Read by Members of the American Musicological Sociey, 1939* (Richmond, Va.: The William Byrd Press, Inc., 1944), p. 155.

[76]Smijers gives no less than twenty-four sources for this work. The first printed source is dated 1519, the last 1558. *Motetten*, II, vii-xi.

[77]*Motetten*, II, 42; the c.f. is the well known antiphon, *Ave Maria, LU*, p. 1679.

[78]*Motetten*, II, 58; the psalm tone can be found in *LU*, p. 646. Reese discusses the allusions to Gregorian psalm tones in Josquin's settings of the psalm texts. The tenor motive *Miserere mei Deus* is "undoubtedly suggested by the general nature of the psalm-tones." *Renaissance*, pp. 247-248.

[79]*Motetten*, I, 140. The first part of the text is an acrostic on Josquin's name. See Introduction, *ibid.*, p. x. Van den Borren has attempted an interpretation of the second verse in the same manner. The first letters of the twelve lines are A C A V V E S C A U G A, and he reads them: A—from; CAW or CAWE—the village of Cantaing, or Cantin; ESCAU or SCAU—the river Escaut; GA—*gouw* or region. Since Josquin wrote the first part of the poem as an acrostic, it is reasonable to assume that he wrote the second part as one also, but whether van den Borren's interpretation is correct I cannot say. It is given in his "Une hypothèse concernant le lieu de naissance de Josquin Des Prez," in *Festschift Joseph Schmidt-Görg . . .* (Bonn: Verlag des Beethovenhauses, 1957), pp. 21-25.

[80]*Motetten*, III, 26. Osthoff gives the date of this motet as 1502 in the article "Josquin Desprez," *MGG*, VII, col. 204.

[81]The c.f. starts in the bass, m. 118, moves to the superius, m. 125, and then to the tenor, m. 130. At m. 133, the alto repeats the tenor phrase. The superius takes it at m. 136, and at m. 148 the tenor repeats the superius phrase. The superius has it at m. 152, (the tenor at m. 162?) and proceeds very freely to the end.

[82]*Motetten*, I, 110. The simple relation between syllables and notes is in notable contrast to the solmization tenor of Ockeghem, *Ut heremita solus*, with its tortuous canonic involvements. See p. 236 above.

[83]*Motetten*, I, 21. The first five parts of the motet are in the same volume, p. 41. Text in *Analecta hymnica*, L, 568. The hymns—with citations in *Hymns Anc. & Mod.*—are *Exsultet coelum laudibus* (p. 274); *Jesu, nostra redemptio* (text, p. 250; melody p. 238); *Aeterna Christi munera* (p. 291; the melody of *Exsultet coelum laudibus* is used, rather than the one usually associated with this hymn); *Conditor alme siderum* (p. 54); and *Beata nobis gaudia* (p. 252; the melody used—not the one commonly associated with these words—is that of a related hymn for Pentecost, *Iam Christus astra ascenderat*). Smijers gives references to the text of the sequence, *Christum ducem*, (Josquin *Motetten*, II, introduction, p. xv) but does not give a melody. Even so, it seems quite clear that a melody with repetitions like a sequence is carried by the superius and tenor, with the other voices partaking of it occasionally in imitation. Jacquelyn Mattfeld has shown that the text of the first five parts of the motet "is an integrated series of texts, or one long one, traditionally associated with the Office of the Commemoration of the Passion." "Some Relationships Between Texts and Cantus Firmi . . . ," pp. 175-176.

[84]*Motetten*, I, 85. The bass has the text of the respond *Ave Maria*, but after m. 49 the melody differs from the Vatican version (*Vesperale*, p. 123*). The tenor presents

the entire solemn tone of the *Pater noster*. Cf. *Missale Romanum* (Turin: P. Marietti, 1921), p. 269.

[85]*Motetten*, I, 136. The chanson of Ockeghem is given by Smijers as Appendix II to the *Missa D'ung aultre amer* (Josquin, *Missen*, II, 140). *De tous biens pleine* occurs in Hewitt, ed., *Odhecaton*, p. 263, *Victimae paschali laudes* in *LU*, p. 780. For further uses of *D'ung aultre amer* see p. 358, above.

[86]It is taken first by the tenor, migrates to the bass at m. 14, and returns to the tenor at m. 20. At the beginning of the second part the alto takes the c.f., preceded by a short imitative entry in the bass. It returns to the tenor at m. 60 and then to the alto at m. 70. The alto statement continues to m. 78, but in the meantime the tenor has entered with the next phrase at m. 76, so for these three measures there are three voices concerned with c.f. There is another overlapping migration (m. 86-87) when the c.f. returns to the alto. At m. 90 the tenor takes it once more and retains it to the end. There is a short imitative entry in the alto at m. 101.

[87]*Motetten*, I, 105; the two Marian antiphons are given in *LU*, p. 273, 274.

[88]*Motetten*, I, 1; the sequence is found in *Var. Prec.*, p. 46.

[89]*Motetten*, I, 29; the antiphon is given in *LU*, p. 443.

[90]The c.f. is dropped at the end of *Virgo prudentissima* also, another work in which the tenor is the chief c.f. voice even though the Gregorian melody appears in the others because of imitations. (Josquin, *Motetten*, I, 133; c.f. given on p. 174.) It is not always possible to determine with any degree of certainty whether a c.f. is dropped and the composition continues freely, or whether the melody used by Josquin differs from the one available for comparison. For instance, the motet *Ave Maria* (*ibid.*, p. 12) uses the well-known antiphon for about twenty-four measures, but after this point the melody can no longer be followed. Since the text also deviates later in the motet, it is quite possible that an unidentified c.f. is used. The same is true of the *Ave Maria* melody in *O bone et dulcis Domine Jesu*, which, as mentioned above, departs from any melody available to me but nevertheless has the appearance of Gregorian chant from beginning to end.

[91]*Motetten*, I, 14. The c.f. is given by Smijers, *ibid.*, p. 171; also in *Var. Prec.*, p. 133.

[92]It appears least of all in the alto, which usually is conducted freely, presenting c.f. chiefly in a few short imitations. It can be traced best in the superius, m. 1-23; the bass, m. 22-26, repeated by the tenor, m. 25-34; superius, m. 34-38, repeated by the bass, m. 38-42. Superius and tenor imitate freely in m. 42-53. The alto carries it in m. 56-60, the tenor in m. 60-68. There is imitation in all voices in m. 70-77; the tenor has it in m. 78-87 and the bass in m. 91 ff. The superius and alto have it in a duet, m. 98-123; the tenor then takes it to the end of the *prima pars*. In the *secunda pars* the tenor carries it from m. 1-16, the bass from m. 17-39, and the tenor from m. 39 to the end.

APPENDIX

[1]These are presented in the articles "Die Kolorierungstechnik der Trienter Messen," *Studien zur Musikwissenschaft*, VI (1920), 5-47, and "Die frühen Messenkompositionen der Trienter Codices," *ibid.*, XI (1924), 3-58.

[2]For Bukofzer's criticisms, and for references to those of others, see his *Studies*, p. 52 and n. 19.

[3]Ficker himself says that it does not completely agree with previously observed usages. "Die Kolorierungstechnik . . . ," p. 10.

[4]The reasons for the omission of c.f. reference cannot always be given, but for the most part they can be attributed to carelessness or ignorance on the part of the scribe.

[5]*DTO*, 53, pp. 95-100.

[6]See ex. 29, above.

[7]"Die Kolorierungstechnik . . . ," p. 9.

[8]The intermittent use of a c.f. has been illustrated before, in ex. 33. This Alleluia is certainly an example of very free treatment of the c.f., although it may be that Liebert used a form of the chant somewhat different from that given in the Rouen gradual. However, Ficker has not suggested this as a possibility.

[9]"Die Kolorierungstechnik . . . ," p. 9; my translation. ("Manche Teile der Oberstimme des Alleluia zeigen demnach eine gewisse Unabhängigkeit vom Cantus firmus, eine Feststellung, welche für die Beurteilung der komp.-technischen Faktur des Gloria und Credo der Messe von Wichtigkeit ist.")

[10]He does not make this Alleluia crucial to his succeeding arguments, since he comments that the c.f. usage he finds in the Gloria and Credo "does not fully agree with that otherwise observed" ("mit jener bisher festgestellten nicht völlig übereinstimmt"). *Ibid.*, p. 10.

[11]*Ibid.*, pp. 40-44, and *DTO*, 53, pp. 99-100.

[12]"Die Kolorierungstechnik . . . ," pp. 10-11.

[13]*DTO*, 14, Plate IX, *Et in terra*. Dufay uses the Gloria of Mass XI (*LU*, p. 46), presenting it alternately in polyphonic setting (c.f. slightly elaborated in the superius) and monophonically for "chorus" (without elaboration).

[14]"Es besteht daher nur die Möglichkeit, dass die Melodie dieser Oberstimmen entweder frei erfunden ist, oder dass ihr eine Cantus firmus-Technik zugrunde liegt . . ." ("Die Kolorierungstechnik . . . ," p. 10).

[15]With regard to the Tournai Mass he says: "Die Verarbeitung des Chorals ist hier viel deutlicher zu verfolgen, wie in den entsprechenden Sätzen der Liebertschen Messe, wo bereits die freie Erfindung einen bedeutend grösseren Raum in Anspruch nimmt." (*Ibid.*, p. 22). He also says of the Liebert Mass, "Sie gehört daher bereits einem fortgeschritteneren Stadium im Entwicklungsprozesse der Emanzipierung von der Diskantkolorierung zur freien Erfindung an" (*loc. cit.*).

[16]Apparently the Tournai and Machaut Credos belong to this category, since both begin with a short quotation from the Gregorian Credo I. In trying to fit a c.f. to them throughout, Ficker seems to be pushing the practice of discant coloration too far back. Very early instances of c.f. statement in the discant have been discovered (c.f. Bukofzer, *Geschichte des englischen Diskants und des Fauxbourdons*, p. 115). However, Professor Bukofzer has told me that in these cases the c.f. is not elaborated but quoted note for note. The earliest preserved examples of c.f. *elaboration* in Continental music known to me are found in the group of hymns of the Apt manuscript, which dates from the last quarter of the fourteenth century. (See ex. 17, *Christe Redemptor*, c.f. elaborated in the middle voice.) Discant coloration, as a general practice, is apparently a development of the fifteenth-century English and Burgundian schools.

[17]"Die Kolorierungstechnik . . . ," pp. 24-25. Since the publication of the compositions of Old Hall we are in a better position than Ficker was, to evaluate the c.f. usage of the English in the early fifteenth century. The music gives the clearest possible evidence that, instead of being in full bloom in England c. 1400, the practice of elaborating a c.f. was being developed at that time. It is true that it developed rather rapidly in the conductus, possibly within the space of a couple of decades, and that the English may have been ahead of the Continentals in the practice, but it cannot be shown that they were so far in advance of them that they must have made the significant developments Ficker supposes. Furthermore, they elaborated the c.f. in the middle voice frequently, but rather seldom in the treble. Discant coloration in the strict sense is much more characteristic of Continental music of a slightly later date.

The high esteem in which the English were held by their contemporaries on the Continent can be accounted for very well by the "pan-consonant" style of Dunstable, Pyamor, and their fellow musicians, since this represents a radical departure from the methods of dissonance treatment of the *Ars nova*. As Ficker has pointed out, the English were apparently the first to write c.f. Mass cycles, but their treatment of the cantus firmi does not depart from the ordinary methods in any respect except the use of the same borrowed melody in more than one movement. These cycles do not bear out the treatment he champions.

[18]*Ibid.*, p. 27. (My translation; the italics are Ficker's.) In the case of *O rosa bella III* (DTO, 22, p. 28) there is no doubt that the tenor of the Dunstable chanson *O rosa bella* (DTO, 14, p. 229) is used as tenor of the Mass. Ficker's problem is to show that the superius of the chanson is also quoted *throughout* the work. (Portions of it are clearly present in the superius of the introductory duos.)

[19]*Ibid.*, pp. 45 ff.

[20]See m. 2 and m. 8-9 in ex. 138a-b. The omissions are of little importance at the cadences (m. 8-9), since the essential tones, the leading tone and the tonic, agree exactly.

[21]This is a subtlety not envisaged in Ficker's type of analysis, where the object is solely to find literal correspondences. The effect of these omissions is quite different, for instance, from those found in ex. 137a, m. 19. Here the missing notes are of some melodic importance in the chanson and, despite the fact that there are only a few of them, their absence makes the contratenor seem quite remote from the original melody.

[22]There is no proof that composers did not reverse c.f. notes as Ficker supposes. It is perfectly possible that they occasionally did, although experience shows that there is very little need to go on that assumption. Furthermore, the use of reversed notes in Ficker's analyses seems to be purely opportunistic. Apparently, the only factor with which it correlates is the unlikelihood of the presence of c.f. The more troublesome the task of demonstrating that borrowed material is being used, the more often the analyst has to fall back on it as a way out of difficulties.

[23]It seems even more improbable than in the Liebert Mass, where at least the same attitude was maintained throughout a complete movement.

[24]The tenors of the chansons *Se la face ay pale* and *L'homme armé* contain similar triadic figures which are used in imitation in the original works and also made the basis of imitations in the Masses derived from them. The points of imitation are often made much more complicated in the Masses than in the originals. (See Busnois, *Missa L'homme armé, Mon. Pol. Lit.*, I:1, fasc. 2, p. 7, and Regis, *Missa L'homme armé, ibid.*, fasc., 5, p. 7.)

[25]See the analysis of this work, p. 138. The same objections to Ficker's analysis of *O rosa bella III* apply to the short analytical sketches he gives of the two other Masses of that name, to Dufay's *Se la face ay pale*, to Faugues's *Le serviteur*, etc. "Die Kolorierungstechnik . . . ," pp. 36-39.

[26]Ficker analyzes an early work of the type, Dunstable's isorhythmic motet *Veni Sancte Spiritus* (*ibid.*, p. 33), but misses the fact that the fourth line of the hymn is paraphrased in the fourth duet, so that the orderly plan of the work escapes him. He does say, quite truly, that the quotations in the discant are separated by free insertions, but he does not go on to say that these insertions coincide with the tenor statements and that the paraphrased quotations exactly fill up the spaces where the tenor rests.

However, during a statement of the tenor he finds eight notes of the third verse quoted very clearly in the discant, with no omissions and no ornamentation (DTO, 14, p. 206, m. 158-162). Here there are too many notes of the hymn for one to insist categorically that the correspondence is accidental. Also, it is not my intention to maintain that two *cantus firmi* were never used simultaneously at this period, since they occasionally were. If all Ficker's evidence were as clear as this passage, or even approached it in clarity, it would never be questioned. However, even if Dunstable does use c.f. simultaneously in the tenor and discant of this work, this still does not give much support to Ficker's contention that the technique was in widespread use by the English at this time. The passage is very short and is incidental to the over-all plan of alternating statement.

[27]Ficker's analysis can be seen in *DTO*, 61, p. 114. Asterisks are used to mark the c.f. tones. The "repetition" begins at m. 67, p. 115.

[28]As mentioned before, the tonal schemes of compositions of the fifteenth century are generally simple, with a great number of cadences falling on the first and fifth degrees of the mode. It is to be expected that a certain number of these cadences will correspond in the first and second halves of any composition at that time.

[29]Ficker discusses this Mass pair, Dunstable's *Jesu Christe, fili Dei vivi*, in "Die frühen Messenkompositionen . . . ," pp. 52ff.

[30]*Ibid.*, pp. 36 ff. The whole group of English compositions published in *DTO*, 61, is discussed in this section of Ficker's essay.

Incidentally, it seems that the method of finding musical relationships by means of note names only is still alive. In a recent book, H. C. Wolff makes use of it to support his contention that a technique of melodic variation was used much more extensively by the "old Netherlanders" than has been realized up to the present. Hellmuth Christian Wolff, *Die Musik der alten Niederländer* (Leipzig: Breitkopf & Härtel, 1956). As in the case of Ficker's analyses, some of Wolff's are convincing and some are not. For instance, he contends that Dufay proceeded according to a consistent and far-reaching plan of variation in the superius of the *Missa Se la face ay pale*. *Ibid.*, pp. 30 ff., and ex. 6. But in order to do so, he is forced to ignore some significant points of similarity and stress insignificant ones. (This is, of course, my own opinion. I find some clear instances of isomelism which Wolff leaves out of account altogether, apparently because they concern only two or three movements instead of all five, and because he is interested in showing that the superius of the *entire* work is an expanding series of variations of the superius of the Kyrie. I would suggest that the interested reader strip the example of the analytic apparatus of braces and establish for himself the points that are similar in the passages Wolff quotes.) Wolff also finds evidence of variation technique, but of different types, in the *Missa Ecce ancilla Domini* of Ockeghem and the *Missa Maria zart* of Obrecht. *Ibid.*, ex. 12, p. 36, and ex. 20, p. 42. The method of establishing relationships by note names is unreliable—as it always was and always will be—because it leaves out of account the fact that there are other features, too, which give a musical idea its character. (See pp. 426 ff., where I comment on other theories of variation in fifteenth century music; also the general commentary, pp. 63 ff.)

[31]Compare *DTO*, 61, p. 90, m. 1-20, and p. 91 m. 92-106. There are some points of structural similarity also. Compare the cadences at m. 23 and m. 107, m. 32 and m. 115, m. 67 and m. 137, etc.

[32]With reference to the English Mass movements published in *DTO*, 61, Besseler says: "Für die Sätze Nr. XLVIII bis L und einige später folgende hat Ficker, m. E. überzeugend, eine Diskantkolorierung nachgewiesen, die im Gegensatz zur italienisch-burgundischen als *konstruktiv* bezeichnet werden muss. Merkwürdigerweise ist die zugrundeliegende Melodie, ausser beim burgundisch kolorierten Gloria Nr. LVII, nirgends zu identifizieren. Mag nun ein c.f. oder etwa der frei geschaffene erste Teil als Vorlage gedient haben: der Komponist hat dieses Gerüst in der Tat als blosse Tonsummation behandelt und es mit einem Melos von ganz neuer Gliederung und Gewichtsverteilung umkleidet—nach dem bisher zugänglichen Material zu urteilen, eine spezifisch englische Praxis." ("Von Dufay bis Josquin," p. 5.)

[33]Judgment on other compositions analyzed in *DTO*, 61, will have to be more cautious, since the similarities are not so clear as in the two Credos. However, Besseler considers the Credo on *Alma Redemptoris Mater* (*Ibid.* p. 92) a convincing example of discant-tenor technique ("Von Dufay bis Josquin," pp. 5-6). The Leonel Gloria and Dunstable Credo (*Ibid.*, pp. 104, 117) seem very doubtful.

[34]Dunstable, *Works*, p. 189.

[35]The movement also appears in Tr 90 (no. 943) and Tr 93 (no. 1774). It is anonymous in both these cases.

[36]The Sanctus is also found in Tr 90 (no. 971, *Dumpstabl*) and Tr 93 (no. 1802,

anonymous). The Agnus follows immediately in both codices (nos. 972 and 1803) and appears as well in Codex 92 (no. 1451) in incomplete form.

[37]Nos. 905 and 1715.

[38]Since the tenor of the Cooke Gloria shifts to a tonic of D in the second half (not quoted in ex. 142f), it lacks the element of repetition which is part of Ficker's system. For this reason, if no other, it seems that it can have no relation to the Dunstable-Leonel Mass in any way and that those correspondences which have been found must be truly accidental.

[39]It must be said in favor of Ficker's argument that it is just in this place—the first few measures—that the c.f. is most faithfully presented in English Masses which have named c.f. See exs. 37a-b, 39a-b, and 40a-c.

[40]One must assume extensive omissions, repetitions, and other rearrangements of phrases. Ficker says that the four movements of the *Rex saeculorum* Mass of Leonel(?) display these same peculiarities ("Die frühen Messenkompositionen . . . ," p. 56), but this statement does not correspond with the facts. The four movements of the *Rex saeculorum* Mass are indubitably connected. The tenors all start with the same notes, the extensions and interpolations are not so numerous or lengthy, and there is no question that the c.f. notes dominate the line. (See Dunstable, *Works*, pp. 47 ff.)

[41]"Die frühen Messenkompositionen . . . ," p. 56.

[42]In addition to the comments made above, it can also be pointed out that there are sixteen different copies of the four movements—four of the Gloria, three of the Credo, four of the Sanctus, and five of the Agnus—in the manuscript sources. (Lists of sources, Dunstable, *Works*, pp. 189 ff.) There are six attributions to composers, but not a one to a c.f. This does not prove anything, although it is rather indicative, since scribes were as careful to give c.f. sources as composers' names. It seems likely that had there been a c.f. it would have been mentioned at least once.

[43]In no case is the conclusion that these movements form a musical unit, and hence can only be the work of a single musician, acceptable as proof that Dunstable and Leonel are the same man. (Ficker, "Die frühen Messenkompositionen . . . ," p. 55). Besseler points out that Leonel and Dunstable are not mixed up in the good manuscripts. Most of the double attributions are concerned with Trent, which is not too reliable a source. ("Von Dufay bis Josquin," p. 6.)

[44]*Musik des Mittelalters*, p. 202. (Translation mine.)

[45]*Ibid.*, ex. 140. This corresponds to ex. 97d-e, above.

[46]The Sanctus and Agnus immediately following the Gloria and Credo in Tr 90 (i.e., nos. 1100-1101) were rejected as having no musical relationship. (Ficker "Die frühen Messenkompositionen . . . ," pp. 56 ff.) The *Benedicamus Domino* (no. 216) is not printed by Ficker but it does belong with the cycle. It is placed in Tr 88 immediately after the Credo; the music is a repetition of the final section of the Gloria.

[47]See ex. 63a-b, above.

[48]The musical style of the *Missa Deuil angouisseux* and its place in the younger Trent codices both indicate that it was written after the middle of the century.

[49]"Die frühen Messenkompositionen . . . ," p. 57.

[50]"Von Dufay bis Josquin," p. 6.

[51]This seems to be the general trend of the argument although there is no single, inclusive statement. For instance, Ficker says: "Unfortunately, too few Masses of the pre-Trent era have been published to allow us to survey the gradual transition of the tenor technique into the discant technique which comes to full bloom in the first half of the fifteenth century" ("Die Kolorierungstechnik . . . ," p. 23.) In another place he says: ". . . they removed the c.f. into the tenor in all movements, whereupon this voice again received its old significance, of which it appeared to have been almost completely deprived" (*ibid.*, p. 29); and, finally: ". . . at the same time, this voice, the colorated tenor, was made to move much more quietly than the colorated discant, so that in time, especially in the French-Netherlandish school, it takes on

again the forms of the rigid c.f., which is kept the same in all movements" (*ibid.*, p. 34). (Translation mine.)

[52]One instance is his theory that fauxbourdon developed out of parallel $\frac{5}{3}$ triads, which Bukofzer dismisses as "speculative." *Geschichte des englischen Diskants und des Fauxbourdons,* p. 5.

[53]Jacques Handschin, "Zur Frage der melodischen Paraphrasierung im Mittelalter," *Zeitschrift für Musikwissenschaft,* X (June/July, 1928), 513-559. Handschin's thesis is that the practice of melodic paraphrase of the fifteenth century stems ultimately from the methods of trope composition of the St. Martial epoch, even though the line of descent is not always very clear. The tropes are supposed to have been developed out of the melodies of the Ordinary by a method of melodic paraphrase which he illustrates at some length. Melodic expansion of this type was not cultivated by the central French school of the thirteenth and fourteenth centuries, since the chief interest was in the development of rhythmically organized polyphonic compositions, but it was continued by peripheral schools, e.g., by the English in their conductuslike compositions. It is perfectly possible that the English and central French traits came together in the Avignon school in the late fourteenth century and that the paraphrase technique then regained its former leading position.

[54]Bukofzer, *Studies,* p. 52. See also Besseler, "Von Dufay bis Josquin," p. 3. Rokseth accepts Handschin's opinion with regard to the tenor *Domino* (ex. 145a), without comment on his method. She mentions, however, that this is the only motet in which this *Benedicamus Domino* chant is so modified, and also notes that Gastoué and Ludwig do not believe that the tenor is actually based on it. Yvonne Rokseth, ed., *Polyphonies du XIIIᵉ siècle. Le manuscrit H 196 de la Faculté de Médecine de Montpellier* (Paris: Editions de L'Oiseau-Lyre, 1935-1939, IV, 196.

[55]Jacques Handschin, "Gregorianisch Polyphones . . . ," *Kirchenmusikalisches Jahrbuch,* XXV (1930), 60-76. The superius of this work appears as a late addition in old Hall, so there is no evidence that it antedates the repertory of the early Trent codices as Handschin believes. *Ibid.,* p. 63.

[56]"Gregorianisch Polyphones . . . ," pp. 62-63. (Translation mine.)

[57]*Handbuch der Musikgeschichte,* II:2, 113-115.

[58]Bukofzer, *Studies,* p. 63.

[59]Dunstable, *Works,* p. 103. The superius carries the c.f. in the duo, m. 72-106. The Gregorian melody is given by the editor, p. 161.

[60]"Die frühen Messenkompositionen. . . ," p. 31. (Translation mine.)

INDEX

489

Francisci patris (second verse of hymn *En gratulemur*), 44, 45 ex. 14
Free tones in the c.f. *See* Melodic paraphrase
Frottola, 345
Frye, Walter, 458 n. 85; *Sospitati dedit*, 75-79 and ex. 33 (441 nn. 43-45), 240; *Ave Regina caelorum*, 255 ex. 92, 306-307 (469 n. 21); *Tout a par moy* (chanson), 361-366 and ex. 126f-g, 479 n. 41; *Missa Summae Trinitati*, 455 n. 66

Ganassi, Silvestro di, 45
Gaude Virgo, Mater Christi, Josquin, 340
Gaudeamus omnes in Domino, 320
Gemblaco, Johannes de, 447 n. 21
Ghisi, Federico, 455 n. 64
Ghizeghem, Hayne van, *De tous biens pleine* (chanson), 208, 250-251 and ex. 91, 288, 395
Giesbert, F. J., 456 n. 72
Glareanus, Henricus, 268, 287, 474 n. 54, 481 n. 70
Gloria: melody, 139, 329, 361; Anglicanus, *Alma Redemptoris*, 447 n. 21; anon., 17 ex. 4c, 37, 424 and ex. 145b-c, d, 439 n. 26, 444 n. 12; Ciconia, 95; Cooke, 420 and ex. 142f; Dufay (*Spiritus et alme*) 70, 426, 438 n. 24 (*in modum tubae*), 448 n. 8; Dunstable, 438 n. 24; Excetre, 435 n. 39; Pugnare, Ave Regina, 447 n. 21
Gloria, laus, et honor, Binchois, 54-55 and ex. 21, 57, 437 nn. 14, 15
Gombosi, Otto, 351, cited: 456 nn. 72, 80, 463 nn. 32-33, 37, 468 nn. 11-12, 469 nn. 19-20, 473 n. 46, 474 n. 54, 475 n. 64, 477 nn. 3, 5, 7
Gothic style, 68, 85, 155, 260. *See also* Ars nova; Irrational procedures
Gottlieb, Louis, 452 n. 30, 455 n. 66
Gradual, 61, 91, 93, 140
Grossim, *Missa trompetta*, 95, 446 n. 18
Gymel, 66, 67

Haberl, Franz X., 458 n. 91
Haec Deum caeli, Obrecht, 304-306 and ex. 107 (475 n. 68), 381
Handschin, Jacques, 403, 424-426 (488 nn. 53-55), 427, 432 n. 10, 435 n. 33, 436 n. 4, 445 n. 20
Harmonic idiom, 10-13, 16, 18, 23, 29, 40, 87, 104, 192, 193, 195, 202-203, 209, 212, 217 chap. viii passim, 219-222, 239-240, 298, 361, 382
Harrison, Frank Ll., 7, 8, 36, 38, 40; cited:

431 n. 2, 432 n. 6, 433 n. 18, 435 n. 37, 444 n. 16
Hayne van Ghizeghem. *See* Ghizeghem, Hayne van
Head motive, 121, 127, 128, 138, 139, 155, 272, 274, 355, 378 ff., 412, 416, 446 n. 9, 450 n. 21, 456 n. 70, 472 n. 44. *See also* Identical closing passages; Motive, initial
Hemiola, 224, 230, 393. *See also* Rhythm
Henry IV, King of England, 35
Hewitt, Helen, 343, 344, 438 n. 20, 478 n. 17, 461 n. 6
Heyns, Cornelis, *Missa Pour quelque paine*, 171-172, 240
Hexachord, 313, 328, 354, 392, 393, 394
Hilf und gib Rat (unidentified), 208
Historical sense, 85
Hocket, 37
Homo quidam fecit, Josquin, 384-385 and ex. 129
Hopper, Vincent Foster, 443 n. 6
Huc me sydereo—Plangent eum, Josquin, 383-384 (481 n. 56), 392
Hughes, Dom Anselm, 7, 8, 34, 431 nn. 1-2, 432 nn. 6, 10
Huizinga, J., 447 n. 26
Humanism, 344
Husmann, Heinrich, 431 n. 2
Hymn, 44, 48, 53, 54, 60, 75, 107, 207, 212, 336 ff., 373 ff., 395, 436 n. 2, 475 n. 68

Identical closing passages, 129
Illibata Dei Virgo nutrix, Josquin, 393 (482 n. 79), 481 n. 56
Imitation, 37, 62, 65, 104, 112, 113-114, 115, 119, 123, 127, 129, 133, 136, 140 (438 n. 22), 148-150, 153, 156-157, 163, 167, 189, 193, 197, 198, 202, 203, 206 (462 n. 26), 212, 217, 219, 226 ff. (464 n. 6), 254, 257, 263, 264, 272, 275, 276, 278, 288, 291, 300, 302, 304 ff. (476 n. 78), chap. x passim and 368 ff., 373 ff.; freely introduced, 173-177; parodistic, 177-181, 355, 415-416; close (stretto), 229-231, 232 ff., 258-259; initial and continuous, 114, 167, 173, 174-178, 189, 229, 293, 303-304, 307, 310-311, 314, 319, 339-340, 396 ff., 462 n. 26; 478 n. 21; fugal, 300; syntactic, 345, 478 n. 20. *See also* Counterpoint, non-imitative
In hydraulis, Busnois, 217 (463 n. 40), 222-223, 230, 236 (465 n. 17), 333, 392, 461 n. 9, 463 n. 37, 464 n. 7